NORMAN BIRKETT

By the same author

The Rise of Castlereagh
The Empress Catherine and Princess Dashkov
Londonderry House and its Pictures
Princess Lieven
Judge Jeffreys
Mexican Empire: The History of Maximilian and Carlota of Mexico
A Victorian Historian: Letters of W. E. H. Lecky
Privacy and the Press
John Law
The Trials of Oscar Wilde
Mr and Mrs Beeton
Cases that Changed the Law
Carson: The Life of Lord Carson of Duncairn
The Trial of Craig and Bentley
United in Crime
The Strange Death of Lord Castlereagh
Sir Patrick Hastings: His Life and Cases
The Trial of Sir Roger Casement
Recent Developments in Historical Method and Interpretation
Simla and the Simla Hill States under British Protection
The Quiet Canadian: The Secret Service Story of Sir William Stephenson
Oscar Wilde: The Aftermath
A History of Pornography

With the Marchioness of Londonderry, D.B.E.
The Russian Journals of Martha and Catherine Wilmot
More Letters from Martha Wilmot: Impressions of Vienna

With G. R. Falkiner Nuttall
Air Defence and the Civil Population

With John Kisch
An International Case Book of Crime

NORMAN BIRKETT

THE LIFE OF LORD BIRKETT

OF ULVERSTON

BY

H. MONTGOMERY HYDE

HAMISH HAMILTON

LONDON

First published in Great Britain, 1964
by Hamish Hamilton Ltd
90 *Great Russell Street*, *London W.C.*1

PRINTED IN GREAT BRITAIN
BY EBENEZER BAYLIS AND SON, LIMITED
THE TRINITY PRESS, WORCESTER, AND LONDON

TO

RUTH LADY BIRKETT

CONTENTS

ILLUSTRATIONS

Illustrations in the Text

PREFACE

THE first time I set eyes on the subject of this biography was one afternoon in the Law Courts in London, more than thirty years ago. He was appearing for a Hungarian diplomat in a running-down case, which I have briefly described in the following pages (pp. 377–9). Norman Birkett seemed to me then to be everything the model advocate should be, alert, courteous, of impressive bearing and possessed of a most melodious speaking voice. As it happened, the voice failed to win a verdict on this occasion for his client; but I have never forgotten it, nor its owner. I am glad to think that, although he is no longer alive, his voice has been recorded on several long-playing records, which include his well known talk on the art of advocacy, originally broadcast in the B.B.C. Home Service in 1961.

From time to time I heard him in other cases, when he was at the height of his reputation as an advocate before the last war. Later, at the International Military Tribunal in Nuremberg, in 1946, I watched him on the Bench making notes in his diary which forms the basis of a revealing chapter in this book. My personal acquaintance with him, however, was slight. We corresponded on various subjects of mutual interest, and he was good enough to contribute Forewords to two of my books which interested him, *Judge Jeffreys* and *Sir Patrick Hastings.* He had intended to write his autobiography. Eventually, when he realized that this was not possible, he expressed the hope that I should be asked to assist in the preparation of a memoir based on the records of his cases and other papers which he had carefully preserved. It has been a privilege and a pleasure for me to have been able to respond to this invitation.

To the many people, who have helped me in the work, I wish to express my gratitude.

First, there are the members of Lord Birkett's family, his widow, Ruth Lady Birkett, and his two children, the Hon. Mrs. Cliff Hodges and the present Lord Birkett. In particular, Ruth Lady Birkett, to whom I am indebted for unrestricted access to and permission to quote from her husband's private papers, has shown the greatest kindness, patience and understanding of the problems of an official biographer, in the course of our many discussions. I should also like especially to thank Lord Birkett's cousin, Mr. Henry F. Birkett, for the detailed information about Lord Birkett's early life, and for letting me see his important collection of letters and other documents, as well as for recounting his personal recollections for my benefit.

I wish to thank Mr. A. E. Bowker, who served Lord Birkett for many years both as barrister's and judge's clerk, for answering my questions, and for allowing me to make use of his own valuable publications, *Behind the Bar* and *A Lifetime with the Law.*

I also wish to thank Mr. John Freeman and the British Broadcasting Corporation for supplying me with the script of his interview with Lord Birkett in the 'Face to Face' series in 1959, and for allowing me to quote from it. I am indebted to the B.B.C. for similar facilities regarding Lord Birkett's discussion with Miss Margaret Lane, on the occasion of the Dickens Birthday Celebrations, which was broadcast shortly before Lord Birkett's death.

I am grateful to the editor of the *News of the World* for the text of Dr. Buck Ruxton's confession, the original of which is in the possession of that newspaper.

Mr. Cecil Roberts, an old friend of Lord Birkett's, has kindly read the proofs and made a number of suggestions for the improvement of the book, of which I have been glad to take advantage. I am also grateful to him for putting his files at my disposal. The help I have received at every stage from my secretary, Mrs. R. Roberts, has likewise been invaluable.

As for the others who have contributed in various ways, particularly with information, I must tabulate my gratitude to them in alphabetical rather than quantitative order. They are as follows:

Mr. Leonard M. Alfred, Mr. Henry Annett, Mr. A. C. Baggley, Mr. Leslie Beckett, the Rev. Alfred Bellerby, Mr. Louis Blom-Cooper, Mr. David Bolton, Mr. Joe Burroughs, Mr. Laurence Cadbury, Mr. K. Campbell-Cullen, Mr. P. F. Carter Ruck, Mr. H. Cartmell, Judge Norman A. Carr, the Rev. E. G. Chapman, Lord Chorley, Q.C., Mr. R. W. P. Cockerton, Mr. F. E. Cook, Mr. Ashley Courtney, Mr. Frank Crompton, Mr. John Dowty, Mr. G. G. Eastwood, Mr. Justice Elwes, Mr. Morris L. Ernst, Sir Edward Ford, K.C.V.O., Mr. Justice Finnemore, Judge Arthur Forbes, Mr. Arthur Garner, Mr. Anthony Gishford, Mr. Overton Harris, Mr. Arthur E. Henley, Mr. B. C. Hilliam, Mr. Will Hinson, Mr. Gavin Cliff Hodges, Mr. T. V. Hoyle, Dr. W. G. Humphrey, Mr. Jeremy Hutchinson, Q.C., Mr. Donald Hurst, General Sir Henry Jackson, Miss M. S. Johnson, Mr. Frank Jordan, Lady Jowitt, Mr. E. C. Kennedy, Mr. Ludovic Kennedy, Mr. E. Kershaw, Mrs. E. Lawden, Sir Shane Leslie, Mr. Emile Littler, Mr. D. M. Low, Mr. Miles Malleson, the Rev. A. J. Mangold, the Rev. Michael McCormick, Mr. R. E. Millard, Mr. Birkett Moore, Mr. J. E. Morpurgo, Mr. L. Nott, Mr. R. A. Paget-Cooke, Mr. Edmund Park, Mr. G. P. O'Neill Pearson, Mrs. B. L. Potts, Mrs. Helen M. Rait-Kerr, Mrs. E. M. Roberts, Mr. H. Rollinson, Mrs. K. Saintsbury, Mrs. Helen Sheehan-Dare, Mr. Wilfred Shepherd, Mr. Ernest E. Sheppard, Mr. E. L. Shirley Smith, The Rev. A. G. Stewart, Mr. J. M. L. Stone, Mr. Peter D. Sugden, Mr. Hugo Tyerman, Mr. Russell Vick, Lord Wakefield of Kendal, Mr. Claude F. Westell, Mrs. Margaret Wharton, Mr. G. B. Williamson, Mr. James Wilson, Mrs. Erica Woodhouse, Mr. Nigel Wright, Mr. Ron Yeomans, Mrs. E. York, and Mr. W. H. Young.

Finally, I wish to thank those who have given permission for the reproduction of copyright photographs, particulars of which will be found beneath the relevant illustrations.

H. MONTGOMERY HYDE

Lamb House,
Rye, Sussex.
June, 1964.

NORMAN BIRKETT

CHAPTER I

EARLY YEARS

I

'If it had ever been my lot to decide to cut up a lady in small pieces and put her in an unwanted suitcase,' the late Sir Patrick Hastings once remarked, 'I should without hesitation have placed my future in Norman Birkett's hands. He would have satisfied the jury (*a*) that I was not there; (*b*) that I had not cut up the lady; and (*c*) that if I had she thoroughly deserved it anyway.'

This is a characteristically generous and witty tribute from a man who was himself one of the most successful advocates of his generation, and was frequently Birkett's opponent in the courts between the two world wars. Indeed, the reputation with juries which Birkett built up during this period was truly phenomenal. One learned judge, long since dead, is reported to have said of him that his powers of persuasion were 'a positive menace to the administration of justice!'

In a fragment of his unfinished autobiography, which he began towards the end of his life, the first Lord Birkett of Ulverston wrote as follows:

> It is true to say that until I retired in 1956 from the office of Lord Justice of Appeal I had never had any time in which I could have contemplated writing my memoirs. For many years I had been urged to do it because it was thought that I had had an exceptionally full and exciting life. Nobody knows as well as I do what a wonderful life it has been, but I have always shrunk a little from the task because to write about what one has done in a frank way, as one ought to do if one undertakes the task at all, is to make people think that one is vain and conceited and boastful.
>
> Now I know that I am none of these things, and nobody

has ever charged me with them. But I am naturally proud of the fact that I managed to make my way from behind a draper's counter to positions of considerable dignity and power and, I hope, usefulness. And I want to set down some record of my life before I leave it, first of all for my own satisfaction, and because it might be an encouragement to others.

It is no use regretting it, but I cannot help feeling sorry that I was seventy-three years of age before I had any time to set down the true account of my life. It is true that for many years I have kept diaries and full records of the many exciting law cases, but it is difficult to recapture the first fine careless rapture, and writing well is an accomplishment that either comes naturally or is slowly and painfully acquired.

Of the memoirs he had hoped to write, all that Lord Birkett left at his death in 1962 was an uncompleted draft of one chapter briefly covering his early life to the time he left his father's drapery business and began to study for the Methodist Ministry before going up to Cambridge as an undergraduate at the unusually late age of twenty-four. Nevertheless, he regarded these years as the most important of his life, in which he acquired his initial fluency as a public speaker. 'All subsequent years have been influenced by them,' he wrote. For his biographer, particularly, it is fortunate that some account, however slight, of this formative period should have survived in his own words.

I was born on September 6, 1883, at 4, Ainsworth Street, Ulverston in Furness, in the county of Lancashire. I was the fourth child of my parents. My mother died when I was three years old and I have no recollection of her at all. I have heard from some of my uncles that she was a woman of great character, of homely speech and great good humour, and many of her sayings in the dialect have been repeated.

My father was a draper and when I was born was just beginning to build up a substantial business which in due course became very widely known through the whole of Furness. 'Birketts of Ulverston' was the name by which the business was known, and when in 1898, I went into the business, I soon realized what a strong and resolute man he was.

The little town of Ulverston in Furness is naturally very

dear to me. I spent the first twenty-four years of my life there and the streets and buildings are known to me in the most intimate way. The portion of the county of Lancashire known as Furness was always a little inaccessible, and even today it is outside the main business stream.

Before the coming of the Ulverston and Lancaster railway in 1857, it was reached by crossing the sands. This was the way John Wesley went to the town, and it was the way that George Fox went to his trial at Lancaster Assizes before Mr. Justice Twisden, who is remembered chiefly for his unfeeling attitude to Elizabeth Bunyan when she pleaded with him and Sir Mathew Hale at Bedford Assizes for the release of her husband John Bunyan, then writing 'A Pilgrim's Progress' in Bedford gaol.

It has always appealed to me as a most romantic and exciting thing that the main way into the town for many years was by way of the sands, and there is a considerable body of writing about it.

From boyhood Norman Birkett knew by heart the description of the crossing from Cartmel to Ulverston, which the Lakeland poet William Wordsworth had written in his *Prelude*.

Without me and within, as I advanced
All that I saw, or felt, or communed with
Was gentleness and peace. Upon a small
And rocky Island, a fragment stood
(Itself like a sea-rock) of what had been
A Romish Chapel, where in ancient times
Masses were said at that hour which suited those
Who crossed the Sands with ebb of morning tide.
Not far from this still Ruin all the Plain
Was spotted with a variegated crowd
Of coaches, Wains and Travellers, horse and foot,
Wading, beneath the conduct of their Guide
In loose Procession through the shallow stream
Of inland water; the great Sea meanwhile,
Was, at safe distance, far retired.

'A great family town' was how Birkett liked to describe his birth-place, when he occasionally revisited it in later life as one of its most distinguished sons. 'Everyone knowing everyone. Everyone rather friendly.' Throughout his life what he called 'its lovely surroundings' —'Ulverston is a town set in one of the loveliest spots of all England, the Furness Fells'—whose unspoiled beauty he most effectively strove to preserve, exercised a powerful attraction for him. 'That's one of its secrets of its hold on people,' he remarked on one of these visits. 'Within a few minutes of leaving the town by either of the two ancient ways of Soutergate or Daltongate, you are in the authentic English countryside, and you are surrounded by a wonderland of beauty. If, instead of turning in to the cricket field, you climb on past Gamswell to Kirkby Moor, you will get what I've always maintained is the finest view in the British Isles, with the Duddon estuary, and Black Combe, and Coniston Old Man with its fellows on the one hand, and on the other, the long sweep of Morecambe Bay, the distant view of the Pennines, and the magical beauty of the Lakeland hills.'

As for the little town itself, with its grey stone walls and houses, it remained his real home to the last. 'I know every street in it. I know every building in it,' he told a gathering of Ulverstonians when he opened the town's new library the year before he died. 'The moment I catch sight of the Monument I say to myself, "At last I am home again".' The Monument, it may be explained, is the town's most conspicuous landmark, set in the form of a lighthouse on the summit of an adjacent hill.

> The young folk of Ulverston today will find it hard to believe when I say that I remember the town when there were no films, no radio, no television, no motor cars, no aeroplanes. I remember the first aeroplane that flew over the town and landed on the cricket field; and I remember when Dr. Ashburner of Cavendish Street drove his steam carriage through the streets and everybody came to their doors to see him.
>
> But there were great compensations. When you went for a tour of the Lakes, you were met at Ambleside by a coach with four splendid horses. It's true that you walked up the hills to spare the horses, and walked down the hills because the laden coach was too heavy for the skid pans, so you didn't get a lot of riding; but at any rate you were in the open air! There was a marvellously good amateur dramatic society where two brothers,

John and Sim Clayton, were the two best comedians I think I ever saw; and there was a wonderful Choral Society under Mr. Edmund Telfer, and a Lecture Association that brought many celebrities to the town.

The truth is that Ulverston was always an old country market town with a charm and a character peculiarly its own. . . . There used to be a Town Crier in uniform going through the streets making his public announcements after ringing a large bell, and the announcements always seemed to begin with 'To be sold by auction' or 'Lost, stolen or strayed'. In those days the County Hotel stood where the Coronation Hall now stands, and brightly painted buses from the County and the Sun Hotel met every train at the railway station, the 'Boots' standing on a broad step half way up the back of the bus. Sim Clayton of happy memory was the 'Boots' at the Sun and was a man that Dickens would have loved.

Ulverston seemed rich in 'characters' or 'worthies' then. Bobby Casson who wrote a book about Furness 'worthies' was one of them himself, and many's a time I've heard him sing his favourite song.

> 'Now I likes a drop o' good beer, I does,
> And I'se fond of a drop of good beer, I is;
> Let gentlemen fine sit down to their wine,
> But I'll stick to my beer, I will.'

I remember too how busy the Market days were on the Thursdays in each week. On those days, the carriers' carts used to stand in King Street and carried goods from Ulverston all over the countryside. And on fair days, when the farm servants stood round about the Market Cross with straws in their caps to show they were looking for a new place, the whole town was in a state of excitement; and the Gill filled with roundabouts and sideshows and exuberant life. . . .

'I never wanted to leave the little town,' Birkett admitted long afterwards. 'I delayed it until it was almost too late, and I have always felt the handicap of the years when I might have been making my way. As it was, I was thirty when I was called to the Bar and went into chambers at 27, Temple Row, Birmingham. . . .'

2

Norman's father, Thomas Birkett, and his grandfather, Mathew Birkett, came from the neighbouring village of Haverthwaite, about seven miles along the road from Ulverston to Lake Windermere. Grandfather Mathew was a cooper and was employed in a local gunpowder factory, the Lowood Gunpowder Works, later taken over by Imperial Chemical Industries Ltd. He lived in a cottage called Woodside, opposite Haverthwaite railway station, with his wife Agnes, whom another of their grandsons, Henry Birkett, remembers as 'a tall, forbidding woman', standing near the porch of their home. According to the same source, Mathew Birkett was 'gentle and easy-going, a very popular grandfather'. He was also apparently quite content with his job, enjoyed his quiet life in Haverthwaite and had no idea of what was generally known as 'getting on'. It was his wife, born Agnes Carradus, who determined that her children should be encouraged to progress up the social and economic ladder and 'make good'. 'I am sure it was her drive that lifted the family,' her grandson Henry has recalled. 'I was always frightened of her.'

Thomas Birkett, one of twin sons, was born at Woodside, Haverthwaite, or Wood Cottage, as it was then called, in 1854. His first job, a part-time one, he got while still a schoolboy, when he and his brothers helped with the building of the tunnels on the railway at Haverthwaite. By the eighteen-sixties Ulverston was already noted for its linens and checks and ginghams, and so it came about that Tom Birkett was apprenticed to 'the drapery' at Mr. T. Mashiter's shop, known as the Bee-Hive, in King Street. On completing his time, he went south to London, where he found work in the warehouse of Cook, Son and Company, St. Paul's Churchyard. But his health was not good and it got worse the longer he stayed in London. So he returned to Ulverston, found himself a wife with a little money, and at the age of twenty-four started for himself as a draper in small premises in Market Street, where he and his wife lived 'over the shop'. His business prospered, and a few years later he opened a tailoring business and then, in December, 1899, he acquired large additional premises in County Square, which were to remain the headquarters of a most successful family concern until some years after his death when the Birketts were bought out by the Co-operative Society.

These facts are considered worth recording, since it was sometimes said of Norman Birkett at the height of his professional success that his family was poor and that as a draper's assistant his circumstances were necessarily humble. On the contrary, his father was in a comparatively good way of business almost from the beginning—at one time he employed eight assistants and twenty dressmakers—and if the family background was characterized by a measure of plain living and high thinking it also exhibited a considerable degree of solid middle-class comfort.

In 1877, the year before he began in business, Thomas Birkett met and married Agnes Tyson, daughter of Moses Tyson, a local butcher. She was twenty-three, the same age as her husband.[1] The house at 4, Ainsworth Street, where they went to live soon afterwards, was a dignified three-storey dwelling, with large windows, the best in the short street. Here their five children were born. There were Edith, the eldest, and Gilbert, and another son who died in infancy. Norman, whose full names were William Norman but was often called Norrie, came fourth. Another girl, Ellen (Nellie) followed a little later. Here too, after a comparatively short married life, Mrs. Agnes Birkett died, of tuberculosis, on April 16, 1887.

In the following year, the widowed Thomas Birkett married again. His second wife, thirty-six-year-old Agnes Dodding, was a farmer's daughter from Wyresdale, near Lancaster, but at the time of her marriage was living in Ulverston as companion to a widowed lady, Mrs. Worsdell.[2] In due course they had a child of their own, a girl named Mary. The second Mrs. Birkett was always a good stepmother to Norman and the others, who evidently liked her in spite of her strictness with them. Although she came from an Anglican family, 'she was a great Wesleyan and ran the home very much in accordance with Nonconformist views,' Norman's cousin Henry Birkett has recalled. 'I never knew why my father and my uncles became Nonconformists, but suspect it was because they all married Nonconformist wives!'

There was quite a strong Nonconformist tradition in Ulverston, particularly amongst the business community, and it is more than

[1] They were married on October 15, 1877, in the Parish Church of Ulverston by the Rev. F. G. McNally.

[2] Thomas Birkett married Ann Agnes Dodding on June 18, 1888, in the Parish Church of Over Wyresdale, Lancashire. The bride's father, Bartle Dodding, is described in the marriage register as 'Gent'.

likely that even before his marriage Thomas Birkett fell under its influence as a young man serving his time in the Beehive Drapery store. George Fox, the first Quaker, who is mentioned above by Norman Birkett, had lived at nearby Swarthmoor Hall, and the evangelists John Wesley and George Whitefield had preached in the neighbourhood. In the Birketts' time, Ulverston boasted of the old Wesleyan Chapel, built in 1814, a new Wesleyan Chapel, whose erection was promoted by Thomas Birkett, a Mission Chapel, a Congregational Church, a Baptist House, two Friends' Meeting Houses and an Independent Methodist Chapel. Encouraged no doubt by his wife, Thomas Birkett became the most prominent layman in the local Wesleyan congregation. He was a steward and a trustee for various chapels in the Ulverston circuit, and he appeared as the lay representative at the annual Wesleyan Conference. He was also a manager of the Wesleyan Day School in Ulverston, at which his son Norman became a pupil.

Generally speaking, the Nonconformists supported the Liberals in politics, since the Conservatives were regarded as the mainstay of the Established Church. With the redistribution of seats in the House of Commons, which took place in 1885, Ulverston became part of the new constituency of North Lonsdale. The local Liberal Association, which Thomas Birkett joined, was an active organization. The elder Birkett was soon elected a member of its Executive Committee and also in due course became President of the Ulverston Liberal Club. He was an ardent political worker and campaigned vigorously for the Liberal candidate from nearby Holker Hall, the Hon. Richard Cavendish, who was returned twice at the head of the poll as a Liberal Unionist and who, as will be seen, did not forget the service rendered by this particular supporter.

In local government, too, and its numerous parochial concerns, Thomas Birkett played a useful part. For three years he filled the office of Chairman of the Ulverston Urban District Council, being known popularly as 'Mayor', and for several years more he presided over the deliberations of the Council's Health Committee, becoming quite expert on such matters as drains and sewage. In the council chamber Councillor Birkett had the reputation of being 'a straightforward outspoken man', who 'ruled the deliberations firmly but with fairness and justice to every member'. He was in the chair during the two Coronation years, Edward VII in 1902 and King

George V in 1911, and organized the celebrations which appropriately marked these events in Ulverston.

Thomas Birkett again became a widower when his second wife died of pneumonia in 1901, and his late wife's sister, Barbara Dodding, known in the family as 'Aunt Barbara', who had come to live with them at the time of his second marriage, always kept house for the Birketts in the various houses they occupied after leaving Ainsworth Street, first at Craiglea, a detached house in Kilner's Park on the outskirts of the town, where new building was going on, then at 14, Queen Street in the town, and finally at Nithsdale, a large brownstone house in Kilner's Park, which remained the family home until Thomas Birkett's death. His nephew Henry Birkett has written of him in these words:

> In the eighties and nineties Norman's father had really established himself as a leading man in the town. He was, rightly, looked upon as a successful business man, he was a strong and assertive member of the local Town Council and the School Board, an outspoken Liberal in a town predominantly Conservative, a leading Methodist—in fact in all his activities he was a leader. . . . His Liberalism was a protest, and many said it would ruin his business, at any rate with the Conservatives, and the Liberals were supposed to be Co-operatives and no good for private business. It did not ruin him, but won him support at the various local elections where he always polled well. His moves of residence announced to the world of Ulverston that the young man from Haverthwaite was 'getting on', as indeed he was, although his health was far from good.

Thomas Birkett died of a sudden heart attack on October 1, 1913, when he was in his sixtieth year, leaving almost £15,000 besides a good business to be carried on by his eldest daughter, Edith. He was laid to rest beside the remains of his two wives in Ulverston cemetery. His son Norman caused Browning's verse to be inscribed on the headstone of his grave.

> One who never turned his back but marched
> breast forward,
> Never doubted clouds would break,

Never dream'd, though right were worsted,
  wrong would triumph,
Held we fall to rise, are baffled to fight better,
    Sleep to wake.

3

From his father Norman Birkett inherited a determined character, a prodigious memory and a head of sandy-red curls, which caused him to be known at school alternately as 'Carrots' and 'Copperknob'. On the other hand, his health as a child was 'delicate' and in this he took after his mother. The Birkett children's 'nanny', who lived to be over ninety, recalled long afterwards how she once took her charges to pick daffodils and bluebells at Newland Bottom, where young Norrie collapsed with fatigue and had to be carried pick-a-back all the way home. It was feared that the child had developed his mother's chest trouble, and for a time he was made, on the doctor's advice, to sleep in the open air in the garden, a form of treatment designed to strengthen his lungs. He was fortunate to survive this drastic medical experiment.

As a very young child he showed signs of precocity. When he was about four years old, a new Infants' School was opened a few houses away in Church Walk and he went to this kindergarten. But only for a short time, as one day he came home with a note to the effect that he had absorbed all they had to teach him. The next step in his education was to the Wesleyan Day School, beside the old Wesleyan Chapel, where he was enrolled early in 1889, before his sixth birthday. This academy was run by the steward of the chapel, Mr. E. F. Hibbert, and his wife, for both of whom Norman developed a considerable affection, although Mr. Hibbert was quite a strict disciplinarian and did not hesitate to use the cane in correcting his pupils.

More than fifty years later, when he had become Lord Birkett, the former youngest boy at the school could remember the hymn with which lessons were opened—'My God the spring of all my joys'—and that with which they closed—'Silently the shades of Evening'. He also recalled the grammar lesson in the big schoolroom when the master wrote a line from the poet Gray on the blackboard —'There at the foot of yonder nodding beech'. Young Norman was awarded at least one school prize—for handwriting. He was also good at elocution, since he was put on in the school concert to recite a poem called 'Going on an errand', which he did in the presence of a large audience which included his father and grandfather. Religious instruction was naturally emphasized, and when a particularly good preacher came to the chapel, the school would adjourn to hear a sermon specially delivered for the occasion. Then there was Sunday school, and on Sunday evenings they would all sing hymns together at Nithsdale. The five years he spent at the Wesleyan Day School in Ulverston Norman Birkett always regarded as a most formative influence on his life. 'It was as I look back, a time of great happiness,' he wrote to Mr. Hibbert on the occasion of the master's retirement fifteen years later, 'and I shall always think with affection of the school and chapel and home.'

The old Wesleyan chapel and the school, both still used, were situated at the bottom of a hill, near the Market Place, about ten minutes' walk from Ainsworth Street and a little longer from Kilner's Park. It is difficult to overestimate in Norman Birkett's early life the significance of the Wesleyan Methodist faith, with the powerful emotional feelings which it engendered in its followers and which permeated school and home. The chapel was, of course, the focal centre of the local religious community, in which preaching played the principal part. Great store was placed on the sermon, whether preached by the Minister or a lay preacher, and these sermons were often extremely moving and dramatic in effect. At Ulverston there was a new Minister every three years, and the farewell service taken by the departing Minister was apt to be a tearful affair for the congregation. Norman Birkett has recorded that he 'cried his heart out' on one such occasion, when the congregation sang 'God be with you till we meet again'. 'I was always a homesick boy,' he noted sixty years later, 'and the thought of the Minister starting a new life amongst strange new people made me very sad indeed. I remember to this day a preacher of genius (as I thought then) who took for his text "How shall we sing the Lord's Song in a strange land?" and spoke in a language of such haunting beauty that I not only recall today the emotions of that time but words that the preacher said, and whenever I read the words I have that same dreadful sense of homesickness that afflicted me then and still has power to do so.'

Each of the family pews in the chapel had dimity curtains at the side, which would be drawn apart to allow the occupants to enter and leave. The pew in front of the Birketts was occupied by a Welshman who was the chief clerk at the railway station. Immediately behind sat the manager of the local branch of the 'Co-op', which was eventually to acquire Birkett's County Stores some years after Thomas Birkett's death. Across the aisle were the pews of the local corn and seed merchant and also of the butcher, a man named Hodgson, the memory of whose home-cured bacon and pickled tongues made Norman Birkett's mouth water after half a century. Under the leadership of a Cornishman, Jacob Pearce, who acted as choir-master, the congregation sang the psalms and hymns with vigour, and Norman would join in with a will, for he had quite a good singing voice. There were lighter moments too during the service, such as when Norman and his brother Gilbert would make paper-boats which they would attach to a string and 'sail' across the aisle during the prayers to their friends in one of the opposite pews. The boys' father happened to open his eyes during one of these exercises and saw what was happening. Punishment followed on their return home, one suspects of a corporal character; at all events, the boys never offended in this manner again.

The Birkett family was a happy and united one. Although the religious background was strong, the parents were not killjoys, and allowed their children plenty of healthy amusements and outings, which they all enjoyed together. In the summer there was swimming and boating on the lakes, cricket and picnics to nearby woods, and in the winter walking and skating. Once, when Norman was about seven, the whole of Windermere froze over hard, there was skating from Lakeside to Ambleside, and horses and carts made the journey across the ice, an unusual sight which stayed with him as a vivid memory for long afterwards. As has been noted above, Norman and his stepmother got on well together and she would sometimes send him for a holiday to her father's farm at Wyresdale. For his part he took care to flatter her vanity. Once, when convalescing at his cousin Harry's home at Dalton-in-Furness after an accident—while playing outside the Wesleyan Day School he had been struck by a passing cart which ran over his leg, breaking it—he wished to prolong his stay. Accordingly he wrote for permission to do so from his stepmother, whom he suitably flattered, telling her that she was a good cook. As a result the requested permission was granted. As his cousin put it, 'he succeeded in getting his verdict even then!'

4

Soon after his eleventh birthday Norman Birkett left the Wesleyan Day School in Ulverston for the Higher Grade School at Barrow, where he was enrolled along with his brother Gilbert. This institution, which had the advantages of a technical institute with those of a secondary modern school, had only been in existence for a few years and was quite up-to-date in its teaching and equipment. There was a large science lecture room and a laboratory in the basement, and there was also provision for lessons in such technical subjects as metallurgy, pattern-making, turning, fitting, forging, engineering, plumbing and sanitation. On the main floor there was a large assembly hall and four classrooms, with glass partitions, which allowed the headmaster a good view of what was going on. The headmaster, James Harris, known familiarly among the pupils as 'Boss' Harris, was a bearded patriarchal figure, with a pronounced paunch and a squeaky voice, whose movements were marked by the gravest dignity, even when wielding the cane, which he did with frequency and vigour.

According to Norman's cousin Henry Birkett, 'Boss' Harris was an outstanding headmaster and he had a first-class staff. Among the latter there was H. E. Brooks, known to the boys as 'Snobber' Brooks, the mathematics master, who would sometimes turn aside from the complexities of quadratic equations to discuss such out of the way topics as stag-hunting and the growing of a particular rose; there was 'Porkie' Gower, who taught chemistry and was credited with a particular passion for sulphuretted hydrogen because it 'smelt worst'; and there was Tom Hird, with whom the boys read English literature and who instilled into Norman Birkett a love for good prose and poetry which he never lost.

Of these assistant masters, perhaps Brooks was the most brilliant. Like the Birketts' father, 'Snobber' Brooks voted Liberal at elections, and he had a tremendous reverence for William Ewart Gladstone, the Liberal leader, who had been four times Prime Minister. Norman Birkett was in his last year at the school, when the Union Jack was flown at half-mast from the school flagpole to mark the passing of the 'Grand Old Man', and the mathematics master turned to Norman and said: 'The greatest man in all England is dead.'

One subject in which Norman always got high marks was Practical Chemistry. But he was not so interested in the theoretical branch of the subject, and his attention used sometimes to wander during 'Porkie' Gower's classes. Once, when the master caught him day-dreaming, he called him out in front of the class, and remarked with an air of heavy sarcasm: 'If you think you could give this lesson better than I can, Birkett, you'd better take my place.'

'I wouldn't mind having a shot at it,' the culprit replied, and so they changed places, Birkett taking the master's place behind his desk and the master sitting down with the other boys.

After questioning several of his school fellows in turn, Birkett put a question to the master, who answered it. 'Wrong,' said Norman. 'Come out for the stick.'

This remark produced a roar of laughter in the class. But the master now thought that the joke had gone too far. He thereupon resumed his customary role, and it was Norman who got the caning.

There were no boarders at the Barrow Higher Grade School, the day scholars being divided into 'town boys' and 'train boys'. The latter, which included Norman and his brother, numbered about fifty, and they made the journey each day by train from Ulverston, which covered the ten miles to Barrow in about half an hour, with only one intermediate stop, at Furness Abbey, where the railway company had a hotel. Norman soon became the leader of the 'train boys', and consequently something of a terror to the other passengers and the railway officials. The carriages consisted of several adjoining compartments, connected by a lavatory between the two communicating doors. The boys would often occupy these adjoining compartments and rival factions would raid each other's territory armed with cans of water and other lavatory furnishings. 'Copper-knob' Birkett was in the forefront of these forays, which were sometimes so boisterous that other passengers became apprehensive of travelling when the 'train boys' were on board. On other occasions, Norman would occupy a first class carriage, travelling on a third class ticket, and when the train approached Ulverston station would lean out of the window and shout 'Porter', Porter', in an affected southern drawl. This exhortation would send the station porters scurrying towards the door, expectant of a large tip for handling lots of baggage, while Norman would quietly open the door at the other side and jump out on to the line and make rapidly for home.

Like many schoolboys then and since, Norman Birkett indulged in some surreptitious smoking on the daily rail journey. Once, when leaning out of the window as the train was approaching Ulverston station and having a last few puffs of a cigarette, he was espied by the manager of the railway, who happened to be travelling in the guard's van, which in those days had a projecting window, which gave a full view of the length of the train. As the train drew to a stop, the manager quickly descended on to the platform, determined to catch young Birkett and haul him off to his father for punishment. But Norman had already seen the manager, and as a result he jumped out of the other side, ran under the station subway and so got safely home. However, he was eventually caught by his father with a pipe, which he had been smoking right up to the front door of his home and which he foolishly stuffed into the pocket of his jacket while it was still smouldering. The tell-tale smell proved his undoing. Whatever punishment followed must have been salutary, since his father had strictly forbidden him to smoke. Whatever it was, Norman Birkett did not smoke again as a schoolboy.

As befitted the leader of the 'train boys', he was up to all kinds of boyish pranks, by no means free from danger, and he was lucky to escape any serious accident. On one occasion, he alarmed an old lady in the same carriage, who had warned him against leaning out of the window, which he was doing, having pulled down the sash. Suddenly the train entered a tunnel and when it emerged several minutes later there was no sign of Norman. The old lady almost went into a fit of hysterics. In a few moments the train entered another tunnel, and when it emerged in due course, there was the mischievous boy sitting demurely in the opposite seat with an impish grin on his face. He had been hiding in the luggage rack above the old lady's head.

In those days, the railway coaches were lit by oil lamps, the lamp being let in to a hole in the roof of the compartment. They could be removed for cleaning and were attached to the base of the aperture by a short length of chain. Once he got several of the other boys to hoist him up on their shoulders, so that he could put his head through to the other side of the roof. However, his ears protruded so far that the feat proved impossible. It was just as well for Norman that they did, since his weight made the boys let go of him. Otherwise his ears might have been torn off, or he might even have been strangled. 'Me lugs were in t'way,' he used to say afterwards, laughingly describing the incident in the Ulverston dialect.

The Furness Abbey tunnel was the scene of another diverting episode. At the end of each day in school, homework questions were written up on the blackboard in the main classrooms, and the boys would distribute the work of copying them among each other. One boy, whose name was Lloyd, for some reason refused to part with the history questions, which meant that the others would be unable to prepare their history lesson. A beating seemed almost sure to follow, since the master was not inclined to accept any excuses. Fearing the vengeance of his companions, Master Lloyd deliberately got into a compartment where there was an adult passenger, a commercial traveller, and where he consequently felt fairly safe. Norman and the others entered the adjoining compartment, and after some discussion decided to chastise their erring classmate when the train was in the tunnel by 'roughing him up', and seizing his cap and satchel. The plan was duly put into execution. But unfortunately Norman and his friends attacked the wrong person, for when they had returned to their compartment they discovered they had the commercial traveller's check cap and sample case. A minute or two later, the irate commercial traveller appeared minus his collar and part of his shirt and there and then gave his assailants what he afterwards described as 'the finest hiding they'd ever had'.

The Barrow Higher Grade School was co-educational, and there were about twenty girls who made the train journey from Barrow as well as the boys. The girls also had their adventures. When Norman saw that one of them was being bullied by an older girl, he went out of his way to protect the younger one, an action which the latter always remembered. 'He was such a *balanced* boy,' another contemporary has recorded, 'such a compound of mischief and responsibility, politeness and spirit, courage and compassion, charm and simplicity. He could behave himself without being a prig. He could assert himself and yet consider the feelings of others. He had exceptional intellect and yet could enjoy the rough-and-tumble of a boy's life.' One of his school reports, which his father kept, shows that at Christmas, 1897, he stood seventh in his class of thirty-one boys. His two best subject were Spelling and Practical Chemistry ('Excellent'), while his two worst were Euclid and Algebra ('Poor'). Described as 'Good' were his Penmanship, Composition, French and Physics, both Theoretical and Practical. Attendance and attention to home work were both 'Excellent', and his conduct generally was described by the form master, Mr. Brooks, as 'Very Good', while the Headmaster agreed that he was 'a very bright and intelligent student'.

Day schools in those times did not provide their pupils with a midday meal, so that those boys who lived at some distance from school would bring a sandwich lunch with them. This they would eat in the Coffee House near the school, where they could buy a penny cup of tea or cocoa and, in summer, a bottle of ginger 'pop' to go with their sandwiches. After this quick meal, Norman and Gilbert would often fill in the remainder of the lunch break by going to the docks to see the ships, particularly when a vessel like H.M.S. *Powerful*, which was to be the largest armed cruiser in the world, was being built for the Royal Navy in the Vickers yard. Then there were the timber ships discharging their cargoes for the local paper-pulp factory and also the tramp steamers constantly coming and going. 'The sight of them,' Henry Birkett has recalled, 'stimulated our romantic ideas of a life of adventure.'

Gilbert, the elder brother, had set his mind on becoming a pharmaceutical chemist. But it was always assumed that Norman would go into his father's business, likewise his cousin Harry, whose father was also a draper. Indeed the two boys were considered to be among the lucky ones at school, having secure careers mapped out for them in advance. The only alternative, their respective parents had explained, was to 'go into the ship-yard'. Uncle Will, the eldest of old Mathew Birkett's sons, had done this and was now chief engineer in one of the Peninsular and Oriental Steamship Company's vessels. If they did not have any aptitude for engineering, then they might become draughtsmen. Neither Norman nor his cousin Henry fancied Vickers' yard. Nor for that matter were they particularly enthusiastic about the family businesses. But at least they were safe; the two boys would have the parental roof over their heads, and one day they might be in a position to take over the running of the businesses from their parents.

During the summer holidays in 1898, the last before he began his apprenticeship to 'the drapery', Norman Birkett had a narrow escape from drowning. With several other boys he went to bathe on Ulverston sands. Finding the tide was out, they waded across the channel near the viaduct, where they had undressed, to the sandbank on the other side. After playing about for some time, they saw that the tide was coming in fast and so they started to wade back towards the viaduct. But they found the sand slippery and anyhow the tide was too strong for them, so they were compelled to retrace their steps. Norman and most of the boys managed to reach the sandbank safely, though only just in time. One of the party got into difficulties and was dragged to safety by the others. But another was missing, a lad named Penny, whose father sat on the Ulverston Council with Thomas Birkett. They all thought that he had reached the other side, but in fact he was overwhelmed by the onrushing water. Norman and the others were eventually rescued by a fisherman; young Penny's body was recovered later. At the inquest the Coroner had some caustic things to say about the lack of warning signs; apparently there had been over twenty fatalities within a year. He added that the survivors had narrowly missed death.

Shortly after his fifteenth birthday, in the autumn of 1898, Norman Birkett entered his father's drapery business in Ulverston as an apprentice, at the modest weekly wage of four shillings.

5

Thomas Birkett already had three shops in Ulverston, two in Market Street, one for drapery and the other for millinery, and the third, for the tailoring side of his business, in New Market Street. (In his will Thomas Birkett described himself as 'tailor and draper'.) It was during Norman's first year as a draper's apprentice that his father began negotiations which resulted in the purchase of the large building in County Square, and which combined the separate drapery and millinery branches, subsequently becoming known as 'The County Stores'. The transfer has been recalled by Norman's cousin Henry. 'I well remember the day, with the sumptuous tea provided by my Aunt Agnes for the staff, who had done the removing!'

At this period County Square was almost in the country and Market Street still very much the commercial centre of the town, so it looked as if this was a speculative move. However, the speculation was justified, as the elder Birkett rightly foresaw the future development of Ulverston in that direction. In his first year in the new premises, the turnover increased by a thousand pounds. This may not seem a great deal today, but in fact it represented twelve and a half per cent. of the total sales at the previous three shops.

Meanwhile cousin Henry had joined the firm as an apprentice. He also kept the books, but received no additional pay as book-keeper, an apprentice's wage in the trade being then four shillings a week for the first year, five shillings for the second, six shillings for the third, seven-and-six for the fourth, and ten shillings for the fifth. Shop hours were long in those days, and when they were not serving behind the counter the apprentices spent many boring hours rolling calico, tying up parcels, untangling skeins of wool and clearing out the stockroom. 'If we are not fishing,' Thomas Birkett used to say, 'we are mending nets.' Henry Birkett has recalled that Norman's father was 'a great disciplinarian and with a true Victorian sense of duty saw that Norman and I were not favoured in any way because we were "in the family" '.

Business was naturally at its briskest on the weekly Market Day, when the farmers and their wives would come into town to shop. The wives would sell the farm produce, such as butter and eggs, and by custom would keep the proceeds which they spent on housekeeping. This was always a good opportunity for the drapers to dispose of their oddments and remnants. To stimulate sales the custom in the Birkett shops was for a small sum known in the vernacular as a 'spiff', usually a penny or a halfpenny, to be marked on the sales ticket. On effecting a sale the assistant or apprentice would keep the ticket and duly receive the amount marked as a special commission. On market days Norman would set himself a target of half-a-crown or even five shillings. He usually reached it, and invariably did so with a certain woman customer who had a weakness for remnants and bargains. She would come from the remote hamlet where she lived in the early autumn to get sewing materials for the long winter nights and would buy considerable quantities of shirtings, towellings, flannels and flannelettes, skirtings and calico, all for the garments she was going to make at home. 'Ready made' clothing was still quite a novelty in the shops. Henry Birkett and the other apprentices used to listen to Norman's 'sales talk' with admiration. 'It was an anticipation of modern advertising methods,' according to his cousin, 'much imagination mixed with the description of the goods, not all of it strictly true.'

The firm employed two 'travellers', who were more or less

constantly 'on the road' with samples. They would send in their orders twice weekly for despatch to the outlying country districts by carrier. 'In a shop like my uncle's,' Henry Birkett has recalled, 'a good proportion of the business was done on credit in this way, and I know the amount owing was often very heavy—too heavy, I thought for the total annual business. In the days before the First World War our gross profits were very low and I suppose we managed to make the business pay by the smallness of the wages paid and the strictly economical expenses.'

Sometimes the two cousins were in a state of mutual enmity, but on the whole they were good friends both at work and play, in spite of Norman's liking for practical jokes at the other's expense. Once, in the shop, they joined forces in a window dressing competition which had been organized by a firm of women's corset manufacturers. The cousins' joint effort, which incidentally won the prize of two guineas, was the occasion for one of Norman's characteristic jokes. The central feature of the display was a pair of the firm's rustless corsets immersed in water. Thus it was necessary to procure a container, and the boys decided that the best thing for this purpose would be the kind of glass dome then extensively used to cover artificial flowers placed on graves. Henry was accordingly despatched to a local florist to borrow one of these articles. After some argument the florist consented to part with it but only after repeated warnings that the utmost care must be taken of his property and that Henry must pay for it in the event of its being damaged or broken. Henry retailed these admonitions to Norman as soon as he got back to the shop. He then handed the article over to his cousin to clean, whereupon Norman disappeared downstairs to the cellar. A few minutes later Henry was horrified to hear the sounds of breaking glass. With visions of having lost at least one month's wages, he rushed below to discover the worst. There was his cousin Norman sprawled across several rolls of carpet which were stored in the cellar, 'laughing immoderately and broken pieces of glass everywhere'. Then Henry suddenly realized that the glass belonged to some other quite worthless object and that the precious graveside covering was intact!

On another occasion, a customer who did some spare-time soldiering left in his volunteer's scarlet tunic to be repaired or 'let out'. One of the other shop workers 'dared' Norman to put on the tunic and walk down Market Street to the tailoring branch. Norman accepted a wager of sixpence and set off in his borrowed plumes. The first person he met in the street was his father who eyed him sternly but otherwise gave no sign of recognition and passed on in silence.

On one or two nights a week after the day's work in the shop was finished, Norman would go to night-school classes, where he studied a variety of subjects from shorthand to physiology. He also began to read English literature and he went in for literary competitions of the kind which had been pioneered by the Harmsworth brothers in their publications, and he contributed articles to the local press. Indeed he was barely seventeen when he scored his first success in open competition and was awarded a prize by the local journal *The Ulverston Advertiser* for an article on 'How to Attract Visitors to Ulverston'. His suggestions included railway excursions from Manchester—there were none available to the day tourist at that time—the composition of a booklet setting forth the attractions of the town, the provision of adequate sea bathing facilities, coaching and driving tours in the area, and suitable amusements in Ulverston, such as concerts and band performances in the open air. Excellent ideas, which were all in due course discussed by Councillor Birkett and his colleagues on the Urban District Council.

But it was not all hard work for the two industrious apprentices. They both had successes in various literary competitions and the prize money they won was put into a holiday fund, augmented from parental sources and drawn upon when occasion demanded. One such occasion was the International Exhibition held in Glasgow in 1901, when the Birkett cousins made up a party with another Ulverston draper and his son and a very progressive local printer who had recently acquired a linotype machine which had greatly impressed them. From Glasgow the party took a trip to the Trossachs, taking in Loch Katrine and Loch Lomond. This excursion used up most of the two Birketts' spare cash, so that they had to sit by the loch shore eating buns from a paper bag while the others went to a nearby hotel for a three-and-sixpenny lunch, which (in Henry's words) 'looked an awful lot of money to us'. An even more costly excursion, amounting to a guinea or so, obliged the cousins to cry off and content themselves with a cheap trip down the Clyde to Rothesay, where they searched for Sir Thomas Lipton's yacht

Shamrock among the boats moored in the river. They all returned by way of Edinburgh, where they saw the sights, and Henry, who had brought his camera along, took a photograph of Norman on the Parade Ground in Edinburgh Castle.

The visit to Scotland cemented the friendship between the cousins. They would debate possible future holidays and tours, only a few of which were to materialize, since, to quote Henry again, 'lack of funds generally put paid to our dreams'. They would both have liked to go up to London for the coronation of King Edward VII, just as they would have liked to see Queen Victoria's funeral. But both these projects were ruled out on grounds of expense. However, Norman was able to see the new sovereign and his beautiful consort during their short tour in the spring of 1902, when the King and Queen on board the royal yacht *Victoria and Albert* called at the Isle of Man and a local steamship company ran a three-day boat trip from Barrow to Douglas for the occasion.

On his return home, Norman Birkett wrote an article for *The Ulverston Advertiser*, while the scene in Douglas was fresh in his mind.

> The clock fingers slowly crept on, until at five-fifty, right at the top of Buck's Road, a forest of hats rose, and a wild tumultuous cheer ran slowly down the long dense line. Then the livery of the coachmen appeared, and presently the open landau was coming down the road. For some reason the King did not stay at the House of Keys, and as the road was blocked the Royal carriage perforce had to stop.
>
> I had a magnificent view of the King. I was so near that I could have touched the Royal carriage. The King was lifting his hat all the time during this stoppage, and I had a splendid opportunity of noting his appearance. He wore a light grey overcoat and a light grey felt hat. His face appeared to me to be very grave, and though, of course a smile played upon his features, yet the eyes looked so deeply grave, and his whole look appeared to me to be careworn.
>
> And the Queen! Truly a queen, 'a lady with the secret of perennial beauty'. She was bowing from side to side, smiling graciously and looking radiantly happy.
>
> It is impossible for me to adequately describe my feelings.

> To have seen my Sovereign, to have been so near to note the minutest particulars! Truly this was a scene of a life-time. The blood quickened within me, and I felt an indescribable thrill, and as the carriage moved off, I raised my weather-beaten Panama and cheered for very excess of feeling. Then a short cut through the back streets, and a hard run the full length of the electric car station, where boarding an electric saloon, the greatest monarch of the earth passed out of sight, smiling to the last, amid a cheer, the like of which I have never heard, and the uppermost thought of everybody's heart was—The King, God Bless Him.

Councillor Thomas Birkett was Chairman of the Ulverston Council that year, and in this capacity made elaborate preparations to celebrate the King's Coronation, which was due to take place in June, about two months after the Royal visit to the Isle of Man. Norman and Harry were allowed time off from work to put up flags and bunting in profusion outside the shop in County Square. Then one morning, shortly before the appointed date, Thomas Birkett returned to the shop from a Council meeting and told the boys to take everything down as the King was to have an operation for appendicitis and the Coronation was postponed. Eventually the celebrations were ordered to go on, which they did in somewhat muted fashion, at least in Ulverston, and the King recovered sufficiently to attend the ceremony in the following August.

It was about this time that Norman Birkett became a local preacher on the Ulverston Methodist circuit. At first, he went the round with an established preacher, being provided with what was colloquially known as 'a note to preach' and gaining experience. His admission in due course as a fully-fledged lay preacher was welcome, since the Ulverston circuit was a scattered one, extending from Askham on the borders of Cumberland to Arnside in Westmorland. 'Between these two extremes we have thirteen preaching places in all,' young Birkett noted at the time; 'some standing in quiet country lanes, where the music of the river that runs nearby can almost be heard in the pauses of the sermon; some standing close to the borders of the voiceful sea, and others erected in the midst of comparatively large populations.' The circuit had been founded in 1810, and 'it is a fact upon which we pride ourselves that the first minister stationed here, the Rev. John Bedford', who incidentally built the first Wesleyan Chapel in Ulverston, 'became, in due course, President of the Conference'. However, the circuit had to rely principally on the 'locals' for conducting the chapel services, many of whom were farmers. One wonderful preacher, whom Norman Birkett long remembered, was said to be unable to read or write and was commonly supposed to memorize the lessons from the Bible.

His cousin Harry Birkett, who used to accompany the new preacher, has recalled how popular he soon became on the circuit and how greatly he was sought after. He seemed to have derived considerable help from the compositions of the great Methodist preacher, Morley Punshon, whose published lectures he found an invaluable standby. Writing to a friend in 1950, Norman Birkett remarked: 'I have a MS. book of sermons I preached some forty-five years ago, and I was interested in looking through it again to see that there were many passages from Punshon of a highly rhetorical nature incorporated in the sermons without the slightest acknowledgement of their source. My country congregations must have been astonished at the range of my vocabulary and the majesty of some of my sentences.' This was certainly the effect they had on his cousin, who has recorded how the preacher once referred in a Harvest Festival sermon to 'the superb theocracy of the Levitical economy'. But he quickly became an established success in the circuit. He took great pains in the preparation of his sermons, which he wrote out word for word, practising their delivery in the privacy of his room at home.

'In view of his subsequent career,' his cousin has noted, 'there is no doubt that this early experience of the power of the spoken word led to the development of his great gifts. Norman was a very good singer and often sang "gospel songs" when he was "planned" at the country chapels and this added to his popularity.'

In the Connexional Local Preachers' Examination for the year 1904, in which he was one of one hundred and fifty candidates from all over England and Wales, the name of W. N. Birkett was bracketed first in the Honours List. These successes seemed clearly to point the way to a ministerial vocation for Norman Birkett, and his father was quite agreeable to his devoting his whole time to studying at home to achieve it, for by this time the elder Birkett had come to the conclusion that his son would 'never make a good draper'.

'When at the age of twenty-two I left my father's business,'

Norman afterwards wrote, 'it was with the firm intention of entering the Wesleyan Methodist Ministry. . . . The sermons I preached in the chapels of the Ulverston circuit were apparently acceptable to the congregations. . . . To be a Wesleyan Minister and perhaps one day become President of the Conference was a sufficient ambition at that time.'

6

His father gave Norman a room of his own in Nithsdale to work in, and here he began to prepare for the Ministry. At first he felt very lonely after the companionship of the shop, as he plunged into the details of Biblical history and theology. But he soon found a compensation when he began to form a modest collection of books, 'my dear little library as a young man' he called it, looking back long afterwards. They included Palgrave's *Golden Treasury*, George Saintsbury's *Short History of English Literature*, Ruskin's *Sesame and Lilies*, A. W. Kinglake's *Eothen*, most of the works of Froude, Macaulay, Matthew Arnold, Thackeray, Dickens and Hazlitt, *John Halifax, Gentleman* by Mrs. Craik, and *The Private Papers of Henry Ryecroft* by George Gissing—this last work with its expressive descriptions of the English countryside was a particular favourite. George Gissing, as he afterwards found Henry Ryecroft to be, appealed to him most, because, as Birkett put it, 'he was a book-lover through and through, and was a believer in a library of one's own, although he was so poor that he had to starve himself to buy a book he wanted.' What first stimulated his interest in English literature was a paper he heard a local Church of England clergyman read on 'The Pleasures of the Imagination'. About the same time his father gave him a copy of Archbishop Trench's book *On the Study of Words* which he read and reread many times. Besides Gissing, the contemporary novelists who most attracted him were R. L. Stevenson, Rudyard Kipling, Thomas Hardy and J. M. Barrie. Indeed he started a correspondence with Barrie and used to lecture on his fiction to the local Mutual Improvement Societies.

His most popular literary lecture, however, was on Charles Dickens, for whom his admiration remained life-long. He first gave it at Arnside, where he used to go to be coached by the local Methodist minister, the Rev. C. E. Bedale. 'Grand time. Room full. Spoke fifty minutes. Many commendations,' he noted in the diary he began to keep at this period. He was often to repeat this lecture with similar success during the next few years. His skill as an interpreter of Dickens also found expression in the series of 'Dickens Competitions', which were then a feature of *T.P.'s Weekly*, the popular literary journal which was edited by the Irish Nationalist M.P., T. P. O'Connor, and sold for a penny. In these contests Norman Birkett seems to have carried off most of the awards. One of his successful contributions, on Dickens' 'local colour', brought him an enthusiastic letter from a Church of Ireland clergyman, which Birkett carefully preserved. 'I read the eight essays, some of which were very good,' wrote the Rev. L. Ackland from Mitchelstown, Co. Cork, 'but yours left me such a genuine glow of pleasure that I felt I should like to write and say so. In the very limited space of 180 words you have caught the great wide living charm of the most human and tender of all our writers.'[1]

Besides his preaching and lecturing, Norman Birkett joined the Liberal Party—his father was President of the Ulverston Liberal Club—and began to speak at Liberal meetings in the North Lonsdale constituency. The sitting Member, the Hon. R. F. Cavendish, later Lord Richard Cavendish, had originally been elected as a Liberal-Unionist under the leadership of Joseph Chamberlain with Conservative support. But he had disagreed with Chamberlain's tariff reform policy, and in the General Election which took place at the end of 1905 he stood as a Liberal and Free Trader against the official Conservative and Unionist Candidate who had been adopted

[1] DICKEN'S 'LOCAL COLOUR'

I am not at all certain that Dickens introduced any 'local colour' into his work in the ordinary connotation of that term.

The name of Hardy brings visions of Wessex loam; the name of Thackeray—wigs and wimples; but the name of Dickens brings visions of—what? Windy autumn nights; blazing village forges; thronging, surging streets; winding country roads; quiet village inns; ivy-covered churches; but they do not belong to any well-defined locality; they belong to the broad, universal world.

Dickens, then, had this supreme power: he made the 'local' universal, but he also made the 'universal' local. He took scenes, strange and unfamiliar, and, by his wizardry, made them the familiar scenes of all men.

The market-day in *Chuzzlewit* is the market-day of every place; the Spitalfields and Bethnal Green of *All the Year Round* are as our native air; and we find Gadshill Lanes running past our very doors.

Thus, in reading, we are not conscious of 'local colour'; we only find a subtle delineation of places, in which, as wayfarers, we sojourn.

in his place. Norman Birkett organized his meetings and campaigned vigorously for him in the Ulverston area. Although the election resulted in a Liberal landslide throughout much of the country, the Conservatives succeeded in winning the North Lonsdale seat.

After it was all over, the defeated candidate wrote to his young supporter in Ulverston:

St. George's Hill,
Byfleet,
Weybridge.
January 28, 1906

Dear Mr. Birkett,

Just a line to thank you very much indeed for all that you did for me during the Election. I cannot say how much I appreciated the way you worked, and I am sure you will feel almost as disappointed as I do at the result.

I am very grateful to you for the manner in which you organized the meetings; they were all arranged extremely well, and they went off without a hitch.

I am so sorry to think that your first experience in political work should have met with a reverse, but I hope it will not discourage you from taking an active part in the future.

My wife wishes to join with me in thanking you for all that you have done for us. Will you please also thank your father from us both for his very practical support and sympathy. I hope that we shall in the future have an opportunity of working together again.

I am,
Yours very truly,
R. CAVENDISH

In fact, Cavendish had been greatly impressed by Norman's appearances at the various meetings at which he spoke, and in view of his obvious abilities and attractions as a public speaker it seemed to him that the young man should go to the Bar. The next time he saw Thomas Birkett, he mentioned the idea to him, and he repeated it to Norman. But at that time the Bar was a profession about which neither Norman nor his father had the slightest knowledge. Anyhow Norman was quite happy to carry on working for the Methodist Ministry, and this was what the elder Birkett also wished. Although

Thomas Birkett had sat on the magistrates' bench when Chairman of the Urban District Council and his son had occasionally been in the Ulverston Police Court, Norman had never heard a barrister plead a case in a superior court until one day, early in 1907, when he happened to be in Manchester and the Assizes were being held. There for the first time he heard part of a criminal trial and saw the prisoner stand up in the dock and the judge sentence him to seven years penal servitude. 'Awful!' he noted in his diary. The experience haunted him for days afterwards and distracted him from his theological studies.

At the first quarterly meeting of the Ulverston Methodist Circuit held in the same year, Norman Birkett was warmly recommended as a candidate for the Ministry, and it was decided to send forward his name to the Wesleyan Conference. Nevertheless the decision worried him and he wondered whether it was the wise thing to do. His doubts seem to have stemmed from purely mundane causes. He was peculiarly susceptible to the charms of the opposite sex and at this time had several sweethearts whom he courted with enthusiasm and even delight. One of them, a girl called Frida, who was still at school, he had met on the hockey field and he had fallen violently in love with her. He confided his doubts and heartaches to his diary.

> *Easter Monday: April* 1, 1907 . . . How very irrevocable everything seems! It is so very, very hard to believe that the governance of the world is in the hands of a loving God! Help me! Or I perish!

*

> *April* 3 . . . My life is one long battling with an aching heart. God! How very dark the valley is!

*

> *April* 6 . . . Saw Frida at night and after I left her the old impending dread came with a frightful intensity. If the Ministry means giving up illicit delights, such as seeing Frida in a clandestine meeting under the wall, or kissing her dear, dear lips in the starlight, then the Ministry must be put upon one side. I do not believe that God intended me to forego delights such as these. They are a tiny fragment of Heaven sent into my lonely soul: the fruits of earth are well lost for such things. . . .

It was Frida's last term at Springfield Girl's School, and she was soon to leave to finish her education in Germany. Norman felt the parting very keenly and his anguish found expression in a stream of sentimental verses which he sent anonymously to the *Ulverston Advertiser* and which that journal was pleased to publish.

Today my Lady went away,
And, with her, went the light of day:
There was no sunshine anywhere,
I could but grimly stand and stare
Down the forsaken, garden way.

Fortunately the Methodist Minister at Arnside, Charles Bedale, who was coaching Norman in Biblical History and Hebrew, now put up a novel suggestion which strongly impressed his pupil and to some extent, at least, turned his attention from his departed love. He was shortly due to take his qualifying examination for the Ministry, said Bedale. Why not then go up to Cambridge and read for a degree in History and Theology? The idea immediately appealed to Norman. He already knew something of the University and its atmosphere from having corresponded with A. C. Benson, Fellow and later Master of Magdalene College, whose *From a College Window* and other literary studies had made a deep impression on his mind. So Norman invited the Minister over to Ulverston to have a talk with his father at Nithsdale.

'If Norman goes up to Cambridge, will he go into the Ministry?' Thomas Birkett asked. 'Why not?' replied Bedale. 'I did.' The upshot of this conversation was that Thomas Birkett agreed to finance the project if the University would take his son, since Norman would soon be twenty-four and thus somewhat older than was usual for admission as an undergraduate. It was decided that he should apply to Emmanuel College, a choice no doubt dictated by the ecclesiastical aims of the pious founder of this society, where so many theologians and divines had been educated. In due course, the college authorities, having satisfied themselves from Bedale on the score of academic attainments, agreed to admit him provided that he passed the college entrance examination. He was also informed that he would have to take the University's Previous Examination or 'Little Go', if he wished to work for a Tripos.

Several months of intensive 'cramming' with Bedale followed.

'I worked hard and steadily,' Norman recalled later, 'but I had left school at fifteen and had spent seven years behind the counter of my father's shop. . . . To learn enough New Testament Greek and Classical Greek and Latin for the examination was no easy matter.' But Bedale, whom his pupil described as 'young, handsome and scholarly', was an excellent coach. After leaving Cambridge he had studied under Dr. James Moulton, the distinguished Orientalist, who was regarded as the foremost expert in New Testament Greek, in which subject he was tutor at the Wesleyan College, Didsbury, Manchester; Bedale now hoped that Birkett too would eventually be guided by Moulton.[1] In fact, Birkett was soon to make Moulton's acquaintance, when he went to Didsbury in July, 1907, to take the Preliminary Examination for candidates for the Wesleyan Ministry. The written part lasted for two days, the first being devoted to papers on theology and the Bible and the second to literature, which included English, French, German, History and Geography. On the third day there was an oral examination, at the conclusion of which he was told that he had passed with distinction, having secured eighty-seven per cent. in the theological and biblical papers and seventy-two per cent. in the literary subjects. 'Many commendations,' he proudly noted in his diary, after despatching telegrams to his father and Bedale. Shortly afterwards, he received a letter from the secretary of the Wesleyan Conference to the effect that his 'offer for the Ministry' had been accepted and that he had been given permission to go to the University for three years.

There remained the hurdle of getting into the Cambridge college to be overcome in the following October. This is how Birkett recalled it in the fragment of the autobiography which he wrote fifty years later:

> I remember most vividly the morning I set out for Cambridge to take the Entrance Examination at Emmanuel College. I had a large leather trunk with my initials painted upon it, and in the trunk were all the things the College had said it was

[1] James Hope Moulton (1863–1917), who was a nephew of the judge John Fletcher Moulton, later Lord Moulton, was drowned during the First World War, when the ship in which he was returning from India was torpedoed in the Mediterranean. From 1908 until his death he was Greenwood Professor of Hellenistic Greek and Indo-European Philology in the University of Manchester. He was also a noted Iranian scholar and exponent of Zoroastrianism.

necessary to provide, such as silver-ware. My father had had them all engraved with my initials, some of which I still possess, because, dear man, he never dreamed that his son might fail to pass the examination and so have to come back home again. But I remember that morning for the sense of great responsibility that rested on me, and for the terrible sense of homesickness I experienced as I went down Station Hill to the train which was to take me to Bletchley where I would change for Cambridge.

I was given rooms in the main court at Emmanuel looking out on the lovely Wren front of the college chapel, and for several days sat in the lecture room taking the Entrance Examination.

The entrants were seated in alphabetical order, and the name of the man next to Birkett was Bellerby. Alfred Bellerby was to remember his companion for long afterwards as a rather tall, lanky young man with a north country accent and red hair.

Strolling out into Emmanuel Paddock in an interval between papers, Birkett asked Bellerby what his ambition was on coming up to Cambridge. After some coaxing, Bellerby admitted with not much conviction that it was to get a 'Blue'.

'What's yours?' he countered.

Without any hesitation, Birkett replied: 'To be President of the Union.'

Later that week, the list of successful candidates was posted on the college screen and Birkett scanned it nervously. When he saw that his name was there, he ran all the way to the Post Office to telegraph the good news to his father, 'who had done so much for me'.

Both Birkett's and Bellerby's ambitions were destined to be fulfilled. Bellerby indeed achieved a 'Double Blue', while Birkett in due course was elected to the office on which he had set his heart.

CHAPTER II

CAMBRIDGE AND BIRMINGHAM

I

WITH its particular religious and clerical tradition, Emmanuel College appeared a thoroughly congenial place for any young man who like Norman Birkett was thinking of the Ministry as a career. The oldest portion of the college buildings had once formed part of a Dominican Friary in Cambridge and the college itself had been founded by a Low Churchman, Sir Walter Mildmay, who was Chancellor of the Exchequer in the reign of the first Queen Elizabeth, his object being to provide a school for the education and training of clergy of the Reformed Church in England, 'that from this seed-ground the English Church might have those that she can summon to instruct the people and undertake the office of pastors, which is a thing necessary above all others'. The story is related of the founder that, on his return to court after opening the college in 1585, the Queen said to him, 'Sir Walter, I hear that you have erected a Puritan foundation.' To which he replied, 'No, Madam; far be it from me to countenance anything contrary to your established laws; but I have set an acorn which, when it becomes an oak, God alone knows what will be the fruit thereof.' The college's internationally best known son, as Birkett soon discovered, was John Harvard, who gave his name to the university in Cambridge, Massachusetts, which bears his name.

At the time Birkett became an undergraduate, the Master of Emmanuel was William Chawner, who had the reputation of being an atheist. He was the first lay head of the college to be appointed, his predecessors having invariably been clergy of the Established Church and having included among their number the celebrated William Sancroft, the Archbishop of Canterbury who defied the power of King James II, and as leader of the 'Seven Bishops' was imprisoned with his colleagues in the Tower of London. (Sancroft also presented the greater part of his fine collection of printed books and manuscripts, including an extremely valuable MS. of Herodotus, to the College Library, of which Birkett was to make considerable use during his time at Emmanuel.) Apart from an invitation to breakfast in the company of the other freshmen of his year, Birkett saw very little of the Master except when he appeared at dinner in hall. But he frequently came across the Senior Tutor and Chaplain, the Rev. F. W. Head, who was responsible for the undergraduate teaching of History.[1]

Birkett later described his first experiences as a freshman at Cambridge in the following words:

> After the Entrance Examination at the College I sat for the Little Go, and in the following term I took what was called the Additional Subjects. Then I settled down to the college life. I had decided on Bedale's advice to read History, but although I enjoyed reading history I soon realized that I was not the material out of which scholars are made. I was much too interested in too many things.
>
> First of all, there was the College Debating Society and the Union. I was, of course, a few years older than most of the undergraduates and I had had some experience in public speaking. When, therefore, I made my first speech at the Freshmen's Debate at the College Debating Society I had a very gratifying reception. It was a political debate and as I was an ardent Liberal I spoke I suppose with conviction; but I had taken pains with the things I intended to say and the form of the speech I was to make. I became a regular attender at the debates, taking part at judicious intervals and becoming in time the Secretary and then the Vice-President. . . .
>
> But it was the Union on which my ambition was set.

Incidentally, Birkett made no deliberate attempt to change his northern accent; when he went up to Cambridge and began to take part in discussion groups and debates, he found that he automatically slipped into what he called 'the ordinary groove of standard English'.

[1] Frederick Waldegrave Head (1874–1941) afterwards became Chaplain to King George V and subsequently Archbishop of Melbourne.

As he was later to express it, 'had I tried to force my accent away, it would have been the most lamentable thing I could have done. Nothing is worse than the artificial veneer some people adopt in order, they think, to give an impression of breeding and education. Exaggerated speech in order to create an effect is ridiculous.'

Like its Oxford counterpart, the Cambridge Union Society, founded in 1815, has enjoyed a special reputation as an undergraduate debating society and has been linked with many of the foremost names in British public life. No wonder, therefore, that Norman Birkett was ambitious to become its President. The man who had occupied the presidential chair in the previous term and was still up in Birkett's first year was a brilliant speaker, F. D. Livingstone, destined to be killed fighting in France in the First World War.[1]

> I myself came to the University a little later than most men. I was twenty-four years of age. I did not bring much with me, for I had little to bring. But I had some knowledge of a certain kind of public speaking, and a close acquaintance with the cadences of the Authorized Version of the Bible. When I first attended the Union debates I heard speaking of a kind I had never heard before. When I first saw and heard F. D. Livingstone I sat under a kind of spell. He had the prestige that belonged to Ex-Presidents, and revealed the beauty and power of the spoken word in the most memorable way. . . .
>
> I was content for some time to attend the debates with complete regularity but to take no part in them. Truth to tell I was a little overawed. This splendid arena was somewhat different from any previous speaking of mine. In my first year I heard many Ex-Presidents with the same kind of prestige about them, men like J. K. Mozley, J. M. Keynes, H. G. Wood, A. C. Pigou and others. I remember a speech made by Pigou on the subject of tariffs as a memorable example of the highest quality of sheer debating. He annihilated the previous speaker, and at the end of the closely-reasoned speech he ended with a peroration that I can quote to this day, and which roused the House to the wildest enthusiasm.[2]

[1] F. D. Livingstone was a brother of Sir Richard Livingstone, the classical scholar and President of Corpus Christi College, Oxford.

[2] Cited by Percy Cradock: *Recollections of the Cambridge Union* (1953), pp. 95–6.

The Union had its own premises, including a smoking room, library and a debating hall arranged somewhat on the model of the House of Commons, with the President taking the place of the Speaker, and serried rows of benches facing each other for the members, while visitors including women, who were not then admitted to membership, were accommodated in the galleries. Debates were held every Tuesday during term time, beginning at 8.15 p.m. and lasting until towards midnight. The four principal speakers, occasionally increased by visiting politicians and guests from other universities, whose names appeared 'on the paper', as the agenda was called, took up the time until about ten o'clock when the House would be open to general discussion of the motion being debated. A newcomer seldom had a chance of 'catching the President's eye' and being called upon to speak before eleven o'clock, and as a rule had to confine his remarks to not more than five minutes. But if he acquitted himself reasonably well, he would be called again at future debates, where continued success would justify his being proposed for membership of the six-man committee responsible for the general running of the Union's business. The candidates for the Committee were elected by ballot, and a committee member would in due course run for the offices of Secretary, Vice-President and President, which were held for one term.

Birkett made his maiden speech at the Union in his second term when he spoke to the motion 'That this House would welcome the Disestablishment of the Church of England', proposed by Hugh Dalton of King's, the future Labour politician and a leading member of the University Fabian Society. Birkett spoke twelfth, and, although he was not called until after eleven o'clock, he was satisfied with the result judging by the entry in his diary: 'Good I think. Feel rather happy.'[1] *The Cambridge Review* described his contribution as 'a most interesting speech', and he was further encouraged when he read the account of the debate in the undergraduate journal *Granta* a few days later: 'Mr. Birkett (Emmanuel) tried to be impartial. We hope to see such a rare phenomenon as an impartial critic on the paper.'

Mozley made a career in the Church, becoming Canon of St. Paul's Cathedral; Keynes, later Lord Keynes, was the well-known banker; Wood became the first Professor of Divinity at Birmingham University; and Pigou was Professor of Political Economy at Cambridge for thirty-five years.

[1] February 11, 1908.

He did not speak again at the Union during his first year, although he did try without success on one occasion to catch the President's eye. But he was busy in other directions. He preached regularly on the Cambridge Methodist 'circuit' and also at the Leys School. He read papers at the Mildmay Club, the college literary society, and he also sang at the college concert, when he was encored six times and the Rev. F. W. Head came up to him and said: 'I am proud to be your tutor.' Thus by the end of his second term he had already made his mark at Emmanuel.

So far as physical recreation was concerned he played rugby football and golf. He also tried rowing but dropped it when he realized that he had not the makings of a good oar. In the summer he preferred to go for walks rather than play cricket, a sport in which he was to take a very considerable interest in later life, but for which he showed no aptitude at Cambridge.

With others who were reading in the Historical Tripos, he took the customary inter-collegiate examination at the end of his first year. On the eve of the examination, he wrote to his father a letter in which he described his work and academic prospects.

Emmanuel College,
Cambridge.
May 31, 1908

. . . I welcome this opportunity of being able to write to you without anyone else seeing it, because I want to put the position with reference to the Exams. quite clearly.

In the first place, it is just one year since I commenced working for the University at all, and that after an arduous six months preparing for my ministerial examination. Since then I have passed the Greek and Latin Exams., the Mathematical Previous, and advanced French. The Exams. of this week in History comprise:

1. Ancient Greece from 3000 B.C. to 318 B.C.
2. Greco-Macedonian History from 318–167 B.C.
3. Roman History from 2000 B.C. to A.D. 423.

All this is included in one paper of six questions, to be answered in three hours. So it may well be that I shall get a question or two I know nothing about: on the other hand I may be fortunate.

Then we have a paper on English Economic History, which includes Industrial, Agricultural and Commercial History from the Roman Occupation to the Budgets of Mr. Gladstone.

Then we have a paper on our Special Period, which is of course the Liberal Movement in France and Southern Europe from 1815–1830. In connection with this, there are three huge French authorities which have to be known, Chateaubriand, Metternich and Gentz. They have nearly 3,000 pages altogether, but we only get five paragraphs, so luck is operative there too.

Then we have the Essay, and Economic Theory.

That, in outline, is the scope of the Exam., which commences at nine o'clock on Friday. At four o'clock on Saturday all will be over, for good or ill.

Well, in Economic History I should do—*Well.*
In Liberal Movement I should do—*Very Well.*
In Essay I should do—*Excellently.*
But in Ancient History—*Well.*

Seventy per cent. is wanted in every paper for a first, and eighty per cent. for a first with Scholarship. You must remember that *no firsts at all* were given last year, and a *second* in this exam. means an almost certain first in the Tripos next June: and furthermore that my Greek kept me back last Michaelmas.

Only one Scholarship is given at Emmanuel, and there are fifteen of us trying for it, but our marks are given in comparison with men from Trinity, Caius, Pembroke, etc. Personally I am regarded as the most likely candidate for the Scholarship, but there are two men, who, in my judgment have a better chance. . . . Of course, if nobody gets eighty per cent., nobody gets a Scholarship.

Now I think I have put the matter fairly before you. I have thought of nothing else for some time, and I am beginning to feel the continuous strain of eighteen months hard brain work. I had hoped that if I worked hard and got a Scholarship I might with a good conscience spend some money on a good holiday somewhere. But it is an increasing burden to me that I am helpless and earning no money. I have never worked harder in my life than since I left the shop, and although I have some honours at Emmanuel which I prize dearly, yet one feels so useless. The fact of Harry's approaching marriage only emphasizes the isolation of my position. But as Browning says—

> 'God's in his Heaven.
> All's right with the world.'

Don't think I am complaining at all: I shall have to thank you whilst my body has breath for all you have done for me—both things that I knew, and things that I knew not: things remembered and things forgotten: things numbered and things numberless.

But I have a growing feeling that I am a dead weight, a burden to you.

But if God gives me Health and Strength the coming years may alter the situation. In any case, nothing can ever shake my sense of debt and loyalty to yourself.

You will not forget me on Friday morning I know, and I, I *shall do my best*!

To God I leave all the rest. . . .

P.S. Upon reflection, taking everything into consideration, I think I should get a good second, and *with very great luck*, a first. . . .

P.P.S. My Mildmay Essay was a very great success. I had to entertain members to coffee, fruit, cake, etc., though.

In the result he got a 'second' so missing the Scholarship. So also did the two other Emmanuel men who he thought were more likely winners.

2

Birkett returned to Cambridge at the beginning of his second year, determined to work harder than ever and full of ambitious plans. He put down the following four resolutions in his diary:

Resolved—

1. To work a good eight hours a day.
2. To read, at least, a book per week.
3. To win everything I can lay hands on.
4. To remember why I am at the University, and to seize every opportunity.

He began the term well by being elected top of the Emmanuel Debating Society's Committee. A week later he spoke at the Union in a debate on Home Rule for Ireland.[1] The note he put in his diary afterwards ('Good, I think. Feel happy about it.') was endorsed by *Granta*, which observed: 'Mr. Birkett (Emmanuel) has a good vocabulary and a wide grasp of quotations. . . . He should certainly speak again, and incidentally much louder.' He evidently heeded this advice, as he did speak again, in the following month, on 'The Liberty of the Press', to such effect that *Granta* wrote that he 'should be put on the paper without delay'.[2] A few days later, at an inter-collegiate debate with Caius College, Arnold McNair of Caius, who was Secretary of the Union, agreed to propose him for the Committee at the end-of-term elections.[3] In the event, he was not one of the first six in the poll and so was not elected. But McNair, with whom he had become friendly and who was favourably impressed by his backbench performances, got him 'put on the paper' at the first debate in the following term. He spoke third, in support of the motion which condemned the recent action of the House of Lords in rejecting the Licensing Bill after it had been passed by a large Liberal majority in the Commons.[4] 'Great success,' he noted briefly in his diary, while *Granta* wrote: 'Mr. Birkett is to be congratulated on his first appearance on the paper. His matter was good, and his vocabulary better, but he should show a little more emotion.'

He seems to have rectified the omission during the succeeding months, when he spoke on such subjects as cruelty in sport ('Mr. Birkett seemed angry'), secular education ('He is becoming one of our best speakers'), the partisan tactics of the Conservative Opposition in the House of Commons on the Navy ('He was at his best'). When the motion, 'That this House is of the opinion that the Kaiser is a menace to the peace of Europe', was debated, he spoke against it ('Mr. Birkett made his points very concisely and clearly'), remarking that its supporters had not tried to realize the German point of view and that 'the days were past when the opinions of any one man could affect the peace of Europe'. (In recalling this debate many years

[1] October 26, 1908.

[2] November 24, 1908.

[3] Afterwards Lord McNair, the well-known international jurist and President of the International Court of Justice and the European Court of Human Rights.

[4] January 19, 1909.

later, Birkett noted: 'I paid for that particular folly, I suppose, by sitting for twelve months as one of the British judges at Nuremberg when the major war criminals were indicted before the International Military Tribunal in 1945.')

His big chance at the Union came towards the end of the Summer Term in 1909. His friend McNair, who was now President, invited him to propose the motion, 'That this House would welcome a revival of the Puritan spirit in English life.'[1] It was opposed by Hugh Dalton of King's, who had as his seconder on this occasion Raglan Somerset of Queen's. (The latter, popularly known as 'The Heavy Villain', reported the Union debates for the *Granta* with a fairly caustic pen, although he usually treated Birkett with kindness.[2]) The subject was very much to Birkett's taste at this time, and although the motion was defeated, when the division was called at the end of the evening, his performance made a considerable impression and ensured his election to the Union Committee shortly afterwards.

The Cambridge Review gave the following account of his speech:

> Mr. BIRKETT, in moving his motion, remarked that Puritanism was in its origin a revolt, an antagonism, and no one could demand a revival of the old spirit in its primitive form. Puritanism was elastic enough to have a message for every age. It may have been intolerant, but there were times when intolerance was needed. It may have destroyed many innocent pleasures, but it had often rebuked a nation wallowing in the mire of iniquity. Luxuries were on the increase, and the expenditure on drink and gambling was largely the cause of the prevailing mammon-worship which was draining the life-blood of the nation. Relief could only be brought to the suffering millions by a renunciation of private indulgence. Modern fiction and journalism afforded illustrations of the degraded taste of the public.
>
> Mr. Birkett has in a comparatively short time placed himself in the very front rank at the Union. His speech was sincere, fluent and rich in literary culture.

After sitting for the Historical Tripos Examination, Birkett

[1] May 25, 1909.

[2] Raglan Somerset (1885–1956) edited the *Granta* when he was at Cambridge. He was a journalist and literary critic of some distinction and later went to the Bar, becoming a Queen's Counsel and Recorder of Gloucester.

planned to stay up at Cambridge for a third and possibly a fourth year, reading in subjects likely to help him towards a career in the Methodist Ministry. Law, more History, and Theology were possible choices, and he wrote to Dr. James Moulton for advice. Moulton replied after consulting the Principal of the theological college:

Didsbury College,
Manchester.
5.6.'09

I am very glad to have the opportunity of advising you on a matter of such importance. I have had a word with Dr. Moss, who quite agrees with me that Law is decidedly off the lines which are likely to be of service to you. Between History and Theology it is less easy to choose: both are excellent in themselves, and I must frankly confess that the advantage of Theology is rather diminished in my eyes by the 'crammy' character of the Theological Tripos—unless indeed it has materially altered since I looked at it and went back to Philology twenty-three years ago! But then it does at least involve Old and New Testament languages and exegesis, and I am thinking of future possibilities.

We want in our ministry, and for other purposes as well as the ultimate possibility of teaching posts, men who can do their share in Biblical study; and the training which combines History and Theology would I think be the very best possible. So I should decidedly advise this, with the fourth year if in any way possible. . . .

I entirely approve of the Union also: I found it invaluable myself. It happens that only this week Bedale was telling me about a Religious Discussion Society at Emmanuel, in which you have been *Athanasius contra mundum*. I am very sorry for the *mundum*—and astonished to hear that your well-known though not (it must be confessed) very scholarly Master is of them—but that it is excellent for Athanasius's training there is no doubt whatever. The *mundus* is extra aggressive in these days. I am acutely conscious of it today after spending a morning correcting a proof for the *Hibbert*!

One other matter before we meet. I write entirely for myself, but I always want to be keeping open eyes for Assistant

> Tutors here. I will talk of it further when you come, but just now only want to ask you to note my mention of it should any other College propose it. I don't know what we are going to do this year, or when we shall have our next vacancy, but I mention it as a preliminary.

Birkett was placed in Class II in the Historical Tripos in May, 1909. 'It was quite a satisfactory second class, your weaker side apparently being shown in the Economic History,' his tutor wrote to him. 'You have done well in your first Tripos: now go on with similar success to your second.' At the same time he won the college English Essay Prize 'with a very good essay' on political satire in English poetry, an achievement which he was to repeat in the following year with an essay on James Boswell, which he wrote during the ensuing Long Vacation. 'Let me hear how you get on with Theology and if I can help you at all,' added Mr. Head. 'It is nice to think that we shall have you with us for two years more.'

Before Birkett went down for the Long Vacation in 1909, he learned that he had been awarded a grant of five pounds from the Tutor's Gratuity Fund. 'It is a very small sum,' the Senior Tutor told him, 'but the fund is small. We wanted to show you thereby that we appreciate you.'

3

Birkett came up to Cambridge for his third year to find himself less interested in attending lectures on the eschatology of St. Paul than in advancing the position he had won for himself at the Union where he had been elected at the head of the Committee. The great constitutional struggle between the Lords and the Commons was mounting at Westminster, and its course was arousing intense interest throughout the country. Consequently Birkett spoke to an exceptionally large gathering when he proposed, in the first Union debate of the term, 'that this House would strongly condemn any interference with the Budget on the part of the House of Lords.' After a very long debate to which many more members than usual contributed, Birkett succeeded in carrying his motion by sixteen votes. 'Spoke well for thirty-five minutes,' he noted in his diary the same night, and on this occasion he seems to have been widely complimented. 'The task of presenting a case so much canvassed during the last few weeks was a hard one,' *The Cambridge Review* commented; 'but Mr. Birkett is never commonplace. What he has to say is always worthy of attention, and his manner and expression always secure it. There is no speaker who may be more sure of pleasing the House.'

Praise from the undergraduate journals was not always undiluted with criticism. When he spoke later the same term on another extremely topical subject, 'votes for women', *The Gownsman* while admitting that he argued seriously and well against female suffrage took him to task for the use of 'that tiresome formula "I submit", which all subsequent speakers exercised to the full'. ('I have also paid handsomely for this piece of folly,' he remarked many years later when he had become a judge, 'for I now have to listen every day of my life to a more tiresome formula—"in my respectful submission"—and I confess I weep secret tears of remorse and contrition.')

A debate on the same subject organized by Birkett in his college debating society was the occasion of a brilliant undergraduate hoax, in which Birkett played a leading part. The hoax was by way of revenge for what happened in an inter-collegiate debate with Caius earlier in the year when the Emmanuel men were completely taken in. This debate which had taken place in Caius, was on the motion 'that Alcohol and Tobacco are the twin evils of the Nation', and it was announced beforehand that the motion was to be proposed as guest speaker by Mrs. Carrie Nation, a notorious American Prohibitionist who went about smashing saloon windows in the United States with a hatchet. But the guest speaker turned out to be a Caius undergraduate and 'Rugger' Blue, who was appropriately dressed up in women's clothes, declaring, 'Smash the bottle, or it will smash you.' On the occasion of the suffragette debate, which was held in the Emmanuel College Hall on Saturday night, November 13, 1909, it was announced that the question would be opened by Miss Beatrice Thomas, a woman undergraduate from Girton, who as guest speaker would put the case for the suffragettes, that Mr. W. N. Birkett as Vice-President would oppose, and that after two more men from Emmanuel and three from Caius had spoken, the debate would be summed up by Mr. G. B. Haddock, the Conservative M.P. for North Lonsdale, who had accepted the Vice-President's invitation to be the second guest speaker. The Caius men were naturally on their guard when they entered the Emmanuel Hall on the night of the debate, and they subjected the Girton undergraduate to a close scrutiny. But there was no doubt that she was a woman and the person she purported to be. It did not apparently occur to anyone to question the *bona fides* of the other guest speaker.

The truth was that Birkett had persuaded another Emmanuel man, Miles Malleson, who was a clever amateur actor (and subsequently a successful professional one) to impersonate the North Lonsdale M.P. For this purpose Malleson had gone to London earlier in the day and there been 'made up' by Willie Clarkson, the famous wig-maker, with a grizzled, grey moustache, heavy side-whiskers and florid cheeks and nose. He had spent several hours in town, exercising his capacity for acting and deceiving everybody from tea-shop waitresses to railway guards. By the end of his journey back to college he felt so bold as to lean over in the railway compartment to another old gentleman and ask, 'Is this Cambridge?' A hansom cab took him to Emmanuel College, where the porter, with much bowing, showed him the way to Birkett's rooms, where a photograph was taken. Before the debate there was a dinner, at which the three Caius speakers were present; and, although one of them gazed long and earnestly at the principal guest, his suspicions were allayed, and it was not until afterwards that 'Mr. Haddock' was discovered to be really 'a cod'.

When it came to his turn to speak, Malleson played his part to perfection and gave a superb imitation of the average M.P.'s platform manner. He began by saying that he was in the unfortunate position of not knowing which lobby in the House of Commons he would walk into if there was a division on the question tomorrow. (Cheers and cries of 'Shame' and 'Cheer up, Sir!') 'It seems to me,' he went on, 'that the spheres of man and woman are so essentially different that it would be dangerous to force their energies into the same channel.' (At this point there was loud laughter joined in by the waiters who were serving coffee in the hall.) He continued, twirling the end of his moustache: 'I do not say that there are not women of the very highest political intelligence. ('Hear, hear!' from Mr. Birkett.) No one can deny that there are. But it seems to me that woman should be the goddess of the household and the presiding deity of the home. Once you grant women the vote, you let loose a body of voters who cannot bear their share of the ultimate responsibility.' Then, suddenly remembering that he was expected to be impartial, the speaker concluded with these words which fairly brought down the House: 'I put forward these points, not so much to prove the arguments against the motion, but as points to be considered, and finally my earnest appeal to you all is to consider!—to think!—and in doing so to be true above all to yourselves!! Only so can the solution of this great problem be found.'

It was during the division which followed—the motion was lost by 52 votes to 97—that the secret of the pseudo-M.P.'s identity leaked out. But Malleson carried through the joke to the end. Escorted by Birkett and the other committee members to the secretary's room, he leaned out of a window and pretended to address his constituents. 'Gentlemen of Emmanuel,' he said in true parliamentary manner, 'I thank you from the bottom of my heart for the reception you have accorded me today. Today has been the most extraordinary day in my life. Since I left Mr. Willie Clarkson's shop at half-past one this afternoon I have had a most extraordinary existence.' Whereupon the irrepressible Miles Malleson disappeared from the window and was seen no more in his whiskers.

Everyone took the hoax in good part and it was generally agreed that Emmanuel's honour had been satisfied. In fact, the only person who did not appreciate the joke was the real Mr. Haddock's agent who threatened to sue the culprits for impersonation. But fortunately wiser counsel prevailed, and the Member for North Lonsdale, who had a sense of humour—in spite or possibly because of his name—ended by sending the Birkett-Malleson partnership a telegram of congratulation.

Apart from the office bearers, Birkett was the most outstanding figure in the Union in the Michaelmas Term of 1909. At the President's invitation, he represented Cambridge at an inter-university debate at the Manchester University Union, where he successfully moved a motion approving the policy of Mr. Asquith's Liberal Government. It was thus in the nature of things that he should run for the office of Secretary at the end of term.

In those days the offices of President and Vice-President were uncontested, so that the Secretary could normally look forward to being automatically elected to the two higher offices in succession. The unsuccessful candidate in the immediately preceding contest for the Secretaryship was Hugh Dalton, and it might have been expected that he would again be a candidate for the office. But 'Comrade Hugh', as the editor of the *Granta* used to call him in his reports of the debates, had been defeated on an earlier occasion, and in the circumstances he was unwilling to expose himself to the humiliation of a third defeat. Had he done so and been successful, he would have become the first Socialist President of the Cambridge Union. As things turned out, Norman Birkett, flying the Liberal colours, was elected by only six votes in a straightforward fight with a Conservative, H. P. W. Burton of St. John's—the voting was 245 to 239—a narrow enough margin, everything considered.[1] Nevertheless it meant that the achievement of his greatest ambition at Cambridge was now but a matter of course.

The pleasure which he felt at his success was not unclouded during the Christmas Vacation which he spent at home in Ulverston. For the first time he began to have serious doubts as to whether he was right in going on for the Wesleyan Ministry, and he seems to have communicated at least a hint of this development to his father. At all events he returned to Cambridge in a rather heavy-hearted mood. 'I think I shall go on with my work and get my degree in June,' he wrote to his father (January 19, 1910): 'it would break my heart to do anything you didn't approve. You have done everything for me, and my only wish is to try and make you proud of me in return. I have had the most miserable experience this last day or two: everything seems so dark: but Light must break.'

Norman had left his home in the middle of the General Election, which had been precipitated by the House of Lords rejecting Mr. Lloyd George's Budget. As the leading Liberal in Ulverston, Thomas Birkett was in charge of the local Liberal candidate's campaign against the sitting Conservative Member, the real Mr. George Haddock, who supported the Lords' veto. 'I am thinking a great deal of you in North Lonsdale,' Norman wrote to his father on the eve of the poll, 'and I hope all your work will get its reward.' However, the result was disappointing for the Liberals. The Conservatives and Unionists regained over a hundred seats, incidentally holding North Lonsdale, and Mr. Asquith found his majority in the House of Commons at the mercy of the eighty-two Irish Nationalists.

[1] Burton was elected Secretary the following term and eventually succeeded Birkett as President. He later went into the Church and became a Canon of Lincoln Cathedral.

The new Secretary of the Union was the natural choice to propose a motion of 'unabated confidence' in Mr. Asquith's Government in the first debate of the Lent Term in 1910.[1] 'Our commercial policy,' he declaimed in the best style of Union oratory, 'cannot be controlled from the bathchairs of Brighton or from the Cathedral stalls of Salisbury and Exeter.' He was supported by an undergraduate from Trinity, who spoke third. This was J. F. Roxburgh, future Headmaster of Stowe School, where Birkett was to send his only son to be educated. On this occasion, Roxburgh spoke wittily and well, but Birkett's speech was the success of the evening. 'We have only one remark to make about Mr. Birkett,' wrote *The Gownsman*; 'he was splendid. There was, as always, a high note of integrity running through his speech.'

As Vice-President in the following Summer Term, it fell to him to move the resolution making Theodore Roosevelt an Honorary Member of the Society.[2] The former U.S. President had come to Cambridge to receive an honorary degree, and his visit to the Union gave the young Birkett an opportunity of pronouncing upon a theme which was subsequently to become an abiding interest—the promotion of Anglo-American relations.

> I, for my own part, as a member of Emmanuel College, experience this honour in a deepened sense if that be possible. For Emmanuel is justly proud of its intimate connection with Harvard University, and it is to me a matter for personal congratulations to welcome, in the name of this House, one of Harvard's most distinguished sons.
>
> It is a good thing for us to think, sir, that for the future the ex-President of the United States of America will be associated with this House; but we also like to think that this day's proceedings are significant of the very cordial relations which have existed and which I trust will continue to exist between this country and the country of the distinguished visitor. . . . For our part, we can but trust that it is the sign and symbol of yet closer friendship between the two great countries.

In the course of his remarks, Birkett referred to the fact that another great American name, that of Oliver Wendell Holmes, was

[1] January 25, 1910.
[2] May 26, 1910.

already on the Union's short list of honorary members. When Roosevelt made his speech in reply, he spoke of the gratification he felt at having his name linked with that of Oliver Wendell Holmes. Then, he suddenly broke off, and turning to the President, asked: 'By the by, Mr. President, was that the younger or the elder Oliver Wendell Holmes?' Without a moment's hesitation, and with the most courtly bow, the President, Geoffrey Butler, said: 'The younger.' The distinguished guest then went on to say that he had had the pleasure of appointing the younger Holmes to the Supreme Court of the United States. However, Butler, who was a brilliant historian with a 'double First', had made a slip, for his answer should have been, 'The Elder.' 'I have always thought this to be a perfect example of what to do in a crisis,' wrote Birkett, recalling the incident long afterwards, 'to show no hesitation or doubt, but right or wrong to give the impression of perfect assurance.'[1]

Before the debate, Roosevelt paid a short visit to Emmanuel, where Birkett and his friends presented him with a 'teddy bear', with an outstretched paw, which the ex-President laughingly shook. Birkett then accompanied Roosevelt to the college picture gallery, where he was shown Harvard's portrait and signature, and to the rooms which Harvard was reputed to have occupied about the year 1630.

In the same term Birkett sat for the Theological Special Examination and was placed in the First Class. A 'Special' was not of the same standing as the Tripos, but as he had already got through the Historical Tripos the addition of the 'Special' enabled him to take the degree of Bachelor of Arts. He also won the Emmanuel College Essay Prize, for the second year running, with his essay on James Boswell.

To Thomas Birkett

University Union Society, *Cambridge*, *June* 16, 1910 . . .

I am glad to have got my degree, and to have got a First Class in the Special. Of course, it isn't the same as the Tripos, but many men fail altogether. Marley has at last got a third in it, and with less time I have beaten all the men at Emmanuel.

[1] Cradock, p. 101. Sir Geoffrey Butler (1887–1929), Lecturer in History at Cambridge and Fellow of Corpus Christi College, was M.P. for the University from 1923 until his death.

Now with regard to what I am to do in the future. I don't want to do anything that is not in accordance with your wish, and in everything I will be guided by you.

After long thought, I think it would be wiser if I did not enter the Wesleyan Ministry. The prospects at Didsbury are not high, and to be compelled to struggle all my life with comparative poverty is not inviting. I am afraid, also, that I should find the Ministry rather cramping, and, in general, feel that I am scarcely fitted for it. I know that to make a change now is to invite strong criticism and possible misunderstanding, but it is well to count the cost.

I have had a long talk with Mr. Head, and he was not surprised that I desired a wider field. He favoured the idea of going to the Bar, and sent me to the Secretary of the Appointments Board, who gets appointments for men. I told him that whatever happened, *I must earn my living at the end of next year*, and he seemed to think that that could be managed quite well. He thinks I might get a post as Private Secretary to a Member of Parliament, or a post on a newspaper, or at the offices of the Board of Education.

But in all these cases I should be able to read for the Bar at the same time.

Mr. Heseltine of Emmanuel, the Law Reader in the University, is going to talk the whole question over with me at nine o'clock tonight, and I will write you again tomorrow. What I shall learn from him will be the nature of the Examinations for the Bar, the time it will take to be called to the Bar, and other information possible.

Mr. Head thinks I should take Part II of the Law Tripos next year, and in that case would come up to Cambridge about July 6th for the Long Vacation Term, because there are many Law Lectures then. . . .

Of course, all this is very very serious and anxious, and I am simply worn out with anxiety, but it is necessary to face things boldly. I shall be glad of a rest.

Write and tell me what you think, and I will write tomorrow.

June 17. I saw Mr. Heseltine and Mr. Head together last night, and they were both agreed that I should do well to go to the Bar. Heseltine said it was perfectly feasible to earn my living at the end of next year and read for the Bar at the same time. He said in three years from now I should have passed all the Bar Examination, and should have been called.

The expenses would not be too heavy, and he thought a poor man could do it quite well.

I should have to keep twelve terms at the Inner Temple, but that means merely eating four dinners per year, one dinner counting as a term.

I should have to go into Chambers for six months and that would cost a little, but that and the actual expense of being called to the Bar would be the only drain upon you . . .

You can't think how very depressed I am at worrying you so, and being such a strain on you: but given good health, some day I will pay it all back with interest. I like to think that I have done something at the 'Varsity already which reflects honour on you: and Heseltine says there is every hope of a good future career.

He was quite enthusiastic last night, and if you like I will ask him to write to you.

The elder Birkett was naturally disappointed when he heard his son's news about abandoning the Ministry. He suggested that as soon as Norman got home they should go off for a holiday together and discuss the situation. Norman wrote to his father on the same day as he took his degree.

Saturday, June 18, 1910. Many many thanks for your very kind letter.

Of course, it would be a disappointment to you, but one has to face all the facts. I should never sever my connection with Methodism, and I shall remain on the Plan. It is at moments like this when the future is unknown that one has need of all faith and guidance.

I sincerely wish to do what is right, and would willingly enter the Ministry if I thought I was right in so doing. But when I talked to Harvey here the other night, he told me that the life of a Wesleyan Minister was a dog's life. He has been in the Ministry for some years, and feels he is too old to do anything else now. But what a dreadful life his must be now; with no heart to go on.

But I will get everything clear for when I come, so that we shall know exactly where we are.

I have been troubled all day about your disappointment. It makes everything doubly hard for me. But I feel so clearly that I could never make an ordinary Minister, that I am afraid I should be in Harvey's position some day, earning very little and not happy. I pray that you may be spared till I succeed, and am able to make some small return for all your goodness to me.

I am particularly glad we are going to have a holiday: I feel so ready for it. And it will do you good, and we ought to have a really good time.

I got my degree this morning, and was loudly cheered as I went up to the Vice-Chancellor for it . . .

Shall be home about four-thirty Monday.

Norman and his father went to the Isle of Man for their holiday; there they talked long and earnestly together, and eventually Thomas Birkett accepted his son's decision. He also remembered the advice of Lord Richard Cavendish that the boy should try for the Bar. A fortnight later Norman was back in Cambridge and had begun to prepare for his new career.

4

The change involved Norman Birkett in considerable emotional stress, and he was greatly worried by the fact that he was a financial liability upon his father. 'Since I came up this term, I do not think I have ever been so oppressed before with the difficulty of my position,' he wrote to his father after he had been back for a week or so. 'I grudge every penny I spend, because when I think of Gilbert and the girls working hard and earning money, I feel like a useless drag on everything. Of course, other people see the bright side of one's life (and I have everything to be thankful for) but they don't see the loneliness and the hours when one is sick with fear and difficulty. Law is very hard, and the books want mastering, but I am perfectly confident of my power to get the LL.B. comfortably. . . . I am sorry to be such a great burden: it makes me dreadfully unhappy: I am never free from the weight and trouble of it: but do remember that I try to be careful in a dozen little ways and will try harder.'

The mood persisted and he felt miserably dejected. After a further brief visit home in September, he returned to Cambridge for the beginning of the Michaelmas Term, when he was to occupy the Presidential chair at the Union. He confided the following to his private diary:

> I start on my new life tomorrow, feeling tonight bankrupt financially, spiritually and mentally, and above all utterly devoid of any hope! Nothing could be worse than this awful mental misery. Father has my love, but oh! he tries it hard. All my life is an effort to please him, and this is my reward—a gnawing hopelessness of his making!
>
> Let me hold fast to such faith as I have!
> God pity me and lead me on!
> And so—the Great Unknown.

But he was soon caught up in the stress of affairs in what was to be his busiest term at the University. He confessed to feeling 'very nervous over the ordeal of a huge First Debate House' when he took the chair for the first time in the Union. But everything 'went off splendidly without one disturbing feature'. He duly enrolled himself as a student in the Inner Temple and began to eat the requisite number of dinners, although his perusal of the *Student's Guide to the Bar* 'brought on the old feeling of dismay'. He continued to preach in the local Methodist chapels and he also addressed Liberal meetings in Cambridge with such effect that he was invited by the Cambridge Liberals to become the official candidate at the next Election with a guarantee of all expenses paid. 'But, as I pointed out, having no private income to live on were I returned, I refused it,' he told his father, adding, 'it is much better to go slowly, and I am sure the way will open.' He also refused the Presidency of the University Liberal Club ('a great honour') on the plea of work. 'I have a very busy life at present and frequently go to bed quite tired out.'

His Presidency of the Union involved him in some entertaining, since by custom the President had to dine the speakers on the paper. ('The dinner is 2/6 each and there is the wine they have. But £5 or £6 should cover that.') To make up for this he economized in other directions.

> I am giving no lunches at all so ought to save £2 there. The men who came to lunch were the men that I now give dinners to at the Union . . .
>
> I am providing my own breakfasts as I go along, except when I have men in. Of course they ask me back so that squares things. I get Commons from the College (butter, bread, milk at 6d per day) and I buy 2 eggs (4d) so I get a cheap breakfast, whereas the cheapest breakfast from the College is 8d, and Commons would have to be got just the same.

As President of the Cambridge Union, Birkett led a party to debate with the Society's counterpart at Oxford, where he proposed a motion on the familiar topic of Puritanism and the desirability of a larger element of it in English social life. 'Great success,' he noted briefly in his diary, after which he and his friends climbed Magdalen Tower where he recorded that they remained until 1.30 a.m. 'in snow and moonlight'. Among those whom he met on this occasion, and who impressed him as outstanding speakers, were Philip Guedella and R. M. Barrington-Ward, both future Presidents of the Oxford Union. Consequently for his last debate in the chair at Cambridge, which took place in December 6, 1910, during the second General Election to be held in that year, the President invited these two Balliol men to come to Cambridge. The motion on the paper, which Birkett himself moved, was 'That in the opinion of this House the Political Liberties and true Prosperity of the Nation can only be assured by the return of the Liberal Government to power at the present Election'.

Although the Liberals were to succeed in winning the Election, their supporters in the Cambridge Union on this occasion were defeated by a majority of forty-three, in spite of a brilliantly witty speech by Philip Guedella. 'The speech he made that night still lingers in my memory,' wrote Birkett more than fifty years later.

Guedella began by deploring the fact that visitors from Oxford were required to make epigrams and 'an epigram is only another name for a platitude on its night out'. Other quips Birkett remembered were: 'Any stigma is good enough to beat a dogma with,' and, 'What three-quarters of Lancashire says today, England will say tomorrow.'

Like Birkett, both Guedella and Barrington-Ward were eventually called to the Bar; but, unlike him, they left it after a while, the former to devote himself to the writing of history and the latter to journalism and the editorship of *The Times*. Of Guedella, Birkett had this to say in his brief unpublished autobiography:

> His ambition was to succeed at the Bar. I used to see him at luncheon at the Inner Temple Hall, and for ten years he persisted at the Bar but without any success worth talking about. Then, like so many others, he had to make the great decision whether to continue or to seek some other way of making a living and he left the Bar.
>
> It is one of the fascinating questions why men succeed or fail at the Bar. Guedella with every gift—brilliant in speech, highly intelligent, industrious—and yet he failed. My own view is that he was *too* clever and gave the impression of being a little superior to the ordinary run of men.

Thomas Birkett came to Cambridge to hear his son's retiring speech as President of the Union ('Much moved. Great success') and Norman found time to show his father round the colleges ('The most impressive thing in Cambridge for him was when we walked under the windows of King's Chapel and heard the choir singing "Now thank we all our God" '). They returned together to Ulverston for the last few days of the Election. Norman delivered four major speeches in different parts of the constituency in two days, which left him 'dead tired', with a feeling of 'blank, hopeless misery'. His stint in the Liberal Central Committee Rooms on Polling Day further exhausted him ('Terribly handicapped for lack of vehicles') and after the declaration of the poll he felt 'very dispirited', although the Conservative candidate, who was the celebrated Mr. Haddock, only defeated the Liberal by 74 votes.

The remainder of the Christmas vacation was divided between preaching, reading his law books and paying family visits. His cousin Harry Birkett, with whom he had served his apprenticeship at the shop, was now happily married, and this provoked further disquieting thoughts as the New Year opened. He wrote in his diary:

> *January* 1, 1911 . . . Felt very deeply my own lack of the domestic element in my life. People are settling down to love and domesticity, and I am a wayfarer, a sojourner in life. God

FATHER AND MOTHER

Stearn

NORMAN BIRKETT AT CAMBRIDGE

EMMANUEL COLLEGE DEBATING SOCIETY COMMITTEE

Miles Malleson, who impersonated Mr. G. B. Haddock, M.P., at a debate in Michaelmas Term, 1909, is wearing a false beard. Birkett, who planned the hoax, is sitting second from the left.

CAMBRIDGE UNION SOCIETY, MAY 26, 1910

Birkett (*centre*) moves the resolution proposing the election of ex-U.S. President Theodore Roosevelt as an Honorary Member of the Society. Roosevelt, who had just received an honorary degree, can be seen in academic robes seated on the left.

> grant that in this New Year I may fight bravely and well: there is much against me, but by God's favour my mountain may stand firm. And so—forward again to the great and wonderful Unknown.

If Birkett's last two terms at Cambridge were something of an anti-climax, he enjoyed the prestige of an ex-President of the Union. His portrait was specially drawn for *The Gownsman*, and it appeared in that undergraduate journal with an appropriate comment.

> 'Those who have heard him at the Union, where today he undoubtedly bears the palm for oratory; those who have had the honour of his benevolent acquaintance; those who have the delight of his friendship, will all agree that to attempt to describe him . . . would be impertinently foolish or foolishly inadequate. Suffice it to say that those Conservatives who hear him declare his Liberalism, and those Anti-puritans who hear him declare his Puritanism, are irresistibly driven to think, "*O si sic omnes*". After all the fact that the appearance of his portrait calls for no tittle of excuse, *is* a tribute of sorts.'[1]

The last public occasion in Cambridge in which Norman Birkett declared his Puritanism called forth the warmest praise. It was at an inter-collegiate debate at Jesus College, where his host J. H. Allen, who was also Vice-President of the Union, slipped him a hurriedly scribbled note after he had sat down. 'You were most excellent!' Allen wrote. 'How I wish I could speak! You can; I can see you talking to 10,000 people and bringing out their affections.'

Of the many friends Birkett made during his time at Cambridge, perhaps the closest and the one whom he most admired as a speaker was another Emmanuel man, H. D. Henderson, later Sir Hubert Henderson, Professor of Political Economy at Oxford and Economic Adviser to the Government. They saw a great deal of each other during Birkett's last two years. When Birkett's sister Edith came up for May week in 1910, he introduced them, possibly hoping that a romance would develop. But this did not happen, although Birkett used to send his sister news of Henderson and his progress in the Union. Shortly after Henderson's premature death in 1952, Birkett was to write the following account:

[1] *The Gownsman*, March 14, 1911.

A little junior to me at Emmanuel was H. D. Henderson. At the college debates he seemed to me to show qualities as a debater of the most unusual kind. I am glad to think that I encouraged him to speak regularly at the Union, and in due course he became President. I naturally took great pride in his subsequent career. He became a world famous economist, and had he lived he would now be the Head of a famous Oxford College; but I shall always think of him as the best pure debater that I heard in my time. He had a habit of crooking a long forefinger at his immediate opponent as though he had got complete possession of him, and he certainly never let him go until he had reduced him to the equivalent of pulp. Relentless, pugnacious, inexorable, I scarcely know the right words to employ, but it was all done with consummate grace and ease, and as the victim expired, Henderson never failed to produce a most radiant and indulgent smile. It is sad to think that his great gifts are now lost to Oxford and the nation.[1]

The Tripos Examination was drawing nearer, and as yet Birkett had found no work to keep him financially independent of his father until he should have been called to the Bar and begun to practise. First, he tried for a job on a Liberal newspaper, going to Manchester to see C. P. Scott, editor of the *Manchester Guardian*, and to London to call on J. L. Garvin, editor of *The Observer*. Both editors were sympathetic but had nothing to offer in the way of an opening at the moment. He also considered doing social welfare work in the East End of London and made inquiries at Toynbee Hall, which had been founded some years previously for this purpose under the trusteeship of the University Settlements Association. But nothing came of this project either. Eventually, after he had sat for the Law Tripos and was anxiously waiting for the result in the first days of June, the Appointments Board put him in touch with Mr. George Cadbury Junior, who was looking for a private secretary.

Cadbury was a son of the well-known cocoa and chocolate manufacturer, Quaker philanthropist and social reformer, and he shared his father's interests both in the factory at Bournville, outside Birmingham, and in the various adult religious and educational institutions which the elder Cadbury had founded at Selly Oak

[1] Cradock, p. 102. Sir Hubert Henderson (1890–1952) was appointed Warden of All Souls College, Oxford, in 1951, but died before he could take up the appointment.

nearby and which were known as the Selly Oak Colleges. One of these, called Fircroft, 'where working men may go into residence for a varying number of weeks, and study social and religious questions, and generally increase their knowledge and enlarge their horizon,' had recently been opened by the younger Cadbury and was his particular interest.[1] He now invited Birkett to visit him and spend the night at his home, Primrose Hill, at Selly Oak. Birkett did so. The two men had a long talk and took to each other immediately. George Cadbury Junior explained that he hoped to stand as a candidate for the Birmingham City Council at the next local government elections and he particularly needed help in collecting information on such subjects as public health, education, housing and the like. Next day Cadbury showed him round the Bournville works, which were a model of their kind from the standpoint of industrial hygiene and the welfare of the employees, pension schemes and so forth. 'While municipal problems would be your chief work,' Cadbury told him, 'there would also be other social questions upon which I should want help.' When Birkett pointed out that he had never been a private secretary and did not know anything about the duties, Cadbury replied: 'That suits me. I have never had a private secretary before.'

In the result, Birkett was offered the job at a salary of two hundred pounds a year, with six months notice on either side should one or the other wish to terminate the arrangement. 'Of course,' added Cadbury, 'there will be no difficulty about your Bar business.' Birkett was very glad to accept and agreed to start work towards the end of July. Certainly the salary was not a princely sum and he would have to pay for rooms and his keep out of it. But he could manage to live on it with the exercise of great care and economy, and he would at last be independent of his father's bounty.

A few days after returning to Cambridge, the Tripos results were announced and he learned that he had got a Second Class in Part II of the Law Tripos.

If he had been cheered when he received his B.A. degree a year previously, this time, so he recorded in his diary, he 'got an ovation in the Senate House when I took my LL.B.'. Next day he spent

[1] See the lecture given by Mrs. George Cadbury Senior (later Dame Elizabeth Cadbury) on 'Adult Schools' at Birmingham University: J. H. Muirhead. *Birmingham Institutions* (1911), at p. 221.

saying good-bye to various friends, beginning with John Allen, who had succeeded to the President's chair at the Union. Then he caught the train for Ulverston. 'And so four years ended. . . .'

5

After a month at home which seemed to pass far too quickly, Norman Birkett packed his bags and left by train for Birmingham. It was a miserable journey, and he was 'on the verge of tears all day' due to a combination of homesickness and a terrible longing for a girl called Ruth Hindle with whom he had been playing golf and had fallen violently in love. He reached Selly Oak about tea-time and sent his bags up to his lodgings in a cab, while he completed the journey on foot 'with the most awful feeling of desolation I have yet experienced'. To add to his misery the rooms which had been taken for him proved a disappointment, as they were very small. How he settled in to his new job he described in letters to his father.

To Thomas Birkett

124, *Oak Tree Lane*, *Selly Oak*, *Birmingham*. July 20, 1911.

I thought you would like to hear how the first day went. I roamed round Selly Oak last night. It is similar to Dalton with one straggling street, so you can imagine I felt pretty lonely, not knowing anybody.

I wish I could get rid of these simply dreadful attacks of homesickness: but it is something to be as fond of home as I am.

I saw Cadbury this morning, and had a long conversation with him. A typist does his correspondence, and the correspondence I shall have to deal with will be that relating to his public work which has not yet commenced. I talked with the organizer of education and the organizer of the social work. That took me till one o'clock. Then I read all the pamphlets they gave me on the matters, and I have just been into Birmingham with Cadbury in the car and been introduced to many people. My work is to keep abreast of modern things in education and town planning, etc., and to put it into short shape for him.

My only capital is my brain, and I must work it hard.

I have been invited to the Adult School on Sunday at seven-thirty and have promised to go.

The rooms here are small, but the ones into which I shall move next week are larger. The food is good and plentiful and when the strangeness wears off I should settle down.

But at present the work is vague, and I don't feel confident of myself.

However, a stout heart goes all the way, and I'm here to win, and if effort can do it, I shall come out all right.

July 23. I wrote on Thursday, and I now take up the record from Friday. In the morning I saw Mr. Cadbury at Bournville and he gave me £5 for expenses, such as Blue Books, postages, etc. I have to keep a Petty Cash a/c in a small book with regard to it. Then he asked me if I had a cycle. I said I had waited until I saw if I wanted one. He then said, 'Go and get a good one and put it down to me.' I said I ought to pay for it myself, but he said 'No: I shall want you to do a good deal of cycling for me. But get one of the best: not a cheap one.' I thanked him and went into Birmingham and ordered a B.S.A. throughout, 3-speed gear etc. £10.13.6. They lent me one until my new one comes. Then I went back and got to work on various Birmingham schemes, when Laurence Cadbury came and asked me to go up to Northfield (the old man's home) for tennis at 4 o'clock. I knew him at Cambridge and we had some good sets.[1] A lot of people were there: Miss Cadbury partnered me and we won . . . She was very nice to me.[2] Then I came back about 6.30 and got some more work done. . . .

I am beginning to see my work take shape; I have got files for separate subjects and am at present engaged on an enquiry into Juvenile Employment Bureaux in Birmingham, London, Edinburgh and Leicester. The work is interesting and extremely valuable for me, and I am going to put my best efforts into it.

Of course, fears come. I have been oppressed with the feeling that I might not satisfy Cadbury, or that he might suddenly die and leave me stranded. But I am sure that is silly, and I look on the brighter side.

The Cadburys have done all they can to make my first

[1] Laurence Cadbury, half-brother of George Cadbury Junior was the eldest son of George Cadbury's second marriage.

[2] Dorothea, Laurence Cadbury's eldest sister.

days happy, and I shall never forget their kindness at a time when kindness was precious to me.

July 30. I've seen nothing but wealth since I came, and the next best thing to having it is to enjoy the benefit of it in these grounds and houses. . . .

August 2. On Monday morning I was at the office at eight-thirty with the morning papers read and marked for Cadbury. He said nine o'clock would be more convenient so I get a little more time in the morning. I have not missed rising at seven o'clock since I came a fortnight ago, and I have never been a minute late for any appointment anywhere. . . .

On Tuesday I saw Cadbury at nine o'clock. He gave me a cheque for £10.13.6. for my cycle and one for £5.16.0. being salary from July 20–31. . . . He further said he was struck with the quick way I was adapting myself to the Birmingham problems, and said I should be of great service to him. . . .

I enclose (via Edie) a little present we arranged *out of my first earnings. It gives me infinite pleasure to send it* and I hope it will give you pleasure too. It is for Llandudno.

Now don't say 'He'd better save his money'.

I'll save money alright and shall be as careful as possible. At Xmas I'll produce my books!

When I've sent this, paid my landlady, my laundry and all other expenses, I've saved 20/– in 10 days, so I can give myself the pleasure of giving you a special burst at Llandudno!

It's only a little, but I wanted to give you something out of my first earnings to mark my love for you, and for all you've done for me.

May you have a good holiday and better health to enjoy it—and God bless you very much!

The sense of homesickness which he showed in these letters persisted with Norman Birkett for the next two years during which he worked as Cadbury's secretary, although all the Cadburys treated him practically as one of the family and did everything to make him feel at home with them. He used to count the days carefully until he could get back to Ulverston for his next holiday, and his diary was punctuated with such statements as 'ninety-seven days gone: fifty-nine to come'. He was depressed, too, by the knowledge of his father's increasing ill-health—his holiday at Llandudno did not seem to do him any good. Neither was he encouraged by the news of his elder brother Gilbert, who was not prospering as a pharmaceutical chemist and was soon to emigrate to South Africa. The realization that he was now the family's main hope inspired Norman to work harder than ever and to save every penny he could. Indeed in his first year at Bournville he was able to put by nearly half his salary, and in doing so he did not go short of food, since his lodgings all found cost him less than thirty shillings a week. He closed his diary for this first twelve month period on a note of mingled thankfulness, regret and hope—'thankfulness for mercies received, regret for opportunities wasted, but still some slight hope of growing up into a learned and a distinguished man.'

Fortunately there were plenty of opportunities for recreation at Bournville. A typical entry in his diary for a Saturday in winter reveals that he played golf in the morning, took part in a rugby football match in the afternoon, scoring two tries, and attended a social evening at the Bournville estate, where he sang two songs and afterwards acted the part of Sergeant Buzfuz in a mock trial based on the case of Bardell versus Pickwick in *The Pickwick Papers.* ('Your wig suited you,' the Cadburys told him after the performance.)

Besides Fircroft, the working men's college at Bournville, where Birkett was expected to lend a helping hand in organizing various activities, such as lectures and discussions, there was a Junior Adult School at Cregoe Street, a poor quarter in Birmingham, in which Birkett also took part. Here his principal duty was in helping George Cadbury Junior to run a Sunday school, which began with a breakfast at 7 a.m. followed by hymn singing and Bible study.

The elder George Cadbury had eleven children, of whom George Cadbury Junior was the second son of his first marriage, and Birkett was constantly asked to one or other of their houses. Besides the tennis courts at the Northfield Manor House, the elder Cadbury had a private golf course on which Norman was invited to play whenever he liked. There was also a swimming pool, where he would bathe to the accompaniment of shouts of 'Ginger pelt' from the younger Cadbury brothers. The latter's mother, later Dame Elizabeth Cadbury, always made him welcome in the friendly household with its fine Quaker traditions, and when she died in 1951, at the age of ninety-three, Norman Birkett, then Mr. Justice Birkett, delivered an address at her memorial service, in which he recalled her great qualities of character. 'Forty years ago, when I lived in Bournville village,' he said, 'I was privileged to see and to share in some degree the family life at the Manor House. Dame Elizabeth knew the enormous value and influence of family life, and throughout her life she sought in every way to enrich and strengthen it and maintain it; and when on her ninetieth birthday there were thirty-seven grandchildren and forty-nine great-grandchildren, her happiness was intense. . . . She was a most forceful and effective public speaker, and was extraordinarily well-informed on all the many subjects in which she was interested and on which she spoke. I have cause to remember that, for I had the temerity once to debate with her at the Bournville schools.[1] Her perennial youthfulness of mind enabled her to speak with great acceptance to the young, and it was to the moulding and shaping of the young life that she devoted so much care. When she was approaching her ninetieth year she spoke to the Girls' Athletic Club at Bournville, when I was present, and again she revealed the ease with which she bridged the years, and entered into the hopes and aspirations of her young audience.'[2]

Polling in the Birmingham Municipal Elections took place on November 1, 1911, and for the preceding fortnight Birkett was out canvassing on most nights in Selly Oak with his employer's brother Laurence, and also speaking at factory meetings. For this he was made much of at the Manor House, where one speech was hailed as 'magnificent', particularly by Miss Dorothea Cadbury. His electioneering efforts left him physically exhausted, but he had the satisfaction of seeing George Cadbury Junior returned at the head of the poll. Nor did Cadbury fail to appreciate his private secretary's services. At Christmas he sent him a cheque for fifty pounds as a present, and at the end of his first year he increased his salary to two hundred and fifty pounds. 'You put me on the Council and kept me there,' he told him when they finally said good-bye. Further increases of salary were offered if he wished to stay on, and had he done so no doubt an attractive opening would have been found for

[1] This debate, which took place at the Infants' School, Bournville, on December 2, 1913, was on the subject of women's suffrage. It was held under the auspices of the Birmingham Women's Suffrage Society (Non-Militant). The Rev. R. A. Aytoun presided.

[2] Communicated by Mr. Laurence Cadbury.

him in the business at Bournville. But his mind was now firmly set on going to the Bar, and so he gave in his notice at the end of eighteen months.

He was politically active in other ways at this period and started a branch of the League of Young Liberals at Selly Oak. His first big speech at a Liberal meeting in the District was undertaken at two hours' notice on behalf of J. W. Wilson, the M.P. for North Worcestershire, where he took the place of the Scottish Lord Advocate, who had been billed as the principal speaker but was unable to come. ('Great time. Brought the house down. Established my reputation for ever in North Worcestershire as a speaker.') Forty-six years later, he was able to remind Mr. Ernest Sheppard, the local Liberal Agent, of the quotation with which he had begun his speech.

'As in a theatre, the eyes of men,
After a well graced actor leaves the stage,
Are idly bent on him that enters next,
Thinking his prattle to be tedious.'

According to the Agent, Birkett held an audience of a thousand for an hour and 'Mr. Wilson, who had not met him previously, was thrilled'.[1]

However, this progress towards the achievement of a barrister's wig and gown was not without setbacks. Those who believe that success in the courts of law depends little upon facility in passing written examinations will take comfort from the fact that, when Norman Birkett sat for Part I of the Bar Examination, he failed in the paper on Real Property. But he got through all right next time and also duly passed the Final. On the night of June 4, 1913, he was called to the Bar at the Inner Temple, the Bencher who proposed him being Mr. J. F. Rawlinson, K.C., Recorder of Cambridge and M.P. for the University. 'Strangely unmoved,' he noted in his diary, when he returned to Birmingham. 'Back with wig etc. at midnight.' The ceremony as was the custom, took place in the Hall of the Inn after dinner, and his father was particularly pleased by something Norman told him beforehand. 'I felt very proud to read that you were going to drink the judges' health in water,' the elder

[1] Communicated by Mr. Ernest Sheppard. The meeting took place on December 14, 1911.

Birkett wrote to his son. 'I appreciate the compliment very much.'

The newly fledged barrister had a photograph taken of himself in his wig and gown and sent it to Nithsdale, where it was eagerly scanned by the family. 'We all admire it very much,' wrote his father. 'Mary said, "Doesn't he look learned!" Nellie said, "Isn't it lovely?" and Edith said, "Isn't it charming?" and Father said in his heart, "May God bless the lad." '

Meanwhile he had been looking around for a good junior barrister's chambers where he could be taken in as a pupil and where perhaps there would be a chance of his staying on at the end of his twelve months' pupilage. For this purpose he went along to the House of Commons to seek the advice of a well-known Liberal M.P. and Chancery 'silk', Stanley Buckmaster, who was shortly to become Solicitor-General and later Lord Chancellor. Buckmaster had represented Cambridge as a Liberal in the 1906 Parliament, and Birkett had campaigned for him during both Elections in 1910 when he had unsuccessfully recontested the seat. Buckmaster strongly advised him to start in Birmingham, as he had already established some useful connections there, such as the Cadburys, and was getting known as a speaker at Liberal meetings in the area. Various names were mentioned, among them that of J. G. Hurst, subsequently Recorder of Birmingham. John Hurst had originally practised as a solicitor in Birmingham before transferring to the Bar, and was a leading junior on the Midland Circuit at this time, and Birkett promised to go and see him with Buckmaster's recommendation. The result was that Hurst said he would be willing to take him into his chambers at 27, Temple Row, Birmingham, 'if he can get a room for me'.

One man who thought Birkett's decision to go to the Bar was the right one was the Warden of Fircroft College, Tom Bryan. 'You are cut out for great things,' Bryan told him.

CHAPTER III

JUNIOR BARRISTER

I

On leaving Bournville, Norman Birkett took a prolonged holiday at the family home in Ulverston, where he was made much of by his father and sisters. He returned to Birmingham after two months to begin his pupilage with John Hurst and wait for briefs. As soon as he had settled himself in his lodgings and had met his new master, he gave his father a full account of the situation and future prospects.

To Thomas Birkett

125, *Bristol Road*, *Edgbaston*, *Birmingham*, *September* 23, 1913.

I have seen Hurst this morning, and really he is quite hopeful.

He has not yet got [larger] chambers but he is expecting a favourable reply from some chambers two doors away, where he will be able to get a set of four rooms, one for himself, one for the clerk, one for Coley (the man reading with him) and one for me. If he gets these, he will be into them quite soon, and I shall have my name on the door at once.

I am starting with him in earnest on Monday next, but he has an important case on Thursday and Friday of this week, which is a case about electric bell-pushes which was referred from the last Assizes to an expert Trade Arbitrator, and he expects it to last two days, and I am going with him to it. Then on Saturday morning I am going into chambers with him to look through his briefs for the following week. The next week is an important County Court week, when all cases involving £20 and upwards are referred to this week from all the sittings of the County Courts, and he expects to be in Court almost all week. The following week is Sessions and he expects to be in Court all that week too. After that we ought, if all goes well, to be settled in our new chambers.

I talked with him about taking briefs and I am glad to say his view was the same as mine. He said I ought to get a good many briefs in my first year, but I ought to wait a month or so, in order to get practical experience: but after that I might take simple cases in the County Court and elsewhere.

He also said that frequently he had cases which took him longer than he thought, and he wanted someone to keep them going whilst he went over to his chambers to see clients, and this work he thought I might do. It would involve the examination-in-chief of a witness or something like that.

He told me he had talked with his clerk about remuneration, and the clerk said the usual practice was a guarantee and fees. There is a scale of fees fixed. For example, if I get a brief marked £1.1.0 the solicitor would pay £1.3.6d, the 2/6 being for the clerk. Similarly with bigger briefs. The guarantee is £26 per year or 10/– per week payable on Saturdays. I saw the clerk and talked with him, and this is what we agreed to—that I am to pay him £26 per year for the next year. The clerk said I would make it easily in the year, if I could do the work, for he had to refuse pounds worth of work in a year, because Hurst was so busy.

He said he was very glad I was coming for it would mean more for him. He said that already he had had enquiries about me from solicitors' clerks, and I said I wanted a little practical experience first, and he agreed.

Hurst got £52.10.0 marked on his brief for [a recent prosecution] and 30, 20, 10, 5, 4 guineas are marked on briefs I saw, so there is money to be made. The clerk's business is to get me briefs, so he is certain to get them when it means fees for him. So I anticipate making a small amount. . . . He is getting me a Fee Book etc. for when we get in to the new chambers. So that is how matters stand at present. He is getting me information about the Circuit, and I believe there is a small fee on joining that. I am afraid my little stock of money will dwindle, but with G[eorge] C[adbury] J[unio]r's £100 I hope to be almost abreast at the end of the year.

I am going fully robed to Sessions the week after next.

I had quite a comfortable journey yesterday . . . I got a taxi at New Street and transported my luggage and myself for 2/3 to my new rooms, which looked a bit cheerless with all my belongings in boxes. I set to work and unpacked, and things are getting a bit more ship-shape. Your photograph made me a bit more homesick and I had the 'Lord's-song-in-a-strange-land' feeling!

. . . I met Coley who knew me at Cambridge. He will be called in January next, and he has been with Hurst since April and likes it very much. His father is a solicitor here, and Coley said there were a few young barristers waiting for work, so I shall have to fight—and I mean to!

Thomas Birkett replied to this letter by return, pleased that 'everything looks very promising' and adding that he was paying the amount of his son's pupil fee (100 guineas) into his bank account 'so that you can make it all right with Hurst'. Long afterwards the son admitted that there was one sentence in this letter which made him keep it. 'It was prophetic.'

I have no doubt long before the year has gone by you will have addressed his Lordship with that truly legal tone which will at once command his attention and respect.

The reference was to Lord Ilkeston, the Birmingham Stipendiary Magistrate; and the very next day Norman Birkett received a brief to appear before 'his Lordship' at the Police Court. It was an application for an order to compel an apprentice to fulfil the terms of his indenture, and the young barrister was instructed to represent the employer, a building contractor. The arrival of the brief naturally excited him, and he immediately wrote off to his father with the news, saying he wanted to accept the brief but would be guided by Hurst's advice. Thomas Birkett replied as follows:

Nithsdale, *Ulverston.*
September 27, 1913.

My dear Boy,

Many thanks for letter to hand this a.m. You have not been long in getting your first brief. You are quite right. Do exactly as Hurst would suggest in the matter because he has had a wide experience and knows how best to act under such circumstances.

I have not been very grand this week. It has been my stomach and indigestion has caused me a lot of pain so I saw Dr. Bowman who gave me a bottle and I am feeling somewhat better but he says he will come up again tomorrow morning and re-examine me.

You have had a very full week and it seems more than a week since you returned. I need hardly say how much interested I am in all you do and how much I enjoy reading your letters.

I thought a short letter better than a postcard.

With much love,

Ever your affectionate father,

THOS. BIRKETT

P.S. Don't worry about me. It is only for extra precaution that I saw Bowman.

This was the last letter that Norman Birkett received from his father. Four days later a telegram from Ulverston informed him of his father's sudden turn for the worse, and he caught the first train north, arriving home just in time to clasp his hand before he died. It was a great shock for the whole family, since Thomas Birkett had not passed his sixtieth birthday, and although he had been in indifferent health for some years he continued to work at his business almost to the end. He was tremendously proud of his younger son and had quite overcome the feelings of disappointment he experienced when Norman announced that he was not going on for the Wesleyan Ministry. Although Norman had sometimes found his father a source of trial, he for his part was devoted to him and often worried himself about his health. 'Now don't worry unduly about me,' Thomas Birkett wrote in one of his last letters. 'I shall take every care and precaution that I can and leave the rest to Our Father, whose power cannot fail.'

Norman Birkett returned to Birmingham and the new chambers which his master, John Hurst, had secured at 41, Temple Row. He discussed the question of the brief with Hurst and after some coaching the latter agreed that he should take it. He consequently prepared the case with the greatest care, writing out his speech beforehand, even to the opening words, 'May it please the Bench, I appear for the Plaintiff in this case.' The essence of the complaint was that the apprentice did not keep proper working hours, 6.30 a.m. to 6.0 p.m., which were customary in those days. Apparently he had joined the Carpenters Union and the union instructed him to work only from 7.0 a.m. to 5.30 p.m. and he had been doing this. Having heard the evidence, the Stipendiary said he did not think he could rule that the employer's commands were unlawful and he thought they ought to be obeyed. He accordingly made an order to enforce the terms of the indenture.

For some months the apprentice conformed to the order and then began again to come in late and leave early. This conduct prompted the employer to take out a summons against the apprentice to show cause why he should not be committed to prison for not obeying the order. Birkett again appeared for the employer. The Stipendiary adjourned the case for eight weeks so as to give the apprentice another chance of obeying the order, otherwise he would go to prison. 'I think the hours are very long,' said Lord Ilkeston, 'but I don't think it is my duty to interfere with them on this particular summons.'

After consulting his lay client, Birkett informed the Court that 'as a matter of grace' the plaintiff would agree that in summer the hours should be from 6.30 to 5.30 and in winter 7 o'clock to 5.30, the latter hours being those demanded by the trade union. And so the matter was presumably disposed of, since no further complaint was made against the apprentice. Birkett argued it well and the case was fully reported in the local press.[1] There can be little doubt, however, on which side the advocate's sympathies lay in this case and that he agreed with the magistrate's remarks about the length of the apprentice's working hours.

The original brief was marked at one guinea, with the customary half-crown for the clerk. The day was to come when the figure of one thousand guineas was written on a brief for Mr. Norman Birkett, K.C., to appear at the circuit Assizes. As this was generally believed at the time to be a record fee for a circuit case, a friend of his wished to photograph it. But the 1,000 guinea brief, as Birkett told the law students of Birmingham long afterwards was 'as

[1] *The Birmingham Gazette*, February 17, 1914.

nothing' compared with that which earned him the first 'magical figure' of £1 3*s*. 6*d*.

Birkett's next step was to join the Midland Circuit, so as to enable him to appear at Assizes and at those Sessions which were restricted to members of the circuit. 'You fellows,' said Hurst to the other members in the robing room in his general breezy manner on the opening day of the next Birmingham Assizes, 'I want you to meet a man who is to be a member of our circuit; he's come into my chambers—Norman Birkett.' Thus the introduction to the circuit was characteristically effected by Hurst, and his pupil was duly elected at the Bar Circuit Mess on November 27, 1913. There were eleven Assize towns on the Midland Circuit—Aylesbury, Bedford, Northampton, Peterborough, Leicester, Oakham, Lincoln, Derby, Nottingham, Warwick and Birmingham—which the judges who went the circuit visited in that order, to hear and determine cases and to clear the gaols. Birmingham, with its modern Victoria Law Courts, reputedly the finest outside London, always had the heaviest list at Assizes. The senior practising member of the circuit was the Leader, to whose position Birkett was one day to succeed. In 1913 the Leader was Marston Clarke Buszard, K.C., Recorder of Leicester (known as 'The Bird'), who had been called to the Bar in 1862, when executions were still carried out in public. Buszard was a vigorous personality with a quiet voice, who could say incisive things in spite of his age. To Birkett he extended a very warm welcome in the Circuit Mess, having already proposed him for election. The other leading 'silks' on the circuit included Hugo Young, Rydal Adkins, and J. S. Dugdale, the then Recorder of Birmingham. The juniors in a good way of practice besides Hurst were Henry Maddocks, who had seconded Birkett's election to the circuit, Henry McCardie (later the well-known judge), Henry Joy, Arthur Ward, Norman Winning, Maurice Healy, Paul Sandilands, Richard O'Sullivan and St. John Field. The strongest local Bar on the circuit was at Birmingham, where the numbers were between forty and fifty practising barristers at the time Birkett joined. 'We all wished him the best of luck,' said Arthur Ward later recalling Birkett's introduction, 'the general impression being, after a few minutes' chat, that he was a very nervous fellow of a very few words.'[1]

Then there was that important court official, the Clerk of Assize,

[1] Arthur Ward. *Stuff and Silk* (1949), at p. 57.

who was responsible for the drawing of the indictments, arraigning prisoners, taking the jury's verdict, fixing the amount of counsel's fees and generally ensuring the smooth working of the legal machinery of the courts. By a coincidence a new Clerk of Assize for the Midland Circuit had been appointed two days before Birkett joined. This was George Pleydell Bancroft, son of the famous actor-manager Sir Squire Bancroft and his wife, the actress Marie Wilton. George Bancroft and Birkett immediately took to each other and became close friends. When Bancroft wrote his reminiscences a quarter of a century later, Birkett, who had by now become the Circuit Leader, introduced them in a Preface, in the course of which he remarked: 'When I first appeared as a shy and nervous Junior, George Bancroft was already the Clerk of Assize. . . . There is not a judge on the Bench who has not found in George Bancroft a wise, patient, and faithful adviser, practical, resourceful and considerate. There is not a single member of the circuit who has not found in him the staunchest of friends, through good and evil report, kindly, far-seeing, and understanding. . . . To hear him read His Majesty's Commission at the opening of the Assizes is a thing never to be forgotten, and it is already one of the traditions of the circuit which he has created. "Doing that which to Justice doth appertain" when spoken by him in his strong and vibrant voice springs to life with dignity and meaning and great power.'[1]

Among his other duties the Clerk of Assize had to arrange for the defence of prisoners, who could not afford to pay for counsel to defend them, under the Poor Prisoners' Defence Act. Bancroft had not been the Clerk for long when there was what he described as a 'hopeless murder' at Bedford Assizes, where the accused's guilt was clear from the outset. The prisoner who was charged with the murder of his wife, had almost severed her head with a chopper and there was no question of insanity being pleaded as a defence. 'I was anxious about it,' Bancroft later recalled. 'And finally, after meeting a young man for the first time at the Bar Mess, whom I had never met before nor seen in robes, I decided to take the big risk of entrusting him with the brief solely upon the strength of his conversational powers. That was Norman Birkett. . . . It was his first

[1] G. P. Bancroft. *Stage and Bar* (1939), at p. 11. Bancroft was Clerk of Assize for the Midland Circuit for thirty-three years. He was also the author of a successful play, *The Ware Case*. He died in 1956, aged 88.

Poor Prisoner's defence . . . and a most ingenious and able defence it was. Mr. Justice Shearman was the judge, and in the opening sentences of his summing-up to the jury paid the highest compliment I have ever heard paid to a young counsel. I think I am right in saying that it was the flying start in his successful race.'[1]

Later, when Birkett came to be widely known as a defence counsel, it was commonly said that he had never failed to secure an acquittal in a murder case. This was not so. The case at Bedford was his first capital one and his defence was unsuccessful, although he was warmly complimented upon it by the judge.

Besides defences under the Poor Prisoners' Defence Act, Birkett had more than his fair share of 'dock briefs'. By long established custom, a prisoner who has been charged and is in the dock may pick out any barrister who happens to be in court and robed at the time to defend him, and by the etiquette of the Bar the barrister must accept the brief for the fee of £1 3*s.* 6*d.*, which sum must be paid in cash on the spot. The feature of Birkett which prompted a prisoner to point to him was the colour of his hair, which appeared conspicuously from under his wig. 'I'll 'ave the bloke with the red 'air,' the man in the dock would say more often than not when Birkett was in court. Thus the feature, which Birkett always felt to be a hindrance at school, turned out to his advantage. 'When I was a lad,' he once admitted, 'I worried and was absolutely ashamed because of the colour of my hair. . . . Well, I have found that it has added to my success, for work has come my way because I have red hair.' This was particularly true in his early days on the Midland Circuit, when he could say in the words of the judge's song in *Trial by Jury*:

All thieves who could my fees afford
  Relied on my orations,
And many a burglar I've restored
  To his friends and his relations.

One of Birkett's best lay clients was an old man with a white beard and a deceptively courtly manner, named Tommy Evans, a professional pickpocket, whose acquittal Birkett secured on three occasions. Happening to meet Tommy at a railway station, where he

[1] Bancroft, 295.

was catching a train, Birkett admonished the pickpocket to mend his ways, as he could not rely on him to get him off a fourth time. While they were talking, Birkett, whose mind was on the departing train, felt for his watch and discovered to his annoyance that he had forgotten to bring it with him.

'What's the matter?' asked Tommy Evans. 'Haven't you got a watch?'

'No, confound it—I must have left it at home.'

'Wait here a moment, guv,' said Tommy with his usual innocent-looking air. 'I'll get you one!'

Fortunately the whistle blew at this moment, and Birkett was glad to bolt for his train.

Thus, in little more than a year, when he was scarcely out of his pupilage in John Hurst's chambers in Birmingham, Norman Birkett had made some headway as an advocate on the Midland Circuit and briefs with his name on them were arriving in increasing numbers in Temple Row, although the fees were small. But it was an encouraging beginning.

2

At first the chambers at 41, Temple Row, Birmingham, consisted of John Hurst and his two pupils, Norman Birkett and Colin Coley. After about a year they were joined by another young Birmingham barrister named Donald Finnemore, later Mr. Justice Finnemore. Then there was the clerk, George Newey, and the junior clerk, a lad called Rollinson, who still wore short trousers. Young Rollinson used to play football for a local Boys' Brigade team formed by Finnemore, while Birkett would cheer from the touch line. 'He always appealed to me as he was so considerate and generous,' the former junior clerk has recalled. 'I remember the first suit I had with long trousers. Mr. Birkett gave the senior clerk, Mr. George Newey, the money to pay for it and also put a golden sovereign in the pocket.'

On the outbreak of the First World War, Birkett tried to join the army but failed to pass the medical examination. In fact, he was twice rejected as physically unfit for any form of active service between 1914 and 1918. He was keenly disappointed and showed it when he was turned down on the second occasion, and Finnemore was accepted and went off to serve with a field unit of the British Red Cross in France. At this time Birkett was threatened with tuberculosis, but refused to go into hospital for treatment and so take up a bed which might be needed for a war casualty. Instead he went back to Ulverston where he spent six months being nursed back to health by his sisters. During his convalescence he went on a walking tour with his cousin Harry, putting up among other places at the Ullswater Hotel, where the sight of two young men not in uniform was unusual. 'We were both rejects for the army and naturally felt rather out of it,' Henry Birkett has recalled, 'not that either of us wanted to be soldiers. There were few young men about anywhere and we rather felt our position. Norman was lame with rheumatism and I had a nasty skin trouble. We attended the Keswick Wesleyan Church on the Sunday morning, but the service had little value for us after a hymn beginning, "Jesus, regard our joint complaint" was announced. This was a joy for years and often recalled.' It was during this tour that Henry Birkett first came to realize his cousin's remarkable powers of memory. When they were in Keswick, Norman bought a copy of G. K. Chesterton's volume of verse, *Wine, Women and Song*, which he presented to his companion, whom he astonished by reading a page or two and then quoting a poem in full and with absolute accuracy.

Throughout the war Birkett did voluntary work for the Belgian refugees and subsequently received the personal thanks of the King of the Belgians. He sat too on a tribunal in the Birmingham City Hall, which examined the cases of those who claimed exemption from military service on the ground of conscientious objections. At the same time, he preached regularly at the Wesleyan People's Chapel in Great King Street, Birmingham, and he also continued to run his Sunday school class at the Junior Adult School in Cregoe Street, which duty he shared with his old employer George Cadbury. He also kept in touch with the family at the Northfield Manor House. These, among other visitors, were the novelist Archibald Marshall (at this time Paris correspondent of *The Daily News*, which was owned by George Cadbury Senior) and his Australian wife and eleven-year-old daughter Betty. The latter took a strong fancy to Norman, who was very kind to her, as indeed he always was to children. One Christmas, when she was staying with her parents at Northfield, he sent her Charles Dickens's *A Christmas Carol*, together with a letter which she found charming. She carefully treasured it.

Birmingham,
December 22, 1915

Dearest Betty,

If you have room for one more book after all your gifts of Saturday, I send you the second best Christmas story in the world.

You know the First Story and will hear it read again I'm sure this Christmas. I wish that I could come and hear it read with you, and hear you and Ursula sing the Christmas hymns.

For Christmas was made for you and Ursula and Knox and all boys and girls—and the grown-ups really get their Christmas from you! So you see you must enjoy yourselves or else the grown-ups won't enjoy themselves at all!

Do you have a stocking? If so, you must sleep soundly on Christmas Eve!

A Merry Christmas!

With love,
from
'B'.

Another literary acquaintance he cultivated at this period was the actor-playwright and poet John Drinkwater, who managed the popular Birmingham Repertory Theatre, which Drinkwater had helped Sir Barry Jackson to found when working as a clerk in an insurance office in Birmingham. Birkett and Drinkwater had first met at Bournville, where Drinkwater regularly produced an open-air pastoral play for the annual Works Summer Party. In Birmingham Birkett was one of the audience for the first performance of *Abraham Lincoln*, the play which established Drinkwater's fame as a dramatist overnight when it was later produced in London; and Birkett wrote an enthusiastic notice under his own name in the local newspaper, in which he forecast the play's subsequent success. 'We congratulate Mr. Drinkwater and the whole of the Repertory Company on a most memorable performance; they help to make us citizens of no mean city, for no other city has yet given us such a theatre and such a play as *Abraham Lincoln*.'[1]

[1] *Birmingham Gazette*, October 14, 1918.

A member of the Cadbury family not hitherto mentioned, who with his wife was very kind to Birkett at this period, was William Cadbury, a nephew of George Cadbury Senior. Birkett was a frequent guest at his house, Wast Hills, near Birmingham; indeed they had political interests in common, since William Cadbury represented the King's Norton ward on the City Council, which formed part of the parliamentary constituency of North Birmingham, for which Birkett, as will be seen, had become the Liberal candidate. At this time William Cadbury took an action, which was bound to be unpopular for a man in public life but which commanded Birkett's admiration. For many years he had been on friendly terms with Sir Roger Casement, having strongly supported his exposure of the rubber atrocities in the Congo, but Cadbury had had no communication with him since his defection to the German side at the beginning of the war. Nor did he approve of Casement's behaviour in this respect. However, after Casement had been captured following his unsuccessful landing from a German submarine on the Irish coast and was charged with high treason, Cadbury sent his solicitor two hundred pounds towards the cost of his defence, as he understood Casement had no money and he wished him 'to have every opportunity of stating his case'. After Casement had been found guilty and executed, Birkett formed the view that he had both had a fair trial and had been properly convicted. On the other hand, he applauded Cadbury's generous action which had enabled the prisoner to have the best counsel to defend him, and he seems to have agreed with Cadbury—at any rate, in private—that the Government would have done better in view of all the circumstances to have reprieved this unfortunate Irish patriot instead of making a political martyr of him.[1]

After his illness and convalescence in the Lakes in 1916, Birkett returned to Birmingham and was soon picking up more and more work. He gradually acquired an air of self-assurance, although he was always nervous when he went into court and got on his feet. His circuit colleague Arthur Ward was to note that, when he took off his coat and waistcoat in the robing-room after the hearing of a case, his shirt was often wet from the effects of nervous strain and tension, a feeling which never left him throughout his career as an

[1] William Adlington Cadbury was Lord Mayor of Birmingham from 1919 to 1921.

advocate, although his clients in the court room seldom noticed it. No one's services for 'dock defences' were more in demand among the more recently called members of the Midland Circuit, and as his work increased this sometimes proved a cause of embarrassment. On one occasion, at Birmingham Assizes, when the prisoner had pointed him out as his choice for a dock brief, Birkett had to throw himself upon the mercy of the Bench. 'I'm most awfully sorry,' he said pathetically, 'but I'm due in the Nisi Prius Court at this moment. Still, perhaps, Mr. Coley would take the case on?' With the assent of the prisoner and the judge, Birkett's fellow barrister in chambers did so to such effect that, although he was opposed by the experienced Rydal Adkins who prosecuted, Coley put up a brilliant defence and secured his client's acquittal, thereby laying the foundation of his own subsequent successful career at the local Bar.

Outside the Circuit Assizes and Sessions, Birkett's work lay chiefly in the local county courts and police courts, with an occasional trip to London when a case came before the Court of Criminal Appeal or the High Court. Once, when arguing an appeal before Mr. Justice Darling, he neatly turned the tables on that judge, who fancied himself as a wit. Darling, who seemed to have forgotten where he had spent his salad days in the law—he had been articled to a Birmingham solicitor before going to the Bar—interrupted Birkett with the remark: 'All this took place in Birmingham, where they are never tired of declaring how much cleverer they are than other people.' 'I hope counsel are not included in that category,' promptly retorted Birkett. This remark, which for once put the usually irrepressible Darling in his place, gave considerable pleasure in Birmingham, where it was widely repeated.

Court reporters now took to watching for quotable remarks from the striking red-headed junior barrister, and they were seldom disappointed. In one case at the Birmingham Police Court which concerned a fight between two rival Italian groups, prosecuting counsel observed: 'These aliens ought not to be allowed to carry loaded firearms.'

'These aliens!' Birkett, who appeared for the defence of the Italians, echoed scornfully: 'If my learned friend had been defending instead of prosecuting, they would have been "Our Glorious Allies"!'

One lesson which the young barrister learned was to be patient, particularly when dealing with a difficult witness. A good example of his exercise of this quality occurred in the course of an action brought in the Birmingham County Court by a Solihull farmer against a neighbour, whose sheep, which were stated to be of a particularly hungry Welsh breed, had one night entered the plaintiff's field and done exhaustive justice to his crop of clover, incidentally trampling down part of a field of barley on their way to the clover. Birkett, who appeared for the defendant farmer, spent a considerable time cross-examining one of the plaintiff's witnesses, a shepherd, and trying to extract an important piece of information from him, namely that the clover crop might have been destroyed by rabbits. The witness admitted that rabbits frequently visited the clover field, but he added that they had now all been shot.

'What did you do with them?'

'Ate some of 'em,' the witness admitted.

'And did they taste as if they had eaten clover or barley?' Birkett continued.

'Well,' the shepherd replied, 'they didn't taste as if they had been drinkin' beer!'

'And naturally you view this damage from the standpoint of one who is accustomed to place great value on small things?'

'Well, now,' said the shepherd, 'that's just what the old Squire used to tell me.'

And so, like Sam Weller, the witness stepped down from the box, having said as little as he possibly could for the other side and earned the reputation, as far as the plaintiff's counsel was concerned, of being 'a fine example of a humorist, but little else'.

One war-time case brought him a much valued souvenir. One of his colleagues on the circuit, Henry Maddocks, lost his son, who was killed at the Front. Shortly afterwards, the son's batman came home on leave and got into trouble, as a result of which he was faced with a serious criminal charge and asked Maddocks to defend him. Maddocks appeared for the batman at the police court, where he was committed for trial at the next Birmingham Assizes. But Maddocks had not the heart to continue with the case—he was 'afraid of it', he said and asked his friend Norman Birkett to take it on for him, explaining that the man was poor and could not afford any brief fee. Birkett willingly obliged, defended the man brilliantly and got him off. Whenever he went into court afterwards, he could be seen with a fine gold pencil case. It was a present from Maddocks to mark his gratitude for his friend's action on this occasion.

The case which first drew general public attention to Birkett on the Midland Circuit occurred at Nottingham Assizes before Mr. Justice Shearman during the last months of the war and ended with a remarkable demonstration by the spectators in court. Birkett was briefed to defend an army captain charged with abducting a girl under fifteen years of age, who was a clerk in the Army Pay Corps in Nottingham and whose father was a Staff-Quartermaster-Sergeant. Evidence was given by the latter that he found her in the prisoner's flat in Maida Vale, London, and the prosecution suggested that he had inflamed the girl's mind with words, wine and money and his description of life in the metropolis. The captain had also promised marriage, according to the girl, but this was hotly denied by the captain who had previously declared his belief to the police that she was over sixteen. He also produced her letters to show that the idea of going to London originated with her, and in addressing the jury Birkett described her as 'fast, forward, frivolous, romantic, adventurous, a confessed liar, and lured by khaki'.

The judge summed up strongly against the prisoner. While discrediting the girl's story about a promise of marriage and accepting her letters, he directed the jury that initiative had nothing to do with it and that the prisoner was guilty of abduction if he took an active part in persuading her to leave her parents. Nevertheless, such was the effect of Birkett's appeal that the jury acquitted the captain of the charge.

Immediately the verdict was announced, there was an amazing scene in court, the first time such a thing had happened as the result of Birkett's successful advocacy on behalf of a client, though by no means the last. There was a loud outburst of applause and people began to cheer. Such behaviour deeply shocked Mr. Justice Shearman, who ordered the court to be cleared and did not hide what he thought of the defendant. 'It astonishes me,' he said. 'This man has broken up the home of a good man, the home of a soldier and of his wife, and yet there are people who can applaud over it. It makes me astonished and ashamed. Let everybody leave the court at once.'

This sensational acquittal was much talked about at the time and as a result more and more briefs for the successful defending barrister flowed into the chambers in Temple Row. After barely five years in practice, Norman Birkett was becoming quite a name on the Midland Circuit, and his success brought him the customary mark of recognition from the Leader of the circuit in the shape of a red bag in which to carry his briefs instead of the blue one, with which the junior barrister begins his career at the Bar. 'Will you accept the accompanying Red Bag to which I think you are thoroughly entitled?' the octogenarian circuit Leader wrote to Birkett on May 15, 1917. 'It has been on several occasions a pleasure to me to hear you conduct a case and I doubt not you will go on and prosper. I hope the Bag will always have plenty of briefs and that you will find it a convenience. That you may have a prosperous career on the Midland Circuit and in the profession generally is the sincere wish of your friend Marston C. Buszard.'

3

While he was making his way at the Birmingham Bar and on the Midland Circuit, Birkett maintained his interest in the political cause of Liberalism. His great speech in North Worcestershire in December, 1912, before an audience of a thousand, when he took the place of the principal speaker at two hours' notice, had created a great impression in local Liberal circles, and this achievement coupled with his known identification with the Cadburys' schemes of social reform, adult education and industrial welfare, clearly pointed the way to an early parliamentary candidature. A few months before the outbreak of the First World War, he agreed to become the prospective Liberal candidate for North Birmingham, and at the public meeting at which he opened his campaign he made a declaration of political faith in terms of deep conviction.

'I desire to say in the clearest and most explicit way,' he proclaimed, 'that the only thing for which I am going to fight in North Birmingham is not in any sense personal advancement, but I am going to fight with all the power that in me lies for that great body of people who are unable to fight for themselves,' namely, 'the toilers and dwellers in these crowded streets.'

'I am on the side of those who are opposed to privilege,' he proceeded in outlining his policy. On one side, he pointed out, there was enormous wealth, and on the other abject poverty. This was clearly inequitable, and politics could do something to equalize matters, and bring about a better and more equitable distribution of the wealth of the country. Half the land was owned by a few thousand people, and the rest of the millions had to make do with the other half. Furthermore, there were five millions of people living in slum areas. Was this fair and equitable? Then, in regard to infantile mortality, it was, in St. Mary's Ward, higher than in any other ward in the city. The Medical Officer's Report showed that it was 172 per thousand, while in the residential suburb of Edgbaston (where Birkett himself lived) it was only 62 per thousand. 'In this campaign I am going to fight for political freedom for Ireland, Welsh disestablishment, and all those measures which will bring about a brighter and happier day for the great masses of the population of this country.'[1]

The war put an end for the time being to party political rivalries and postponed the General Election until after the Armistice had been signed with Germany. Speaking at the Annual Meeting of the Birmingham Liberal Association in Birmingham on May 21, 1917, Birkett had this to say about the future treatment of that country:

> There are people in this country and other countries who still cherish the idea that Germany shall be crushed, peace dictated in Berlin, and ideas of that kind. I want to speak my mind, having considered the matter as best I can; and having brought it all the judgment I have, I am bound to say that the policy of crushing Germany, using those words in the ordinary sense, seems to me to be a fatal policy. It is the language of the man who still regards Europe as a cockpit. It seems to me that if that policy is followed, then no sooner is this war over, no sooner is this danger removed, than all the nations prepare for the next war. And of all things that is the calamity which has got to be avoided. . . .
>
> *If by some inconceivable catastrophe the position was reversed, and Great Britain was crushed, is there a man who would deny that the one thing Great Britain would do would be to set to work and prepare and struggle for the day when the memory of that insult would be wiped out?* It is just as well for us to confess that

[1] *Birmingham Gazette*. May 5, 1914.

> that particular policy is not conducive to liberty, but the reverse. But you say partition her, dismember her, change her Government. The answer is that the stability of Europe is not advanced by any of these things. They have been tried elsewhere and without much success. For look at the Balkan States, look at Italy, look nearer home, look at Ireland, and then ask yourself is it a judicial policy, is it a wise policy, having regard to the issues at stake?

Prophetic words, indeed! How abundantly they were to be justified, the history of the Versailles settlement, the crushing reparations policy inflicted upon Germany by the Allies and the rise of Hitler and the Nationalist Socialist Party were to show in the course of the next twenty years.

Meanwhile the electoral divisions of Birmingham were being redrawn and the number increased. In the consequent redistribution much of the old North Division was comprised in the new King's Norton Division, including Bournville and Selly Oak, and it was this division that Birkett contested as the official Liberal candidate at the General Election in December, 1918. But the situation had changed considerably since the last Election eight years previously. It is true that the Prime Minister, Mr. Lloyd George, was a Liberal and the Election was fought on a new franchise, which amounted in effect to universal suffrage and admitted women both as voters and candidates for the first time. But the Prime Minister headed a Coalition Government made up of Liberals and Conservatives, which he was determined to keep in power, and he had the assent and support of the Conservative leader Mr. Bonar Law. Candidates, whether Liberal or Conservative, who supported the continuance of the Coalition, were given a certificate or 'coupon' by Lloyd George as a badge of their loyalty. The rump of the Liberal Party continued to be led by Mr. Asquith, who had been ousted as Prime Minister by Lloyd George during the war, and he claimed the allegiance of the Birmingham Liberals.

Birkett's opponent with the 'coupon' in King's Norton was the Conservative Sir Herbert Austin, later Lord Austin, the well-known motor manufacturer and a public figure of considerable consequence, as well as of personal power and influence. In addition, the Co-operative Society put up a candidate, Mr. Thomas Hackett.

The latter, who was a works foreman, and who sat on the Birmingham City Council, also had the backing of the local Labour Party. Indeed Birkett had once spoken for him during the municipal elections before the war. But, even without Hackett's intervention, Birkett stood no chance against the Coalition candidate, who had an absolute majority in this three-cornered contest. The actual voting figures were:

Sir Herbert Austin (Coalition Unionist)	8,809
T. Hackett (Co-operator)	4,917
W. N. Birkett (Liberal)	2,435

This disappointing result, with the Liberal well at the bottom of the poll, was reflected in the composition of the new House of Commons, to which the Prime Minister and the Coalitionists were returned with a strength of 478, while Labour secured 59 seats and only 27 of Mr. Asquith's Liberal followers reached Westminster.

When it was all over, the defeated Liberal candidate for King's Norton sat down and wrote to his supporters and workers, thanking them for their efforts.

> The result of the Election was, in some measure, a disappointment, but there is no cause for discouragement or dismay; and I hope that no worker will feel anything but pride for the campaign which we fought together.
>
> We stood for things which do not change even in electoral defeat—the unrestricted right of free speech, the extension of the bounds of Freedom, the expulsion of things alien to Liberty, and the extension of the reign of Justice in matters social, industrial, national and international for all mankind.
>
> If these things are true—and they are true—one day shall see their final triumph; and in that day of triumph it will now be a good thing to remember with that pride with which I now write, that in the days when popular feeling was insensible to them, we still fought a good fight for them, and inflexibly kept the Liberal faith.
>
> For myself, I retain the gracious recollection of fine loyalties, generous enthusiasm, splendid sacrifice, and noble encouragements given and made by those I may now call my friends in King's Norton, and wherever I may go in the world,

> and whatever the future may bring, it can bring with it nothing which will ever remove the abiding sense of grateful thanks I am now so happy to acknowledge.

Indirectly this Election campaign was to provide Birkett with a source of deep and lasting happiness. Among those who heard him address an open-air meeting at the Bournville works was an attractive Swedish girl, Ruth Nilsson, whose parents had come over from Malmö to settle in Glasgow, and who had recently joined the welfare side of the staff at Bournville as an instructress in physical culture, a subject in which Mrs. George Cadbury Senior (Dame Elizabeth Cadbury) had long taken a special interest. Shortly afterwards they were introduced in the house of a mutual friend in Bournville and a warm friendship developed between them. But that was as far as their relationship went.

Meanwhile Birkett's practice continued to grow. On the eve of the short Easter Vacation in 1920, when Birkett was about to take a short holiday, his clerk George Newey wrote to him: 'Yours surely is a very hard life and what little recreation or change you get is well merited. I feel *very guilty often* that I am the cause of a lot of it, but as you know it is very difficult for me to make your yoke lighter and your task easier under present conditions with everybody wanting you and saying "I must have him, nobody else will do".'

So far as his work went in the criminal courts, Birkett now began to be instructed by the Crown solicitors and to receive briefs to prosecute as well as to defend prisoners. While he always preferred the role of advocate for the defence—it was in his nature that he should—he took his share in the allocation of Crown briefs among the circuit members, as indeed professional etiquette required. Curiously enough, it was an incident arising out of one such prosecution which first made Birkett wonder whether he ought to remain in Birmingham.

The case in question, which was tried at the Assizes by Mr. Justice Atkin, was a somewhat complicated one of fraud against the Inland Revenue involving stamps which it was alleged had previously been used. The prisoner, who was defended by Arthur Ward, was a most impressive little man, who appeared in the dock in a double-breasted frock coat similar to those formerly worn by Victorian Cabinet Ministers. In the course of giving evidence, he made a great parade of his religion, much to the annoyance of most people in court including his own counsel who could see what an effect it was having on the jury, who subsequently convicted him. 'It was a case with any amount of detail and one very difficult to present to a jury,' Arthur Ward later recalled. 'But Birkett's opening was a masterpiece of clarity, as was his conduct of the prosecution right through to the end.'[1]

This was also the view of Mr. Justice Atkin, who sent a note to Birkett from the Bench inviting him to dine at the Judge's Lodgings. When they met for dinner, the judge came straight to the point.

'It's time you left Birmingham. You have cut your teeth, but you have learned all you can and all you ever will here. You must go to London.'

'That is all very well, Judge,' said Birkett, 'but I have only been at the Bar for a few years and I am at least known and earning a living here in the Midlands. Competition in London is on quite a different scale, and, if I failed there, I would have lost everything I have built up here.'

'You won't fail,' the judge assured him.

'And another thing,' Birkett went on. 'I haven't got any private means to keep me going while I get established in London.'

'You won't need any,' said Atkin, adding that in a short time Birkett ought to be in a position to apply for a silk gown, in other words to become a King's Counsel.

Birkett thought over the judge's advice long and anxiously. It was certainly an unusual step for a successful provincial barrister unless he had previously 'taken silk', like his old master John Hurst who had gone south and found a place in the chambers of the great fashionable leader of the day, Sir Edward Marshall Hall. On the other hand, Birkett knew that if he stayed in Birmingham there would be no chance of the Lord Chancellor granting his application for silk until he had been in practice as a junior for fifteen years, at the very least. For the moment he could not make up his mind what to do. However, events soon shaped his decision.

[1] Ward, 58.

4

At Leicester Summer Assizes in 1920, Norman Birkett received the junior brief for the Crown in a remarkable murder trial, popularly known as 'The Green Bicycle Case'. In this he was led by the Attorney-General, Sir Gordon Hewart, K.C., M.P., and his old circuit friend Henry Maddocks, by then also a 'silk' and in Parliament. The leading counsel for the defence was Marshall Hall, who had been briefed 'special'—that is to say, he had an extra fee of fifty guineas marked on his brief in addition to his normal fee and daily 'refreshers', since Marshall Hall belonged to another circuit, and by the etiquette of the Bar was only permitted to accept a brief to appear on the Midland Circuit if the brief was so marked.

It was not the first time that Birkett had found himself up against Marshall Hall. Once during the war, they had been in a case in Birmingham involving a violation of the food and drugs regulations, when the young Birkett had appeared for the prosecution and Marshall Hall was for the defence. Marshall Hall had a Senior Clerk, A. E. Bowker, who had once worked in a Birmingham barrister's chambers but on this occasion was absent on war service. On Bowker's return at the end of the war, Marshall Hall said to him: 'By the way, while you were in France, I did a case in your old haunt, Birmingham, and ran up against a most offensive young man; but he did his case very well and he will go far. Of that I am sure.' Bowker was sufficiently interested to turn up the records to find out the name of the man who had prosecuted Marshall Hall's client. A little later, Bowker happened to go into the Lord Chief Justice's Court and was 'arrested by a voice full of music'. The clerk listened to the argument for a few minutes and then asked an acquaintance who it was. 'Norman Birkett,' came the whispered reply, 'a fellow from Birmingham.' Bowker instantly remembered his conversation with Marshall Hall. He also realized that in reality there was nothing offensive about Birkett's handling of the case: it was simply that he had got the better of his more experienced opponent on the earlier occasion. Bowker was again reminded of the incident when he saw Birkett in the Assize Court in Leicester Castle and he made a mental note of his performance, although as a junior, who was led by two K.C.s, Birkett's role in the trial of Ronald Light for the murder of Bella Wright was a relatively minor one.

Westminster Press Provincial Newspapers

NORMAN BIRKETT, K.C., M.P.

As the result of structural repairs carried out during the 1929 Parliament, Birkett was able to acquire the piece of the old fabric of the House of Commons on which he is sitting. He subsequently installed it as a well-head in the garden of his country home, Challens Green, in Buckinghamshire.

Radio Times Hulton Picture Libr.

SIR EDWARD MARSHALL HALL, K.C.

It was the first murder case of note in which Birkett appeared, and naturally every detail of the trial was afterwards imprinted upon his memory.

> I shall always remember the moment when Marshall Hall came into court at Leicester Castle. He brought with him a strange magnetic quality that made itself felt in every part of the court. The spectators stirred with excitement at the sight of the man whose name was at that time a household word, and a faint murmur ran from floor to gallery. Marshall came, of course, with all the prestige of the greatest criminal defender of the day, and every eye was fixed upon him. He was a very handsome man, with noble head and a most expressive face, and F. E. Smith's comment is not to be bettered: 'Nobody could have been as wonderful as Marshall Hall then looked.' When he addressed the judge it was seen that to his great good looks there had been added perhaps the greatest gift of all in the armoury of an advocate—a most beautiful speaking voice. He had in this case a terrible task before him.[1]

The trial began before Mr. Justice Horridge on June 10, 1920, and lasted for three days. 'Who was the man with the green bicycle?' the Attorney-General asked in his opening speech to the jury. He thus echoed the question which the police and the public had been asking for the past year, since the man was believed to have murdered Bella Wright, a factory girl who had been found dead with a bullet through her head but otherwise unmolested, in a country lane on the evening of July 5, 1919. The Attorney-General suggested that the man was Ronald Light, a Cheltenham schoolmaster and ex-army officer, who after shooting the girl had panicked and thrown the bicycle into a nearby canal where it was later accidentally dragged up and was proved to have been bought by the prisoner. Although there was no witness to the actual murder, several people had come forward and deposed to having seen Bella and the man with the green bicycle together on the fatal evening. At the time of his arrest Light had denied that he ever owned a green bicycle, but he later admitted it on being told that a mechanic who had repaired his gear chain had identified him. The difficulty, however, from the prosecution point of view, was the absence of any motive, since the girl had

[1] Lord Birkett. *Six Great Advocates* (1961), at p. 12.

been neither robbed nor raped. Of course, it was not necessary for the prosecution to establish motive to prove its case, but failure to do so was bound to have an effect upon the jury when they came to consider their verdict.

The first day was taken up with the Attorney-General's opening and examination of the earlier Crown witnesses; nor, it may be added, was the principal Law Officer of the Crown in a particularly good temper on this occasion, since he was still smarting under a feeling of considerable annoyance due to one of the leading barristers' clerks having gained access to his room in the Bell Hotel on the previous night and made him an 'apple pie' bed.

Shortly after the court rose, Hewart received a telegram from the Prime Minister, asking him to return to London immediately on urgent political business. Henry Maddocks and Birkett were accordingly left to carry on the case for the Crown, and next day they divided the examination of the remaining witnesses between them. Thus it fell to Birkett to examine Muriel Nunney, a fourteen-year-old schoolgirl living in Leicester, who had been cycling with another girl on the night of the crime.

Instead of beginning by asking the witness what she had been doing the previous July, Birkett made the mistake of asking her whether she had been out cycling with her friend on July 5th. This immediately brought Marshall Hall to his feet with a protest to Birkett that he should not 'lead' the witness. The prisoner's counsel added that the two girls were not called upon by the police to make statements until more than eight months later. Mr. Justice Horridge followed this up with an implied rebuke to Birkett when he informed the jury that they must remember that counsel had suggested a date to the witness, and he must see that a date was not suggested to the next witness.

In the resumed examination, Miss Nunney said the man she and her companion saw on the road that day and who had spoken to them she had identified out of a parade of twelve men. He had a green bicycle 'with funny handle-bars', a light suit and carried a raincoat over his shoulder.

There was a tense moment when Birkett, addressing the witness, asked, 'Do you see that man in court?'

The little girl pointed at the dock and replied with emphasis, 'There, sir!'

Marshall Hall's brief cross-examination provided Birkett with a brilliant object-lesson, which he never forgot, of how to discredit a witness's testimony in the eyes of the jury.

MARSHALL HALL: Did you hear about what was called 'The Green Bicycle Case'?
WITNESS: Yes, sir.
MARSHALL HALL: And I think you saw the photographs?
WITNESS: Yes, sir.
MARSHALL HALL: You knew about this poor girl being found dead in the road?
WITNESS: Yes, sir.
MARSHALL HALL: You read it in the papers, I suppose?
WITNESS: Yes, sir.
MARSHALL HALL: You were asked whether you had seen this particular man on the 5th of July?
WITNESS: Yes.
MARSHALL HALL: They (the police) gave you a date?
WITNESS: Yes, sir.

The inference was obvious. After so many months had elapsed, how could the girl in the circumstances be sure about the date unless it had previously been put into her mouth and the newspaper photographs of the accused had implanted themselves in her mind?

After the Crown case had been closed, Marshall Hall put the prisoner into the witness box. In his evidence, which he gave convincingly and well, Light admitted to owning the bicycle and also the revolver holster which had been found, but he swore that he had left his revolver at a casualty clearing station in France. As for the dead girl, he admitted having been with her for a short time the evening she died but had parted from her at a certain fork in the road near where her body was found. He frankly admitted that he had made a grievous mistake in not telling the police when he read about her murder, but he had kept on hesitating and then drifted into doing nothing at all, and to spare the distress of his invalid mother, he had disposed of the bicycle, the holster and even the clothes he was wearing on the fatal evening. He stuck to this story throughout and remained completely unshaken under cross-examination by Maddocks, in spite of the fact that, according to Marshall Hall's biographer, Edward Marjoribanks, Maddocks had sat up most of the previous night with Birkett carefully preparing his line of questions.[1]

While Marshall Hall was making his final speech to the jury, a most unusual occurrence took place, the like of which Birkett had never seen before or for that matter was ever to see again in an English court of justice. The judge happened to look up for a moment at the gallery and detected a man at the back in the act of taking a photograph. He ordered the man to be brought down to the well of the court, where he admonished him severely and told him he was fortunate not to be committed to prison for contempt.

This unfortunate interruption put Marshall Hall quite out of his stride and broke the spell of his eloquence. Nevertheless he had said enough to persuade the jury, when the time came for them to retire, to find the prisoner not guilty. But it took them over three hours to return this verdict.

The mystery of 'The Green Bicycle Case' has remained unsolved, although several ingenious solutions were subsequently put forward by amateur criminologists. One of these, which intrigued Birkett, pointed to a dead raven which was found near the scene of the crime and it was suggested that instead of gorging itself to death from a surfeit of Bella Wright's blood, as had originally been assumed, the bird had been shot with a rook rifle by a reckless marksman, probably a boy, as it sat perched on a gate, the bullet had passed through its body and then entered the head of the girl who happened to be riding past the gate at that precise moment and in turn passed through her head ending up on the road. It is an attractive but somewhat far-fetched conclusion. The truth will probably never be known.

A few weeks later, Birkett went to London to argue a case in the Court of Appeal. Against him was his old master and friend J. G. Hurst, now a silk and practising in Marshall Hall's chambers at 3, Temple Gardens. After the appeal had been decided, incidentally in favour of Birkett's client, the two counsel walked back to chambers for tea, accompanied by the clerk, Edgar Bowker.

'I am thinking of coming to London and would like to get into chambers with J.G.H. here,' he said to the clerk. 'I wonder whether you could find room for me?'

Although the chambers in Temple Gardens were fairly full up,

[1] Edward Marjoribanks. *The Life of Sir Edward Marshall Hall* (1929), at p. 405.

Bowker replied that he would be most happy to accommodate him, provided that Marshall Hall, who was the tenant, agreed. At tea time the matter was put to Marshall Hall and he did agree. Later it was settled that Birkett should join them by the beginning of the next term.

The decision to move to London having been made, Birkett went back to Birmingham to pack up. The first person he told was his friend Ruth Nilsson at Bournville. Once or twice previously Birkett had thrown out a hint that they should get married; but so long as he remained in Birmingham Miss Nilsson was quite happy to continue just friends and carry on with her own work. However, Norman Birkett's news had changed the situation completely for her and she in turn was faced with an important decision to make. After thinking it over, she decided to give up her post with the Cadbury firm, and become his wife.

But before doing so, Ruth Nilsson, who was known to her family and friends as 'Billy', had to pay a visit to Sweden to tell her relatives the news of her engagement. She stayed with her uncle Hugo Lindgren and his wife in their villa in Malmö, where her fiancé joined them a little later for a round of calls so that he could meet the various members of the Nilsson and Lindgren families. They also had a short walking tour through some of the beautiful wooded country of southern Sweden, and they made plans for the future. At times, in spite of his happiness at the thought of their approaching marriage, Norman Birkett had fits of depression, wondering whether he was really wise in making the move to London. 'Don't be depressed ever about London,' his fiancée reassured him. 'You really have no reason to be depressed, and you know quite well that you need never be anxious about me, even if you failed absolutely and entirely, because I'll only just love you extra hard to make up, as I've already told you.'

Their wedding, which took place at St. Pancras Registry Office in London on August 25, 1920, was an extremely quiet affair, with no friends or even relatives present, the bride having previously taken a room at the Euston Station Hotel in order to obtain the necessary residence qualification in the St. Pancras district.

After a short honeymoon of ten days, spent touring Devon and Somerset, the couple returned to London and their new home in Bigwood Road, Golder's Green, or Hampstead Garden Suburb, as it was coming to be known. Next day Norman Birkett went along to the Inner Temple, where he saw that his name had been newly painted on the door at 3, Temple Gardens, under those of Sir Edward Marshall Hall and Mr. J. G. Hurst.

5

That great lawyer, Lord Simon, had a favourite recipe for success at the Bar. 'You must have a good clerk and a good digestion.' Fortunately Norman Birkett had both. What he lacked when he joined Marshall Hall's chambers in Temple Gardens were established connections with London solicitors, who could be relied upon to keep him in regular work. Indeed he was practically unknown in London at that time. However, Edgar Bowker, who was a jewel among barristers' clerks, had the feeling, as he put it, that 'here was a winner', and he was as determined as Birkett that he should succeed in spite of the intense competition in the Temple for briefs. 'We shall have to put a minimum of twenty-five guineas for you to go out of town, sir,' Bowker said to him in one of their early talks. 'I think you must concentrate on London work.'

The assiduous clerk began by getting him briefs from some of Marshall Hall's professional clients, to appear in cases where a leader was likely to be instructed as well, but who could only participate, as required by the etiquette of the Bar, when he was accompanied by junior counsel. In civil cases the junior's task was to deal with the preliminary paper work in chambers known as 'settling the pleadings', and in criminal matters to appear, usually without his leader, at the Police Court proceedings where the accused would be committed for trial. Also, the junior would help his leader generally with the conduct of the case in court, examining witnesses and deputizing for him if for any reason the leader should be called away.

One of Birkett's earliest briefs in London came from the firm of solicitors which acted on behalf of St. Dunstan's Institution for the Blind. It was for the defence of a young ex-soldier, blinded in both eyes on active service in France, who was charged with the murder of his wife. The story was pathetic. After the birth of a baby daughter, whom he had never seen, she had left him to lead a gay life, although he still loved her and continually begged her to return to him. This she refused to do, but she would occasionally visit him, as she wanted the daughter to live with her. Finally she called one day to tell her husband she was going abroad. He blocked the doorway to prevent her leaving, then seized her by the throat. There was a struggle, and suddenly he felt her body go limp. Only gradually did he come to realize that he had killed her whom he dearly loved. Then he tried to kill himself with a razor. 'Let me die,' he said afterwards. 'What is my life? What have I got to live for?'

Birkett represented the prisoner at the Police Court, an experience which moved him deeply. While the prosecution was outlining its case and describing the blind man's love for his wife and child—one of the witnesses described how he looked after her, 'dressing her and keeping her clean, much better than a man who could see'—the unfortunate individual in the dock began to weep. Birkett, greatly touched, leaned back in his seat in front of the dock and handed him his own pocket handkerchief with which to wipe his blinded eyes. In the words of Edgar Bowker, who was present at the time, 'the gesture was natural and unobtrusive but none the less impressive.'[1]

At the subsequent trial at the Central Criminal Court—the Old Bailey—Marshall Hall led Birkett for the defence. The facts could probably have been relied upon in any event to reduce the charge from murder to manslaughter. But Marshall Hall called expert medical evidence to prove that the dead woman suffered from the relatively rare condition of *status lymphaticus*, or enlargement of the thymus gland, which rendered her capable of dying as the result of excitement alone. The jury accepted this explanation and after retiring for only a few minutes found the blind prisoner not guilty of either murder or manslaughter.

'This was the first time that Marshall Hall and Norman Birkett were teamed up together,' their clerk was later to recall, 'and it struck me then that with such a combination in chambers we had a pair almost unbeatable.'[2]

Another case in which Birkett was paired with Marshall Hall at this period also concerned a man who had been blinded but from a very different cause. It was a civil suit for damages of considerable interest to golfers and arose out of the action of a player at a course in Kent hitting a ball into a nearby road where it struck a passing

[1] A. E. Bowker. *A Lifetime with the Law* (1961), at p. 64.
[2] A. E. Bowker. *Behind the Bar* (1947), at p. 90.

motorist and put out his right eye. The motorist, who was a taxi-driver named George Castle, brought the action not only against the golfer, Mr. Marcus Chapman, who by the time the case came to trial had gone to Australia, and was not represented at the hearing, but also against the golf club, where the accident had occurred, the St. Augustine's Links at Ebbisham. The trial took place before Mr. Justice Sankey, afterwards the Lord Chancellor, sitting in the King's Bench Division without a jury, in May, 1922. Marshall Hall and Birkett appeared for the taxi-driver.[1]

In opening the plaintiff's case, Marshall Hall described the accident as 'the irony of fate', since Castle had served throughout the war as chauffeur to General Plumer and had encountered every sort of danger from shells and bombs but had emerged without a scratch. On being demobilized, he had bought a taxi with which he hoped to make a living and barely two months later he had suffered this misfortune, losing one eye and the sight of the other being affected so that he was unable to continue driving. The accident had occurred at the thirteenth hole, a short hole of 140 yards, which ran parallel with a much used highway. There was no warning anywhere in the club or its precincts or on the road itself, and the club had taken no precaution to prevent such an accident such as erecting a high fence.

After the plaintiff had told his story, his brother, who also owned a cab, went into the witness box to be examined by Birkett. He stated that about three weeks previously he was driving past the links when a player drove a ball in front of his car. He interviewed one of the club directors and informed him that unless care were exercised someone else would be hit. This was the only main road to Sandwich, Folkestone and Dover.

'Have you yourself seen golf balls driven across the road?' Birkett asked.

'Yes, and I have also seen the caddies looking for balls,' the witness replied, adding, amid some laughter, 'they take them back to the links again and sell them to the players.'

In giving judgment, Mr. Justice Sankey said he was satisfied that 'slicing' a ball such as happened on this occasion was an incident in the game of golf—the only player who did not sometimes 'slice' was the very bad player and that was because he never hit the ball—and

[1] *Castle* v. *St. Augustine's Links, Ltd. Daily Mail*, May 4, 1922.

the club directors ought to have known that balls driven from this tee frequently landed in the road. Consequently he held the club to be liable. On the question of damages the judge observed that no money would put the plaintiff where he was before the accident, but on the other hand he felt that he could not make the club pay thousands of pounds 'for a regrettable occurrence'. He therefore awarded the sum of £450 and costs against both defendants. One good thing might arise out of this case, added the judge—and here Birkett as a keen golfer himself warmly agreed—any golf player or club, if they had not done so already, would be able to insure against a risk of this kind for a very small sum.

It was as the result of another case which came before Mr. Justice Sankey at this time that Birkett's name found its way for the first time into the official Law Reports. The case, *Rex* versus *Wheat and Stocks*, had led to a conviction for bigamy at Derby Assizes, and the Crown considered that such a novel and important point of law was involved that the Attorney-General, Sir Gordon Hewart, was instructed to lead for the Crown when Birkett appeared for the appellants in the Court of Criminal Appeal.

While Thomas Wheat, a twenty-six-year-old miner, was serving with the Royal Engineers in Palestine during the First World War, his wife went away with another man, with whom she continued to live and by whom she had two children. Wheat, who had meanwhile returned home and discovered what had happened, began divorce proceedings under the Poor Persons Act. At the same time he was living in the house of a young woman named Marion Stocks, and as he was illiterate she conducted the correspondence with the solicitors for him. When she told him that she was pregnant by him, she sent a telegram at his request to the solicitors asking them to expedite the divorce, and they replied that they hoped to send the necessary papers to him for signature in the course of the next day or two. 'Thank God my divorce has come through,' he told a friend. Three weeks later he went through a ceremony of marriage with Stocks.

After Wheat, who wore the Mons Medal and suffered from shell shock, had gone into the witness box, the trial judge asked the jury to say whether they thought the accused believed in good faith and on reasonable grounds that there had been a divorce. The jury replied that they did. However, Mr. Justice Sankey held that this was not a good defence in law, and formally directed them to return a verdict of guilty, leaving the legal point to be decided by the appellate court. He sentenced both defendants to one day's imprisonment.

The Offences Against the Person Act, 1861, (section 57), repeating an earlier statute of James I, declares it to be a felony to marry any other person during the lifetime of a husband or wife, but provides for a presumption of death after seven years' absence and recognizes divorce. In his argument before a bench of five judges in the Court of Criminal Appeal, Birkett submitted that a presumption of divorce was equally applicable and afforded a complete answer to the charge, relying on a judicial statement in an earlier case that 'at Common Law, an honest and reasonable belief in the existence of circumstances which, if true, would make the act for which the prisoner is indicted an innocent act, has always been held to be an innocent act'.[1] The Attorney-General, on the other hand, argued that death and divorce were two things which must be kept distinct. In the former case the excuse of absence was only valid if there was no knowledge on the part of the accused that the spouse was alive, but in the case of divorce, there was no presumption, 'because it was an artificial thing the truth of which was ascertainable with mathematical precision.'

In a reserved judgment, delivered by Mr. Justice Avory, the Court accepted the Attorney-General's argument and dismissed the appeal, thus holding that the trial judge had been right in law. 'We are of opinion that a *bona fide* belief on reasonable grounds that the accused has been divorced, when in fact he has not been divorced, affords no defence to the charge of bigamy, although it may afford good reason for the infliction of a nominal punishment.' At the same time, although he failed, Birkett was widely complimented on his argument in this case, which immediately became a leading one in the law of bigamy.[2] Indeed, after Birkett had sat down in court, H. D. Roome, the Junior Treasury Counsel, who was in the case with the Attorney-General, sent him an enthusiastic note of congratulation. 'If you will allow me to say so,' wrote Roome, 'the case could not have been more clearly or forcibly argued. It was a treat to listen to your handling of it.'

[1] Per Cave J. in *R.* v. *Tolson*, 23 Q.B.D. 168, at p. 181.

[2] *Derby Daily Express*, November 11, 1920; *The Times*, February 1, 15, 1921.

At Nottingham Assizes in 1921, Birkett led the prosecution, having another junior, Mr. T. L. Winning, with him for the first time. The accused, an ex-Guards officer and a man of some means, was charged with manslaughter by running down a pedestrian when he was riding a motor cycle and sidecar combination.[1] He was defended by two K.C.s, Marshall Hall and John Hurst, the former having been briefed 'special' to lead the defence; but on this occasion the eloquent Marshall Hall pleaded in vain and the defendant was found guilty. Birkett's handling of the prosecution on this occasion won the praise of the Clerk of Assize, George Bancroft. 'Your speech was a model of what a speech for the prosecution should be,' Bancroft scribbled on the back of an envelope. 'Its conciseness too was very effective. My congratulations once more. I feel you will tire of receiving them.'

The first case which Birkett conducted on his own at the Old Bailey was a long and extremely complicated one of conspiracy to defraud in connection with the shares of a company called The Jubilee Cotton Mills Ltd. The ringleader of the conspiracy was the notorious financier and share-pusher, Ernest Terah Hooley, whose father had been a poor Nottingham lacemaker, and who had made and lost several fortunes in the course of his spectacular career. At this time he was sixty-two years of age and an undischarged bankrupt, and he had already served one prison sentence for obtaining money by false pretences. Nevertheless he managed to live in considerable style in a fine mansion set in its own grounds, Riseley Hall, Derbyshire. Along with his partners, John Macdonald and Llewellyn Demery, who dabbled in real estate, he had recently been dealing in shares in large quantities. Within the space of twenty months he had floated no less than twenty-six companies with a capital of £18 millions, so that it was hardly surprising that he should be popularly known as 'The Modern Midas'. The others indicted were his solicitor, Alfred Wallis, and his secretary, Bertram Breakspear; also Thomas Fletcher, who owned the Jubilee Cotton Mill in Lancashire, by means of which the frauds were perpetrated, and who (according to the prosecution) had received from Hooley as the first proceeds the sum of £20,000 in cash together with the promise of a substantial share allocation in the company which was to be formed. Fletcher, whom Birkett defended, was a respectable old gentleman

[1] *R.* v. *Stubley. Nottingham Guardian*, June 15, 16, 1921.

of seventy, a former Mayor of Derby and a local magistrate. Naturally he felt his position very keenly, since he had been perfectly honest if somewhat careless in all his business dealings and had only accepted Hooley's offer because he was in financial difficulties.

The Senior Treasury Counsel, Sir Richard Muir, was in charge of the prosecution, which opened at Bow Street Police Court, and which after a hearing lasting seven days resulted in all the defendants being committed for trial. Birkett recorded his impression of Hooley in a letter which he wrote to his wife at the time:

> Hooley *is* a charming man, and I like him very much. . . . He smiled now and then with quite a *radiant* smile: I can well understand how he got his money from susceptible people. And sometimes when Muir (who is a silly, pompous, self-opinionated, vain, hard, emotionless, despicable ass!) made some alleged cutting reference to him, Hooley whispered something to his companions [in the dock] which doubled them all up, even though they were on trial!

The trial of Hooley and his five companions began at the Old Bailey on March 9, 1922, before the Common Serjeant, Mr. (later Sir) Henry Fielding Dickens, who was a son of Birkett's great literary idol, and it lasted a month. Fifteen counsel in all were briefed. They were Sir Richard Muir and Mr. Roland Oliver (later Mr. Justice Oliver) for the Crown; Mr. Henry Maddocks, K.C., Mr. H. H. Joy and Mr. Maurice Healy for Hooley; Sir Ernest Wild, K.C., and Mr. Walter Frampton for Demery; Mr. T. Hollis Walker, K.C., and Mr. H. D. Roome for Wallis; Serjeant Sullivan, K.C., Mr. Norman Winning and Mr. H. H. Maddocks, Jun., for Macdonald; Mr. Norman Birkett and Mr. Richard O'Sullivan for Fletcher; and Mr. G. D. Roberts for Breakspear.[1]

It is unnecessary to describe the long drawn out proceedings, in which there were over fifty Crown witnesses and 164 documentary exhibits, except insofar as they affected Birkett's client, against whom the Crown did not have a particularly strong case. Indeed the case against Fletcher merely amounted to his having been in financial difficulties and having sold the mill to a company which he must have known to be a fraudulent concern. When his turn came to go into the witness box, Fletcher frankly admitted that he was in need

[1] *The Times*, March 10, 1922.

of cash, having lost about £200,000 over his mills in Russia, owing to the Revolution. Answering his counsel, he said he did not know that a public company was to be formed with a capital of £150,000 and £30,000 debentures. The only company talked about when he sold the mill to Hooley was a private one with 60,000 ordinary and 30,000 preference shares. Nor did he know of the document transferring the mill to the company until the latter had been wound up, and he did not authorize Wallis to act for him.

'How came your signature on that document?' Birkett asked him.

'I suppose Wallis brought it to me, and said it was all right, simply carrying out the arrangement between me and Hooley, and I signed it,' Fletcher replied. 'I did not read it, and I am very sorry I did not do so.' The witness added that, when the dividend of $33\frac{1}{3}$ per cent. was proposed, he opposed it, saying there was no money to pay a dividend with, but he was assured by Hooley that the money for the dividend and for working capital would be forthcoming.

'And is the net result of the deal that you got £22,608 6*s*. 8*d*. for your mill, which was worth at least £55,000?'

'Yes.'

'From first to last, had you the slightest intention to deceive anybody in any way at any time?'

'No.'

Sir Richard Muir's cross-examination of this witness was prefaced by the sharpest clash which Birkett had ever had with an opponent in court; and, in view of his previously expressed opinion of the Senior Treasury Counsel, it was not surprising.

'Now, Mr. Fletcher,' Muir began, 'we will have the truth!'

Birkett immediately jumped up. 'I object, my Lord,' he appealed to the Bench. 'That is not a question, and it is charged with the most improper and unwarranted prejudice.'

But the Common Serjeant, who was accustomed to this kind of expression from Muir, who had been prosecuting at the Old Bailey for over thirty years, was not inclined to interfere. He allowed Muir to continue.

'Now, Mr. Fletcher, I repeat—we will have the truth!'

Again Birkett was on his feet protesting. During the next few minutes he interrupted Muir seven times. Eventually the Senior Treasury Counsel bellowed at him, 'Will you sit down, sir!'

'No. I will not sit down,' Birkett retorted with some heat. 'I will not sit down while my learned friend so grossly misconducts himself.' Then, addressing himself to the Bench, he added, 'I insist that a note be made by your lordship of my protest, and I say here and now that, whatever the outcome of this trial, it is likely to be held as invalid by the Court of Criminal Appeal in consequence of the impropriety of the remarks made by my learned friend.'

Fortunately Muir did not persist and the cross-examination proceeded quite peacefully. In the result, all that could be elicited from the witness was that to pay a dividend of $33\frac{1}{3}$ per cent the company would have to earn a profit of £50,000 and in the circumstances 'this was hardly to be expected'.

During the trial all the defendants were on bail, and every morning before the sitting of the court Birkett and his clerk used to meet them in the big upstairs hall of the Old Bailey. Poor Fletcher dreaded each day's ordeal and the very idea of going into the dock was sheer torture. He aged visibly and Hooley made matters worse by his cheerful banter, although Birkett did his best to reassure his client that on the evidence he stood every chance of being acquitted. 'Now, don't you worry about anything, Tom,' Hooley would say. 'You just leave it to me. Once we get inside I know the ropes, and I'll see what I can do about getting you a job in the prison library.' And Tom would writhe in anguish.

Hooley kept this up, and, as the trial drew to its close, he would turn to Fletcher and remark casually: 'Well, Tom, only another few days of liberty, and then it's us for the high jump! Now, don't forget what I've told you—*if* there isn't a job going in the library, you just ask the prison M.O. if he will recommend you for the laundry or kitchens. You can always wangle a bit more grub in the kitchen, you know, and you're not strong enough to sew mailbags. That's heavy work—for the hardened old lags!'

Fletcher need not have worried after all. As Birkett anticipated, the jury found him not guilty, as they did Hooley's secretary, Breakspear. The rest of the defendants were convicted, Hooley receiving the heaviest punishment. 'Ten years ago you did twelve months' imprisonment for a bad fraud,' the judge thus addressed Hooley in passing sentence. 'Nothing has been known against you since, but you, of course, were the ringleader of this swindle, and you brought down some good men. You must go to penal servitude for three years.'

From the point of view of Birkett's client, this case provided an important object lesson in demonstrating the folly of signing a document without first reading it through carefully and understanding its real purpose. It so shocked the judge that he said he had never been a company director and after hearing this case he certainly never would be. Birkett was inclined to agree with him.[1]

A few weeks later, the Common Serjeant who had tried this case, received a knighthood in the King's Birthday Honours List. Birkett sent him a few lines of congratulation in which he mentioned his devotion to the works of Charles Dickens, who was the judge's father. Birkett's gesture produced the following reply.

8, *Mulberry Walk,*
London S.W.
June 14, 1922.

My dear Birkett,

I have an enormous number of letters to answer but yours is couched in such warm and even affectionate language that I cannot answer it by a mere formal reply.

I rejoice to know that you are a great admirer of my father and I am proud to feel that I have won your esteem and regard. The feeling of sympathy which exists between myself and the Bar is inexpressibly welcome to me.

Your advocacy of Fletcher was quite admirable. Up to a certain point of the case I had difficulty in dissociating Fletcher from the others—a cross-examination by you of not more than a quarter of an hour first opened my eyes and from that time I followed his case very closely. Your speech quite satisfied me and I rejoiced in his acquittal.

You possess tact and great earnestness both of which are essential to success as an advocate.

I wish you the utmost success.

Sincerely yours,
HENRY F. DICKENS

6

In spite of the rule which Birkett's clerk had laid down that he would not accept a brief for his master to go out of London which was

[1] *The Times*, April 10, 1922.

marked at less than twenty-five guineas, work continued to come in from every town on the Midland Circuit. This involved many tedious train journeys and he often had to sit up far into the night working on his briefs and papers for the following day's cases. Here he was fortunate in having the help of a devoted wife as well as the services of a highly efficient clerk, not to mention a digestion which could endure the irregular meals and long hours. 'I have three cases to get up tonight for tomorrow and one urgent set of papers to do,' he wrote to his wife from his old chambers in Birmingham, which his friend Donald Finnemore had now taken over. 'I have conferences at 9.30 in the morning. I got up at 5.45 this morning too!' From the beginning of their married life, Ruth Birkett acted as his private secretary and was able to relieve him of numerous small chores and details, unimportant in themselves but always time-consuming for a busy man coming more and more into the public eye. For this he was grateful and it gave him particular pleasure too that she went down so well with his own family and friends. After they had spent one Christmas with his cousins the Henry Birketts in Ulverston, he wrote: 'I was made very happy by the way everybody welcomed my dear Billy. She ain't a great converser, but she is a great appreciater!' Their happiness was completed by the appearance of a baby daughter, who was born on June 27, 1923, and given the Swedish name, Linnéa.

'Linnéa thrives and is real bonny and wonderfully fascinating!' he wrote when his daughter was two months old. 'Marriage can be a wonderfully mellowing influence.' It was due at least in part to his wife that his outlook on feminist questions underwent a marked change, and the man who in his undergraduate days at Cambridge had strongly opposed female suffrage now became a stout champion of women's rights, particularly in his chosen profession. 'We have just finished the Bar Meeting where they decided not to admit women to the Bar Mess, although electing them to the circuit,' he wrote to his wife at this period. 'The men were very much against it and were impatient of speeches, but I am glad to think that I spoke in favour of equal rights and won one or two votes.'

Birkett was such an essentially human and warm-hearted person that he was liable to be considerably upset by court incidents which left others comparatively unmoved. In those days a woman who killed her newly born child was guilty of murder even though it could be shown that she had not fully recovered from the effects of giving birth and that her mind was not normal at the time. Of course, the death sentence was invariably commuted, but the distraught prisoner was not to know this when the judge assumed the black cap. Once at Leicester Assizes Birkett had to prosecute a factory girl and unmarried mother who had suffocated her baby within a matter of minutes of its birth by tying a lace camisole round its mouth. The doctor who was called in gave evidence that in his opinion it was perfectly possible that the girl was unconscious through the pain she suffered and that she might not have realized what she was doing. Nevertheless the jury on the judge's direction convicted her of murder and she was duly sentenced to be hanged by the neck until she was dead. Then followed the most harrowing scene which stamped itself indelibly upon Birkett's memory. The poor moaning creature was literally carried out of the dock, almost unconscious and crying, 'I am very sorry—I didn't intend doing it.' Since then, mercifully, the law has been changed by the Infanticide Act, and a woman in such circumstances no longer has to hear the judge pass sentence of death upon her.

Indeed prisoners of all kinds often showed signs of great emotional stress when they went into the dock, and Birkett took the humane view that as a rule they ought to be allowed to be seated except at certain solemn moments in the trial such as when they were called on to plead to the charge and during the giving of the verdict and passing of sentence. While this is the general rule today, at the time in question the more old-fashioned among His Majesty's judges opposed it. On one occasion, when Birkett was defending a railway time-keeper charged with forgery at Nottingham Assizes, and the case had proceeded for some time, he asked the judge, Mr. Justice Horridge, if his client might be seated in the dock.

'Why?' inquired his Lordship sharply.

'I think the prisoner is under some strain,' Birkett replied.

'Not unless there is some special reason,' the judge rejoined. 'We are getting really too delicate in our habits towards people who are being tried.'

The result was that, when the judge came to pass sentence—six months' hard labour—the prisoner fainted in the dock and had to be revived and assisted below.

The incident had an interesting sequel at the next assize town, which was Derby. Here another circuit member, Maurice Healy, made a similar application on behalf of a prisoner, which the judge again refused. But he allowed Healy to argue it, which that witty and urbane Irishman did with courage as well as courtesy. Birkett was greatly impressed by Healy's masterly argument, as indeed was the whole Circuit Mess including the Clerk of Assize.

> The prisoner comes to the bar as an innocent man and is to be regarded as an innocent man. He is entitled not only to every right but to every privilege which is granted to every other person in court. When your Lordship comes into court we all stand up because your Lordship represents the Majesty of the King, and when your Lordship sits down we are all allowed, by that courtesy, to resume our seats in such ease as enables us to perform our respective duties, and I submit that that courtesy should be extended as much to an unconvicted prisoner as to anybody in court.
>
> I am extremely sorry that I should make a demand which is unpleasant to your Lordship, but there is something which all counsel must do, and that is that they should have courage in defending the rights and in defending the liberties of their clients, and the constitution of this country has never been more jealous than in pruning all relics of harsh and cruel treatment of prisoners. For these reasons I submit that as a matter of right the prisoner, unless there is danger of his escape, should be allowed to be seated.

At first Mr. Justice Horridge was adamant, but after Healy had opened his case and called one or two witnesses, the judge relented and allowed the prisoner to have a chair. Nor, it must be admitted, did he bear any malice in the matter, either towards Healy or Birkett. And the fact remains that from the date of these incidents, which received fairly wide publicity, the invariable practice of every trial judge has been to direct that the prisoner be seated immediately after he has been 'given in charge' of the jury.[1]

Another interesting case in which Birkett appeared at this time involved a different aspect of the administration of justice. He came before the bench of magistrates in the Nottingham Shire Hall in defence of a number of small shopkeepers from Hucknall, who

[1] Bancroft, 311–15.

were accused of contravening the Sunday Observance Act, an old statute which had been passed in 1677 'for the better observance and keeping holy of the Lord's Day'. The first of the defendants, whose case served as a test for the others, was a widowed woman, who opened her shop on Sunday for the sale of bread, sweets, newspapers and the like. The summonses were taken out at the instigation of the president of the local Free Church Council and Sunday School Union.

A police officer testified that he had visited the woman's shop one Sunday morning and warned her that she was committing an offence by selling two loaves and a wax taper to a boy who was on the premises. 'Surely you are not going to stop me opening my shop?' she said. 'I am a widow, with an invalid father to keep, and if I have to close the shop on Sunday I might as well close it for the whole of the week.' Then she added, 'I might just as well go to court and be fined as go there for debt.'

'Did you buy a paper there last Sunday?' Birkett asked the policeman in cross-examination.

'No, sir.'

'Have you ever bought a Sunday newspaper?'

'We had one in our house once.' (Laughter.)

'Don't you have newspapers delivered at your house every Sunday?'

'Yes, sir.'

'Did you know you were aiding and abetting the breaking of this law every Sunday of your life?'

The witness did not reply.

'If you were,' continued Birkett, 'can you tell us of the justice that you, an officer of the law at Hucknall, can go scot free, but a widow who has her living to get should be brought here on a charge of this kind?'

Again there was no answer.

'Have you ever bought cigarettes on a Sunday?'

'I may have done,' the policeman replied, looking rather shamefaced.

'On a hot summer's day have you ever bought ginger beer?'

'I'm not very partial to it.' (More laughter.)

'On Sunday, during licensed hours, I suppose you have had a drink of beer?'

'Yes, sir.'

In addressing the Bench, Birkett said that as far as the interests of true religion were concerned he was anxious to maintain them as much as anyone in the country. But the Sunday Observance Act was 'monstrous', because it was passed during a time of great religious intolerance, and those who infringed it, if they were unable to pay the fine imposed, were placed in the stocks for two hours. Conditions of 1677 did not apply today and he claimed that the Act had fallen into disuse. Why, only the previous week at the Church Congress a speaker had advocated Sunday games, and in a newspaper for that very day there was a photograph of a vicar organizing a game of football in his park on Sunday.

At this point one of the magistrates hearing the case interrupted Birkett to say 'Shame!'

'I am very glad to get that interruption,' observed Birkett. 'It shows what I have to deal with. On the other hand, there is the modern spirit which we are finding inside the Church Congress, and we have the Bishop of Birmingham advocating tennis and golf on Sunday.'

'Excuse me,' the magistrate again interrupted. 'He has mistaken his calling.'

'The merit of any law is that it must be equal,' Birkett went on. 'But where is the justice in raking up this Act of 1677 against a widowed woman who has to get her livelihood by this means? The Lord Chancellor (Lord Birkenhead) writes in the Sunday newspapers, and the Prime Minister (Mr. Lloyd George) uses them as a vehicle for communications to the public, and people are supposed to buy them. Is it just that a poor widow who kept her shop open in a bye-street at Hucknall in order to pay her rates and taxes should be brought here and punished, and others more fortunate and in a better position should be allowed to go scot free?'

The Bench retired to consider this momentous matter, and after an absence of ten minutes they reappeared and the Chairman announced that they had come to the conclusion that an offence had been committed against the Act, but 'taking all things into consideration', they had decided to dismiss the case on payment of four shillings costs. The other cases were similarly dealt with, and thus was English justice done.

At this period, besides Marshall Hall, the other particularly fashionable leader was Sir Henry Curtis-Bennett. The two were frequently opposed to each other in big court cases, just as Sir Rufus Isaacs and Sir Edward Carson had been in an earlier generation of barristers and Sir Patrick Hastings and Birkett himself were destined to be in the ensuing decade. Although 'Curtis' was perhaps not of the same calibre as the others, nevertheless Birkett came to realize that it was a mistake to underestimate his abilities with a jury. On one occasion, Birkett prosecuted a motorist on a manslaughter charge at Lincoln Assizes, when Curtis-Bennett was briefed 'special' for the defence. The case came on late in the afternoon and the prosecution had not concluded its case by the time the court rose for the day. Birkett returned to his hotel and wrote a note to his wife:

> *The White Hart*, *Lincoln. Thursday*, *February* 1, 1923.
>
> We were not reached until 3.30 this afternoon, and I then opened the case. I took 40 minutes and did it rather well! We sat until 6.30 and I am going to try and get a breath of air before dinner. It was very oppressive in the Court. Curtis-Bennett is not very much to fear! I rather think it will be Saturday night before I am through. . . .

As events turned out, the jury were impressed by Curtis-Bennett's eloquence and acquitted the motorist. Also, owing to a curious happening, Birkett found he had to remain in Lincoln until the following week.

While the jury were out considering their verdict in the manslaughter case, another prisoner was put up. The charge was one of shooting with intent to kill a gamekeeper who had caught him poaching. On entering the dock, the poacher, who apparently had the sum of £1 3*s*. 6*d*. with him, asked the judge if he could have a 'dock defence'.

The judge, who was Mr. Justice Sankey, signified his assent, whereupon the prisoner looked round the court room and promptly picked out Birkett. 'I'd like him,' he said.

'Mr. Birkett,' said the judge, 'I know you are very busy. Would you like to be excused?'

'No, my Lord,' Birkett replied. 'I think it is my duty in accordance with the traditions of the Bar to accept.'

When Birkett later telephoned his clerk in London to say that he would not be returning next day as he was staying on in Lincoln for a 'docker', Bowker was furious, since they were snowed under with work in chambers at the time, and the clerk had to cancel various appointments.

The case lasted the rest of the day and the best part of the following day. But Birkett had the satisfaction of getting the charge reduced to one of unlawful wounding, so that his client received a sentence of six months' imprisonment instead of a term of penal servitude.

No doubt there is some truth in the old adage that one good turn deserves another. At all events, this particular one had an interesting sequel for Birkett some years later, as will be related in its proper place.

7

During this period, Birkett appeared for the defence in three murder trials. Although none of them aroused nation-wide interest, like 'The Green Bicycle Case', they all deserve mention.

The first, which was tried before Mr. Justice Rigby Swift at Leicester, was one of those comparatively rare cases where the jury's verdict was clearly wrong. A young ex-service man named John Boss was indicted for the murder of his sweetheart, Miss Rose Foster. They had gone for a walk together and her body was discovered near a reservoir where there was no doubt they had been together. She had been strangled but not otherwise interfered with; indeed, according to the medical evidence, she died a virgin. The suggestion put by the prosecution to the jury was that the prisoner attempted to force the girl and she successfully resisted, and that in holding her the prisoner killed her, although he may not have intended to do so. Birkett pleaded insanity and called medical evidence to prove his client's abnormality going back many years to a head injury incurred in childhood. Indeed he was without doubt a manic-depressive and the doctor who had recently treated him had warned his father that it might be necessary to have him confined in an asylum.[1]

In those days, legal insanity was strictly defined by the so-called M'Naghten Rules, and Birkett consequently submitted to the jury

[1] *Leicester Mercury*, October 27, 1921.

that Boss was suffering from such a disease of the mind at the time that he did not know what he was doing or, in the alternative, if he did know what he was doing, then he did not know that it was wrong, arguing that a person with the prisoner's abnormal mentality and mental case history was quite likely to strangle the object of his desire in a moment of sexual excitement without appreciating the consequences of his action.

After retiring for less than half an hour, the jury rejected Birkett's plea and found the prisoner guilty of murder, instead of finding him not guilty but insane, as Birkett had hoped. The Court of Criminal Appeal was unable to interfere, since there had been no misdirection by the trial judge in his summing up, although the court felt the judge had not sufficiently drawn attention to the prisoner's medical history. However, the appeal was dismissed. But the Home Secretary immediately stepped in and granted a reprieve, at the same time directing the prisoner to be sent to Broadmoor Criminal Lunatic Asylum, as the institution was then known.

The second case was one in which the prisoner, a serving soldier named Henry Johnson, whose home was near Nottingham, took the law into his own hands and strangled his wife with a velvet ribbon under the provocation of her gross immorality and infidelity while he was on active service in Egypt—'a most immoral, unfaithful young woman' was how Mr. Justice Swift described her—the wife having had an illegitimate child of which a man named Edward Mitchelson was the father.[1]

Birkett put the prisoner into the witness box and asked him about his wife's general behaviour. In reply Johnson said that on his return to England he forgave her, but she was always saying she could go back to Mitchelson. On the morning of the murder he reproached her for 'playing about' with a group of young fellows, but she said she would do as she liked. They quarrelled about it in the afternoon. 'And then,' the prisoner continued, amidst breathless silence in court, 'I went upstairs. She followed me and started slurring me about these fellows, and she said she would go to them if she wanted to. She said she would fetch her illegitimate child back from Dr. Barnardo's Homes, and have Mitchelson to live with her again.'

'Is that all that was said before she died?' Birkett asked.

'Nothing more.'

[1] *Nottingham Guardian*, October 7, 1921.

'What effect had it on your mind?'

'When she mentioned the word "Mitchelson", I flew into a rage and got hold of her throat, and threw her on the bed. At first I released her. She then said she would go and leave me.'

'What did you do?'

'That was the end.'

'And the velvet ribbon?'

'I tied it round after she lost consciousness.'

Speaking in impressive tones, Birkett asked: 'If the things that had happened when you were on active service in Egypt had not happened, and if the things she said had not been said, would you have laid violent hands on your wife?'

'No,' the prisoner firmly replied.

In his speech to the jury, Birkett described the affair as an appalling tragedy. Both these people were mere children, yet one was dead and the other was on trial for his life. 'Yours is to speak the word of life or to speak the word of death,' he said, in asking the jury for a verdict of manslaughter and not of murder. Although prosecuting counsel had argued strongly that the provocation here had been discounted in advance, since the prisoner had previously forgiven his wife, and it was therefore insufficient to reduce the crime to manslaughter, the jury acquitted Johnson of the capital offence and returned the verdict which his counsel demanded. Mr. Justice Swift sent him to penal servitude for seven years, a severe sentence measured by present-day standards. But the prisoner might well have gone to the gallows like the soldier whose fate inspired Oscar Wilde to write *The Ballad of Reading Gaol* and whose crime like that of many others was strikingly similar to Johnson's.

> The man had killed the thing he loved,
> And so he had to die.

The third trial, which also took place at Nottingham Assizes, was that of a nineteen-year-old coal miner named Byron Berridge who was charged with murdering his father. According to the mother, who had been married for thirty-six years and had eleven children living, her husband consistently behaved badly to her, using foul and threatening language and accusing her of consorting with other men, and that her son Byron always interposed on her behalf, on one occasion snatching a dagger from her husband's hands as he was about to stab her. The prisoner denied that he intended to kill his father. What had happened, he said, was that he pulled a jack knife from his pocket, unsheathed it, and showed it to his father to frighten him and to keep him away from the cupboard. The father then made for his son and fell on the blade which entered his chest.[1]

'Did you at any time with that knife in your hand strike a blow at your father?' Birkett asked him.

'I did not, sir,' answered the prisoner.

The judge, who was Mr. Justice Roche, suggested to Birkett that he ought to keep in mind at least alternatively the question of manslaughter. 'If a man draws an open knife in the face of a man who has not got a weapon——'

'I respectfully submit,' interrupted Birkett, 'that if a man draws a deadly weapon or an extremely efficient knife, in the hope of deterring another, who had threatened him, from using a deadly weapon, and that man meets his death, it is death by misadventure.'

'It all depends on the circumstances,' observed Mr. Justice Roche. 'If a man is in a corner or on the brink of a precipice, it is one thing, but if he is in a room with an easy way out, it is another.'

In his speech to the jury, Birkett argued with such effective persuasiveness that the killing was accidental that the jurors acquitted Berridge of both murder and manslaughter. The announcement of this verdict was followed by an outburst of applause among the spectators, and the judge, who was annoyed that the prisoner had not been convicted of manslaughter and seemed determined to send someone to prison, called on the police to arrest the culprits. But the police were unable to find them.

Birkett also had some striking successes in the civil courts. One of them worth noticing briefly was an action for breach of promise of marriage, which came before Mr. Justice Sankey at Derbyshire Assizes in February, 1923. The plaintiff, a lady from Matlock named Clara Froggatt, sued William Hoyland, a chemist's assistant, alleging that the promise had been made in writing in 1914, although they had known each other since 1907, and that 1,400 love letters had passed between them. According to Hoyland, he confessed to his fiancée in 1916 to having committed adultery with a married woman over the previous four years, and when he met Miss Froggatt she struck him with her clenched fist and called him 'Dog', 'Pig' and

[1] *Nottingham Evening Post*, November 8, 1923.

'Swine'. After this it was hardly surprising that the engagement should have been broken off. She waited for over five years before bringing the action, by which time her ex-fiancé had married someone else. At the trial Birkett appeared for the defendant, while the jilted woman was represented by Mr. Norman Winning, at that time one of the leading juniors on the Midland Circuit.[1]

Birkett decided to employ daring tactics, sometimes used with deadly effect by Sir Edward Carson and other great advocates, but apt to be risky, particularly when employed by an inexperienced counsel. That is to say, he decided to call no evidence, but to rely on the effect which his cross-examination of the plaintiff and his speech to the jury might have, since the fact that he put no witnesses into the box entitled him to the last word with the jury.

On this occasion he began his cross-examination by asking Miss Froggatt why she had waited so long before commencing proceedings. She replied that she did not have the money.

'I suggest you brought the action out of spite?'

'No.'

'Not at all?'

'No.'

'You knew that the defendant was married when you issued the writ?'

'Yes.'

'Did the fact that you learned that he married in 1920 influence you?'

'No. I did not know where he was.'

'Did you think it was a kind thing to bring the action and so pain an innocent wife as well as the husband, the defendant?'

'I did not know where he was before.'

'Why didn't you ask his mother where he lived, for he only lived a hundred yards away?'

'You could not expect me to ask her.'

When Birkett came to address the jury, he stressed that no one condemned the defendant's immoral conduct more than he did, but it was irrelevant to the case, since there had been a rescission of the engagement at Christmas, 1916. The real reason for the present action after five years and five months, he said, was to gain publicity and do the defendant as much injury as she could.

[1] *News of the World*, February 25, 1923.

Among the spectators in court was a local solicitor, Mr. R. W. P. Cocking, then a young articled clerk, upon whom the occasion made a memorable impression. He has recorded his recollection of it after forty years:

> I well remember Winning's address to the jury, which was a masterpiece of ordered cogency, with all the facts and arguments presented in proper sequence. Then Norman Birkett went into action and held the jury almost spell-bound, while he ranged over the facts and arguments not in the same ordered sequence, but frequently returning to emphasize some fact which he had previously mentioned. Not understanding the psychological background of such a speech, I was inclined to assign the honours for legal cogency to Winning and the honours for an impassioned address to Birkett.
>
> The jury retired, and coming back into court found for the lady plaintiff with damages of twenty-five pounds.
>
> Up rose Birkett to his feet and said, 'That, my Lord, is the exact amount which my client has paid into court and I ask for costs since the date of payment in.'[1]

Mr. Justice Sankey agreed and awarded the subsequent costs of the action to the defendant. Of course, these amounted to considerably more than twenty-five pounds and must have been a very small solace to the unfortunate Miss Froggatt who would have been better advised never to have brought the action at all.

By this time Birkett had developed a particularly engaging manner in the conduct of his cases which impressed judges and juries alike. Even when he had to argue a bad point of law, as happens to every practising barrister, he put the best face possible upon it. In one such case he represented some Lincolnshire justices who had convicted two amusement caterers who kept their stalls open on the beach at Skegness after closing time under the Shops Act. The stall-holders appealed to a King's Bench Divisional Court on the ground that their stalls were not shops within the meaning of the Act as no retail trade or business was carried on there, but were merely places of amusement. One of the games in which chance appeared to predominate was called 'The Slippery Bears', in which each player tried

[1] Communicated by Mr. R. W. P. Cocking.

to get a 'teddy-bear' to the top of a pole by turning a handle before the other players could get their bears there.[1]

'Is the Casino at Monte Carlo a shop?' the Lord Chief Justice, Lord Hewart, asked Birkett, who appeared for the respondents.

'It might be for the purpose of this Act,' answered Birkett amid laughter.

'The "tallest man" and the "fat lady" might also come within the definition,' observed Mr. Justice Roche.

When Birkett went on to point out that the businesses carried on by the appellants were those of amusement caterers, the Lord Chief Justice asked: 'What did they retail?'

'Amusement,' said Birkett.

'How do you distinguish between retail and wholesale amusement?' asked Mr. Justice Roche. 'By the encores?'

Birkett's reply was drowned by the laughter which this judicial sally produced. However, it was plain that an amusement caterer was not a shopkeeper, and the Court quashed the conviction.

Birkett also became noticeably quick at repartee. Once when defending one of several men charged with housebreaking before the Recorder of Birmingham, Sir Rydal Adkins, he told the jury that his client was certainly innocent, as he had a good alibi, and that the real culprit might well be still enjoying his liberty. 'For all I know,' he said, 'he may be sitting in the gallery listening to this case.'

'Why in the gallery?' interrupted the Recorder, amid laughter.

'That occurred to me as I said the words,' Birkett replied. 'He may be anywhere in the world; he may be sitting in counsels' seats.'

Only very occasionally did Birkett consent to appear for anyone with whom he had more than a passing acquaintance. There is no rule of practice or professional etiquette against this, but it is as well that he should not do so unless there is a strong reason to the contrary. However, one case in which Birkett successfully did so at this time was when he defended his old friend from Cambridge and Bournville days, Laurence Cadbury, before a local bench of justices on a charge of dangerous driving. He accepted the brief no doubt because he had frequently driven with Cadbury and was convinced that he was always a most careful driver. Indeed his first introduction to motoring had been a day or two after he first came

[1] *Dennis* v. *Hutchinson. The Times*, January 19, 1922.

to work for Cadbury's elder brother George at Bournville in 1910 when Laurence Cadbury had called to take him for a game of tennis. It was in the early days of motoring when the body was usually made by a separate firm from that which made the chassis, and on this particular occasion the body had not arrived and Cadbury had to make do with a soap box as driver's seat, to which the end of the bonnet had been loosely attached. Birkett had not forgotten the comical scene as they were going down Griffin Hill and a gust of wind suddenly whipped off the bonnet, which flew past their heads and landed with a resounding clatter on the road behind them. 'Hey, mister!' shouted a local inhabitant who had seen what happened. 'You've dropped something!'

The accident which led to the summons for dangerous driving occurred when a bus emerged from a side road near a place where repair works were going on and Cadbury had scraped the side of the bus with his own vehicle. No one was injured, and Cadbury swore that he was only doing five miles an hour at the time, although one of the road repair workers estimated that his speed was thirty-five miles an hour and that he had never slowed up at all ('Positively an insult' was Birkett's comment). The magistrates came to the conclusion that Cadbury had committed an error of judgment. But Birkett, in what the local newspaper described as 'a lengthy and powerful address', persuaded them that an error of judgment did not amount to a criminal offence, and the magistrates accordingly dismissed the case after a four-hour hearing.

Birkett's continued appearances on the Midland Circuit in addition to his increasing work in London imposed a heavy strain on his physical powers, and he would often confide to his wife how exhausted he felt. After one particularly heavy week at Birmingham Assizes, he wrote to her: 'I have had some great successes, and Swift J. told me last night that he was sure I would be a judge! So there are compensations!'

CHAPTER IV

MEMBER OF PARLIAMENT AND KING'S COUNSEL

I

AFTER his defeat at King's Norton in the General Election of 1918, Birkett continued as the prospective Liberal candidate and devoted what time he could spare to nursing the constituency, although the sitting Conservative Member, Sir Herbert Austin, was so firmly entrenched that there seemed little chance of being able to win it for the Liberals. However, when he made the move to London in 1922, he felt that as he was beginning to build up another practice he could not devote the necessary time to King's Norton, and so he resigned. Thus it happened that on the break up of the Lloyd George Coalition Government in the autumn of the same year Birkett was not a candidate at the ensuing General Election, which returned the Conservatives to office under the leadership of Mr. Bonar Law.

The new parliament, which saw the resignation and death of Mr. Bonar Law and the succession of Mr. Stanley Baldwin as Conservative Prime Minister, lasted barely twelve months. By the time it had reassembled in the autumn of 1923, after the long recess, Mr. Baldwin, who had always been a protectionist, had come to the conclusion that the best solution of the country's economic difficulties, particularly mounting unemployment at home, lay in the policy of tariff reform. Unfortunately for him, his predecessor had given a pledge that there should be no change in the general fiscal arrangements during the lifetime of that Parliament. He consequently felt that the only course open to him was to ask the King for a dissolution. This he did contrary to the advice of many of his colleagues. His Majesty reluctantly granted his request towards the middle of November.

A few days later, literally on the eve of the opening of the General Election campaign, Norman Birkett was adopted as the Liberal Candidate for East Nottingham. His last-minute adoption came about in this way. Mr. Cecil Roberts, the poet and novelist, who was then editor of the *Nottingham Journal*, had been the Liberal candidate but was obliged to withdraw from a bye-election owing to illness. The dissolution still found the East Nottingham Liberals without an official candidate. As it happened, Birkett was well known in the constituency through his appearances at Nottingham Assizes, so that when Roberts suggested to the Eastern Divisional Liberal Committee that he should be invited to stand, the suggestion was immediately acted upon. Although there was barely a fortnight before polling day, Birkett willingly accepted and plunged into a whirlwind campaign with his wife. Fortunately he was not faced with a three-cornered contest but had a straight fight with the sitting Conservative Member, Mr. (later Sir) John Houfton, a local mining engineer.

The election was fought almost entirely on the issue of Tariff Reform versus Free Trade, and in support of the latter the Liberal followers of Mr. Lloyd George and Mr. Asquith temporarily sank their differences and united. In Nottingham, where lace making was a principal industry, Birkett argued that its prosperity largely depended upon the export of the manufactured product, and if exports were to be continued at a high level the entry of foreign goods into the country must not be restricted. Tariffs too would mean dearer food for the housewife. 'This election is almost the most important within living memory,' he said at one of his meetings, 'because if Protection comes it will mean harder conditions for those who find life difficult enough as it is.' He went on to point out that Joseph Chamberlain had given the country three years to think about Tariff Reform, and the country killed his proposals. 'The present Government, composed of lesser men, said, "Three years killed it: let us try three weeks".'

By making a personal attack upon the Liberal candidate and his wife, Birkett's Conservative opponent did himself no good. According to him, the issue before East Nottingham was whether they were to be represented by a business man or a barrister. Of course a barrister must have 'the gift of the gab', but according to Mr. Houfton a man with the gift of the gab was an infernal nuisance in Parliament. He was always getting up on his hind legs, whereas the real work was done quietly in committee by members like the Conservative candidate. 'I have not only to fight Mr. Norman Birkett, but his charming wife,' Mr. Houfton continued. 'I think it's a bit impudent of a lady who doesn't know Nottingham ladies to come here and give them advice.' Anyhow, the speaker added, 'I always thought I was their candidate.' Finally, he flung a cheap gibe at his Liberal opponent. 'The alternative to voting for me is voting for a man who knows nothing of finance except the fees he takes when the Assizes are on.'

The result in East Nottingham was declared shortly after 11.0 p.m on the day of the poll, December 6, 1923. The figures were:

W. N. Birkett (L)	11,355
J. P. Houfton (C)	9,919
Liberal Majority	1,436

It was one of the first Liberal gains to be announced—there were forty-one in all—and an overwhelming victory, since the Conservative majority in East Nottingham at the previous Election, also in a straight fight, had been in the region of four thousand. 'I have been defeated by a cleverer man, but not a more honest one,' said Mr. Houfton to his disappointed supporters in the Constitutional Club. 'The dear food bogey has frightened the workers; that is the explanation, I am sure, for our defeat.' Meanwhile the victor was addressing his cheering followers at the nearby Reform Club. 'In this moment of very great and perhaps historic triumph,' said the new M.P., 'the predominant feeling in my mind as I stand here tonight, with this responsibility laid upon me by this great constituency, is that it makes my heart quieter and it makes me a more sober, sensible man, to think that the cause which we have at heart has so signally triumphed.' These words were immediately echoed by Mrs. Birkett. 'If my husband feels humble and proud,' she said, 'I feel infinitely more so . . . I, in the little way I can, shall do my level best to help.'

The composition of the new House of Commons was unprecedented, consisting of 258 Conservatives, 191 Labour Members and 158 Liberals. Thus no one political party had an absolute majority over the other two, and any Government could only rule with the support of one of the other parties. The key was held by the Liberals, who could either keep the Conservatives in office or else turn them out in favour of Labour. It soon became clear that the Liberals intended to follow the latter course. Meanwhile Mr. Baldwin's inclination was to resign immediately rather than face inevitable defeat in Parliament. However, the King dissuaded him, pointing out that the Conservatives were still the largest single party in the new Commons and that it was his duty to meet the assembly so as to allow the elected representatives of the people to decide whether they would support his Government or not. Consequently the King opened the new Parliament on January 15, 1924, with Mr. Baldwin still Prime Minister, and the customary Debate on the Address followed. This ended with Mr. Asquith moving a hostile amendment, which the Labour Members supported as well as the Liberals. It was carried by 72 votes, and Mr. Baldwin's resignation was now accepted by the King, who sent for the Labour leader, Mr. Ramsay MacDonald, and entrusted him with the formation of the first Labour Government in English history. The new ministers took their places for the first time on the Government Front Bench on February 12, with their Labour supporters ranged behind them, and the Liberals, who included two ex-Prime Ministers in the persons of Mr. Asquith and Mr. Lloyd George, occupying the benches below the gangway.

Barely a week later, Birkett rose to make his maiden speech. The occasion was a debate on a motion proposed by a backbench Labour Member in favour of State pensions to all widows with children and to wives and mothers whose breadwinner had been incapacitated. 'I support this Motion with all my heart,' he said, 'because not merely will it remove the haunting sense of insecurity with which so many widows are faced today, but it is a very practical charter for the children. . . . A widow is left, and she has to shift and fend for herself, to go out to work, or, to use a common phrase, "to manage somehow". In such a case the children have no father or mother at all.' Indeed Birkett went further than the proposer of the Motion and expressed the hope that consideration would be given to the unmarried mother, the deserted wife, and in some cases the divorced wife. 'At any rate they are points for further discussion.'

No one who has addressed the House of Commons for the first time can ever forget the experience. For the House is perhaps the most critical assembly in the world as well as the most sympathetic

5

and informal. By parliamentary convention a maiden speaker who asks for the indulgence of the House is never interrupted and for the first and only time in his or her parliamentary career the Member is listened to in complete silence. The experience is apt to be an unnerving one, since much may depend upon the initial impression which is created. A lawyer suffers from an additional disadvantage, since his parliamentary colleagues will be quick to detect and to resent any tendency on the part of the speaker to harangue them like a jury or to speak 'down' to them. Marshall Hall's maiden speech had been a disastrous failure for this reason, and he never got over it. Indeed he always affected to despise the House. 'It is all repetition without variation there,' he used to say. Unlike Marshall Hall, Birkett treated the House with great respect and it in return appreciated his obvious sincerity. But in some ways it was a pity that he did not choose a more important occasion such as a big debate when the House was crowded, as F. E. Smith (Lord Birkenhead) had done, rather than a Private Member's motion late at night when many of the benches were empty, although of course the subject was of great importance and it touched his heart very closely. But if the national dailies failed to notice his speech, at least he had the satisfaction of reading in the *Nottingham Journal* next day that he had made 'a most excellent impression'. According to that newspaper's parliamentary correspondent, 'his charming voice, choice language and warm human sympathies won him an audience which the House gives only to the most promising of its younger Members.'[1]

Although another Liberal M.P. and ex-Cabinet Minister, Mr. C. F. G. Masterman, described him as 'a possible future Lord Chancellor', Birkett, unlike F. E. Smith, had no political ambitions. With him his profession as a barrister came first and Parliament second. But he obeyed the Liberal Whip and was conscientious in his attendance at Westminster, in spite of the physical strain involved. In one week in April, for instance, he remained in the House for an all-night sitting which ended at 6.0 a.m., was conducting a case in the courts a few hours later, then went to the House for another long sitting ending in the early hours of the following morning, and later the same day delivered a speech on the Guardianship of Infants Bill. He also visited his constituents regularly in Nottingham. But on the whole his interventions in the debates were too infrequent and, as

[1] *Nottingham Journal*, February 21, 1924.

will be seen, his parliamentary career was too brief to have enabled him to make a lasting impact upon the House. On the relatively rare occasions when he did speak, on subjects which for one reason or another interested him, he was always listened to with polite attention.

Once Birkett raised a curious matter at question time when he drew the Home Secretary's attention to the publication in a Sunday newspaper of the reminiscences of the late public executioner containing morbid details of the last moments of condemned prisoners, and he asked that revelations of this kind should be stopped. He also objected to the admission of Press representatives to executions, as had happened on a recent occasion, pointing out that under statute the powers of the Home Secretary were absolute, although the Under-Secretary in his reply had said that the matter was one for the discretion of the Sheriffs. The Under-Secretary also stated that there was no power to prevent ex-officials from writing about such matters, a most unsatisfactory reply which produced a leading article in the *Nottingham Journal* ('Food for Ghouls'), incidentally praising Birkett's observations.[1] When a Labour M.P., David Kirkwood, asked, 'Is not all this evidence that the consensus of opinion of the House is that capital punishment should be stopped?', there were cries of 'hear, hear' in which Birkett joined, although loud counter-cries of 'No, no' came from the Conservative benches.

Being in Parliament prompted Birkett to take an important step in his professional career. He applied to the Lord Chancellor, then Lord Sankey, to be made a King's Counsel, knowing that his application must stand a good chance of success, since it has always been the custom that a junior barrister who is also an M.P. and asks for permission to exchange his stuff gown for the silk gown of a K.C. usually has his request granted. On this occasion the Lord Chancellor took longer than usual over the applications. Birkett was asked to speak at a Liberal rally at Ulverston in April and, as he told his cousin Henry, 'I had hoped, and still hope, to be able to put on the bills—Norman Birkett, K.C., M.P.—but the Lord Chancellor delays!'

When the list of twelve new 'silks' was published on April 15, 1924, Birkett's name was the last on the list, since he was the most junior in point of call, having been in practise for less than eleven years. The same day, arrayed in his silk gown, knee breeches and

[1] *Nottingham Journal*, August 1, 1924.

full-bottomed wig, he was sworn in and made the customary declaration before the Lord Chancellor in the House of Lords 'well and truly' to 'serve the King in his matters. . . .' A few days later he made the round of the courts with the other newly appointed 'silks', who included another member of his circuit, H. H. Joy.

Two high court judges and a commissioner of assize sent him enthusiastic letters of congratulation. 'I feel that you will do excellently,' wrote Mr. Justice McCardie, 'and that you will continue in ample manner your honourable and successful career;' while Mr. Justice Greer, later Lord Fairfield, wrote: 'Unless my judgment is very much astray, you will quickly acquire a leading place in the front row;' and William Finlay, afterwards Lord Justice Finlay, assured him: 'I am confident that you will rise to the top of the profession and I shall very greatly rejoice when my confidence is justified.'

Birkett and his clerk were on their way to Birmingham when the telegram arrived at his chambers in Temple Gardens from the Lord Chancellor's office announcing the name of the new K.C., and the news was promptly relayed to the court where Birkett was appearing in a number of licensing cases.

'Well, Bowker,' said a solicitor client named Willison when he heard the news, 'I suppose this will go to your head. You'll soon be asking fifty guineas to come here.'

'In twelve months we shall want a hundred guineas, Mr. Willison,' the clerk replied confidently.

'Then you won't get another brief here,' said the solicitor.

But he was soon proved wrong. Indeed within eighteen months this Birmingham solicitor had marked a brief to Birkett at two hundred and fifty guineas. 'Dammit, Bowker, you were right,' he handsomely admitted to the clerk, when the latter reminded him of his previous prediction. 'Norman Birkett's a great man.'

2

There is always a certain element of risk for a successful junior counsel who takes 'silk', since his former solicitor clients may be reluctant to incur the additional expense which instructing him involves. For one thing the etiquette of the profession requires that as a 'leader' he must always be accompanied in court by a 'junior', who undertakes the preliminary work in the case, settling the pleadings and so on, for which the junior receives two-thirds of his leader's fees. A new K.C.'s former clients may prefer wherever possible to dispense altogether with the luxury of a leader and leave the whole conduct of the case in the hands of junior counsel. But Birkett need have had no fears. According to his fee book, his earnings in 1923, his last full year as a junior, amounted to just over £4,300, a figure which was more than doubled during his first year in silk.

His first brief as a K.C., delivered within a few days of his appointment, was what is known in the Temple as a plea, that is to appear on behalf of a client who has pleaded guilty to a criminal charge, and to put forward for the judge's consideration before sentence whatever mitigating circumstances there may be in the case. Here the accused was a solicitor, who came before Mr. Justice Greer at the Old Bailey, having admitted that he had fraudulently converted to his own use a sum of approximately £4,800, which had been entrusted to him by a client. In his speech in mitigation Birkett pointed out that this was not, as in so many other solicitors' cases, the culmination of a series of frauds committed over a long period of time, but an isolated instance where the solicitor utilized some of the money in his charge to pay for the heavy expenses of his wife's illness and had been unable to hand over the amount when the time came since he could not realize certain of his securities on which he relied. This plea had some effect, since the judge did not send the man to penal servitude, although he found it impossible to treat him leniently, because, as he put it in sentencing him to twenty-one months' imprisonment, 'if a man of education and position got off with a light sentence, it would be impossible to justify sentence against an ignorant and poor man.'[1]

Yet almost a year was to go by before Birkett had his first big chance as a 'silk' in a sensational society case which attracted much public interest, although he did nothing which might be described as spectacular during this period. He had his share of 'running down cases', a type of action by no means free from difficulty but one which sometimes has its lighter moments. Birkett's clerk, Edgar Bowker, has recalled one such case in which Birkett appeared soon after he had become a K.C.[2]

[1] *R.* v. *Best. The Times.* May 2, 1924.
[2] Bowker. *Behind the Bar*, pp. 94–5.

It was a claim for damages against a motor cab company, and the plaintiff, who was Birkett's client, had been rather seriously injured when being driven in one of the defendant company's taxis from Waterloo Station to King's Cross. In his evidence, the plaintiff said that the taxi was driven much too fast in view of the greasy state of the roads, and other evidence was given to like effect. Then the taxi driver went into the witness box to give evidence for the defence. He was a typical cheery Cockney, and he told the jury in his examination-in-chief that far from driving fast he was going at a very slow pace the whole time.

Birkett's cross-examination which followed is a good example of how effectively he could, in his peculiarly quiet and even gentle manner, lead on an unsuspecting witness by a combination of charm and subtlety.

BIRKETT: You say you were travelling quite slowly?
WITNESS: Yes.
BIRKETT: Not fast at all, but quite slowly?
WITNESS: That's right.
BIRKETT: And you drew out to pass another vehicle?
WITNESS: Correct.
BIRKETT: Still not going fast?
WITNESS: Yes.
BIRKETT (after a pause): Let us just see, Mr. ——. You skidded slightly?
WITNESS: Yes.
BIRKETT: Mounted the pavement?
WITNESS: Yes.
BIRKETT: Hit a plate glass window and smashed that?
WITNESS: Right.
BIRKETT: Knocked over two or three stalls, loaded with fruit and vegetables outside a shop?
WITNESS: Correct.
BIRKETT: Knocked down one policeman and two pedestrians?
WITNESS: I'm afraid I did.
BIRKETT: And finally knocked down a lamp-post?
WITNESS: Yes.
BIRKETT (after a further pause): Well, now, I wonder if you would like to estimate how much more damage you might have done if you had been going fast?

After this characteristic display of advocacy, Birkett had no difficulty in persuading the jury to find for his client.

Birkett also had his House of Commons work to attend to at this time and regular visits to his constituency, where eventually he found himself facing the expense of a second parliamentary election within ten months.

The downfall of the Labour Government, which precipitated the General Election, was occasioned by what T. P. O'Connor the 'Father' of the House of Commons, described as a 'miserable tempest in the tiniest little teapot ever introduced into political life', namely, the action of the Attorney-General, Sir Patrick Hastings, in first authorizing and then withdrawing the prosecution of John Campbell, the acting-editor of the Communist *Workers' Weekly*, on a charge of sedition. The Conservatives, who put down a motion of censure on the Government, discovered in the course of the debate that they could not count upon Liberal support, since Sir John Simon for the Liberals moved an amendment calling for a Select Committee to investigate the circumstances in which the prosecution had been withdrawn. The Conservatives thereupon went into the division lobby in support of the Liberal amendment which the Government had refused to accept. Birkett voted with the majority of 166, which was recorded against the Government. The Prime Minister, Ramsay MacDonald, thereupon advised the King to dissolve Parliament. This was done and the Election campaign took place during the second half of October.

Birkett hurried off with his wife to East Nottingham for his adoption meeting. This appeal to the country, he told his supporters who unanimously adopted him as the Liberal candidate for this division, was 'unnecessary and unwanted'. He had voted for the Committee of Inquiry into the withdrawal of the Campbell prosecution because, as he put it, 'once you have raised in the minds of men —rightly or wrongly—a suspicion that the administration of justice can be interfered with by anybody for party purposes, it is a clear duty to see that the allegation is sifted to the bottom.' He had been told, he added, that by voting for an inquiry he would injure his political prospects. 'But I did so,' he went on amid loud cheers, 'whatever the consequences.'[1]

[1] *Nottingham Journal*, October 16, 1924. A detailed account of the Campbell case can be found in the present writer's *Sir Patrick Hastings* (1960), p. 141 *et seq.*

In his election address he summarized his brief parliamentary record as follows:

> I have fought on the floor of the House of Commons for Widows' Pensions, and Pensions for Mothers where the Breadwinner is incapacitated. I have spoken in and out of Parliament for Political, Legal and Economic Equality between Men and Women: *I have striven to obtain Justice and Fair Play for all Ex-Service Men and for the Widows and Dependents as many in Nottingham can testify*: and I have supported all those measures of the Labour Government which had as their object the improvement of conditions of living.

Birkett suffered from several disadvantages which had not been a feature of the previous election campaign. In the first place, the Conservatives had a much stronger candidate in the person of Mr. (later Sir) Edmund Brocklebank, who fought cleanly and did not resort to the cheap personal attacks of his predecessor, Mr. Houfton. Secondly—and this was much more serious—the intervention of the notorious Communist Tom Mann as a candidate in East Nottingham made the contest three-cornered, thus promoting a split in the Liberal vote. Furthermore, as the campaign developed, the Liberals began to attract more and more odium to themselves for having originally put the Socialists in office and kept them there. Finally, a few days before the electors went to the polls, an incident occurred which caused a country-wide stampede to the Conservatives. This was the publication of the so-called 'Red Letter', which was alleged to have been addressed by Zinoviev, a prominent Moscow Communist, to the British Communist Party and designed to provoke disaffection in the armed forces of Britain and to organize risings in Ireland and the British colonies. Consequently the Liberal waverers throughout the country, fearful of the 'Socialist menace' transferred their allegiance in thousands to the Conservative candidates.

Polling took place on October 29, 1924, and resulted generally in a Conservative landslide. In East Nottingham the Communist candidate lost his deposit, but he drew sufficient support principally from the local miners to let the Conservative in on a majority vote. The actual figures were:

C. E. Brocklebank (C)	11,524
W. N. Birkett (L)	10,078
T. Mann (Com)	2,606
Conservative majority	1,446

For the Liberals generally the results were catastrophic. In all they lost 118 seats and were never to recover from this staggering electoral blow. Thus the Conservatives returned to power with a majority of more than two hundred over the combined strength of the other two parties, the Liberals having been reduced to a mere forty seats.

Among the messages of sympathy in the hour of defeat which Birkett received was a letter from an unknown working-class supporter, and he was to treasure it carefully. 'I do hope you are not downhearted,' this man wrote, 'as there are many humble people who will cherish the memory of witnessing someone who has fought, clean, honourable and manly, and what is more, now it is over many people feel as though they have lost a loved one; and more than that, the opposition cannot find fault. It is a great pity it was three cornered, but . . . apart from political views we feel you were part of us. You would never have received a word from me if you had got in; but I just send this word now to cheer you up.' The letter concluded with a prediction which was destined to be fulfilled: 'You will win easy later on, although they are fickle and are like a reed in the wind.'

There was some consolation for the defeated Liberal condidate for East Nottingham in returning to his chambers in Temple Gardens. He found his clerk in high spirits, and with some cause. There on his table lay a brief marked at 1,000 guineas, the first but by no means the last brief he was to receive with four figures on it. It was the outcome of a short motion Birkett had argued for a small fee as a junior in the Chancery Court in an action brought by Mr. Woolf Barnato, the son of Barney Barnato, the South African financier and diamond merchant, against two of his cousins, Mr. J. B. ('Jack') Joel and Mr. S. B. ('Solly') Joel. The claim, which arose under two wills and concerned the plaintiff's interest in the family mining business, turned out to be one of considerable complexity and was referred to arbitration in which Birkett received the 1,000 guinea brief to lead for Barnato. The latter was so pleased with his leading

5*

counsel's handling of the case that, after its successful conclusion from Barnato's point of view, he presented Birkett with a gold cigarette case on which he had inscribed the initials 'W.B.' and the words 'Little acorns into oak trees grow'.

To Henry Birkett

3, *Bigwood Road, Golders Green, N.W.*11. *December* 29, 1924. . . . We depart today for the Tregenna Castle Hotel, St. Ives, Cornwall, for a week or so, and hope to have fine weather and golf and the sea.

This last year has been most eventful: it saw me made K.C. and it saw me lose M.P. It has also been a terribly expensive year, with an extra election thrown in following on so quickly the other: and my brief tenure of Parliament cost me little less than £2,000, what with getting in, staying in, and getting out! But Providence sent me a brief marked 1,000 guineas, and added another for January with 1,000 guineas on it, so I shall wipe out the overdraft soon! Then I shall hope to settle down and save for the new house. I should like to get settled in my permanent abode, if any earthly tabernacle can be called permanent, before this real earthly tabernacle dissolves!

. . . I am nerve-weary at the end of Term and feel what a tremendous demand Life makes on one. And nerve-weariness brings apprehension and fears and general 'corners down' for no apparent reason. But a day or two by the sea—and Life is rosy once more. . . .

3

The year 1925 proved to be of supreme importance in the professional career of Norman Birkett, since it saw him securely established both as a lawyer and as an advocate among the leaders of the English Bar. And this position was achieved within twelve months of his becoming a 'silk', largely through his appearance in two cases which received a great deal of attention in different quarters. One of the cases was of the sensational 'society' kind, in which a considerable amount of dirty linen is washed in public, and his conduct of it at once included him in the select band of fashionable advocates whose services are constantly in demand in cases of this kind. The other case, which he argued in the Court of Criminal Appeal, was of particular importance to the medical profession and has since become a leading case in the law of negligence.

The facts of the latter case were as follows. On the night of July 23, 1924, Dr. Percy Bateman, who had a panel 'slum' medical practice in Deptford, was called to attend a woman in childbirth named Mary Ann Harding, the thirty-three-year-old wife of a builder's labourer. The delivery of the child was exceptionally difficult and, after administering chloroform, he attempted to deliver the child by the use of instruments, but without success. He then tried to perform manually the operation of 'version', that is turning the child inside the mother, and after an hour's strenuous work, the child was born dead. When the placenta or afterbirth was removed, part of the woman's uterus came away. Mrs. Harding consequently became very ill. On three occasions the midwife in attendance urged the doctor to send the woman to hospital, but each time he refused, his reason being that to take the woman down four flights of stairs would be immediately fatal. However, the doctor eventually decided to take the risk, and on July 28 Mrs. Harding was removed to hospital where she died two days later. After the inquest, Dr. Bateman was arrested and charged with manslaughter by negligently (1) causing internal ruptures in performing the operation of 'version'; (2) removing part of the uterus with the placenta; and (3) delaying the removal of the woman to hospital. He was tried at the Old Bailey and, although he was eloquently defended by Sir Edward Marshall Hall, who called two expert medical witnesses to show that they would have done the same in similar circumstances, the doctor was convicted of manslaughter and sentenced by Mr. Justice Shearman to six months imprisonment. He thereupon appealed against his conviction. The appeal, which was heard by the Lord Chief Justice, Lord Hewart, Mr. Justice Salter and Mr. Justice Fraser, opened in the Court of Criminal Appeal on February 8, 1925, and lasted for two days, most of which was occupied by Birkett's argument for the appellant.

Birkett began by pointing out that at the trial the prosecution had never really suggested any negligence by Dr. Bateman in his actual treatment of Mrs. Harding during the birth, which treatment was carried out in a room which was badly lit owing to the incandescent gas mantle being broken. As for the suggestion that she should have been removed to hospital earlier than she was, the doctor's course was perfectly justified, since in the very few recorded cases of a similar nature the longest the woman had lived after her admission to hospital was forty minutes, and in one of these three cases the woman had actually died on the way to hospital.

The crux of Birkett's argument was that in his summing-up to the jury the judge had failed to make any distinction between civil and criminal negligence. While it might not have been possible to take exception to the summing-up, if it had been in a civil action for damages against a doctor, this was a criminal case, and Birkett submitted that the omission was fundamental and was fatal to Dr. Bateman's conviction. In his summing-up, Mr. Justice Shearman had told the jury that they could only convict the doctor if he 'fell below the standard of skill which is the least qualification which any doctor should have'. To speak of degree of skill in a criminal case was quite irrelevant, Birkett argued. 'The question was whether Dr. Bateman had been negligent in exercising such skill as he possessed.'

Here the Lord Chief Justice interposed with a question. 'You say, then, that even where a man holds himself out as qualified to perform a difficult and delicate operation, he is not to be judged as regards skill by any objective test, but by reference only to such skill as he possessed in each particular test?'

'I submit the latter,' said Birkett, emphasizing that there was a vital distinction between civil negligence where the injury was to a private person and criminal negligence where the injury was to the State.

'Mr. Birkett,' Lord Hewart again interrupted, 'is there no injury to the State if an unskilled person undertakes to perform a delicate operation and death follows?'

'If a quack holds himself out to do that which he knows he has no skill to do, the State would be right in saying that that was a crime,' counsel replied. 'But here there was a fully qualified medical man doing that which by law he was entitled to do. The mere fact that he might fall below the general skill of the profession has no relation to crime. Where a man has done his best he can never be guilty of manslaughter.'

On the question of the woman not being removed earlier than she was to hospital, Birkett pointed out that two expert medical witnesses had been called by the defence and had testified that they would have done exactly as Dr. Bateman had done, agreeing with his opinion that her removal would cause her immediate death.

By the end of the day the Court was clearly inclining to Birkett's view. 'The question arises,' said the Lord Chief Justice, 'whether a medical man can be convicted of criminal negligence for doing that which two eminent members of his profession say that they would do in similar circumstances. Apparently the removal of the uterus like this is a very rare thing. Is a man expected to know that, if such a rare thing happens, all risks must be taken and that the patient must go to the hospital?'

'I submit not,' Birkett replied.

Next day the Lord Chief Justice returned to the point he had previously put to Birkett, whether it was not open to the jury to say that the doctor must have known by the amount of force which he had to use that what he had got hold of was not the afterbirth. 'Here was a healthy woman, and the doctor, in delivering the infant, pulled away the uterus. Could not the jury say: "*Res ipsa loquitur*—negligence"?'

'That is the danger which should have been guarded against and rendered necessary a very careful summing-up,' said Birkett.

'But might they not legitimately say it?' Lord Hewart persisted.

'I think they might say it, but not legitimately,' Birkett answered. 'In my submission there was a grave danger to be guarded against—namely, that in a case which would horrify and shock anyone, there was not a man on that jury who had not been in the position of Mrs. Harding's husband, waiting outside the room and hoping that all would be well. They might conceivably say that, as such a thing did not occur in the ordinary course of things, it must be due to the negligence of Dr. Bateman.'

'What ought to have been said?'

'I should submit that, after the jury had been directed on the difference between civil and criminal negligence, they should have been warned to put entirely from their minds any thought of convicting Dr. Bateman merely because the uterus was pulled away.'

In conclusion, Birkett reiterated that the evidence of the two expert witnesses called by the defence completely exonerated the appellant from any charge of negligence. 'The members of the medical profession are called upon to confront emergencies at all hours of the day and night and they give all their time and skill to those circumstances. When an untoward thing like this happens, which may be said to be almost unknown in the history of the profession, and when two of the most eminent physicians and surgeons in this country said that they would have done what this man did and that to do otherwise would have caused immediate death, to say that that man shall be found guilty of manslaughter would be to place the members of that profession in a very hazardous situation which would deter men from entering the medical profession.'

After hearing argument from Crown counsel, the Court announced their decision that the appeal ought to be allowed and the conviction quashed, but that on account of the importance of some of the questions raised they would take time to consider their judgment which would be delivered at a later date. Meanwhile thanks to Birkett's efforts on his behalf, the doctor was ordered to be set at liberty, and he returned to the dock area of south-east London to resume his practice among the poor of Deptford.

When he came to give judgment, the Lord Chief Justice recalled that Mr. Justice Shearman had been invited at the trial to withdraw the first and second charges of negligence from the jury, but that he had declined to do so and the jury had returned a general verdict of 'Guilty'. In the opinion of the Court there was no evidence to support the first charge in regard to the manner in which Dr. Bateman had performed the operation of 'version', and if this charge had in fact been withdrawn, it was impossible to say that the jury would certainly have convicted, particularly in the light of the strong defence presented on the third charge, which related to the delay in sending the patient to the hospital. For that reason the conviction could not stand.

At the same time, Lord Hewart laid down the principles of negligence in manslaughter cases, and these, as has been seen, owed something to Birkett's argument. To support an indictment for manslaughter by negligence, the prosecution must prove four things: (1) a duty to take care; (2) failure to discharge that duty; (3) that death was due to that default; and (4) that the negligence amounted to a crime. In a sense it was a question of degree, and it was for the jury to draw the line. 'To establish criminal liability the facts must be such that, in the opinion of the jury, the negligence of the prisoner went beyond a mere matter of compensation between subjects, and showed such disregard for the life and safety of others as to amount to a crime against the State and conduct deserving punishment.'[1]

The other big case in which Birkett was concerned at this time was one where, curiously enough, he played a secondary and supporting role until a crucial stage in its development and he only stepped into the limelight as the result of an accident. Yet it was to make his name as widely known to the general public as the case of *R.* v. *Bateman* had done with the medical profession. It was a civil action, and at the time the writ was issued and issue was joined between the parties, Birkett was still a junior in Marshall Hall's chambers. In fact, all the preparatory work on the case had been done by him in this capacity, which explains how he came to be led by Marshall Hall when the case came to trial.

The matter arose in this way. One day the telephone rang in Bowker's room in Temple Gardens. A lady was on the other end of the line and she asked to speak to Marshall Hall. She turned out to be Almina, Countess of Carnarvon, the wealthy widow of the egyptologist who had discovered the tomb of Tutankhamen, and she had been a close personal friend of Marshall Hall's for many years. Marshall Hall happened to be out, and the clerk asked if there was anything he could do.

'Oh dear,' said Lady Carnarvon, 'I want to know the name of a good, young solicitor, one on whom I can rely. Someone I can trust. And a good fighter. You know the sort of man I have in mind. Can you recommend one?'

'No, your Ladyship, I'm afraid I mustn't do that,' Bowker replied. 'I'm not supposed to recommend any solicitor. You must know plenty of people to go to.'

But Lady Carnarvon was not to be put off. In fact, she was so insistent that before Bowker knew where he was the name of a solicitor of the kind she needed had slipped out. This solicitor's managing clerk was a particular friend of Bowker's, and so in due course the solicitor's instructions arrived in Temple Gardens briefing Marshall Hall and Birkett for the defendant in the celebrated case of Dennistoun against Dennistoun. It was to form a principal topic of conversation in London clubs and drawing rooms for many weeks.

The plaintiff, Mrs. Dorothy Dennistoun, was the former wife of

[1] *The Times*, May 26, 1925.

the defendant, Lieutenant-Colonel Ian Dennistoun, ex-Grenadier Guards, whom she had married in 1910, when they were both young, and had divorced on the ground of desertion and misconduct in 1921. She was an attractive woman of strong character, much stronger than her husband's; indeed, her husband had alleged that, since he was unable to satisfy her physical demands, she had indulged in a series of affairs with, among others, a Hungarian nobleman, a Polish major, a Spanish bull fighter and a high ranking English army officer, who was referred to discreetly by her counsel in opening her case as General 'X', and to whom Colonel Dennistoun was said to have owed his promotion and appointment to a good staff job in the War Office. At the time of their divorce, both husband and wife were in debt, the husband considerably so, and he was unable to make provision for her maintenance. But, according to her, he promised to do this when he became solvent on condition that she refrained from petitioning for alimony.

Shortly after the divorce went through, Mrs. Dennistoun was staying with Lord and Lady Carnarvon, with whom she was on friendly terms. One day, when Lady Carnarvon was going to Paris, she asked her to bring back some small articles belonging to her which her husband, who was then living in France would deliver to her. Lady Carnarvon carried out the commission and immediately there sprang up a sympathy between her and Colonel Dennistoun. A strong friendship developed, with Lord Carnarvon's knowledge and approval, since there was no hint of impropriety in it. However, after Lord Carnarvon's death, which occurred soon afterwards, they proceeded to get married. Now Lady Carnarvon was a wealthy woman in her own right and Colonel Dennistoun had nothing except his clothes, and even these he owed to his new wife since she paid his tailor's bill. Accordingly, in a rare gesture of Quixotic devotion, the Countess handed over the sum of £100,000 to her new husband for the purpose of making a marriage settlement; in her husband's lifetime she had already given him £20,000 and a furnished flat.

On learning of these transactions, Mrs. Dennistoun, who was in some financial difficulties herself, decided to claim the alimony which she considered him morally bound to pay in accordance with his promise. She also claimed several comparatively small sums amounting to about £470 which she said she had lent him, in addition to £616 which she said was borrowed at his request in 1913 and expended in paying his debts.

In view of the relatively trifling amount of money involved, it may well be wondered why Colonel Dennistoun did not quietly pay up and so put an end to the matter. Indeed Marshall Hall, who had represented Mrs. Dennistoun in other litigation, and who consequently knew how much dirty linen could be produced by each party, strongly advised the defendant to settle on these lines. The trouble was that, although he was now nominally well off, Colonel Dennistoun's money in reality belonged to his second wife, and Lady Carnarvon would not hear of a settlement. This was blackmail, she said, and she was determined that the first Mrs. Dennistoun should not get a single penny. As has already been seen from her conversation with Bowker, Lady Carnarvon was accustomed to getting her own way, and in this instance she got it.

What followed was described by Mr. Justice McCardie, who tried the case, as the most bitterly conducted litigation he had ever known.

4

The Dennistoun case began before Mr. Justice McCardie, known as the 'bachelor judge', and a special jury in Court IV of the King's Bench Division of the High Court on March 3, 1925. Sir Ellis Hume-Williams, K.C., the leading divorce practitioner of the day, and Mr. St. John Field, later a County Court judge, appeared for the plaintiff, Mrs. Dorothy Muriel Dennistoun; and Sir Edward Marshall Hall, K.C., Mr. Norman Birkett, K.C., and Mr. A. H. Davis, represented the defendant, Lieutenant-Colonel Ian Onslow Dennistoun. The case, in which a good deal of evidence of a scandalous nature was given, aroused the greatest public interest, particularly in 'society' circles. It lasted for seventeen days and the costs which the parties incurred in bringing it into court, amounted to over thirty thousand pounds. Furthermore, by a fortunate accident, as will be seen, it was to provide Norman Birkett with the greatest opportunity for professional advancement to have hitherto come his way.

In opening the plaintiff's case, Sir Ellis Hume-Williams remarked that the statement of defence, that is the written pleadings, which in their original form had been settled by Birkett, had subsequently been amended six times, and 'the alterations had exhausted all the colours of the spectrum'. The practice is for amendments to the printed or typewritten pleadings to be made in different coloured inks to distinguish them, and in this instance black, red, green, purple, blue and yellow ink had been used.

'A new school of impressionists,' commented Mr. Justice McCardie, in a nice example of judicial wit, at which the various counsel and solicitors engaged in the case laughed politely.

Mrs. Dennistoun's leading counsel argued that Lieutenant-Colonel Dennistoun was prepared to accept any sacrifice from his wife, even to a state of misconduct between her and General 'X' and other lovers from whom she received favours including money, of which the defendant had the benefit. Indeed he had always accepted them with gratitude.

Sir Ellis Hume-Williams proceeded to read a letter full of 'baby-talk', which Colonel Dennistoun had written to his wife in May, 1916, when her affair with the General was developing.

> My own girl,
>
> I could not phone to you as things are moving a bit, and I must get busy. Darling heart, take great care of yourself; you seem sometimes such a tiny, small, brown mouse. Me feels just like a tiger in a cage behind great big iron bars. Oh, girlie darling, I hate you using that lovely body of yours as a gift.
>
> You are all I have got in this world. It makes me despise myself and everything I do. I can't help it; there it is. Why should you be made a fool of, which is the worst of all? Don't go further than you want—life is so short and I want you so dreadfully. Me wishes me were back in the little wee house. Good-night, precious. One big kiss.
>
> TIGER

The General took rooms in a Paris hotel for himself and Mrs. Dennistoun, Sir Ellis continued, and it was clear from the correspondence in the case that not only was the husband encouraging his wife in her association, but he was trying to safeguard her and giving her hints on the way to behave in a quarrel with the General so as not to lose him. 'I know what you object to,' he wrote in one letter, 'but I am sure it is best and the only way to get on, and all I hope is that we can stick it.' It was even suggested that the defendant had inspected the rooms which his wife and the General were to occupy in the Ritz Hotel in Paris.

After the war, Colonel Dennistoun retired from the army and established his domicile in France, a fact which led his wife to take proceedings for divorce under French jurisdiction on the grounds of desertion and misconduct. According to Sir Ellis, before the divorce went through, Mrs. Dennistoun saw her husband in Paris and informed him that she had been advised to obtain alimony or maintenance from the French court. She also reminded him that he owed her a great deal of money. 'You know quite well I cannot do anything for you now, because I have not a penny,' he was alleged to have told her. 'Don't press for alimony now, either here or in England, and I will give you my word of honour that I will support you and provide for you as soon as I am in a position to do so.'

Consequently Mrs. Dennistoun did not petition the court for alimony nor was she awarded any sum by way of maintenance. Even after the divorce she continued to send the defendant money, £20 on one occasion and £100 on another, in response to his pathetic appeals. 'I am just busted to the world,' he wrote a few months after the divorce. 'I have hawked my fur coat all round. I have sold my enamel cigarette case for 400 francs.' He then asked her to send him £100, which she did. It was towards the end of the same year, in December, 1921, that Mrs. Dennistoun, who had left some belongings in the Paris hotel where she had been staying, was told by Lady Carnarvon, who was going to France, that she would get them for her. Mrs. Dennistoun accordingly asked her husband to secure the articles and give them to her friend. As has been seen, this was how her husband first met Lady Carnarvon, whom he subsequently married.

However, while Colonel Dennistoun's financial affairs took an appreciable turn for the better, his ex-wife's progressively deteriorated. Señor Bolin, the Spaniard whom she hoped to marry, had failed to come up to scratch, the General was dead and in any event had rather turned against her at the end, while her other ex-lovers did not come forward with offers of assistance. It was now her turn to appeal to her former husband, which in view of his marriage to the wealthy Countess of Carnarvon she had now no compunction in doing. By the year 1923 she was in severe financial straits. 'Tiger, for God's sake, give me help,' she begged him in a pathetic note. 'I don't even ask to see you . . . I am desperate now. It is more urgent than you realize.' Eventually he gave her six hundred pounds, a relatively small proportion of the thousands she had given him during the period of their marriage. To her further appeals he turned a deaf ear. Finally in a curt letter he told her that any further communications she had to make to him must be through his solicitors, since 'our lives are definitely severed'.

Any man with heart and mind, Sir Ellis Hume-Williams remarked caustically, would scarcely believe that that letter was written by a man who was once 'down and out', in response to appeals which had been made to him. 'He is the man who in the first half of 1923 had £7,000 paid into his account, and in the second half of the same year £42,650, and who was willing to owe his advances to his wife's paramour. At that time, presumably, he would have called himself an officer and a gentleman.' Finally, on the very day the writ was issued, Sir Ellis added, indignantly throwing his brief down with a bang on the bench in front of him, Colonel Dennistoun had closed his account at the Westminster Bank by drawing a cheque payable to 'self' for £51,695.

'The most extraordinary pleadings were raised by the defence, and they did what I suggest was a scandalous thing,' Mrs. Dennistoun's counsel concluded. 'Having denied the existence of the agreement, they put in at the eleventh hour a plea that, if the agreement was entered into, there was an implied term that the plaintiff should live a chaste life, although not a word was said about it. That is absolute nonsense. Whoever heard of a case in which, after a wife had divorced her husband, and they met to agree that the husband should provide for his wife, in the agreement there should be an implied term that the wife should live chastely? This lady has been pursued by detectives. Everything they could do to go into her past life has been done to keep her out of this action, and this defence about the implied term of chastity is made the excuse for allegations against her in regard to seven different men.'

Mrs. Dennistoun was the first witness to be called. As she stepped into the box she was seen to be wearing a sealskin coat and a turban, a dress combination then in the height of fashion. She showed the most complete self-assurance, as she recited her story in answer to her counsel's questions, cutting a very different figure from the 'small, brown mouse' of her ex-husband's letters. Only once did her habitual composure desert her for a moment. This was when she described how Colonel Dennistoun had inspected the rooms at the Ritz where the General had taken rooms in which to commit adultery.

'And did you pay the price?' Sir Ellis Hume-Williams asked quietly.

The witness was seen to tremble slightly, as she answered in a low voice, 'Yes.'

Another touch of drama was provided by the judge when he put a question to Mrs. Dennistoun. 'You lived at an hotel in Paris with a general we have called X?'

'Yes.'

'Who was it?'

'General Sir John Cowans,' the witness answered in subdued tones. This answer created a considerable sensation both inside and outside the court, when it became known, since Sir John Cowans had filled with distinction the post of Quartermaster-General of the British Army throughout the First World War.

Sir Edward Marshall Hall's cross-examination, although it too had its dramatic moments, was perhaps the least successful of his forensic efforts. For one thing, he was plainly ill, suffering from phlebitis of the leg, which made him unusually irritable and prone to lose his temper. Then, the fact that he was in the case at all was due to his life-long friendship with Lady Carnarvon, who insisted against his better judgment in his going on with a case which should have been settled out of court. Finally, he antagonized the jury, not to mention his fellow barristers, by revealing information which he had obtained in confidence when he had appeared for Mrs. Dennistoun in another matter connected with General Sir John Cowans. In particular, his friendship with the defendant's present wife 'warped his independence and I think his judgment', as Sir Ellis Hume-Williams put it in recalling the case afterwards. 'Personally, I have always made it a rule not to appear for anyone with whom I had more than a casual acquaintance. To appear for a friend means to be nervous and over-anxious—neither of which tends to good advocacy, added to which, if you win you get little praise and if you lose all the blame.'[1]

[1] Sir Ellis Hume-Williams. *The World, the House, and the Bar* (1930), at p. 157.

'You heard the opening of the case?' Sir Edward began.

'Yes,' replied the woman in the box.

'You heard the terms in which Sir Ellis spoke of your husband?'

'Yes.'

'You heard the condemnation that he thought fit to utter of him?'

'Well, he said, I suppose, what most people would say.'

'Did you hear the specific charge that he had forfeited the right, if he ever had it, to call himself a gentleman, and had lived on your immoral earnings?'

'I heard it said.'

'Do you approve of it?'

Mrs. Dennistoun went pale, as she answered falteringly, 'I think it is a very unfair question.'

'Madam,' thundered Sir Edward, 'fair or unfair, I propose to repeat it. Do you approve of that charge?'

'I was fond of my husband,' was all Mrs. Dennistoun could say.

Marshall Hall's next question contained the suggestion that the witness had gone in for blackmail. 'How much do you think a woman who loved her husband would pay not to have this case in open court?'

'It is a great deal harder for me than my husband thinks. I am a woman alone, and he is a man.'

'A woman alone?' counsel queried in an incredulous tone intended to suggest to the jury that the wicked woman in the witness box was surrounded by a bevy of lovers.

'I am a woman alone,' Mrs. Dennistoun repeated with a decided hint of pathos in her voice, 'and have no man to protect me!'

'Is that true?' Sir Edward Marshall Hall was still dubious.

'Absolutely and entirely.'

'If the woman who has married your husband is a rich woman, a very rich woman, how much do you think that he would be prepared to pay to avoid a case like this being opened in open court?'

'I have never thought of it in that light at all.'

'If you had married a man and loved him, if you can imagine it,' counsel continued cuttingly, 'how much would you have paid to prevent an attack on this man?'

'If the man cared for the woman he married, he would not want to expose the woman by himself,' Mrs. Dennistoun parried the thrust neatly. 'I asked him to provide for me, and only asked for a small sum—his pension. It did not seem a large sum of money.' Then, throwing a contemptuous glance at her husband's leading counsel, she added, 'The rest of your question was not considered or thought about.'

'Do you not think that Lady Carnarvon and your husband having married on December 19, 1923, there was some sort of reason why she would not sooner pay than have this case in court?'

'Such a thing never entered my head. I thought my husband would keep his promise.'

When Marshall Hall asked her about an action she began to recover a Minerva car from a London garage in 1921, she said, 'You must remember, as you did it all for me.' She then explained that General Cowans gave her the car, but the garage refused to hand it over, since they had an order from the General shortly before he died instructing them not to do so. The General's executors were concerned with the action.

'If you wish me to tell the court what you told me,' said Marshall Hall, 'I am prepared to do so.'

'You persuaded me not to go on with the case.'

'You said that you did not want a certain name brought into it, and I withdrew the case at your wish.'

Needless to say, this observation created a most unfortunate impression in court, since it is an inviolable rule of the Bar that counsel must not disclose information supplied to him by a client in confidence, nor must he volunteer remarks, such as the above, which amount to his giving evidence himself. But Marshall Hall was undeterred.

'At that time you were living at Lady Carnarvon's house?'

'Yes, I had just gone there.'

'Do you know it was at the special request of Lady Carnarvon?'

Mrs. Denistoun could not resist the opening which this question provided. 'Yes,' she said with malice in her voice. 'She paid you.'

'You know I was never paid a penny,' Marshall Hall protested warmly. 'I did not receive one farthing, but as Lady Carnarvon's friend I consented to advise you, introduced by Lady Carnarvon.'

And so it went on, the questions ranging from Mrs. Dennistoun's amorous activities in Budapest to mixed bathing in Majorca.

'How many men in your life have been devoted to you?'

'I don't know.'

'A good many, I suggest. Shall I give you a list of the names?'

The idea that Marshall Hall was about to produce a catalogue of conquests like Leporello in *Don Giovanni* alarmed the judge, who immediately interposed, 'You had better postpone the list, Sir Edward.'

'You have had a great success in your life with men, haven't you?' Marshall Hall persisted.

'You seem to like to put it that way,' Mrs. Dennistoun replied calmly, 'but it is your own way.'

The witness denied allegations of misconduct with a young officer called Oscar Senhouse who was subsequently killed in action during the war. But she admitted sleeping with General Cowans and her husband at the same period.

'You never loved your husband in a marital fashion at all?'

'I do not think he has ever had cause for complaint.'

'Since 1916 he has never had relations with you at all?'

'That is absolutely untrue.'

Here the judge interrupted to ask, 'You had relations with Sir John Cowans and then with your husband?'

'If you put it that way.'

So far as Mrs. Dennistoun was concerned she more than held her own with the famous advocate. Once, when Marshall Hall appeared to suggest that she had sent to a certain registry of domestic servants for a copy of a character she had given her maid the previous day, she denied it emphatically. When confronted with a document which Marshall Hall handed to her, she immediately recognized it as a character she had given the servant six months previously. Sir Edward at once declared that he did not wish to suggest that she wrote it on the previous day, a remark that evoked a chorus of 'Ohs!' some of which came from the jury box.

The plaintiff rebutted with equal emphasis Marshall Hall's suggestion that she had said that Lady Carnarvon would pay £100,000 rather than that this case should come into court. 'I never said anything of the sort. It is a lie.'

Finally, in answer to a question about the costs she had paid her solicitor, Sir George Lewis, she said they only amounted to £100 or £150, she did not remember which. 'What it has cost Colonel Dennistoun for detectives to follow me about,' she added, 'having me hunted everywhere, must be thousands of pounds.'

'Yes,' Marshall Hall conceded, 'it has been an expensive action.'

Later, when Sir George Lewis was giving evidence, Marshall Hall made the foolish mistake of losing his temper with one of the most experienced solicitors in the profession. This evidence concluded the plaintiff's case, which it now seemed clear that Marshall Hall's unfortunate cross-examination had if anything strengthened rather than damaged.

It was his clerk Edgar Bowker who thought of a way to retrieve the situation, when they had returned to chambers. After the veteran leader had had a cup of tea, Bowker went into his room. Marshall Hall was lying exhausted on his couch. They had a little desultory conversation about how the case had gone that day in court, and then Bowker tactfully broached his plan.

'Sir Edward, I think you are tired,' the clerk said. 'Why not let Mr. Birkett open the case and save yourself for the final speech to the jury at the end? As a clincher?'

For a moment or two, Marshall Hall sat still, staring in front of him. There was a flash of resentment in his eyes as he looked at his clerk. But it vanished almost at once. Suddenly he sprang up from the couch and hurried into Birkett's room next door. The clerk followed.

'Norman,' he said, 'I've just had a great idea. You open tomorrow and I'll make the closing speech. I think it will be first-class tactics.'

As the faithful Bowker has recorded, this was Norman Birkett's great stroke of luck.

5

When Birkett rose to open Colonel Dennistoun's defence next morning, he faced a crowded, tense and expectant court, besides a jury which was noticeably hostile towards his client. 'Members of the jury,' he began, 'at last the moment has come when you will hear for the first time what my client has to say. . . . There is only one phrase to describe what Colonel Dennistoun and Almina Lady Carnarvon have passed through during the past few days—unspeakable anguish. You may think this case might have been settled for a payment less than was expended to defend the case. Then there would have been no daily anguish of seeing column after column of this in the daily papers. Why did they fight? They took the view that if they gave way they would never be free from demands. Colonel

Dennistoun and Lady Carnarvon said: "This means the loss of everything dearest to me, but, though I am pilloried every day, I needs must fight, because I cannot do otherwise".'

Birkett picked up a newspaper and proceeded to read an extract from an article in which it was stated that one of the most potent weapons of the blackmailer was to bring proceedings in court, with the consequent threat of publicity. 'That,' said Birkett, emphasizing the word, 'puts into a concise form what the position really will be in this case, if it is found that there never was such an agreement as Mrs. Dennistoun alleges. The only reason this action was brought was because Almina Lady Carnarvon married Colonel Dennistoun and both are living in wealth. An action like this would form a weapon that no man would face; he would do anything and everything to avoid it.'

As for the suggestion that his client owed his military preferment to Mrs. Dennistoun's liaison with the Quartermaster General of the Army which he condoned, Birkett brushed it aside with scorn. 'It was precious poor preferment to give your wife from 1916 to 1920 to another man in order to become a major in the Labour Corps,' he remarked. 'Preferment indeed! There was not a single thing that the colonel got that he would not have got in the ordinary turn of events. What if Mrs. Dennistoun, as a woman who since 1910 had been fond of pleasure, dress and excitement, had gone to Sir John Cowans for the sake of the position, for the opportunities it would give her of living life in a fuller sense than she was able to do with her husband? . . . The truth is that Mrs. Dennistoun went to Sir John Cowans of her own free will; there was never any bargain about it. She was a wilful, impetuous, pleasure-loving wife, and her husband could not control her or persuade her to do what he wanted.'

Finally, there was the point that if an agreement was made in Paris between husband and wife on the question of alimony, it must be an implied term that Mrs. Dennistoun must be chaste. 'How can the court make any order if it is told that at the material time Mrs. Dennistoun was living in open adultery with other men?'

Birkett had opened the case for his client with considerable effect, which did something to dispel the unfavourable impression of Colonel Dennistoun which Sir Ellis Hume-Williams's remarks had created in the minds of the jury. Edgar Bowker, Birkett's clerk, described the speech as 'magnificent', and in recalling it afterwards he remarked as he listened that he felt that it marked the turning point in Birkett's career. However that may be, his real triumph as an advocate in this difficult case was to come later.

Before Colonel Dennistoun went into the witness box, evidence was given by various hotel employees who had been brought over from the continent and kept in England at enormous expense to show what kind of a woman the plaintiff was. One of them related how she had seen Mrs. Dennistoun and Señor Bolin in the bathroom without clothes, and another told of the Spaniard making a hurried exit when Sir John Cowans arrived unexpectedly. One of these witnesses, a Swiss chambermaid, who spoke no English proved a source of considerable merriment in court by her answers. After four minutes had been spent in an attempt to make this lady repeat the oath, Sir Edward Marshall Hall put two or three questions to her. It was evident, however, that the witness was not going to be a success.

Sir Ellis Hume-Williams fared little better when he questioned her through an interpreter and received completely unintelligible replies. He then addressed a question to her himself in French.

'Have you learnt your deposition by heart (*de coeur*)?'

'*Oui*,' replied the chambermaid, amid a roar of laughter.

At this the judge intervened to tell counsel that his French was too classical for the witness. '*De coeur* means something entirely different from what you mean, Sir Ellis.'

Sir Ellis tried German without success, and then Mr. Justice McCardie asked her whether she spoke Italian. She did not, and the judge dryly observed that it was not advisable to introduce too many languages.

The conclusion was swift, and drama followed on the heels of comedy. Sir Edward Marshall Hall rose to re-examine, and speaking in French, of which language he had a fluent mastery, said to the witness, pointing in the direction of Mrs. Dennistoun: 'Do you see that woman there?'

'Yes.'

'What is her name?'

In loud, clear tones the chambermaid replied, 'Madame Bolin.'

When his turn came to go into the witness box, Colonel Dennistoun appeared the typical ex-Guards officer, tall, erect, with a toothbrush moustache. He suffered from deafness, which did not make him an easy witness to examine; apparently this disability was the result of pneumonia which he had contracted in South Africa before his marriage, having run away from Eton to that country where he had served in the Rhodesian Volunteers and later the Cape Police. Answering Birkett, who conducted his examination-in-chief, Colonel Dennistoun stated that his marriage to the plaintiff was not consummated until five months after the honeymoon.

'Why was that?'

'Because my wife was of a nervous temperament.'

Here the judge interrupted to observe that she had already admitted this and that 'details already admitted need not be repeated, particularly if they are sexual'.

Birkett passed on to one of the witness's letters to his wife, in which he had written: 'I have given way to you rightly or wrongly in everything. You loved someone else within a few months of our marriage and took him to our home when I was away on guard.' This referred to Oscar Senhouse, he said, adding that when he spoke to her about it at a later date 'she acknowledged that she was very fond of the boy and had committed misconduct with him.'

'Your wife has sworn that the statement in your letter that I have read was untrue. Is it true?'

'Absolutely.'

'Now, when she told you in 1911 of her relations with Senhouse, what did you do or say?'

Colonel Dennistoun began to look embarrassed. 'I don't remember what I said,' he replied, hesitating as if at a loss for words. 'She gave me to understand that I was not—I don't know how to put it—that she required more than one man.'

'What attitude did you take towards the disclosure she had made?'

'It was not much use taking any attitude, as she was very much more the dominant figure than I was. She had made up her mind that she was going to know him and be friends with him, and she told me where she had been to with him on various occasions and what she did.'

'What age was he?' the judge intervened to ask.

'He was her age. He was a young man.' (Mrs. Dennistoun was twenty-one at the time.)

'Why didn't you take a strong line about it?' continued Birkett.

'I did not wish to do that,' answered Colonel Dennistoun, who went on to explain that he had married against his father's wishes and that his father had objected to his wife because of 'certain family affairs' he knew about. Although he could have divorced her in 1911, 'I had a certain amount of pride . . . I had no intention of letting my father know that things had gone wrong. I protected her then. . . .'

The witness was then questioned by his counsel about the letter in which he had written to his wife: 'Oh, girlie, darling. I hate you using that lovely body of yours as a gift,' and asked to explain what he meant by this. 'It has been suggested that the letter showed your earlier knowledge of the Sir John Cowans matter and your desire that it should go on for your benefit?'

'I deny that entirely,' said Colonel Dennistoun. 'This letter was written after I had seen her in London. I knew nothing of anything happening between Sir John and her up to the time that she wrote a letter to me. I then had an interview with her, and she told me what she had done, and dropped on me for having left her in Paris, and so on. It was all the same thing. I had forgiven her a dozen times. I loved the woman, and would go on doing it, and probably would do it now.'

'Was it possible for you in May, 1916, to stop your wife going with Sir John Cowans if she wanted to?'

'No.'

'Was she in the habit of doing things that you did not wish?'

'If she wanted to do a thing, she did it. If I suggested anything to her that she did not want to do, she jolly well didn't do it.'

'After the communication by your wife about Sir John at the beginning of May, 1916, had you any further relations with your wife?'

'No.'

'In fact she said she did not wish any further relations, though you saw her at intervals from that date down to May, 1921?'

'Yes, very often.' For example, shortly before the divorce proceedings began, she came to see him when he was ill in bed in Paris and unable to provide himself with sufficient food, and gave him some money, saying 'Here, boy, there is another present!' There was no suggestion that it was a loan. Indeed, said Colonel Dennistoun, she had never made him a loan in her life. In this instance, he had not asked her for the money; she had given it to him 'off her own bat'.

Under a most searching cross-examination by Sir Ellis Hume-Williams, Colonel Dennistoun stuck to his story that the real explanation for his seeming complaisance was his desire to protect his wife as long as he could.

'You wanted to protect her?' Counsel raised his eyebrows, while his tone of voice indicated incredulity.

'I did not want everyone to know that my wife was an adulteress.'

'But, surely Colonel Dennistoun, you could have protected her without telling everyone that your wife was an adulteress?'

The witness shrugged his shoulders. For a moment or two he did not reply. Then, looking counsel straight in the eye, he said, 'What would you do?'

Hume-Williams regarded him coldly. 'What would I do?'

'Yes.'

Every eye in court was fixed upon the figure of Sir Ellis Hume-Williams, who suddenly flushed, as he declared in ringing tones: 'I would have told my wife that if she did it again I would divorce her. I would then have gone up to London and assaulted General Cowans—and to hell with my career!'

For several moments there was complete silence. Then someone coughed and there was a sound of shuffling of feet, while Sir Edward Marshall Hall could be heard muttering in amazement, 'Assaulted General Cowans!'

Mr. Justice McCardie further broke the silence by dryly observing that there were some occasions on which emotion was permissible but he did not think Sir Ellis should put it in that way.

Counsel immediately put it in another way. Colonel Dennistoun, he said, had called his wife 'the little brown mouse who wanted so much care and love,' and this was the way he showed it—by accepting appointments from the man who was guilty of committing misconduct with her.

'I could not stop her,' said the witness quickly.

'Why, if you were a man, did you not write to your wife saying, "You see the terrible trouble you are getting me into. Why don't you stop it and leave General Cowans?"'

'I suppose, if I had been a strong man, I should have done that before, in 1911. I should have divorced her in 1911.'

'It is not a question of strength or weakness, but of ordinary decency and common sense. Why didn't you write to her and say it?'

'The only answer that I can give is that I did not do that.'

'Is not the reason that you were content that she should live in misconduct with General Cowans as long as you could profit by it?'

'No.'

'What other reason was there?'

'I could not stop her,' was all the wretched Colonel Dennistoun could say. 'She was always dominant over me.'

Colonel Dennistoun was followed into the witness box by his wealthy second wife. Lady Carnarvon, who was dressed in a black frock and wore a black cloche hat, gripped the rail of the box with the fingers of her left hand on which two wedding rings were plainly visible. Examined by her old friend Sir Edward Marshall Hall, she was asked to explain how she had come to provide the defendant with twenty thousand pounds and a luxurious flat during her first husband's lifetime. 'I found him in Paris,' she said, 'in an attic that not one of my servants would be seen in. There was no fireplace, no hot or cold water, only a very small window overlooking a courtyard. He looked like death. A thin, emaciated, poor creature. His clothes were shiny, and he looked as though he had not had food enough to keep body and soul together.'

She went on to explain that the large sums in Colonel Dennistoun's banking account were paid in by her from the sale of some family pictures and that she used her husband's banking account as she had heavy expenses of her own to meet at the time and she did not wish to pay the death duties on the pictures immediately.

'Had Colonel Dennistoun any authority to spend any of that money for any other purpose except with your approval?'

'Had he done so, he would have been a blackguard.'

'Although the account was in his name, whose money was it?'

'Mine.'

'Whatever has been said about Colonel Dennistoun, are you very fond of him?'

'I love him with all my heart, soul and body.'

This answer caused some laughter at the back of the court, but it was promptly suppressed. It made Marshall Hall look round and exclaim: 'It may be a matter of laughter to some people, but it is a solemn statement.'

'Too sacred even to discuss,' Lady Carnarvon broke in, raising her head slightly and closing her eyes.

'She is going to faint, quick!' her counsel exclaimed, as his client clutched the sides of the witness box. 'I'm all right,' she said weakly.

The usher then brought her some smelling salts, which she sniffed. After a few moments she was able to continue her evidence. She was not cross-examined. 'I have no questions to ask you, Lady Carnarvon,' Sir Ellis Hume-Williams was considerate enough to say.

The plaintiff's counsel then requested leave, which was granted, to call another witness to prove receipt of a copy of a letter from Colonel Dennistoun to his wife which the plaintiff had sent him. He was Major Guy Paget, late Scots Guards, a relative of Mrs. Dennistoun, and a former M.P.

'You have been in court nearly every day during the hearing of this case, sitting with Mrs. Dennistoun?' he was asked by Marshall Hall.

'Yes.'

'And I don't think you disguise the fact that you have a very strong hostile feeling against Colonel Dennistoun?'

'Well,' this witness declared, 'I should think every decent man has.'

6

The arrangement will be remembered whereby Marshall Hall was to make the closing speech for the defence in the Dennistoun case. Accordingly, after the last witness had given evidence and the Court had risen for the day, the leader went off to his flat to prepare what he would put before the jury on the following morning. In fact, he was to take no further part in the case.

Shortly after Bowker had reached his home in Chiswick, the telephone rang. It was Marshall Hall. 'Bowker,' he said, 'my leg is so bad that I shan't be able to attend Court tomorrow.' In fact, a vein in his leg had burst.

'I'm sorry to hear that, Sir Edward.'

'Doctor's orders. Mr. Birkett will have to take over. Will you arrange matters?'

The clerk immediately telephoned Birkett and gave him the news. He then returned to the Temple to collect the brief and all the voluminous papers connected with the case which Birkett had left in chambers in the fond belief that his work was finished. He then went off to Birkett's house in Golders Green, picking up Arthur Davis, his junior, on the way.

The task which confronted him was much more formidable than on the occasion when he prepared the opening speech at short notice.

COLONEL DENNISTOUN AND LADY CARNARVON

MR. JUSTICE McCARDIE

Then all he had to do was to follow his brief, set out his client's case, summarizing the proofs of evidence of the various defence witnesses, which were attached to his instructions. Now he had to range over the whole of the plaintiff's case and attempt to demolish it to the jury's satisfaction in the light of all the evidence that had been given, seizing upon and analysing the weak points in his opponent's case as well as emphasizing the strong points in his client's.

When his junior and the clerk arrived at his house, Birkett was not in the least put out. All he said, after Bowker had handed over the huge bundle of papers, was: 'Well, it's been a frantic rush for you, Edgar. Now go home and get some rest. We're going to be busy.'

Birkett and Davis got down to work, sustained throughout the night by sandwiches and repeated cups of black coffee which Mrs. Birkett prepared. Mrs. Birkett also helped with the documents, marking and 'flagging' those to which her husband might need to refer. After some hours Davis began to nod his head and become drowsy. Mrs. Birkett thereupon put him to bed in their guest room, leaving her husband to labour on alone. Shortly after seven o'clock, he broke off for a bath and breakfast. Two hours later he and his junior were in their places in court, Birkett looking quite fresh beside Davis who still showed signs of weariness.

As soon as the judge had taken his place on the Bench, Birkett rose and explained that owing to unexpected illness, his leader was unable to be in court. 'His illness has incapacitated him entirely,' he said, 'and it was not until ten o'clock last night that I knew I should have to take his place—Sir Edward has been suffering all the time from very considerable pain and it was only his great courage that caused him to attend until yesterday.'

'Members of the jury,' he continued, after apologizing for the absence of his leader, 'if this action had been brought on the simple issues of money lent and an agreement to support, it would have been laughed out of court. Other issues, however, have been inextricably bound up with these. My client, Colonel Dennistoun, has married a wealthy countess, and you cannot disguise from yourselves the fact that, whatever else you may say about him, Colonel Dennistoun has been about as weak, about as vacillating, about as infatuated a man as you have ever either heard of or read of. But I suggest that he is not a liar. He is many things, but not that. The words which my learned friend, Sir Ellis Hume-Williams, has not hesitated to use to Colonel Dennistoun in his cross-examination would have made any ordinary man shrivel; but now the story is told and the real state of affairs laid bare, it has been shown that in plain terms there was blackmail.'

Birkett then launched into the most scathing denunciation of Mrs. Dennistoun, calling her 'heartless', 'a traitress' and 'a liar of the first rank'. Her conduct was 'the absolute negation of every quality that calls for respect', particularly when it was borne in mind that she could do anything with her weak, vacillating husband that she pleased.

Pointing at Mrs. Dennistoun, he went on:

> She comes into court and, in order to extort money from the poor weak husband and from Lady Carnarvon, says that Colonel Dennistoun arranged for her to go with General Cowans. The use of misconduct committed from choice and because she wanted to do it, as a means of getting money from Lady Carnarvon, is in the last grade of unforgivable sins!
>
> . . . I suggest that it is an extraordinarily dangerous woman with whom you have to deal. She lied with readiness, with resource, and with ingenuity, and every time she had a moment's breathing space to realize that she had made a mistake she cleverly tried to recover. Sometimes, in trying to recover, she implicated herself more deeply.

Birkett went on to refer to Mrs. Dennistoun as speaking untruths, 'consciously, and, oh, so cleverly.' He then said that he wanted to put before the jury one or two aspects of the Cowans matter which had not been previously put before them.

> Sexual matters are matters of hot blood, not of cold, calculated bargains. If General Cowans was of the sort he is said to be, why did he not misconduct himself with Mrs. Dennistoun on the night the bargain was made instead of waiting for six weeks?
>
> Mrs. Dennistoun has said that she was fond of General Cowans, that she admired him, and that her affection was increasing. Has this woman ever thought of the attack she has made on General Cowans? She says that she was fond of him, but now that he is beyond the grave she defames him. She makes this a matter of world-wide interest because of the position that

great Quartermaster-General held. She does not hesitate to drag the name of the dead General Cowans through the courts. Am I right if I characterize that conduct as heartless?

Mrs. Dennistoun says that she lived with General Cowans in order to gain military preferment for her husband. That conduct is just the opposite of love. If a woman wanted to do things for her husband, that is just the thing she would never do.

Mrs. Dennistoun kept all the letters which have been produced. She it was who controlled the correspondence before the court. I shall produce the original documents showing the way in which passages used by my learned friend, Sir Ellis Hume-Williams, with such effect were marked by Mrs. Dennistoun.

The real truth, I submit, is that Mrs. Dennistoun pursued her own course, and that Colonel Dennistoun, who was without 'guts' in this matter, did not make any stand against her, but did his best to look after and shield her as far as possible. He was so infatuated with his wife, so in love with her, that a course which would seem to the ordinary man truly repugnant was to him a matter in which he acquiesced, and he did his best to look after and shield her. . . .

Never for one moment did Mrs. Dennistoun dream that this case would be fought out to the end with such intensity. It was her intention the action should be settled.

One remark made by Birkett in the course of his speech produced a piece of advice from the judge which Colonel Dennistoun's counsel accepted in good part. It was when Birkett remarked, 'There are men on the jury who are older than I am.'

'You mustn't say that,' Mr. Justice McCardie interrupted him. 'If you want to flatter the jury, you must say, "There are young men among you with a wide knowledge of the world".'

Birkett explained the purpose of his original remark by observing that he did not want to disguise the fact that his client was 'weak beyond all expression', and if the jury saw that position aright they would have an explanation of the whole matter.

Mrs. Dennistoun knew that at all material times Colonel Dennistoun never had a penny that did not come from Lady Carnarvon. Is it to be expected that Lady Carnarvon should

> say, 'I will give you my money and you shall give it to the woman who has divorced you'? That would be repugnant to morals, to common sense, and to everything else. . . . There was never a word of any legal claim until Colonel Dennistoun's marriage with Lady Carnarvon, until the countess's fortunes were linked with those of the man with whom she stands or falls and to whom she showed such wonderful devotion in the witness box yesterday.
>
> I have not shrunk from using the hideous term, 'blackmail', in connection with this action. Blackmail takes many forms, but this is about the most dreadful form that it can take. There are issues in this case of exceeding gravity. People in the position of Lady Carnarvon do not face the ordeal of publicity during nearly three weeks for nothing.

This speech, which occupied the greater part of the day, was most moving in its effect. It reduced Almina Lady Carnarvon to tears. She sat in her place at the solicitors' table for most of the time with her face buried in a white-gloved hand, occasionally raising a handkerchief to dab her eyes. It made headline news on the front pages of the evening papers. If his opening speech had been 'a brilliant piece of advocacy', then, in the words of his delighted clerk Edgar Bowker, 'this final address rose to heights of eloquence rarely heard in a court of law. No reading of it can convey its effect, for stripped of Birkett's voice and manner—a blend of harmony and reason—the words lose their magic. When he had finished, Mr. Justice McCardie and Sir Ellis Hume-Williams congratulated him. He left the Court that day at the top of his profession.'[1]

It should be added that the compliment paid him by Sir Ellis Hume-Williams was of the barbed variety. Sir Ellis began by saying that, although he regretted the absence of Sir Edward Marshall Hall, he thought Colonel Dennistoun had had the advantage of having had 'a very clever speech made on his behalf by Mr. Birkett', and he did not think the Colonel had 'lost anything'. He then went on to say that as an older man he welcomed Birkett to London 'from the provinces, where he has been practising for some years', and predicted for him 'a great and successful future' at the Bar in London.

These remarks produced some apt editorial comment from one

[1] A. E. Bowker. *A Lifetime with the Law*, pp. 69–70.

London newspaper. 'Considering how long Birkett has been practising in London, and with what success', wrote the *Daily Graphic*, 'no lady barrister could have said more of any other lady barrister.'[1]

In his summing-up, Mr. Justice McCardie observed that, in view of the charges levelled by each side against the other, he did not regret one hour that had been spent on the hearing of the action. At the same time he clearly stated his opinion of the parties. 'I recognize and feel that the conduct of Colonel Dennistoun in permitting his wife's liaison with Sir John Cowans is conduct which is greatly to be condemned,' he said. 'It discredits him in a very grave measure, but on the other hand you will remember this: that when a man has been guilty of unmanliness such as this and letters exist, you ought to weigh the case with even greater care.'

As for Mrs. Dennistoun, the judge went on, 'I myself have formed the view that the plaintiff, Mrs. Dennistoun, is one of the most adroit and ingenious witnesses that I have seen in the witness box for thirty years. If she had decided to invent the claim against Colonel Dennistoun, whether for maintenance or otherwise, then she would be one of the most dangerous women that I have seen in the witness box for thirty years. She has a quick brain, absolute composure, a resolute will, and a wonderful mastery of answer.'

While the judge agreed with Birkett that Mrs. Dennistoun did not contemplate bringing her action until after her former husband had married her friend Lady Carnarvon, Mr. Justice McCardie gave the impression that in his view the mainspring of the action was not so much blackmail on Mrs. Dennistoun's part as the sentiment expressed by the dramatist William Congreve in the following lines:

> Heaven has no rage like love to hatred turned,
> Nor Hell a fury like a woman scorned.

The judge put ten questions to the jury, which it took them three hours and forty minutes to answer. Briefly, they found that at the time he was divorced in Paris, in 1921, Colonel Dennistoun had entered into a verbal agreement to 'assist to support' his wife, Mrs. Dennistoun, in her customary station of life provided that he was in a position to do so. However, they found that the agreement was not made in the form set out by Mrs. Dennistoun in the pleadings. The jury also found that Mrs. Dennistoun had made certain payments on

[1] *Daily Graphic*, March 25, 1925.

Colonel Dennistoun's behalf as loans, and assessed damages due to her under the agreement at five thousand pounds.

The jury's answers to the questions were so confusing that opposing counsel both asked for judgment in their favour. In regard to the agreement, Birkett said he could not follow exactly what the jury intended. On that point the judge enlightened him: 'You are entitled to the verdict.'

In his reserved judgment, which he delivered ten days later, Mr. Justice McCardie deprived Mrs. Dennistoun of the £5,000 damages which the jury had awarded her under the agreement on the ground that the alleged verbal agreement was 'too vague to be enforceable by law', being 'a conjecture, unsupported by any evidence'. Mrs. Dennistoun also failed on the claim for the return of the £616 expended on paying her husband's debts in 1913 on the ground that it was barred by the Statute of Limitations, but she succeeded in recovering £472, the amount of the later loans. Thus, on balance the judgment was in favour of Birkett's client, although Mrs. Dennistoun was awarded what was termed the general costs of the action as distinct from the special costs on the various individual claims which were roughly divided between the parties. The net result, however, was that neither side gained a single farthing and a great deal of dirty linen was publicly washed, so much so that Mr. Justice McCardie was moved to observe that 'cases like the present do not in any way represent the general way of life of well-to-do people in England. They give a wholly false impression of English social and family life.'

For Birkett the case constituted the biggest milestone so far in his career. The *Daily Mail*, which enjoyed the largest circulation of any English national newspaper of that period, hailed him as 'the great legal discovery of the year'. Congratulations reached him too from many friends and colleagues at the Bar. 'I hardly looked at the reports of the Dennistoun case,' wrote Maurice Healy: 'but my heart must have been cold indeed if it had not throbbed again and again with affectionate pride as I heard your praises on every tongue. You have scored a magnificent professional achievement, and my only tinge of regret is the thought that we shall rarely see you on circuit, which means I shall see very little of you. I wish you a series of as important but more savoury cases. May you always continue to wear your honours in their newest gloss.'

CHAPTER V

GLADSTONE'S DEFENDER

I

THE publicity which he received from the Dennistoun case quickly proved of the greatest professional advantage to Birkett, since it brought his name to the attention of many leading London solicitors, who had not previously briefed him. During the next few months, Birkett's table in 3, Temple Gardens was piled high with sets of papers, and the flood of briefs was to increase. One case, in which he appeared at this time for a well-known catering firm against a Fascist British General, deserves brief mention as indicative of the reckless and untrue anti-semitic statements which were beginning to be bandied about and which Birkett loathed.

The defendant, Brigadier-General Cyril Prescott-Decie was an elderly 'blimp' who unfortunately combined a fine military record with a profound hatred of the Jewish race. He was also something of a crank and was in the habit of carrying a revolver with him at all times: he had once let it off at a drawing-room meeting at Brighton, when he declared that it never left him day or night as he expected to be assassinated at any moment. At a meeting organized by the Loyalty League, forerunner of the League of Empire Loyalists, he accused J. Lyons & Co. Ltd., of prior knowledge that Mr. Snowden, the Chancellor of the Exchequer, was going to take fourpence a pound off the tax on tea in the 1924 Budget and of consequently unloading all their tea on the retailers, who lost money on the resale. The plaintiffs, for whom Birkett appeared, sued the general for slander and libel. It was stated in evidence on their behalf that they had supplied their customers with tea at the reduced price immediately after Mr. Snowden's Budget speech at a loss to themselves of about £20,000. Birkett's old colleague on the Midland Circuit,

Sir Henry Maddocks, who represented the General, tried to persuade the jury that the words complained of, if they were spoken, were really a compliment to the business capacity of Messrs. Lyons & Co. But as the Lord Chief Justice, Lord Hewart, put it in his summing up, some people might say it was good business when something particularly mean was done, but language of that kind was 'a great affront to the commercial community'. In the result, the jury found for Lyons and awarded £600 damages against the General, which Birkett's clients immediately donated to charity.[1]

The beginning of the Long Vacation found him pleased with how his practice was going; he had made £8,000 in the first seven months of 1925, but he was nervously exhausted.

To Henry Birkett

3, *Bigwood Road*, *Golders Green*, *N.W.* 11. *August* 3, 1925.

I am in the throes of deciding what to do for a holiday, having been so busy with work that I have made no arrangements. But we leave here on Tuesday for Bristol, and thence for a week or so to Egbert Cadbury's new country house in Hampshire. After that the gods decide, but I think it will be this country. It may be for a short time in the Lakes, I don't know. . . .

I have had a very good term, with lots of very good work, and everything seems very favourable. I have had one or two good briefs—800 guineas, 500 guineas, 500 guineas, 350 etc.—and from really first class firms. I finished with one which lasted 7 days, re the fraudulent firing of an American ship for the insurance money.[2]

Truth is I'm very ragged in nerves at present. But I appear to be fairly well established in the front row of silks. . . .

Before visiting the Lakes he and his wife went to France for a fortnight. But no sooner was he there than he felt an acute nostalgic longing for England.

Hotel Majestic, *Grenoble*, *August* 24. We're on the Continong! So there! Where everybody speaks a beastly patois!!! But the hills are fine, and there's snow on the top of 'em even so far

[1] *The Times*, July 16, 1925.

[2] *Empire Steamship Co. Inc.* v. *Threadneedle Insurance Co. Ltd.*, reported in *The Times*, July 25, 31, 1925.

south as this. And we're going to Monte Carlo and Nice because the Casino is closed!!!

We left London on Sunday morning and reached Paris in the afternoon, and left Paris by sleeper that night, but there was an accident to the train in front, and we were delayed 6 hours!! It's all very fine and wonderful and thrilling and all that . . . but there's a spot down by Beck Bridge. . . .

And I wonder what Surrey have done with Yorkshire at the Oval today. . . .

And then the Hotel Majestic is a barn and the disgusting patois is unseemly . . . and oh! for 'rosbif' and 'amandeh'!

They finished their holiday with his cousin Henry in Ulverston, 'lil 'Oostan', as he called his native town, where he played golf and tennis with all his old enthusiasm. Then he went on to the Nottingham division which he was still nursing as Liberal candidate, and where he spoke among other topics on the charm of modern poetry. Then back to London where he confessed he found it hard to settle down again to work. He was now saving hard for a new house on which he had set his heart.

To Henry Birkett

3, *Bigwood Road*, *Golders Green*, *N.W.*11. *October* 30, 1925.

. . . I've been very busy this term since I came back and have had a case each Saturday as well! I got 250 guineas for the first Saturday case, so it was worth missing tennis. The important cases don't get reported, and I have had some very good ones already. I have a big list already for the remainder of this term and the new house looks a certainty for next spring, if health holds good and I don't get biffed by a motor-bus!

I managed to transfer £1,500 in my first fortnight this term to the 'New House a/c' from old fees paid this term and hope to transfer another £1,500 before Christmas! I want £6,000 before we move, for house, furnishing and our Vauxhall car, but I shall get something for this house, and I think, if all goes well, we shall have a nice house for a permanent home in spring. . . . At any rate, we'll have a place where thee and thine can come and be comfortable, which ain't quite the case here with our lack of space and Linnéa all over the shop.

Among the cases in which he appeared during the Michaelmas Term, 1925, was a libel action brought against Odhams Press Ltd., the publishers and proprietors of *John Bull*, the outspoken weekly, which had been founded by Horatio Bottomley, backed by Odhams, although Bottomley had ceased to have any connection with it several years previously. The plaintiffs were two amusement caterers named Laycock and Bird, who had formed a company for the purpose of operating various side-shows at the British Empire Exhibition at Wembley. In an article under the heading 'Gigantic Wembley Scandal', *John Bull* accused the two men of duping and tricking various firms into doing work for them and then contriving that none of them should be paid by putting the company into liquidation. The defendants admitted publication, but pleaded justification, that is that the words were true in substance and in fact. For many years Marshall Hall had held a 'general retainer' from Odhams, but for some reason he was not available to go into court on this occasion. As Birkett was in the same chambers, it was agreed that he should have the brief.

The trial, which took place before Mr. Justice Horridge and a special jury, lasted for eight days.[1] Laycock, whose counsel described him as 'a man who knew everything that there was to know about amusements', was certainly a man of considerable experience in the business, while his partner, who incidentally did not choose to go into the witness box, was said to be 'the cleverest and most successful engineer of gravity rides in Europe'. The plaintiffs' argument, which Birkett found it difficult to meet, was that their company failed, not on account of any fraud but because the numbers of people attending the Amusement Park at Wembley were considerably below the official estimate. However, Birkett was able to show in his cross-examination of the first plaintiff that Mr. Laycock's commercial history was not altogether unblemished. He had been bankrupt, as also had his partner, and he had later gone to Canada on a gold mining venture, which the *Canadian Mining Journal* had called 'an unmitigated hoax'. Before going in for the Wembley concessions Laycock admitted that he had speculated in shipping and property deals.

'Would it be right to say that you have a speculative mind?' Birkett asked, with apparent guilelessness.

[1] *The Times*, December 3, 4, 5, 8, 9, 10 and 11, 1925.

'I think there is no doubt about it,' the witness replied.

The next question was of the 'loaded' variety. 'Do you think that it would be very wrong to indulge the speculative habit at other people's expense?'

'I do.'

There never had been an exhibition so big as Wembley, nor an amusement centre so extensive, said Birkett when he came to address the jury. The plaintiffs must have appreciated at once the tremendous risks involved. 'Their whole scheme from start to finish was that they stood to win large profits; they anticipated a golden stream if all went well.' When *John Bull* made inquiries and found that the plaintiffs had not paid their debts, were they not justified in their remarks? Was it not right to say that the plaintiffs were playing a 'large and scandalous part' in the Exhibition when poor struggling traders, who thought they were doing work at the great Exhibition for which they would be paid, had in many instances not received a penny, and £20,000 or £30,000 were still owing?

Mr. Justice Horridge did not accept this view in his summing up, nor for that matter did the jury when they returned their verdict. The jury were not there to decide whether the best methods were followed, Mr. Justice Horridge told them. The law allowed limited liability companies to be formed, and, indeed, without such a law the financial operations of the City could not go on. There was no doubt, in the judge's opinion, that Laycock set out with the intention of doing extremely well. 'A man did not go in for such a thing without expecting it to be remunerative. Mr. Laycock said that he knew it was a speculative matter, but that he thought that the speculation was reduced to a minimum because of all the circumstances.' On the question of damages, the judge added, newspapers like *John Bull* existed for profit very largely by means of things which attracted the public eye, and they must not howl if they had got to pay when they went wrong. If it were not a case where the jury might think that the abstention of Bird from going into the witness box affected the question, then they 'ought to give substantial damages'.

In the result, the jury found for the plaintiffs and awarded £250 damages. That the sum was not considerably larger was due at least in part to Birkett's handling of the defendants' case. Anyhow that was how it appeared to Odhams, who were so pleased with the result that they transferred their general retainer from Marshall Hall, who was glad on grounds of health to relinquish it, and appointed Birkett to be their standing counsel. 'So I shall be in all their cases,' he told his cousin gleefully. In addition, the editor of *John Bull* sent him a cabinet of six hundred large Corona Corona cigars (about £50 worth), as a Christmas present, 'in appreciation' of his efforts.

2

In 1925, which was his first full year as a 'silk', Birkett made £12,000 in fees. In the following year his earnings at the Bar were in the region of £16,500. If there was nothing of the sensational character of the Dennistoun case in his fee book for 1926, there were several cases which deserve mention, in particular three actions of defamation, one of insurance concerning the destruction of a valuable painting, and one relating to an assault which provided some lighter moments in court. His first murder defence as a 'silk', which occurred in that year, is also noteworthy.

In the assault case a company director named Harold Dole sued the door attendant of the Regent Palace Hotel in London and his employers. The attendant was a man called Wackett, 'a very appropriate name,' said the plaintiff's counsel, since his duties included those of 'chucker out'; the plaintiff claimed that he and a Greek friend called Papanicoly had been ejected by Mr. Wackett from the Palm Court of the hotel with such violence that his (the plaintiff's) back was injured and his friend's umbrella was broken. It appeared however, that Papanicoly had previously had a dispute with the hotel and been told not to frequent its premises in future. The defendants, for whom Birkett appeared, claimed that no more force than was necessary had been used to eject the two men.

Cross-examined by Birkett, the plaintiff admitted that he and his friend had once conversed at the Lyons Corner House in Coventry Street until three or four o'clock in the morning.

'Discussing what?' interrupted the Lord Chief Justice, Lord Hewart, who was trying the case. 'The foreign exchange?'

'Greek philosophy sometimes,' replied the plaintiff.

'What department of Greek philosophy did you discuss?' the judge queried further.

'Mr. Papanicoly thought that the Greeks were responsible for the civilization of the world,' answered the witness, adding amid laughter, 'except the Regent Palace Hotel!'

Birkett raised a further laugh when he asked the witness, whether, when Wackett was speaking to him in the Palm Court, he (the witness) did not shout at his friend, 'I am surprised at your coming into this bloody synagogue!' 'Certainly not,' declared the aggrieved Mr. Dole.

The plaintiff's doctor also gave evidence and was cross-examined by Birkett.

'Did you tell him to lead a quiet life?'

'I told him to take care of himself.'

'Would you consider that he was taking care of himself if he often stayed up until four o'clock in the morning?'

'Discussing Greek philosophy!' Lord Hewart could not resist another interruption, adding, 'It may have a tranquillizing effect on the nerves.'

'It would not make much difference to the cure of his back,' observed the doctor to the accompaniment of more mirth.

In his summing up, the Lord Chief Justice pointed out that, although a considerable amount of humour had been imported into it, the case was an important one. Licensees had duties to perform, and by statute they could turn out any person who was drunk, violent, quarrelsome or disorderly. He then put certain questions to the jury, as a result of which the jury found that the plaintiff had been asked to leave the hotel with reasonable care, that he had refused, and that no more force than was necessary was used for the purpose of ejecting him. Accordingly, they brought in a verdict for Birkett's clients, the defendants.[1]

The insurance action was a claim by Lady (Rose Marie) Thomas, the wife of a Welsh baronet and Member of Parliament, Sir Robert Thomas, against a Lloyd's underwriter, being part of a total claim for £20,000 for the loss by fire of a picture said to be an Old Master under an insurance policy. The picture had been purchased some years previously by Sir Robert for his wife from an art dealer in London for £25. It was subsequently believed to be the 'Madonna del Pozzo' (Lady of the Well) by Raphael and was appraised at £20,000 by expert valuers. The case came before Mr. Justice McCardie and a special jury in February, 1926, Sir John Simon, later

[1] *Dole* v. *Strand Hotels Ltd. The Times*, January 27, 28, 1926.

Lord Simon, leading for the plaintiff and Norman Birkett leading for the defendant.

The defence alleged that the picture in question was a copy and not a Raphael as claimed, and that the circumstances of its purchase were not disclosed to the underwriters when the insurance was effected. This prompted Sir John Simon to remark in his opening speech that the words 'by Raphael' in the insurance policy were not words of guarantee. 'Supposing I insured the works of Shakespeare and they were destroyed by fire,' said Sir John, 'and the insurers refused to pay, alleging that the author was Bacon?'

'I think they would rather pay than take the trouble to attempt to prove that,' the judge replied, amid laughter.

There was more merriment when Sir Robert Thomas went into the witness box, particularly when he told his counsel that if he had died he had no doubt the Inland Revenue authorities would have required payment on the value of £20,000. Cross-examined by Birkett, Sir Robert stated that he first began to take an interest in pictures when he was a young man. 'A great deal of my time is also taken up by business and politics, I am sorry to say,' he added. He also stated that he had never made an inquiry of the art dealer how he got the picture.

'Even after you thought you had a £20,000 picture for £25?'

'No.'

'It was one of the best investments you have made?' Birkett continued.

'Well,' replied Sir Robert, who was obviously proud of his business ability as well as his knowledge of art, 'I have made one or two good ones in my life!'

'Where did you get the value of £20,000?' interposed the judge.

'After experts had valued it,' answered the witness, who also stated that he would gladly pay £20,000 if he could get the picture back again.

'If it were proved that your picture was not a Raphael, would you still require the £20,000?' asked Birkett.

'Certainly,' said Sir Robert, who was himself an underwriting member of Lloyds, 'I paid the premium on it.'

When another of the plaintiff's witnesses, an insurance broker, stated that he had forty-six years' experience, Sir John Simon commented, 'A longer experience than Raphael had of painting.' This was capped by Birkett after the same witness had referred under cross-examination to an early edition of the Scots poet Robert Burns, which he had picked up for three shillings and insured for £100. Asked where he had bought it, the broker replied, 'Berne, in Switzerland.'

'Ah,' said Birkett, 'I thought you did not get it in Scotland!'

These light-hearted exchanges were brought to an end by a whispered consultation between opposing counsel. The plaintiff intimated that she was willing to compromise, and the case was accordingly settled on this basis, Lady Thomas agreeing to accept and the underwriter to pay an undisclosed sum less than the total amount claimed.[1]

The first of the defamation cases was also settled out of court. It deserves a passing reference if only by reason of the fact that it was the first case in the English courts in which any question of defamation by way of broadcasting had arisen. The action was for slander and was brought by Williams and Norgate Ltd., the publishers of *The White Chateau*, a play by Reginald Berkeley. It arose out of a broadcast statement by the British Broadcasting Company, the forerunner of the Corporation, to the effect that owing to labour troubles copies of the work were not obtainable from the plaintiffs. This statement was wholly incorrect, as Birkett admitted on behalf of the Company, at the same time apologizing and intimating that his clients would pay the publishers an agreed sum by way of damages and costs. 'I am so glad,' said Mr. Justice McCardie from the Bench on this occasion, 'that so novel an action has been settled in so friendly a way.'[2]

The two other defamation cases in this year worthy of mention had one unusual feature in common—in each case the jury awarded the plaintiff the sum of one farthing damages. The first was a slander action brought by Mr. Lionel Martin, the well known racing motorist and designer of the Aston Martin car, for whom Birkett appeared, against a fellow director of his company.[3] It is unnecessary to go into the facts of the case except to say that the words complained of imputed dishonesty to the plaintiff in his business activities. At the last moment, as the plaintiff admitted in congratulating

[1] *Thomas* v. *Marshall. The Times*, February 25, 26, 1927.

[2] *Williams & Norgate Ltd.* v. *British Broadcasting Co. Ltd. The Times*, April 24, 1926.

[3] *Martin* v. *Benson. The Times*, October 14, 16, 19, 20, 21, 22, 23, 1926.

his counsel, Birkett 'pulled the case out of the fire' on the seventh day and wrung a verdict from the jury for his client, even though the damages were nominal. 'I really do not know how even to begin to thank you for all you have done for me,' Martin wrote in a letter which Birkett preserved: 'I am only just beginning to realize that all the strain and anxiety of months are over, and that, thanks to you, I can still look men in the face. It really seems like a miracle after the condition at which we had arrived yesterday morning. I do hope you understand that I know and deeply appreciate the self-sacrificing devotion which you gave to the case: without it I could not have succeeded. . . . I hope one day we may meet again under happier circumstances—perhaps at Brooklands!'

The other defamation case was an action for libel brought by Mr. James Agate, the dramatic critic, against the editor and publishers of *The Guardian*, an old Church of England publication, in respect of a review of a book of essays written by the plaintiff and entitled *Agate's Folly*. In the review, the writer, whose name was Ellis Roberts, after stating that Mr. Agate had 'neither taste nor style', went on:

> Mr. Agate's chief interest is in the theatre: and the fact that he is now regarded as one of our leading dramatic critics illustrates how pitifully that important branch of criticism has deteriorated, and explains a great deal that is wrong with the modern stage.

The defence put forward by Birkett on behalf of the journal was that the words complained of were a fair and *bona fide* comment and criticism and that there was no evidence on which the jury could find that it was unfair or dishonest.

During his cross-examination of the plaintiff, Birkett read out a flattering description of Mr. Agate from the 'jacket' of the book, and Mr. Agate caused some laughter by saying that he could not have written it better himself. He added that anyone reading the book would be entitled to say, 'The style in which this book is written is poor,' but not 'See how dramatic criticism has fallen.' Replying further to Birkett's questions, the plaintiff said that he did not know the writer of the review and had never met him; but he did not think it was a perfectly honest and candid expression of opinion of an educated man who understood the work of James Agate.

'Have you any reason to doubt that Mr. Ellis Roberts, when he wrote the review had any personal bias against you?'

'No educated man without personal bias against me could write such an article.'

Mr. Agate went on to admit that he was 'frank and free' in his own criticisms of plays he did not like, and he did not object to others criticizing him with equal severity 'provided what they said was relevant'.

'When you put yourself before the public in a book,' Birkett continued his questions, 'you cannot dissociate yourself from your position as a dramatic critic, can you?'

'Why not?' countered Agate.

'Because you are a dramatic critic,' said Birkett. 'Has the reviewer of your book to forget entirely that the author is a dramatic critic?'

'He is not entitled to attempt to blast my career as a critic because he cannot get it out of his mind.'

'You say that the data upon which this article is written is insufficient?' Birkett asked sweetly.

'Exactly,' agreed Agate.

'If the writer had read all your published works and had said that, judged from them, criticism had deteriorated, would you have complained?'

'I should have taken counsel's advice,' was the retort, which gained Agate a loud laugh from the onlookers in court.

'If a dramatic critic exhibits in a book lack of taste and want of manners,' persisted Birkett, 'would it not be right to say that criticism had deteriorated?'

But Agate refused to go as far as that. 'Certainly not,' he said, 'when there are other books upon which he could found a judgment, and which he conceals from his readers.'

Three well-known theatrical producers, who had read the review, said they understood it to mean that Agate was a bad critic, unworthy of his position and one whose criticism had led to the degradation of the theatre. They were J. B. Fagan, Nigel Playfair and C. B. Cochran. When Birkett indicated surprise that Cochran, who was known for the 'young ladies' in his revues, should have read the notice, Cochran replied that he did not read *The Guardian* 'as a rule', but when producing *The Miracle* he had become 'well acquainted with ecclesiastical journals'.

'Are you on the side of the "highbrows" or the "lowbrows"?' Birkett asked.

'I am what is called a "high lowbrow",' was the reply which also drew a laugh.

Although Ellis Roberts declared in the witness box that the article was an honest expression of his opinion and that he had not the slightest animus or feeling against Mr. Agate, and although the judge, who was Mr. Justice Avory, summed up strongly in the defendants' favour, nevertheless the jury brought in a verdict for the plaintiff. But they only awarded him a farthing damages and added a recommendation that each side should pay its own costs, which the judge seems to have accepted. So the outcome was really a moral victory for Birkett.[1]

'The case is of some importance to the Press in this country,' wrote the Liberal *Daily News* in an editorial afterwards, 'for it seems to us that if the sort of comment made upon Mr. Agate in this instance is really actionable it would hardly be safe for any editor to criticize adversely any person who wrote a book of doubtful merit or occupied with doubtful distinction a conspicuous position in letters, art or public affairs. . . . How many honest writers of criticism are there who have never said anything more severe than this about the subject of their criticism? Has Mr. Agate, who is not notorious for any tender flinching from the self-imposed duties of blunt and vigorous controversy, never done so? At all events, he will get his farthing. It is not much.'[2]

3

The Agate libel action ended on a Friday and Birkett went home where he planned to spend a leisurely week-end in the knowledge he need not hurry to the Temple on Monday morning, since he had not to be in court that day. But as events turned out, he was to find himself leading for the defence in a murder trial that same Monday morning.

Late on the Sunday evening, the telephone rang at his house in Golders Green. It was Bowker. Would Mr. Birkett take Marshall Hall's brief for the defence at the Essex Assizes? The case had been

[1] *Agate* v. *Guardian Publications Ltd. The Times*, November 5, 6, 1926.
[2] *Daily News*, November 6, 1926.

specially fixed by the judge as the last in the list and was due to open on Monday at Chelmsford, but Marshall Hall was feeling so unwell that he simply could not travel down to Chelmsford. (In fact, Marshall Hall was suffering from an attack of influenza, which he never succeeded in shaking off and which led to his death a few weeks later.) Now Chelmsford was not on Birkett's circuit and to take the case would involve him in being briefed 'special' with a special fee of one hundred guineas, in addition to the fee marked on the brief. When Birkett pointed this out, Bowker told him not to worry as it had all been arranged, which indeed it had by the enterprising clerk. It may be added, by way of explanation, that if Marshall Hall had been able to conduct the defence, no special fee would have been necessary in his case, since Chelmsford was on his circuit.

It had been some years since Birkett as a junior had appeared in a murder case, and as a 'silk' he had never done so. Hence Marshall Hall did not think of Birkett when he first told Bowker that he was too ill to go to Chelmsford. He asked the clerk to try to get hold of one of the leaders at the criminal Bar such as Sir Henry Curtis-Bennett or Mr. Roland Oliver. But both these leaders lived out of town and Bowker knew that it would be impossible to get the brief delivered to them in time. The brief was marked at two hundred guineas and in the event of Birkett taking it the fee would have to be divided, making the brief fee one hundred guineas and the special fee one hundred guineas. Marshall Hall's junior in the case was Mr. Walter Frampton, later a Metropolitan Magistrate, and before proceeding any further Bowker rang him up on the telephone and explained the situation.

'I have decided to take the brief to Mr. Birkett,' he said. 'Of course, it will mean him going off his circuit and that will necessitate dividing the fee by marking the brief a special fee. I have not been able to get in touch with the solicitors and wondered what you thought of the idea.'

To the clerk's intense relief, since it involved the junior in accepting a smaller fee for himself, Frampton replied, 'A splendid way out.'

Bowker than hastened off by taxi to Golders Green with the papers, which he placed in Birkett's hands with some trepidation, since it was now quite late and it meant that Birkett would have to study the brief well into the night and then get up early in the morning so as to be at Liverpool Street Station by 8.30 a.m. to catch the train to Chelmsford.

The clerk never forgot what he called his master's 'serene calm' as he scanned the brief. 'Of course, Edgar,' Birkett said, 'I'll be at Liverpool Street at eight-thirty.'

When he came to study the brief closely, Birkett saw that it revealed a tragic story of a wife who was indicted for the murder of her husband at their farm near Clacton. The accused woman, Mrs. Harriet Crouch, had been a widow at the time of her marriage to Frank Crouch six years previously, at which date she was fifty-three and he was forty. She was also the owner of a fancy goods business in which her second husband worked as a commercial traveller. Shortly after Crouch took the farm, in 1925, for which his wife advanced him £1,100 of the purchase money, Dorothy Smith, the twenty-three-year-old daughter of a stockman, who occupied an adjoining cottage, came to work at the farm as a domestic servant. The relations between Dorothy Smith and Frank Crouch became closer than is usual between master and servant. He taught her to swim, play tennis and drive a car, and from letters which she wrote to him it appeared that there had been an affair between them as a result of which she thought she was pregnant. Mrs. Crouch not unnaturally became jealous of the attentions which her husband was paying their servant. This led to quarrels and finally a physical struggle in the course of which the husband was fatally shot. 'I have shot my husband, but it was not my fault,' the accused woman told the doctor who was called in. 'He knocked me down and kept on hitting me. While on the ground I drew my revolver from my right hand jacket pocket and fired at him. We struggled and he took the revolver from me. I have been worried for twelve months by his attentions to Dorothy Smith.'

It had been arranged that the two defending counsel with Bowker should meet the instructing solicitor at Liverpool Street Station and that they should all travel down to Chelmsford together. Bowker and the solicitor, a young man named Cecil, were the first to arrive. 'Where's the chief?' Mr. Cecil asked Bowker.

The solicitor's face fell when Bowker broke the news about Marshall Hall. 'What in the world are we going to do?' he asked the clerk. 'What have you done about it?'

The solicitor was further dismayed when he learned the name of the substitute, for he had obviously not heard of Birkett's triumph in the Dennistoun case. 'Birkett?' he kept asking plaintively. 'Who's he? I've never heard of him. Is he any good?'

Fortunately at this moment Walter Frampton arrived on the scene, and Bowker suggested that they should have a chat. Frampton took the nervous young solicitor by the arm and walked him up and down the platform for a few minutes. By the time Birkett appeared the solicitor looked somewhat reassured. They found a carriage to themselves and the guard obligingly locked them in so that they could talk undisturbed on the journey.

As they left the train an hour or so later at Chelmsford, the solicitor took Bowker aside and whispered in his ear: 'Well—he certainly knows all about it. He has not only read the brief, but he has some first-class ideas of his own.'

Later on, during the luncheon adjournment, the solicitor again took the clerk on one side. By now he looked quite pleased. 'Don't worry any more,' he told Bowker. 'It was a bit of a shock not having Marshall Hall, but I'm more than satisfied with the substitute.'

The trial of Mrs. Crouch for the murder of her husband opened before Mr. Justice Mackinnon and a jury in the Assize Court at Chelmsford on November 8, 1926, and lasted for two days. The prosecution was led by Mr. J. D. Cassels, K.C., later Mr. Justice Cassels, who emphasized in his opening speech to the jury that 'no such thing as jealousy could possibly avail as an excuse for murder'. The principal witness for the prosecution was the servant girl Dorothy Smith, and Crown counsel took her over her version of the events leading up to the tragedy.

'Was the supposed relationship between you and the prisoner's husband the cause of words between you whenever such words occurred?'

'Yes.'

'Was there any truth in any association on your part with the prisoner's husband?'

'Well, he showed me great respect, but nothing further.'

Having asked these final questions of the witness, Cassels sat down and Birkett rose to begin his cross-examination. It was a crucial test of his skill. Would he try to dominate the girl, as Marshall Hall would undoubtedly have done with his handsome presence, almost bullying her into admissions of friendliness and even intimacy with the dead man? On the contrary, Birkett's performance was an admirable example of restrained questioning, which immediately impressed the jury in his favour.

'You are twenty-four,' he began very quietly, 'the prisoner is sixty and her husband was forty-six?'

'Yes.'

'Was the prisoner extremely unhappy because of what she thought was going on between you and her husband?'

'Yes.'

'Would it be right to say it completely changed her?'

'It did change her.'

'Did you do one single thing to try to comfort her, or did you defy her?'

'I did all I could.'

Birkett eyed the girl sternly, as his next question revealed what he thought of her efforts. 'I suggest that you were brazenly defiant to this poor woman?'

The witness looked down and did not reply.

Birkett did not repeat the question or press the girl further. He had made his point quite simply and without any fuss or bother—the suggestion of provocation over a considerable period. He then passed on to other matters, including her master's teaching her to play tennis, to swim and to drive his car. Did she not think it strange that her master should teach her, a servant, to do these things? No, she said, because they had treated her as a companion rather than as a servant.

'When you went there first, was Mrs. Crouch a quiet, kindly, gentle woman?'

'Yes.'

'Do you doubt that the whole of that change was due, rightly or wrongly, to what she believed about you and her husband?'

'No.'

'Did you call Mr. Crouch "Frank"?'

'Perhaps so.'

'He taught you to swim, play tennis, and drive the car, and you never called him "Frank"?'

'No.'

Asked about the letters beginning 'My darling', Miss Smith

denied it was a love letter; neither were the others she had written to the dead man.

'What was the purpose of that letter if it was not a love letter? Can you answer?'

'No.'

'Why didn't you tell Mrs. Crouch that they were business letters and not love letters?'

'I would have done so if she had not been abusive. I did not wish to have anything to say to her.'

'You knew her life had been a misery for two long years?'

'Yes.'

'And here you are writing secret letters to her husband. Do you say that you did not think it was wrong?'

'No.'

'Then you thought it was right?' asked Birkett quickly.

The unfortunate girl in the box looked confused. 'I don't think it was exactly right,' she managed to say after a pause.

'Did you think there was an element of wrong about it?'

'Yes.'

'Then why did you do it?'

There was just a hint of sharpness in Birkett's voice.

Once more the witness hung her head and said nothing.

It was a masterly cross-examination, in which Birkett with his deceptive quiet manner was at his best. Its effect was not to upset the witness by attempting to discredit her testimony, but to build up from her answers a measure of sympathy for his client in the dock.

The only witness whom Birkett called for the defence was the prisoner herself. A pathetic looking woman dressed completely in black, Mrs. Crouch related the story of her unhappy marriage, of her quarrels and separation and reconciliation with her husband, and how she caught him kissing the servant girl in the scullery.

'Whenever your husband assaulted you at any time was it always in connection with something relating to Dorothy Smith?'

'Yes.'

She went on to describe how, on the day of the shooting, she had passed Dorothy Smith's cottage and had thrown a clod of earth at the window, thinking her husband might be there, and the window had been broken. Then her husband followed her home, and coming into the sitting room, said, 'What have you been doing at the cottage?' He then knocked her down and kept on hitting her, using abusive language. She was on the floor and he was bending over her and knocking her head from side to side. She kept trying to get up, she said, but he would not let her. She felt the revolver in her pocket and pulled it out, intending to let him see it and thinking that he would then leave off hitting her.

'Had you any intention of firing at him?' Birkett asked her.

'It never entered my head,' Mrs. Crouch replied.

'Either to wound or kill him?'

'No.'

She went on to describe how her husband grasped her wrist, after the revolver went off the first time, and the bullet entered the ceiling. Then when he grasped her wrist, the revolver went off again, and in the excitement she must have pulled the trigger. This was the shot that killed Frank Crouch.

'Was there any aim on your part?'

'No.'

'Was there any intention or desire on your part to injure or wound or hurt him in any way?'

'Not in the least.'

The prosecution had made a good deal of the fact that, when the doctor arrived, she was smoking a cigarette on the porch of the house, as if she were callously indifferent to the shooting. Birkett threw a very different light on this incident by asking her a simple question which drew forth a simple answer.

'Why did you light a cigarette?'

'Because I was so shaken. I wanted to steady my nerves.'

The accused woman was equally convincing when cross-examined by counsel for the prosecution. 'If Miss Smith had been guilty of such unpardonable conduct,' Cassels asked her, 'why did you have her back over and over again?'

'Because I could get no one else,' was the reply. 'People would not let their daughters come because the scandal was in everyone's mouth.'

Re-examined by Birkett, Mrs. Crouch said sometimes she thought misconduct had taken place between her husband and Miss Smith, and sometimes she thought it had not. But she came to the conclusion that there had been misconduct on a certain day in the preceding April.

The text of Birkett's concluding speech to the jury has not survived. All we know is from the local newspaper that it was an eloquent and moving plea, and from Edgar Bowker that at one stage the woman in the dock burst into tears, when Birkett was speaking of how hurt she was at her husband's persistent conduct. What happened on the day of the tragedy, he said, was 'something directly alien to the woman's will.'

It did not take the jury very long to make up their minds. After an absence of a quarter of an hour they returned to court, and the foreman announced their verdict: 'Not Guilty'.

A remarkable scene followed. The spectators in court cheered and applauded, while Mrs. Crouch was so overcome by the result that she blew kisses to the jury, as she was being discharged.[1]

Mrs. Crouch's acquittal was a great triumph for Birkett. Unfortunately admiration was mixed with jealousy on the part of Marshall Hall, for he had never envisaged Birkett as a great criminal advocate. Now it seemed that his mantle was about to descend upon the younger man, for Marshall Hall felt that the shadow of death was near. 'Somehow I feel that I shall not live much longer,' he said to a friend in a moment of premonition. 'Do not grieve for me too much. I am very, very tired.' A few weeks later he collapsed while conducting a case in court and struggled home to bed. He never put on his wig and gown again. And then in February, 1927, Bowker brought Birkett the news of the end, the flag over the Inner Temple flew at half mast, and Birkett joined the rest of the Bench and Bar to do honour to his memory in the Lord Chief Justice's Court.

Marshall Hall was sixty-eight when he died in harness, and Birkett, who had spent the last seven years in his chambers, had seen him still at the height of his wonderful powers. Thirty years afterwards, Birkett was to recall these powers in a broadcast tribute to his memory.

'We shall not look upon Marshall's like again,' Birkett said on this occasion, 'for the age that produced him and gloried in his spectacular triumphs in the courts, has passed away for ever. The advocate no longer plays the part in our public life that he once did. The fashionable divorce suit, the sensational libel action, the great murder trial—they are no longer the dramatic events that once

[1] *Essex Weekly News*, November 12, 1926.

occupied public attention to the exclusion of almost everything else. The television star and the film actor or actress, idolized by millions, now take pride of place. But men must be judged by the standards of the age in which they lived and worked. Marshall Hall was one of the great figures of his world. He was one of the greatest advocates when he was at his best. . . . He had sympathy and understanding; he could enter fully into the lives of other people almost naturally; he had fire and passion and zeal; he was dramatic and histrionic; he could speak simply and most attractively to ordinary people; and, as his outstanding quality, he could rise to heights of pure eloquence and sway the hearts and minds of men. But he had grievous shortcomings that might so easily have destroyed a lesser man. He was the strangest mixture of perfections and imperfections that I ever knew at the Bar.'[1]

4

Early in 1927, Birkett appeared for the defence in a libel action which aroused the greatest public interest. Of the long line of cases, both civil and criminal, in which Birkett appeared in his career at the English Bar, none gave him a deeper sense of personal satisfaction in regard to its outcome than the case of *Wright* versus *Gladstone*. The main point at issue in this case was the sexual morality of the Liberal statesman and leader, William Ewart Gladstone, who had been four times Prime Minister of Britain. Although the 'Grand Old Man' had died when Birkett was fifteen, his memory had continued to be almost piously revered in the Birkett household and it had certainly inspired Norman Birkett's own political beliefs as well as his father's. Any charge affecting the private life of his boyhood hero might be expected to touch him keenly and move him to aid in the vindication of his hero's reputation, should it be assailed.

Slanderous allegations against the Liberal leader had long been current. According to his son, Viscount Gladstone, they had originated as long ago as 1876, when the statesman was still alive, and his family knew of them, for the most part, through anonymous letters. They arose largely through his interest in rescuing prostitutes from the dangers of their profession and his habit of talking to

[1] Lord Birkett. *Six Great Advocates* (1961), at pp. 9–10.

prostitutes in the streets and sometimes of visiting them in their rooms. No chance of taking action to refute these allegations was given to the family until 1925 when a book of essays appeared under the title, *Portraits and Criticisms*, by Captain Peter Wright. 'Gladstone founded a great tradition since observed by many of his followers and successors with such pious fidelity', wrote the author of this volume in what was a passing allusion to the G.O.M. in an essay on Lord Robert Cecil and the League of Nations, 'in public to speak the language of the highest and strictest principle, and in private to pursue and possess every sort of woman.'

In this passage, the charge hitherto uttered surreptitiously by word of mouth or innuendo and consequently difficult to pin down, was embodied positively in print for the first time. At this time the dead statesman's surviving sons were Mr. Henry Gladstone and Viscount Gladstone, aged seventy-four and seventy-two respectively. What could they do? Their father had been dead for thirty years and anyhow their solicitors advised them that a statement libelling a dead person was not actionable in the English civil courts. Of course, they might have brought a private prosecution against Captain Wright for criminal libel, but to obtain a conviction they would have had to prove that the author intended to provoke a breach of the peace or to injure the Gladstone family, and of this they were advised there was no evidence. They could also have given Captain Wright a horsewhipping or at least attempted to do so, but even if the circumstances might have been thought to warrant taking the law into their own hands in this manner, a summons for assault would not have enabled them to adduce the facts and information they desired. On the other hand, if they took no action, it would have been open to the author of the libel or anyone else to say that the charges were true because two of Mr. Gladstone's sons were alive when they were made and dared not take any action. Such statements would have the appearance of truth.

'We held that if we did nothing, we should fail in our duty as sons,' wrote Lord Gladstone afterwards. 'Moreover, we had reason to know that the allegations were disturbing the minds of many of those who revered Mr. Gladstone's memory. Doubts and apprehensions would grow in the course of time; we could see that the charges had impressed the minds of those without personal knowledge of him. My brother and I, being of advanced years, realized that when we were gone there would be no one to give the evidence we alone could give.[1]

After taking the best advice which his solicitor, the Hon. Charles Russell, could give, Lord Gladstone with the concurrence of his elder brother decided to write Captain Wright a letter in the most insulting terms, and so as to force him to bring a civil action for libel against them, they sent copies of the letter to his publishers and also to *The Nation*, a weekly journal which had strongly criticized Wright's book when it came out and asked how a reputable publishing house could allow such a gross statement about Mr. Gladstone to appear.

The letter read as follows.

> Mr. Peter Wright.
>
> Your garbage about Mr. Gladstone in 'Portraits and Criticisms' has come to our knowledge. You are a liar. Because you slander a dead man you are a coward. Because you think the public will accept invention from such as you, you are a fool.
>
> GLADSTONE
>
> I associate myself with this letter.
>
> H. N. GLADSTONE

The letter was addressed to Captain Wright, care of his publishers, Eveleigh Nash and Grayson Ltd., who forwarded it to Wright's club, The Bath Club. When he had read the letter, Captain Wright replied to Lord Gladstone in equally offensive language.

> My Lord,—I am in receipt of your Lordship's outburst dated July 22.
>
> I attributed to Mr. Gladstone the character of a hypocrite in matters of sex. I have evidence of his conduct as good as any that exists about events in the past. I wrote what I did on the authority of the late Lord Milner; to use Milner's own phrase, Mr. Gladstone was 'governed by his seraglio.' This foible had considerable political effects. One affair turned Mr. Gladstone from being a friend of Turkey and an enemy of Russia as he was in the fifties, into being a friend of Russia and an enemy of Turkey, as he was in the eighties.

[1] Viscount Gladstone. *After Thirty Years* (1928), 435. Lord Gladstone died in 1930, and his brother in 1935, both without heirs.

Mr. Gladstone's hypocritical character (which in no way detracts from his merits as a public financier) is the common, though it may not be the official reputation of him that has descended to us. It was crystallized in Labouchere's famous epigram, 'that Gladstone might be caught playing cards with a fifth ace up his sleeve, but he would only explain that God had put it there.' This contemporary reputation is strikingly confirmed by the circumstances of the Parnell case as we now know them. Gladstone not only connived at Parnell's illicit relations with Mrs. O'Shea, but utilized them for his own political purposes. Parnell's sin was Gladstone's opportunity. As soon as the misconduct was made known and public in divorce proceedings, Gladstone was foremost in denouncing its immorality.

This hypocrisy in the case of another is more heinous than any hypocrisy in the case of himself. Strong temptations might excuse his own departure from his own avowed principles; no such excuse can be found in the case of another. Knowing he could commit the greater offence, I do not find it difficult to believe he could commit the former.

These various considerations prompted the remarks about Mr. Gladstone at which you take offence. Thus based, my views are unshaken even by the impact of your Lordship's controversial language, which, if I may say so without impoliteness, must rather have been acquired by practice in your Lordship's pantry than by the exercise of your Lordship's talents for debate in the House of Lords.

PETER E. WRIGHT

Captain Wright thereupon sent a copy of Lord Gladstone's letter with his reply to the *Daily Mail.* The reason why he did this, as he subsequently explained, was that he was unaware that other copies of Lord Gladstone's letter had been sent elsewhere, and he considered that there could be no actionable libel in the letter since, so far as he knew, there had been no publication to anyone but himself.

When they heard about it, the publishers excused themselves by saying that, when the book was accepted, it did not contain the objectionable words, which the author had inserted when the work was in proof, and they expressed their regret to Lord Gladstone that the words should have escaped their notice when the proof was returned to the printers.

On July 27, Lord Gladstone wrote to Mr. John Wilson Taylor, the secretary of the Bath Club, to which Lord Gladstone also belonged.

> Dear Wilson Taylor,
>
> Mr. Peter Wright appears to be a member of the Bath Club. In a book he made a foul charge against my father. He elaborated this in a letter to the *Nation* in the issue of, I think, July 2, in the preceding week. He wrote on Bath Club notepaper.
>
> My brother and I wrote and told him that he was a liar and a coward, the law, in the case of a dead man, giving no remedy.
>
> In a letter published this morning by the *Daily Mail* he amplified his slander and his lies, not daring apparently to face us in Court. Again he writes on Bath Club notepaper. It seems to me that this is a matter for the Committee.
>
> Sincerely yours,
>
> GLADSTONE

In a postscript Lord Gladstone mentioned that he had just heard from Wright's publishers with their explanation about the passage being inserted in the proof. 'This shows the sort of man he is—he is a *foul* fellow.'

Four days later, Lord Gladstone again wrote to the Bath Club secretary to the effect that he did not wish to take part personally in any discussion or action of the committee with reference to Captain Wright. 'I wrote to you because I was so indignant that the fellow was sheltering in my old club, which, for my brother, myself, and my wife becomes uninhabitable so long as it is polluted by his presence.'

The committee of the Bath Club, having met and considered Lord Gladstone's complaint, decided to expel Captain Wright, which they proceeded to do without hearing what he had to say on his own behalf. He then issued a writ against them and obtained damages of £100 for loss of the amenities of the club and £25 as damages for injury to his reputation.[1]

[1] This action has been described by the present writer in *United in Crime* (1955), pp. 77–80.

During these proceedings, Lord Gladstone's letter to the club secretary was disclosed, and it was in respect of this letter that Captain Wright issued a further writ for libel against Lord Gladstone. This tardy action was what Lord Gladstone had wanted all along, and he immediately prepared to defend the action. He pleaded four defences: (1) that the words complained of were not libellous and did not injure the character of the plaintiff; (2) privilege; (3) justification; and (4) fair comment. At the same time he made it clear to his solicitor that he wanted above all a verdict on the third of these defences.

The action came before Mr. Justice Avory and a special jury in the King's Bench Division of the High Court on January 27, 1927, and lasted for five days. Mr. Boyd Merriman, later Lord Merriman, President of the Divorce Court, and Mr. St. John Field appeared for the plaintiff, while Mr. Norman Birkett, K.C., and Mr. Theobald Mathew represented Lord Gladstone.[1]

In opening the case for Captain Wright, Mr. Merriman stated that his client was forty-six years old, educated at Harrow and Balliol College, Oxford, and had held various staff appointments in France during the First World War, including that of joint secretary and interpreter to the Executive Committee of the Supreme War Council. He also wrote for the newspapers and was the author of several books which had been published. In the case of public men who were alive, the plaintiff's counsel continued, the test was—what is the effect of the man's private weakness on the public service? But with regard to the dead, some different considerations must obviously apply.

'Even the most ardent Jacobite would, at this distance of time, not be affronted by being reminded that the King's Road led to Nell Gwynne's cottage at Chelsea,' said Merriman. 'I suppose that even the family of Lord Nelson are not hurt if reference to Lady Hamilton is coupled with reference to Trafalgar. Coming even nearer to our own time, we were reminded yesterday of the forty-second anniversary of the death of General Gordon, with whose fate Mr. Gladstone was so intimately bound, and in respect of whom, and other eminent Victorians not much earlier than Mr. Gladstone, a new form of biography has been introduced which makes no bones about exposing such human weaknesses as there were

[1] *The Times*, January 28, 29; February 2, 3, and 4, 1927.

without any public reprobation or notorious consequences for the author.'[1]

If Captain Wright believed his statements, his counsel urged, he was justified in expressing his belief. Manifestly, in the case of a man who died at the age of eighty-nine, practically thirty years ago, the actual facts could be neither proved nor disproved with strictness. What other people thought did not matter. The issue in the case was what Captain Wright thought.

'The question is whether he had the right to say it,' the judge interposed, '—not what he thought.'

'Whether he had the right to say it,' counsel qualified his previous remark, 'having regard to what he thought.' Merriman added that Lord Gladstone's attack on Captain Wright was an attempt to curtail the right of free discussion which no filial piety could for a moment excuse.

The plaintiff then entered the witness box, where he was to spend more than ten hours. He appeared a man of medium height, clean shaven, with hair turning grey, deep-set tired eyes, and a monocle which he would let fall from time to time from his right eye and with which he never ceased to play. Below him, a few yards away, sat the distinguished looking figure of Lord Gladstone. These were the two principals in the case. But to everyone in the crowded court it was obvious that there was a third principal, the dead statesman whose unseen presence seemed to haunt the court room, while his son's counsel struggled valiantly to clear his name from a terrible imputation.

'At the time when you inserted in the proofs the passage about Mr. Gladstone, did you or did you not believe it to be true?' Merriman asked his client in examination-in-chief.

'I certainly believed it to be true, and I still believe it to be true,' Captain Wright answered confidently.

'You are charged with being a liar. What were the grounds existing at the time which you considered justified you in making these statements?'

'Things I had read and things I had been told.'

'Who was the first person from whom you heard anything of this sort?'

[1] Counsel was referring to *Eminent Victorians* by Lytton Strachey, in which General Gordon was depicted as a chronic alcoholic.

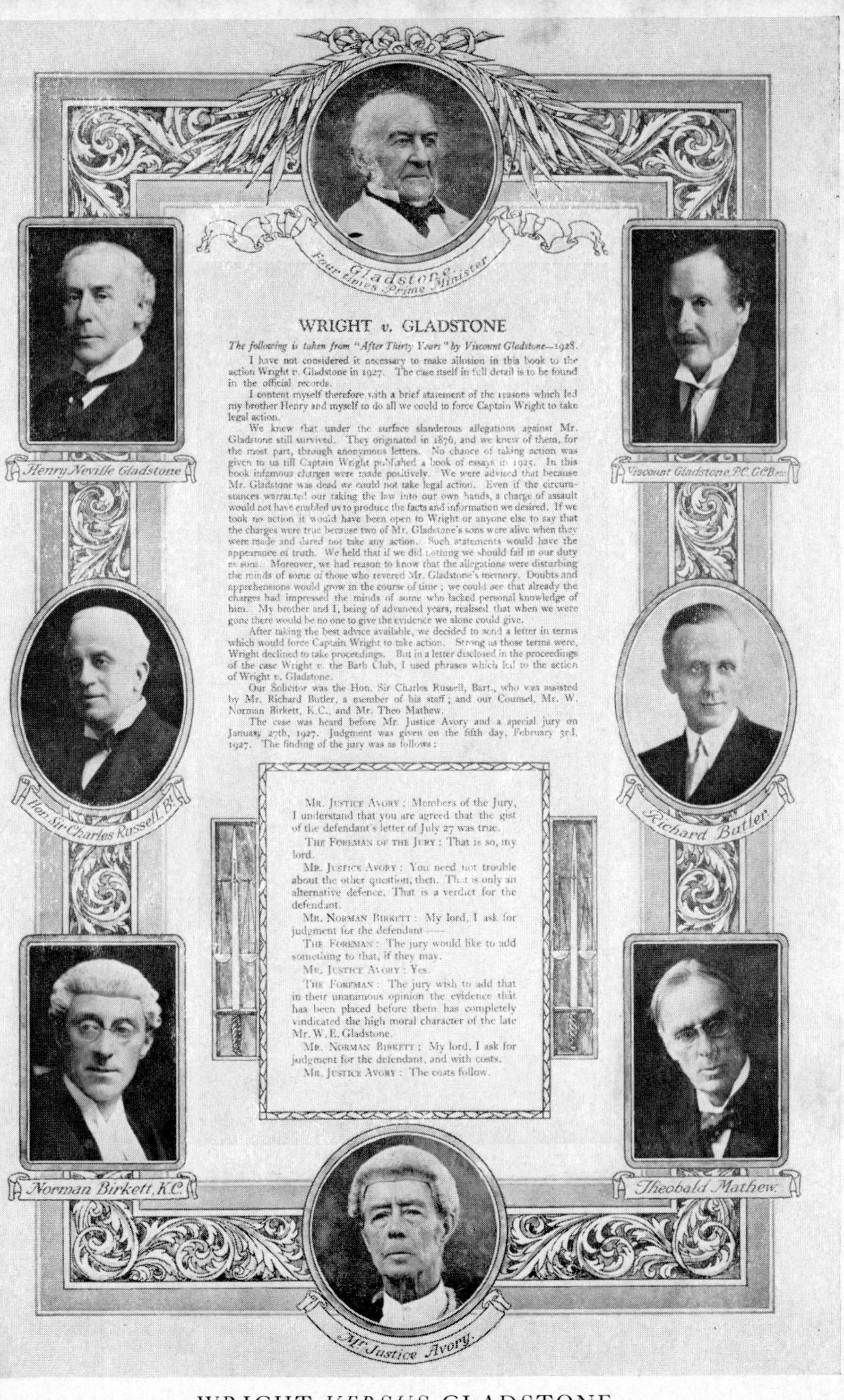

WRIGHT *v.* GLADSTONE

The following is taken from "After Thirty Years" by Viscount Gladstone—1928.

I have not considered it necessary to make allusion in this book to the action Wright *v.* Gladstone in 1927. The case itself in full detail is to be found in the official records.

I content myself therefore with a brief statement of the reasons which led my brother Henry and myself to do all we could to force Captain Wright to take legal action.

We knew that under the surface slanderous allegations against Mr. Gladstone still survived. They originated in 1876, and we knew of them, for the most part, through anonymous letters. No chance of taking action was given to us till Captain Wright published a book of essays in 1925. In this book infamous charges were made positively. We were advised that because Mr. Gladstone was dead we could not take legal action. Even if the circumstances warranted our taking the law into our own hands, a charge of assault would not have enabled us to produce the facts and information we desired. If we took no action it would have been open to Wright or anyone else to say that the charges were true because two of Mr. Gladstone's sons were alive when they were made and dared not take any action. Such statements would have the appearance of truth. We held that if we did nothing we should fail in our duty as sons. Moreover, we had reason to know that the allegations were disturbing the minds of some of those who revered Mr. Gladstone's memory. Doubts and apprehensions would grow in the course of time; we could see that already the charges had impressed the minds of some who lacked personal knowledge of him. My brother and I, being of advanced years, realised that when we were gone there would be no one to give the evidence we alone could give.

After taking the best advice available, we decided to send a letter in terms which would force Captain Wright to take action. Strong as those terms were, Wright declined to take proceedings. But in a letter disclosed in the proceedings of the case Wright *v.* the Bath Club, I used phrases which led to the action of Wright *v.* Gladstone.

Our Solicitor was the Hon. Sir Charles Russell, Bart., who was assisted by Mr. Richard Butler, a member of his staff; and our Counsel, Mr. W. Norman Birkett, K.C., and Mr. Theo Mathew.

The case was heard before Mr. Justice Avory and a special jury on January 27th, 1927. Judgment was given on the fifth day, February 3rd, 1927. The finding of the jury was as follows:

MR. JUSTICE AVORY: Members of the Jury, I understand that you are agreed that the gist of the defendant's letter of July 27 was true.

THE FOREMAN OF THE JURY: That is so, my lord.

MR. JUSTICE AVORY: You need not trouble about the other question, then. That is only an alternative defence. That is a verdict for the defendant.

MR. NORMAN BIRKETT: My lord, I ask for judgment for the defendant——

THE FOREMAN: The jury would like to add something to that, if they may.

MR. JUSTICE AVORY: Yes.

THE FOREMAN: The jury wish to add that in their unanimous opinion the evidence that has been placed before them has completely vindicated the high moral character of the late Mr. W. E. Gladstone.

MR. NORMAN BIRKETT: My lord, I ask for judgment for the defendant, and with costs.

MR. JUSTICE AVORY: The costs follow.

WRIGHT *VERSUS* GLADSTONE

his illuminated extract from Lord Gladstone's book, *After Thirty Years*, with photographs some of the principal characters concerned with the case, was presented by Lord Gladstone to Birkett as the leading counsel for the defence.

Associated Newspaper

CAPTAIN PETER WRIGHT

'I first heard this fact when I was still at Harrow from Mr. James Haslam, a friend of my family who lived in Paris and was a collector of pictures and prints.'

'What did he tell you?'

'He told me that Lily Langtry had been the mistress of Gladstone.'

'How old were you at this time?' Mr. Justice Avory intervened to ask.

'Seventeen.'

'And of what age was this man Haslam?' continued the judge.

'About the age I am now, forty-six.' The witness added that Mr. Haslam was now dead.

'Who was the next?' Merriman went on.

'When I was twenty-one, Dr. Greatorex, who had a considerable West End practice, told me that he had had women patients who had told him that Gladstone had tried to make their acquaintance in the street. About then I had first read of Gladstone's connection with Laura Bell, the most famous courtesan of the nineteenth century.'

Wright went on to say that he must have heard about the same time of Gladstone's relations with Olga Novikoff and he always understood that she was Gladstone's mistress. He had gathered this tit-bit from a Mr. Walter Morrison, but that gentleman was also dead.

'In making your statement about Mr. Gladstone did you rely on any other verbal communications?' Merriman then asked his client.

'About fourteen years ago I saw at Eastbourne a man named Cecil Gladstone whose resemblance to the statesman was unmistakable,' Wright replied. 'I was told he was an illegitimate son, but I cannot identify my informant.

'Of what kind was the resemblance?'

'Facial,' said Wright. 'I should say that he was a larger and inferior edition of Mr. Gladstone.'

'Was he inferior in point of intellect?' interposed the judge.

'He had not the distinguished air of the statesman.'

Answering further questions by his counsel, the plaintiff mentioned a French actress named Brassin with whom (so a Frenchman in Paris had told him) Gladstone had had an intrigue during a visit she paid to London with a French theatrical company. Also, an amateur steeplechase rider, Charlie Thompson, had told him that

Gladstone had once tried to make the acquaintance of a lady whom he (Thompson) had left for a moment at a shop. On Thompson's return, Mr. Gladstone had fled, and the lady subsequently complained that he had been making advances to her.

As for the written statements on which Captain Wright relied, they included among others a statement by Lord Granville, who had twice served under Gladstone as Foreign Secretary, that he had known five of Queen Victoria's Prime Ministers, all of whom had committed adultery. As he read the passage, the witness said that it meant that all the Prime Ministers of Queen Victoria, of whom there were nine, had committed adultery.

Captain Wright also referred to a book about the pleasures of London's underworld with illustrations by Phil May which he had read and which contained a picture of a man at a stage door with a bouquet and a very amorous air. The man was obviously Mr. Gladstone and he was waiting for Lily Langtry.

A copy of the picture was handed up to Mr. Justice Avory, who looked at it carefully. 'You seriously believed when you saw this that Mrs. Langtry was the mistress of Mr. Gladstone?' Mr. Justice Avory asked the witness.

'I had been told that,' was the reply.

'And this confirmed your opinion?' There was a distinctly incredulous note in the judge's voice.

'Yes, my Lord,' the plaintiff agreed blandly. He then repeated that when he wrote what he did about Mr. Gladstone he believed it to be true.

5

Birkett began his cross-examination of the plaintiff in his customary quiet manner. 'Captain Wright, do you regard yourself as a serious journalist?'

'I try not to be dull.'

The witness's attempt to be smart was capped by Mr. Justice Avory, who had begun to take an unfavourable view of his behaviour. 'Does that mean that all serious people are bores?' he asked.

When the laughter caused by this judicial sally had subsided, Birkett continued: 'Do you regard yourself as a responsible journalist?'

'I speak the truth.'

'Would you answer the question? Do you regard yourself as a responsible journalist?'

'Certainly,' answered the witness. 'The newspapers treat me as one, and I conclude that I am one.'

'Do you agree that the charge you make is about as horrible a charge as can be made against any man?'

'No, because it has been made against innumerable great men.'

'Is it not a charge which reflects on all the women who honoured Gladstone with their friendship?'

'No, certainly not. He might behave very well at Carlton Gardens, but not elsewhere.'

'How many times did you see him?'

'I saw Mr. Gladstone once when I was a boy.'

The witness went on to explain that when Gladstone played a part he played it so well that he became the real thing. When he was religious, therefore, it could not be said that he was completely insincere.

'Does it mean that he was the rankest kind of hypocrite?'

'Yes, but, being a wonderful sort of man, he was a wonderful hypocrite.'

'Does it follow from that that his professed religion was a simple mockery?'

'No.'

'Why not?'

'Because he was such an actor and he threw himself so entirely into the part that he became it.'

'I take it that these assertions are based upon the evidence you have given us?'

'You cannot say he disbelieved what he said. When he acted, he believed it. It was not merely in the matter of sex. Take anything else. He was always doing acts of jobbery and then condemning them.'

Birkett then read a passage from Morley's *Life of Gladstone*, recording the ideal married life of Mr. and Mrs. Gladstone, which he put to the witness. 'Take it on the footing for a moment that it was an ideal domestic life. Is this charge of yours that Gladstone was faithless to his wife for sixty years?'

'Of course, it is,' Wright continued to answer with characteristic brashness. 'Men who are very fond of their wives are often faithless to them.'

'Are you ready to believe that there are millions of people in this country who believe that this charge is a horrible one?'

'I should not have thought so.'

'Do you regard immorality in a man as an ordinary thing?'

'No, I regard it as culpable.'

'But not horrible?'

'No.'

'If such a charge were made against a man falsely, would you not regard it as a foul charge?'

'Yes, most certainly.'

'And the man who made it would be a foul man?' Birkett pressed his attack.

'Hardly,' the witness parried, 'for a person who makes such a charge is not necessarily dissolute—that is the meaning of the word foul.' That was Lord Gladstone's bad English, Wright went on. 'And I can't talk bad English to please you, you know,' he added.

'If a person made a foul charge against you or your dead father,' Birkett continued, this time in a tone of withering sarcasm, 'what would you call him in your beautiful English?'

'I should call him intemperate.'

This reply produced some laughter in court, which was by no means all on the side of the witness.

'Is that the best you can do?' Birkett went on, after a pause. 'Were you intemperate in that charge against Mr. Gladstone?'

'I think that is the worst that can be said of it,' Wright admitted. 'It is a slightly intemperate phrase.'

'If a man made charges which were false, and without evidence on which to make them, what would you call him?'

'I should call him a liar.'

Birkett had not got very far in his cross-examination when the court rose for the day. But his questions had already made an impression on the jury, and that impression was not by any means in the plaintiff's favour. This may have been why Captain Wright appeared rather more subdued when he took his place in the witness box next morning to face his opponent's leading counsel.

'When a writer makes a serious charge against a dead man, would you regard that as a responsible task?'

'A serious writer ought to regard all he writes as a responsible task.'

'A responsible journalist would regard it as his duty to verify the facts before making a serious charge against anybody?'

'Not if he thought he knew them,' Wright answered incautiously; 'otherwise he could never write anything.'

'He might proceed upon information given to him without verifying a single thing if he had formed a decided opinion?'

The witness now began to hedge. 'In this case my charge against Gladstone is primarily one of hypocrisy,' he said. 'If a man has formed that opinion, and the reason is there, why should he go through some process of verification? It would paralyse him.'

Birkett let this pass without comment. 'Let me take what you said about Lord Milner and the use of the phrase that "Gladstone was governed by his seraglio". Was that the best evidence you had?'

'What I heard from Lord Milner,' Wright replied, 'was the most reliable and best evidence I ever had.'

'There is no question that it is the conversation with Lord Milner that you regard as the most reliable authority you have got?'

'It clinches the opinion I had formed long before.'

Replying to further questions, Wright agreed that the solicitors for the executors of Lord Milner had written to him asking what was the authority for his statement about Lord Milner's expression and that he had replied that the statement was made to him in a conversation at Versailles towards the end of the war. He had also written that, if the solicitors would refer to Mr. T. P. O'Connor's obituary notice of Lord Milner in the *Daily Telegraph*, they would find that Lord Milner had used that phrase forty years ago.

'When you made the reference to the obituary notice,' Birkett continued, 'you knew full well that in that notice Mr. O'Connor was referring to Gladstone's devoted wife and daughter as "the seraglio"?'

'I was quite candid,' Wright replied, 'and I referred to the notice to show that Mr. T. P. O'Connor used the same words. "Seraglio" could not mean wife and daughter . . . it was impossible.'

'I put it to you plainly that when you wrote your letter to the executors' solicitors you wanted them to believe that you were corroborated by Mr. T. P. O'Connor?'

'That is childish; they could see the article for themselves,' said the witness, his voice rising in annoyance. 'I have Murray's *Dictionary* here, and if you turn to "seraglio", you will find that it does not mean wife and daughter.'

'Don't shout please!' the judge interrupted.

'Don't you think that the word could be used in jest without a serious meaning?' Birkett went on.

'No!' Wright persisted. ' "Seraglio" in the mouth of a man like Lord Milner, who was a great literary artist, even when he was a young man, could not mean wife and daughter.'

Lord Gladstone's counsel then passed to the question of Mr. Cecil Gladstone, whom the plaintiff had once seen at Eastbourne and who, so he had been given to understand, was the statesman's illegitimate son.

'Did you make any inquiries about Cecil Gladstone?'

'I did not deliberately make inquiries. I should never write anything if I did.'

'You believed what you heard, and acted upon it?'

'I did.'

At this point Birkett handed the witness two documents. The first was the birth certificate of Cecil Thomas Gladstone, which showed that he had been born in 1856 at Highgate, his father being described as 'William Gladstone, general merchant'. The second was a marriage certificate, from which it appeared that Cecil Thomas Gladstone had been married in 1902, his father being described as 'William Gladstone (deceased), merchant'.

'So those two documents would appear to show the birth of Cecil Thomas Gladstone?'

'Yes, to William Gladstone.'

'You want to emphasize the "William" to the jury?'

'Yes. They both have the same Christian name and surname.'

'You mean that William Ewart Gladstone was also a William?'

'Yes.'

'The certificates would appear to show that Cecil Gladstone was the son of William Gladstone, a merchant?'

'A general merchant, yes, a very large category of people.'

'Do you think that a Prime Minister is covered by that description?'

'I don't know that it does not. You are trying to show that Cecil

Gladstone cannot be the son of the statesman, but I am not certain whether your proof is quite conclusive.'

Birkett then handed up a copy of Cecil Gladstone's death certificate, which was signed by his widow. According to this, he had died at Eastbourne, aged sixty-eight.

'Is the widow alive?'

'I don't know.'

'Do you know whether she lives in Eastbourne now?'

'I do not.'

'You have never made any inquiry about it?'

'No. I was only showing the process of thought by which I arrived at my conclusion.'

'Do these documents influence your judgment at all?'

'They don't seem to be quite so very conclusive on your side, because if Gladstone had an illegitimate son this is rather the way he would deal with it. It does not seem completely to refute my view.'

'In your view these documents are forgeries reeking with false information?'

'They might be.'

'Given by the Prime Minister of this country?'

'If he had an illegitimate son. But he was not Prime Minister at the time. In 1856 Gladstone was apparently excluded from politics altogether.'

'You think the certificates are full of false information?' Birkett repeated his previous question.

'Yes,' the witness now answered more definitely, 'by a Cabinet Minister who did not dare to speak the truth.'

By this unfortunate admission, Captain Wright had fallen into the simple trap which Birkett had set for him, as the counsel made clear by his next move. This was to hold up a large volume lying in front of him.

'Do you know a publication known as *Lodge's Peerage*?' he asked the witness.

'Yes,' Wright replied, 'but I have not studied it to such an extent as to be aware that it gave a genealogical tree of the Gladstone family and its branches.'

'Do you know that William Ewart Gladstone had a first cousin named William, who is fully dealt with in this work?'

'No, I do not.'

'Did you ever make any inquiry?'

'No,' said the witness, 'and when this case arose, what did it matter? What mattered were my processes of thought.'

The copy of *Lodge's Peerage* was handed up to the witness box, where Captain Wright carefully scanned the entries to which Birkett directed his attention. He agreed, when they were put to him, that the entries bore out the certificates.

'Do you still say that Cecil Gladstone was the illegitimate son of William Ewart Gladstone?'

'No, not now,' replied Captain Wright, for the first time looking somewhat deflated if not shamefaced.

'Do you now withdraw what you said?' the judge broke in.

'Certainly, my Lord. That book convinced me at once.'

'Don't you think you should be more careful before you make suggestions?' Mr. Justice Avory went on. 'When you saw the birth certificate, did it not occur to you that it was not usual for an illegitimate son to be registered in the name of his father?'

'It did not,' Wright answered. But he admitted that, if a child were the illegitimate son of a statesman, it would not be registered in his name.

'You now agree that the information on which you acted was quite unreliable?' Birkett asked, rubbing in the judge's stricture.

'Yes,' retorted the plaintiff, trying to appear unabashed. 'But I thought I was right at the time.'

Next, Birkett questioned the plaintiff about the French actress named Brassin who was supposed to have known Gladstone.

'To what theatrical company did this actress belong?'

'I don't know.'

'At what theatre did she act?'

'Let me see——'

'What play was she in?'

'I cannot tell you that.'

'She is dead now?'

'I should think so.'

'You never troubled to inquire?'

'No.'

'Did you ever see her act?'

'Yes, when I was quite young.'

Birkett looked doubtful. 'You are quite sure she existed?'

'Oh, yes,' answered the witness. 'I saw a reference to her in a book quite recently.'

'That is not conclusive,' the judge broke in.

'In what year did she come to London?' continued Birkett.

'I cannot say.'

'Apart from the fact that a man, now dead, told you as a lad of twenty that an actress twenty years before had an intrigue in London with Gladstone when he was seventy-two, you made no further inquiries?'

'No. Why should I?'

Captain Wright's self-confidence was astonishing. The trouble was that he always thought he was right, and unfortunately the majority of his informants were no longer available, as Birkett reminded him. 'Lord Milner is dead, Haslam is dead, Dr. Greatorex is dead, Morrison is dead, Novikoff is dead, Laura Bell is dead, Sir Francis Burnand is dead, Labouchere is dead, and Lord Morley is dead?'

'Yes,' came the cocksure reply: 'and Gladstone was born six years before the Battle of Waterloo.'

'It is difficult when people are dead to get at the exact facts?'

'Nearly every character in history is dead. I don't know whether you have observed that, Mr. Birkett!'

Birkett let this impertinent remark pass without comment. Instead he abruptly switched his line of questioning to other specific individuals.

'Where is Charlie Thompson? Is he alive?'

'I don't know.'

'Mrs. Langtry is alive, is she not?'

'Yes. She lives on the Riviera.'

'Do you think some of the answers you have given in the witness box might cause grievous pain to her?'

'I am afraid so. It very much annoys me that it should be so. I am very sorry about it—more than I can say. I would have done anything I could to avoid it.'

'You don't like reflecting on a living person?' the judge interrupted.

'Not a woman.'

When Birkett suggested that the offending sentence about Mr.

Gladstone was not essential to an article which dealt primarily with Lord Cecil and the League of Nations, the witness replied: 'Digression is one of the arts of essay writing. This is an essay, not an affidavit.'

'It appears to be as unreliable,' the judge observed aptly.

Birkett had not concluded his cross-examination on that Friday afternoon when the court adjourned until the following Tuesday. When it sat again, the defendant's counsel had a surprise for the court. He held a telegram in his hand which he asked permission to read. The telegram was addressed to him personally, and he had received it on the previous day. It had been handed in at Monte Carlo and read as follows:

> 'Strongly repudiate slanderous accusations by Peter Wright.
> LILY LANGTRY'

'Captain Wright seems to have believed that what he was told was true,' Birkett added, 'and I am content that the telegram should be before your Lordship and the jury as strongly repudiating a slanderous assertion. I understand that my learned friend, who appears for the plaintiff, agrees to that.'

'Absolutely,' said Merriman. 'The issue is whether the plaintiff believed the statement to be true. I am content that the telegram should be put in, and I shall not comment upon it.'

Over the week-end, Birkett had been rereading Boswell's *Life of Johnson*, and when he resumed his cross-examination he drew the witness's attention to a particular passage, which he made him read out:

> We surely cannot but admire the benevolent exertions of this great and good man. . . . He has sometimes suffered me to talk jocularly of his group of females and call them his 'seraglio'.

'Now it is quite clear that the use of the word by Boswell was a jocular use?'

'Yes.'

'Do you agree that a man might use the word jocularly?'

'Boswell might jest, but Milner did not. . . . He was not a jester,' Wright persisted.

'Looking back upon all that has transpired in this litigation since the publication of the passage in your book,' Birkett asked in conclusion, 'do you now regret the publication?'

'Yes, of course I do; and if Lord Gladstone would withdraw his charge, I would say, "I am extremely sorry that I hurt your feelings!"'

'You regret publication?' Birkett repeated.

'I regret most emphatically hurting the feelings of Lord Gladstone and his family,' Captain Wright replied, emphasizing each word by striking the front of the witness box with his clenched fist, 'and if they had given me anything of a chance I would have said so. I would say it now.'

'Don't knock the furniture about!' the judge mildly reproved the witness.

After a short re-examination, in which he repeated that he relied primarily on Lord Milner's words as the basis of his charge, the plaintiff stepped down from the witness box. His counsel called no further witnesses.

6

'Captain Wright has brought an action for libel against Lord Gladstone,' said Birkett, in opening the defence. 'But who is the libeller and who is the libelled? Members of the jury, the libeller is Captain Wright who libels the dead, and the real plaintiff in the action is Lord Gladstone, who is the defender of his father's memory and reputation. Strong words have been used by Lord Gladstone about Captain Wright. But is there a word used which is a whit too strong? He has been called a liar. . . . Captain Wright has said that Mr. Gladstone, not in youth or middle age, but in old age—in extreme old age—was an evil liver, yet he could not bring a single living witness to prove it. He is a liar when he desecrates the grave and when he robs the dead of that one thing which spurs men throughout life to win for themselves, by things which are honourable and of good repute, a reputation which may live after they are gone and give them an immortality which they may leave as a heritage to those who come after them.

'You have seen Captain Wright in the witness box. You have heard the kind of thing that he says. Do you think that "liar" is a bit too strong?'

Birkett's speech, which lasted two hours, occupied the remainder of the day and held the packed court spell-bound, as he mercilessly exposed the flimsy nature of Captain Wright's allegations, for instance, regarding Mlle Brassin and Mme Novikoff. 'It is not usual for a man of seventy-two to start an intrigue with a French actress,' said Birkett scornfully. 'The year the plaintiff doesn't know, the theatre he doesn't know, the play he doesn't know, but "someone told me". It is shameful, shameful!' As for Mme Novikoff, she had corresponded with Gladstone for twenty-three years and her letters had been brought into court for the jury to see, but none of them contained a single reference pointing to an adulterous intrigue. 'I propose to put Lord Gladstone in the box,' his counsel added, 'and he will tell you he knew Mme Novikoff and of the opportunities he himself had of observing the general position.'

Next morning the defendant was examined by his leading counsel. He was the fourth and youngest son of Mr. Gladstone, he said, and until his father's death in 1898 he had lived with him, in London either in Carlton House Terrace or in Downing Street, and in the country at Hawarden. He first entered the House of Commons in 1880 and in the same year was appointed private secretary to his father. Other offices he held during his father's lifetime were Lord of the Treasury, Financial Secretary to the War Office, Under-Secretary for Home Affairs, and First Commissioner of Works. After his father's death, he had served as Home Secretary and finally as the first Governor-General of South Africa.

'With regard to the positions which you held down to your father's death, did they bring you into close relationship with him?' asked Birkett.

'Some of them, most certainly,' Lord Gladstone replied.

'Having regard to your position as a son and to the offices you held, what do you say about this passage in Captain Wright's book?'

'It was a revolting passage which made me angry to an almost ungovernable extent.'

'What was the cause of your anger?'

'I knew it to be false.'

'As a son living at home, will you tell my Lord and the jury what was the relationship between your father and mother in the home during the years that you were there?'

'It was absolutely perfect.'

'Did the knowledge of that have any effect upon you when you read this passage in the book?'

'It had a great effect.'

'You called the accusation a foul charge?'

'Certainly. It was a charge which made out my father to be a foul sensualist and a foul hypocrite. Those were lies, and the charge, therefore, was a foul one.'

'After listening to the evidence which Captain Peter Wright has given, do you wish to qualify or withdraw the expression "foul"?'

'Most certainly not!' Lord Gladstone emphatically declared.

Birkett then questioned the defendant about his father's interest in the work of rescuing prostitutes, in which his mother also took an active part. Mr. Gladstone had helped to found the Church Penitentiary Association for the Reclamation of Fallen Women, the St. Mary Magdalene Home in Paddington and similar missionary institutions. He was also on the management committee of Millbank Penitentiary, where arrested prostitutes were detained, and Lord Gladstone remembered being taken there once as a boy by his parents and waiting for his father there.

'What was the main social work of your father and mother?'

'It took the form throughout their lives of rescue work."

'In that connection, and from your own knowledge, do you know whether your father spoke to such women in the street?'

'I did not happen to see it myself, but I know it.'

'And the passage in Lord Morley's *Life* that your father's actions were open to misconstruction, but that he pursued them—was that passage confirmed by your own knowledge?'

'Certainly. He kept to his resolution with iron tenacity.'

Questioned about Mme Novikoff, Lord Gladstone said that he first met her at a political meeting in 1876, but got to know her better after he entered Parliament. He and his wife had dined at her house. There was no secret about his father's communications with her.

'Captain Wright says that because of some adulterous intrigue with Mme Novikoff your father changed his Eastern policy?'

'If it was not concerned with so serious a charge, it would be a matter for laughter.'

'From your knowledge of your father, from your knowledge of Mme Novikoff, and from the correspondence you have read, is there the slightest basis for any allegation of any impropriety of any kind?'

'Absolutely none. I have never heard a whisper against Mme Novikoff. There were other charges against her, but not of immorality. It is an infamous charge.'

'Was your father's policy changed?'

'I can easily prove that it was not. The correspondence with Mme Novikoff began in 1873 and she was a perfect stranger when she first wrote.' Lord Gladstone added that her early letters, which she wrote when his father was reappraising his Eastern policy, did not refer to the Eastern Question at all, but to another matter in which Mr. Gladstone was deeply interested at the time, namely the possible union of the Roman Catholic and the Greek Orthodox Churches.

'With your knowledge of the facts, is there the slightest ground for saying that Mme Novikoff induced a change in the policy advocated by your father?'

'No, not the slightest.'

'So, apart from the serious charge of adulterous relations, which you say is false, the second is also false?'

'Absolutely.'

It was the same with the charge that Mr. Gladstone had connived at Parnell's illicit relations with Mrs. O'Shea and utilized them for his own political purposes. First of all, Lord Gladstone explained that Mrs. O'Shea had only acted as an intermediary between Parnell and his father for a short time in 1882, when relations between the Liberals and Irish Nationalists were strained, and they only met on three occasions.

'Had you yourself at that time any idea that Mrs. O'Shea was Parnell's mistress?'

'No, not of the exact position, but rumours grew.'

'When did you personally have knowledge that it was alleged that such an intimacy existed?'

'I never heard any definite statement of that kind. I heard rumours, but I never heard anybody say that Parnell was living with Mrs. O'Shea until later.'

'When?'

'In 1890, when there was the actual petition for divorce.'

'To the extent that your personal knowledge goes, did your father have any knowledge of the matter before that date?'

'No. He did not know so much as I did.'

'You remember your father's expression about the news coming to him as a thunderclap. That has been characterized by Captain Peter Wright as Gladstonian humbug. What do you say about that?'

'What my father said was true.'

'Is there, so far as your personal knowledge goes, any ground for saying that your father connived at the relationship between Parnell and Mrs. O'Shea?'

'There was absolutely no connivance. It is a lie to say so, and Mrs. O'Shea's book proves to a fair minded person that there was no connivance.'

Birkett's final questions were directed to Mr. Gladstone's religious beliefs. 'Was your father a man who believed in religion?'

'Religion was the deepest passion of his life from first to last,' answered the witness.

'And with your knowledge as a son living at home and seeing the visitors there, did people of a like mind visit him?'

'Certainly.'

'If somebody was in fact religious-minded and invoked the aid of Mr. Gladstone on religious matters, would he be ready to give it?'

'From my knowledge of him I know that any man or woman who asked for his advice and for his help never got a refusal, and particularly on questions of religion and morals.'

Under cross-examination, Lord Gladstone's evidence was quite unshaken. For instance, when asked about Mrs. O'Shea's book *Charles Stewart Parnell*, he agreed that Mrs. O'Shea had said that Mr. Gladstone had known all along of her association with Parnell. However, he absolutely denied the truth of that charge. The book was written thirty years afterwards with a vindictive purpose, Lord Gladstone added, and it contained many inaccuracies.[1]

'Have you anything to add to the explanation you have given of the phrase "foul fellow" in your letter?' he was asked by Captain Wright's counsel.

1 'The statement that Mr. Gladstone knew the facts of her relationship to Parnell is a falsehood. No one knew, not even Captain O'Shea . . . Mrs. O'Shea acted absolutely under the direction of Parnell, and the last man to whom he desired to convey information, so carefully concealed from his own colleagues, was Mr. Gladstone.' Viscount Gladstone. *After Thirty Years* (1928), at p. 304.

'I will sum up what I said,' Lord Gladstone replied. 'He made a foul and loathsome charge against my father, and it was a deadly insult to every member of my family—a charge so loathsome that it could only be made by a foul-minded man—and I say that because of that he was a foul fellow. That is my last word.'

Birkett's re-examination was brief and to the point. 'Is it any pleasure to you to come into public and discuss these matters about your dead father?'

'At the age of seventy-two,' said Lord Gladstone, 'I have to face all this muck that is thrown by Captain Peter Wright and deal with it as if I were a scavenger. Do you think that that is a pleasant duty?' Then, he added with a touch of sadness in his voice: 'We had to do it, because my brother and I knew that if we passed away Captain Wright might say in a future publication that Mr. Gladstone's two sons were living when he made these statements and that they dared not take any notice of them.'

Besides Mr. Eveleigh Nash, the publisher, who testified that the offending words were inserted in the proofs of Captain Wright's book without his knowledge, the defendant was supported by several distinguished witnesses, who spoke to Mr. Gladstone's high character. They included Lord Phillimore, Mr. Henry Gladstone, Mr. T. P. O'Connor, M.P., and Lady Gwendolen Cecil, daughter of the Conservative leader Lord Salisbury.

When Lady Gwendolen left the witness-box, it was generally assumed that the defendant's case would now be closed. But Birkett had another surprise. 'I will now call my last witness,' he announced dramatically. 'Mr. Charlie Thompson.'

The buzz of interest which this statement caused was heightened when Birkett added that his clients had only got into touch with Mr. Thompson early that morning.

'How many times in your life have you seen Captain Peter Wright?' Birkett asked this surprise witness.

'Once,' replied the steeplechase rider.

'When was that occasion?'

'About a year ago.' The witness added that he could not fix the date or time exactly, but it was when the talk was going round about Captain Wright and the Bath Club.

'Where did he see you?'

'At my flat.'

'Did you know that he was coming to see you?'

'I am not sure whether I was advised by a man named Voigt that he was coming or whether he came and announced that he had been sent by Voigt.'

'What did he say?'

'He said that Voigt had repeated something to him that I had said.'

'Did you repeat it to Captain Wright?'

'Yes.'

'Tell my Lord and the jury what you repeated to him?'

'I told him that one day I was walking down Jermyn Street with a lady and she wanted to see a photograph which I had in my chambers in Jermyn Street. I told her that I could only have men in my chambers and if she didn't mind waiting in the street while I ran upstairs I would not keep her more than a few minutes. I fetched the photograph and found her outside. She then said, "Do you see that old gentleman over there?" I said, "Yes, it's Gladstone." She said, "Is it? Why, he has been trying to get into conversation with me." '

'What did Captain Wright ask you to do?'

'He asked me to write to the secretary of the Bath Club something to that effect.'

'What did you say?'

'I told him that I did not wish to have anything to do with the matter and that I did not know him very well. I said that I would consider the matter.'

'Did you consider it?' Birkett went on.

'Yes,' said Charlie Thompson. 'I sent a letter to Captain Wright saying that on consideration I did not propose to write the letter which he suggested because, in the first place, I objected to maligning a dead man, and that, besides that, Mr. Gladstone was a man—however much my politics and his might differ—who was considered by the majority of his countrymen to have done a great benefit to his country. In addition, the lady who had given me the information was of doubtful character and what she said might be open to suspicion.'

In his final speech to the jury, Birkett began by saying that, whatever the result of the trial might be, Lord Gladstone and his brother by their conduct had dignified and exalted the name of sonship. Had they not done what they had, they would have been unworthy to bear the great name they had. Lord Gladstone and his brother, with the memory of their ideal home life, of their relationship to Mr. Gladstone and of his character, were moved by righteous indignation in the truest and fullest sense, an indignation which was based on absolute, direct and personal knowledge. Captain Wright, on the other hand, had spoken on hearsay and rumour which, in every matter where they could test it, had broken down hopelessly.

'I ask you to give me your verdict for Lord Gladstone on the plea of justification,' said Birkett. 'Once you give me that verdict nothing else matters. I have tried to make it clear that, so far as Lord Gladstone is concerned, there never has been a moment when he has not said that the one thing which he desired above all else is that this foul charge against his father's memory should be put to the arbitrament of a British jury. I ask you to give me that verdict on the ground that there never was a case tried in these Courts in which a verdict of justification for the defendant would be more just. You have heard the evidence. If I could judge your minds or consciences, I am sure that I should see that there is not a man or a woman sitting in that box who will not say that this charge, made against a great figure who died thirty years ago, was a foul charge. It may be that, long after we are gone, the result of this case will be discussed. You have a great opportunity to strike a resounding blow for the purity of public discussion, to secure that men will no longer be permitted to traduce or defame the dead on garbage such as has been produced in this case. More than all, I ask you by your verdict to vindicate the memory of a great Englishman.'

Since no witnesses had been called for the plaintiff apart from himself, this meant that his counsel had the last word with the jury. But there was little that Merriman could do to alleviate the impact of Birkett's cogent eloquence. In his speech, Merriman emphasized that the issue in the case was what was the state of mind of Captain Wright when he wrote the passage about Mr. Gladstone. It was not true that the real plaintiff in the case was Lord Gladstone, he argued, nor that the real issue was Mr. Gladstone's reputation. The tributes which had been paid to Mr. Gladstone on his death had been rightly described as unreliable from the historical point of view. How could there be entirely reliable evidence of matters which occurred after so many years? He begged the jury not to be overawed by a great name and a great tradition. Throughout the case Captain Wright had played a pretty lone hand, and it was for them to see that he had such reparation as a much injured man was entitled to.

Mr. Justice Avory, in summing up, made no attempt to disguise his prejudice against the plaintiff, although his analysis of the evidence was fair enough in itself. He reminded the jury, which contained three women, that Captain Wright had said that the real charge he had made against Mr. Gladstone was one of hypocrisy, and that the allegation of pursuing and possessing every sort of woman, was of quite secondary importance, and asked them which they thought was of greater importance to the memory of a dead man. 'When Captain Wright shifted his ground in that way, was it not, to use his own words, a forensic trick?' Again, Captain Wright had said that a writer who had formed his opinion—no matter on what material—was not bound to fortify it by making elaborate inquiries, and that if he did so it would paralyse his writing, and history would never be made. 'If history is to be made of the tittle-tattle of the Upper Tooting tea tables,' said the judge, indulging in one of his characteristic alliterations, 'you will no doubt consider whether it would not be better that history should not be made at all. In writing what he did, did Captain Wright act recklessly, not caring whether what he wrote was true or false?'

There was certainly no doubt in the mind of Mr. Justice Avory that the illustrations which had been given, such as Lily Langtry, Lord Milner, Mme Novikoff and the Parnell–O'Shea affair, were sufficient to bring the plaintiff within this definition. 'Is not a man who slanders the dead a coward?' he went on to ask the jury. 'Is not a man who stabs another in the back a coward? What is the difference between stabbing a man in the back and slandering a dead man in a way which it must be known would bring the greatest pain to his descendants, knowing it would be almost impossible technically to disprove the charge?'

The final words which Captain Wright complained of, said the judge, were 'a foul fellow', upon which he had chosen to put an extravagant meaning—that he was a person of dissolute and vicious life. But the primary meaning of 'foul' was 'unclean', and a secondary meaning was that a foul fellow was one who used scurrilous or abusive language, or one who indulged in foul play. Was not that the sense in which the word was obviously used by Lord Gladstone? Shakespeare, whom the plaintiff 'would no doubt deem to be no less eminent than himself', had also used the word in that sense when he wrote:

> Is't not enough thou hast suborn'd these women
> To accuse this worthy man, but, in foul mouth
> And in the witness of his proper ear,
> To call him villain?

And with this telling quotation from *Measure for Measure* ringing in their ears, the jury retired to consider their verdict. The time was 4.45 p.m. They had listened to a slow, deliberate review of the case, in which Mr. Justice Avory had not concealed his opinions, and most people in court thought the nine men and three women would not be absent for more than a quarter of an hour at the most. After half an hour had gone by, the spectators began to wonder what the jury could be doing and counsel got up to leave, followed by Captain Wright, who put on his hat and coat and found his umbrella. After an hour and then another hour had passed, whispers went round that the jury had disagreed and there would be a new trial. Meanwhile Birkett did his best to comfort his clients and assure them that all would be well; but even he began to grow anxious, and his anxiety was increased when Captain Wright returned with a much more confident air than he had shown when he left, fixing his monocle in his eye and examining the packed court row by row, while the two Gladstone brothers sat side by side with their solicitors in nervous silence.

At last, when the hands of the court room clock pointed to a quarter-past-seven, the door behind the witness box suddenly opened, the jury filed back into their places, and Mr. Justice Avory returned to the Bench. The judge had just received a message from the foreman of the jury, which was now repeated in open court.

MR. JUSTICE AVORY: Members of the jury, I understand that you are agreed that the gist of the defendant's letter of July 27 was true.

FOREMAN OF THE JURY: That is so, my Lord.

MR. JUSTICE AVORY: You need not trouble about the other question, then. That is only an alternative defence.[1] That is a verdict for the defendant.

BIRKETT: My Lord, I ask for judgment for the defendant——

FOREMAN: The jury would like to add something to that, if they may.

MR. JUSTICE AVORY: Yes.

At this point the spectators in the public gallery began to applaud and stamp their feet. They were sternly silenced by the judge.

MR. JUSTICE AVORY: I will not have any noise in court. If anybody makes a noise after this warning, I will commit them for contempt.

FOREMAN (*amid deep silence*): The jury wish to add that in their unanimous opinion the evidence that has been placed before them has completely vindicated the high moral character of the late Mr. W. E. Gladstone.

MR. BIRKETT: My Lord, I ask for judgment for the defendant, and with costs.

MR. JUSTICE AVORY: The costs will follow.

Lord Gladstone and his wife and brother were all in court to hear the verdict, and their friends now crowded round to congratulate them. The victorious defendant was quite overcome with emotion and gratitude. 'Everything is all right now,' was all he could say. 'We are all happy.'

Another very happy man that evening was Norman Birkett. And his happiness was completed next day when he received the following letter, which he was to treasure until his death.

4 *Cleveland Square,*
St. James'.
February 4, 1927.

My dear Mr. Birkett,

I could not tell you last night what I felt. At our first consultation—you were only just back from your holiday—I found to my intense satisfaction that you had already grasped the whole position and knew my own particular difficulties. I told my brother who was not present, 'It's all right. We have got the man'.

[1] The defence of privilege.

Never was any one more fortunate in his legal advisers. Your sympathy and insight were invaluable. Your command to stand to my guns and never to withdraw one inch was an inspiration. What I feared most was the plea that I had written in haste.

The restraint and temper in your masterly cross-examination I admired more than I can say. Your handling of the whole case gave me a confidence which carried me through the long and trying delay at the end. To me it was the most trying episode in my life and the burden was almost too great. But thanks to you we won triumphantly on the big issue and it is a great pleasure to me to think that your name will always be brilliantly associated with an historic case.

I can only express to you my real and heartfelt gratitude and in this my wife and brother most warmly join.

Believe me most truly yours,

GLADSTONE

It is only fair to Captain Peter Wright to add that immediately the trial was over he made an unqualified apology in writing to Lord Gladstone and sent a copy of it to the *Daily Mail.* 'I formally say to you now what I would have said to you in July, 1925, if you had given me the opportunity to do so,' he wrote. 'I regret that a crude phrase of mine about the late Mr. Gladstone should give you and your family pain and annoyance. If any more copies of the book are printed, I shall alter it so as to remove what offends you.' Lord Gladstone replied with a formal acknowledgement.

Thus ended what the successful defendant had rightly called an historic case. Of the many cases in which Birkett appeared as an advocate, he considered that for him the Gladstone Libel Case was the most rewarding of his whole career, though not in the financial sense.[1] For not only did he win it, but he did so most conclusively, as the jury's emphatic rider had demonstrated to the world.

[1] Birkett's brief in this case was marked 400 guineas, and in addition he received three daily 'refreshers' of 100 guineas each. The total costs which Captain Wright had to pay were estimated at £5,000.

CHAPTER VI

'A POLICEMAN'S LOT IS NOT A HAPPY ONE'

I

ALTHOUGH his name was now firmly established in London as a leading 'silk'—his fees for 1926, his best year so far, had amounted to £16,500—Birkett continued to take his share of less remunerative work in the shape of Crown cases on circuit and he also appeared from time to time in cases heard under the recently introduced Poor Person's Act, for which of course he received no fee at all. Two trials in which he appeared for the prosecution at this period deserve mention, one for attempted murder and the other for murder. The first of these took place at Nottingham Assizes in February, 1927, and 'it was there,' to quote Birkett's clerk Bowker, 'that we met as brave and courageous a man as it has ever been my privilege to meet.' This was a twenty-six-year-old officer of the local county constabulary named Thomas Dainty.

There had been several complaints of assaults on women in the Newark area by a masked man driving a small car. Police Constable Dainty had just come off duty one foggy night in January when he received such a complaint. Hastily donning a civilian jacket over his uniform trousers, the constable made a search and came across a man seated in a Morris Cowley by the roadside. He told him that he was a police officer making inquiries respecting a young girl who had been assaulted on the road by a motorist driving a car of this description, and that he was going to search the vehicle. While the constable was doing so, the engine was suddenly started and accelerated rapidly. Dainty thereupon seized the steering wheel with one hand and put his other arm under the driver's chin. Then the constable felt something poked into his body, and the driver fired two shots at him at point blank range. Undaunted though hit, Dainty clutched the steering wheel with both hands and drove the car against a wall. Again the driver fired at Dainty, this time the bullet missing a vital artery by a hairbreadth. He also fired three more shots which went through the hood of the car. There was a further struggle during which the car gained speed, and Dainty finally dropped exhausted to the road bleeding profusely. Even then he managed to hold on to the back of the car and was dragged for a short distance before he finally collapsed. He was barely able to crawl to the nearest police box where he gave the alarm. Fortunately he recovered and was later able to limp painfully into the witness box and tell his story.

Meanwhile the gunman had been arrested in London and he proved to be a twenty-nine-year-old commercial traveller from Lincoln named Edgar William Smith. His Morris Cowley car had also been found in a Lincoln garage with three bullet holes in the hood. Several weeks later a further important discovery was made in the neighbourhood when a schoolboy came upon a brown attaché case at the bottom of a dyke near his home. The case contained among other articles two motor number plates, a false moustache, a black velvet domino mask and a cigarette case bearing the initials 'E.W.S.'

Smith's defence was that the man who stopped him was gruff and peremptory and did not disclose that he was a police officer. 'I did not like him and did not know him, so I slipped in the clutch,' said Smith, adding that he only fired at the constable to frighten him. He denied all knowledge of the attaché case and its contents. He also denied Birkett's suggestion in cross-examination that the real reason he did not report the matter to the police was because he thought he had a chance of getting away undetected.

Birkett's style of cross-examining was deceptively mild.

'You always carried a revolver for protection?'

'Yes.'

'What happened that night, according to you, was that you believed you had been attacked by some ruffian on the road?'

'Yes.'

'And you were fortunate in escaping?'

'That is so.'

'And you were of a nervous disposition, much agitated and distressed?'

'I was very upset by the whole affair.'

'How many police stations did you pass before you got home?'

'I could not tell you.'

'Did it ever occur to you that night to acquaint the police?'

'If I had been in a normal frame of mind and calm, I should no doubt have gone straight to the nearest police station and reported the whole affair.'

'You had been grossly and wantonly attacked by a ruffian on the road. Had it ever happened before?' Birkett went on to ask with apparent incredulity.

'No,' said the prisoner.

'You had shot from your revolver six live cartridges. Did you know whether they had hit the man?'

'I did not know.'

'Had you any reason to suppose they had?'

'No.'

'Had you any reason to suppose they had not?'

'Yes, because I saw him going away.'

'But so far as you knew he might have been mortally wounded?'

'I did not know, but he could not have got away if he received a mortal wound.'

'Is it a fact that you never mentioned the dreadful thing that had happened to a living soul?'

'I did not mention it. I had driven the ruffian off, and that was all I cared.'

At this point the judge interposed. 'This ruffian—as you say—was at large, and might have attacked someone else who did not have a pistol?'

'That did not enter my mind,' the prisoner replied.

'Did you sleep well that night?' continued Birkett.

'Yes.'

'Next morning did it occur to you that you really ought to go to the police?'

'My one idea was to go to London where my wife was.'

'I suggest that Dainty was right when he said he opened a conversation with you by saying he was a police officer?' Birkett went on.

'He did not say that.'

'Your whole behaviour showed you knew he was a police officer.'

'I do not agree.'

'How did you shoot Dainty in the side?'

'It must have happened in the struggle,' said Smith. 'After I fired three shots in the hood two shots were fired. Where they went I do not know. . . . I would far rather have frightened the man than actually shot him. If I had intended to kill Dainty, I could have blown his brains out at the start when I produced the revolver.'

Birkett then reminded him of what he had done. 'You poked the revolver into his body near the top waistcoat pocket and fired, the bullet coming out of the back of his body. Is not that shooting to kill?'

'I don't agree with you,' was all the prisoner could reply. 'It would not kill him. That is quite evident.'

'You say that Dainty never mentioned to you that he was making inquiries about a girl who was assaulted?'

'Never.'

'You say you fired three shots to frighten him—two were fired accidentally, and one deliberately?'

'Yes, that is so.'

'You did not care what happened to the constable afterwards?'

'No, I did not, so long as I got away,' Smith answered callously. 'I thought he was a ruffian.'

Summing up, Mr. Justice Branson, who was the trial judge, told the jury that if they accepted the word of the constable they had no course but to return a verdict of attempted murder. And this is exactly what the jury did after an absence from court of less than a quarter of an hour.

Asked if he had anything to say, the prisoner in the dock declared: 'I am not guilty. If I had known Dainty was a policeman, I should not be standing here, my Lord.'

'The evidence given could lead to no other verdict,' said Mr. Justice Branson. 'I entirely agree with the verdict of the jury. You shot this unfortunate man, who was attempting to do his duty, three times. There is only one penalty I can inflict, and that is penal servitude for life.'

Smith reeled against the dock, staggered by the sentence, which had not been passed in a similar case for thirty years. 'Can't you have mercy, my Lord, and reduce it, if not for myself, for the sake of my wife?' he pleaded. 'It is a terrible sentence.'

'It is a terrible sentence,' Mr. Justice Branson agreed. 'But you have done a terrible thing, and it is only by the mercy of God that you are not charged with murder.'

After the prisoner had been removed, the judge called the gallant P.C. Dainty before him and said: 'At the conclusion of this case, I wish to express publicly to you the gratification I have felt in listening to the details of your courage in attempting to arrest the man I have just sentenced. No one could have blamed you if, seeing that he was armed and having got one bullet wound through your body, you had ceased to continue to try and arrest him. But, notwithstanding that, it took two more shots put into your body before you ceased your efforts to do your duty. It is a record of which any man could be proud, and I hope your future in the police force will reflect the glory of the beginning.'[1]

The murder trial in which Birkett led for the prosecution later in the same year took place before Mr. Justice Rigby Swift at Birmingham Assizes. The accused was a brutal looking individual named James Joseph Power, aged 36, who had formerly belonged to the Birmingham police force but had been discharged for unsatisfactory conduct. He stood indicted for the murder of a young factory worker, Olive Turner, whose body was found in the canal at Winson Green. He had also been charged with rape, assault and attempting to obtain money by menaces.

The story which Birkett unfolded for the Crown was that Miss Turner and her sweetheart, Charles Bromhead, went for a walk one evening along the tow path on the canal bank, which although private property was a favourite promenade for courting couples who lived in the industrial quarter of Birmingham. They were stopped by Power, who pretended to be a plain-clothes policeman and told them that he would have to take them in charge since they could not prove that their names and addresses which they had given him were correct. As they walked along, Power said to Bromhead: 'You know you can square me. It is up to yourself.' Bromhead offered him fourpence for a drink, which Power refused saying, 'Fourpence is no good to me.' Bromhead then told the girl to go home, and she started to run. Power immediately ran after her closely followed by Bromhead. When Bromhead caught up with

[1] *The Times*, February 19, 21, 1927. P.C. Dainty was deservedly awarded the King's Medal by King George V for his gallantry in this case.

him, Power turned round and struck him a fierce blow on the jaw which knocked him down. The young man was dazed by the blow for a minute or two; he then picked himself up, but the other two had disappeared. A little later another courting couple saw Power and the girl, and the man asked Power what he wanted with her. Power said he was a police officer and put his arm round Olive Turner's waist. She seemed distressed and exhausted, and she was led away by Power in a half-fainting condition. That was the last that was seen of her alive. The time was 11.30 p.m. About five minutes later a woman heard terrifying screams coming from the direction of the canal, and shortly afterwards another woman saw a man climb over a wall adjoining the tow path. When the man saw her he stepped backwards, hesitated a little and went quickly into the street, at the same time pulling down his cap to hide his face. The girl's handbag and a hat and fur she was wearing were later found by Bromhead on the canal bank near the spot where her body was recovered. Exactly how she met her death is uncertain, but it appeared that she either jumped into the canal to escape from Power or else she was pushed into it by him.

Power went into the witness box and denied murdering the girl. He had been to a public house with a friend that night, he said, and got home about ten-thirty. He swore that he did not leave home again. His counsel had said he intended to call Power's wife to prove that he was in bed at the time of the girl's disappearance. It was as well that he did not, since the prosecution had in their possession a statement from her to the effect that her husband did not come home until nearly midnight.

Birkett began his cross-examination of the prisoner by producing a cap which had been found in his possession at the time of his arrest and asking him about it.

'Do you look very different in a cap, Power?'

'No.'

'Is this cap yours?'

'Yes.'

'Were you wearing it that night?'

'I may have been.'

Birkett handed the cap to a warder to pass to the prisoner in the box.

'Put the cap on, Power!'

Power placed it on top of his head.

'Put it on, sir,' said Birkett sternly, 'and pull it down over your eyes.'

The prisoner pretended to try, but without success. 'I can't pull it down without hurting myself,' he said. 'It's too tight.'

Birkett was not as a rule given to theatrical demonstrations in court of the kind Marshall Hall used to indulge in with such effect before a jury. But on this occasion he did something quite in the character of his old leader. 'Warder,' he said to the figure standing beside the witness box, 'pull the cap down over the prisoner's eyes.'

The warder immediately did so, having first released the stud in the peak of the cap. This simple but dramatic gesture effectively disposed of the prisoner's alibi.

After the jury had returned the inevitable verdict, Mr. Justice Swift addressed the prisoner. 'For the crime of which the jury have found you to be guilty,' he said, 'our law knows but one punishment, and that punishment is death.'

'I quite understand that,' Power interrupted the judge. 'I don't want any sympathy from you!'

And when the judge had finished, the prisoner, with a final touch of defiance, declared: 'I will appeal against that sentence, you know.'

He did so, but it made no difference. The appeal was dismissed, and Power was duly hanged for what Birkett had rightly described as a brutal and callous murder.[1]

2

Birkett's fee book for 1927 showed over eighteen thousand pounds and fully justified his leaving the house in Golders Green, where he had lived since his marriage, and moving into a new and considerably larger property in Buckinghamshire. 'Challens Green' was a modern house built on an eminence with a fine view across open country to the Chiltern hills. There were two acres of land and garden attached to it, which Birkett and his wife planted enthusiastically and where later he was to construct a swimming pool. The place was about one mile from Chalfont and Latimer railway station, from which there was a good train service to London. Also, it was on the edge of a golf

[1] *Birmingham Post*, December 8, 9, 10, 1927; *The Times*, January 13, 14, 1928.

course, for Birkett kept up his golf and still played off a handicap of ten.

To Henry Birkett

Challens Green, Chalfont St. Giles, Bucks. December 19, 1927.

. . . Our garden alterations are complete, and next spring you must not fail to pay us a visit as we anticipate a great sight. We have put in £150 worth of new bulbs and shrubs. The new terrace and rockery ought to be very fine. . . .

December 26. . . . We had a quiet Christmas this year and the rest has done me good. I needed it greatly, and have a very hard and strenuous term before me.

Three murder cases, which always take a lot out of me. I cannot tell you what it means to me when the Black Cap goes on. DOOM comes striding in suddenly! . . .

I did a record year last year just finished, but the house and super tax on January 1st makes me quail and reduces me to a very humble frame of mind!

January 10, 1928. . . . I am not certain of Easter plans yet, and may not come north: but the rush of Term is really overwhelming, and I cannot find time to think of the joys of Easter yet!

But the crocuses are out in the garden and £100 worth of new bulbs coming up!!!!

Birkett devoted three days of the first week of the new term, in spite of great pressure of other work, to giving his services free to a poor litigant. It was a complicated case in which the woman plaintiff, whom Birkett represented, claimed the return of a substantial sum of money from the man she had lived with for more than twenty years as cook-housekeeper. The money, she alleged, had been handed over to him so that they could have a nest egg when he got his divorce and they were able to marry; but, instead the defendant had cast her adrift. Birkett was able to obtain a settlement by which she was paid a satisfactory sum with a contribution towards her costs.[1]

In announcing this settlement, Mr. Justice Swift, who had heard

[1] *King* v. *Ball. Daily Mail,* January 19, 1927.

the case, publicly thanked Birkett for his work. 'It is gratifying to those who have to administer justice to know,' he added, 'that if a person has a claim, which on preliminary investigation seems to the proper officers to be a claim that should be brought to court, that person is able to be provided with the assistance of counsel without having to find a farthing towards their fees.'

'My Lord,' Birkett modestly replied. 'It is a pleasure to do for nothing something that some years ago a barrister could not do.'

In January, 1928, Birkett defended a well known figure in fashionable London society on a charge of manslaughter arising out of an illegal abortion which he was alleged to have performed on a young married woman. The accused, Charles Jackson Palmer, carried on a practice as a medical electrician, which today might be called that of a radio-therapist. This was perfectly legitimate, being licensed by the London County Council. He had no professional medical qualifications, although he had studied anatomy at University College; he got his patients partly through doctors of his acquaintance and also through friends such as the Duke of Westminster, who was in a sense his patron and who sent people to him for treatment for pains and aches resulting from falls in the hunting field. The electrical treatment in which Jackson Palmer specialized may also in certain circumstances have been capable of helping to induce a miscarriage in a pregnant woman. At any rate the 'medical electrician' had been under suspicion for some time by the police as an abortionist, but they had been unable to find anything to prove their suspicions, although L.C.C. inspectors had frequently visited his premises.

About five o'clock one afternoon in the previous November, the young married woman, Mrs. Alice Goldsmith, went to Palmer's consulting rooms off Grosvenor Square, and at six o'clock or thereabouts she was dead. She had recently returned from her honeymoon to find herself pregnant, and the prosecution alleged that her death had been caused by an injection of soap and water given her by Palmer for the purpose of procuring an abortion. After Palmer had informed the dead woman's husband, the police were called in and Palmer was arrested. At the police court he was charged with murder, but this was altered to manslaughter after he had been committed for trial. The case was tried at the Old Bailey by the

Lord Chief Justice, Lord Hewart, with Mr. Percival Clarke leading for the Crown. As might be expected, it created a considerable public sensation.[1]

The dead woman's husband went into the witness box and told how Palmer had telephoned him and how he had gone to his consulting rooms where he saw his wife lying on a couch with a napkin over her face. Her body was still warm. 'Good God, is she gone?' he asked Palmer, 'Can't you bring her round?' 'I have tried everything,' the prisoner had said to him. 'I have sent for a doctor. I was giving her treatment when she suddenly sat up and clenched her hands, and it was all over. I have been giving treatment for years and have never had an accident.' Mr. Goldsmith added that Palmer did not give him any details of the treatment he had administered to his wife, nor did the witness ask for them. He gave the impression in the witness box that his wife did not wish to have a baby. Replying to Birkett in cross-examination, Mr. Goldsmith said that he did not know his wife was pregnant. He understood that she went to Palmer for treatment for her nerves—to 'buck her up', in fact—and it was her fifth visit to him.

The doctor, whom Palmer had sent for and who had tried without success to revive Mrs. Goldsmith, said the accused told him that most complaints were amenable to electricity.

'Did he say what he was treating this woman for?' asked the Lord Chief Justice.

'Yes,' answered the doctor. 'For anaemia, muscular weakness, and nervous debility.'

He added, when cross-examined, that the prisoner offered no objection to his communicating with the police and the coroner. So far as the doctor could see, there were no suspicious circumstances at all.

Unfortunately for Palmer this evidence was not confirmed by the expert medical witnesses called by the prosecution.

Dr. H. B. Weir, who conducted the post-mortem examination said that on opening the body a soapy fluid began to escape. The dead woman was three months advanced in pregnancy. In his view, the cause of death was syncope and shock from the introduction of this fluid which took place immediately before she died. This was corroborated by Sir Bernard Spilsbury, the Home Office pathologist,

[1] *R.* v. *Palmer. The Times*, January 24, 25, 26, 27, 28; February 1, 1928.

SIR PATRICK HASTINGS, K.C., M.P.

MISS RADCLYFFE HALL

who said the fluid found in the body was a strong solution of soap in water.

'Did you find anything to indicate anaemia?' he was asked by Percival Clarke.

'No,' Sir Bernard replied. 'I found no evidence of disease in any part of the body.' He then went on to say, referring to an abrasion which was found on the body, that in his opinion it was produced by the nozzle of a syringe, and that it was made only a few minutes before death. Death was caused by shock, he added. An injection of soapy fluid might cause a shock, and such a shock was occasionally fatal. He made it clear that he based his conclusion on the amount of fluid found.

3

In opening his defence of Jackson Palmer, Birkett begged the jury not to be carried away by the glamour of a great name. It would be an evil day, he said, if in a criminal court, merely because of distinction and attainments, the word of an expert were accepted as final and conclusive. The word of Sir Bernard Spilsbury was not the final word. Sir Bernard Spilsbury's name was a great name, but where his evidence was in the region of speculation, where there was a margin for error, and where he might be wrong, he reminded the jury that they must give the benefit of the doubt to the man accused. The case for the defence simply was that the prisoner did not put the fluid into the woman's body. Someone else must have put it there, but the prisoner did not know who it was. Birkett suggested that it was the woman herself who did it.

The prisoner then went into the witness box and described the various methods of electrical treatment he employed. A current from an induction coil apparatus was what was applied to Mrs. Goldsmith. The machine would produce a voltage of up to forty volts when the patient was in circuit. When Mrs. Goldsmith first came to see him, he went on, she looked pale and said she had been suffering from anaemia for a long time. She also said she felt depressed and asked him if he thought he could relieve her of her nervous condition and enable her to get over her depression. It was arranged that she should have a course of electrical treatment extending over three months at an approximate cost of thirty-five guineas, of which she paid thirty pounds in advance. Her treatment on November 21 was the fifth she had received from him.

'It was no new thing to her on November 21?' asked the Lord Chief Justice.

'No, my Lord.'

Continuing his evidence, Palmer said that about 5.30 p.m. on that date he saw her and gave her treatment similar to that on her previous visits. It consisted of placing a pad down the spine and inducing an alternating current through the body in the region of the abdomen. 'The treatment lasted about twenty minutes,' he said, 'and as I got towards the end of it she seemed to get a sudden cramp, partially sat up, then lay back and looked rather faint. I immediately switched off the current and crossed the room to get some smelling salts—aromatic ammonia. I could not get the box open, and I had to go back and get another box. I placed the aromatic ammonia to her nose. She did not revive, and as I found that she did not appear to be breathing I ran upstairs to see if the doctor who had been to see my wife was still there. I found that he was not. I then tried artificial respiration, but without effect.'

When the prisoner came to describe what passed between the dead woman's husband and himself following his telephone call to Mr. Goldsmith, the Lord Chief Justice suddenly interrupted him, pointing to the court room clock: 'You see what time it is. It is eleven thirty-four.' Lord Hewart added that he drew attention to the time for a reason which would subsequently appear.

'Did you at any time know that Mrs. Goldsmith was pregnant?' Palmer was asked at the conclusion of his examination-in-chief.

'No, I did not.'

'Did you ever inject any fluid, soapy or otherwise, into Mrs. Goldsmith?'

'No, never,' the prisoner answered slowly and deliberately.

'Did you in any treatment you gave her do anything at all which could have resulted in any fluid being introduced into her?'

'No. I did not.'

Cross-examined by Percival Clarke, Palmer repeated that he never knew that Mrs. Goldsmith was pregnant and he never asked her.

Again the Lord Chief Justice intervened. 'Have you any doubt after her husband's evidence that this young woman ardently desired to avoid having a baby?'

'No,' Palmer was obliged reluctantly to reply.

'And do you tell the jury and me that nevertheless she said nothing about it?'

'She never mentioned it to me,' the prisoner persisted.

Besides the accused, two other witnesses gave evidence for the defence. One was a member of the Institute of Electrical Engineers, who said that it was not voltage alone which would produce shock, but the current also. He had tried to stand the intensity of the full current obtainable from the induction coil apparatus, and he was not able to stand it. He had conducted many experiments with exactly similar machines as to the force given out, and it was capable of throwing a man off his legs or off a bed on which he might be reclining.

The other defence witness was Professor F. J. Browne, Professor of Obstetric Medicine at London University. He said that he examined the pelvic organs of the dead woman in the presence of Sir Bernard Spilsbury and Dr. Weir, and he had also examined parts of the body under a microscope. He differed from the opinion given by the two pathologists that death followed immediately on the injection of soapy fluid. There were indications that a miscarriage had been going on for several hours. He thought that it was quite possible that Mrs. Goldsmith had induced this herself. Finally, he agreed, when the question was put to him, that she might well have died of shock from electricity of low voltage.

On the last day of the trial, when Birkett knew he would have to address the jury, he woke up to find he was suffering from an acute attack of laryngitis and that he could only speak in little more than a hoarse whisper. The news was broken to the Lord Chief Justice, who immediately suggested an adjournment, but Birkett said he would try to carry on. For this purpose he was allowed to leave his usual place in counsel's seats and stand close beside the jury box when he made his speech. He spoke for two hours.

In spite of his physical handicap, Birkett put forward the most powerful plea on behalf of his client, the effect being heightened by the Lord Chief Justice who intervened from time to time to ask him if he would not like to rest for a few minutes. He began by submitting that what he had said in opening the defence had been abundantly justified and that the case for the prosecution against Palmer had broken down in every vital particular. He had submitted that upon the non-medical evidence, if it was examined critically and dispassionately, it would be true to say that every fact was quite consistent with Palmer's innocence, and to that submission he adhered. 'In dealing with the medical evidence,' he went on, 'you are in a region where an eminent man said one thing and an eminent man on the other side said, "I say the contrary." Both are honest men, and both are distinguished men. One says this, and the other says that.' As for Palmer's evidence, he submitted that it had been quite unshaken in cross-examination. He concluded by begging the jury to discharge their 'clear duty on the evidence' which was to return the only verdict that they ought to return, and that was one of 'Not Guilty'. 'It is for that verdict that I appeal,' he finally gasped out, as he returned exhausted to his seat in court.

Unfortunately Birkett's speech was only very briefly reported, and it is impossible to convey the impression that he made upon the jury. That he must have moved them greatly is clear from the judge's summing up, in which he reminded the jury that it was according to the evidence, and not according to the eloquence of learned counsel on one side or the other, that they had to give their verdict. 'There may be a danger, when you hear fine sentiments uttered, to attribute the responsibility for them to a wrong quarter, Lord Hewart warned them. 'One cannot help reflecting very often in a court of law that the merits, and it may be the charm, of the advocate are unconsciously imputed to his client. Members of the jury, you are not trying Mr. Norman Birkett. When you listened to his remarkable and brilliant speech, full of so much earnestness, pathos, and eloquence, you might think at the time that it would be almost a breach of a moral duty not to accept the argument that was being made. But your task and my task is to examine this case according to the evidence.'

As might be expected from his interjections in the course of the trial, the Lord Chief Justice summed up strongly against the prisoner. Incidentally, he explained why he had drawn attention to the time by the clock when Palmer was in the witness box.

> Mr. Goldsmith in evidence has said that when Palmer informed him of his wife's death he had asked him if she had

really gone and if Palmer could not bring her round. I waited, and I am sure you waited, to hear what questions this youthful husband, married two months before, then put to the defendant about the tragic death of his young bride. Not a question. The defendant did not tell him the various steps which had proceeded between five-thirty and six o'clock, nor did Mr. Goldsmith ask; and when the defendant himself came into the witness box I waited again to hear what he would have to say on that matter.

You will recollect that Palmer went into the witness box shortly before the close of the hearing on the day before yesterday. He went into the witness box again yesterday morning. He gave his evidence with the deliberation and consideration which you remember. There was no hurry. There was no occasion for hurry. It was not until eleven thirty-four that it happened, a complete hour after he had been in the box yesterday morning, that he reached and disposed of that interview.

Not one word to contradict the statement of the husband that the defendant did not tell him what was being done, what had been done during the period when the wife was in the consulting room. Not a word to contradict the statement that the husband asked no questions.

It took the jury just under an hour and a half to find Jackson Palmer guilty of the manslaughter of Mrs. Goldsmith.

An Inspector from Scotland Yard then informed the court that there were no previous convictions against the prisoner. For some years, according to the inspector, he had conducted a genuine business as a medical electrician among well-to-do people. Until about eighteen months previously nothing had been heard either derogatory to himself or his business. Since then, however, from information which the police had received, there was reason to believe that he had been a party to performing illegal operations. It was the custom of the L.C.C. to visit the premises of such people once a year, but his premises had been visited on many occasions, and it was because of certain suspicions that his premises had been visited so frequently.

Asked by the Clerk of the Court whether he had anything to say before sentence was passed, Palmer replied: 'I am not guilty of this charge.'

To this the Lord Chief Justice observed that in his view the jury had convicted Palmer on evidence which was 'so clear as to be quite overwhelming' and which 'approached the certainty of mathematical demonstration'. The judge then announced that he would consider over the week-end what would be an appropriate sentence to pass upon him, and that Palmer should be brought up to receive it on the following Tuesday.

When the convicted man again appeared in the dock, Lord Hewart showed him no mercy. 'Charles Jackson Palmer,' he addressed him in the severest tones, 'the officer who gave his evidence so fairly concerning you mentioned on Friday certain suspicions that you had for some time past been carrying on the trade of abortion. I deliberately put out of my mind suspicions and rumours of suspicions. It is right that I should direct my attention to the evidence and to the evidence in this case alone. That evidence convinces me that you were carrying on the trade of abortion.

'It was as a person carrying on the trade of abortion that you were consulted by Mrs. Goldsmith. Such persons no doubt subject their clients or patients to very grave risks, and it is right that all of them, wherever they may be in this country, should understand that they incur grave risks themselves. The law must have regard to human life, even though the particular life in the individual case may not be of the highest consequence.

'In the public interest it is necessary that you go to penal servitude for seven years and pay the costs of the prosecution.'

It was a peculiarly savage sentence, in view of the police evidence that Palmer had carried on a legitimate practice for many years and in view, too, of the fact that the prosecution suggested that he should pay only a part of the costs. So far as the latter were concerned, the Duke of Westminster came to the rescue with his cheque book, and he also gave Palmer financial help to begin life afresh when he was released from prison. But there was no appeal against the sentence which stood and which was served out.

4

It was at this period that Birkett's name first appeared alongside the name of another advocate, who had already made his mark in the Law Courts. This was Sir Patrick Hastings, with whom Birkett had sat in Parliament, and they now began to be regularly pitted against each other in much the same way as Edward Carson and Rufus Isaacs in the previous generation and more recently Edward Marshall Hall and Henry Curtis-Bennett had been. Hastings had retired from politics, deeply disillusioned by his treatment over the Campbell Case when he was Attorney-General in the first Labour Government.[1] He had also suffered a serious illness, which had kept him away from the courts for some time. But he had recently returned to the Temple and was beginning to rebuild his practice in the most successful and spectacular manner.

The differences in the forensic methods employed by the two advocates were clearly reflected in their respective styles of cross-examination. In its way each was equally effective and produced similar results. Hastings, with his beetling eyebrows, would fix an unfortunate witness with a severe look. 'Now, let me see, Mr. A.,' he would say and proceed to fire questions at him in such quick succession that he sometimes laid himself open to the charge of bullying. His friend Roland Pertwee, with a euphemistic touch, has described his manner in handling witnesses in court as 'cool, concise and gently cynical'. Birkett, on the other hand, had a more suave and polished approach, as well as perhaps a deceptively friendly one. 'I wonder if you can help me, Mr. A.?' he would usually begin. But the admissions which he gradually and eventually elicited, as indeed has been seen above, could pulverize a prevaricating or untruthful witness as completely as Hastings's more robust methods of questioning.

The first of the long line of cases in which Birkett and Hastings appeared together oddly enough found them on the same side, and it was one of the very few such cases in which Birkett was led by Hastings. The plaintiff, whom they both represented, was a professional explorer, Mr. F. A. Mitchell-Hedges, who sued the *Daily Express* newspaper for libel, alleging that the newspaper had published articles to the effect that he was a liar and a hoaxer on account of a bogus highway robbery which the explorer had faked in order

[1] See above, p. 125.

to draw attention to himself, and also to advertise a certain commercial product. The case was tried by the Lord Chief Justice, Lord Hewart, and a special jury, Mr. William Jowitt, K.C., later Lord Jowitt, leading for the *Daily Express*.[1]

In his opening speech to the jury, Sir Patrick Hastings related how the plaintiff had dined with a friend, Mr. Harry Edgell, one evening in January, 1927, at the National Liberal Club in London, and after dinner they both went down to his house in Dorset in a chauffeur-driven car. Near Cobham on the Ripley road, the car was stopped by a man, who emerged from the side of the road and told them that someone had been injured. The chauffeur went down a lane to investigate, and as Mr. Mitchell-Hedges and his friend were following several men jumped out and set upon them. After a short skirmish the men ran away, after tying up the chauffeur with ropes. The attackers also removed an attaché case from the car belonging to the explorer and containing valuable papers and some 'reduced or desiccated' shrunken heads which he had collected in the course of his travels. (The case was afterwards returned to him.) Mr. Mitchell-Hedges and Mr. Edgell informed the police of what had happened, but they declined to prosecute their assailants when their identity was revealed. It was suggested by the *Daily Express* that the whole affair was a hoax and that the explorer was a party to it all along.

'The truth about the battle on the Ripley road,' wrote that newspaper, 'is that it was planned as a publicity enterprise for the identifying device known as Monomark. The originator of the conspiracy was Mr. Clifford Bagot Gray, who kept the joke going by introducing himself to the public as the leader of a young gang of Liberal desperadoes.' According to Mr. Bagot Gray and others, the plaintiff had known about it the whole time and had 'entered into the fun with great gusto'.

When he went into the witness box, Mr. Mitchell-Hedges flatly denied that he had any prior knowledge of the hold-up. But, as the case continued, the hold-up tended to recede into the background, and the defence, directed with what the plaintiff afterwards called 'ruthless brilliance' by Mr. Jowitt, developed into an attack on the veracity of the explorer's expeditions and discoveries.

[1] *Hedges* v. *London Express Newspaper Ltd. The Times*, February 9, 10, 14, 15, 1928. For a fuller account of this case, see Montgomery Hyde, *Sir Patrick Hastings: His Life and Cases* (1960), pp. 166–75.

Since Hastings made both the opening and closing speech for the plaintiff to the jury and also examined and cross-examined most of the witnesses, Birkett had very little work to do. However, he did examine one of the plaintiff's witnesses, Mr. Edgell, who had been with the explorer in the car at the time of the alleged attack.

'Had you any inkling that the hold-up was a pre-arranged affair?' Birkett asked.

'Absolutely none.'

Here the judge interrupted. 'Do you know now that it was a pre-arranged affair?'

'Yes, I do.'

'What was it?'

'I understand that it was arranged by Mr. Bagot Gray as a publicity stunt for Monomarks.'

'Not for the National Liberal Club?' the Lord Chief Justice queried with a chuckle. (Lord Hewart was a Conservative in politics.)

'No, my Lord.'

At this point Birkett suggested that it should be explained to the jury what a Monomark was.

'I have been wondering myself ever since this case began,' the judge observed amid laughter.

The witness was able to satisfy his Lordship's curiosity. 'It is an identifying device which enables lost property to be returned to its owner,' he told him.

'Does it apply to shirts?' asked Lord Hewart.

Finally, Mr. Edgell, who was a member of the Liberal Party Executive, said that he would never have associated the National Liberal Club and the Party organization with any scheme to advertise Monomarks or anything else. After the hold-up he got tonsilitis owing to the wetting which he had received.

Unfortunately for Mr. Mitchell-Hedges, one of the defence witnesses made it so clear that the affair was a hoax—he described how the chauffeur even put his hands behind his back so as to enable him to be tied up more easily—that the jury returned a verdict for the *Daily Express* without leaving the jury box.

The verdict came as a great shock to Mr. Mitchell-Hedges. 'The result of the case, in plain language, was that I was branded as a fraud, a modern Baron Munchausen,' he wrote in his autobiography, *Danger My Ally*, over a quarter of a century later. 'I left the court with my mind in a whirl. I had been proved a liar when I was telling the sober truth. My small reputation had been blasted; many of my so-called friends knew me no more, and my faith in British justice and the ways of the law had received a blow from which—I will be frank—it has never recovered.'

The unsuccessful plaintiff afterwards complained that his leading counsel were half-hearted in their conduct of the case, and also that various witnesses were not called to testify to his meritorious achievements as an explorer. But it was difficult to see what more Hastings and Birkett could have done for their eccentric client. As for the anthropologists and other witnesses of the plaintiff's expeditions, who were not called to give evidence on his behalf, it was because their evidence was quite irrelevant to the truth or otherwise of the alleged libel.

This case provides a salutary example of the dangers of rushing into ill-considered litigation, where the most brilliant counsel are powerless to win a verdict for the reckless plaintiff. The fact is that he would have done better to have simply issued a denial of the newspaper story and left it at that. If he had done so, at least he would have saved his reputation as an explorer.

5

The retainer which Birkett had from *John Bull* now involved him in a curious case concerning the activities of a matrimonial agency which had been exposed in the pages of that journal. The plaintiff, Thomas Owen, who ran a monthly publication called *The Matchmaker* in connection with his business, complained of three articles by a journalist named Sydney Moseley attacking him and his agency in *John Bull*, and sued the owners, Odhams Press Ltd. and the author of the article for libel. The trial took place before Mr. Justice Avory and a special jury in the King's Bench Division.[1]

The articles were headed 'Will Anybody Marry Me?' 'Amazing Marriage Mart', and 'Infamous Editor Exposed'. In them Mr. Moseley said that it occurred to him to go in search of a wife, and then the plan of finding one by advertisement was suggested to

[1] *Owen* v. *Odhams Press Ltd. The Times*, May 17, 18, 19, 22, 1928.

him. As a result he discovered that behind most of these 'lonesome' advertisements were matrimonial agencies which inserted them as a bait, a business which he described with perhaps some hyperbole as 'the greatest scandal of modern times'. After giving particulars of the method of introduction employed by the plaintiff's agency, he concluded with an account of an interview which he said he had had with a 'City Typist', whose name Mr. Owen had sent him and who was referred to in the trial as 'Miss X'. According to Mr. Moseley, this lady had told him that the first man who had called to see her in response to her advertisement in *The Matchmaker*, was nothing like the picture of the man she had dreamt about. He was old enough to be her grandfather, and besides this, he was fat, smelt of drink, and certainly did not want to get married. The next man who called rather shocked her, since he turned out to be a half-caste Mexican. For a moment her blood seemed to turn to ice, and then not surprisingly she bolted.

'Miss X', who went into the witness box rather reluctantly to give evidence for the plaintiff, said that she had seen an advertisement in *The Matchmaker* and had replied to it, since her object was to get married and go abroad. She paid three guineas and was given an introduction to a man described as 'a bachelor, thirty-six, Spanish descent, owning a large farm in South America'. She arranged to meet him in the street near the office where she worked, but when she saw him she did not like the look of him and 'passed him straight by'. She denied that she subsequently told Mr. Moseley that the man looked like a half-caste from Mexico. She disputed other details given in the articles including the one that she was a 'City typist',—she 'did statistical records', she said. As a result of another introduction, she became engaged to a man called Newman, whose home was in Australia. But the engagement was broken off as she was 'not so keen about going out to Australia'.

'I am going to suggest that you are the kind of girl who ought to have somebody to save you from yourself,' Birkett said to her in cross-examination. 'You were nineteen then and, without your parents' consent, you wrote to *The Matchmaker*, because you wanted to get away from home and go abroad?'

'I did not want to get away from home,' answered the witness a little disingenuously, 'but I wanted to travel.'

'For all you knew you might have been ruined by some ruffian or adventurer whom these people might have sent you?'

'That was not likely.'

'What was Mr. Newman?'

'A marine fitter and engineer.'

'Where is he now?'

'I don't know and I don't care.'

'Did it ever occur to you that Newman might have been an adventurer who wanted to take advantage of you?'

'It did not occur to me, but I have never given a thought to him from that day to this.'

'Do you realize that you were on the brink of a very great tragedy for yourself?'

'I am afraid I do not.'

'Miss X' was followed into the witness box by the enterprising Mr. Owen, who said he was fifty-one years old and was a married man living at home with his wife and family. He had been carrying on *The Matchmaker* for five years. Down to the time when he had dealings with Mr. Moseley he had never introduced a male client who did not want to marry any of his female clientele who wanted to marry.

'You mean that the male clients said that they wanted to marry?' Mr. Justice Avory intervened to ask. 'How do you know whether a male client wants to get married?'

'I can only take his word and how he impresses me at the time,' answered the witness. 'If I don't think he is quite genuine, I make inquiries before proceeding further. No man can do more.'

He admitted having received ten pounds registration fee from Mr. Moseley along with his application form, but he denied receiving any letter at the same time in which Mr. Moseley was alleged to have written that he was a married man and did not get on well with his wife.

The plaintiff went on to state in his examination-in-chief that he had attended between two and three hundred weddings in London as the result of his introductions. He gave value for their money to all who came on his register for the purpose of getting married, and he strenuously denied fleecing his women clients. The only two classes of business he dealt with, he said, were 'matrimony and platonic friendship'.

Asked by Birkett in cross-examination when the fashion of platonic friendship had sprung up in his business, this amazing matrimonial agent said he did not know. But he denied that that side of the business had only been referred to in his journal since the present action began.

Birkett then read out several advertisements from *The Matchmaker*, which he put to the witness. The first was as follows:

> Gentleman, age 37, medium height, heavy build, fond of motoring, own car, practically single, independent means, wishes to meet young lady of refinement, not over 30, strictly for companionship only.

Asked what he supposed the advertiser meant when he described himself as 'practically single', the plaintiff replied: 'I can only think that he had had a divorce, and was waiting for the decree to be made absolute.'

' "Strictly for companionship only"?'

'Until the decree was made absolute,' the plaintiff answered without much conviction.

Birkett next read an advertisement by 'a widowed lady, aged 83, who desires to marry an independent gentleman about her own age,' and asked: 'Do you think that is right?'

'I think that there is more righteousness about my paper than there is about the paper and the people you represent!'

Letting this remark pass, Birkett went on to quote from two more advertisements in *The Matchmaker*. The first was by 'a business man (41), with money to spend on a frolic; generous, kind, and debonair, who wishes to meet a young lady who would teach him dances.' The other ended with the couplet:

> Kind hearts are more than coronets
> And simple faith than Norman blood.

The plaintiff said that that was 'a genuine advertisement by a titled lady'.

'I suggest that this platonic business is all nonsense and that these men advertising in *The Matchmaker* wanted to get in touch with women for immoral purposes?'

'I deny that.'

Questioned about a man named Thompson whom he had

introduced to Mr. Moseley, the plaintiff explained that Mr. Thompson wanted to get up a small party to visit Italy.

'Would it surprise you to learn that the address given by Mr. Thompson could not be found?'

'I am surprised at nothing,' said the plaintiff, adding that he had introduced women clients to Mr. Thompson and that they all desired platonic friendship.

'Is it necessary to go to Italy to find it?' the judge interrupted.

'No,' the plaintiff agreed. 'It was an unusual bargain.'

Answering further questions by Birkett, the plaintiff said that he had known of engagements to take place in less than six days.

'What is the record time for two people to meet, fall in love, and be engaged? Five minutes?'

'I have known people to be introduced on Monday and marry on Wednesday.'

When it was his turn to go into the witness box, Mr. Moseley admitted that he had written to the plaintiff and told him that he was a married man, although the plaintiff denied ever having received his letter. But this was 'in the nature of a test', since in fact he was a bachelor. If the agency had been genuine, he said, he would have been turned down on his letter, and he thought that he would have been turned down.

In his summing-up, Mr. Justice Avory said he supposed that no one with any knowledge of human nature, or what might be learned of it from history, would deny that there might be such a thing as purely platonic affection, as it was called, between a man and a woman. What, however, did a pure platonic friendship care for the questions in the advertisements whether a woman's eyes were dark or a man's hair curly; whether he had grey eyes, sometimes blue, or whether the woman's figure was good or a full one? He asked the jury to consider whether it was not merely throwing dust in their eyes to say that those advertisements were intended to promote pure platonic friendships. Did they not, on the very face of them, bear out the defendants' allegation that a part, at all events, of the plaintiff's business was of that dangerous nature which was undoubtedly a menace to the public, of promoting and procuring the introduction of men to young women, some of whom might be perfectly honestly desirous of trying to find a lawful husband, but others of whom wished to find someone to 'come and have a cup of tea' in the afternoon, as one advertiser put it, because they were lonely. If they believed that the plaintiff received the letter which Mr. Moseley said he sent him with his ten pounds, the damning evidence was that the plaintiff, knowing him to be a married man, sent him the names and addresses of six young women. If that were so, the substantial and grave allegation made against the plaintiff would be thereby established, and no wonder the plaintiff had taken the line of saying that the letter was never received. Finally, the judge asked the jury whether they could 'accept that euphemism of platonic friendship which was introduced by the plaintiff to cover up what, to any man or woman of the world, was calculated to lead to immoral relations being established between persons who advertised in *The Matchmaker*.'

After reflecting for two hours, the jury found that they could not accept the plaintiff's story, and they returned a verdict for Odhams Press and Mr. Moseley, whose successful justification of their libel, with Birkett's aid, had the effect of bringing the undesirable activities of one London matrimonial agency to an end.

6

In the summer of 1928 there occurred a sensational official inquiry into methods used by the English metropolitan police in interrogating private individuals. For some time there had been complaints that officers from Scotland Yard were employing 'third degree' tactics, and these complaints came to a head in the Savidge Inquiry, in which both Birkett and Sir Patrick Hastings played leading parts, this time on opposite sides. The inquiry arose out of certain actions taken by the police following the dismissal at a London Magistrate's Court of a charge of indecency affecting a well-known public man, Sir Leo Chiozza Money, and a young woman named Irene Savidge.

Sir Leo, whose father was an Italian called Chiozza, had been born in Genoa and came as a young man to England, where he adopted his present surname. He was an author, journalist and economist, and he also wrote poetry. For a dozen years he had sat as a Liberal in the House of Commons, where he had attracted the attention of Mr. Lloyd George, who appointed him his Parliamentary Private Secretary. He later held two junior ministerial posts and was knighted for his public services. Afterwards he resigned and joined the Labour Party but failed to win a seat in the Labour interest. He was fifty-eight years old at this time, married and had a daughter. About 9.45 on the evening of April 23, 1928, he and Miss Savidge were sitting under a tree near the Albion Gate entrance to Hyde Park, when they were suddenly arrested by two police officers in plain clothes and taken to the nearest police station, where they were charged with committing an indecent offence contrary to the Parks Regulation Acts. 'We are both respectable people,' said Sir Leo, in denying the charge. Next morning they were brought up at Great Marlborough Street Police Court and remanded for a week on bail. During this period Miss Savidge was medically examined, with negative results.

At the next hearing Sir Leo Money, who was defended by Sir Henry Curtis-Bennett, K.C., went into the witness box and repeated his denials of the charge. Evidence was also given by the police that a man in the park had run after Sir Leo with his umbrella, but that the officers who made the arrest did not ask him for his name. At this the magistrate remarked that the man must have been pretty close to the couple at the time of the arrest. The police constable replied that it never entered his head to take the man's name and address.

The magistrate said he had come to the conclusion that the defendants were not guilty and he dismissed the case, with costs against the police. He did so after he had listened to Sir Leo Money's evidence and without hearing what Miss Savidge had to say, as he did not think anything could be gained by exposing her to the ordeal of going into the witness box. At the same time the magistrate criticized the police on two grounds: first, for not taking the opportunity they had of obtaining corroborative evidence, and secondly, for not sending their reports immediately to Scotland Yard so that the Commissioner might, if he thought fit, proceed by summons instead of the accused being charged straight away and taken to the police court next morning. 'If that had been done in this case,' said the magistrate, 'I think that the case would never have been brought and a great deal of pain would have been spared the defendants.'

Sir Leo Money immediately got busy through his connections in official quarters. A few days later the matter was raised in the House of Commons, when it was suggested that the police evidence was perjured. The Home Secretary, Sir William Joynson-Hicks, later Lord Brentford, was asked whether in view of the results of recent prosecutions in such cases he was 'satisfied that sufficient care is taken to establish the trustworthiness of the evidence before the charge is made'. The Home Secretary replied that he would have to consider with the appropriate authorities whether the police officers concerned in this most recent case were guilty of perjury or other breach of duty. He added, in words which caused considerable amusement, both inside and outside Parliament, that, in view of the suggestion that Sir Leo and Miss Savidge had been discovered kissing, 'it is not illegal for any young member of the community to take any equally young lady to Hyde Park to sit in the park, and it is not illegal to salute her with a chaste embrace.' Cartoons appeared in the press showing the embrace taking place, with 'Jix' in the guise of Cupid making a careful inspection assisted by two constables with flashlights.

Meanwhile the Home Secretary instructed the Director of Public Prosecutions to make a full investigation into the possibility of perjury, and the Director, through the Metropolitan Police Commissioner, in turn instructed Chief Inspector Collins to see Miss Savidge, then Miss Egan, the lady who Sir Leo Money had stated in the police court had introduced him to Miss Savidge, and finally Sir Leo himself, in that order.

Next day, two police officers and a policewoman called at Miss Savidge's place of work, and took her to Scotland Yard for questioning. What happened there was raised two days later by a Labour M.P. in the House of Commons on a motion for the adjournment, when it was alleged that during a five-hour interrogation by Chief Inspector Collins Miss Savidge had been subjected to 'third degree' treatment, and allegations of familiarity on the part of the officers present at the questioning were further supported by an affidavit by Miss Savidge which was read out. An immediate public outcry followed, which the Government wisely made no attempt to resist. The Home Secretary promised the fullest inquiry, and shortly afterwards appointed a Tribunal 'for inquiring into a definite matter of urgent public importance, that is to say, the action of the police in connection with their interrogation of Miss Savidge on May 15 1928'.

Sir John Eldon Bankes, a former Lord Justice of Appeal, was

appointed Chairman of the Tribunal; the other members were a Conservative M.P., Mr. J. J. Withers, and a Labour M.P., Mr. H. B. Lees-Smith. The Tribunal commenced its public sittings in the Law Courts on June 6. Sir Patrick Hastings, Sir Henry Curtis-Bennett and Mr. Walter Frampton appeared for Miss Savidge, while Birkett led Mr. H. B. Roome for the police.

Opening the case for Miss Savidge, Sir Patrick Hastings said she was twenty-two years of age and lived with her parents in New Southgate. She was employed by the Standard Telephone Company in testing wireless sets at the company's New Southgate factory. When the police officers arrived at the factory shortly after the lunch break on May 15, they invited her to accompany them to Scotland Yard 'to clear up a few matters about the Leo Money case'.

Miss Savidge then went into the witness box. She was a girl of slight build and was dressed in sober black. It may be remarked in passing that, although she worked in a factory and ordinarily moved in quite a different social circle from Sir Leo Money, she was thoroughly respectable and indeed bore no resemblance to the typical 'good time girl' who would allow herself to be casually 'picked up' by men. Fortified by a bottle of smelling salts, which the usher had considerately placed on the ledge in front of her, she answered her counsel's questions in a low tone and with recurring pauses. She related how Sergeant Clarke and another officer had come to the factory where she worked.

'Did you want to go to Scotland Yard?'

'No, I did not.'

'Why did you go?'

'Well, I felt frightened, and Scotland Yard is a big place. But I thought that I would have to go and the questions would have to be answered.'

'Was anything said by anyone about a woman?' Sir Patrick Hastings continued.

'Yes,' replied Miss Savidge. 'Sergeant Clarke said, "You will be quite all right. There is a lady outside to chaperone you in the car".'

The lady turned out to be a metropolitan policewoman, Miss Lilian Wyles, who had been one of the original women members of the force to join when women were first admitted ten years previously and was indeed an excellent officer.

On arrival at Scotland Yard, Miss Savidge was conducted to a room where Chief Inspector Collins was seated. Turning to Miss Wyles, the Inspector said, 'I don't think we shall need you any more. We will have you to escort Miss Savidge home again.' Miss Wyles, who would gladly have remained, thereupon withdrew, leaving a telephone number at which she could be reached in case she was needed.

'What did Inspector Collins say to you after Miss Wyles had gone?' Sir Patrick Hastings asked.

'He said, "Look here, Miss Savidge, we have you here to tell us the truth, and if you don't tell us the truth you and Sir Leo Money will suffer severely." That was how he started. His manner towards me was very threatening.'

According to Miss Savidge, the Inspector went on to say that she had not been in the witness box at the police court and sworn before God, and he asked her if she did not realize that the police officers had the best of characters and had their wives to think of. Miss Savidge said she had told him that it would be quite easy for her to tell the truth. 'Ah, not always when you are in a tight corner,' the Inspector remarked, to the accompaniment of a titter of mirth in the court room. 'I know that myself.'

Asked by her counsel if anything was said about how much the police knew about the matter, Miss Savidge answered, 'The Inspector said that perhaps I was not aware how clever a man I was speaking to, and that they knew everything.'

Later the Inspector's manner became quite friendly, she said, and even familiar. Most of the interrogation which began at 2.50 p.m. and ended at 7.40 was concerned with her acquaintance with Sir Leo Money. Some tea was brought in at four o'clock. Seeing there was only one spoon on the tray, Sergeant Clarke, who had been employed taking down notes of the interrogation, was said to have offered it to Miss Savidge with the remark, 'Now Irene will spoon with me.' It was an ill-timed jest, which Miss Wyles very rightly described afterwards as not in keeping with the austere atmosphere of a police headquarters, and it created an unfortunate impression, although Sergeant Clarke subsequently insisted that what he had really said was, 'Now Irene will use this spoon with me.' But worse was to come. According to Miss Savidge, the Inspector said to her, 'You are a good girl, and you have never let a man have you.' He then told her that she need not be afraid to tell them, as they were both married men and in addition were 'fond of a good time'.

The sensation, which these revelations produced, was increased when Miss Savidge went on to describe how both officers had told her to stand up and questioned her about the length of her clothes and in particular the colour of her petticoat. Inspector Collins then invited her to give them what he called a 'demonstration' of the episode in the park. The Inspector placed two chairs side by side, on which they both sat, at the same time putting one of his arms round her waist. He suggested that Sir Leo was embracing her in this manner, which she denied. At that moment someone came into the room and interrupted them, whereupon the Inspector drew back and seemed uncomfortable. He then suggested that Sir Leo's right hand was holding her left hand and rested on her left leg.

'Did he ask you whether Sir Leo had done anything with his hand?'

'He suggested that Sir Leo had put his hand up my clothes.'

'Was anything said about sinning?'

'Yes. He went on to say that there were so many things you could do without really sinning.'

At the end of the interrogation, she had signed the statement, which had been drawn up by Sergeant Clarke on the understanding that it would not be made public. She was driven home by the two police officers, who continued to question her, but on the return journey she was not accompanied by Miss Wyles, who had been told on the telephone that she would not be needed. She said she had reached home feeling completely exhausted.

Birkett now rose to cross-examine Miss Savidge on behalf of the police. His first questions were designed to put her at her ease.

'You felt that you had been through a very great ordeal?'

'Yes.'

'Was the statement you made at Scotland Yard a true statement?'

'No, it was not.'

'Is it what you said?'

'No.'

'They have put things down which you did not say?'

'Yes.'

Birkett went on to suggest in a series of skilful questions that Miss Savidge had shown by her conduct that she was perfectly well able to look after herself.

'You are able to take care of yourself?'

'Ordinarily, but I do not understand all this.'

'Is it true, for instance, that you ordinarily come home very late at night?' Birkett stressed the word 'ordinarily'.

'No.'

'Is it true, which is contained in the statement, that, when you met Sir Leo Money, you would get home quite late?'

'Sometimes. But I explained that that was because of my living some way out and of the bad train service.'

'Before this you had spent about half a dozen evenings with Sir Leo Money?'

'It might have been eight or ten.'

'Spread roughly over six months?'

'Yes.'

'And on all these occasions you would arrive home after midnight?'

'Sometimes.'

'By yourself?'

'Yes.'

'Not nervous?'

'No. I know where I live and I am used to the roads.'

'During that six months you knew that Sir Leo Money was a married man with a daughter?'

'Yes.'

'You dined with him, took wine with him, went either to a cinematograph house or to a theatre with him, and then arrived home after midnight?'

'Yes.'

'That indicates that you are an independent sort of girl?'

'I suppose so.'

'In addition to that, you had a young man all the time and you were deceiving him?'

'Yes.'

'For six months you kept up that deception?'

'Yes.'

'After all the publicity you posed to have your photograph taken for the newspapers?'

'Yes.'

Then came the important question to which Birkett had been

gently leading up. 'You knew perfectly well what was happening on May 15?'

'No, I did not,' she replied emphatically. And on this she remained unshaken.

'I am going to put to you,' continued Birkett, 'that you were quite bright and cheerful and ready to go to Scotland Yard?'

'No, I was not,' said Miss Savidge. 'I tried to hide my feelings, but inwardly I was very frightened. It frightened the life out of me when I knew I had to go to Scotland Yard.'

'Was it not made plain from the earliest moment that your visit to Scotland Yard was in respect of a prospective charge against the two constables?'

'No, it was not.'

'If you have been done a grievous wrong and Parliament wants to put it right,' Birkett asked in his sweetest tones, 'why should you not go and tell the truth?'

'It wasn't Parliament that asked me, but Scotland Yard.' This answer produced some laughter, as Miss Savidge went on, 'They didn't say anything about Parliament wanting to put it right!'

'These two constables had made a grievous mistake and done you a grievous wrong. If the desire was to inquire into the matter to see whether what had been done had been done wickedly or falsely, so that they might be punished, would you not have gone readily and told the truth?'

'It wasn't put in that way. When I got there it was not mentioned how bad they might be, but what good characters they had. Even if it had been made clear, I would not have gone, because I was "fed up" with it all and wanted to forget it. I had been acquitted and wanted to be left in peace, and not made to go through all this.'

Questioned further about what happened with Sir Leo Money in Hyde Park, Miss Savidge persisted that Sir Leo had kissed her only once in the park and not several times before the police appeared, and that she had said this after the Inspector had told her there was no harm in kissing. 'It was just a peck at that,' she added, 'not a passionate kiss.' As for her statement, containing the passage about Sir Leo's hand resting on her left knee, she denied that had in fact happened, but the Inspector had suggested it and she had let it go as she was 'fed up' by that time and felt 'awful' and would have signed 'anything to get away'.

Mr. Lees-Smith from the Bench asked Miss Savidge whether the questions put to her at Scotland Yard were like those of Sir Patrick Hastings or those of Mr. Norman Birkett. Her reply caused a roar of laughter. 'It was a mixture between the two,' she said. 'They didn't keep on at me like Mr. Birkett.'

7

Miss Savidge, for whom this was her second ordeal by question, spent altogether five-and-a-half hours in the witness box. When she stepped down to rejoin her mother outside the court, she was observed to be looking extremely pale. Sir Patrick Hastings had intended to call Mrs. Savidge next, but after a whispered word from the solicitor who hurried into court, he informed the Tribunal that Miss Savidge was in a state of acute hysteria and her mother would not leave her.

The girl's father, Mr. John Savidge, was consequently called instead. He described how Sir Leo Money arrived at his house about midnight on the day of his daughter's interrogation. When Sir Leo asked why she had gone to Scotland Yard, Irene, 'who did not seem to know what she was doing', threw a box of matches at him, rushed towards the door, and then fell to the floor in another fit of hysterics. Her father then carried her up to bed.

'The arrest of your daughter must have been a very great shock to you?' Birkett began his cross-examination with characteristic courtesy.

'It was,' answered Mr. Savidge.

'I should like to say,' Birkett went on, 'how very much one sympathizes with you about the matter.'

Asked about his daughter's association with Sir Leo Money, the witness said that he had known about it since it began seven months previously.

'Did you approve of it?'

'I did not disapprove of it.'

'You knew that her age was twenty-two and his fifty-seven, and that he was married?'

'Yes.'

'And that he had a daughter.'

'Yes.'

'Your daughter has an independent outlook?'

'Yes.'

'Has she got a will of her own?'

'Yes.'

'Suppose you had said to your daughter, "I forbid you to go out with a married man that I do not know"?'

'She would have argued with me.'

Mr. Savidge added that he supposed it was vanity that his daughter was sufficiently interesting to attract a man whom he (the witness) knew to be a public man and a gentleman. His daughter had told him that Sir Leo was 'a perfect gentleman and that he always treated her as a gentleman should treat a lady'.

'Did she get back sometimes after midnight?' Birkett asked pointedly.

'I did not altogether approve of it,' Mr. Savidge admitted. 'But she had her own ideas and was prepared to defend them.'

After Mrs. Savidge had briefly confirmed her husband's evidence and the solicitor to whom Miss Savidge had made a different statement next day had confirmed this, Birkett rose to open the case for the police. After submitting briefly to the Tribunal that what had to be considered was whether there ought to have been any interrogation at all, and if so whether it had been properly conducted, Birkett put Chief Inspector Collins in the witness box. With his dignified bearing and white hair, the Inspector certainly looked the personification of a kind and even fatherly investigator rather than the bully accustomed to use 'third degree' methods. His record of thirty-two years service in the force was excellent, he had been publicly commended by several judges and had risen to be Chief Inspector of the C.I.D. at Scotland Yard. After repeating his instructions from the Director of Public Prosecutions, he stated that when he saw Miss Savidge in his room at Scotland Yard, she said she would be pleased to tell him anything and she never departed from this attitude. According to Inspector Collins, she was very cheerful, self-possessed and quite normal throughout the questioning. He denied that he had exercised any threats towards her at any time, nor did he use any blandishments.

'From first to last,' Birkett asked him, 'have you consciously done anything which you did not conceive to be your duty owing to the instructions which had been given to you?'

'No,' the Inspector replied most emphatically.

Birkett resumed his seat, satisfied that his witness had made a good impression.

Hastings began his cross-examination with a most pertinent question, to which there could be but one answer.

'You would agree, wouldn't you, Inspector, that on May 2 Miss Savidge was acquitted of a most loathsome charge which was likely to have a most terrifying effect on a girl of her age?'

'Yes, I would.'

Hastings then passed to the events of a fortnight later.

'On May 15 a motor-car, which I think is known in the Force as the fast car—the most important police car—arrived where Miss Savidge works with two policemen and a policewoman in it and another policeman awaiting it?'

'Yes.'

'It arrived without the slightest indication to her parents or any of her friends that they were coming?'

'Yes.'

'Was it intended to take that girl to Scotland Yard if possible?'

The Inspector paused for a moment before replying, and began to look slightly uncomfortable.

'Very well, sir, yes.'

'I suggest to you that you knew as well as anyone in this court knows it that, if you had told Miss Savidge or her mother of the arrival of that car, you had not the faintest chance of getting Miss Savidge to Scotland Yard?'

'I did not know that.'

'Do you think that anyone sitting in these benches'—Hastings indicated the rows of counsels' seats with a sweep of his hand—'would allow his daughter to go along alone to Scotland Yard to be questioned?'

'Yes.'

The Inspector agreed that he had interviewed Miss Savidge's friend, Miss Egan, at home. Why had he not taken the same course with Miss Savidge? 'It was a matter for me,' replied the Inspector.

To the many searching questions put to him by Hastings about the extent of his interest in Miss Savidge's relations with Sir Leo Money, the Chief Inspector invariably replied that he was only doing his duty.

'Do you not consider it a most impudent thing to ask this girl a lot of questions about the length and colour of her clothes?'

'From the point of view of a police officer, no. I have asked many women far more delicate questions than that.'

'I am sure you have,' was Hastings's sarcastic comment. 'Do you think that she would have gone to Scotland Yard if she had known that all these questions would be asked her?'

'She came of her own free will.'

'Did you ask her to stand up?'

'No.'

The Chief Inspector went on to say that from his point of view the length of her clothes was not important. ('It was important to get the colour and the texture.') At the same time she had it in mind that the dress she was wearing in Hyde Park was shorter than the one she had on the day she went to Scotland Yard.

'She told you that the dress she was wearing on April 23 did not come over her knees when she was sitting down? And no one asked her?'

'Yes,' said the witness. 'And she was bold in doing it! Her anxiety in telling me how she was dressed was to show me how the two officers had made a mistake.'

'I suggest that your main object was to clear the character of the two police officers?'

'No, sir. I have had to investigate the conduct of officers before. I was impartial.'

It was now nearing the end of the third day of the hearing, and Inspector Collins was feeling the effects of his long drawn-out and most pointed cross-examination. Beads of perspiration stood out on his forehead, for he realized that not only was his own career at stake but the honour and reputation of the C.I.D. as well. He stoutly denied that he had ever said to Miss Savidge, 'You are a good girl, you have never had a man.' 'It would have been a most disgusting thing for anyone to say,' he replied, 'let alone a police officer.'

Hastings resumed his cross-examination next morning. 'Do you agree that, if you are going to cross-examine three persons, the most important is the one you get first?'

'Yes.'

'And then you cross-examine the other two persons on the statement you have got?'

'We endeavour to do that.'

'Is it a coincidence in this case,' Hastings continued, 'that the first witness, the most important witness, is the only one who could be persuaded to go to Scotland Yard?'

'No,' answered the Chief Inspector. 'Sir Leo Money was asked to go to Scotland Yard.'

'But you didn't get him?'

'That was a matter for him.'

'Is it merely a coincidence that the first witness was the only one who had no opportunity of consideration?'

'No. She had the opportunity of refusing.'

'Was it deliberate in her case the police came to her without warning?'

'Certainly not.'

'Merely a coincidence?'

'No, the ordinary practice.'

'What is the ordinary practice?' Mr. Lees-Smith asked from the Bench.

'The ordinary practice is that an important witness is asked to go to Scotland Yard or to a police station.'

This was one of the most vigorous and unrelenting cross-examinations conducted by Sir Patrick Hastings in the whole of his professional career, and in the circumstances it is remarkable that Chief Inspector Collins came out of it as well as he did. The other police witnesses included Sergeant Clarke and Miss Wyles. The sergeant, in addition to giving his version of the spoon incident when the tea was brought in, explained that the Inspector did the questioning and dictated each sentence which Sergeant Clarke took down and embodied in the statement which Miss Savidge subsequently signed. He confirmed that this was the ordinary practice. Miss Wyles testified that Miss Savidge had appeared to be composed during the journey to Scotland Yard, and answering Hastings about a suggestion she made that Miss Savidge should powder her face she said that she only did this so that the girl might be 'comfortable'. This led Hastings to allude to this witness sarcastically as 'the comforter', although she denied Hastings's suggestion that it was necessary to lull Miss Savidge 'into a sense of comfort'.

'You did not know that she was going to have an unpleasant time?' Hastings asked the policewoman.

'No,' said Miss Wyles. 'I do not think that she ever did have one.'

The Tribunal called a number of other witnesses including the Metropolitan Police Commissioner and the Director of Public Prosecutions, as well as the young woman, Marie Egan, who had also refused to go to Scotland Yard and was seen by Inspector Collins at home. Her account of the interview differed in some particulars from that given by the Inspector, particularly as regards her insistence that her brother should be present.

Most of the final day of the hearing was devoted to counsel's concluding speeches. Birkett, who spoke for three hours, submitted that Miss Savidge was never in the category of a suspected person, that she was willing to go to Scotland Yard and that she made no request that was not complied with. His principal contention was that the whole situation was changed when Sir Leo Money arrived at her home on the same night. 'If Sir Leo Money had gone into the witness box,' he said, 'he would have shed a great deal of light on the conversation which took place when he saw Miss Savidge at midnight on that day, the conversation at the solicitor's office next day and the why and wherefore of it all. He arrived at midnight, he asked her why she had gone to Scotland Yard and he told her there was no necessity to have done so. It is plain that Sir Leo Money wanted to let the matter drop. Up till the moment he went to her house that night, Miss Savidge never thought for one single moment that she had been subjected to any treatment which she resented in the smallest degree.' It was not until she went to the solicitor's office on the following day that she swore that certain things were put down in her statement to the police which she had not said, all of which were matters affecting Sir Leo Money.

'The issues raised in this case cannot be over-emphasized,' said Birkett in his peroration. 'The case, as presented is one that two police officers entered into a conspiracy to defeat the ends of justice at the expense of a girl. . . . If there has been a conspiracy, the Members of the Tribunal should say so; but, if on a view of the whole facts of the case, you find that the charge has not been made out, I am sure that it will be your pleasure to exonerate the police. The vigilance of the public is a very salutary thing. The liberty of the subject must be quite unimpaired, and that liberty is best preserved by the police not being attacked unfairly.'

The Tribunal then went into private session to consider its findings. Meanwhile, Birkett received the following letter from the Metropolitan Police Commissioner, Sir William Horwood.

New Scotland Yard,
*London, S.W.*1
June 14, 1928.

My dear Mr. Birkett,

Now that the hearing of the Tribunal on the Savidge case is at an end, I would like personally and on behalf of all members of the Metropolitan Police—especially those whose actions were impugned—to thank you most sincerely for the wonderful way in which you conducted our defence. Your summing-up was, if I may say so, magnificent.

I have on all sides been congratulated on the way in which you presented our case. The contrast between our attitudes put forward by you, and the attitude adopted by the leading advocate on the other side has, I feel certain, been appreciated by every fair-minded person. It has certainly been appreciated here and by the many who have written and spoken to me on the subject, congratulating me on our fortune in obtaining your services as advocate. . . .

Again with very many thanks and the real gratitude of all members of the Metropolitan Police,

Believe me,
Yours sincerely,
W. HORWOOD

The findings of the Tribunal announced a month later, were not by any means unanimous, since a sharp difference of opinion between one of its members and his two colleagues arose on the credibility of Miss Savidge's evidence, which resulted in the presentation of a majority report and a minority report. The majority report, which appeared over the signatures of Sir John Bankes and Mr. J. J. Withers, completely exonerated the police and did not accept Hastings's submissions of what had happened. Miss Savidge, according to the majority findings, was not intimidated into answering questions and was treated with no lack of propriety at Scotland Yard; the alleged 'demonstration' did not take place nor was the alleged remark about her being 'a good girl' made by Chief Inspector Collins; neither were Miss Savidge's answers, which she approved at the time, misconstrued or improperly recorded. 'We are unable therefore to accept Miss Savidge's statements on the material matters as to which there was a conflict of evidence between her and Chief Inspector Collins, and we acquit him of any improper conduct during the taking of Miss Savidge's statement. We are satisfied that the interrogation followed the lines indicated to him by the Director of Public Prosecutions and was not unduly extended.'

In his minority report, Mr. Lees-Smith, who agreed with Sir Patrick Hastings, blamed the police, and in particular Chief Inspector Collins, for the method by which Miss Savidge's presence was secured at Scotland Yard. The Inspector also incurred censure for having sent Miss Wyles away, particularly as her presence in the car had been used as an inducement to Miss Savidge to come to Scotland Yard. As to what happened after she arrived, there was a clear contradiction between the two versions of what occurred, and little corroboration could be obtained of the story told by either side. 'The test is the credibility of Miss Savidge on the one side, and the two police officers on the other,' observed Mr. Lees-Smith. 'My conclusion is that Miss Savidge is the more credible witness. The impression that she made in the witness box was that of a frank, simple and somewhat child-like witness, whose evidence remained unshaken under cross-examination. The police officers did not give the impression that they were equally frank in their evidence, but denied both the probable and improbable with equal force. The mechanical precision with which the chief police witnesses corroborated every detail of each other's statements cast suspicion upon their evidence. . . .'

This momentous Inquiry, in which Birkett was opposed by Hastings for the first time, had the effect of introducing three important changes in police methods in interrogating persons who might be witnesses or even defendants in subsequent criminal proceedings. These changes, which had the support of the whole Tribunal, were, first, that the person to be interrogated should in future be clearly informed beforehand of the nature of the statement and the possible consequences involved in making it; secondly, that the statement should be normally taken at the person's home and not at his or her place of employment; and thirdly, that in cases in which a statement to be taken from a woman by the police 'involves matters intimately affecting her morals', a woman should always be present unless the woman being interrogated expressed a desire to the contrary.

As a Liberal, Birkett no doubt approved of these reforms since as he put it in his concluding speech to the Tribunal 'a blow struck at the integrity of the police is a blow struck at the whole fabric of the State'.

CHAPTER VII

THE CREST OF THE WAVE

I

IN the summer of 1928 Birkett led the defence in a poison murder of exceptional public interest. The case was tried at Gloucester Assizes, and it was necessary for Birkett to be briefed 'special' since the assizes were not on his circuit. It was the first case of its kind in which he appeared, and it was incidentally to lead to an important change in the law relating to coroners' inquests.

The story began six months previously in a bleak and lonely cottage at Coleford in the Forest of Dean, where a quarryman named Harry Pace lived with his wife and five children and died after an extremely painful illness. The funeral procession was just about to move off to the cemetery when the coroner's officer suddenly appeared and stopped the burial. The coroner had acted as the result of information laid by the dead man's brother, Elton Pace, and an inquest was ordered. A post-mortem examination was immediately carried out, and this revealed the presence of nine grains of arsenic in the dead man's body, that is over four times the amount of the minimum fatal dose.

When asked by the coroner how her late husband could have got such a large quantity of this poison in his body, the widow, Mrs. Beatrice Annie Pace, could only repeat in a broken voice, 'I cannot tell you! I cannot tell you!'

At the conclusion of the inquest, which occupied twenty-two hearings and extended over four months, the coroner's jury found that Harry Pace had met his death by arsenical poisoning 'administered by some person or persons other than himself and that the case called for further investigation'.

To this the coroner observed that only the committal of a person

WITH HIS SON MICHAEL

WITH LADY BIRKETT

London Express Pictures

KING CAROL AND BARBU JONESCU

Associated Newspapers

MAUNDY GREGORY

Associated Newspapers

MRS. PACE

after a coroner's inquest could bring about an investigation, and that if anyone was to be charged the jury must name the person in question. Whereupon the jury retired again and twenty-five minutes later returned a verdict of wilful murder against Mrs. Pace. She was then arrested on the coroner's warrant and charged accordingly.

The long drawn out coroner's proceedings, which showed that Harry Pace was a thoroughly unpleasant individual and that he had treated his wife most cruelly, aroused considerable public sympathy for 'the tragic widow of Coleford', as the newspapers described her. Mr. A. A. Purcell, Labour M.P. for the Forest of Dean, whose constituent she was, set about collecting funds for her defence from the local people, and it was at his suggestion that the Gloucester firm of solicitors, Wellington and Mathews, who had represented Mrs. Pace at the inquest, approached Birkett to lead the defence at her trial. Birkett agreed to do so and his clerk accepted the most reasonable fee which he could in the circumstances, namely 100 guineas in addition to the 'special' fee of 100 guineas on the brief, with no 'refreshers'.

Like most quarrymen in the Forest of Dean, Harry Pace kept some sheep. But he was not a sheep farmer in the accepted sense of the term, although by dint of saving from his small wages as a quarryman he had managed to accumulate a flock of eighty. These sheep were his dominating passion. He would personally attend to their dipping from time to time, and for this purpose quantities of an arsenical powder compound used as a sheep dip were kept in his cottage.

The accused woman was only seventeen when they got married, and from the beginning she was most unhappy. According to the statement she made to the police after her arrest, in which she also suggested that he had poisoned himself, her husband beat her throughout their married life, which, incredible as it may appear, lasted for nineteen years, although she did leave him from time to time and returned to her father's house. On one occasion Pace tied her to a bedstead with a rope, 'apparently for nothing', and left her there all day while he went out to work, untying her when he came home. He repeatedly threatened to murder her with a razor, and on one occasion he attacked her with a hatchet, but she managed to elude him. 'We have been in our present house nearly four years,' she said, 'and on two occasions my husband thrashed me severely, one about two years ago and again in March before I was having my baby. The first time was with a strap and the second time with a stick. In the early part of last year he threatened to shoot me and I sent for the police.' As a result Pace was fined, but he persuaded his wife who had left him to return under promise of behaving better in future. But things were no better. He had an ungovernable temper, and once he picked up his wife's Pomeranian dog and dashed out its brains against a wall after one of his sheep had been killed on the railway line. 'On this occasion I think he was quite mad. He went and got bricks and threw them at the chimney pots, knocking them off.' Another cause of her unhappiness was her husband's association with other women. 'He was a very lustful man,' said Mrs. Pace, adding that he was twice in trouble for indecently assaulting girls.

The trial of Mrs. Pace for the murder of her husband by the administration of arsenic opened before Mr. Justice Horridge in the Assize Court at Gloucester on July 2, 1928. In accordance with custom in poison cases, the prosecution was led by a Law Officer of the Crown, who in this instance was the Solicitor-General, Sir Boyd Merriman, K.C., M.P., later Lord Merriman. He had with him as junior counsel Mr. St. John Micklethwait and Mr. H. M. Giveen, while for the defence Birkett was assisted by Dr. W. G. Earengay, who had represented Mrs. Pace at the committal proceedings in the police court.

In his opening speech to the jury, the Solicitor General pointed out that sixty-five per cent. of sheep dip consisted of sulphur, and when the powder was mixed with water the arsenic was easily soluble, whereas the sulphur was not. This meant that a colourless fluid could be drawn off. 'I want you to bear this in mind because it is a vital factor in this case,' said the Crown counsel. 'If sheep dip were taken as sheep dip, without the fluid being drawn off and the sulphur left, and taken in powder form, you would necessarily find in the body something like three times as much sulphur as arsenic. No sulphur was found in the dead man's body. Large quantities of arsenic were found, but no sulphur. One can easily understand anyone seeking to poison a victim with arsenic taking care not to put him on his guard by giving something which was indicative of sheep dip by the presence of quantities of sulphur. On the other hand, it is not so clear why a man so minded to administer sheep dip to himself in order to put an end to himself, should take the trouble of getting rid of the sulphur before taking the mixture. . . . If you are satisfied that arsenic was administered in such a form that there was no sulphur in it, and if you are satisfied that that man was not in a position, at any rate during the forty-eight hours before death, to get rid of the sulphur himself, that is an end of the theory of suicide.'

The first witness was the Paces' ten-year-old son Leslie, who was sworn after he had told the judge that he knew the difference between telling the truth and telling lies. Without hesitating the boy said he remembered his father dipping some lambs in a tub before he went to hospital the previous summer. 'Daddy got the powder out of the kitchen to put into the water,' he explained. 'The powder was in a packet in a newspaper and he did not use it all. I remember Daddy took what was left, screwed it in a piece of paper, and put it in his box downstairs.' Later, at Christmas time, when his father was in bed upstairs, he asked him (the witness) to bring him the box which also contained books and papers. His father removed the papers, and then, finding what he was looking for, took the box away.

'What was it he found?' asked Birkett in cross-examination.

'Something wrapped up in paper,' the boy replied.

The next witness was the dead man's mother, Mrs. Elizabeth Porter. She said that during the first part of his illness Pace complained of pains in the stomach and tried to vomit. While he was in bed she offered him a cup of water from the bedside. After tasting it, he said he could not drink it. She then tasted it and found it 'salt and nasty'. She said that she had seen her son alone about a month before his illness began.

Birkett immediately picked on this admission when he cross-examined. 'Did you say before the magistrates that you had not been to your son's house before July for about six months?'

'I cannot remember.'

'Then why do you say a month here today?'

'I think that was about the time.'

'Did you give evidence at the inquest and tell the coroner you had hardly been to your son's house before July, 1927?'

'I suppose I did.'

'You realize the immense importance of being accurate if you can?'

'I am saying the truth.'

'Do you say you never saw your son alone?'

'Not when he was ill.'

'When did you see him alone?'

'I cannot remember.'

'Did you ever ask to see him alone?'

'No, sir.'

Further cross-examined about an illegitimate son of hers, she at first refused to answer Birkett's questions until the judge told her that she must, however painful it might be. She then admitted the fact.

'Do you know that he shot himself while of unsound mind?' Birkett asked.

'I do not know anything about it,' she replied. 'That is the first time I have heard of it.'

'Do you not know that this son is dead?'

'No, sir.'

Mrs. Porter was followed into the witness box by one of her legitimate offspring, Elton Pace, who showed great animosity against his sister-in-law. He stated he had heard the accused say that she wished she could get rid of 'the old bastard', and on one occasion she remarked that she could poison him. Once when he went to see his brother who was ill in bed, he found Mrs. Pace lying across his chest and crying out, 'Harry, Harry, you be dying. We shall not see you much longer.' She was impeding his breath, so he got hold of her by the back of the neck and pulled her off. The witness also related how on one occasion she sent him a note saying the doctor would be at the house at one thirty when he was really there at eleven thirty. The witness called her 'a bloody liar' and she ordered him off the premises.

Cross-examined by Birkett, this witness agreed that he was watching the house at the time.

'What you are seeking to convey is that Mrs. Pace sent a note with the wrong time so that the doctors would come and go before you knew it?'

'It was to keep my mother from the consultation.'

'Did you not trust the doctors?'

'I trusted the doctors, but I did not trust my brother's wife.'

'I put it to you plainly,' Birkett chose his words with some deliberation, 'that this matter of the alleged false time is untrue?'

'It is true,' the witness shouted.

'Did she seem distressed?'

'Distressed!' Elton Pace answered in a tone of contempt. 'No, she did not. She can stand more than that.' He added something inaudible, whereupon the judge sternly told him not to pass comments but to stick to the facts.

'You have just said that she has a bad reputation,' Birkett continued, for the witness had suggested that she went with men.

'Do you say that now to injure her while she sits in the dock on her trial for murder?'

'Well, facts are facts.'

'I suggest that the things you call facts are not facts?'

'It is a fact,' the witness persisted stubbornly.

At this point the woman in the dock broke down and began to sob convulsively. Birkett paused in his cross-examination while she was attended by a nurse.

When she had recovered, Birkett went on with his questioning of her brother-in-law. 'Did Mrs. Pace say, "You are not going to die. You will soon be better"?'

'Nothing of the sort,' the witness replied. 'She was as unconcerned as this here box.' With these words he thumped the rail of the witness box in front of him.

Asked what Mrs. Pace was doing, when he came in response to a message from her that his brother was dying, he replied that she was upstairs making a bit of a row. 'She was unconcerned and play-acting again.'

'What was she doing?'

'She was shouting, "Harry's dead! Harry's dead!" and said she would have one of the best coffins made for him.'

Elton Pace then confirmed that it was in consequence of what he said that the coroner had stopped the funeral. 'I can see now,' he added, 'that I had good cause for saying what I did.'

In his evidence for the prosecution, the Pace family doctor stated that, while Pace was in hospital, he told Mrs. Pace that the hospital authorities thought that her husband's paralytic condition was due to arsenical poisoning contracted during sheep dipping.

'From start to finish of the time that this man was under your care,' Birkett asked the doctor in cross-examination, 'did the prisoner appear to be a devoted nurse and wife?'

'Yes.'

'And, so far as your directions were concerned, did she appear to do all she could to get him better?'

'Yes,' said the doctor. He added that Pace left the hospital at his own request and against his wife's wishes.

Of the other medical witnesses, Sir William Willcox, an expert on arsenical poisoning, who testified that all the post-mortem findings in this case were consistent with death being caused by arsenic, was briefly but brilliantly cross-examined by Birkett.

'Arsenic may find its way into the body through the mouth?'

'Yes.'

'Sometimes through the skin?'

'If the skin is broken.'

'You have from time to time pointed out cases of accidental poisoning from certain preparations such as sheep dip, which contain arsenic?'

'Yes.'

'Also that there was a danger of suicidal death from this preparation?'

'Yes, there is, of course, a danger,' the expert agreed.

'You have pointed out there is a risk of chronic arsenical poisoning from arsenical rashes to those who carry out sheep dipping processes.'

'Yes.'

'If the most perfect methods of cleanliness were not followed during the process, some of the arsenic might be absorbed when taking food?'

'If there were rashes on the hand and the person did not wash his hand.'

The witness added that the arsenic might get into his food in this way. He agreed that the poison might also be absorbed into the system by a man who bit his nails.

The case for the Crown was closed just before the luncheon adjournment on the fifth day of the trial. Immediately the Court reconvened, Birkett rose to submit to Mr. Justice Horridge that there was no case to go to the jury on the indictment. 'The scientific evidence is consistent with administration of the poison by the deceased equally with any other theory,' he said. 'The fact that there was arsenic in the body, the quantity found, the effect upon the organs, all these are consistent with self-administration. The burden on the Crown is that they must exclude it, and that, in my submission, they have not done. Of the Crown evidence there is a very considerable body of positive evidence against administration by the prisoner. Dr. Du Pré said that on every opportunity he had of observing the prisoner she exhibited the demeanour of a devoted wife and nurse.'

Birkett went on to say that the Crown had asked who else had the opportunity of administering the arsenic. 'Every wife in the country has opportunity,' he declared. 'If it is said the prisoner alone prepared the food, that will not do. There was no one else to prepare the food, and that kind of argument would lead to this—that every innocent thing the ordinary person may do becomes some evidence of guilt.' So far as the amount of sheep dip purchased went, the quantities were precisely the same in 1927 as in the preceding five years, and the only Crown evidence of possession was the evidence of that in the box, which had been known to the deceased but unknown at the time to the prisoner.

The judge then delivered his ruling. 'No case has been more thoroughly investigated,' he remarked, 'and no case could have been conducted with more scrupulous fairness by the prosecution than this. I think the Solicitor-General did quite right in leaving this matter to me, and I am of the opinion that it would not be safe to ask the jury to proceed further with it.'

Mr. Justice Horridge thereupon directed the jury to return a formal verdict of Not Guilty, which was accordingly done.

Mrs. Pace received the verdict sitting in the dock with her head bowed and weeping. For a moment she seemed dazed, then her solicitor turned round and, reaching across the dock rail, grasped her by the hand. Then, as soon as the judge had left the court, she shook hands with Birkett. 'And that's that,' said Birkett. 'I'm so glad, Mrs. Pace.' This action was the signal for a great outburst of cheering. Men in the gallery waved their hats and the women their handkerchiefs.

Birkett and his clerk stayed during the trial at the King's Arms Hotel at Cleeve Hill, outside Cheltenham, and each morning a car would take them to the court and call again to collect them at five thirty in the afternoon. As the case finished at three o'clock, they had a wait for the car, and to fill in the time they decided to walk to a nearby café for a cup of tea. Immediately he appeared in the street Birkett was recognized, and there was more wild cheering. 'Edgar,' he said to his clerk, 'this is a most embarrassing moment!'

This popular tribute to Birkett's successful advocacy was echoed by the local M.P. who had sat in court throughout the trial. 'Mr. Norman Birkett's conduct of the defence was magnificent and masterly,' said Mr. Purcell afterwards. 'It will be a classic in criminal annals. . . . It is personally very gratifying that I was able to secure his services on behalf of the tragic widow.'

It may well be that Harry Pace accidentally killed himself. Nor can there be any doubt that in the circumstances the trial jury returned the right verdict in this case, although some observers may possibly have been tempted to adopt the opinion expressed by a distinguished surgeon with regard to a similar case of poisoning forty years previously that, 'once it was all over, she should have told us, in the interests of science, how she did it.'[1]

One immediately satisfactory result of the Pace case was the passing by Parliament of the Act which limits the duty of a coroner to finding the cause of death and debars him from specifically naming any individual as being responsible.

2

The same month of Mrs. Pace's dramatic acquittal witnessed a significant literary event with which Birkett was to be professionally concerned. This was the publication of *The Well of Loneliness*, the now well-known novel by Miss Radclyffe Hall on the theme of female homosexuality. Miss Hall was a writer of distinction, who had won two literary prizes in England and a gold medal in America for an earlier novel called *Adam's Breed*, and her latest work was naturally appraised by the critics with some care. It was indeed a sincere and dignified plea in the form of fiction for the toleration of Lesbianism, and it contained passages of considerable power and

[1] Sir James Paget, Sergeant-Surgeon to Queen Victoria, on the case of Adelaide Bartlett, who was acquitted of poisoning her husband by chloroform in 1886, after a coroner's jury had recorded a verdict of wilful murder against her.

beauty, as was recognized by the more serious journals which reviewed it, including the *Daily Telegraph*, the *Sunday Times*, and the *Times Literary Supplement*. 'I wrote the book from a deep sense of duty,' explained the authoress, who was herself an invert. 'I am proud indeed to have taken up my pen in defence of those who are utterly defenceless, who being from birth a people set apart in accordance with some hidden scheme of Nature, need all the help that society can give them.'

At first it seemed that *The Well of Loneliness* would escape the attention of the popular press. But this was not to be. On August 19, 1929, the *Sunday Express* came out with a sensational article by James Douglas attacking it with characteristic invective. 'It is a seductive and insidious piece of special pleading designed to display perverted decadence as a martyrdom inflicted upon those outcasts by a cruel society,' Mr. Douglas fulminated. 'It flings a veil of sentiment over their depravity. It even suggests that their self-made debasement is unavoidable because they cannot save themselves. . . . I would rather put a phial of prussic acid in the hands of a healthy girl or boy than the book in question. . . . What then is to be done? The book must be at once withdrawn.'

Fearing that a prosecution would follow this outburst unless prompt action were taken to forestall the possibility, the publishers, Jonathan Cape, Ltd., wrote to the Home Secretary, Mr. Joynson-Hicks, offering to withdraw the book. 'Jix', who personally shared the Puritanical feelings of James Douglas, advised withdrawal as the best course, and the publishers acted accordingly. However, in the following month, a publishing firm in Paris, the Pegasus Press, reprinted the book in its original English text and proceeded to import copies into England. Whenever these were detected at the ports of entry, they were seized by the Customs acting on the Home Secretary's instructions, and the Government was consequently accused in various quarters of instituting a censorship. Finally, the matter came to a head when the Director of Public Prosecutions applied for an order under the Obscene Publications Act, 1857, commonly called Lord Campbell's Act, which gave magistrates power to order the destruction of 'any obscene publication held for sale or distribution on information laid before a court of summary jurisdiction'.

The proceedings began before the Chief Magistrate, Sir Chartres

Biron, at Bow Street Magistrate's Court of November 9, 1928, the publishers being summoned to show cause why such an order should not be made. The Senior Treasury Counsel, Mr. Eustace Fulton, appeared for the Director of Public Prosecutions, while Jonathan Cape, Ltd., and Mr. Leopold Hill, the English agent for the Pegasus Press, had as their leading counsel Mr. Norman Birkett, K.C., and Mr. J. B. Melville respectively.

It may be noted in passing that Lord Campbell's Act did not create any new offence and nobody could be convicted under its provisions. It merely provided a summary procedure which authorized the police to search for and seize obscene material; and then by due process of law, if the case was made out to the satisfaction of the magistrate, the objectionable material could be destroyed. Thus, as the law stood, neither the authoress nor for that matter anyone else could be called to give evidence as to the literary value of the book.

For the prosecution Mr. Fulton submitted that the theme of *The Well of Loneliness* was obscene and that 'a person who chose an obscene theme could not but write an obscene book'. He then called Chief Inspector Prothero from Scotland Yard. This witness, who had bought a copy of the book, said briefly and simply that he considered the whole theme offensive because it dealt with physical passion. 'The book is indecent because it deals with an indecent subject.'

In opening the case for the defence Birkett made it clear that the Chief Inspector's evidence was a considerable over-simplification of the issue involved. The book, he said, was concerned not with perversion but with what the medical profession called inversion, that is emotions and desires which with most people are directed towards the opposite sex but here are directed towards their own.

'Do you mean to say,' the magistrate asked, 'it does not deal with unnatural offences at all?'

'I say not,' replied Birkett. 'Nowhere is there an obscene word or a lascivious passage. It is a sombre, sad, tragic, artistic revelation of that which is an undoubted fact in this world. It is the result of years of labour by one of the most distinguished novelists alive, and it is a sincere and high minded effort to make the world more tolerable for those who have to bear the tragic consequences of what they are not to blame for at all.' After referring to the views of the critics, 'which constitute a chorus of praise from those well qualified to speak upon matters affecting literature in general.' Birkett added that there were in court 'people of every walk of life who desire to go into the witness box and to testify that this book is not obscene, and that it is a misuse of words for the prosecution to describe it as such.'

At this point Sir Chartres Biron again interrupted from the Bench: 'The test is whether it is likely to deprave or corrupt those into whose hands it is likely to fall. How can the opinion of a number of people be evidence?'

'I want to call evidence from every conceivable walk of life which bears on the test whether the tendency of this book was to deprave and corrupt,' Birkett explained. 'A more distinguished body of witnesses has never been called in a court of justice.'

'I have the greatest doubt whether the evidence is admissible,' the magistrate retorted.

'If I am not allowed to call evidence, it means that a magistrate is virtually a censor of literature,' Birkett protested.

'I don't think people are entitled to express an opinion upon a matter which is for the decision of the court,' said the magistrate.

Birkett then called Mr. Desmond MacCarthy, a leading literary critic, and he went into the witness box. Mr. MacCarthy said he had read the book.

'In your view is it obscene?'

'No, I shall disallow that,' the magistrate interrupted. Then, fortified by Mr. Fulton's opinion that it was entirely a question for the magistrate to decide whether a book was obscene or not, Sir Chartres Biron continued: 'It is quite clear the evidence is not admissible. A book may be a fine piece of literature and yet obscene. Art and obscenity are not dissociated at all. There is a room at Naples to which visitors are not admitted as a rule, which contains fine bronzes and statues, all admirable works of art, but all grossly obscene. It does not follow that because a work is a work of art it is not obscene. I shall not admit the evidence.'

Birkett then formally tendered thirty-nine other witnesses. 'The evidence which a number of them would have given is identical with that of Mr. MacCarthy,' he submitted. 'In a second category are distinguished authors and authoresses who would have said that they had read the book and in their view it was not obscene. Other witnesses include booksellers, ministers of religion, social workers, magistrates, biologists, including Sir Julian Huxley, educationists, including the Registrar of Durham University, medical men and representatives of the London libraries.'

But Sir Chartres Biron was not in the least moved by this impressive catalogue. 'I reject them all,' he exclaimed testily.

Birkett next requested the magistrate to state a case for a higher court on the question of the admissibility of the expert evidence he wished to call, since (in his submission) the test of obscenity was not the magistrate's personal view but the view of reasonable men. But this the magistrate refused to do.

Finally, Birkett asked that the summons should be dismissed. 'The contention for the defence is that the treatment of that theme in this book cannot possibly offend against the law or, indeed, good taste,' he urged. 'It is done out of a sense of duty, with a high-minded desire to deal with it as a fact of life. I submit that the theme of the book is a theme which ought to be discussed just as any other phase of life ought to be discussed in order that it may be understood. Therefore, I submit, I have shown cause why the summons should be dismissed.'

But the magistrate could not agree. 'With regard to the point that the book is well written and therefore should not be subjected to these proceedings, that is an entirely untenable position,' he said in the course of his judgment. 'I agree that the book has some literary merits, but the very fact that the book is well written can be no answer to these proceedings because otherwise we should be in the preposterous position that the most obscene books would be free from stricture. It must appear to anyone of intelligence that the better an obscene book is written the greater the public to whom it is likely to appeal. The mere fact that the book deals with unnatural offences between women does not make it obscene. It might even have a strong moral influence. But in the present case there is not one word which suggests that anyone with the horrible tendencies described is in the least degree blameworthy. All the characters are presented as attractive people and put forward with admiration. What is even more serious is that certain acts are described in alluring terms.'

Sir Chartres went on to quote extensively from the book. While he was dealing with a passage which described how 'some women of standing and position, engaged as ambulance drivers at the front' in the First World War 'were addicted to these practices', Miss Hall could not contain herself any longer. 'I protest,' she shouted from her place at the solicitors' table. 'I emphatically protest.'

'I must ask you to be quiet,' the magistrate rebuked her.

'I am the author of this book——' But she was not allowed to finish the sentence.

'If you cannot behave yourself in court,' Sir Chartres broke in, 'I shall have to have you removed.'

'Shame!' cried the indignant Radclyffe Hall, who never lacked courage.

The magistrate concluded by declaring that he had no hesitation in finding that the book was an obscene libel and that it would tend to corrupt those into whose hands it might fall. He then made an order for the seized copies to be destroyed and awarded twenty guineas costs against each of the two defendants. This decision was upheld on appeal to Quarter Sessions, where the Chairman, Sir Robert Wallace, described the book as 'most dangerous and corrupting'.[1]

In excluding evidence of literary merit as he did, Sir Chartres Biron was no doubt correct in law. But to hold *The Well of Loneliness* to be obscene, as he likewise did, Birkett always thought to be demonstrably wrong. Writing shortly after the amendment of the law thirty years later, which now permits expert evidence of literary merit to be given, Birkett had this to say about the case:

> 'I was counsel for the defence of the book and had perforce to read it with a most critical eye, keeping in mind at all times the wording of the Act of Parliament. I felt then, and feel now, that there was no word of obscenity in that book from the first page to the last, and that to call it an obscene publication was a dreadful misuse of language. Sir Chartres Biron condemned the book because it described a certain relationship between women, and Miss Radclyffe Hall, who wrote the book, had not stigmatized this relationship as being in any way blameworthy. . . .
>
> 'It is an indication of the world of rapid change in which we live and of the vagaries of taste that *The Well of Loneliness* is now on sale in every bookshop without the slightest

[1] *The Times*, November 10, 17, 1928.

interference from the police or the Director of Public Prosecutions or anybody else. The phials of prussic acid can be taken freely without apparent injury to the citizen or the State.'[1]

3

Two other cases, in which Birkett was on the losing side at this period, must also be mentioned here. They were both libel actions. The first arose out of an article on capital punishment by Miss Helena Normanton, a leading woman barrister of the day, in the magazine *Good Housekeeping*. Arguing that the Mosaic Law of an eye for an eye and a tooth for a tooth was out of keeping with modern conditions, Miss Normanton wrote:

> 'Up to a few months ago, was there not always Sir Edward Marshall Hall, K.C., in the offing, who might cheat the gallows of its prey? . . . Nowadays, after nineteen centuries of Christian teaching, it may be that the nearest relative is far from wishing for a crude and personal revenge. After one of the most recent of our murder trials—the Stella Maris case—the murdered man's wife expressed her personal relief at the acquittal of the man who had been tried. So here again the basis has altered in a sense which makes the Mosaic Law less applicable than ever.'

Alfonso Austin Smith had been defended by Marshall Hall on a charge of murdering by shooting him a man named John Derham who had fallen in love with Mrs. Smith, the jury accepting defence counsel's plea that the shooting was accidental. Smith now sued the publishers of *Good Housekeeping* for libel, and claimed that what Miss Normanton had written conveyed the impression that he was guilty of murder, although the jury had found he was not.

'You say that "cheating the gallows of its prey" means "saving the guilty"?' Birkett asked the plaintiff in cross-examination.

'It must mean that,' Smith replied.

'Is not the idea of the word "prey" something innocent wrongfully taken—the lion's prey, for example?'

'I don't think so.'

Birkett was bound to agree with Mr. Justice Horridge, who tried the action, that the only question for the jury was whether the article

[1] C. H. Rolph. *Does Pornography Matter?* (1961), pp. 2–3.

bore the meaning that the plaintiff had been guilty of murder. He further agreed that, if the jury came to the conclusion that it did bear that meaning, he (counsel) could not contend that it was fair comment.

The jury did so find for the aggrieved Mr. Smith, and awarded him £500 damages and costs.

The second libel action concerned a notorious solicitor named William Cooper Hobbs, who had been sentenced to two years imprisonment in 1925 for his part in a blackmailing conspiracy, as the result of which the Maharajah of Kashmir, Sir Hari Singh (originally referred to as 'Mr. A.') had been defrauded of £150,000. While he was in prison, various newspapers published highly coloured accounts of Hobbs's lurid past, alleging that as a solicitor's clerk he had touted for clients, that he had financed burglaries, fleeced wealthy young men, promoted doubtful oil companies, instituted a passport office for criminals, received stolen property, associated with the worst race gangs and run a gambling den in Paris. As soon as he was released, Hobbs issued writs for libel more or less broadcast. The first of his actions to come before the courts was against the proprietors of the *Liverpool Evening Express*, for whom Birkett appeared, while Hobbs engaged the veteran Irishman, Serjeant A. M. Sullivan, as his leading counsel. The action was tried by the Lord Chief Justice, Lord Hewart, who throughout the trial showed the most pronounced hostility towards the plaintiff, to Sullivan's annoyance and Birkett's embarrassment.[1]

Cross-examined by Birkett, the sixty-four-year-old plaintiff admitted that he had brought the action 'to show the world and his children that the stories which had been told about him were absolute concoctions, and to get damages.'

'I am glad that you added the last words,' observed Birkett sweetly. 'Have you brought twenty-three actions before this against newspapers?'

'Yes.'

'Is this the first one that has been fought?'

'Yes.'

'Did you issue the writ in this action after you had settled with other newspapers?'

'I could not issue them all at once.'

[1] *Hobbs* v. *Tinling*. *The Times*, December 5, 6, 7, 1928.

'Have you more on your waiting list?'

'I think that there are one or two.'

'Do you seek to suggest to the jury that, apart from this unfortunate matter with the Maharajah, you have had a blameless life?'

'I have always tried to do right, and I have always done right.'

'Do you agree that a man who attempts to blackmail another is a man who has no character?'

'I am not in a condition to answer that.'

'Physically or mentally?'

'Both.'

'Do you mean,' the Lord Chief Justice interrupted, 'that your physical and mental condition is such that you cannot express your opinion of a blackmailer?'

'I think he ought to be shunned,' Hobbs had to admit.

'Have you heard judges say that morally blackmail is often worse than murder? Do you agree with that?'

'I do.'

'Can you conceive a worse case of blackmail than the "Mr. A." case?' Birkett continued.

'Yes,' Hobbs answered. 'Persistent blackmail is worse than that.'

'You agree that a blackmailer ought not to get damages from a jury?'

'Once a man is convicted there is no justification for raking up a pack of lies about him. Nothing can justify what has been done to me.'

Birkett was still cross-examining the plaintiff at the end of the second day when the court adjourned. On taking his seat on the Bench next morning, the Lord Chief Justice announced that he had received an intimation from the jury that they were unanimously agreed that they had heard sufficient evidence in this case.

'Do you mean by that intimation,' Lord Hewart then asked them, 'that, on the plaintiff's own evidence, you are prepared to find a verdict for the defendants?'

'Yes, my lord,' replied the foreman.

'May I take it as a consequence that if, as a matter of law on these pleadings, it is necessary that there should be a verdict for the plaintiff for some amount of damages, your verdict would be for the smallest possible amount?'

'Yes, my lord.'

'In other words, for a farthing?'

'Yes, my lord.'

Serjeant Sullivan immediately jumped to his feet. 'Before that result is arrived at,' he said, 'I should insist on addressing the jury.'

'You would insist?' the Lord Chief Justice queried. 'That is a strange phrase to use.'

'I conceive that I am entitled to address the jury.'

'Please do not use the word "insist".'

'Of course, I did not do so against your Lordship,' said Serjeant Sullivan, who went on to submit that on the plaintiff's evidence there was nothing to disentitle him from recovering substantial damages.

Birkett then said that he had no objection to Serjeant Sullivan addressing the jury, but he would leave the matter in the judge's hands. In these circumstances, he did not propose to continue his cross-examination.

Serjeant Sullivan was now allowed to address the jury, which he proceeded to do in his characteristic, rich Irish brogue. But he had not got very far when Lord Hewart interrupted him in tones of biting sarcasm.

'Are you addressing the jury as counsel, or are you summing up to them as a judge?'

'My Lord,' said the Serjeant, who had some difficulty in controlling his temper, 'I am explaining to the members of the jury the basis on which I consider that they erred when they expressed an opinion without hearing the case out.'

'Then I am bound to point out to you as a matter of law,' the judge remarked, 'that your observations entirely fail to give effect to the numerous admissions which the plaintiff has made in the course of his evidence.'

Asked by Lord Hewart at the end of Serjeant Sullivan's speech if they were still of the same opinion that they had already expressed, the jury agreed that they were. 'We wish to find for the defendants so far as the law allows us,' said the foreman.

But the Lord Chief Justice showed himself unwilling that the plaintiff should get even one farthing by way of damages. 'No doubt,' he said, turning to Birkett, 'where written as distinct from spoken words are defamatory, the law presumes some damage, but can that presumption not be rebutted? May a plaintiff not obviously be so worthless a person that it is impossible for him to suffer damage from any libel?'

'I can conceive the possibility of such a case,' Birkett replied. Then he added, causing some laughter, 'But as the present defendants have paid twenty shillings into court—nineteen shillings and elevenpence three farthings too much—a verdict and judgment for the plaintiff for a farthing would, from a practical point of view, be a judgment for the defendants. I know of no case where a plaintiff who has been entitled to damages has failed to get a farthing.'

'You ask for judgment for the defendants on the footing that the jury have found a verdict for the plaintiff for one farthing?'

'Yes, my lord.'

After the jury had returned a formal verdict for the plaintiff, the Lord Chief Justice directed that judgment should accordingly be entered for the defendants, with costs after the date of the payment into court.

The next case on the list was a similar action brought by Hobbs against the proprietors of the *Nottingham Journal* in respect of an article in substantially the same terms as that published by the *Liverpool Evening Express* with the same counsel on each side. As soon as the case was called, Serjeant Sullivan applied for an adjournment so that his client could consider his position.

To this, of course, Birkett could not assent, since there were about thirty witnesses waiting to give evidence for the defendants. 'I object most firmly,' he said.

'Certainly,' the Lord Chief Justice agreed. 'You need not say a word. I never heard of such an application. If the case is to be gone on with, it must be gone on with now.'

Sullivan then submitted that the case should not be heard by the same jury as the previous case. It happened that no other special jury had been empanelled for that day, and it was a question of either adjourning or going on with the same jury, to which Hobbs now added his objections through his counsel. Had the Lord Chief Justice insisted that the case should be heard by the same jury, Serjeant Sullivan intended to challenge each juror as he was sworn and then cross-examine him on his knowledge of the plaintiff. (This was a common practice in Ireland, where Sullivan had formerly practised, but it was rarely followed in the English courts.)

However, in view of the objection—'I say nothing about its merits' —Lord Hewart agreed that the case should go over until the following day.

Next morning, at the sitting of the court, Sullivan renewed his application which led to a head-on collision between him and the Bench.

'In my opinion there is no reason for an adjournment,' said the Lord Chief Justice, 'and the application is refused.'

'May I apply for liberty to appeal?' Sullivan now asked.

'I do not think you want liberty to appeal,' the judge rejoined in surly tones. 'If you do, I do not give it to you.'

At this Serjeant Sullivan threw down his papers and walked out of court followed by his junior counsel and the plaintiff himself.

Asked by the Lord Chief Justice whether he could account for this curious conduct, Birkett said he was not certain whether the two barristers had left the court to consult with their client or whether it was part of a fixed procedure. 'If the latter,' he went on, 'it is interesting to remember that when this case was fixed in your Lordship's list the ground of the application by the plaintiff's counsel was that Mr. Hobbs should meet with speedy justice. It seems a strange way of obtaining it to leave the court when the case is called on. I must assume they have left the court of set purpose.'

'It looks like part of a transparent manœuvre,' the judge remarked.

Birkett then asked for judgment for the defendants with costs. After this had been given, he applied for the payment out to the defendants of twenty shilings which had been paid into court.

'Are you entitled to twenty shillings, or to nineteen shillings and elevenpence three farthings?' the Lord Chief Justice asked; to which Birkett replied, amid laughter, 'To twenty shillings today—to nineteen shillings and elevenpence three farthings yesterday!'

And this is what he got with the verdict. Meanwhile Serjeant Sullivan had not been idle. It was not long before the Lord Chief Justice learned that Sullivan had been given liberty to appeal to the Court of Appeal against Hewart's refusal to grant an adjournment in the second case. At the same time Sullivan entered notice of appeal against the verdict and judgment in the first.

Six weeks later, the appellate court allowed the appeals 'with regret' and ordered a new trial in each case, the 'regret', in Lord Justice Scrutton's words being 'occasioned by the consideration that it was quite possible that a jury, properly directed on relevant evidence, might properly arrive at the conclusion as had already been arrived at, and the Court would not be able, even if it wanted to, to disturb their verdict.' In short, the Court did not think that Hobbs had had a fair trial according to the rules of law by which a man was entitled to be presumed innocent until he was proved guilty. 'Hobbs is entitled to justice,' said Scrutton, L.J., 'and I hope he will get it.'[1]

In fact, Hobbs got more than justice. He got £17,000, since there were no new trials, the newspapers preferring to settle the actions out of court for this combined sum. It may be added that Sullivan shared Birkett's opinion of the ruffianly Hobbs. 'For half the money,' Sullivan later wrote recalling the cases in his memoirs which it amused Birkett to read, 'I will give leave to any paper that cares to publish any libel that it pleases about me.'[2]

4

There was a prophetic note in the customary Christmas and New Year greetings which Birkett's faithful chief clerk Edgar Bowker sent to his master at the close of that year. 'May 1929 bring you everything you desire,' he wrote. 'I am sure there is nobody who is more proud than I am that you have risen to the height that you have and have firmly established yourself there, and I'm prouder still when I hear on all sides, "And he hasn't changed a scrap!" It's a fine thing to have said of anyone, and it gives me the most intense gratification to feel that I have in any way assisted your rapid strides. Soon there will be no fresh fields to conquer, but the thoughts of the few years as junior, the anxieties of "silk", and then the advance over all comers to the front, will always be a happy memory. . . . I hope you will . . . return . . . to what I foresee will be a record-breaking term.'

In fact, the Hilary Law Sittings were the prelude to a record-breaking year, for Birkett's fees for 1929 amounted to £33,500, a figure which they were never to reach again, although they always remained close to the £30,000 mark. It was during this term too that Birkett received a brief marked 1,000 guineas with daily refreshers

[1] *The Times*, February 9, 12, 13, 14, 15; March 12, 1929.
[2] A. M. Sullivan. *The Last Serjeant* (1952), p. 308.

of 100 guineas to defend a wealthy man on a homosexual charge at Derby Assizes. Briefs were, of course, often marked higher than this in civil actions in the High Court in London, but the fee Birkett got at Derby was believed to be a circuit record at the time.[1]

One day at this period Birkett was travelling home from the Temple on the Underground and he happened to sit down beside his old friend from Cambridge days, the actor Miles Malleson, who was coming from a rehearsal. After exchanging reminiscences,—they had not met for some years—Birkett turned to his companion and said: 'Do you know, Miles, I am making more money than I thought existed in the world!'

A touch of ingenuousness characterized this admission. Although he welcomed his financial prosperity for the sake of his family and relations to whom he was extremely generous, Birkett cared nothing for money for its own sake. It has already been seen how he was always ready to take on poor person's cases for virtually nothing in the way of fees, a practice which did not invariably commend itself to his clerk.

The year 1929 proved an *annus mirabilis* for Birkett. Not only was it a record for fees, but it also saw him re-enter Parliament for his old seat in East Nottingham. Finally, his pride and joy were crowned by the arrival of a son and heir to whom his wife gave birth in London on October 22, and whom they named Michael.

The Parliament elected in October, 1924, following the General Election at which Birkett had lost his seat in East Nottingham, was now nearing the end of its natural term, and the Conservative Prime Minister Mr. Baldwin decided to appeal to the country for a fresh mandate in the spring of 1929. The three political parties combined to put up a record number of candidates, about 1,500 in all for 615 seats in the House of Commons. Meanwhile the electorate had been increased by some five millions mainly as the result of the extension of the women's right to vote, the so-called 'flapper franchise', for which the candidates now had to compete. There were, for instance, 10,000 new women voters in East Nottingham. The main issues concentrated on mounting unemployment at home and the problem of international disarmament abroad. For their election slogan the Conservatives led by the pipe-smoking Mr. Baldwin chose the sedative 'Safety First': the policies of the Liberals and the Socialists

[1] *Daily Mail*, March 6, 1929.

were more dynamic and on this occasion the majority of the country favoured them.

In East Nottingham, Birkett, who had nursed the division as best he could for the Liberals during the preceding four and a half years, was readopted as the official candidate. Again he had to face a three-cornered contest, but this time he was much better known than either of his two opponents. The sitting Conservative Member, Mr. Edmund Brocklebank, who had defeated him in 1924, did not seek re-election. His place was taken as Conservative candidate by a young barrister, Mr. (later Sir) Louis Gluckstein, who was a stranger to the division. Mr. Gluckstein was also to some extent handicapped by his un-English name and Jewish origin, as also was the Labour candidate Mr. J. H. Baum. Birkett, on the other hand, was widely known and in particular appealed to the women voters largely on account of his success in securing the acquittal of Mrs. Pace, for whom sympathy had been nation-wide.

The campaign was conducted in perfect weather, and the blue skies and sunshine encouraged Birkett's campaign organizers to hold most of their meetings in the open air. As a rule he would speak for anything up to half an hour, followed by another half or three quarters of an hour for questions. That Birkett encouraged questions and replied to them freely gave him an additional advantage over his opponents, neither of whom did so.

At one of these first open-air meetings, Birkett came in for some severe heckling, and for a few minutes it looked as if the meeting would break up in disorder. Then a remarkable thing happened. A burly figure of a man was seen pushing his way through the crowd, at the same time demanding silence in the most powerful tones. As soon as he reached the edge of the platform, he turned round to face the hecklers, and pointing at Birkett said: 'Now, you people, listen to me! This gent looked after me when I was in trouble at the Assizes and saved me from a "lagging". From now on anyone who tries to interrupt him will have to reckon with me and I'll knock his block off. Understand?'

In the sudden silence which followed this outburst, Birkett recognized the poacher, whom he had defended on a dock brief at Lincoln some years previously. The poacher had not forgotten his benefactor and thereafter constituted himself a bodyguard, attending all Birkett's subsequent meetings and keeping a watchful eye open for any further trouble. As he invariably made himself known among the crowd, needless to say no further trouble occurred from hecklers.[1]

Polling took place on May 31, 1929. The result in East Nottingham was as follows:

Norman Birkett, K.C. (L)	14,049
L. H. Gluckstein (C)	11,110
J. H. Baum (Lab.)	9,787
Liberal Majority	2,939

Thus Birkett won back for the Liberals the seat which he had held in their interest in the short 1924 Parliament. 'Well done, East Nottingham!' he said from the steps of the City Hall when the result was declared. 'It is one of the most remarkable victories in the country. I have always been proud of East Nottingham, but I have never been prouder than I am today.' It was indeed one of the fifty-nine Liberal victories in the country and the only one among the four Nottingham divisions.

The Liberals polled five million votes, as against eight million each which went to the Conservative and Labour parties, but this proportion bore little relation to the distribution of seats in the new House, thanks largely to the vagaries of the English electoral system. The final figures showed that Labour was now the strongest single party in the Commons with 287 seats, the Conservatives came next with 261, while the Liberals succeeded in capturing 59, only nineteen more than they gained in the disastrous 1924 election, although they had polled nearly one quarter of the total number of votes cast.

As soon as he arrived at Westminster, Birkett went to the library where he sat down and wrote his wife the following characteristic note.

House of Commons,
2 *June*, 1929.

My very dear darling,

His first letter from the House must be to his Private Secretary!

He sends her all his love.

Her loving M.P.

NORMAN

[1] See above, pp. 107–8.

Since the Conservatives were no longer the largest single party in the Commons, unlike the position after the 1923 election, Mr. Baldwin decided he ought to resign immediately without waiting to meet Parliament, as he had done on the previous occasion. Accordingly he delivered up his seals of office to the King, who immediately sent for the Labour leader Mr. Ramsay MacDonald to form a Government. Its principal members were sworn in at Windsor Castle on June 10.

While Mr. MacDonald had little difficulty in filling the principal departmental posts, the appointment of the two Law Officers presented a difficulty, since there were virtually no experienced Labour lawyers in the new House of Commons. Sir Patrick Hastings, who had been Attorney-General in the first Labour Government in 1924, had retired from politics in disillusion and was thus no longer available. To the general surprise and, it must be added, the disgust of his Liberal colleagues, Mr. William Jowitt, K.C., M.P., who had sat in two previous Parliaments as a Liberal and had been elected to the new one under the same colours, suddenly decided to join the Labour ranks in order to qualify for the post of Attorney-General which had been offered to him by the new Prime Minister.

At the same time, according to a London evening newspaper, Birkett was approached on behalf of the Prime Minister with the tentative offer of the office of Solicitor-General if he would follow Jowitt's example. 'He replied in effect that he for one could not change his politics in twenty-five minutes. The view of those who know him best is that even if the Liberal Party should disintegrate completely he would not be seen taking refuge in the Labour ark.'[1]

As in 1924, the MacDonald Government was hampered by the fact that it ruled by favour of the Liberals who could combine with the Conservatives to defeat it at any moment. Hence its domestic legislative programme was tentative and vague and the Bills it introduced were apt to be either drastically amended or else completely blocked as the result of Liberal tactics. As for the Liberal Party leadership it was in effect a duumvirate with Asquith nominally leading it from the Upper House to which he had recently been translated as Earl of Oxford, while in reality Lloyd George was trying to lead it from the Commons in spite of his differences with Asquith's supporters and the fact that the nominal Deputy Leader

[1] *Evening News*, June 8, 1929.

was Mr. Herbert Samuel, who had returned as an M.P. after an absence of ten years.

Owing to the enormous progress which he had made in his profession since the previous Parliament in which he sat, Birkett's name meant much more to the House than it had done then, and when he did rise to speak he was heard with much greater attention. But on account of the demands of his practice, he could still only follow the rule he had set himself five years previously, that was to speak but seldom and then only on subjects which touched him deeply. One of these occurred during the first few weeks of the new Parliament and in fact arose from an incident in the election.

The incident concerned a thirteen-year-old boy named Wilfred Carpenter on election day in the Yorkshire division of Barnsley, where he was minded to wear political colours. 'They happened to be the Liberal colours,' said Birkett who introduced the subject on the motion for the adjournment, 'but I trust that whatever colours they had been I should have raised this matter had I had an opportunity in this House.' Two men who supported the Labour candidate pursued the boy and told him to discard the colours. When the boy refused, one of the men twisted his arm so severely that he broke it, an assault which Birkett rightly described as 'unprovoked, unjustifiable, brutal and cowardly'. The men were prosecuted at the local police court, but the Justices merely fined the man who broke the boy's arm the sum of two pounds and his companion one pound. The facts of the case had occasioned a great amount of disquiet in the public mind, Birkett went on, and much of it arose from the fact that 'the political complexion of the Bench was the same as the political complexion of the defendants'.

This revelation caused cries of 'Oh!' from the Ministerial benches. It also led the Speaker to intervene and warn Birkett that he must be careful not to criticize a judicial decision in a particular case. 'I only mentioned the matter,' said Birkett apologetically, 'lest it might be said that a most material factor had been omitted and that I had misled the House.' He concluded by suggesting to Mr. Short, the Under-Secretary for Home Affairs, who answered for the Government, that the Home Secretary should order an inquiry or at least he should send the papers in the case to the Lord Chancellor for his consideration. This latter action the Minister promised to take.

Speaking from the Opposition Front Bench, Mr. Winston Churchill on behalf of the Conservatives approved this move, while Mr. Lloyd George also gave it his blessing. 'We are here dealing with a judicial matter where the facts are not in dispute,' said the former Liberal Premier, 'and the Under-Secretary has acted in a way which is exceedingly gratifying, not merely to honourable Members here, but to all who desire that our Elections should be conducted in a manner in which brutality and violence shall not overcome judgment.'

Fortunately, as the Minister said in congratulating Birkett on the skill and effort with which he had discharged his task, 'such incidents are rare in our election contests' and 'our political fights are carried on with good conduct and good sense'. Nevertheless liberties once won must be preserved and on this occasion Birkett proved himself a vigilant guardian of one of the most important in English political life.[1]

5

Most of the cases in which Birkett appeared were widely noticed in the newspapers by reason of their public interest at the time, although many of them have now been forgotten. Comparatively few, however, found a place in the official Law Reports, since these cases were mostly heard before special juries where the matter at issue was usually one of fact and seldom involved an important or novel point of law. But one of his cases at this period did become a leading case in the law of libel after it had gone to the House of Lords for a final decision. This was the case in which Mr. Cyril Tolley, the amateur golf champion sued J. S. Fry & Sons Ltd., the well-known firm of chocolate manufacturers, in respect of an advertisement inserted by the firm in sixty-four newspapers, which Tolley claimed had infringed his amateur status.

The alleged libel consisted of a caricature of the champion playing a stroke while a caddy looked on. Below the picture appeared the following limerick:

> The caddy to Tolley said: 'Oh, Sir!
> Good shot, Sir, that ball see it go, Sir.

[1] Hansard. *Parliamentary Debates, House of Commons*, July 23, 1929.

My word, how it flies
Like a Cartet of Fry's
They're handy, they're good, and priced low, Sir.'

Cyril Tolley complained that the advertisement meant that he had allowed his portrait to be exhibited for the purpose of advertising the defendants' chocolate; that he had done so for gain and had thus prostituted his reputation as an amateur golfer. The defendants admitted publication but denied the innuendo and said that the words were incapable of constituting a libel. The action was tried before Mr. Justice Acton and a common jury in the King's Bench Division, Mr. Rayner Goddard, K.C. (later Lord Goddard, Lord Chief Justice) appearing as leading counsel for the plaintiff and Birkett leading for the defendants.[1]

The plaintiff, who presented as formidable a figure in the witness box as on the golf course, said he was a stockbroker by profession and that he had won the Amateur Golf Championship in 1920 and again in 1929. He had no idea whatever that the cartoon was being prepared, he said, and emphasized that in his view such an imputation on a golfer's amateur status was likely to prevent him from playing in the amateur championship. However, when he was cross-examined by Birkett, he admitted that he had won the championship since the appearance of the advertisement.

'You are a public figure?' Birkett went on to ask.

'I suppose so,' the champion admitted.

'Is it not the delight of the public to picture you as bigger than you are?'

'It is one thing they can caricature about me.'

In reply to further questions from Birkett, the witness admitted that other well known people had been caricatured in similar advertisements including several Cabinet Ministers. 'But they are professionals,' was the amateur champion's comment when the Minister's names were put to him.

'You don't complain of the drawing, do you?'

'It is not a particularly good swing,' said the witness, 'and I don't think it's a very good limerick. The presence of a packet of chocolate in my pocket insinuates that I chew chocolate when I play golf!'

[1] *The Times*, July 24, 1929.

'That is hardly libellous,' Birkett rejoined. 'It has been made quite plain, I hope, that you received no payment, were not consulted, and gave no approval whatever to this cartoon. It is well that that should come from the defendants.'

In the circumstances all that Birkett could do was to argue that the case was not really one of libel but of the unauthorized use of the plaintiff's name. But the judge could not agree with this submission and ruled that there was a case to go to the jury. In due course the jury returned a verdict for the plaintiff and awarded him one thousand pounds damages.

The defendants appealed, and the Court of Appeal unanimously allowed the appeal, Lords Justice Greer and Slesser on the ground that the advertisement was not *prima facie* defamatory and Lord Justice Scrutton on the ground that the damages were excessive. But the House of Lords reversed this judgment by a majority of four to one and held that the trial judge had been correct in allowing the issue to be decided by the jury. Thus this interesting case, which Birkett argued unsuccessfully from the court of first instance to the highest court in the land, is an authority for the important proposition in the law of libel that language or conduct which in its natural or ordinary meaning is innocuous may be rendered defamatory by reason of the special circumstances in which it is published.[1]

It was in 1929, too, that Birkett was instructed for the defence in two separate cases involving large-scale frauds by company directors in the City of London. The cases were initiated, as such cases often are, by the action of chartered accountants, and both cases were prosecuted to conviction at the Old Bailey, so that once again Birkett was on the losing side. In the first, a fifty-year-old self-made man named Charles Albert Brandreth was charged with publishing a false balance sheet relating to a company he had founded named

[1] *The Times*, March 24, 1931. 'I find that the caricature of the plaintiff, innocent in itself as a caricature, is so to speak embedded in an advertisement. It is held out as part of the advertisement, so that its presence there gives rise to speculation as to how it got there, or in other words provokes in the mind of the public an inference as to how and why the plaintiff's picture, caricatured as it was, became associated with a commercial advertisement. The inference that is suggested is that his consent was given either gratuitously or for a consideration for its appearance. . . . It seems to me that all this is within the province of a jury to determine. The idea of an inference in the circumstances is not so extravagant as to compel a Judge to say it was so beside the mark that no jury ought be allowed to consider it.' See *Tolley* v. *Fry*, Law Reports [1931] A.C. 333, *per* Lord Dunedin, at p. 342.

Ner-Sag Limited, and with making false entries in an invoice book of the company.

Brandreth was by trade a motor mechanic and he had spent most of his working life as a fitter at the bench, although he had also had a confectioner's shop in Nottingham. Some years previously he had invented a mattress support and patented the invention. At first he had very little money and he and his wife made the supports at their house in Ilford. But the business prospered and he eventually turned it into a limited company. Although he pretended to be a child in matters of company finance, he proceeded to speculate in the shares of Ner-Sag Ltd., by which he enriched himself to the extent of £110,000. Meanwhile the £1 shares of the company had risen to £9 on the Stock Exchange, and in order to keep up the price Brandreth was alleged to have deliberately invented bogus orders purporting to be from other companies in which he and his wife had a controlling interest. When the investigation by a firm of City accountants was ordered following upon a shareholder's complaint at a company meeting, the subject was taken up by the Press and Brandreth was pursued by every kind of inquiry. This caused him to take fright; he altered his appearance by shaving off his moustache, assumed the names of Gordon Bell and moved secretly into another house. He was eventually traced and charged with fraud.

Brandreth gave evidence in his own defence. However, he did not cut a very convincing figure in the witness box and the jury refused to accept Birkett's plea that he had acted foolishly as the result of a great business being suddenly thrust upon him but that he had never acted with intent to defraud. In the event the jury found him guilty and the Recorder of London, Sir Ernest Wild, sentenced him to four years penal servitude. In passing this sentence, the Recorder made it clear that, if it were not that 'up to a point' Brandreth had had an honest business, he would have given him the maximum sentence.[1]

The other big fraud case in which Birkett was concerned at this time did involve the maximum sentence. It began with a telephone call one Friday in September, 1929, from Sir Gilbert Garnsey, a well-known City accountant, to Sir Archibald Bodkin, the Director of Public Prosecutions. Sir Gilbert said that he had with him a group of company directors whom he had advised to see Sir Archi-

[1] *The Times*, April 23, 24, 25, 26, 30; May 1, 2, 1929.

bald urgently. Bodkin asked what they wanted. 'To confess to fraud,' was the answer.

'Fraud?' queried the Director. 'What sort of fraud? What have they done?'

'It is fraud and forgery, as far as I can see,' the accountant replied. 'And the amount involved is stupendous. How much? It may well be in the order of £20,000,000!'

Next morning the members of the group were shown into Sir Archibald Bodkin's office. Their leader gave his name as Mr. Clarence Hatry.

6

Clarence Charles Hatry was forty years old at this time. A brilliant financier, he had personally launched many prosperous companies in the City of London in the nineteen-twenties and he had had a hand in many other floatations. He was ahead of his time in realizing how industries could be 'stream-lined' by the profitable amalgamation of a number of separate concerns, and he had carried through various successful company mergers notably in the fields of glass and jute. He next turned his attention to steel, and the successful promotion of Allied Ironfounders Ltd., a £3 million combine of light castings manufacturers, early in 1929, led to Hatry being invited to undertake the 'rationalization' of the heavy steel industry. Hatry's own principal company was Austin Friars Trust Ltd. which had been incorporated in 1927 with a capital of £300,000. After its formation it had raised over £4,000,000 in respect of the sale of shares in the steel companies which it had bought. The money came in part from pledging the shares and in part from the activities of certain syndicates, but there was more than enough to pay the shareholders the full purchase price of their shares. However, about £1,500,000 of the £4,000,000 which was raised had been initially used by Hatry and his business associates for purposes other than the immediate reimbursement of the steel companies' shareholders, namely to keep up the price of the shares in Hatry's companies, and it was the need to recover this sum and apply it to its proper purpose which led Hatry and the other directors of Austin Friars Trust and associated companies to embark on a peculiarly unfortunate course.

A directors' meeting was held one Sunday in June, 1929, at

Hatry's London house. Besides Hatry, there were present Edmund Daniels, Hatry's right-hand man, who had once been a bank clerk and was now only thirty-two years old, John Dixon, who had risen from being an office boy, Albert Tabor, a relative junior on the board, and John Gialdini. The last named was an Italian and it was this director who made the suggestion which when acted upon was eventually to bring Hatry and his fellow directors, except Gialdini himself, to the dock at the Old Bailey.

One of the companies in the Hatry group was Corporation and General Securities Ltd. In fact, it was next in importance to the Austin Friars Trust. Although it was unpopular with the older-established underwriters, it had a genuine and lucrative business in handling loans for municipal corporations. The latter included the Corporations of Swindon, Gloucester and Wakefield, and stock for amounts of up to £500,000 had been issued by Corporation and General Securities on behalf of each of these corporations. In an attempt to find a way out of the group's financial difficulty, Gialdini now proposed to have some additional bearer scrip certificates relating to the stock printed for use as security for bank loans. They could be redeemed later, he urged, when the situation became easier and funds were available. Otherwise the steel merger would fall through and they would all be ruined.

Hatry and the others were at first somewhat taken aback by this daring proposal and some of them it appears were reluctant to accept it. But when Gialdini threatened to blow out his brains before their very eyes 'rather than face disaster' Hatry in a weak moment assented and the rest followed. After all, he reassured himself and his associates, the duplicated stock would be redeemed immediately the steel negotiations went through, and everything would be all right. In Birkett's words, 'there was no thought of ultimate fraud. It was a great gamble in which Hatry pledged his liberty and reputation and everything that made life worth living so that he might save from ultimate loss a great many innocent people.'

Unfortunately everything was not all right. Additional certificates to the face value of over £1,600,000 were printed, of which £789,000 were used to borrow money. In addition, £200,000 of the unauthorized stock was exchanged for genuine Birmingham Corporation stock. Shortly afterwards unpleasant rumours about the Hatry companies began to circulate in the City, and the apparently large amounts of scrip certificates relating to the Wakefield stock in particular that were being dealt in began to arouse suspicions. The upshot was that the Stock Exchange suspended dealings in the shares of the Austin Friars Trust, and the company was eventually put into compulsory liquidation. At this time Sir Gilbert Garnsey, the accountant, estimated that its liabilities were in the region of £19,000,000, while its assets amounted to only £4,000,000. It was immediately followed up by a petition for the winding-up of Corporation and General Securities, in whose name the additional scrip certificates were issued and whose principal asset was a claim against Austin Friars Trust for £2,700,000, of which only £500,000 was secured. Meanwhile Hatry had heard that Sir Gilbert Garnsey had been instructed by certain banks to make investigations into the affairs of his group and he made up his mind to go to the accountant and make a clean breast of the whole sorry business. He was accompanied on his mission by Daniels, Tabor and Dixon, but not by Gialdini, the real instigator of the fraud, who had fled to Italy on the first signs of approaching trouble. 'I wish to say there are irregularities,' Hatry told the accountant. 'We want to make a complete statement before the investigation is begun.'

It was on the strength of this statement that the accountant arranged for the men to see the Director of Public Prosecutions, who in turn handed them over to the police. Unfortunately for Hatry his reference in the statement to 'fictitious Corporation stock' suggested that municipal bonds had actually been forged. This was misleading, since the unauthorized scrip certificates were issued in the name of Hatry's company, Corporation and General Securities Ltd. which as sponsor of the municipal loans in question it was entitled to do. Of course, the scrip certificates could be exchanged for genuine municipal corporation loan stock. In the result, Hatry and his associates were charged with fraud and remanded in custody to appear before the magistrates in the Guildhall.

The proceedings in the magistrate's court were protracted by reason of the complicated nature of the charges, and the four accused men were brought up five times before being committed for trial at the next Old Bailey sessions. On each occasion the presiding magistrate refused to grant bail. After a similar application had been made to a High Court judge in chambers and likewise turned down, Birkett, who had been instructed in Hatry's defence, renewed his application on October 15 in open court before a bench of two other judges. He pointed out that earlier in September, Hatry, who possessed a passport, had been in Paris with Daniels, and he could easily have absconded then, but he preferred to return to England with his colleagues and render every assistance he could in the matter of the investigation which Sir Gilbert Garnsey was making. He had made no attempt to evade arrest. On the contrary, it was of very great importance, as Birkett stressed, that the genesis of the whole proceeding was Hatry's voluntary surrender to the authorities. If the Court refused bail because the present case was a serious one, a precedent would be set up and no man in the future who was charged with a serious offence would be able to obtain bail. 'A denial of bail to Mr. Hatry,' said Birkett, 'would be a denial of true justice.'

But their Lordships could not agree. 'If I was satisfied that, when they went to the Director of Public Prosecutions, the defendants knew what they might be charged with on the statement which they made, it might have induced me to come to a different conclusion,' said Mr. Justice Branson in rejecting the application. 'But I am not satisfied that these men at all realized the gravity of the offence with which they could be charged and what, in these statements they were confessing. Consequently, although no doubt at that time they were prepared to face the Director of Public Prosecutions and put themselves into the hands of the police, I am by no means satisfied that they would be of the same opinion now, should they be granted bail and given an opportunity to evade trial for which they are being held in custody.'

And so Hatry and his three fellow directors went back to Brixton Prison, there to await their trial which the prosecution was not ready to begin until over three months later. Unhappily for the defendants, the preliminary proceedings, and indeed the trial itself, could not have taken place at a more unfortunate time. While they were under arrest and awaiting trial, the New York stock markets collapsed, and the terrible losses incurred on Wall Street were necessarily reflected on the London exchange. Many small investors blamed the 'Hatry crash' for the drastic marking down of their holdings, although Hatry's dealings had nothing to do with these later market trends.

The trial opened before Mr. Justice Avory at the Old Bailey on January 20, 1930. All the defendants were charged with conspiring with Gialdini and other persons unknown to forge municipal scrip certificates. Hatry was further charged with obtaining money and valuable securities by false pretences for Austin Friars Trust and his other companies. They pleaded Not Guilty to these charges. No less than eleven counsel were engaged in this sensational case. Hatry was defended by Mr. Norman Birkett, K.C., M.P., and Mr. St. John Hutchinson; Daniels by Sir Henry Curtis-Bennett, K.C., and Mr. Christmas Humphreys; Dixon by Mr. Cecil Whiteley, K.C. (later Common Serjeant), and Mr. Walter Frampton; and Tabor by Mr. Roland Oliver, K.C. (later Mr. Justice Oliver) and Mr. Russell Vick. The Attorney-General, Sir William Jowitt, K.C., M.P., led Mr. H. M. Giveen and Mr. H. D. Roome for the Crown.

So multifarious and complex were the financial transactions involved in the charges against the defendants that it took the Attorney-General four full days to present the case for the prosecution. During this time a procession of bankers, accountants and other experts followed each other into the witness box and gave evidence which made the spectators' heads reel with the vastness of the figures with which they dealt. As Birkett's clerk Edgar Bowker put it, millions of pounds were glibly mentioned as though they were so many bus tickets. All that Birkett could do in cross-examining these witnesses was to try to demonstrate Hatry's reputation for financial integrity in all his previous dealings in the City. Among them was the manager of the Threadneedle Street branch of Lloyd's Bank, which were the Hatry group's bankers. This witness agreed with Birkett that the amount of money going through the bank on the group's account was in the neighbourhood of £100 millions.

'Was all the business which was done by those companies with you conducted regularly and properly?' Birkett asked.

'Yes,' said the manager, 'nothing ever came to our notice.' But he added that in the spring of 1929 the companies appeared to be short of money.

'Many admirable and excellent people are short of money,' Birkett commented amid laughter.

'And so are many others,' Mr. Justice Avory broke in ominously from the Bench.

Hatry's solicitor for the past sixteen years, Mr. Stanley Passmore, was another of the Crown witnesses. Cross-examined by Birkett, he agreed that in order to save an older company, the Commercial

Corporation of London, which was in difficulties, Hatry had used the whole of his personal fortune of some £750,000 to pay the company's liabilities.

'Did Mr. Hatry thereafter, and in addition to the payment of the £750,000, take over all the liabilities of the Commercial Corporation of London and make himself personally responsible for them?'

'For the greater proportion of them, if not all.'

'After 1920 did Mr. Hatry float many companies?'

'Yes.'

'Amounting in capital to many millions of pounds sterling?'

'Yes.'

'The majority of those companies are today sound and flourishing concerns?'

'Many of them are.'

'From your personal knowledge of Mr. Hatry during all those years,' Birkett went on to ask the solicitor, 'did you form the opinion that he was a capable man of business?'

'A very brilliant man,' Mr. Passmore was obliged to admit.

'And carried through many important and complicated financial matters?'

'Yes.'

Sir Gilbert Garnsey also gave evidence for the Crown and was cross-examined by Birkett. He described the meeting in his office with the defendants. What Hatry told him came as a great shock, but he was satisfied that the financier realized its gravity and its consequence.

'Did he put himself in your hands as to the course he should take?'

'Yes.'

'Is there any doubt that on that morning he was exceedingly anxious to do all he could to limit the area of the damage?'

'Yes.'

'Throughout the whole period from September to today, has he rendered you every assistance in his power?'

'Yes.'

'Without his assistance would you have found your investigation of much greater difficulty than you have?'

'Yes.'

'It has been a most difficult and complex investigation?'

'Most involved.'

'Without Mr. Hatry's help it must have been much more prolonged?'

After the accountant had agreed that this was so, Birkett put the vital questions to which he had been skilfully leading up.

'Without the confession made to you on September 19, it would have been very difficult for any charges of a criminal nature to be formulated for a considerable time?'

'Yes.'

'The charges made against him were formulated on his statement?'

'Yes.'

Questioned about Hatry's projected steel venture, the accountant admitted that in conception it was 'very fine' and immense profits might have accrued to Austin Friars Trust.

'Quite apart from the Hatry crash, there have been immense losses in all sorts of companies all over the world.'

'Yes.'

'The Hatry crash coincided with a great depression of share values?'

'Yes.'

'And a great deal was attributed to the Hatry crash which should not have been?'

'Possibly,' the accountant agreed.

'Certain banks, stockbrokers, and financial houses have been losers,' Birkett continued, 'but have you formed any idea of the loss suffered by the outside public?'

To this question the accountant replied that the total of publicly held shares in the Hatry companies amounted to £1,200,000, about equally divided between financial institutions and the outside investor. He added that his investigation had confirmed his opinion that 'the defendants had not received a penny piece from any of the money which has been irregularly raised'.

The last witness for the prosecution was the police officer who had arrested the men in the office of the Director of Public Prosecutions and at the same time had taken a statement from Hatry. In this Hatry had admitted that some of the stock in respect of which scrip was issued was non-existent and that there were 'irregularities' in other companies with which they were connected, and that they 'wished to give all assistance'. Hatry had further stated that he was 'personally and primarily responsible' and that none of his associates had benefited in any way; in fact, they had lost. 'There was no intent to defraud,' he had said when formally charged.

The Crown case was closed at the end of the fourth day. Consequently the Old Bailey courtroom was densely thronged next morning when Birkett rose from his place, as many of the onlookers thought, to open Hatry's defence and put his client into the witness box. Instead Birkett briefly addressed the Bench, explaining that he and his junior counsel had had a conference with Mr. Hatry on the previous evening during which many matters which had to be borne in mind 'had received the most anxious and prolonged consideration'. As a result they had tendered 'certain advice' to Mr. Hatry, who 'now desired, fully realizing the nature of the advice . . . and the responsibility which it entailed, to ask permission to withdraw his plea of "Not Guilty" and to substitute a plea of "Guilty" to all the counts in the indictment.'

Hatry's companions in the dock also intimated through their counsel that they wished to take this course, and so all the pleas were formally changed to 'Guilty'. It now only remained for Mr. Justice Avory to pass sentence after the prosecution had accepted the pleas and defending counsel had been heard in mitigation.

For an hour and a quarter Birkett employed all his eloquence in pleading that some clemency might be shown to his client. 'Hatry does not attempt to defend what he has done,' he said, 'but he says that, when he did it, the circumstances were such that he thought that it would be only temporary. He did it in a moment of great and overwhelming temptation, when great projects and great enterprises seemed near fulfilment, and it appeared that by taking that wrong step, it would be possible to avert a disaster which would bring on many thousands of innocent people a loss that they could hardly bear. It was at a moment when failure was never envisaged that the fatal step was taken. . . . In a very true sense no punishment which your Lordship can inflict on Hatry can fill the cup of suffering from which he has most bitterly to drink more full than it now is. He has been four months in prison with time to think, to brood, to reflect, to see what might have been, and what now is. . . . The appeal I make is that you should impose such a sentence as will vindicate the law and will make it manifest that no interference with the integrity of credit will be permitted; but a sentence which by reason of its elements of seasoned mercy, will not crush, or break, or destroy, but will permit Mr. Hatry to maintain the hope—which is the last earthly thing he has—that one day he may live to redeem that career which has been so finally and tragically shattered.'

Birkett's words brought tears to the eyes of his client in the dock who immediately wrote a note of thanks to his defender. ('That speech was wonderful. Again I am deeply grateful.') His example was followed by Sir Gilbert Garnsey, who, although he was the chief witness for the prosecution, felt he had to 'express my admiration for your most eloquent speech'.

Other judges might have been moved by this appeal, but Mr. Justice Avory showed no mercy to Hatry when he came to sentence him. 'You stand convicted on your own confession of the most appalling frauds that have ever disfigured the commercial reputation of this country,' the judge addressed Hatry in a rasping voice like the crackling of dry parchment, 'frauds far more serious than any of the great frauds on the public which have been committed within the last fifty years, for they have been carried out by means of wholesale forgeries of bearer securities in trustee stocks which neither banker, nor broker, nor any member of the public would ever dream of suspecting of being otherwise than genuine. . . . I am asked to take into consideration in mitigation of your offence the fact that, on September 19, you made a voluntary confession. I do not think there is much if any merit in that confession, because you knew at that time that investigations were on foot and that . . . these forgeries must be inevitably discovered. . . . Therefore in making that confession you were merely succumbing to the inevitable.'

Nor was the judge at all favourably impressed by Birkett's plea that in June, 1929, Hatry was engaged on a large financial transaction on which he hoped to reap considerable profit. 'What does that plea amount to when stripped of the rhetorical language in which it has been put forward? It is nothing more or less than the threadbare plea of every clerk or servant who robs his master and says that he hoped to repay the money before his crime was discovered by backing a winner. Except that your crime was on a large scale, there is no difference between that excuse and the excuse which is daily made by the dishonest clerk or servant. Therefore I can give no effect to that.'

When the actual sentence was pronounced, the judge's words sent a gasp of amazement round the crowded court room—fourteen years penal servitude, the maximum possible under the law. Not content with that, the judge recalled Hatry twice to the dock to be sentenced in respect of other charges, these sentences to run concurrently. His companions were then dealt with, Daniels getting seven years, Dixon five and Tabor three. The first two years of each sentence were to be served at hard labour.

To Hatry's family and friends, as also to his counsel, the sentence was regarded as one of savage and unmitigated severity. 'I shall never forget your speech in his defence,' Hatry's son Cecil wrote to Birkett after the trial. 'That the case has been prejudged and the sentence given as an example is unfortunately obvious. If the chief points in his favour are again put before the public in the appeal, a reduction of his sentence at some future date must, I suppose, be our only hope.'

Two months later Birkett appeared for Hatry in the Court of Criminal Appeal, where he argued as eloquently as he did in the Old Bailey for a reduction of the sentence. 'The suffering he is undergoing is difficult to conceive and beyond my power to depict,' said Birkett, and went on to quote Oscar Wilde's celebrated words in *De Profundis*, 'All trials are trials for one's life, just as all sentences are sentences of death.' The appeal was dismissed, the Lord Chief Justice, Lord Hewart, declaring that in the view of the Court the sentence was 'not one day too much'. Birkett's request that the sentence should be allowed to run from the date of Hatry's conviction, instead of from the date the appeal was dismissed, was also refused.

When they met immediately afterwards in the solicitors' room, Hatry held out his hand which Birkett took. 'It's a terrible sentence, but I'll do it,' the financier said with dogged determination. 'And one of the thoughts that will help me through is the remembrance of the great fight you put up for me.'

But Birkett's fight was not over. Not only did he write regularly to Hatry and visit him in prison, but it was largely due to his efforts that Hatry was released after serving nine of his fourteen years sentence and he was able to begin successfully to rebuild his ruined career when he was still on the right side of fifty.

For much of his imprisonment Hatry remained the object of hostile and ill-informed prejudice. At the beginning of 1933 he wrote to Birkett:

It was not only very charming of you, but, if I may say so it was a very big thing to have written to me again this Christmas. I do not forget that in the eyes of my fellow men I am an outcast, while you are one of our great public men occupying a very enviable position.

. . . I am more than ever convinced that the day will come when my name commands universal respect . . . I constantly see my name in books of every description, novels, biographies, etc. I shudder each time I see it and get horribly depressed, for nearly always it is a sordid motive attributed to my actions. I could not be more maligned if I had put a fortune into my pocket, instead of depriving myself and family of every penny I possessed. But what is much worse than these references in books is the fact that since the trial a score of people, at the very least, have taken advantage of the fallacious belief that the failure of my companies caused widespread loss and ruination to investors all over the country, and have put down their particular troubles (often to obtain the clemency of a Judge or Magistrate) to me. The Press without investigation have invariably referred to these thoroughly dishonest persons as 'Hatry Victims' with prominent headlines. . . . The most serious of these inaccurate accounts in the Press have been stories of suicide due to alleged losses in the 'Hatry Crash'. There is not a particle of truth in a single case of any sort so far reported, as our investigations have proved. . . .

. . . I still feel that public opinion would be much less critical if the real nature of the documents were understood and if it were generally known how it comes about that they can even be called forgeries—a term which conveys a very different meaning from that which took place to the man-in-the-street.[1]

[1] Further details of the background to the Hatry case will be found in the account given by his son Cecil Hatry in *The Hatry Case: Eight Current Misconceptions* (1939). In the Foreword to this publication, which was signed by eighteen well-known persons, including solicitors, accountants, stockbrokers and six M.P.s, it is stated:

> We give way to none in our insistence upon the need for unwavering adherence to the highest standards of honesty and integrity in financial and commercial affairs. We know that Mr. Hatry in these respects erred, and in seeking to retrieve his error did much that should not have been done. But he never was a reckless adventurer of the vulgar legend. He is a man of high quality and notable achievement, who was caught in a world of depression, and hoped, by taking risk to win through, not for himself but for his enterprises. By the narrowest of margins he failed. He

7

No practising barrister can invariably be on the winning side in a civil action any more than he can invariably secure his accused client's acquittal on a criminal charge, no matter how eloquent his advocacy may be. It is perhaps in the nature of things that public attention should tend to concentrate more on the advocates' victories than on his defeats in the courts. If the latter are not so often recalled by newspaper readers, they are sometimes remembered by the unsuccessful litigant with more gratitude than the victorious party shows his professional advisers. Certainly many of Birkett's lay clients who had verdicts or judgments given against them never forgot his efforts on their behalf and would come back to him as their leading counsel whenever they were in a position to do so. In this context three civil actions, which were tried in the same year as Hatry's conviction and in which Birkett appeared for the unsuccessful party, deserve some mention.

The first was an action for libel brought by a Rumanian named Barbu Jonescu, a friend of King Carol of Rumania, against the London *Evening Standard*. Carol had recently lost his throne and was living in exile with his attractive red-headed mistress Madame Magda Lupescu; while in England M. Jonescu was their host at his country house in Surrey. The Foreign Office could not take any exception to this *ménage*, however morally irregular it might appear; but when evidence reached Downing Street that the ex-King was plotting with his adherents in Rumania to regain his throne, he was asked to leave the country. Carol had no choice but to comply with this request. Shortly afterwards it was suggested in the 'Londoner's Diary' in the *Evening Standard* that the activities of M. Jonescu 'in relation to this matter' called for close examination. Was not he, as a foreigner, also enjoying the hospitality of this country? The writer of the column went on to state that his name was not originally Jonescu, nor again was he of Rumanian nationality. In fact, he was a Pole, who first came to England with the refugees from Belgium at the beginning of the First World War. After M. Jonescu had issued a writ for libel, the newspaper in its plea of justification alleged that

has taken harsh punishment. We are glad it is at last to be ended; and we commend to the reader this booklet which clears his name of unjustified calumny.

his real name was Moritz Leiba, that his parents were of Jewish faith and his father of Polish descent.

The trial of the action opened before Mr. Justice Horridge and a special jury in the King's Bench Division on February 4, 1930, and it lasted for thirteen days. Serjeant Sullivan, K.C., led for the plaintiff and Birkett for the newspaper.

M. Jonescu gave evidence at great length and his cross-examination by Birkett occupied four days. But his main contention that he was not Moritz Leiba but the son of a Rumanian farmer named Virgiliu Jonescu remained unshaken, although he could not produce his birth certificate and it appeared that the register of births had had two pages removed by the Rumanian Secret Police for the month in which he claimed to have been born. He freely admitted that when he arrived in England he was very poor and had worked as a waiter, a cinematograph operator and a cigarette seller in a London restaurant before becoming a person of considerable means. The weakest feature of his evidence was that he could not produce any convincing particulars of his early life in Rumania, which covered twenty-seven years.

Where were his schoolfellows, Birkett asked in opening the defence, the people he met at church or chapel, at the club, at games, presents on his birthday, inscriptions on the fly leaves of books, letters written by him or sent to him? There was not one letter, not one word for the whole of the twenty-seven years. 'The thing we state is true,' said Birkett, 'and we shall prove it.'

Two Rumanian witnesses, one a doctor and the other a barrister, whom Birkett called, swore that they had been at school in Bucharest with the plaintiff, and that his name then was Moritz Leiba, and that he changed his name to Leibovici to make it less Jewish sounding and more Rumanian.

Unfortunately for the *Evening Standard*, Serjeant Sullivan sprang a surprise witness, which he was allowed to interpose among the other defence witnesses. This turned out to be a man who gave his name as Marcel Aldeanu and claimed to be a brother of Moritz Leiba, having no doubt changed his name for the same reason as it was suggested that his brother had done. This surprise witness was positive that the plaintiff was not his brother Moritz. His real brother he believed had gone to the war and been killed.

This unexpected testimony, reinforced by the witness standing beside M. Jonescu in the court room, was apparently conclusive in the eyes of the jury. At all events, they returned a verdict for the plaintiff and awarded him the relatively large sum of £12,000 damages. A similar action brought by M. Jonescu against the *Evening Standard*'s sister newspaper, the *Daily Express*, was settled out of court.

The Jonescu libel case had a curious personal sequel for Birkett. Among the spectators of the trial was a woman named Mrs. Elizabeth Cruesman, who was quite unknown to Birkett but who now wrote him an enthusiastic letter of congratulation with the result that a kind of 'pen pal' relationship developed between them, kindly on his side and admiring on hers. 'Above all,' she wrote in her first letter, 'did I admire your opening speech for the defence, quite the finest I have been privileged to hear in the Law Courts. The care and clarity and forensic beauty of your address were sheer mental joy to the listener; but when a man speaks with such conviction and puts so much effort and sincerity into a speech of that kind, one cannot but feel that the ultimate result must bring a very human disappointment.'

The second case which Birkett's clients in effect lost, although it was the subject of a settlement out of court, was an action for alleged conspiracy to cheat and defraud brought by the United Diamond Fields of British Guiana Ltd. against Mr. S. B. ('Solly') Joel and other defendants forming the famous South African Diamond Syndicate which controlled the world output of diamonds. The plaintiff company alleged that, when it had a contract with the Diamond Syndicate under which the syndicate undertook to buy all the output of the company's fields in British Guiana, Mr. Otto Oppenheimer, who had been appointed technical adviser to the company at the instance of the syndicate, instructed his representatives in British Guiana to take steps which would (and in fact did) result in cutting down the prices paid to the company and so lessen its power to purchase from the natives and consequently reduce its output. The defence was a denial of the allegations of conspiracy and fraud.

The case was tried before Mr. Justice McCardie and a special jury. It lasted for ten days and might have continued much longer but for the settlement which was reached. Sir Patrick Hastings led for the plaintiff company, while Birkett appeared as leading counsel for Mr. Oppenheimer, who had been joined as a defendant with the members of the syndicate. In spite of its complexity, the case threw some interesting light on the workings of the diamond industry.

'What was the motive of the Diamond Syndicate in wishing to ruin your company?' Birkett asked one of the United Diamond Fields directors in cross-examination.

'The Diamond Syndicate is very reluctant to see new producers of diamonds coming into the field,' the director answered. 'There are already too many diamonds in the world. If the demand for diamonds doubled tomorrow, the syndicate could immediately produce all the stones it wanted from its own mines. Any new producer that comes into the market is a nuisance to the syndicate and is called a bone in its throat. If it cannot stop a new company being formed, it gets a contract to control its output. And, if the opportunity presents itself, the syndicate quietly does away with it and buries it.'

Now the contract between the company and the syndicate provided that the price payable by the latter for the company's diamonds could be reduced at the expiration of any six-monthly period upon an accountant's certificate being given that the value of the diamonds held by the company in stock and unsold had fallen. For the purpose of the certificate the value of the unsold stock was to be arrived at by taking the price realized by the Diamond Syndicate at the last sale immediately preceding the date of the certificate. However, since the company was not permitted to inspect the books of the Diamond Syndicate, in the event of a fall in the value of diamonds the company was bound by the certificate and was in effect entirely in the hands of Mr. Oppenheimer, who regulated the price paid by the syndicate for all stones purchased from the company.

It was the final cut of ten per cent in the price that had brought the plaintiff company to the brink of ruin. The relevant certificate furnished by Mr. Oppenheimer was based on a sale to a Mr. Van Antwerpen, but it now emerged that the latter gentleman had been dissatisfied with his bargain and that Mr. Oppenheimer had taken back the diamonds and rescinded the sale. After the disclosure of these facts, Birkett's client became ill and the Diamond Syndicate intimated its willingness to meet the company's claim on a settlement basis provided the charges of fraud were withdrawn.

This was accordingly done, the company accepting that Oppenheimer's conduct was not dishonest, since (as Birkett emphasized) he believed that a drop in the world prices of diamonds at the period in question justified a reduction of the prices which were to be paid by the Diamond Syndicate to the company. For the Diamond Syndicate it turned out an immensely costly settlement.[1]

The third of the losing cases which Birkett fought at this time also involved millions and was equally expensive in respect of its legal costs. Known as 'The Portuguese Banknote Case', it must rank as one of the most amazing frauds ever perpetrated, involving as it did the fabrication and distribution throughout Portugal of banknotes to the face value of more than £1,000,000. The notes were printed in London, but so ingenious was the deception practised that only the printers could tell the difference between genuine notes of the same denomination and those which were in effect forgeries.

The story begins on December 4, 1924. On that day a Dutchman, who gave his name as Mr. K. Marang Van Ysselveere, of The Hague, presented himself at the offices of Waterlow's, the well-known firm of printers in the City. He looked about thirty-five years old and was described as 'an ingratiating foreigner with beautiful manners'. Mr. Marang carried with him a letter of introduction from a firm of printers of high standing in Holland addressed to Sir William Waterlow, the chairman of the English firm. The letter stated that its bearer wished to place an order for the printing of banknotes which might best be executed by Waterlow's. Incidentally, Waterlow's had previously printed notes for the Bank of Portugal.

Mr. Marang explained that the finances of the Portuguese colony of Angola were in a bad way, and that a Dutch syndicate of which he was a member was, at the request of the Portuguese Government, going to the colony's assistance. The syndicate proposed to subscribe £1,000,000 sterling and the Bank of Portugal was prepared to help. Marang accordingly asked if Waterlow's would print some of the Bank's notes for circulation in Angola. After delivery the notes would be overprinted in the colony with the word 'Angola' on their face. The High Commissioner was leaving for the

[1] For a more detailed account of this interesting case, which was a great triumph for the plaintiff company's leading counsel, see Hyde, *Sir Patrick Hastings*, pp. 197–206.

colony in about two months' time and would take the notes with him, the plausible Mr. Marang went on, so that there was no time to be lost. He added that the matter must be treated as strictly confidential.

Sir William Waterlow does not seem to have regarded this request as unusual. Anyhow he had once worked in his country's secret intelligence service and was no doubt accustomed to 'undercover' operations. But he naturally asked for time to consider the proposition and an appointment was made for about a fornight later. On this occasion Marang brought with him various legal documents which had been duly authenticated by a Portuguese notary. One of them was a contract by which the Bank of Portugal seemingly authorized the Government of Angola to arrange for the printing of the notes.

Sir William Waterlow informed the visitor that his firm could not supply the notes without the authority of the Bank, since it owned the plates from which the printing was done. He would, therefore, write to the Bank for their authority, which, after consulting his colleagues and having also taken legal advice, he was satisfied would put the matter in order. Mr. Marang, who said he happened to be going to Lisbon next day, offered to take the letter with him, and to this Sir William Waterlow agreed.

Marang returned to London a few weeks later, bringing with him a reply purporting to be signed by the Governor of the Bank. It was written on notepaper bearing the Portuguese national arms in the corner, and though it was not the kind of paper which the Bank used, its style was sufficient to impress Waterlow's. It contained the necessary authority and requested the British firm to deal directly with Marang on matters of detail. It was, however, written in English and not Portuguese, in which language the Bank had previously communicated with Waterlow's. Also the seals were different from those formerly used. These points escaped attention at the time, and the bogus letter was accepted and acted upon by Waterlow's in good faith.

Waterlow's now set to work to fill the order. Two hundred thousand notes in denominations of 500 escudos (approximately £5) came off the printing presses as a first instalment. Each note bore the portrait of Vasco da Gama, the great Portuguese navigator, and to all except the expert eye of Waterlow's themselves were identical in appearance with the notes previously printed by Waterlow's for the Bank.

Early in February, 1925, Marang took delivery of the consignment, collecting the notes in a large suitcase, which he subsequently deposited for the night in the cloakroom of Liverpool Street station ('Fancy all that for one and sixpence!' he remarked about the modest cloakroom charge.) An even larger printing, some 380,000 notes, was executed by the firm some months later. None of the notes ever reached Angola. But the equivalent of more than £1,000,000 passed into circulation in Portugal.

To facilitate this process the conspirators, who included a brother of the Portuguese Minister in The Hague, obtained permission for the Ministry of Finance in Lisbon to found a new bank, the Bank of Angola, and it was through its medium that the bulk of the false notes reached the public. But gradually suspicions were aroused. Eventually, the police searched the Bank of Angola premises in Oporto and found several large bundles of new Vasco da Gama notes, which were neither numbered nor packed in accordance with the practice of the Bank of Portugal.

On December 5, 1925, the Bank of Portugal suddenly decided to withdraw the whole Vasco da Gama issue from circulation. The public were allowed three weeks to exchange any of the notes for others, after which they would become valueless. The directors did not cable Waterlow's until a week or so later, and although Sir William Waterlow immediately hurried to Lisbon to explain how the spurious notes could be distinguished from the genuine ones—a magnifying glass revealed a small letter on the stalk of the lily in the design, which did not appear on the plate previously used—the bank insisted on carrying out the withdrawal *in toto*. This naturally involved a great rush on the bank and greatly increased the measure of damages subsequently claimed against Waterlow's. Meanwhile, Marang and his associates were arrested, tried and sentenced to terms of imprisonment. In the excitement, even the Governor and Vice-Governor of the Bank of Portugal were also arrested, but they were released almost immediately.

The Bank of Portugal now issued a writ against Waterlow's in the English courts, alleging breach of contract and negligence and claiming £1,106,691, being the face value in sterling of the notes they had paid out in exchange for the notes of the Vasco da Gama issue which had been called in. The action opened before Mr. Justice Wright in the King's Bench Division on November 24, 1930 and lasted twenty-one days. Mr. Stuart Bevan, K.C. appeared with two other 'silks' for the Bank, while Birkett led Mr. H. Bensley Wells and Mr. Theodore Turner for Waterlow and Sons Ltd.

Birkett and his two juniors spent a considerable amount of time in acquainting themselves with the details of Portuguese banking practice, before the case came on, in anticipation of having to cross-examine the Bank's witnesses. The latter incidentally provided some of the lighter moments in an otherwise serious action; for instance, when Birkett asked Señor Camacho Rodrigues, the Governor of the Banco de Portugal, about a decoration bestowed upon Mr. Marang by the Portuguese Government, the Order of Christ, which Birkett suggested was the highest order which the Government could bestow.

'No,' replied the Governor indignantly. 'It is a comparatively inferior order.' The Governor went on to say, raising another laugh, that the counsel who prosecuted Marang in Portugal was the man who had recommended him for membership of the Order. 'That,' Señor Camacho added, 'is only one of the incidents in the life of political people!'

Another of the Bank's directors, Dr. Ruy Ulrich, agreed with Birkett that a loan from the Banco de Portugal to the Portuguese Government was effected by the issue of notes by the bank and the use of those notes by the Government for its own purposes.

'Would it be right to say,' continued Birkett, 'that the Banco de Portugal was really a gigantic paper machine to meet the needs of the State?'

'To a certain point, yes,' the director agreed. 'But that is so in the case of all banks.'

'Are we agreed that from 1925 until the present time the Banco de Portugal has been under no liability to pay any of their notes in gold, silver, or other metal coin?'

'Yes.'

'That period of inconvertibility was intended to last for ten days, but it has lasted ever since 1925?'

'Yes.'

'The only liability of the bank is to pay with other notes a note that is presented.'

'Yes.'

'You took your irrevocable step of calling in the Vasco da Gama notes without asking Waterlow's whether they could come and distinguish the authorized notes from the unauthorized ones?'

'Yes.'

'You asked everyone to bring his notes, good or bad, and they would be paid?'

'Yes.'

'You have said that, if the bank had not withdrawn the whole issue of the notes, you would have had a revolution in Portugal. Why a revolution?'

'If you tell the people that they are threatened with the loss of one-sixth of their money, it is not very extraordinary if you do have a revolution.'

'The income of Portugal for years has been less than its expenditure,' said Birkett at this point. 'In private life that sort of thing leads to bankruptcy?'

'Yes,' the banker agreed, pitying Birkett's ignorance of high finance, 'but a State is quite different!'

The mirth which this reply caused swelled in volume as Birkett commented: 'Perhaps they have translated Mr. Micawber into Portuguese!'

When he came to summarize Waterlow's case in his concluding speech, Birkett argued that, since the Portuguese currency was inconvertible, the exchange of one piece of paper for another produced no effect at all on the position of the bank and could not do so until the occurrence of some future contingent event, namely until the régime of convertibility returned. The most the plaintiffs had proved was that there might be a contingent, hypothetical loss which might or might not accrue. There were no assets behind the notes which the Bank of Portugal had put out. 'The loss was all on paper and in paper,' said Birkett. The only measure of damages to which the Bank was entitled, in his submission, was a more or less nominal one arising from the misuse of the Bank's plates to print the unauthorized notes.

Mr. Justice Wright rejected this ingenious argument and found that Waterlow's had fallen short of that standard of care which their contract with the Bank of Portugal required. 'No one suggests for a minute a word of reflection on the honour and good faith of Messrs.

Waterlow or any of the directors,' said the judge. 'It is merely one of those unfortunate circumstances . . . in which the wiles of the swindlers distract the minds of those concerned from the clear sense of what they ought to do in duty to those who have placed confidence in them.' But in entering judgment for the Bank against Waterlow's, he reduced the amount of damages from the sum claimed to £567,421, being the amount of the face value of the notes, less certain deductions.

Both sides appealed—Waterlow's on the ground that the damages awarded were excessive and the Bank on the grounds that they were not enough. In the Court of Appeal, Birkett was led by Sir John Simon, later Lord Simon, who succeeded in getting the damages further reduced to £300,000. The Bank then took the case to the House of Lords, where Birkett had another leader in Mr. Gavin Simmonds, later Lord Simmonds, who adopted Birkett's arguments with similar skill to Sir John Simon. But their Lordships rejected them, setting aside the award made in the Court of Appeal and awarding the sum of £610,392 as damages to the Bank, in addition to an enormous bill of costs.

During the lengthy hearings of the case, Birkett was presented with one of the unauthorized 500-escudo notes appropriately mutilated in case he should be tempted to use it himself. He carefully preserved it as a souvenir of what Mr. Justice Wright had rightly described as a 'fraud unparalleled in the history of commercial swindles' as well as what was probably the most expensive litigation in which Norman Birkett ever participated as counsel.

CHAPTER VIII

'HIS HONOURS THICK UPON HIM'

I

BIRKETT was once discussing the subject of murder trials with a fellow barrister in the Temple. His colleague ventured the remark that to defend a person accused of a capital charge was extremely difficult. 'No, I don't agree,' said Birkett. 'Defences in murder cases are not difficult, provided that three conditions are satisfied. First, there must be a good background to the case; secondly, the accused must be of previous good character; and thirdly, he or she must be able to go into the witness box and give evidence that a reasonable jury can believe. If they can believe it, they will certainly do so, for no juryman or jurywoman, if they can honestly avoid it, will send an accused person to the gallows.'

The relatively large number of murder cases in which Birkett appeared in his career at the Bar, usually for the defence but sometimes for the prosecution, he liked to cite in support of his opinion. In particular, there were five in the nineteen-thirties. The first of these, in which Birkett led for the Crown, was known as 'The Blazing Car Case'. It was a case which had three distinctly unusual features. For one thing, there was a complete absence of any apparent motive for the crime; again, the identity of the murdered man was never discovered; also, the accused, who could have undoubtedly saved himself from the gallows by keeping silent, was convicted by a series of almost unbelievable admissions out of his own mouth.

About 2 a.m. on November 6, 1930, two young men were returning home from a dance at Hardingstone, a village near Northampton, when they noticed a bright light some distance along the road. Just then a stranger came out of a ditch at the side of the road and walked past them. A few moments later he glanced back and said, 'It looks as if somebody has had a bonfire.' He then walked on down the road, seemed to hesitate as to which way to go and finally turned in the direction of London and disappeared. The two young men ran towards the light and discovered a motor car blazing away by the side of the road. They then ran back to the village to fetch the local constable, and returned with him to the scene of the blaze. After the flames had died down they discovered the charred remains of a man inside, whose face was burnt away and was quite unrecognizable. However, the number plate on the car was intact and on inquiry it showed that the vehicle was registered in the name of Alfred Arthur Rouse. The two young men were subsequently able to identify the stranger whom they had seen walking away from the blazing car as Rouse.

Little was known about Rouse, apart from the fact that he was a thirty-six-year-old commercial traveller, who led an extremely irregular private life. He had served in the First World War and was severely wounded in the head, which may have had something to do with his later extraordinary behaviour. His appearance was not exactly prepossessing, although he might have been regarded as good looking in a weak sort of way. Yet he must have exercised considerable attraction for women, judging by the promiscuous relations and the number of illegitimate children he had. Besides his legal wife, with whom he lived in Finchley on the comparatively rare occasions when he was at home, he had a 'bigamous' wife named Helen Campbell, by whom he had two children. He also had had an affair with a girl called Nellie Tucker, who had also borne him two children. Then there was Ivy Jenkins, a probationer nurse from South Wales, who was pregnant by Rouse at the time of the car fire. In addition there were two other children of whom Rouse was the father, one a boy of fourteen in Paris. In all no less than eighty cases of seduction were traced to him. His salary and commission from his firm amounted to £8 a week, but by the time he had given his wife £2 for housekeeping and paid the hire purchase instalment on his car, a similar instalment to the Building Society on his house, besides sums due on two paternity orders and the wages of a foster-mother for one of Nellie Tucker's children, he did not have much left over with which to pay for his amorous adventures, although one or other of his mistresses sometimes travelled with him.

After the owner of the burnt out car had been traced from the registration number, Rouse was arrested and charged with murder. During the police court proceedings, a good deal was made by the prosecution of the accused's amorous propensities, and a statement which he had made to the police after his arrest when he had asked to see his wife was read out.

> 'She is really too good for me. I like a woman who will make a fuss of me. I don't ever remember my wife sitting on my knee, but otherwise she is a good wife. I am very friendly with several women, but it is a very expensive game. I was on my way to Leicester on Wednesday, when this happened, to hand in my slip on Thursday morning to draw some money from my firm. I was then going to Wales for the week-end. My harem takes me to several places and I am not at home a great deal. But my wife does not ask questions now. I was arranging to sell my house and furniture, I was then going to make an allowance to my wife. I think I should clear between £100 and £150 from the sale.'

Rouse's statements at the time of and before his arrest were equally damaging. 'I'm very glad it's over,' he told the police when he was being charged. 'I was going to Scotland Yard about it,' 'I'm responsible,' and 'I've had no sleep.' Previously, on leaving the scene of the burning car, he had got a lift in a lorry as far as Tally Ho Corner on the Barnet Road. 'I am in a bit of a mess,' he told the driver, 'I lost my car or had it pinched.' He then had taken a coach for Wales, repeating quite gratuitously both to the manager of the transport company and the coach driver that his car had been stolen. When he reached Wales, he had made for the house of one of his 'harem' Miss Ivy Jenkins, where he had told the girl's father, who thought Rouse had married his daughter, that he had had his car stolen in Northampton.

The trial of Alfred Arthur Rouse for the murder of an unknown man opened at Northampton Assizes before Mr. Justice Talbot on January 26, 1931. Mr. Norman Birkett, K.C., M.P., and Mr. Richard Elwes (later Mr. Justice Elwes) appeared for the Crown, while Rouse was defended by Birkett's old Birmingham colleague, Mr. Donald Finnemore.

Briefly the case which Birkett outlined to the jury was that Rouse chose his victim and took him for a ride with the object of staging his own disappearance. At the spot where the charred remains of the car and its occupant were found, he got out, struck his fellow passenger on the head with a mallet, subsequently found at the roadside, and while he was unconscious bundled his body into a position face downwards on the driver's seat. He probably saturated the body with petrol from a can, and then to ensure a steady stream of petrol to feed the flames, he deliberately loosened the petrol union joint so that the petrol seeped into the car. Birkett pointed out to the jury that in all cases of accidental fire the engine must be running, but in this case the engine had been switched off. 'Thus the causes or cause of an accidental fire were missing in this case.'

Birkett, who was not instructed to lead for the Crown until after Rouse had been committed for trial, had taken no part in the police court proceedings. A considerable amount of evidence had been given at the police court about Rouse's sexual irregularities, including the statement to this effect made by Rouse himself and already mentioned. Birkett decided not to use this evidence at the trial, since he felt that, although it had some relevance to the murder charge, it might be unfair or prejudicial to the prisoner to include it; but, of course, he could not remove any impression it might have left on the minds of those members of the jury who had read it in the newspaper accounts of the police court proceedings. The point is worth noting, since Birkett was later accused in certain quarters of pressing the prosecution's case against the prisoner with excessive vigour.

The most important evidence put forward by Birkett was given by two expert witnesses. The first of these, Colonel Cuthbert Buckle, was the managing director of a well-known firm of fire loss assessors. Asked about the cause of the burning of the car he replied that in his opinion the fire was fed continuously from the forward part of the car in the vicinity of the petrol tank. With the aid of a model of a petrol pipe, this witness explained how he had found the union at the carburettor end one whole turn loose. 'I went to the police car and found a union like this on it,' he went on. 'The petrol flowed quite quickly, and it filled an ordinary half-pint tumbler absolutely in one minute twenty seconds.' He added that petrol from a loosened union would flow at considerably more than the normal rate of pressure on to the floor in front of the passenger near his feet.

The other expert witness was the Home Office pathologist, Sir Bernard Spilsbury, who stated that in his view the position of the body was consistent with the man either pitching forward or being thrown face downwards on to the seat of the car from the nearside door. The effect of the overheating would be to shorten and contract the muscles and so cause the limb to be bent.

'Having regard to the fact that you found the left leg doubled up and the right leg extended,' Birkett asked him, 'is there in your view any possibility that he did assume any posture other than what was found?'

'No,' answered Sir Bernard, 'I think the stretch of the right leg rules that out.'

'What do you say about the projection of the right leg beyond where the door was?'

'I think it suggests that the door was open and no doubt both legs were extended in the same way originally.'

When Birkett put it to Spilsbury that the bent up leg protected the clothing, the pathologist agreed that the way in which the limb was doubled up to the body would normally prevent the clothing from catching fire. 'There is only one other explanation,' he concluded, 'and that is that the clothing had become soaked in petrol before the fire started.'

2

The principal witness for the defence was the prisoner himself. He had given an unknown man a lift in his car, he said, and thinking that he was running out of petrol, he had asked the man to empty the contents of the spare can into the tank. According to his story, Rouse then got out to relieve himself. 'I then went some distance along the road and had just got my trousers down when I noticed a big flame from behind. . . . My first thought was that the petrol tank would explode . . . I did not know what to do and I ran as hard as I could along the road where I saw the two men. I felt I was responsible for what had happened. I lost my head. . . .'

'Did you do anything wrong at all in Hardingstone Lane between one and two on that night?' Rouse's counsel asked him.

'Nothing criminal at all,' the prisoner replied. Then he continued after a moment's pause: 'I did wrong very likely in running away.'

'What do you say now about your having run away in panic?'

'Well, I ought perhaps to have tried to help, but thinking of the whole of the circumstances I have come to the conclusion that it would have been impossible for me to give anyone inside the car help in any way.'

'Subsequently you gave explanations, in South Wales, for instance, which were not true?'

'I gave explanations which I thought were most suitable at the moment.'

'Now you know they were wrong, you realize the difficulties. What do you say as to that?'

'It is very unfortunate. That is all I can say.'

'Did you, in fact, intend to do any harm or hurt to the man you picked up?'

'I have not done any harm that I consider to anybody!'

'Do you know exactly just what happened that night?'

'Not in the car, sir.'

Birkett began his cross-examination by asking the prisoner why he had lied. 'When you told my learned friend that the lies you told in Wales were unfortunate, what did you mean?'

'I am not used to telling lies, sir,' Rouse answered. 'At the time I thought it was the best thing to do.'

'Why was lying better than the truth?'

Rouse looked sheepish. He explained that 'it would not be very pleasant with ladies present' to give the real reason for his leaving the car.

'Why tell it at all if it was a lie?' Birkett persisted.

'My name has been clear up to now of lies.'

'Do you think an innocent man might tell the truth?'

'Yes, but I think I did the best possible thing in the circumstances.'

'Is it a fact that to all the people you saw from two o'clock in the morning of November 6 to nine-thirty on the evening of November 7 you never told a word of the truth to any of them?

'I said what I thought was best,' the witness repeated.

'You went to Wales to think it out, didn't you?'

'I went with the intention of seeing Miss Jenkins.'

'Did you not say in your statement, "I decided to leave London so as to think things over, and went to Wales"?'

'Obviously my mind is not a blank always.'

'Were you surprised when the police asked you to get out of the coach?'

'Well, it was in the papers and I was going there to see them.'

'Did you say in your first words, "I am glad it is over"?'

'I was glad I could make a statement.'

'Did you say, "I am glad it is over"?' Birkett repeated the words.

'I do not remember what I said,' Rouse replied feebly. Then he corrected himself, adding: 'It was words to that effect.'

'You could have gone to the police in Cardiff to make your statement. The police station was forty-one yards from where you were staying.'

'I do not know where it was, and if I did I should not have gone there. I would not go to a provincial police station. I wanted to go to Scotland Yard.'

'Would you not go to a provincial station because you distrusted them?'

'I was going to the fountain head.'

'Did you say in your statement, "I am responsible"?' Birkett continued.

'I don't remember the exact words,' he replied. But, almost in the next breath he admitted, 'Very likely I did.'

'Did you say later, "I feel I was responsible for what happened"?'

'Yes.'

'But you were not in the smallest degree responsible?'

'I feel even now that I am responsible. I handed the man a cigar and asked him to put in my can of petrol. I did not know whether he was capable of doing it.'

'Is that all you mean by your responsibility?'

'Yes.'

'You never did anything to try and help him when the car was burning?'

'For one thing I could not see him there.'

Birkett looked intently at the prisoner for a moment or two. 'Do you swear that?'

At these words Rouse stood erect, looking first at Birkett and then at the judge. 'I swear that,' he said, extending his hand slightly as he spoke.

Questioned about his attaché case which he had admitted taking with him when he got out of the car, Rouse said that in those circumstances he would not trust anybody. 'I do not see why I should let myself in to have my things taken, and so I took my case away.'

'Did the man get out at all when the car stopped?'

'No.'

'Do you swear that?'

'Absolutely.'

'You alone got out?'

'Yes.'

'Out of the side door?'

'Yes.'

'Did you close it?'

'I got my attaché case and began to walk away.'

'Did you use the mallet that night with its handle for opening the can?'

'I cannot recall or visualize handling the mallet.'

'Rouse,' said Birkett, addressing the prisoner sternly, 'you are the only person who can tell us how that petrol can was opened. Your passenger is dead. Do you tell the jury you cannot recall such an important matter?'

'I don't remember every motion of my hands and feet,' Rouse replied sullenly.

'When you had unscrewed the cap of the petrol can, what did you do with the mallet?'

'I don't know.'

'You know where it was found. It was found fourteen yards in front of the car and about a foot from the grass edge. So somebody must have carried it there.'

'I don't know.'

'I want you to think.'

'I did not put the mallet on the grass there.'

'And did your passenger never get out of the car?'

'No.'

'Then how did the mallet get there?'

'I don't know.'

'Did you give any instructions to the man about filling your tank?'

'No, I did everything and prepared it for him.'

'You took the cap off the tank, looked into it, and unscrewed the petrol can which you knew to be filled with petrol. Why did you not pour it in?'

'Because it takes some time to pour in.'

'You have heard Sir Bernard Spilsbury describe the extended right foot showing, in his view, that the body had been outside the car. Are you sure that this dead man did not walk some fourteen yards up the road with you, where you unscrewed the can with the mallet?'

'No, he did not get outside the car in my presence.'

'You were the only one to handle the mallet and the can that night?'

'Yes, but I do not know whether the man handled the can after I left.'

'Why did you put a full can on the back seat?'

'I thought it would be easier for him.'

Asked why he had not warned the man against the danger of striking a match in the car, the prisoner said, 'I thought he would have the common sense not to light a match with a can of petrol there.'

'I want to suggest as plainly as I can, Rouse,' Birkett put his last question in slow and measured tones, emphasizing each word, 'that you lit that petrol in that car?'

'I certainly did not, sir,' Rouse answered quietly.

The next defence witness was Mr. Harvey Wyatt, a pathologist who was called to rebut the expert evidence which had been given for the prosecution by Sir Bernard Spilsbury. 'One could draw very definite conclusions from the position of the body when found,' he said in examination-in-chief. 'We know that great heat does contort the limbs and I do not think one can assume safely that the position of the body as it was found afterwards was the same as that in which the body was when death took place.' Mr. Wyatt also advanced the theory that the roof might subsequently have fallen in, pressing on the body. 'It is impossible to say from the position of the body whether the door was open or shut,' he added.

'Do you agree that the man might be overcome and killed quite quickly in a petrol fire?'

'Yes, I do.'

Birkett took up his cross-examination from this point. 'It is clear, is it not, that the man breathed for a short time in the car?'

'A very short time,' the witness agreed.

'He breathed in the car while the fire raged for half a minute?'

The witness nodded.

'Does not all the data point to the conclusion that before that half a minute began he was unconscious?'

'I am very sorry,' answered the pathologist, 'I do not quite follow why that should be.'

Birkett paused and adjusted his wig. 'Let me try to explain,' he said. 'You have seen the mallet in this case?'

'Yes.'

'A blow from that mallet would stun, would it not?'

'Yes.'

'A blow from that mallet upon the skull would not now be traceable because of the effects of the fire?'

'No.'

'You would not have blood or tissue adhering to the mallet?'

'No.'

'Since the fire it is impossible to say whether the skull was originally fractured or not?'

'Yes.'

'The posture of the body which has been described would lend considerable support to the view that the man was unconscious when placed in the car, would it not?'

'I do not quite see why.'

'Take this—the face down in the driver's seat. Very difficult to get prone with your face in the driver's seat unless placed there by some other human agency?'

'I think in a small car you might easily fall into that position.'

'Is it not quite clear that the posture must have been occasioned by the man being placed there?'

'I don't think there is any "must" about it,' said the pathologist, determined to stick to his opinion.

Unlike his friend Marshall Hall, Birkett rarely indulged in theatrical demonstrations in court, least of all when he was on the prosecuting side. But on this occasion, he turned to his junior Richard Elwes, who was sitting behind him, caught hold of his right arm, and gripped it. 'Supposing the man had been flung in by another man holding his right arm,' he asked the witness, 'that would tend to fall inside, would it not?'

'I cannot quite see that,' the pathologist repeated his previous answer.

Birkett persevered, gesturing with his free hand as he spoke. 'Supposing there was an unconscious man who had to be supported as he was thrown into the car, that arm flung across the seat would remain extended?'

'Yes.'

'And that would account not only for the prone position of the body falling helpless that way, but for the extended right arm?'

'It would be a possible explanation,' the pathologist agreed.

'And a reasonable explanation?'

'Yes.'

Among the other witnesses called by the defence was a motor engineer from Cricklewood named Arthur Isaacs, who had voluntarily come forward with an offer to give expert evidence after reading of the case in the newspapers and in particular of the controversy concerning the nut on the union joint in the petrol pipe of Rouse's car—whether it was loosened accidentally or on purpose. He was emphatic when questioned by Rouse's counsel that his experience of car fires was that a fire invariably loosened this particular joint.

'Do I understand you to say,' the judge intervened at this point, 'that the nut is found to be loose invariably as long as the fire is intense?'

'Yes, my Lord,' the engineer replied. This witness then went on to explain that the loosening was caused by the contraction and distortion of the metal threads cooling down after the fire.

This evidence of technical expertise appeared at first sight to demolish a principal part of the structure of the Crown case. But Birkett immediately rose to the occasion. His cross-examination of the Cricklewood engineer was brief but deadly.

BIRKETT: What is the co-efficient of the expansion of brass?
WITNESS: The what?
BIRKETT: The co-efficient of the expansion of brass.
WITNESS: I am afraid I cannot answer.
BIRKETT: Do you know what the question means?
WITNESS: Well, if you put it that way, I don't.

BIRKETT: But aren't you an engineer? You are not a doctor or a crime investigator, or an amateur detective. Aren't you an engineer? Don't you know what the co-efficient of brass is?
WITNESS: No.
BIRKETT: But your company deals with the heat treatment of metal. What do you make?
WITNESS: Springs.
BIRKETT: How many people do you employ?
WITNESS: About seventy.
BIRKETT: Have you any degrees?
WITNESS: No.
BIRKETT: And as a fire assessor did you have any training?
WITNESS: I think so.
BIRKETT: Where?
WITNESS: All over the place, in South Africa, and in this country.

The witness went on to say that after the First World War he had had experience through employment by insurance companies to assess the damage by fire and to try to locate the cause of it. It was part of his firm's work. In the last year he had investigated fifteen to twenty fires. They were all car fires, mostly by the roadside.

BIRKETT: What is the melting point of brass?
WITNESS (after some hesitation): Ah, brass! Oh! about 1,800 degrees Fahrenheit.
BIRKETT: If you took half an inch of brass and heated it to 1,500 degrees Fahrenheit, what expansion would you get?'
WITNESS: I would not like to say.
BIRKETT: Do help me about it. Surely, Mr. Isaacs, you have been giving evidence about the effect of intense heat upon the brass nut. Do you now tell the jury that you have no idea what effect 1,500 degrees of heat would have on a half-inch of brass?
WITNESS: I do not know. I have no need to know.

After some further questions about the effect of heat on metal and the loosening of nuts, Birkett passed on to the witness's theory that the fire might have been started by the passenger's cigar while he was picking up the petrol tank. 'Does it destroy your theory,' he asked, 'to hear that the can was at the back of the car?'

'I do not think so,' the engineer replied, still looking confident.

'Would anything destroy your theory?' Birkett retorted, as he resumed his seat. This rhetorical question produced an outburst of laughter in which even the prisoner joined.

Mr. Issacs was followed into the witness box by another engineer, Mr. Arthur Cotton, from Manchester, who said he acted as fire loss assessor to fifteen different insurance companies. From his experience he had always found the petrol union nuts to be loose after a fire.

'You are an engineer?' Birkett asked.

'Yes.'

'Do you know the co-efficients of expansion?'

'No.'

'But they are in any little engineer's diary?'

'I am a practical engineer, not a theoretical one,' this witness replied, very much on his dignity.

This question, which effectively demolished the evidence of the defence's two expert witnesses, has been cited as the most devastating in its effect of any question ever put to a witness by Birkett in cross-examination. At the time, however, it was criticized in some quarters as a 'trick' question which should not have been asked. But Birkett considered the question quite justified, as he had seen it in the engineer's diary belonging to Colonel Buckle, the expert witness called by the prosecution, and he assumed that a qualified engineer would be familiar with the answer. Asked many years later what he would have done if the witnesses had given the correct answer (0.0000189), he said that he would have gone on to copper, then to aluminium and other metals, eventually leaving the subject as if it were of no particular importance.

Mr. Justice Talbot summed up the evidence very fairly, but he could not conceal his opinion of Rouse. 'There is no doubt that he is by his own confession a most facile liar,' said the judge. 'It is really not exaggerating the matter to say that from the moment when he got on that lorry from the main road which runs out of Northampton to the moment when he got out of the motor coach in London, he told lies about almost every conceivable matter and to almost every conceivable person he saw.'

It took the jury only a quarter of an hour to find Rouse guilty. Asked if he had anything to say before sentence of death was passed, he replied, 'Only that I am innocent.'

But after his appeal had been dismissed and the Home Secretary refused a reprieve, Rouse admitted that even at this solemn moment in court he had again been lying. On the eve of his execution, he confessed that he had strangled the unknown man, who was half intoxicated, inside the car and had then started the fire with a trail of petrol. ('He just gurgled. I pressed his throat hard . . . I ran to the beginning of the petrol trail and put a match to it.') For once, it seems, Rouse had told the truth.[1]

3

'If only people did the right thing in life and all the circumstances of life, the lawyer's occupation would be gone.' Birkett spoke these words in addressing the jury on behalf of Mrs. Sarah Ann Hearn towards the end of her trial for murder. Like the case of Mrs. Pace, which in some particulars it resembled, interest in this trial was nation-wide. Again the case involved a woman who was charged with murder by arsenical poisoning and again Birkett was briefed 'special' to defend the prisoner, who had foolishly disappeared at a critical moment and in circumstances which were bound to reflect strong suspicions upon her conduct.

At this time Mrs. Hearn was a widow in her middle forties. At least she claimed to be a widow, although the newspapers which reported her case searched in vain for her marriage certificate in the official registry at Somerset House. According to her, she married a medical student named Leonard Wilmot Hearn in a London register office in 1919, but they only lived together for a few days after which they parted. A day or two later she read in a Harrogate paper, so she said, that he had died. Although it had no direct bearing on Mrs. Hearn's trial, there was certainly something rather odd about her supposed marriage. It may be that she had no photograph of her husband to show her family and after his death felt that for the sake of respectability she should acquire one. Anyhow she did give her relatives a photograph purporting to be of the late Mr. Hearn, but when it eventually found its way into a newspaper it turned out to be a likeness of Lieutenant Charles Stewart Vane-Tempest, great-grandson of the third Marquess of Londonderry. Lieutenant Vane-

[1] Rouse's confession was published the day after he was hanged. For details see the *Daily Sketch*, March 11, 1931.

London Express Pictures

CLARENCE HATRY

Keystone

ALFRED ARTHUR ROUSE

Keyston

ROUSE'S BURNT OUT CAR

Tempest, it appeared, had been killed in action in 1917 and Mrs. Hearn subsequently bought his photograph.

At first she had lived in Harrogate with an aunt who ran a cookery school there. In 1921 she moved to Cornwall with the aunt and an invalid sister, Mrs. Lydia ('Minnie') Everard, whom she helped to nurse. They shared a home, Trenhorne House, in the village of Lewannick, near Launceston. Unfortunately Mrs. Everard's health did not benefit from the change, her eyes and heart troubled her, she also suffered from severe gastric pains and on one occasion complained to her sister that the medicine she was taking tasted 'too strong'. Eventually, in 1930, she died and was buried in Lewannick Churchyard.

The next door property, Trenhorne Farm, belonged to a small farmer William Thomas, who lived there with his wife Alice ('Annie'). The Thomases felt sorry for Mrs. Hearn, who had lost her sister and previously her aunt and must now be feeling lonely. Mr. Thomas knew, too, that she was far from well off and to help her out temporarily he made her a loan of thirty-eight pounds. Then, on October 18, 1930, he and his wife invited Mrs. Hearn to go to Bude with them in their car for an afternoon's outing. Mrs. Hearn gladly accepted the invitation and prepared some tinned salmon sandwiches. They stopped for tea at a café in Bude and supplemented the meal with the sandwiches which they all shared. On the way home Mrs. Thomas became ill with violent stomach pains and vomiting. Mrs. Hearn stayed at the farm to nurse her, but she did not recover. The abdominal pains grew worse, she was removed to Plymouth Hospital and on November 4 she died. A *post-mortem* examination was carried out and this revealed the presence of 0.85 grains of white arsenic, which was a form that could be obtained from weed-killer. Next day, Mr. Thomas told Mrs. Hearn that one of them was likely to be blamed and that she would be more heavily blamed than he. 'People are saying so,' he told her, 'and a detective may be here at any time.' At the funeral, a brother of the dead woman, Mr. Percy Parsons, made some rather pointed remarks which seemed to associate Mrs. Hearn with his sister's death, after he had asked whether she was responsible for making the sandwiches which were eaten. 'The matter must be cleared up,' he was overheard to remark, as he looked steadily at Mrs. Hearn.

Mrs. Hearn now returned to Trenhorne House and a few days

later Mr. Thomas received a letter from her which suggested that she was about to commit suicide. 'Good-bye,' she wrote. 'I am going out if I can. I cannot forget that awful man and the things he said. I am innocent, innocent, but she is dead and it was my lunch she ate. I cannot stay. When I am dead they will be sure I am guilty, and you, at least, will be clear. May your dear wife's presence guard and comfort you still.' In a postscript she added: 'My life is not a great thing now dear Annie is gone. My conscience is clear. I am not afraid of afterwards. I am giving instructions about selling the things and hope you will be paid in full. That is all I can do now.'

By the time Mr. Thomas received this letter Mrs. Hearn had disappeared. Shortly afterwards her coat was found on the cliffs at Looe, and one of her shoes was later washed up by the sea, which lent support to the idea of suicide. However, far from taking her own life, she had gone to Torquay where she registered in a hotel under an assumed name. A little later she answered an advertisement in a local paper which had been inserted by a Mr. Cecil Powell, an architect, who required a housekeeper. She was duly engaged.

Meanwhile a coroner's inquest had found that Mrs. Thomas had died from arsenical poisoning. The next step was for the bodies of Mrs. Hearn's sister and aunt to be exhumed. Both were found to contain distinct quantities of arsenic. Meanwhile the *Daily Mail* published her photograph and offered a reward of five hundred pounds to any reader who could either confirm her death or give information which would enable the police to interview her. The architect immediately recognized his housekeeper as Mrs. Hearn and informed the police. She was thereupon arrested and charged with the murder of Mrs. Thomas and also of her own sister Lydia Everard.

Mr. Powell now claimed and was paid the reward of five hundred pounds. With characteristic generosity he handed over the sum to an able solicitor of his acquaintance, Mr. Walter West, to enable his housekeeper to have the best defending counsel obtainable. It was in this way that Birkett was instructed to lead the defence of Mrs. Hearn. As junior counsel he had Mr. Dingle Foot, who belonged to the Western Circuit and whose father Mr. Isaac Foot was the local Liberal Member of Parliament and an old friend of Birkett's. Birkett stayed at his home throughout the trial.

The trial opened before Mr. Justice Roche at Bodmin Assizes on July 15, 1931. Although charged under two separate counts in the indictment, relating respectively to Miss Everard and Mrs. Thomas, Mrs. Hearn was actually tried on the second, the murder of Mrs. Thomas, the Crown having the right of election. She pleaded Not Guilty. The prosecution was led by Mr. H. du Parcq, K.C. (later Lord du Parcq), assisted by Mr. Patrick Devlin (later Lord Devlin).

At the end of the first day, almost entirely taken up with Mr. du Parcq's opening statement, Birkett went home with his junior. The latter's father was in the habit of asking his guests, instead of signing a visitor's book, to plant a tree in the grounds of his house. While he was engaged in this operation Mr. Isaac Foot's gardener, who was standing by to help, remarked, 'Well, I suppose she'll get a fair trial.'

'Let's hope that everyone will get a fair trial,' Birkett replied gently.

Some moments of silence followed, while Birkett busied himself in arranging the soil round the tree. Then he turned to his companion and spoke again. 'I expect there is quite a lot of arsenic in this soil.'

'There is no arsenic in that soil,' said the gardener, 'any more than there is in the graveyard at Lewannick.'

The gardener's remarks indicated in some measure the intense prejudice shown locally against Mrs. Hearn at the outset of her trial. Indeed feeling was so strong that it had been found necessary to empanel a jury to try the case from the other side of the county. So far as concerned the soil, however, the gardener was wrong. The earth in the graveyard *did* yield a high proportion of arsenic on analysis, but apparently not higher than one might expect to find in an area where there were tin mines. But the fact that there was any arsenic at all there lent support to the theory which Birkett was to advance that some of the poison might have seeped into the coffin and impregnated the bodies after burial.

Apart from some formal evidence, the first prosecution witness was Mr. Thomas, who described the trip to Bude, the consumption of the sandwiches and his wife's subsequent illness. They had been on picnics together before. Sometimes Mrs. Thomas brought the food, sometimes Mrs. Hearn, and sometimes both of them. He could not remember who took the first sandwich, but he was certain that he himself took one and his wife and the prisoner one each.

'As to the taking of the sandwiches, there was no pushing of the plate or juggling with them?' Birkett asked in cross-examination.

'No, there was no juggling at all,' the witness replied, adding that the sandwiches were placed on the table in two piles, each of which he thought contained three each.

'Did your wife take a second sandwich?'

'I do not remember.'

'Did you know what was in the sandwiches? You had eaten one?'

'Yes, but I did not know what kind of fish it was.'

'Did you tell the doctor what your wife had had for her midday dinner?'

'I cannot remember.'

'Do you remember what you did have?'

'No.'

The dead woman's husband went on to say that it was quite unexpectedly that Mrs. Hearn was asked to go to Bude, and in the same way she was asked to stay at his house. She appeared to him to do her very best for his wife.

'Did you say anything to her about what you knew people were saying?'

'I do not remember.'

'In her letter to you Mrs. Hearn wrote: "I want to go out if I can." I suggest you said to that woman that people were talking?'

'I may have said so.'

'Did you tell her that people were talking about you both?'

'I might have said people were talking about the sandwiches and that my wife had died from poisoned sandwiches.'

'Had the doctor said that to you?'

'Yes.'

'Might you have said, "The blame will come heavier on you than me"?'

'I may have. I do not remember. It was Mrs. Hearn's sandwiches my wife took.'

'Did you say, "A detective might be here at any time"?'

'I said someone might come to make inquiries. I may have said detective, but I do not remember.'

'Did you say, "Whatever there is they will find it out"?'

'Yes.'

'Were you referring to food poisoning?'

'Yes.'

'Did Mrs. Hearn say, "If people think like that I had better go to my own house"?'

'Yes.'

'It is true, then, that she said people were blaming her?'

'I might have said people were talking about the poison in the sandwiches.'

'Poison, sir!' Birkett rapped out the words sharply. 'Did you use the word "poison" to her?'

'No.'

Enough had been elicited from this witness to conjure up in the eyes of the jury the picture of a distressed woman who was a prey to the most horrible gossip. Birkett heightened the effect by putting some quotations from Mrs. Hearn's letter to the dead woman's husband.

'When Mrs. Hearn wrote to you, "Good-bye, I am going out if I can" did you think that she meant she was going to take her life if she could screw up her courage to the sticking point? Is that how you read it?'

'Yes.'

'Then when Mrs. Hearn wrote, "I cannot forget that awful man and the things he said", did you know she meant Parsons?'

'Yes.'

' "I am innocent, innocent." Were those two words underlined?'

'Yes.'

'You knew people were talking about the sandwiches?'

'Yes.'

'Do you think that was the letter of a distraught woman, of a woman very upset and very grieved?'

'I took it that she was upset.'

'What did you do with the letter from Mrs. Hearn?' Birkett asked in conclusion.

'I gave it to the police the same day that I received it,' said Mr. Thomas.

Mr. Parsons, the dead woman's brother, giving evidence, denied that he had accused Mrs. Hearn at the funeral of poisoning Mrs. Thomas, although he admitted saying the matter should be looked into. He also made it clear that Mr. and Mrs. Thomas did not get on well together in their married life. This was relevant to the current rumour that Mrs. Hearn had done away with Mrs. Thomas so that she could marry her husband.

Police-Sergeant Trebilcock of Lewannick then went into the witness box and described how he had arrested Mrs. Hearn in a street in Torquay. While Superintendent Pill was writing down her statement, she had said to the Police-Sergeant in a low voice, 'Mr. Thomas used to come to our house every day with a paper. Of course, that was only a blind.'

'Have you ever heard a sentence of yours not properly caught by the hearer?' Birkett asked in cross-examination.

'Yes, at times,' the Police-Sergeant admitted.

'Your voice is not too clear,' Birkett continued. 'It is possible to make a mistake about what you said?'

'I thought I spoke very plainly.' This answer, given in a strong Cornish accent, caused some laughter in court.

'But this statement of Mrs. Hearn's, do you not think that it was a misunderstanding of what she said?'

'I made no mistake about that.'

'Well, listen to this,' said Birkett. ' "Mr. Thomas used to bring a paper. He was very kind." "Mr. Thomas used to bring a paper. It was only a blind." Don't you think you could have made a mistake?'

'No.'

'I suggest that Mrs. Hearn never said anything of the kind about it being a blind?'

'I say she did.'

4

The chief chemist of the manufacturers of the tinned salmon from which the sandwiches had been made also gave evidence for the Crown. He agreed with Birkett that the sterilization of food by heat might kill the bacteria, but food poisoning by toxins might still occur. He also agreed that the effect of eating food in which there were toxins of a particular group commonly associated with tinned and other foods would manifest itself after an interval of from two to four hours.

'Can you find cases of food poisoning in which one person has been affected and others not although they have all partaken of the same food?'

'Yes.'

Birkett displayed similar skill in cross-examining the other expert witnesses for the prosecution, his object being to satisfy the jury that Mrs. Thomas suffered from ordinary food poisoning as a result of eating the sandwiches and only later from arsenical poisoning, for which Mrs. Hearn could not have been responsible.

On the question of the presence of arsenic in the soil, he got Dr. Eric Wordley, the pathologist who conducted the exhumation of Miss Everard's body, to admit that minute particles could have entered the 'unstoppered' jars containing the organs which were the subject of the *post-mortem* examination carried out at the graveside.

'Am I right in saying that a piece of soil, so small that you could hold it between your fingers, dropped on to the body would make every single calculation wrong?'

'Yes.'

When Dr. Roche Lynch, the senior Home Office analyst, was examined by Mr. du Parcq for the Crown, the analyst retailed much expert knowledge on the effect of arsenic on the human organs. But it was clear that his experience, valuable as it was, had been confined to organs which had been removed for analysis after death had taken place.

'Have you ever examined a living patient suffering from arsenical poisoning?' was Birkett's first question in cross-examination. The witness admitted that he had not.

The prosecution had proved that Mrs. Hearn had once purchased some arsenic weed-killer. According to Dr. Lynch, there must have been about fourteen grains in the sandwiches.

'You say that in your opinion the weed-killer was used in solid form?' Birkett asked him.

'I suggest so.'

'Have you taken a sandwich and put 14.3 grains in it?'

'No.'

'You have shown that arsenic put in Benger's Food discolours the white food?'

'Yes.'

'That is with two grains?'

'Yes.'

'Seven times as much would greatly discolour it?'

'Yes.'

'If you put fourteen grains of blue weed-killer on a sandwich and carried it for hours, I suggest it would be blue?' Birkett continued, in the knowledge that the experiment had already been made by his instructing solicitor.

'I have not tried it,' said the analyst, 'but my opinion, for what it is worth, is that it would not be.'

'*But you have not tried it*,' Birkett went on. 'On the theory of the prosecution, surely it was a most terrible risk to run?'

'Personally I don't think so.'

'If you have sandwiches in two piles of three each—assume for the moment that the topmost sandwich of one of those piles contains arsenic—am I right in assuming that the sandwich with the blue weed-killer would stain downwards?'

'Yes.'

'The white bread, like the white Benger's Food, would make the stains instantly discernible?'

'I agree, and the white bread being more localized, the blue would come through in spots and stains.'

'I am much obliged,' said Birkett, with a glance at the jury to note that they had taken in the significance of this answer. 'And would not the stains also go upwards?'

'Yes.'

At the close of the case for the prosecution, Birkett briefly submitted that there was no evidence to go to the jury. But the judge ruled that there was ample evidence, and so Birkett immediately put the accused woman into the witness box.

Mrs. Hearn proved an excellent witness, speaking in a straightforward manner, as she told the story of her early life, her marriage and her sister's illness, and denied that she had given any poison either to her sister, or to Mrs. Thomas. Explaining her 'flight' to Torquay after the funeral of Mrs. Thomas, she said that she meant, as she declared in her letter to Mr. Thomas, to throw herself over the cliffs at Looe, but could not bring herself to do it. Her testimony was quite unshaken when she was cross-examined by Mr. du Parcq.

In his re-examination, Birkett dealt with the suggestion about her feelings towards the dead woman's husband. Mrs. Hearn said that until that very moment no one in the world had suggested that she wanted to marry Mr. Thomas. There was never at any time in her mind, she emphasized, the thought that she might marry Mr. Thomas.

'I want you to understand,' Birkett put it to her bluntly, 'that it is now suggested that you killed Mrs. Thomas in order to do that. Is there a word of truth in that?'

'Not an atom.'

'Did you ever conceive a passion, guilty or otherwise, for Mr. Thomas?'

'No.'

In order to have the final word with the jury, except for the judge's summing up, Birkett decided to call no further witnesses for the defence. Accordingly, the seventh day of the trial began with Mr. du Parcq's closing speech to the jury.

The Crown counsel had not been on his feet for long when he suddenly collapsed. He was helped out of court by Birkett to an ante-room, where he fainted. The trial was thereupon adjourned, but two hours later Mr. du Parcq returned and told the judge that he had now recovered and was able to continue his speech. This the judge directed him to do while remaining seated. 'It is as well not to make a mystery of these things,' Mr. Justice Roche told the jury. 'Mr. du Parcq's indisposition was perfectly simple of explanation. When the brain is working, blood flows to the head, and, speaking quickly after a meal, blood is thus transferred from the stomach, and digestion is interfered with. This causes pressure by the intestines upon the heart, causing this faintness.' The judge went on to say that it had happened to him once in the early days of his own professional career, adding amidst laughter, 'I am still here, and older than Mr. du Parcq.'[1]

Birkett began his speech to the jury immediately after the luncheon adjournment by paying a tribute to the prosecution. 'I know something of the strain which learned counsel undergoes in a case of this nature requiring all the strength and fortitude that a man may have,' he said, 'and I share with you the regret that my learned friend should have the temporary illness of this morning. I am sure

[1] Mr. Justice Roche, who was 60 at this time, lived to be 86. But Mr. du Parcq who was nine years younger, died at the age of 69.

I share with you and with all our gratification that he has fully recovered. His closing speech lacks nothing of ability and lacks nothing of power because of that interruption. These are matters that are to be observed by all, but one thing I want to do in my particular province as counsel for the accused is to say that the case here for the Crown has been presented by him with conspicuous fairness, and that in every part of it he has shown himself to be in accord with those traditions of the Bar which made the prosecuting counsel truly a demonstrator of justice.'

For upwards of four hours Birkett analysed the Crown's case against his client, which, he said, depended on 'all sorts of coincidences, and rare possibilities'. The suggested motive that Mrs. Hearn murdered Mrs. Thomas so that she could marry Mr. Thomas he dismissed as 'fantastical' and 'fanciful'. As for Dr. Roche Lynch's evidence, 'Dr. Roche Lynch had never attended one living patient suffering from arsenical poisoning, and yet he speaks of symptoms with the same confidence that he spoke of other matters. Let the cobbler stick to his last. . . .' Again, there was no evidence that the weed-killer had ever been taken to Trenhorne Farm, the Thomas's home. But there were some Cooper's worm tablets in the house, and they contained not only arsenic but also copper which the weed-killer did not contain. 'And in the organs of Mrs. Thomas there was found copper.'

Before coming into court Birkett had given some thought to the peroration of his speech. At first, he thought of building it round a quotation from the 14th chapter of St. John, which it had come out in evidence a kindly neighbour read to Miss Everard in the sick-room, 'Let not your heart be troubled, neither let it be afraid.' But he decided to discard this when he heard that the jury on the previous Sunday when given the choice of attending divine service or going for a motor drive had unanimously plumped for the drive.

Eventually he took his cue from a shaft of sunlight which penetrated the windows of the court room. 'For over five months Mrs. Hearn has lain in Exeter Gaol,' he said. 'When the darkness of winter has now come to this lovely light of this June day, for her upon trial for her life it may be said with truth she has been walking in the valley of great shadows. It is your hand and your hand alone which can lead her forth into the light. It is your voice and your voice alone which alone can speak her the word of deliverance. My appeal is that you will speak the word, that you will stretch forth the hand. . . . Your verdict ought to be and should be that she is not guilty. For that verdict I appeal.'

The court now adjourned for the day. The following morning Mr. Justice Roche began his summing up. It was just past three o'clock in the afternoon when he finished and the jury retired to consider their verdict. Birkett, who had been briefed to appear in a case in the High Court next day, did not wait to hear the verdict but left with his clerk to catch a fast train to London.

The train stopped at Plymouth, and Bowker got out to buy an evening paper to find out the result of the trial. But the news had not come through. He did the same at Newton Abbot, still with no result. Finally, at Exeter, which was the last stop before London, the clerk succeeded in getting hold of a paper. Mrs. Hearn had been acquitted after the jury had been absent from court for a little under an hour. She had also been acquitted on the other count in the indictment, which charged her with murdering Lydia Everard, since in view of the first acquittal the prosecution decided to offer no evidence on this count.

Bowker hurried back to the compartment to give his master the good news and to congratulate him. Then a curious incident occurred which demonstrated the fallibility of human memory. The only other passenger in the carriage was an elderly gentleman who now spoke for the first time. 'This is a most remarkable coincidence,' he said to the successful counsel. 'You are Mr. Birkett. I have only seen you once before—that was when you were travelling to Gloucester to defend Mrs. Pace. We travelled in the same carriage then. Now I see you for the second time, and I gather from your friend that your defence of Mrs. Hearn has been equally successful. I think this is a wonderful coincidence.'

Birkett agreed, but neither he nor his clerk said anything further. Later the two men went along to the restaurant car for a cup of tea where they discussed the reason for their silence, since they felt it would be a pity to destroy the stranger's illusions. In fact, Birkett had motored from Bristol to Gloucester for the opening of the Pace trial, and the old gentleman must have travelled with Sir Boyd Merriman, who was prosecuting.

Next morning, Birkett appeared in the King's Bench Division before Mr. Justice Rigby Swift. His case happened to be first in the judge's list, and as he entered court a note was passed down to him from the Bench. Initialled by the judge, it read: 'With his honours thick upon him.' It was a kindly and characteristic tribute.

5

In the circumstances of his busy practice, Birkett kept up his attendance record in the House of Commons as best he could. Along with Sir John Simon he became one of the two leading Liberal spokesmen on the legal aspects of Government legislation. But his speeches were relatively infrequent, as they had been in the 1924 Parliament, and although he would go straight to the House when the courts rose shortly after 4.0 p.m. it was as a rule to vote rather than to speak. He was consequently rather concerned when his defeated Conservative opponent in East Nottingham, Mr. L. H. Gluckstein, attacked his division record, since many divisions of a more or less formal character, such as on the question of the House sitting after eleven o'clock at night, took place early in the afternoon, when Birkett could not be present. For instance, during the first session of the 1929 Parliament, thirty-four divisions were called on the suspension of the 'Eleven o'clock Rule', which Birkett admitted 'quite frankly' to his constituents he had missed through engagements in the Law Courts. 'I can only sincerely hope,' he added with a good-humoured tilt at his fellow barrister, 'that one of these days Mr. Gluckstein will realize what an urgent and personal matter it is when he is overwhelmed with clients.'

His attack upon a far-reaching clause in the Finance Bill of 1930, which he felt greatly infringed the principle of individual liberty, drew tributes from both sides of the House, although the clause was subsequently passed in spite of Birkett's protest. The clause in question empowered the Special Commissioners of Income Tax to call on companies for particulars of the shares and other securities of any taxpayer, the accuracy of whose tax returns they might doubt. Birkett had this to say during the debate on the Committee Stage on the clause which he regarded as 'entirely revolutionary':

> Anybody who resists a clause of this nature would in certain quarters be open to the criticism that he is protecting

the tax evader. I am certain that in every quarter of the House there is not the smallest desire to assist anyone in any way to evade a just and proper duty. But what it is important that the Committee should realize—and I think they do realize after this debate—is that you must not, in order to hit the tax evader, hit, and hit very hardly, a larger number of innocent citizens and innocent taxpayers, and that by attempting to deal with one evil you may possibly do very much greater injury. The whole point of the matter is this: this Clause is a Clause which seeks to give to the Special Commissioners power, the like of which they have never had. It is not enough to say that they have certain powers now under the Finance Act and other Statutes, and that this is a small extension. In reality it is one of the most far-reaching proposals which this Committee has ever had to consider with regard to the power of the Commissioners.[1]

The most striking tribute came from Mr. Winston Churchill on the Opposition Front Bench. 'I have rarely heard a speech more precisely directed to the object under debate, more harmoniously attuned to the character of Committee discussion, than the excellent statement the Honourable and learned Gentleman has just made,' said Mr. Churchill, who had been Chancellor of the Exchequer in the previous Conservative Government. 'It seemed to me that there could hardly be a more damaging speech from the point of view of the Attorney-General himself. Not only were his facts traversed, not only was his legal authority impugned and even controverted, but these sharp arrows were planted in his person by his distinguished legal successor in his old primacy on the Liberal benches. He has been able to answer him in fact and law and leave him a sprawling, a pitiable object.'[2]

In January, 1931, the Labour Government introduced a con-

[1] *Official Report*, June 17, 1930.

[2] 'A well phrased compliment!' was how Birkett's backbench colleague Leslie Hore-Belisha in a newspaper article described Mr. Churchill's remarks. 'One cannot listen to Mr. Birkett, and one cannot know him however slightly, without feeling a most comfortable confidence in his capacity and in his character. Surely it is a miracle that, despite his professional contact with much that is disillusioning in human relations, he has retained so unspoiled a courtesy and understanding.' *Daily Express* ('In the Speaker's Eye'), June 20, 1930.

troversial Trade Disputes Bill designed to reverse the Conservative measure following the General Strike of 1926 which had declared such a strike illegal. It also legalized peaceful picketing, 'contracting out' of paying a political levy instead of 'contracting in', and affiliation of the Civil Service unions with the Trade Union Congress. Birkett was put in charge of the Bill for the Liberals and as the debate on the Second Reading, which lasted three days, coincided with the Rouse trial at Northampton Assizes in which he led for the Crown, he was extremely busy dashing to London after the court rose and returning to Northampton by the midnight or an early morning train. Birkett spoke third from the corner seat on the front bench below the gangway, following the Attorney-General (Sir William Jowitt) who introduced the Bill, and Mr. Baldwin who led the Conservative Opposition. As the parliamentary correspondent of *Punch* put it, 'Mr. Birkett commanded more attention [than either the Bill's proposer or opposer] partly because, though a great lawyer, he is seldom heard in the House, but chiefly because it fell to him to bestow the Liberal blessing—tempered with a strong leavening of Liberal condemnation—on the Bill. He did it in the traditional way, tearing the Bill to tatters in a closely reasoned speech and intimating that the Liberal Party would die in the last Lobby in defence of contracting in, the removal of Civil Servants from politics, and the right of local authorities to employ non-union Labour, and concluding rather lamely by announcing that the Liberal Party would support a Second Reading of the Bill and give it socks in Committee.'[1]

In fact, the Liberals abstained from voting on the Second Reading except for a handful of their supporters who voted for it, thus ensuring its passage by the relatively small margin of twenty-seven votes. As Birkett forecast, the Bill was drastically amended in Committee, where the Liberals, with Conservative support, carried an amendment severely limiting the legality of strikes. In this context Birkett's speech on the Second Reading provided a rich stock of ammunition for the Bill's opponents, among whom was Sir Henry Betterton, a future Conservative Minister of Labour (later Lord Rushcliffe), who sent Birkett a note immediately after he had made his speech. 'May I write a line of warm congratulation on one of the most effective and

[1] *Punch*, June 28, 1931.

deadly speeches I have ever heard in the House,' wrote Betterton. 'The rapt attention with which you were heard—very seldom accorded to the third speech in such a Debate—was of itself a tribute, and so thoroughly deserved. I often think the House a very difficult place to speak in, but you seem to find no embarrassment.'

This was probably the best speech that Birkett ever made in the House of Commons. Certainly he won most acclaim for it. 'I had a great success in the House yesterday,' he told his cousin Henry Birkett next day: 'but it has meant weeks of work—and will!' Above all it impressed the Prime Minister.

Ramsay MacDonald would have been glad to have Birkett as Solicitor-General if he had been willing to join the Labour ranks as Jowitt did. Birkett's refusal to consider this at the time has already been noted. Overtures were renewed in 1930 when the then Solicitor-General, Sir James Melville, was obliged to resign his office on account of ill health. On this occasion Birkett was strongly pressed to reconsider his previous decision, but again he would not hear of it, and the office went to Sir Stafford Cripps. If he was to be a Law Officer, Birkett was determined that he would only fill the post as a Liberal, and there seemed little hope of there ever being a Liberal Government in power again. Yet Birkett did come close to being a Liberal Solicitor-General when Ramsay MacDonald formed his National Government with Liberal and Conservative support in the summer of 1931.

Herbert Samuel, the acting Liberal leader in the Commons, urged the new Prime Minister to offer the post to Birkett, who was prepared to accept it on learning that other prominent Liberals, such as Lord Reading and Lord Crewe, besides Samuel himself, were joining the administration. But a difficulty immediately arose, which Samuel explained to Birkett in the following letter.

35, *Porchester Terrace,*
London, W.2.
29th August, 1931

My dear Birkett,

If you had been in London, I had been hoping to see you at the Party Meeting yesterday in order to have had an opportunity of explaining the position. With the full concurrence of

Lloyd George, I had been very anxious to arrange that the Prime Minister should offer you one of the Law Officerships. I mentioned this at one of my first conferences with the Prime Minister and Baldwin, when we were engaged upon the personnel of the Government, but at that time it was not known whether the former Law Officers would continue or not. Jowitt has now decided to go on, but not Cripps. As the Prime Minister has been away since Thursday, all these matters are in abeyance, but I should think it probable that the Conservatives would put in a claim for the Solicitor-Generalship. As a matter of fact, we already have considerably more than our proportion of offices in the Government, seeing that our Party is less one-fourth as numerous as theirs, though it is not advisable to say very much about that!

I had assumed that considering the claims of your practice you would probably have been unwilling to accept any of the minor offices in the Administration, and did not feel at all sure that even one of the Law Offices would attract you. But I should certainly have pressed that an invitation should be sent to you if both the Offices had been vacated.

We probably have a strenuous session in front of us.

Yours sincerely,
HERBERT SAMUEL

Parliament was recalled on September 8, 1931 to pass the emergency economy legislation which the serious financial situation of the country demanded. Unfortunately for Birkett the post of Solicitor-General had now been otherwise filled. As Sir William Jowitt was one of the few Labour Ministers to pledge support to the new National Government, MacDonald was naturally anxious that he should continue to fill the office of Attorney-General which he had held throughout the Labour administration, particularly since this was desired by Jowitt himself. But in the business of Government making, the Conservatives on whom the new Premier now greatly depended insisted that the other Law Officer should be a member of their party, as Samuel had foreseen. They put forward the name of Sir Thomas Inskip, who had been Attorney-General in the previous Conservative Government, and, as Inskip had no objection to stepping down into the junior position, which he had also previously held, the Prime Minister was reluctantly obliged to agree to his appointment as Solicitor-General. Apart from his own sense of disappointment, Birkett was surprised that Inskip should agree to serve as subordinate to Jowitt. It did not increase his respect for Inskip nor incidentally for Jowitt, who for the sake of office had twice changed his political allegiance in a little more than two years.

Of course, Birkett could have had a non-legal office in the new National Government, and it was conveyed to him that such an office was at his disposal. But for the reason he made clear to his cousin in a letter he wrote on the day Parliament met, he was unable to accept a compromise of this kind.

To Henry Birkett

> *House of Commons. September* 8, 1931. . . . I am back here today. We had a thrilling day, and it was good to be an eye-witness. I was invited to be a Member of the Government, but the Law Officer's post was claimed by the Conservatives: and I could not contemplate a post which meant giving up my practice. . . .

By the National Economy Bill, which was now rushed through Parliament, the deficit was largely met by making cuts in salaries and other benefits and imposing fresh taxation, and the drain on gold caused by foreign withdrawals from the Bank of England was temporarily halted. Unfortunately the alarm felt by foreign investors returned immediately afterwards in increased measure, when the so-called 'Invergordon Mutiny', in which some naval ratings refused to obey orders, was magnified into the symptoms of a national revolution. The drain on the Bank's coffers was resumed with an intensity that compelled the Directors to request the Government as a matter of the utmost urgency to relieve them of their statutory obligation to sell gold, after they had parted with £33 million within four days.

To Henry Birkett

> *House of Commons. September* 17, 1931. . . . The national position is very grave, very grave indeed. There may be a collapse of the Exchanges at any moment—it is freely said

within 24 hours. You have no conception of the panic existing in this House. I have just listened to a speech made privately which has filled us all with complete consternation.

The foundations of the world are rocking!

A few days later Britain went off the Gold Standard, and the immediate crisis was averted. But for the drastic economies imposed by the National Government, a serious inflation of the currency must have taken place and the pound might well have followed the same disastrous course as the German mark had done after 1924. A demand for a General Election now arose, mainly among the Conservatives, since it was felt that confidence could only be fully restored if the Government and its policies were endorsed at the polls. MacDonald reluctantly consented. Indeed under Conservative pressure, added to the desertion of most of his old Labour followers who now accused him of betraying the Labour cause, the Prime Minister had little choice in the matter. Of course, he could have resigned, but the King urged him to stay at his post as a patriotic duty and even intimated that if he submitted his resignation it would not be accepted. Granted the necessity for an Election, the question then was whether the three political parties should fight separately or whether the National Government should go to the country on the basis of a joint appeal.

Mr. Herbert Samuel and his Liberal colleagues had only agreed to join the coalition for the purpose of enacting the emergency legislation, and they expected to revert to normal party politics as soon as the danger to the country's economy had passed. They did not relish the idea of a General Election, which they felt was bound to give the Conservatives a preponderance of influence in the new Government and Parliament. This view was shared by Birkett. But an enterprising and ambitious Liberal backbencher, Mr. Leslie Hore-Belisha, favoured the idea of a joint appeal and he circulated a document among his fellow backbenchers promising continued support to Ramsay MacDonald. When he signed this memorial to the Prime Minister, Birkett did not realize its full implications and the uses to which it might be put.

Accordingly he wrote to Mr. Hore-Belisha as follows:

House of Commons
22nd September, 1931

My dear Leslie,

I find that the document you were good enough to ask me to sign has been given a publicity and a construction which I did not contemplate.

The conception in my mind was a general support of the Prime Minister in his efforts to deal with the Nation's interests at this time of undeniable crisis.

But I now find that it is being interpreted as a general declaration in favour of tariffs, and as a stimulus to a General Election to be fought on the question of tariffs.

The views which have been expressed on the meaning of the document are such that it is impossible to allow my name to remain there: for it was never my intention by a stroke of the pen to subscribe to a policy of tariffs, or to link myself with any movement for a General Election.

I deeply regret this situation which has arisen, and I am quite sure you are not responsible for it: but I cannot allow any misunderstanding to persist which places me in the position of appearing to promise my support to something which is quite opposed to what I thought was the position.

I shall continue to support the National Government, and will be guided at all times in the future by the national interest (and this is no idle word!): but the construction which is being placed upon the document is one which is contrary to my intention, and I should be glad if you could withdraw my name to avoid future misunderstandings.

Yours ever,
NORMAN BIRKETT

Birkett and Hore-Belisha had a meeting the same day, at which Hore-Belisha undertook to communicate the contents of his letter to the Prime Minister personally.

Meanwhile the Liberals and the Conservatives in the Cabinet were at a deadlock on the issue of Free Trade versus Protection. Eventually, at midnight on October 5, a formula was found by which the National Government was to appeal to the country for a 'doctor's mandate', which was to embrace every kind of cure for the country's economic ills, even, if necessary, a cautious dose of tariffs, although it was agreed that the word 'tariffs' was not to be stressed in any appeal the Government might address to the electorate.[1] With this, the King, who had played some personal part in the crisis, dissolved Parliament, and Birkett hurried off to face the electors of East Nottingham for the fourth time in his career.

There he found his old Conservative opponent, Louis Gluckstein, waiting to take the field against him, the local Conservatives having decided to run a candidate on account of Birkett's 'persistent refusal to state clearly that he was behind the Prime Minister's manifesto' and because 'at no time had he given unqualified support to it'. Mr. Gluckstein was a strong Protectionist and this time he was on much better ground than in 1929. There was considerable unemployment in the lacemaking and hosiery trades. Lacemaking had once been safeguarded but the protective duty had been removed by the Labour Government—indeed Birkett as a convinced Free Trader had voted for its removal. Since then lace had been coming into Nottingham from abroad at a price at which the local manufacturers were unable to compete. Cheap hosiery was likewise being imported, while ladies' bags of leather, another local industry, were being dumped by Germany and selling at prices which could not be said to return a profit to their foreign makers even if they were made with sweated labour. On the other hand, Birkett was adamant on the tariff issue. Although he expressed willingness to 'deal with emergency situations by emergency methods', he made it clear that he would never be a party to 'any proposal for any general system of protective tariffs as an integral part of our national system'. The Conservative candidate naturally made the most of this admission, as well as the fact that Birkett had voted for the removal of the lace duty; and in the depressed state of the local industries Mr. Gluckstein soon won the active support of the lace and hosiery workers' organizations. 'I am the National candidate,' said Mr. Gluckstein, 'for I am prepared to give the Government a free hand, while Mr. Birkett only wants a free hand for himself.'

[1] King George V wrote in his diary on October 2: 'Received Sir Herbert Samuel at 10.30. He was quite impossible, most obstinate, and said he would not look at tariffs and that there was a deadlock as regards Conservatives and Liberals in the Government. God knows what can be done! . . . Am much worried by the political situation and can't see a way out.' Cited in Harold Nicolson, *King George V* (1952), at p. 402.

Birkett also claimed to be the National candidate, and the confusion was hardly removed when the Prime Minister endorsed Birkett's candidature in a public statement, since Birkett's withdrawal of his name from the Hore-Belisha memorial was effectively used against him, as well as his reluctance to accept the implications of the Prime Minister's election manifesto.

This election campaign showed a decided swing away from Liberalism compared with the position in 1929; nor was Birkett helped by the appearance of a Labour candidate, who was bound to draw some of the former Liberal votes. Nevertheless, Birkett's supporters were confident that his personal popularity in the constituency coupled with his professional fame would insure his return. Also, he had some enthusiastic meetings. By a slip of the tongue he addressed one of them as 'Members of the jury', hastily correcting himself on the ground that 'evil communications corrupt good manners'. He added, 'You are indeed the members of the jury, but unlike the verdicts of the Court, we take a majority verdict here, and I hope it will be one on the right side next Tuesday.'

But he had a premonition of defeat. 'I think I am beaten,' he wrote to Henry Birkett on Polling Day (October 27). 'An election fought like this might well break a stout heart—but we must keep a smiling and resolute face tomorrow.' His wife, he added, 'has been noble' in her work in the campaign. But to no avail; when the result of the poll was announced, it was seen that he had lost to Gluckstein by over 5,500 votes.

Gluckstein, L. H. (C)	17,484
Birkett, W. N. (L)	11,901
Windsor, W. (Lab)	5,339
Conservative majority	5,583

The general result was a sweeping victory for the National Government candidates. Of these sixty-nine Liberals were returned including most of Birkett's old colleagues in the previous Parliament, although in reality the successful Liberals were split into two sections by reason of the tariff issue. That Birkett's stand on this issue had been mainly responsible for his defeat in East Nottingham he had no doubts. He took his defeat philosophically, despite the fact that its implications affected him personally far beyond the loss of his seat in the House of Commons.

On November 3, he wrote to his cousin Henry Birkett: 'I am informed today that, had I been returned to Parliament, it had been the Prime Minister's intention to make me Solicitor-General. *Hinc sunt lacrimae rerum.* But I couldn't mumble the form of words in which I didn't believe—and so I've a clear conscience and can stand upright.'

6

For Birkett the 1931 Election proved to be his political swansong. The result had left him disillusioned and in the circumstances he felt that he could not continue as the Liberal candidate in East Nottingham. 'After eight years of close association with East Nottingham which on my side has been an association of unbroken happiness, you must know what it costs me to say "Farewell",' he wrote to the President of the local Liberal Association; 'but recent events have made it quite plain to me that I can best serve the interests of Liberalism by taking this course.' Thus he severed his political connection with the division. There was a final reunion at which Birkett and his wife entertained the party workers to a dinner in the constituency and received from them two handsome gifts, a silver tray for Mrs. Birkett, and a silver cigar casket for himself, appropriately inscribed 'as a sincere mark of esteem and affection for him, and in appreciation of his devoted services as Member of Parliament'.

A few months later, Birkett received an invitation to become the Liberal candidate for Torquay, which had returned a Liberal in 1923 and where there seemed a good chance of winning back the seat for the party. This invitation he declined. Shortly afterwards he turned down a more tempting offer from North Cornwall. There the sitting member was the veteran Liberal, Sir Donald Maclean, a former Chairman of the Liberal Party, who had held the seat in 1931 and had joined the National Government as Minister of Education. On his death in June, 1932, the local Liberals offered the seat to Birkett, but he again refused despite the virtual certainty of being able to re-enter Parliament. The truth was that Birkett disliked the manner in which the Liberals had aligned themselves with the

Conservative 'Establishment' under the 'National' label and in an administration with such an avowedly Protectionist wing as that in which Mr. Neville Chamberlain was the moving spirit. For pure Free Traders like Herbert Samuel, Birkett realized the position was rapidly becoming impossible, and he was not surprised when Samuel and his followers resigned from the Government later in the same year.

Relieved to be free from political chores, Birkett devoted all his energies to his practice. Although not yet fifty years old, he had come to be regarded as at the very top of his profession. In spite of the economic depression, his fee book showed no diminution in its figures and briefs were as plentiful and varied as ever.

At this period he appeared for the Stewards of the Jockey Club in a case arising out of the alleged doping of a racehorse called Don Pat.[1] He secured the acquittal of his client in a complicated bank fraud case tried at Leeds Assizes where the indictment contained 149 counts and the trial lasted ten days.[2] He also defended the financier A. J. Klein at the Old Bailey on a fraud charge involving £250,000. This trial occupied eleven days, and, although Klein was convicted, Birkett's powerful speech in mitigation persuaded the judge not to send him to penal servitude.[3] The judge who tried Klein was Mr. Justice Avory, and he was so impressed by Birkett's defence that he sent him the following note after the trial: 'I have assumed you would like to be a Bencher of the Inner Temple and on that assumption have proposed you.' Thus Birkett was at last elected to the governing body of his Inn. It was an honour which, in view of his standing as a King's Counsel, also the fact that he had declined a judicial appointment in the High Court three weeks previously and had narrowly missed becoming Solicitor-General, might have come to him sooner than it did. Jealousy on the part of some of the other Benchers at his phenomenally rapid success as a 'silk' was thought by some of his friends to have been the cause of the delay. As the event turned out, he could not have had a more powerful sponsor than Avory, the senior judge of the King's Bench Division and a Bencher of the Inner Temple for the past quarter of

[1] *Chapman* v. *Lord Ellesmere*. November 28, 1931. For a detailed account of this case see Hyde *Sir Patrick Hastings*, pp. 229–36.

[2] The Batley Bank Case. *Leeds Mercury*, December 8, 9, 10, 11, 12, 14, 15, 16, 17, 18, 1931.

[3] *R.* v. *Klein*. *The Times*, January 26, 27, 28, 29, 30; February 2, 5, 6, 9, 10, 1932.

a century, since no one would openly dare to question Avory's choice.

In February, 1932, Birkett prevailed upon an all-male jury at Hereford Assizes to find the thirty-six-year-old widow, Mrs. Edith May Dampier, guilty but insane of the murder of a handyman whom she employed by shooting him in the kitchen of her house in the Wye Valley. Mrs. Dampier was suffering from venereal disease in an advanced stage, which she had communicated to her son causing him to be blind in one eye, and with the aid of medical evidence Birkett made out a virtually unanswerable case that the accused woman was out of her mind at the time of the killing.[1]

In the same month as Mrs. Dampier's trial, Birkett through his retainer for Odhams Press was involved in proceedings which made legal history and which were the prelude to a most sensational inquiry before a Consistory Court at the suit of the Bishop of Norwich. The question at issue in the preliminary hearing was whether there could be a contempt of an ecclesiastical court punishable under the ordinary law. The matter arose from the conduct of a clergyman in the Bishop's diocese, the Rev. Harold Davidson, Rector of the Parish of Stiffkey, Norfolk, who had been accused, among other charges, of immoral conduct on numerous occasions with a prostitute named Rose Ellis.

The Rector, who had a wife and several children, was in the habit of spending his weekdays in London on the pretext of reclaiming prostitutes, returning to his parish only to preach the sermon on Sundays. Information eventually reached the Bishop that Mr. Davidson's pretended interest in prostitutes was merely a cloak for his own amorous activities. It appeared that he had made improper suggestions to a waitress in Walbrook, he had kissed a girl in a Chinese restaurant in Bloomsbury, he had embraced an actress in her nightdress, and for the past eleven years he had been intimately associated with Miss Ellis, although his original pretext for picking her up in Leicester Square was to rescue her from a life of prostitution.

While the charges were pending before the Consistory Court in Norwich, and while the morally delinquent Rector was preaching sermons at Stiffkey, appropriately on the theme of love, Miss Ellis was interviewed by a reporter from the *Daily Herald*, which was

[1] *The Times*, February 13, 1932.

published by Odhams. An article subsequently appeared in that newspaper and was the subject of contempt proceedings. In that article Miss Ellis was reported as having stated that Mr. Davidson had been very kind to her on numerous occasions, that there had never been anything improper in their relations and that she had been bribed by 'a man and a woman' whom she had met in a public house and when she was under the influence of eight glasses of port wine to make false charges against the Rector. The latter, not wishing to be outdone by his girl friend in publicity, proceeded to give his version of what had happened in another journal, the *Empire News*. Proceedings for contempt of court were accordingly instituted against the publishers of both newspapers, as well as against Mr. Davidson, before a King's Bench Divisional Court presided over by the Lord Chief Justice, Lord Hewart.[1]

In apologizing on behalf of his clients, Birkett said that this was the first time so far as his researches went, 'and they had been very extensive', where it had been sought to attach anyone for contempt of a Consistory Court. This kind of contempt differed considerably, at least to the lay mind, from contempt of the King's Courts such as Assizes, the Consistory Court's jurisdiction arising as it did from the Clergy Discipline Act. He could only plead in mitigation that, whatever might be said of the wisdom or prudence of such stories as had appeared, it might be natural for those responsible to think that their publication in the circumstances could not be a contempt of court.

Giving judgment, the Lord Chief Justice said he had no doubt the Court of King's Bench had jurisdiction over the inferior ecclesiastical court, and that the publications were a gross contempt. As a result the *Daily Herald* was fined fifty pounds and the *Empire News* one hundred pounds.

The amorous Rector now announced to the press that Birkett would defend him at the subsequent proceedings before the Consistory Court. In fact, Birkett did not do so, although he appears to have been consulted at one stage. In the event the Rector was found guilty of immorality, deprived of his benefice and unfrocked. To earn some money he now exhibited himself in a barrel in Blackpool, and was finally mauled to death by a lion in a cage at Skegness Amusement Park where he had also been engaged to do an act, thus

[1] *The Times*, February 23, 1932.

assuming the unexpected role of an early Christian martyr in the Colosseum.

This was the last case in which Birkett appeared for Odhams Press under his general retainer. Unfortunately some misunderstanding arose as to the form of the retainer, as a result of which Birkett, to his sincere regret and even more that of his clerk, ceased to act for them. Thus it happened that when Lady Louis Mountbatten, as she then was, sued another of the Odhams newspapers, *The People*, for libel, Birkett found himself on the side of the plaintiff in the action.[1]

The libel, which Birkett rightly described as 'atrocious and abominable', was published in a gossip column entitled 'Behind the Scenes' in *The People* on May 20, 1932, and written by an annonymous contributor who signed himself 'The Watcher'. It said:

> FAMOUS HOSTESS EXILED
>
> SOCIETY SHAKEN BY TERRIBLE SCANDAL
>
> I am able to reveal today the sequel to a scandal which has shaken Society to the very depths. It concerns one of the leading hostesses in the country, a woman highly connected and immensely rich.
>
> Associations with a coloured man became so marked that they were the talk of the West End. Then one day the couple were caught in compromising circumstances.
>
> The sequel is that the Society woman has been given the hint to clear out of England for a couple of years to let the affair blow over, and the hint comes from a quarter which cannot be ignored.

'It is not too much to say that it is the most monstrous and most atrocious libel of which I myself in all my experience in these courts have ever heard,' said Birkett in opening the case before the Lord Chief Justice, Lord Hewart. 'Your Lordship may think that the word "scandal" at the top of the article coupled with the words, "the hint comes from a quarter which cannot be ignored", puts it beyond all doubt that the writer deliberately intended to defame Lady Louis Mountbatten. It is unnecessary to say that there is not one word of truth in these horrible allegations. Nor is there the

[1] *The Times*, July 9, 1932.

faintest ground upon which these lying rumours could be brought into existence at all.' Birkett went on to say that the defendants were willing to pay damages, and there was not the smallest doubt that a jury would have awarded very heavy damages, but Lady Louis refused to accept one single penny which would be to her 'in the highest degree distasteful'. What she did desire was that there should be a speedy and public vindication of her name in the fullest possible manner, and with this end in view her counsel asked that 'in the very exceptional circumstances of this case', she and her husband might be allowed to go into the witness box. Lord Hewart agreed.

Lord Louis Mountbatten was the first to give evidence. He told the court how, as a naval officer attached to the Mediterranean Fleet, he had been ordered to Malta for two years and it was natural that his wife and children should follow him there for the duration of his appointment. Lady Louis then entered the witness box. Replying to her counsel's questions, she declared that she had returned to this country from Malta solely in order to give evidence in this case.

Birkett held up a copy of the offending journal. 'The second paragraph in this publication deals with a coloured man,' he said. 'Is there one single word of truth in the allegation there made?'

'Not one single word,' Lady Louis answered in ringing tones. 'In fact, I have never in the whole course of my life met the man referred to.'

'Your friends have named to you the coloured man supposed to be referred to in the paragraph?' continued Birkett.

'They have,' admitted Lady Louis.

'And you have never had anything to do with him in any shape or form?'

'The whole thing is a preposterous story.'

'Was it your desire, when the article was brought to your notice, that you should have the opportunity of going into the box to deny this horrible thing on oath?'

'It was my express wish.'

For the defendants, Sir Patrick Hastings made an unqualified apology, coupled with 'genuine and deep regrets', and reiterated the newspaper's willingness to pay damages, which Hastings agreed if awarded by a jury must have been extremely heavy. It was also intimated that the person responsible for the gossip column had been dismissed as soon as the proprietors of *The People* had received Lady Louis Mountbatten's complaint.

'One does not wonder that in these circumstances the plaintiff does not desire damages,' Lord Hewart observed. 'I should have been astonished if she had accepted them because there are some libels which are crimes on the part of everybody concerned.'

In agreeing to Birkett's request that the record should be withdrawn on the terms that the defendants apologized and paid all the plaintiff's costs and expenses, the Lord Chief Justice made it clear that he did so 'with considerable doubt and hesitation' in view of the possibility of criminal proceedings being instituted. As it was, Lord Hewart ordered that a copy of the paper should be kept in the custody of the court, and the editor was fortunate in escaping prosecution for criminal libel.

Another titled person for whom Birkett appeared at this time was a young Indian nawab, Prince Ali Khan of Hyderabad, who was a student at an agricultural college in Devonshire. This young man owned a flashy looking sports car, which he left outside an hotel in Newton Abbot while he was refreshing himself with some friends indoors. A local police constable asked him to move the vehicle as it was causing an obstruction, and at the same time to produce his driving licence and insurance certificate. Unfortunately for the nawab his licence had been suspended for a motoring offence committed several months previously, which meant that the insurance was also automatically suspended. There could, of course, be no answer to either of these offences, and an ordinary individual would have instructed a solicitor to plead guilty and apologize to the court on his behalf when the case came before the local bench of magistrates. It may be that the nawab's fellow students jokingly exaggerated the seriousness of his crime to him, suggesting that he faced a term of penal servitude. Anyhow the nawab became alarmed and communicated his fears to his father, the wealthy Nizam of Hyderabad, who sent instructions to England that no expense was to be spared in getting the best counsel available to defend his son. When the Nizam's solicitor approached Birkett through his clerk the latter was not exactly enthusiastic about the idea of his master going down to 'do a plea' at Newton Abbot police court when he was so busy with big cases in London. When he was asked to name his fee,

Bowker put it at two hundred guineas, which, somewhat to his surprise, was accepted without the least demur.

The prosecution was conducted by the local police Inspector, who was naturally a little taken aback to see such an eminent King's Counsel as Birkett, accompanied by his junior, appearing for the defendant, who had pleaded guilty. After the constable, who had asked the nawab for his licence, had told his story from the witness box, he admitted, in reply to a question from Birkett, that the defendant had an insurance policy, but that liability in respect of third party risks was excluded when the driver was disqualified.

'This young man, when he grows to maturer years—he is now twenty-three,' said Birkett, addressing the court, 'will be charged with the responsibility of administering both the civil and criminal law in the State of Hyderabad under His Highness the Nizam of Hyderabad, and, of course, it is vital that one who is one day to be called on to occupy a position of that kind should pay due regard himself not merely to the laws of his State and country, but to the law of the country which gives him hospitality.' After 'humbly and sincerely apologizing' for his client's behaviour, Birkett pleaded in mitigation that, being an Indian and not so familiar 'with that which is almost second nature to us', the nawab did not realize, 'as he now does, the seriousness and gravity of disregarding any order made by an English court'. He added that the nawab's car was most noticeable, as it was bright scarlet in colour and upon it was the crest of the college. 'Its appearance was the hallmark of youth, and just the kind of car the police would notice, as its colour indicated that it might go a little faster than others.'

Birkett's clerk Bowker reckoned that the luxury of having Birkett and a junior counsel to appear for him must have cost Prince Ali Khan about sixty pounds a minute, apart from his solicitor's expenses. But no doubt he thought it was worth it, since, instead of being consigned to Dartmoor, as he seems to have imagined might otherwise have happened, he was merely fined a total of twenty-six pounds and thirteen shillings including costs.[1]

7

It was at this period that Birkett appeared in a bizarre and somewhat

[1] *Western Morning News.* June 8, 1933.

macabre case in which a spiritualist medium named Mrs. Meurig Morris brought a libel action against the publishers of the *Daily Mail* for exposing her spiritualistic performances as fraudulent and dishonest. The case which was tried before Mr. Justice McCardie and a special jury in the Royal Courts of Justice in April, 1932, caused the greatest public interest. During the eleven days of the trial, when forty witnesses were examined, the proceedings got remarkably out of hand, so much so that the exasperated judge had to adjourn them twice when the medium went into a trance in open court. In the action Birkett represented the newspaper, which had published the defamatory article which the medium complained of.[1]

The article, which described Mrs. Morris's spiritualist sermons at the Fortune Theatre in London, was advertised on the *Daily Mail* billposters as 'TRANCE MEDIUM FOUND OUT' and it appeared under such headlines as 'Power's Sermon Jargon', 'One Talk for all Texts' and 'Is It Hypnotism?' The author was a staff reporter named Charles W. Sutton, and, in the course of the article, he remarked:

> I have heard three of Mrs. Morris's sermons, and at a private seance I had with 'Power', her spirit control, he talked to me a great deal about the other world, and on all four occasions the young medium used the same phrases—many of them almost meaningless—but strung them together in different contexts.
>
> It is now very obvious to me that Mrs. Morris could preach a sermon on any subject, provided she had the text read out to her, and she would use the same phrase every time.
>
> Mr. Laurence Cowen, the playwright, says that Mrs. Morris can deliver sixty or seventy different sermons, but I have found that the only difference is in the stringing together of the sentences and phrases.
>
> So it was last night.

The defendants pleaded justification and fair comment on a matter of public interest.

According to Serjeant Sullivan, who appeared for Mrs. Morris,

[1] *Morris* v. *Associated Newspapers Ltd. The Times*, April 6, 7, 8, 9, 12, 13, 14, 15, 16, 19, 20, 1932. Birkett's brief in this case was marked 500 guineas, and he got a 100 guineas a day refresher.

the thirty-three-year-old medium was the daughter of a Worcestershire market gardener; she went to a village school and had no opportunity of mixing with well educated men and women nor did she have any access to books and libraries. She was married at twenty-three and after the birth of her daughter she had developed marked spiritualist characteristics. For some years she had taken an active part in spiritualist church services, and she now claimed to be one of the ministers of a creed, whose disciples numbered between 200,000 and 300,000.

From childhood, Mrs. Morris declared from the witness box, she had seen 'spirit people whom other people could not see'. Describing her first psychic experience at a seance, she said that she felt she was getting smaller and smaller and seemed to be floating away. At the next seance she experienced a similar sensation and eventually lost consciousness. The sensation of falling under 'controls' was different. With 'Power', who first controlled her in 1924, she began by seeing a yellow light like a searchlight. Then she felt herself get very big and felt a strong personality over her. Then she lost consciousness.

'Is "Power" an individual?' Mr. Justice McCardie asked her.

'Yes, but he will not disclose to us his identity,' the medium replied.

'What do you mean by an individual?'

'He is somebody living on the spirit side, but he will not tell us who he is.'

'Have you ever considered the meaning of the word "spirit"?' the judge went on.

'I have not,' said the medium. 'I have always thought that, when we pass over, we become spirits.'

Birkett began his cross-examination by asking the medium for further particulars about 'Power'. She explained that he had survived bodily death and was living on another plane.

'Do you know the name of the other plane?'

'No, but I have seen it.'

'Is it in time?'

'I cannot tell you.'

'Is it in space?'

'I cannot tell you.'

'Where did you see it?' Birkett pressed her.

'I saw it as I see you,' the witness answered. 'When I see it, it appears to be all round. Physical surroundings disappear altogether.'

'For all we know "Power" is here in this Court?'

'I expect he is.'

Birkett went on to question the medium about her other controls. One of them, known as 'Sunshine' was a child with a round face and a snub nose rather like her own little girl. She described how on one occasion when she was away and had not heard from her little girl she asked 'Sunshine' to go and see how she was. 'Sunshine' came back and controlled her and said that her little girl had been naughty and had walked into a brook and had got a cold. Mrs. Morris's husband then wrote to the aunt with whom the little girl was staying and found out that this was true. Later, the little girl saw 'Sunshine' and said to her aunt: 'I have just seen "Sunshine", and I hope she is not going to tell any more tales about me to Mummy.'

'How do you speak to little "Sunshine" and the others?' Birkett asked. 'With your physical voice?'

'I speak like I am speaking to you.'

'So little "Sunshine" has physical ears?'

'I don't know, I hear them just as if it was physical.'

Pressed for a further explanation, Mrs. Morris suddenly burst out: 'Mr. Birkett, you are very ignorant. I do not mean to be rude, but you do not understand this subject.'

Bidding the medium not to trouble about his state of mind, Birkett went on to ask her about another of her 'controls', a female Red Indian known as the Squaw, who helped to magnetize the medium's body and kept her fit for her services. The 'controls' were in different states of development, Mrs. Morris explained, and the Squaw was on the lower plane.

'What language does the Squaw speak?'

'I don't know; I do not know anybody who has heard her speak,' replied Mrs. Morris. 'She had a band round her head—it looked like a feather.'

'The typical squaw of fiction?' queried Birkett sarcastically.

'I have never read any fiction about squaws.'

Another 'control' was called Sister Annette. She always came in a white kind of dress which sometimes shaded into different colours. 'I do not know why,' added the medium. 'It was a long dress with a girdle round the waist.'

Associated Newspapers

MRS. MORRIS DELIVERING A SPIRITUALIST SERMON

London Express Pictures

(*above*)

LEOPOLD HARRIS

(*right*)

MRS. ETHEL LILLIE MAJOR

'What fashion was it?' the judge intervened. 'Last year's or the year before?'

'I don't know. It was a loose dress.'

Then there was Selina. It was months and months since the medium had seen Selina. She did not know who she was nor what her nationality was. This also applied to 'Power', although people had said that he was a clergyman.

'The "controls" are all in touch with each other?'

'I expect so,' said Mrs. Morris with a serious air. She went on to say that it was wonderful that a discarnate being could control a physical person on earth.

'You had a gramophone record made, which is on sale?' Birkett continued.

'Yes.'

'What price is it?' asked Mr. Justice McCardie.

'Four shillings and sixpence.' Mrs. Morris added that it was a record that 'Power' made.

'In March, 1931,' continued Birkett, 'did you enter into an agreement with the Columbia Gramophone Company Ltd. and were you to get a royalty?'

'Yes, which was to be devoted to the work.'

'Have you a "control" called Zodiac?'

'I have heard of him. He is not my "control", although he spoke to me once. They say that Zodiac was a teacher in the time of our Lord.'

'What language did he speak to you in?' asked Birkett, remembering his theological studies. 'Was it Aramaic or Greek?'

'It was just ordinary English,' Mrs. Morris admitted without much conviction.

Birkett was questioning the medium about one of 'Power's' sermons, which appeared nonsensical and which even she was unable to explain, and suggesting that she might be exploited by others, when the judge intervened to ask whether she would allow herself to be responsible for anything however incomprehensible that 'Power' chose to transmit through her. 'I have perfect faith in him,' she said. 'He would not do anything wrong.'

At this point, the medium proceeded to go off into a trance. Her eyes filled with tears, she clenched her hands and her face twitched. When the court usher moved towards the witness box to help her, as she seemed about to faint, some of her friends called out from the back of the court: 'Don't touch her!' She thereupon burst into tears, murmuring incoherently, 'The Christ. . . . A vision of the Christ came.'

She was then assisted out of court and Mr. Justice McCardie adjourned the proceedings for ten minutes. Eventually Mrs. Morris returned but was unable to continue her evidence. The gramophone record previously mentioned was then played over to the jury, and several other witnesses were called. One of these was a man who described a seance at Mrs. Morris's house at Newton Abbot, at which she was controlled by a Frenchman who had been dead for fifteen years. What made him sure that it was this particular Frenchman, the witness said, was the fact that when he was alive he had a habit of standing with his hands in his trousers pockets, and Mrs. Morris stood in the same way as he used to do and placed her hands where the pockets would have been.

In cross-examination, the witness admitted that he was a Customs and Excise officer.

'Testing spirits?' asked Birkett, amid the inevitable laughter.

'Yes,' the Customs man admitted, to the accompaniment of further hilarity. 'But not the spirits of which we are speaking now.'

8

Another witness, who gave evidence for the plaintiff was the well-known scientist, Sir Oliver Lodge, who was also an authority on psychical research. He said that he had seen Mrs. Morris going into a trance which was undoubtedly genuine. Her 'control' was not her own personality but another intelligence speaking through her. When she went under control, Mrs. Morris stood up, held her dress where the lapels of a man's coat would be, looked quite different, and spoke in a loud masculine voice like an orator or a preacher.

'Was Mrs. Morris honest, or was she playing tricks?' the plaintiff's leading counsel asked him.

'Oh, she was not playing tricks,' said Sir Oliver. 'She is perfectly honest. It is a phenomenon that must be recognized that a person can leave his or her body to be manipulated by another intelligence.' That had not been unanimously recognized by scientific men, Sir Oliver Lodge added. There were a good many sceptics, but the scepticism was being reduced as people were willing to study the subject. Mrs. Morris, in his opinion, was actuated by a sense of duty, lending her body to be used by other powers.

'You say there are many sceptics?' Birkett asked him in cross-examination. 'There are many credulous people, too, in the world, are there not?'

'Yes,' the spiritualist-scientist replied. 'They are more trouble than the other people.'

'The whole history of spiritualism is bestrewn with persons who have made claims which were subsequently proved to be false?'

'I hear about fraudulent mediums, but I have not come across them. I do not think that they are so numerous.' Sir Oliver added that in his view it was very difficult to detect a fraudulent medium. On the other hand, it was easy to think that a person was fraudulent when she was not.

Replying to a question from the judge, the witness said that he thought that the denizens of the other world were resident in space. 'But the fact is,' he added, 'that I do not quite know where they are in space.'

'Do you think that the denizens of the other world have the material comforts which we have?' Birkett went on.

'There are many grades of existence in the other world,' Sir Oliver answered. 'I have been told recently by the denizens of the other world that the state in which they first are is a world of illusion, where they get whatever they want . . . I think that we shall take our faculty of interpretation with us and the other world will seem very like this homely sort of world. In that sense we shall have the material comforts which you mention.'

As an instance of people who had just 'passed over' receiving the comforts of this world, Sir Oliver Lodge mentioned that men who were killed in the last war 'went over' very excited and wanted to go on fighting. They had to be calmed down by whisky and cigarettes. He went on to say that he thought that, when people died, they carried with them to 'the other side' many of the prejudices and ideas which they had here. 'When I have discourses with people who have departed,' he added, 'I have found them very much the same as we are. They know a little more, but I do not accept all that they say for gospel.'

In opening the defence, Birkett stressed the plaintiff's failure to call as a witness Laurence Cowen, the dramatist, who had been organizing Mrs. Morris's public appearances. Then he put Mr. Cowen's former charwoman into the box to tell her story. Mrs. Morris used to come to Mr. Cowen's house, she said. One evening, when Mrs. Morris and Mr. Cowen were together in the library, the charwoman heard a little child's voice say: 'I so happy.' Then she heard Mr. Cowen say: 'I would like that a little louder, my dear.' Mrs. Morris repeated the words until Mr. Cowen was satisfied. 'I thought that they were rehearsing a play,' said the witness.

On another occasion, the charwoman continued, she heard Mrs. Morris speaking in her own voice and then in the voice of another woman. Then it seemed as if she were trying to talk 'in the back of her throat' with a very thick voice. Mr. Cowen asked her to repeat the word 'world' more plainly. She did so and Mr. Cowen said: 'That's better.' Every evening after dinner the same sort of thing used to go on. It seemed as if Mrs. Morris was trying to imitate the powerful voice of a man.

'Do you look on these things as rehearsals?' Mr. Justice McCardie asked another witness, who had testified to overhearing a simulated man's voice talking 'pidgin English' in Mrs. Morris's dressing room at the Fortune Theatre, where she was appearing. 'I thought Mrs. Morris was keeping herself in practice for her public performances,' this witness replied. At this point, Mrs. Morris again broke in. 'It is so dreadful to say this sort of thing against me,' she protested, and was again led sobbing from the court room.

An actress also gave evidence for the defence, saying she did not mind trying to put herself into a trance. 'When you get wrapped up in a part,' she said, 'you can go into hysterics and really feel that you are in hysterics.'

The last defence witness was the *Daily Mail* reporter, Mr. Sutton, who had interviewed Mrs. Morris after several of her 'services'. After coming out of trance, he said, she began to laugh uproariously. She immediately went into another trance, and a man's voice with an Irish brogue came through, saying 'Sure and begorra' twice.

'Do Irishmen say "Sure and begorra"?' Birkett asked him.

'I am told they do not,' the witness replied, adding that when Mrs. Morris came out of her second trance she said she had seen Father O'Keefe, an Irish priest who also controlled her, leaning over

Mr. Sutton's chair and reading the notes that he (the witness) had made of the interview. That was why she laughed, she said.

'Do you charge Mrs. Morris with being a fraud?' Serjeant Sullivan asked in cross-examination.

'I do,' said the reporter.

'What fraud has she practised?'

'I think that she is not what she claims to be.'

'What is the fraudulent practice about which the *Daily Mail* poster announces that the medium has been found out?'

'Mrs. Morris claims to be controlled by discarnate entities, and I say that she is not.'

In making his final speech for the defence, Birkett said that the issue in the case was not whether it had been demonstrated that there was a survival of the spirit after bodily death. The issue was, what view had the jury formed of Mrs. Morris and her claims? Was she genuine, or was she not? As for the evidence of Sir Oliver Lodge, if he were wrong, he would not be the first distinguished man, supreme in his own sphere, who was a child outside it. 'A great scientist can weigh the atom and the star,' he remarked. 'He can tell you about the nature of light and the vibrations of the ether, projecting his mind into space and making the most fruitful suggestions. Yet it would not be the first time that a great mind had gone completely wrong when stepping outside that sphere.' Nor would it be the first time that 'a frail, *petite* emotional woman' like Mrs. Morris had deceived people in the very same way.

Mr. Justice McCardie summed up with an evident lack of relish. 'This action touches the very gravities of life and death,' he declared, 'and I say frankly that I dislike the action from beginning to end and every aspect of it.'

When he came to deal with the case for the defence, the judge referred to the evidence of several of the plaintiff's witnesses who had described the burning through of a rope suspending some lights at the film studio when a talking picture was being made of Mrs. Morris in trance, which they thought had been broken by psychic forces. 'That shows how credulity can operate in cases of this sort,' said the judge, 'and how easily credulity can be exploited to create publicity.'

This was too much for Mrs. Morris. She got to her feet, seized the lapels of her coat and began to address the judge in a deep voice.

'Thou, who art a brother judge, hearken unto my voice,' she began.

'This really must be stopped,' Mr. Justice McCardie exclaimed in understandable irritation. 'Tell her to stop. She knows better.'

'I will say this——' continued Mrs. Morris in the same voice.

'Let her stop,' the judge interrupted her. 'We have had this so often that we are all getting tired of it.' Then, addressing her solicitor, he added, 'You can stop her perfectly well. You can take her out.'

But the medium's booming tones continued, 'Do not touch her until I have left the body.'

At this Mr. Justice McCardie exploded. 'Each day we have had these outbreaks of emotion. Either she should stay out of Court or, if she comes in, she should suppress these things. She can be taken out now. The jury will see now why I say that I dislike every minute of this case.'

Mrs. Morris was then supported out of the court room by two friends for the third time in the case, and the judge adjourned the proceedings for a quarter of an hour.

On resuming, Mr. Justice McCardie, who was obviously distressed by the whole incident, reminded the jury that, whatever emotions were exhibited, whatever dramatic episodes had occurred during the trial, it was their duty to deal with the matter in a spirit of cold, unswerving investigation. 'I hope that I have not upset the feelings of anyone unnecessarily,' he concluded, 'but as a judge I care not for all the incarnate or discarnate spirits in the world. As long as I remain on the Bench, I shall resolutely seek to reach for truth and I advise the jury to do the same, although there may be ten thousand million discarnate spirits around us.'

It took the jury four hours to find for the defendant newspaper on the plea of fair comment, but they did not consider that any allegations of fraud or dishonesty had been proved. The result, said Mr. Justice McCardie, was that there must be a verdict for the defendants. This was not accepted by Serjeant Sullivan for Mrs. Morris, and he took the case to the Court of Appeal and later to the House of Lords on her behalf. But both the appellate courts upheld the finding of the jury in the court below.[1]

Not only did Birkett gain the congratulations of Lord Rothermere,

[1] *The Times*, June 15, 16, 17, 18, 1932; February 8, 11, 21, 1933.

the proprietor of the *Daily Mail*, for his success in this case, but also those of the rival newspaper owner, Lord Beaverbrook. 'I congratulate you most warmly on your verdict in the *Daily Mail* case,' Lord Beaverbrook wrote to him. 'It will have an excellent effect on public opinion. I have no doubt that Judges are coming to the conclusion that justice frequently miscarries where newspapers are concerned. It is your misfortune to be always on the side of the newspapers. But you have made a great job of it, and you ought to be publicly thanked.'

There was a personal sequel. Many years later Birkett was discussing old cases with Cecil Roberts, his guest at Challens Green. He said that one day in the carriage of a train going north a lady looked hard at him and said, 'Are you Sir Norman Birkett?' He replied that he was. 'Ah, I am Mrs. Morris, the medium. You made me lose my case. But I want to tell you that I bear you no ill feeling and that I very greatly admire you.' They talked amicably for the rest of the journey.

'Did you think she was a fraud?' asked Roberts.

'No—in the sense she genuinely believed in and was operated by her own nonsense,' replied Birkett.

CHAPTER IX

ADVOCATE EXTRAORDINARY

I

ONE evening in October, 1932, a man named Harry Thompson was walking along Willows Crescent, in the Cannon Hill district of Birmingham, with his fiancée, when a young woman suddenly appeared in the doorway of a house, shouting, 'Murder! Murder! Fetch the police!' A few moments later she was joined by a slightly older woman, who exclaimed to Thompson, 'Come here and get this strange man out of the house.' 'Who is it?' inquired Thompson, and the woman replied, 'I have never seen him in my life before. He hit me in the mouth. There was a ten shilling note on the table, and when we came down it had gone.'

Thompson then entered the house, where the first sight which met his eyes was the figure of a man standing against the wall in the passage beyond the front door. Thinking he was an intruder, Thompson gripped him by the wrist and asked, 'What's your game?'

'I've done nothing,' the man answered in a weak voice. Thompson began to drag him outside, when the man slowly sank to the ground.

'He's only shamming,' said the woman who had called Thompson into the house. She added, contradicting her previous words, 'He has done that before.'

But the man was not shamming. He was dead. He had been stabbed, as a wound in his breast revealed. The knife, with which the wound was inflicted, was discovered in his overcoat pocket, while the handle was picked up in the passage. A crumpled ten shilling note was also found in one of his pockets.

The younger of the two women was Emily Thay, aged sixteen,

and employed in a warehouse. The other was her twenty-two-year-old sister, Mrs. Marjorie Yellow, a shop assistant who was married to a coloured man from whom she was separated and who was living with a man named Gwinnell in the house at 63, Willows Crescent. Emily was spending the week-end with them at the time of the killing.

Whilst they were waiting for the police, whom Thompson had summoned, Marjorie Yellow related how she was upstairs powdering her nose when Emily returned from buying some cigarettes. According to Marjorie, she then went downstairs and met a man who tried to stab her. Emily corroborated this, adding that she saw the man holding her sister by the throat. Whilst the police inquiries were taking place, Marjorie was alleged to have said to a police officer: 'They don't hang women, do they? Well, you only have to die once. Women go to prison for life, don't they?'

The dead man proved to be a young grocer's assistant, named Sidney Marston, who had been seen in a nearby café a short time before. A memorandum book found in his possession contained the entry 'Miss Gwinnell', and at the inquest, which was held on the circumstances of his death, Marjorie Yellow told the Coroner she had met a young man named Sid a few weeks previously and had given him her name as he had asked her and her sister to go out dancing with him and a friend. In view of the circumstances, the police arrested both sisters and the local magistrates committed them for trial on a joint charge of murdering Marston.

The case, which came before Mr. Justice Humphreys at the Birmingham Winter Assizes, began on December 6, 1932. Birkett's old friends, Maurice Healy, K.C., and Donald Finnemore, appeared for the prosecution, while the defence of the two women was accepted by Birkett under the Poor Persons Defence Act. This meant that Birkett received a fee of fifteen guineas instead of the two hundred and fifty or five hundred guinea fee he could normally have commanded.

According to Maurice Healy, the dead man was 'a fine outstanding type of manhood, five feet eleven inches in height, muscular, well nourished, neat in dress, proud of his personal appearance, and, so far as was known, without an enemy in the world'. Yet, 'he was plunged into eternity without warning and in a twinkling of an eye, and, in the submission of the Crown, he was sent to his death in circumstances which amounted to murder, and the persons responsible were the prisoners at the bar.' Yet, when it came to be analysed, the Crown case was far from strong.

Apart from the police, the principal Crown witness was Sir Bernard Spilsbury, who had carried out the *post-mortem* examination. Giving details of Marston's wound, he said it was a clean-cut, gaping wound, while its direction was downwards and slightly outwards. In his opinion, it could have been inflicted by the blade of the knife found on Marston's body. Judging by the nature of the wound, the weapon must have been withdrawn along the same track by which it penetrated.

'Do you consider that this wound could have been caused by the dead man?' Healy asked.

'It is possible,' Sir Bernard replied, 'but it is highly improbable owing to the strained position of the hand and owing to the great difficulty of withdrawing the weapon along the same track.'

Cross-examined by Birkett, the expert pathologist expressed the view that Marston had received the fatal blow from somebody face to face with him, and he thought there could be no doubt that Marston would know at the time whether or not his assailant was one of the girls. He agreed that Marjorie Yellow had known Marston before, according to the evidence, and that if she was the assailant she must have been looking into Marston's face quite close. The witness went on to say that there were injuries about Marston's face and these indicated that a violent struggle had taken place.

At the conclusion of the Crown case, Birkett submitted that there was no case to go to the jury. Before such a charge as the present one could succeed, he argued, there must be some evidence of a common design and of acting in concert and participation, and there was no such evidence here. In particular, there was not a line of evidence against Emily Thay. The only thing really held against the two sisters was that a man died in the house when they were there. When Thompson had come in and asked Marston what he was doing, the latter could have said at once, 'She stabbed me,' more especially in view of Sir Bernard Spilsbury's opinion that the assailant who caused Marston's death was looking him in the eye at the time. But all Marston said was, 'I have done nothing.' Nor was there any evidence of motive. Also, the evidence that there had been a violent struggle and a knife blow was at variance with the theory that the girls did it, since they were in sight of everyone within thirty seconds of the fatal wounding.

Mr. Justice Humphreys agreed with this submission. There was a *prima facie* case that one or other of the two accused did strike the blow that caused the death. 'But that will not do,' the judge declared. In his opinion there was no evidence at all against Emily, while against Marjorie there was some evidence, but he thought that what Sir Bernard Spilsbury had said told if anything in her favour. Accordingly the judge withdrew the case from the jury and directed them to acquit the two prisoners. This was done and the sisters were thereupon discharged.

The elder sister said afterwards: 'When the judge began to tell the jury that he did not think the prosecution had made out their case, I reached across the dock and gripped Emily's hand. We knew our prayers were being answered in that moment. Mr. Birkett has been wonderful.'

The subsequent career of Marjorie Yellow was not destined to be free of legal entanglements. Less than two months after her acquittal, she was fined in Manchester, where she and her sister had gone to live, for disorderly conduct and assaulting a policeman. Two months after that she was sent to prison for ten weeks for assisting in the management of a disorderly house in the same city. And two years later, she received a sentence of eighteen months' imprisonment for stabbing a coloured seaman with whom she was living. In this case, her defence was that, intending to leave his house, she stood on a chair holding a knife with which she meant to cut down the curtains; he caught her hand and slipped to the floor, and the knife was pulled down on him.

The question remains, who killed Sidney Marston? It is certain that he was killed and did not commit suicide. But exactly how and by whom is a mystery which may never be solved, although it is interesting to speculate about the identity of the killer.

2

Shortly after this, Birkett was instructed for the defence in a curious prosecution, the first to be brought under a statute which had been passed some years previously for the express purpose of checking the abuses which had grown up, notably in the last years of Lloyd

George's Government, over the conferment of political honours in return for the recipients contributing to party political funds. What amounted in effect to trafficking in honours became a national scandal, and after protests from King George V, who was the constitutional fount of all political honours and did not disguise his strong dislike of some of those whose names were put forward for awards, a Royal Commission was set up to look into the whole procedure of recommendations for political honours. As a result the Honours (Prevention of Abuses) Act was passed in 1925. Birkett's client, who was charged with contravening this necessary piece of legislation by touting for honours, boasted an impressive string of names—Arthur John Peter Michael Maundy Gregory. His lavish style of living and wide range of social connections were designed similarly to impress the gullible and ambitious.

Maundy Gregory, as he was generally known, was something of a mystery man and he made the most of the mystery which surrounded him and his plush office in Whitehall. Brought up in modest circumstances, the son of a Southampton clergyman, he was by successive turns an actor, impresario and manager of a detective agency. During the First World War he claimed to have been employed in the counter-espionage branch of the British Secret Service, and may well have been a spy-catcher, as such employment fitted well with his bizarre and eccentric character. In 1919 he had founded the *Whitehall Gazette*, a journal with a spuriously official ring about its title, largely given to puffing diplomats and other public figures who were reputed to have paid Mr. Gregory for the publicity. The principal London clubs and Government offices received complimentary copies; indeed most of its readers seem to have been on the complimentary list, although the nominal price of the publication was half a crown. Besides his Whitehall office, furnished with an odd assortment of signed royal portraits, telephones and buzzers which flashed different coloured lights, Mr. Maundy Gregory had a house in Hyde Park Terrace, another house in the country (where he lived with a mistress named Mrs. Rosse, although he was said to have homosexual tastes), a flat in Brighton and two yachts. He also owned the smart Ambassador Club in London, where he could be seen lunching on most days to the accompaniment of the best brands of champagne and cigars. Outside a taxi discreetly waited; he was the owner of this vehicle, too, which he found facilitated his mysterious comings and goings. In addition to a liking for fine wine, he was also a collector of rare books and manuscripts. Among the curiosities of his collection were an early passport belonging to Mussolini, whom he greatly admired; also the originals of the notorious 'Venice Letters' of that strange writer and pseudo-priest Frederick Rolfe, who called himself Baron Corvo. Maundy Gregory had bought the latter from A. J. A. Symons, a Corvine enthusiast, who was engaged in writing a biography of the self-styled Baron.[1]

Maundy Gregory seems to have first dabbled in honours during the palmy days of Lloyd George, and the passage of the Honours Act did not deter his efforts to exploit the vanity and snobbery of some of his fellow citizens. But the longer he operated in this field, the less careful he and his agents became. In 1932, legal proceedings were begun against him by the executors of a man who had given him £30,000 in anticipation of honours never received, and at the last moment Maundy Gregory was obliged to pay up so as to avoid an inconvenient court case. But for Maundy Gregory it was a question of out of the frying pan into the fire. In December of the same year, one of his agents, a man named Moffat, approached a retired naval officer, Lieutenant-Commander Edward Leake, D.S.O. The latter was subsequently introduced by Moffat to Gregory, who made a proposition amounting to an offer of a knighthood or a baronetcy —Maundy Gregory was not sure which—in return for £10,000. Commander Leake informed the police, and in the result Maundy Gregory was charged at Bow Street Police Court with having attempted to obtain from Commander Leake £10,000 'as an inducement for endeavouring to procure for him the grant of a dignity or title of honour, contrary to the Honours (Prevention of Abuses) Act, 1925'. He pleaded 'Not Guilty' to the Summons.

The case was tried summarily by Mr. (later Sir) Rollo Graham-Campbell. The Attorney-General, Sir Thomas Inskip, K.C., M.P., later Lord Caldecote, and Mr. Eustace Fulton, appeared for the Crown, while the accused man was defended by Birkett and Mr. Valentine Holmes. The fact that the senior Law Officer of the Crown led the prosecution indicated the degree of importance which the

[1] *The Quest for Corvo*, first published in 1934. Birkett, who shared the author's interest in the subject, wrote an Introduction for the edition brought out by The Folio Society in 1952.

Government attached to the case, the first of its kind to be brought under the provisions of the statute.[1]

Giving evidence, Commander Leake, tall, distinguished looking and very much the retired naval officer, described his meetings with Moffat and his principal. He said that he had no previous acquaintance with Moffat who had written to him. As a result of this letter he met Moffat who took him to see Maundy Gregory at the latter's home in Hyde Park Terrace. 'Mr. Gregory said that he very much wanted to meet me because some of the highest authorities in the country were desirous of my accepting some kind of honour,' the witness stated. 'I said it was a very great surprise to me and the only reason I could possibly imagine was some kind of aftermath of the war. Mr. Gregory then told me that, as a matter of fact, that was more or less the bottom of the whole thing. He said, 'Your name, I know, has been mentioned several times in connection with this, and your name is very high in the list at the present moment.' I then said I did not quite understand why it should arise in the way it had, and it seemed to be rather curious but as it was a conversation entirely between gentlemen I would take his word for it.

'He told me these matters had to be arranged, but sinews would be necessary in order to open certain closed doors. I asked what form the sinews would take. He told me that in a case such as mine it could be done for £10,000 but if I could make it £12,000 it would make it easier.'

After describing a further meeting with Maundy Gregory, at which the latter said that the people in authority were willing to arrange the matter for £10,000 and that 'a deposit of £2,000 immediately would make it a certainty', adding that he himself had been instrumental in making such arrangements 'for some considerable time', Commander Leake informed Maundy Gregory that he did not wish to continue the matter, having previously got into touch with the police at Scotland Yard.

At the beginning of the hearing Birkett had asked leave to postpone cross-examination in order to consider the position, and, as the magistrate had agreed to this request, the case was now adjourned. During the adjournment the defendant took the precaution of communicating with several of his friends and getting various sums of money up to £1,000 as a consideration for keeping their names

[1] *The Star*, February 16; *The Times*, *Daily Mail*, February 22, 1933.

out of the case. Fortunately for Birkett, Mr. Gregory had already paid Birkett's fee of three hundred guineas for representing him.

At the resumed hearing, Maundy Gregory's counsel intimated to the court that they had tendered 'certain advice' to their client who had accepted it and consequently now wished to withdraw his original plea and plead 'Guilty'. Inspector Askew of Scotland Yard then went into the witness box and said that the defendant had no previous convictions. He proceeded to state that the police had a number of similar complaints under consideration where people had paid or been asked to pay money to Maundy Gregory in connection with receiving honours. 'But,' said Crown counsel, 'I don't propose to carry it any further than that.'

Addressing the court on behalf of Maundy Gregory, Birkett said that if these further suggestions had been the subject of investigation his client would have been able to render explanations, and it would be fairer to eliminate consideration of these matters. Whatever explanation might be put forward as to Maundy Gregory's intent on the present charge, the substance of this particular complaint was not to be defended. So far as the defendant's activities were concerned, Birkett assured the magistrate that they were now at an end, so that the object of the prosecution had been achieved. 'I am conscious of the figure (£10,000) named in the summons,' Birkett continued, 'but this is not a case in which it is alleged that any sum of money actually passed. I do not think any useful purpose would be served by suggesting explanations as to intent or anything of that kind. In those circumstances I hope you may feel that Mr. Gregory has taken the proper course and that in the difficult circumstances of this case. . . . I hope you will feel that the ends of justice would be met by the imposition of a monetary penalty. I submit that would be a proper ending to this disturbing case.'

But the magistrate could not agree. The offence struck at by the Act was of a most mischievious character, said Mr. Graham-Campbell, in passing sentence of two months' imprisonment in the second division plus a fine of fifty pounds and fifty guineas costs, and doubly so, because anyone who committed an offence under the Act endeavoured to induce some other person to commit a crime, although fortunately on the present occasion the attempt was unsuccessful owing to the very proper attitude taken by Commander

Leake. 'In my opinion,' added the magistrate, 'the maximum fine of £50 would be wholly inadequate to meet this case.'

Maundy Gregory's subsequent history deserves some brief notice. While he was in prison rumours began to circulate that his mistress Mrs. Rosse, who was separated from her husband and had died in the previous summer, had been deliberately poisoned by him. Certainly the circumstances of her death were most suspicious. She had been suddenly taken ill after having had a meal with him and during her illness she had made a will in Gregory's favour, leaving him all her money amounting to about £18,000. After her death, Gregory paid a high fee to have her buried in the churchyard at Bisham a few feet from the river which frequently overflowed its banks. It seems that Gregory expected the churchyard to become waterlogged, which is what actually happened. He had also carefully supervised the interment, refusing to have the normal wooden coffin, preferring instead an unsealed lead shell which was placed in unusually shallow ground. Furthermore, poisons were found in Gregory's country house where Mrs. Rosse died.

As soon as Maundy Gregory was released from prison, he hurriedly left the country for France. His departure was followed by the exhumation of Mrs. Rosse's remains and an inquest, which were ordered by the Home Office at the instigation of the dead lady's relatives. But nothing positive was discovered despite protracted analysis and investigation, and in the end the coroner's jury returned an open verdict.

The possibility that Maundy Gregory murdered his mistress for her money cannot be wholly dismissed. He was faced with a demand for the repayment of the £30,000 he had received from a man who had died before any honours were conferred upon him, and it is a coincidence that the £12,000 he asked from Commander Leake, when added to Mrs. Rosse's money, made up the exact amount of his debt. It may be no more than a coincidence, but it is a remarkable one.

Maundy Gregory ended his days in Paris, supported largely by remittances from some of his former clients as the price for his silence about their business dealings. He went by the name of Sir Arthur Gregory, having given himself the comparatively modest honour of a knighthood, though no doubt in keeping with his somewhat diminished financial circumstances. Being a British subject, he was interned by the Germans after the fall of France, and he eventually died in a Paris hospital during the war.

In his palmy days, Maundy Gregory used to put his Ambassador Club at the disposal of A. J. A. Symons for the annual dinner in memory of Baron Corvo, when he acted as the host, and this was where Birkett first met his extraordinary client. As Symons put it, 'his memory remains like that of an incandescent meteor in the sky of high finance, an acquaintance as fantastic and unlikely as the wildest passage in the books of the weird Baron whom we both admired.'[1]

3

About the beginning of April, 1933, Birkett received an invitation from Mr. Justice McCardie to visit him in his London flat in Queen Anne's Mansions, overlooking St. James's Park. Since they were neighbours—Birkett had a flat in the same block—as well as having common legal roots in Birmingham and the Midland Circuit, besides a common love of literature, Birkett rang the judge's door bell when he got home expecting to have an ordinary social chat, since the judge was a bachelor and Birkett guessed that he might be lonely in the evenings after his day's work in the courts was over.

A widely-read man with a deep social conscience, although somewhat moody and eccentric, Henry McCardie was very much a lawyer after Birkett's heart, and Birkett appreciated his pronouncements on such questions as abortion, birth control, euthanasia and sterilisation, with which McCardie, who was fourteen years Birkett's senior, used to embellish his judgments, notwithstanding that his observations frequently brought him into sharp conflict with his judicial brethren. Rebuked on a recent occasion by Lord Justice Scrutton, who commented tartly on the singularity of a bachelor like McCardie displaying such an intimate knowledge of women's underclothes as he did, the judge had retaliated by proclaiming his intention of withholding any further notes of his cases from any Appeal Court on which Scrutton sat, and the Lord Chancellor had had to intervene to resolve the unseemly dispute.

[1] *The Quest for Corvo* (ed. 1952), at p. 253. For further details about Maundy Gregory, see Gerald Macmillan, *Honours for Sale* (1954).

Birkett had heard that McCardie, who had been on circuit, had been suffering from influenza. But he was not prepared for the sight which met his eyes. Haggard and grey with fatigue and worry, the judge looked a different person from when Birkett had last seen him in court.

'I am in desperate trouble,' he told his visitor, 'financial trouble. Unless I can get help, I am faced with ruin.'

'How much is involved?' asked Birkett.

Instead of a sum running into many thousands of pounds, which Birkett expected, McCardie mentioned a figure of approximately £2,000.

'As far as the money is concerned, you may put your mind at rest immediately,' said Birkett. 'You will have it tomorrow. But I must make one condition. You are a High Court judge, and I am a practising barrister. I cannot take the responsibility of helping you on my shoulders alone. I must have your permission to let me share the knowledge and responsibility with some other member of the Bar.' Birkett mentioned the name of Stuart Bevan, K.C., M.P., who was a friend of his in addition to being a Bencher of McCardie's Inn, the Middle Temple. To this McCardie willingly agreed.

Next day Birkett called on the judge again, this time accompanied by Bevan, and the loan was made.

A terrible sequel occurred a week or so later when McCardie was found dead in his flat with a shot gun by his side. It was clear that he had died by his own hand. Birkett was shocked when he learned the news, and still more when certain other facts about the judge's private life became known to him. The total sum of McCardie's financial indebtedness was far in excess of the relatively small amount which he and Bevan had paid. The truth was that the judge had been gambling unsuccessfully, and his liabilities ran into five figures. Point was also given to Lord Justice Scrutton's remarks when it was discovered that McCardie had been keeping a mistress in the country, while a titled lady in London claimed to be pregnant by him.

The whole truth about the suicide will probably never be known, or exactly why McCardie should have been gambling so heavily, when for many years he had earned over £20,000 a year at the Bar and since 1916 he had drawn the salary of a High Court judge. No doubt an acute fit of depression following recurrent attacks of influenza was the immediate cause. It was rumoured too that he was being blackmailed, and some support was lent to this theory by the subsequent confession of two notorious blackmailers that they had obtained money from him by this vile means.

In the same month as McCardie's tragic death, Birkett appeared for an Irish Senator in a libel action against the *Sunday Times* newspaper. The plaintiff, E. J. Duggan, who was a solicitor by profession, had been one of the signatories of the Anglo-Irish 'Treaty', which terminated the struggle between the British forces and the Irish nationalists and set up the Irish Free State with the status of a self-governing British dominion. The jurisdiction of the new Government extended to the whole of the country except the six counties in the north-east, which preferred to remain more directly under British rule. Senator Duggan, who before being elected to the Senate had sat in the Dail, as the Lower House was called, became a Minister of the Free State Government under the Prime Minister Mr. Cosgrave, remaining in office until Mr. Cosgrave's party was defeated at the polls by Mr. De Valera and his Republican followers in 1932. During the election much controversy centred round the Oath of Allegiance to the British Sovereign provided in the 'Treaty', since the Crown remained a nominal link with Britain, as it did in the case of the other self-governing dominions. Another thorny issue was the land annuities, a debt which it had been agreed should be taken over by the new Irish administration. Mr. De Valera and his party wished to abolish the Oath and cease payment of the annuities to the bondholders, mostly former English landlords. In an interview with Mr. Duggan published by the *Sunday Times*, some paragraphs were inserted from a pro-De Valera organ, the *Irish Press*, which gave the impression that Mr. Duggan's position about the Oath and the annuities was equivocal, whereas he had always thought that the maintenance of the Oath was a vital part of the 'Treaty' and he had fought consistently for the payment by the Irish Government of the land annuities to the English bondholders. In Dublin, Mr. Duggan succeeded in obtaining an injunction against the *Irish Press*, restraining that journal from further publication of the offending paragraphs, and in London the *Sunday Times* apologized, so that the only issue to be decided in court was the amount of damages, if any, which Mr. Duggan should be awarded.[1]

Asked in cross-examination why he had not demanded a fuller apology from the *Sunday Times* if he wanted it, Mr. Duggan replied, 'I had to leave the matter to my legal advisers. I am a busy politician.'

'But you are also a solicitor of many years standing?' asked Mr. Rowland Thomas, K.C., for the newspaper.

'A dangerous combination,' interjected Birkett, to the accompaniment of some laughter.

When the Senator went on to say that he had recently retired from the Dail and been elected a member of the Senate, Mr. Thomas asked him, 'You regard that as an honour?'

'I would rather be in the Dail,' replied Mr. Duggan.

'Perhaps there is more fun there,' was counsel's comment on this admission, and this time Mr. Thomas drew a laugh. But the laugh, at least from the jury, was on Birkett's side, as the jury awarded his client £500 damages. Had it not been for the amends already made by the defendant newspaper, the sum would, without doubt, have been greater.

Birkett's next notable case was a curious murder trial, which had been transferred from Bedford to Nottingham Assizes and came before Mr. Justice Finlay in June, 1933. Birkett was briefed for the defence, and in writing to ask the judge to fix a date for the hearing, he stated that he did not think the matter would take up much time, as the facts were clear and the only possible defence seemed to be insanity.

The accused, William Fountain of Dunstable, aged twenty-nine and a gun-maker by trade, was charged with murdering his wife, Ethel, a faithless creature whose cruel and promiscuous conduct had caused him to leave her; besides incessant nagging and getting him into debt, she had given him a venereal disease which she had caught from one of her lovers.[2] As a result both husband and wife had to undergo clinical treatment, after which the wife returned to her parents' house to live. Left alone, he became morbidly introspective

[1] *Duggan* v. *Allied Newspapers, Ltd. The Times*, April 18, 1933.

[2] *Nottingham Guardian*, July 1, 1933.

and her conduct preyed on his mind. He tried to drown his sorrows in music, and joined the Dunstable Excelsior Brass Band, but as soon as he had finished practice his troubles would return to him. Meanwhile his wife began to pester him to take her back. She threatened that if he would not do this she would 'do herself in'. Consequently Fountain resolved, as he said, 'to take her the means whereby she could let me have a free man's life with my boy Tony'. One might have expected from his trade that 'the means' would have been a gun: in fact it was a dagger, which he brought with him when he called at her parent's house one Sunday evening in the previous May.

She was out at chapel, so he waited, and when she got back they went for a walk together. They reached a stile on which Ethel Fountain sat, while her husband remained standing close to her. What happened then he described in a statement he subsequently made to the police, which he prefaced by swearing that he never intended to do her any harm himself.

> I explained to her that she could never have me, but she turned like a mad woman, and said if I didn't have her she would wreck my life for ever. She said she would make trouble for my next woman and get us parted and try to get my boy away.
>
> It made me see red, my brain I could not describe. . . . My hand flew to my pocket, and I drew the dagger from it and stabbed.
>
> She said, 'Oh, Sid, what have you done?' I think I said 'The only thing possible!'
>
> She then cried, 'Oh look!' (meaning blood), 'don't leave me like this,' and she grasped my hand over the dagger and drove it in again. What I did next I don't know.
>
> Realization came to me of the deed which had been done. I saw she was still alive, and ran to attract attention. . . . I swear once more what I did was never in my mind until my sense of reasoning failed me and the devil himself guided me.

After telling a passer-by that if he went to the stile he would 'see something', Fountain gave himself up to the police.

The first witness was the dead woman's father, who gave evidence of identification. Cross-examined by Birkett, he admitted that his son-in-law was 'one of the best chaps there was, in a rough way, straight, upright, and honest, kind to his wife and passionately fond of his little boy'. He did not know that his daughter had been getting the prisoner into debt, nor that she had been going with other men, but when Fountain told him that he thought he had contracted venereal disease from her, he gave his daughter 'a good talking to'.

'Has he tried to be a good husband?' Birkett asked.

'Absolutely,' replied the witness. 'He was a decent fellow in every way.'

The remainder of the morning was taken up with police and medical witnesses, who testified that there were two wounds when the body was discovered, one under the right shoulder and another between the second and third ribs, through the right lung, which had severed the right pulmonary artery.

Among these witnesses was the doctor who had made the *post-mortem* examination. He stated that in the case of the second wound the dagger went in fully, but in the case of the other it probably only went in half-way.

Cross-examined by Birkett, the doctor admitted that whereas the first, non-fatal wound could not have been self-inflicted, the fatal could have been, although, owing to its position, he considered this was unlikely. Replying further to the judge, this witness said that the less serious wound might conceivably have proved fatal, although the probability was that Mrs. Fountain would have recovered.

Birkett had previously intimated to the court that he did not intend to put the prisoner into the witness box, since he intended to plead insanity when he addressed the jury. But the doctor's admissions had completely changed the situation, and he now realized that there was a chance of acquittal. It was now about 12.45 p.m. and Birkett asked the judge if he would adjourn for luncheon as he wished to consult his client.

The judge agreed, and for the next hour and a quarter Birkett conferred with the prisoner, telling him that he wished to call him as a witness after all and going over his statement with him. He then snatched a sandwich and went back to court as Mr. Justice Finlay was taking his seat on the Bench.

'My Lord, I call the prisoner, William Fountain.' The prisoner then left the dock for the witness box, where Birkett again took him over his statement. After he had repeated exactly what had happened at the stile, the prisoner said that his wife put her hand over his hand on the dagger and forced it towards herself.

'With what amount of force did she force it towards herself?' Birkett asked.

'With almost a mad plunge,' the prisoner replied.

'Had you any power or control to stop that blow?'

'No, I had no power over anything.'

'You had no idea where you stabbed?'

'Not an earthly idea.'

'Up to that moment, when your wife said you should have no future happiness, after all that had passed, and that your boy should be taken from you, had you ever at any time the slightest intention of doing harm to your wife?'

'No, never.'

Cross-examined by Mr. J. F. Eales for the prosecution, Fountain admitted he wanted his wife to get emotional so that he could give her the dagger to use on herself. The idea of this way out of the trouble came to him when she talked about committing suicide at an earlier date. When he met his wife on the night of the tragedy, there was a note of triumph in her voice, suggesting that she had 'won again' and that 'the poor fish had come back'.

'You remember pulling the dagger out the first time!'

'No. I do not remember it. I saw nothing. There was a cloud before my eyes.'

'Did she try to defend herself?'

'Probably. I could not swear to it.'

The dagger was in a sheath, he added, and how it came to be in the sheath when he handed it to the police he could not say.

'Did the idea of giving her the dagger come to you when your brain was in a whirl and people were pitying you?' Birkett asked in re-examination.

'Yes,' said Fountain. He added that the dagger was taken out solely with the idea of giving it to his wife. He had already started divorce proceedings against her and a solicitor had the matter in hand.

As the prisoner was the only witness for the defence, Birkett was able to have the last word with the jury, apart from the judge's summing up. Fixing his eye on a rather emotional woman with a large hat in the jury-box, who was on the verge of tears, Birkett succeeded in building up a deeply moving picture of a man who had been 'most terribly and gravely injured in that which was most intimate and most sacred to most men in their domestic life', of how his wife had associated with other men and had eventually left him, and of how the wretched prisoner had made a great endeavour to console himself and joined the Dunstable Excelsior Brass Band. (Incidentally, Birkett made a great play with the name of the band, which had occurred in the prisoner's statement and which rolled off counsel's lips with a pronounced air of pathos.) To bring in a verdict of wilful murder would be unjust and wrong, Birkett urged. 'The mad plunge was the fatal wound,' he said, and in any event there was such provocation as must reduce the charge at least to manslaughter.

In his summing up, Mr. Justice Finley told the jury that there were four possible verdicts. They could bring in murder, manslaughter, attempted murder, or not guilty of any of them.

To the surprise of many in court, not least the prisoner, who collapsed in a dead faint when he heard the foreman's words, the jury acquitted him on all counts.

Sitting beside Mr. Justice Finlay on the Bench was the Judge's marshal, a young barrister recently called to the Bar named Edward Ford, now Sir Edward Ford, K.C.V.O., Assistant Private Secretary to Her Majesty the Queen. He has recalled how Birkett folded up his papers, tied them up with red tape and handed them to his clerk, and then walked out of court with no more ado than if he had just made an application to the court on some trivial matter. 'But it was as brilliant a piece of advocacy and of opportunism as I've ever heard in a Court. One unexpected answer from the doctor had made Birkett see that he had a chance and by changing the whole nature of the defence, of gaining an acquittal.'[1]

A few days later, Birkett found himself appearing in an interesting civil action in London which was brought against the owners of a so-called 'nature cure' establishment by a woman who had undergone treatment there. Birkett appeared for the defendants, Mr. Stanley Lief and his company, Nature Healing Ltd., while Sir Patrick Hastings led for the plaintiff, Mrs. Eleanor Walton, who sued for personal injuries, negligence and breach of contract. The action came before the Lord Chief Justice, Lord Hewart, and a special jury in the King's Bench Division of the High Court.

[1] Communicated by Sir Edward Ford.

Opening the plaintiff's case, Sir Patrick Hastings said that Mr. Lief undertook to cure her of a skin affection, and she underwent treatment prescribed by Mr. Lief, with the result that her face and scalp had become permanently disfigured. 'I cannot tell you whether Mr. Lief is a medical man or not,' Sir Patrick continued. 'He runs a sanatorium named Champneys, at Tring, in Hertfordshire. He is obviously a man of high qualifications. At his sanatorium he charges twelve or fifteen guineas a week for accommodation, food and treatment, and the diet in Mrs. Walton's case consisted mainly of "natural food", orange juice and fruit.'

Mrs. Walton confirmed this account of the health establishment. 'Mr. Lief told me, most definitely, he could cure me,' she said. 'The first evening I was given a glass of milk and a pear, fruit to get the poisons out of my system.' Next day, a Sunday, she had no breakfast; for lunch she had hot lemon and honey, a peach, an orange and a pear; and for tea, more hot lemon, honey and two plums. 'On the Monday I had no breakfast, and treatment with an electric blanket was given. On other days my total daily meals consisted of three oranges and a grapefruit and a half. Osteopathy and massage were practised on me and the diet gave me indigestion. I also had water in which vegetables had been boiled and the juice of apples.' She added that just before she left the sanatorium at the end of five weeks, she was given a salad and a baked potato. She had one poached egg, but never a real meal the whole time.

Lord Horder, the well-known physician—he was the Prince of Wales's doctor—also gave evidence for the plaintiff. He said he did not think that the nature of her complaint had been realized. 'So few treatments succeed,' he declared; 'so many do harm.'

Cross-examined by Birkett, this witness admitted, 'I realize that there is, just now, a great vogue about starvation, both by those who need it and those who don't. Some people enjoy a mental satisfaction in starving.'

'There is a school of thought about fasting?' Birkett queried.

'I would not call it a school of thought but a fashion,' replied Lord Horder.

'A great many members of your profession subscribe to it?'

'In the case of the City Aldermen, yes.'

'Do you know that very distinguished people have been treated in Champneys?' Birkett continued.

'I believe so,' said the famous doctor. 'They also come to see me.'

Denying the plaintiff's charges, Mr. Lief in the witness box said that when he first examined Mrs. Walton he told her that in his opinion her disease was due to impure blood and intestinal toxaemia, and that the dietary and other treatment was administered to her in the light of past experience. But he had never given her any guarantee of cure, he added. If Mrs. Walton had asked for it, he would have said 'No', since hers was a very difficult case to cure. Answering Birkett, he said that he had practised osteopathy in this country for many years.

'What is osteopathy?' asked Lord Hewart from the Bench.

'It is a method of treatment,' Mr. Lief replied, 'in the belief that disease is produced by certain lesions or interferences in the system.'

Another osteopath, Dr. Sidney Callum, who assisted the defendant at Champneys, said that Mrs. Walton had told him about the disease on her face and he considered she was a proper patient for treatment at Champneys.

'There is no complaint about the treatment at Champneys under your direction?' Birkett asked this witness.

'No,' replied Dr. Callum, 'in fact Mrs. Walton wanted more of it.'

The result of the trial was a win for the plaintiff, but it was qualified by the contemptuous sum awarded by way of damages on the negligence issue—one farthing. The jury did find, however, that there had been a breach of warranty, since in a journal entitled *Health for All* owned by Natural Healing Ltd. and advertising the merits of Champneys it was stated that no disease was incurable there except cancer, tuberculosis and paralysis, and they awarded Mrs. Walton the amount of the bill for her five weeks stay at this remarkable establishment—£123 16s.

From the public point of view the case was important for the jury's rider which was to lead to a change in the law—'that all institutions of this character should be subject to supervision by some Government authority.'[1]

4

Most people are familiar with the detective story of fiction in which the authorities are enabled to track down the criminal through

[1] *Walton* v. *Lief. The Times*, July 7, 1933.

the aid of an outside investigator. Such a story does not often happen in real life. Yet it did happen in the case of Leopold Harris and his gang of fire raisers who were tried by Mr. Justice Humphreys in 1933, and one of whom, an assessor named Adam Loughborough Ball, was defended by Birkett. It was an amazing case in which a London solicitor, by much perseverance and a certain amount of good luck, brought off what must surely be the most sensational feat of private detection in history.

As a result Harris and sixteen other prisoners, including Ball, eventually stood in the dock at the Old Bailey charged with defrauding insurance companies by presenting bogus claims. Their trial lasted for thirty-three days and was the longest, and probably the most complex, which has ever been heard there. Apart from the accused, three men whose names were mentioned in the evidence anticipated their arrest by committing suicide. One poisoned himself with disinfectant, another was found asphyxiated in his garage, while the third threw himself in front of an Underground railway train, after first carefully removing his gold wrist-watch and placing it on the platform.

Harris described himself as an insurance assessor, but it would be more accurate to call him a 'claims-maker', since his function was invariably to represent the victim of a burglary or fire and to prepare the appropriate claim against the insurance company concerned. He operated an intelligence service which kept him posted of fires and burglaries throughout the country. On receiving news of one he would be quickly on the scene, and would offer to prepare the claim on behalf of the insured for a five per cent commission. His claims were always greatly inflated, and he was in consequence much distrusted by the insurance companies. Among those with whom he frequently crossed swords over claims was Mr. William Charles Crocker, a solicitor who specialized in insurance work.

The prosecution of Harris and his confederates was conducted by Mr. Roland Oliver, K.C., later Mr. Justice Oliver, and the tale of the prisoner's misdeeds which he related in court made both judge and jury gasp by reason of their bare-faced effrontery.

Briefly, what happened was this. Harris got tired of presenting claims mainly for the benefit of others, and he decided to use more direct and lucrative methods of swindling insurance companies. His plan, which he carried out on an extensive scale, was to float dummy businesses, put them in the name of a confederate as owner, insure them for fantastic sums in respect of fire loss and 'loss of profits', and having burnt them down and thus destroyed the stock, present huge claims, ostensibly on behalf of his clients but actually on behalf of himself and his fellow conspirators. For this purpose he enlisted two members of his family, his brother David and his brother-in-law Harry Gould (formerly Goldstein), a tailor, who had developed an interest in fires as a buyer of salvaged goods. Gould's firm was the main source from which Harris obtained 'stock' for his warehouses. The two other chief conspirators were Louis Jarvis (formerly Jacobs) and Camillo Capsoni, an Italian who had been in the silk trade.

The first big fire mentioned in the trial occurred in 1927, when the warehouse of Fabrique de Soieries Ltd. went up in flames at Manchester. Jarvis and Capsoni were its nominal proprietors, but in reality Harris had a substantial share in it. Its stock, which consisted of depreciated Italian silk from Gould's firm, was insured for £40,000, though its actual value was only a tenth of that figure. There was also a 'loss of profits' policy with Lloyd's for £20,000. Harris, who had conveniently arranged to be in Manchester on the night of the fire, proceeded to handle the claims, which were eventually settled by the insurers for £29,000.

Thereafter Harris adopted similar methods all over the country, not stopping at bribery to serve his ends. The insurance companies naturally employed their own independent assessors to examine and adjust the claims, but Harris's knowledge of the individual assessors usually retained by each fire office was such that he deliberately placed insurance where he knew that the assessors likely to be sent to investigate claims possessed personal weaknesses of which he could take advantage for his own ends. On the other hand, Crocker, the solicitor, continually contested Harris's grossly exaggerated claims, and in a certain instance was able to effect very substantial reductions, but as yet he had no evidence of fraud.

Then Mr. Crocker had two pieces of luck. First, a man named Mathews, who had been a clerk in Lloyd's and consequently knew of the solicitor's connection with the insurance world, came to him with an amazing story. According to Mathews, a friend of his had been approached by a certain Harry Priest, who told him that a mysterious personage, whom Priest referred to as 'The Prince', would set him up in a bogus business, which in due course was to be burnt down, so that everyone could benefit at the expense of the insurance companies. Crocker's reaction was to tell Mathews to ask his friend to keep in touch with Priest and find out more about 'The Prince', who was, of course none other than Leopold Harris himself.

A little later Mathews returned with the exciting news that Priest had told him that a 'bric-a-brac' shop in Poland Street, off Oxford Street, was being fitted out by 'The Prince' and would shortly go up in flames. Sure enough, in a week or two this is exactly what happened.

With the backing of Lloyd's and one of the principal fire offices, Crocker decided to concentrate on investigating this and similar losses. He found that Priest was a partner in a silk business at Stoke Newington. He then managed to obtain a photograph of him leaving the warehouse, on the pretext of collecting evidence of a motor accident. Crocker also discovered that Priest's partner was the Italian Capsoni who had recently had a fire in another business with which he was associated, the Franco-Italian Silk Company in Oxford Street. Capsoni also turned out to be the source from which the owner of the bric-a-brac shop in Poland Street had acquired £1,400 worth of Venetian glass, which had figured in the insurance claim after the fire there.

Crocker's next stroke of luck was when Capsoni's Scottish wife walked into his office one day not long afterwards. She had been sent by Captain Miles, the head of the London Salvage Corps, an official body subsidized by the fire insurance companies to protect their interests and co-operate with the Metropolitan fire brigades in saving life and property at fires. Miles was one of the select few who had been let into the secret of Crocker's investigations. It appeared that Mrs. Capsoni had in turn been sent to Miles by an insurance official whom she had told that she had seen a photograph of Harris's confidante, Louis Jarvis, as being concerned with a fire at Wembley, and that she had reason to believe that Jarvis had committed arson.

Mrs. Capsoni now made a complete confession. She told Crocker that she and her husband had belonged to the Harris gang, but had lately been troubled with conscientious scruples and they now wished to return to an honest way of life. She then went out and fetched Capsoni, who confirmed her account of how he set fire to the

Manchester warehouse of Fabrique de Soieries in 1927. There is no doubt that the Capsoni's repentance was genuine, but of course as erstwhile accomplices their evidence would require independent corroboration if the jury was to be convinced of the gang's guilt.

In an attempt to obtain further evidence directly implicating Harris, Crocker faked a motor accident to Capsoni, who agreed to say that this was engineered by the gang to 'bump him off', and his wife would warn Harris that he intended to go to Scotland Yard, when he had recovered, unless Harris visited him with an assurance that he was not behind the accident. Concealed microphones at the bedside would record Harris's conversation. Everything went according to plan, except that Harris flatly refused to visit the hospital. Someone or something had occurred to arouse his suspicions.[1]

However, Crocker, who had by this time been instructed by the Director of Public Prosecutions to act as his agent, was able, by following up the files of the insurance companies, and other clues, to establish the complicity of Harris and his gang in no less than twenty fires. The evidence was considered sufficient to justify the arrest of the fire raisers. While they were in custody 26,000 Bank of England notes were traced through their numbers as having passed through the hands of Harris and his agents.

The final scene in the Old Bailey was probably unique. Roland Oliver's brief for the prosecution was two feet high, a room in the court building had to be specially set aside for the accommodation of the documents in the case, and Mr. Justice Humphreys gave permission for a so-called 'whispering telephone' to be put beside Crocker in court. In reality it was an ordinary post office instrument with specially powerful batteries and a tuned-up microphone, which Crocker could use to communicate with the outside world without disturbing the proceedings in court. It was in fact used at the judge's suggestion to recall a witness who had gone to his house at Bognor and was eventually found swimming in the sea.

The prosecution did not suggest that Mr. Loughborough Ball, an educated man, who had been a fire assessor for twenty-two years and had some of the leading London insurance companies as clients,

[1] It later transpired that Captain Miles of the London Salvage Corps was also in Harris's pay and that it was he who had warned his master not to go and see Capsoni in hospital. He was tried later in the year and went to penal servitude for four years.

had been in the conspiracy to set fire to business premises, but it was alleged that he conspired with the other defendants to cheat insurance companies of money in respect of claims which he knew to be fraudulent. 'It is significant,' said Roland Oliver for the Crown, 'that in cases where the assessors were honest, claims were either repudiated altogether or drastically cut down. In claims where there was dishonesty the amounts were paid in full. Where crook assessors are employed this kind of fraud is highly successful.' Thus it appeared that the sum of £206,000 had gone to the gang from crook assessors, whereas only £14,000 had been paid where honest assessors were employed. According to the prosecution, Ball had been introduced to Capsoni by Harris after a fire in an Oxford Street silk shop, and it was suggested that Ball knew the nature of Capsoni's activities.

'In May, 1930,' Birkett asked Capsoni, who was the principal Crown witness, in cross-examination, 'when you started the Oxford Street fire, you had been living a life of crime for five or six years?'

'Yes, if you put it that way,' Capsoni replied.

'How many places had you burned down at that time?'

'Three.'

'And in these crimes had you adopted every form of deceit?'

'Yes, sir.'

Replying to further questions from Birkett, the witness agreed that he obtained about thirty billheads of foreign firms, which he used for faking invoices. Referring to one document, Birkett said to Capsoni: 'You used every conceivable skill and artifice to make it deceive anyobdy and to defy the most critical examination?'

'Yes, sir.'

'Do you assert that Mr. Loughborough Ball never saw this and all the other invoices?'

'Not in my presence.'

Birkett adopted the same line with Harry Gould, another of the Crown witnesses. Gould agreed that he had held a good position in the City and that therefore Ball had trusted him implicitly.

'How long have you been leading this life of crime?'

'A few years.'

'How much money have you had out of it?'

'Not very much.'

'What is the object of your giving evidence today? Do you think it is going to benefit you?'

'I am telling the truth. I do not want to commit perjury.'

'Would it be right to say that for many years you have been engaged in a life which involved deceit at almost every turn?'

'Untrue.'

'It involved knowledge that places were to be burned?'

'Yes.'

'It involved habitual lying?'

'Yes.'

The trial had begun on July 3, but it was not until July 27 that Birkett was able to open his client's defence and to put him into the witness box. It was alleged that without Ball's aid the gigantic fraud might have been stopped, but no one, said Birkett, had ever alleged that Ball had anything to do with the main conspiracy of starting fires. 'Never from start to finish did Ball conspire with anybody to defraud any insurance company in any way whatever. He acted honestly on behalf of the insurance companies.' When he went into the witness box, Ball was emphatic in declaring his innocence. He had often been in conflict with Harris over his claims, he said, and he had constantly advised the insurance companies that they were exaggerated. As for the Oxford Street fire, he had suggested to Gould that they should accept an allowance of twenty per cent. on a quantity of damaged dresses. It was in Gould's interest to keep the prices as low as possible as he was a prospective purchaser of salvage. 'I questioned Capsoni closely about the fire,' added Ball. 'There was nothing fraudulent whatever in my conduct, and in similar circumstances I could not do better today.'

In the end, after Birkett had succeeded in getting certain of the charges against Ball withdrawn, the case against his client amounted to having received £1,150 over eight years in respect of fraudulent claims. 'Would a man ruin himself beyond recovery for such a sum?' Birkett pleaded to the jury. 'This case means more than life to Ball, for an assessor of his standing to be guilty of such an offence is to wither away the whole of his reputation and the whole of his life's work.' Both Capsoni and Gould, Birkett went on, had admitted they did certain things to deceive Ball. And when the conspiracy was at its very height, Ball did not act in a single fire and not one of his companies was involved.

In his summing up, which lasted almost thirteen hours and was the longest ever delivered at the Old Bailey—he uttered in all 100,000 words—Mr. Justice Humphreys, referring to Ball, pointed out that he had been a trusted assessor of an insurance company, which on the strength of his report on the fire at the Oxford Street store, paid out £22,000 for junk supplied by Gould and worth £3,000 at most. Ball's reward for his services was £600; Harris, for his, took £10,000.

The jury returned their verdicts on August 18. Counsel were provided with charts marked with black and white squares not unlike a crossword puzzle, and containing the names of the defendants with spaces in which to record the jury's findings in each of the thirty-two counts in the indictments. The actual delivery of the verdicts lasted half an hour, and all the defendants including Ball were found guilty. Leopold Harris as the ringleader got fourteen years penal servitude and the others were sentenced to lesser terms. Mr. Loughborough Ball, the erstwhile respectable assessor, who was foolishly drawn into the criminal network, was sent down for three years.

When the proceedings were over, the twenty-five counsel engaged in it presented the judge with a silver inkstand to mark their admiration of the way he had tried this legal marathon case. It contained their signatures in facsimile. After the judge's death, it was presented to the Old Bailey Bar Mess by his son, Mr. Christmas Humphreys, who had defended Priest. In associating himself with this tribute to a great criminal judge, Birkett was proud to see among the other signatures such familiar names as Roland Oliver, Henry Curtis-Bennett, Walter Monckton, William Fearnley-Whittingstall, Eric Sachs and Christmas Humphreys, besides that of his own junior, G. D. ('Khaki') Roberts, all of whom like him had in one way or another made their reputations at the English Criminal Bar.

5

Birkett's main outdoor recreation continued to be golf, which he played off a club handicap of nine. He spent the Easter Vacation in 1933 at Turnberry, where he created a sensation by doing the thirteenth hole in one. He and his wife, also a keen golfer, returned to Turnberry in the following Long Vacation, taking in Ulverston and the Lakes on their way. On this occasion he won a guinea prize in a competition run by the Scottish edition of the *Daily Express* for the best contribution from a reader on the subject of 'A Model Grace before Meat', with the following lines.[1]

Over land and sea they fared
  Brought earth's bounty to our board:
For this table so prepared,
  Make us truly thankful, Lord!

He also enjoyed revisiting the Oxford Union, which he did at the invitation of the President, Mr. Michael Foot, the youngest son of of his old Liberal friend Isaac Foot, M.P. As guest speaker of the evening he had to support the motion, 'That the revival of Liberalism offers the only safeguard against war and dictatorship in Europe.' Birkett was always at ease when speaking to an undergraduate audience, and although his eloquence on this occasion failed to carry the motion, which was defeated by thirty votes, it made a fine impression upon the House. 'Abroad in the world today there is a great shadow of war,' he said, conscious that he was speaking in the year Hitler had seized power in Germany. 'Everywhere and in every country, there is fear, anxiety and a kind of intensive nationalism which finds its expression in restricting trade, and in rather selfish monetary policies. That is the situation of the world, and Liberalism is undoubtedly under a cloud. . . . In any definition of Liberalism freedom has an important part to play. Liberalism is therefore opposed to any idea of dictatorship, whether by a party, an individual or an organization, and surely it offers the highest safeguard against war. Surely it is not beyond the bounds of proven and enlightened Liberalism to pass beyond the frontiers of the ordinary sovereign state to envisage a world in which war as such can be made quite unthinkable.'[2]

To Henry Birkett

Challens Green, *October* 25, 1933. . . . I, too, think continually of golf and Ulverston and the Lakes this Summer. It was the best Long Vacation of recent years, and is a great stand-by in the stress of life here in London. The anxiety and strain of the cases grow with the years, and though I continue to win

[1] Published August 18, 1933.
[2] *Oxford Mail*, October 13, 1933.

very remarkable victories—one at Bedford Assizes last week[1] —they are bought with a price! . . .

I had a very good visit to the Oxford Union at the opening of Term, and there is quite a happy photograph in today's *Tatler*. Billy says I look thirty!!!

The names of some of Birkett's clients at this period and the courts in which he appeared for them reflect the variety of his practice. In November, 1933, he defended the Duke of Atholl at Bow Street Police Court on a charge of contravening the Lotteries Act of 1823. The Duke, who was disturbed by the amount of money surreptitiously leaving the country in the purchase of tickets in the Irish Hospitals Sweepstake, devised a scheme called 'The Duke of Atholl's Fund', to which he invited public subscriptions in the form of the purchase of tickets. According to the document announcing the scheme, there was 'no promise of any prizes'. Although it was made clear that the Duke had complete discretion to deal with the money as he thought fit, which included disbursements to charity, there was a plain inference that the purchaser of a ticket thought he was buying a chance of winning a prize. One purchaser selected at random by the prosecution gave evidence to this effect, and, although Birkett argued that there was nothing on the ticket to show that he was buying a contractual right to a chance, the magistrate, Sir Rollo Graham Campbell, convicted the Duke and fined him £25 and £36 15s. costs. 'I find as a fact that the defendant made an offer of a sale of a chance that there might be prizes,' said the magistrate, 'and that if there were prizes the acceptor of the offer might be given one.' Since then, the law has been changed, and the antiquated and complex legislation on lotteries has been swept away, although when he argued the case Birkett did not think he would live to see the day when the Government would sponsor a nation-wide lottery in the shape of premium bonds with a great many more prizes than the Duke of Atholl contemplated in his comparatively modest scheme.

Another titled aristocrat for whom Birkett appeared at this time was the Marquis Alphonse Pallavicini, First Secretary at the Hungarian Legation in London, who sued the London Passenger Transport Board for damages for personal injuries, which, he

[1] This was a running down case where the defendant was charged with manslaughter, characterized by the prosecution as 'a bad case of reckless driving'. Birkett secured an acquittal in the face of strong Crown evidence: *Wellingborough News*, October 20, 1933.

alleged he had suffered by reason of the negligence of the driver of one of the Board's 'Green Line' coaches.[1] In opening the case before the Lord Chief Justice, Lord Hewart, and a special jury, Birkett said that the Marquis was returning to London with the Marchioness of Londonderry in his car, which he was driving, after having dined with the Duke of Sutherland at Sutton Place, near Guildford. He was in collision with the coach on a hill on the Portsmouth road between Kingston and Putney, receiving injuries to his head, chest and thigh, as a result of which he had been compelled to lead the life of a semi-invalid. Lady Londonderry was also injured, her head being forced through the windscreen and one of her thumbs being broken. The Marquis in the witness box said that the coach seemed to descend the hill straight in front of him, but the Board's counsel Mr. Malcolm Hilbery, K.C. (afterwards Mr. Justice Hilbery), put it to him with some effect in cross-examination that he was travelling at high speed in the middle of the road and in trying to get over to his proper side struck the coach with his off-side wheel.

Lady Londonderry, who also gave evidence, did her best to support her companion. According to her, the Marquis's car was always on the proper side of the road. The coach was thirty yards away when she first saw it clearly, and it was then on the wrong side of the road, bearing down on the Marquis's car very quickly. The Marquis braked hard, steering further in the direction of the left, when he was struck by the coach on his front off-side wheel. 'My head went through the windscreen and my face was streaming with blood,' Lady Londonderry added on a dramatic note.

'How was it,' Mr. Hilbery asked her in cross-examination, 'if you were sitting in the front seat on the left of the Marquis, you could have seen the impact on the off-side wheel?'

Such a gymnastic feat would have been physically impossible. But Lady Londonderry was not in the least dismayed by the question. Drawing herself up to the full height of her regal and commanding presence—she was one of the most beautiful and distinguished hostesses of the period—she replied in icy tones: 'The facts are as I have already stated them.' With these words, she gave Mr. Hilbery such a bitter look that he quickly passed on to some other subject.

Nevertheless the case for the defence was plainly the stronger. If

[1] *The Times*, November 25, 1933.

they were to find in favour of the Marquis Pallavicini, Mr. Hilbery told the jury, they would have to accept the suggestion that on a clear road and a clear night the coach came down the road close to its wrong side, ignoring all the empty road on its near side, although an approaching vehicle on its proper side of the road was coming straight at it. Defence counsel then proceeded to reinforce his point by putting the uniformed coach driver and other witnesses into the box, who all swore that at all material times the coach was on its proper side.

On this occasion, Birkett's eloquence failed to get a verdict for the plaintiff. There was a distinct conflict of evidence, and the jury chose to accept the defendants'. In reaching their decision, the jury seemed to have been influenced by the impression they had gained that Lady Londonderry was having a night out with someone who was not her husband, who was moreover a foreigner, and furthermore a particularly dangerous type of foreigner, namely a Hungarian, besides which the couple had probably dined at the ducal table not wisely but too well and were in a hurry to get home. Nor were Lord Londonderry's feelings solaced by having, in addition to his wife's medical expenses as the result of the accident, to pay all the unsuccessful plaintiff's legal costs. Although the Marquis Pallavicini was socially prominent in English society—it was said that he had brought the action at the suggestion of King George V at a shooting party at Sandringham—'Fono' Pallavicini was really an impoverished nobleman and received a mere pittance for his job at the Hungarian Legation.

But fees and fashionable clients were never a prime consideration with Birkett. Shortly after the Pallavicini case, he gave his services free and travelled to Cambridge to defend an undergraduate of his old college who had pleaded guilty to stealing books from bookshops and libraries in the neighbourhood. The undergraduate was the son of a milkman, and his parents had scraped and saved every penny for twenty years in order to send him to the university. The undergraduate was a brilliant student and a prizewinner, who had gone without food and had originally taken the books for purposes of study, although he had continued to do so 'for the mere acquisition of books'. Birkett had personally interested himself in the case and had persuaded the college to take the lad back provided the Cambridge bench of magistrates bound him over. When the Bench learned this from Birkett's lips, and also that all the books had been restored to their rightful owners, they took the merciful course and put him on probation for two years, thus saving a promising career from ruin by a momentary lapse.[1]

In the same month, Birkett appeared for Mr. Edward James, the son of the famous Edwardian hostess Mrs. Willie James, in the divorce suit which he brought against his wife, the Viennese dancer Tilly Losch, on the ground of her adultery with Prince Serge Obolensky. The hearing, which took place before the President of the Divorce Division, Sir Boyd Merriman, occupied eight days and provided a society sensation, both from the nature of the evidence given and the witnesses who included the respondent's fellow dancer, Lady Charles Cavendish (Adele Astaire), Sir Thomas Beecham and Mr. Randolph Churchill. In the event, the petitioner got his decree and the judge rejected the wife's counter-charges of cruelty. The costs in this suit amounted to £10,000, Birkett's share being 500 guineas on his brief for the petitioner and a daily refresher of 100 guineas. On the issue of cruelty, the judge agreed with Birkett's submission that the wife should pay the costs on this issue, and in this connection the President had some severe things to say about Miss Losch's cruelty charges. 'They were pressed ruthlessly,' he remarked. 'They were abandoned, when seen to be hopeless, in a way which was by no means calculated to remove the sting of the charges.'[2]

6

Birkett's services continued to be in demand for every kind of litigation. In the Michaelmas Term, 1934, he appeared for the defence in three sensational trials at Lincoln, Leeds and Lewes Assizes respectively; he travelled down to the small Devon town of Paignton to defend a local bone-setter in the police court on the charge of improperly describing himself as a 'manipulative surgeon'; he also represented *The Star* in an interesting libel action brought against that newspaper by Sir Oswald Mosley in the High Court.

The task of defending Mrs. Ethel Lillie Major accused of poison-

[1] *Daily Telegraph*, July 12, 1934. In addition to giving his services free in this case, Birkett reimbursed the instructing solicitor for his out-of-pocket expenses, so that neither the undergraduate nor his parents had any costs to meet.

[2] *News Chronicle*, July 28, 1934.

ing her husband with strychnine and so causing his death, was one of the utmost difficulty for Birkett, since the case against her was overwhelmingly strong. Nor could he implant any real elements of doubt in the jury's mind, as he had done in the cases of Mrs. Pace and Mrs. Hearn, where the poison used was arsenic. The dead man, Arthur Major, was a lorry driver, and he and his wife had lived at Kilby-on-Main, a small village near Horncastle, with their fifteen-year-old son; but they were not happily married. Mrs. Major complained that her husband drank too much and that he left her too much alone; there was evidence, too, that she was jealous of him and accused him of associating with another woman, a neighbour named Mrs. Rose Kettleborough. Mrs. Major claimed to have found two love letters written by Mrs. Kettleborough to her husband. She showed the letters to her doctor, and according to the doctor, said: 'A man like him is not fit to live, and I will do him in.' Mrs. Kettleborough denied having written these letters, and it may well be that Mrs. Major wrote them herself.

Arthur Major died after a short and agonizing illness, the cause of death being certified as epilepsy. But Mrs. Major seemed in a great hurry to get him buried, and indeed she might have succeeded if an anonymous letter had not reached the police suggesting that Mrs. Major had poisoned her husband. 'Why did he complain of his food tasting nasty and throw it to the neighbour's dog, who has since died?' asked the writer, who signed himself 'Fairplay'.[1]

The upshot was that the funeral arrangements were stopped and *post-mortem* examinations carried out on the bodies of Mr. Major and the dog. They showed on analysis of the organs the presence of 1.27 and 0.12 grains of strychnine respectively.

When interviewed by Chief Inspector Hugh Young from Scotland Yard, Mrs. Major said, 'I did not know my husband had died from strychnine poisoning.'

'I never mentioned strychnine,' the Inspector interrupted her. 'How did you know that?'

'Oh, I'm sorry,' replied Mrs. Major. 'I must have made a mistake.'

Mrs. Major was arrested, charged with murder and duly brought up at the Assizes held in Lincoln Castle before Mr. Justice Charles on November 29, 1934. The case for the prosecution was presented by Mr. Edward O'Sullivan, K.C., and one of the most damning

[1] *Lincoln Echo*, October 29, 1934.

pieces of evidence he produced was the key of a box containing strychnine, which was kept in the house of the prisoner's father, an ex-gamekeeper, who used the poison for the purpose of putting down vermin. The key was found in Mrs. Major's purse, and its shiny condition indicated that it had been recently used.

Birkett did his best with the prosecution witnesses, but his task was hopeless from the beginning. He tried to make the doctor admit that what Mrs. Major had really said to him was, 'Men like that are not fit to live' instead of 'A man like that is not fit to live', but the doctor would not accept this suggestion. The words had impressed him, he said, just as Mrs. Major's other remark, 'I will do him in.'

'Did you regard it at the time as the mere vapouring of a very excited woman?'

'Yes.'

'If you had thought there was any deep significance in it, you would have taken steps about it?'

'Yes.'

The most this witness would concede, when pressed by Birkett, was that Mrs. Major was a very nervous and excitable woman and was 'beyond the ordinary in this respect'.

Birkett did not put the prisoner into the witness box. Nor did he call any other evidence, so that he had the last word with the jury. His hope was to satisfy the jury that the case against Mrs. Major had not been proved beyond all reasonable doubt, and if she were really guilty, he suggested, she would have thrown the key of the box away. Nor would she have given some of the poisoned corned beef which her husband had consumed to the dog, who died immediately after eating it. But Birkett's hope was forlorn. In reality the effective last word had already come from the Crown counsel when he said that 'the case is really on the evidence unanswerable'.

When the jury filed into court after an hour's absence, Birkett knew the verdict before the foreman announced it, since the foreman and his fellow jurors all looked away from the prisoner. Then came the fatal announcement, coupled with the words that 'a strong recommendation to mercy should be given to the prisoner'. But there was no mercy in the words of the judge when he passed the death sentence upon the weeping woman in the dock. 'You have been found guilty of one of the cruellest crimes that you could have committed,' Mr. Justice Charles declared sternly. The prisoner thereupon collapsed and had to be practically carried below. 'I am innocent,' she kept moaning.

Birkett realized that it would be fruitless to appeal. But he associated himself with a memorial got up by Mrs. Major's solicitors and addressed to the Home Secretary petitioning for a reprieve, and which he himself forwarded to the Minister.

But this last effort failed on Mrs. Major's behalf. On December 16, Birkett received an official letter from the Home Office informing him that after considering all the circumstances of the case the Minister had been unable to discover 'any sufficient ground to justify him in advising His Majesty to interfere with the due course of law'. A few days later, Mrs. Major was hanged. While murder by poisoning is no longer a capital offence, in Birkett's time it was considered such a repulsive crime that convicted poisoners were practically never reprieved.

On the same circuit, at Leeds Assizes, Birkett defended another woman charged with murder, on this occasion with happier results. The case was one of so-called 'mercy killing'. Mrs. Mary Brownhill, aged sixty-two, was accused of murdering her thirty-year-old imbecile son Denis by giving him about a hundred aspirins and then placing a gas tube over his mouth and turning on the gas. She was apparently driven to take this desperate step by the knowledge that she would have to go into hospital for a serious kidney operation and there would be no one to look after Denis when she was away. 'I did not do it feloniously or maliciously,' she told the police when charged, 'I mercifully put my boy to sleep.'

In his speech to the jury Birkett described the case as one of extreme poignancy which in all probability they would never experience again. 'Sympathy springs up in our hearts and minds,' he said. 'There was no mean motive. There was no desire to be rid of a helpless son because he required care and attention. There was never such a mother as this. Her whole life was one of care and devotion, and for ten years, day and night, her devotion had been unceasing. Even when she was suffering bodily weakness, with increasing exhaustion and loss of weight, she was still the same devoted mother. Every witness has said that in every change of circumstance and situation her thoughts were always for her boy. There was never a holiday, never any relaxation. Instead her whole life was devoted to the boy.'

The trial judge, Mr. Justice Goddard, in his summing up told the jury that Birkett's words amounted to a recommendation to mercy which they might attach to the verdict that they would probably feel that it was only their duty to return. 'There are no circumstances which amount to justification for the killing of this woman's son,' he said. 'The time may come when it may be the law of this country that an imbecile or idiot may be put mercifully to death. That is not the law at present, and neither you nor I have any right to make law. We have to take the law as it is found. . . . No person has a right to kill another human being because he thinks it would be better for that human being if he should die. Therefore there is no justification for this unhappy act.'[1]

In returning the inevitable verdict of guilty, the jury added 'the strongest possible recommendation to mercy', which the judge had anticipated and which he now undertook to support when forwarding it to the proper quarter. The result was that Mrs. Brownhill was reprieved within forty-eight hours and three months later she was granted a free pardon, which enabled her to return home in time to spend Christmas with her husband.

Does the use of the word 'surgeon' on the name plate of a door imply that the inmate is a registered medical practitioner? This was the question Birkett had to argue when he defended a manipulative surgeon, thus describing himself, on a charge of unlawfully implying that he was registered under the Medical Act. For years controversy had raged round the practice of bone-setting or manipulative surgery, as its celebrated pioneer Sir Herbert Barker preferred more accurately to call it, and it had come to a head shortly before the First World War when a doctor had been struck off the official medical register for acting as Barker's anaesthetist. But, in spite of the dogged opposition of most of the medical profession the value of Barker's work had generally come to be realized even by eminent medical men. But Barker, although he called himself a manipulative surgeon and was usually referred to as such, did not have a nameplate with the words outside his surgery because it was not the practice in London for surgical practitioners to indicate on their nameplates the particular kind of surgery they practised, which might be medical, dental or veterinary. In the case of Birkett's client, Captain Horace Barrow, of Paignton, the prosecution was

[1] *Yorkshire Evening Post*, December 1, 1934.

brought by the Medical Defence Union against Captain Barrow for exhibiting a nameplate calling himself a surgeon when in fact he was not a qualified surgeon. The plate had been outside Barrow's house since he commenced to practise about eight years previously, during which period he had acquired between seven thousand and eight thousand patients, including the Chief Constable of Devon. He had previously practised for fifteen years in other parts of the country. The description he used on the plate read 'Captain H. Barrow, M.M., Manipulative Surgeon'.[1]

'You know that Captain Barrow has the Military Medal,' Birkett asked the police witness who had proved the existence of the plate from a photograph, 'and that qualification at any rate is quite correct?'

'Yes, sir,' the officer agreed.

The prosecution was conducted by a solicitor from Plymouth, Mr. John Woolland, who did not call any evidence to the effect that it was thought that the defendant was a registered practitioner. Instead he relied on the assumption that the use of the word 'surgeon' implied registration.

Birkett made short work of him. 'No such thing,' he declared. 'Suppose Captain Barrow had called himself "Quack Surgeon"? Would that have implied that he was registered? Obviously not. It makes no difference whether he used the word "quack", which cannot possibly bear the implication of registration, or the words "Manipulative Surgeon". Suppose the plate said "Captain Barrow, M.M., Unregistered Surgeon". Clearly the implication of registration is excluded.'

When Captain Barrow went into the witness box, Birkett asked him, 'How long has this phrase "Manipulative Surgeon" been employed by people who are not registered?'

'I saw it when I was a boy and ever since,' Captain Barrow replied. 'About thirty-five years.'

The defendant then produced a copy of *The Times* newspaper for November 25, 1912, in which there was a reference in a leading article to a 'master of manipulative surgery'. That reference, said the witness, was to Sir Herbert Barker.

At this point the Clerk to the Justices took a hand in the proceedings. 'Did Sir Herbert Barker call himself a manipulative

[1] *Paignton News*, November 17, 1934.

surgeon when he was practising,' he asked Captain Barrow, 'or only when he was writing his reminiscences?'

'I think throughout his life,' Captain Barrow answered.

'Why do you use that description?' Birkett went on to inquire of the witness.

'To distinguish myself from a registered practitioner.'

'Have you ever tried to mislead anybody?'

'Never in my life.'

'Do you always charge for your services?'

'No. Sixty per cent. or seventy per cent. of my work is free to people who cannot afford to pay.'

'You regard that as a contribution to public welfare?'

'I think it is a duty, sir.'

Replying to further questions from his counsel, Captain Barrow said he had never been to any college or institution for training, but during his work while serving in France during the last war he had been under the supervision of two doctors. No complaint was made about his work.

'You don't claim to be an osteopath?'

'Not in any way.'

'Does your work go farther than that of an ordinary masseur?' the prosecuting solicitor asked Captain Barrow in cross-examination.

'Entirely different.'

'Does it go further than a bone-setter?'

'Yes, if you define that as setting bones and only setting bones. I not only set bones, but I reduce dislocation.'

Asked by the solicitor whether he had read the Medical Act, Captain Barrow said that he had not. 'I don't mind what they call me,' he added, 'but I think "manipulative surgeon" is the only way to describe my work.'

'Do you intend to continue to use the word "surgeon"?'

'I do until I'm stopped,' answered Captain Barrow with an air of determination.

'If there was a name which described what you did better than the title you used,' Birkett asked his client in re-examination, 'would you use it?'

'Gladly.'

'Have you in fact treated many patients sent to you by medical men?'

'Yes,' said Captain Barrow, adding that they included medical men themselves.

'In the whole course of your life as a manipulative surgeon until you had this letter of complaint from the Medical Defence Council, has anyone objected to your using the title?'

'Never.'

A nineteen-year-old girl then gave evidence to the effect that when she was a child she had had an accident resulting in a double curvature of the spine and a dislocated hip. She had seen twenty-nine doctors before she saw Captain Barrow. He never at any time had said he was a qualified doctor and she did not think he was. She had been in pain for twelve years, and he had effected a remarkable improvement in her condition.

The small court room was filled with other patients willing to testify to the defendant's remarkable curative powers, but they were not called after the Court had made it clear that it was not doubted that Captain Barrow did good work.

Birkett then addressed the Bench. The section of the Medical Act under which these proceedings were brought, he submitted, was designed to protect people against quacks. 'It was never intended, in my opinion, for a case like this,' he added. 'This successful, upright man with thousands and thousands and thousands of patients, after fifteen years is told, "You are using a title which implies that you are registered" . . . I cannot conceive that any doctor in Paignton would think of putting "manipulative surgeon" on his plate. It is not the description of a registered man. It is the description of an unregistered man. This description has been used for a quarter of a century. To do what? To describe an unregistered man. . . . I want this Bench to find there is no evidence here at all upon which it can be said that the title implied registration?'

The magistrates obligingly agreed with Birkett and dismissed the summons against Captain Barrow to the accompaniment of loud applause in court. Thus ended the first and last case brought against anyone properly describing himself as a manipulative surgeon. After all, as Birkett had made clear, the word surgeon qualified the word manipulative—otherwise the manipulator might be the manipulator of anything.

7

'The whole point and substance of the article, in my submission, is this: it is a plea for toleration, a plea for free speech and a plea for liberty of opinion.' With these words Birkett summarized the case for the *Star*, when that London evening newspaper was sued by Sir Oswald Mosley for libel. The action, which provoked considerable public interest on account of its political overtones, was tried before the Lord Chief Justice, Lord Hewart, and a special jury in the Royal Courts of Justice on November 5 and 6, 1934. Sir Patrick Hastings led Mr. St. John Field and Mr. Gerald Gardiner for the plaintiff, while Birkett appeared with Mr. Valentine Holmes for the defendant newspaper.

Opening the case for Sir Oswald, aged thirty-eight at this time, Hastings said that when war broke out in 1914 he was a cadet at the Royal Military College, Sandhurst. He was immediately gazetted to a cavalry regiment, and he served with that regiment and with the Royal Flying Corps in France. After suffering severe injury, he was invalided out of the forces. He entered the House of Commons in 1918, while still a very young man, and, as Hastings put it, like many other young men, his political enthusiasm led him to a certain degree of restiveness towards the party to which he belonged. Originally he was a member of the Conservative Party, then an Independent; he later joined the Labour Party, becoming Chancellor of the Duchy of Lancaster in the Labour Government in 1929. He resigned in the following year, and in 1931 he left the House of Commons in order to form his New Party, which became the British Union of Fascists.

The alleged libel consisted of a paragraph in the *Star*, which purported to report what Sir Oswald Mosley—he had succeeded to his father's baronetcy shortly before—had said at a public meeting on February 24, 1933. The meeting, at which Mr. Lloyd George was in the chair, took the form of a debate, in which Sir Oswald expressed his point of view and Mr. James Maxton, the Independent Labour Party leader, voiced his feelings. In the course of his speech, Sir Oswald Mosley said this:

> Knowing their proposals will bring revolution to this country, Mr. Maxton and his followers are not organized for revolution. They go round this land talking pacifism, hum-

> bugging, deluding, daring the Working Class to believe the remedies they propose will come by peace until Mr. Maxton is prepared to organize the revolution. There we see in them what we also see in the Labour Party—the eternal figures of a shadow, the eternal Kerenskys galloping up to the fence, and stopping short, to leave the nation to fall into the hands of Communism. . . . When they have led us more rapidly to the situation which comes anyhow, but which they precipitate, behind them will emerge the real man, the organized Communist, the man who knows what he wants; and if and when he ever comes out we will be here in the streets, with Fascist machine-guns to meet them.

The *Star* published the following comment on this speech:

> IS IT PROGRESS?
>
> Sir Oswald Mosley warned Mr. Maxton that he and his Fascists would be ready to take over government with the aid of machine-guns when the moment arrived. Mr. Tom Mann was recently thrown into prison on the mere suspicion that he might say something ten times less provocative than Sir Oswald's words.

In the submission of Sir Patrick Hastings, these words could only mean that he was prepared to take over the Government of the country by force and that what he had said was ten times worse than the words used by Mann who had been thrown into prison.[1]

Apart from the formal evidence of a shorthand writer at the meeting and the Clerk of Bow Street Police Court to prove Tom Mann's conviction for sedition, Hastings called no other witness except the plaintiff. His examination-in-chief was necessarily short. Sir Oswald admitted that he had spoken of Mr. Maxton and the Independent Labour Party in the terms quoted by his counsel in his opening speech. What the *Star* had published, he said, was incorrect.

The greater part of the first day of this interesting trial was occupied with Birkett's cross-examination. It was perhaps a somewhat unusual cross-examination, being largely directed to Sir Oswald

[1] In December, 1932, Birkett's old Communist opponent in East Nottingham had been sentenced to two months imprisonment on refusing to be bound over to keep the peace after agitating among the unemployed in London.

Mosley's political credit; but it was no doubt justified in the circumstances, although it seems to have considerably incensed Hastings and it provoked a severe comment from him when he came to address the jury for the second time. At the same time, he was greatly helped by the fact that Sir Oswald Mosley answered Birkett's questions effectively and at times brilliantly.

The plaintiff witness began by denying that the British Fascists were training as a military organization in the ordinary sense. But he admitted that his movement was a disciplined one.

'Have you got Fascist machine-guns?' asked Birkett.

'Certainly not,' replied Sir Oswald.

'Have you got armoured cars?'

'No.'

Sir Oswald added that he only advocated the use of machine-guns in a situation in which it would be legitimate to use them, namely to save the Crown and the State on the occasion of a Communist rising. That was an occasion he thought when any loyal citizen would be justified in using force to protect the State from anarchy.

'Was the purpose of your speech to show that, when the moment comes, the Fascist doctrine will be imposed on the nation?'

'Nothing of the sort, I have never suggested that Fascist doctrine will be imposed on the nation. It will come in only one way—by the will of the people at a General Election.'

'Do you believe,' continued Birkett, 'that there is no organized party except Fascism in this country which could deal with the present situation?'

'Certainly, I do,' answered Sir Oswald. 'Otherwise I should not live the very unpleasant life which I do live by advocating Fascism.'

'Who are you to take machine-guns into the street and shoot people?'

'No more and no less than any other British citizen who sees the State in danger of being overthrown by an anarchist rising.'

'You are organizing to meet that?'

'Only to the extent to which we can do so legally in time of peace. We do not possess machine-guns because it is illegal to have them.'

Sir Oswald further admitted that he thought Mussolini and Hitler had served their countries, but he had no desire to emulate their methods here. He had never said that the British Fascists would obtain power by force. That was a different thing from saying that they would obtain power after force had been used. 'Fascists are ready to meet force used against the State by force,' he declared, 'but not by force to obtain the reins of Government.'

'Is it new for a leader of a political party in this country to say "I will be the judge whom the guns are to shoot"?'

Birkett's question elicited a shrewd reply. 'Lord Carson said things far worse than that when he was a Leader at the Bar.'

The witness agreed that one local branch of the Fascist Movement in Britain at one time formed a flying club and held air rallies.

'What earthly assistance to a political movement is an air rally?' asked Birkett.

'Anything which promotes manly sports helps a movement like ours,' Sir Oswald answered. 'The Junior Imperial League has whist drives. We have air rallies, football matches and boxing contests.'

'There is a great deal of difference between a whist drive and an air rally?'

'Yes, all the difference between Conservatism and the Fascist Movement.'

'Supposing a Communist Government was in power with the consent of the King,' Birkett continued, 'would you still oppose it with guns?'

The witness's prompt reply showed what he thought of this question. 'You might as well ask me what would happen if the King enacted the law of Herod and ordered every first-born in the land to be killed. The question is so hypothetical as to be absurd.'

'Can you answer it?'

'You cannot answer questions which are by their very nature absurd.'

'If the Communist Party were returned to power by the country and its leader was invited by the King to form a Government, would you resist it?'

'By then the Communists would be as mild as Mr. Ramsay MacDonald is now, compared with what he used to be.'

Asked whether the British Fascists had not often been in conflict with 'the Reds', Sir Oswald said: 'Yes, when they have attacked us. We have never interfered with the meetings of our opponents, but when our meetings are violently attacked, we resist attack. If people try to shout down our speakers at our meetings, Fascists are sent to throw them out with their bare hands and nothing more.'

'Do you not issue rubber truncheons to your forces?'

This Sir Oswald Mosley categorically denied. 'The carrying of any weapon is absolutely forbidden in Fascism,' he said. 'Only once, in a very heavy fight in Manchester rubber truncheons were used, after our men had been slashed with razors for weeks. Subsequently I forbade these weapons being used.'

Apart from brief formal evidence about Mann's prosecution and the press report of the Mosley meeting, Birkett called no other witnesses for the defence, preferring to rely on the effect on the jury of his cross-examination of Sir Oswald Mosley and of his own speech. In this he argued that the whole point and substance of the words complained of was a plea for toleration, free speech and liberty of opinion. The article in the *Star* never purported to be other than a summary of what the plaintiff had said, and in that way the words were true in substance and in fact. In his speech at the meeting Sir Oswald, in effect, had said that Mr. Maxton's policy was words, words, words, but that the Fascists would not meet the situation with words, but with machine-guns. Birkett emphasized that in the witness box Sir Oswald had said that he had never envisaged the use of machine-guns unless there was a state of complete collapse in the country and the Communists were going to seize power. 'It is a great pity he did not say so in his speech,' counsel observed pointedly. Dealing with the possibility of damages arising in the case, Birkett suggested that the situation could be met by the award of the smallest coin in the realm.

In his concluding speech to the jury Hastings strongly attacked the defendant newspaper for having 'instructed their counsel to challenge the veracity and probity of Sir Oswald, who had always borne a perfectly honest name'. He felt it was 'infinitely to be regretted' that the plaintiff had been cross-examined for so long as to credit, since the obvious inference was that 'the cross-examination led nowhere and it ought never to have been administered'. In his speech, according to Hastings, Sir Oswald had stated that he and his Fascists would only use force to resist Communist violence, and that only if the situation arose in which Communists had come out and wrecked the country would the Fascists fight back. But the *Star* had suggested that he had done something ten times worse than

Mr. Tom Mann, who was a person about whom the police took strong views and who had rightly been flung into prison. That was tantamount to accusing him of high treason.

'There is really no defence to this action, members of the jury,' said Hastings. 'As for damages, Mr. Birkett's suggestion that a farthing should be awarded is adding insult to injury. I cannot ask for phenomenal damages but I do ask for such damages as will mark your sense of the injustice which has been done to Sir Oswald, first, by writing the article about him, and secondly, by conducting the defence in the way it has been conducted.'

The Lord Chief Justice summed up very much on the side of Sir Patrick Hastings. Did not the words complained of mean that, if Mr. Tom Mann had been thrown into prison, how much more should the Government take steps to throw Sir Oswald Mosley into prison? Was the article, as had been suggested by Mr. Birkett, a plea for toleration, or was not the inactivity of the Government in connection with Sir Oswald Mosley contrasted with its activity in the far less serious case of Tom Mann? Was it not a taunt to the authorities for not prosecuting Sir Oswald Mosley? 'You have been told that this matter which is complained of is really something which amounts to a plea of liberty of opinion. Well, liberty of opinion will become a strange and farcical thing if it means we are prepared only to listen to the opinions of those who agree with us. Toleration of free speech only begins when persons listen decently and fairly to opinions with which they profoundly disagree.' Dealing with the meaning of the alleged libel, Lord Hewart asked the jury whether there could be any doubt that the words imputed to Sir Oswald a criminal offence. 'You must remember the terrible power of the modern printing press by which any matter can be distributed a hundred-thousand-fold.'

With these words fresh in their ears, the jury retired and after a short interval returned a verdict in favour of Sir Oswald Mosley. They assessed the damages at £5,000 and judgment was accordingly entered for the plaintiff in this sum, with costs.

'Will your Lordship grant a stay of execution?' Birkett now asked the Lord Chief Justice.

'No, Mr. Birkett, not on any terms whatever,' Lord Hewart replied. 'If you want a stay, you must go to the Court of Appeal. I entirely agree with the verdict of the jury.'

In the event, there was no stay and no appeal, and the damages were paid at once. A curious footnote to the case was subsequently provided by one of the jurymen who revealed how the sum was arrived at—that each member suggested a figure, and the total was divided by twelve.[1]

Although the Lord Chief Justice acknowledged in his summing-up that the case had been presented for each side by 'two of the best advocates of this or any other generation,' nevertheless Birkett's tactics, particularly in directing so much of his cross-examination to the plaintiff's credit, were afterwards criticized adversely. However, it should be remembered that he was acting on instructions from a newspaper which expressed strong Liberal principles which he himself warmly shared, although in this case the *Star* undoubtedly went too far in contrasting as it did the respective political utterances of the Fascist Oswald Mosley and the Communist Tom Mann, particularly when it appeared that its comment was based upon an inaccurate report of what the British Fascist leader had actually said. Nor can there be any doubt that the measure of damages in this case was enhanced by the line followed by the defence and the skilful manner in which Sir Patrick Hastings and the plaintiff himself combined to rebut it.

8

The last of the three murder trials in which Birkett was briefed for the defence towards the end of the year 1934 has been generally acclaimed his greatest triumph in a capital case. Nor, due to its peculiarly gruesome circumstances, did any of his many cases arouse so much public interest, at least of the morbid type, as the so-called 'Brighton Trunk Murder', where he defended a twenty-six-year-old waiter, with a criminal record, whose real name was Cecil Lois England but who went under a number of aliases of which the most notorious was Toni Mancini.

It was the second 'Trunk Murder' to become known to the police that year. On Derby Day in June, 1934, a woman's torso had been found in a suit-case in the left luggage office of Brighton Railway Station. Next day the legs belonging to the same body were similarly discovered at King's Cross Station in London. Examination of the

[1] Robert Jackson. *The Chief* (1959), p. 248 note.

remains revealed that they belonged to a five-months pregnant woman, aged about thirty, who was in the habit of having her toes pedicured. But her head and arms were never traced. Nor was her identity established in spite of the most extensive police investigations. It remains a mystery to this day.

These investigations were prompted by the disappearance of a relatively large number of girls from Brighton at this time, no less than twenty. Among them was a prostitute in her early forties named Violet Saunders, otherwise known as Violette Kaye. At one time she had been a professional dancer, but latterly she had been sharing a basement flat at 44 Park Crescent, Brighton, with Mancini who had been living on her immoral earnings. On July 14, the police interviewed Mancini, who had moved to other accommodation, but he was able to satisfy them that the remains found in the station left-luggage offices did not belong to his sleazy mistress, who was a dozen years his senior. Nevertheless he was uneasy, particularly as he knew the police were aware of his criminal record.

About a week before Violette Kaye disappeared, Mancini had obtained employment as a waiter at a Brighton café, the Skylark. The last day she was seen alive was May 10, when she visited the Skylark Café and later that afternoon returned to Park Crescent where she was observed standing in the doorway by a man named Kerslake, looking distressed and excited and twitching in the hands and face as if she were under the influence of drugs. Her sister, Olive Watts, who lived in London, had been planning a holiday with her, but on May 11 Miss Watts received a telegram which read: 'Going abroad. Good job. Sail Sunday. Will write. Vi.' The telegram was written in printed capitals and the Post Office officials could not say who sent it. But a handwriting expert was later to testify that the writing bore a striking resemblance to the printed capitals on a menu card in the Skylark Café, which had certainly been written by Mancini.

On May 14, the day that Violette and her sister hoped to start their holiday together, Mancini moved his belongings from Park Crescent to a basement room he had taken in Kemp Street in the near-slum area of the railway station. With the help of another man named Capelin, who also worked at the Skylark, Mancini's effects were transported on a hand truck. They included a large trunk, which was too heavy to move by hand. At the same time Mancini told several people that he had left Violette Kaye who was continually nagging him. She had gone to Paris, he said, to Montmartre. He also admitted that he had 'had trouble with his missus' and had given her the biggest hiding she had ever had in her life. 'I don't suppose I shall see her any more,' he added, 'because when I got up in the morning she had blown,' meaning she had gone away. To another acquaintance he was alleged to have said 'What's the good of knocking a woman about with your fists? You only hurt yourself. You should hit them with a hammer the same as I did and slosh her up.' A charred hammer head was later found among the rubbish at Park Crescent.

The trunk remained undisturbed in the basement room in Kemp Street for the next two months. On one occasion during this period, the landlady called her lodger's attention to some fluid which appeared to be running from the trunk. Mancini replied that it was french polish and that he would see to it.

Immediately after he saw the police on July 14, Mancini decided that Brighton was now too hot for him. The same night he visited a local dance hall, where he told one of the instructresses that he was going to London and that when he did Kemp Street would be famous. In fact, the whole of Brighton would be famous. He then returned to his room, hastily packed a bag, and went with some companions to an all night café, where he remained until he was able to catch the early morning train to London. Meanwhile the Brighton police visited the basement room in Kemp Street. Although their bird had flown, an overpowering stench remained. Its cause was quickly apparent when the trunk which Mancini had left behind was opened to reveal the decomposing corpse of Violette Kaye.

A hue and cry immediately began throughout the country for Toni Mancini alias Jack Notyre. In the early hours of July 17 he was picked up on the London-Maidstone road. The police asked if he was Jack Notyre and said they would like him to answer some questions about the dead woman. 'Yes, I am the man,' he replied, 'but I did not murder her. I would not cut her hand. She had been keeping me for months.' When charged with Violette Kaye's murder, he again denied responsibility. 'All I can say is I am not guilty.'

The *post-mortem* examination was carried out by Sir Bernard Spilsbury, who found a fracture on the right side of the skull, which in his opinion and that of other doctors had been made during life by a violent blow with some blunt object, possibly a hammer. At the same time Dr. Roche Lynch examined Mancini's clothing, where he found human blood on three of his shirts and two pairs of trousers.

It was the height of the holiday season in Brighton when Mancini was brought before the magistrates, and on each occasion disgraceful scenes occurred outside the court in the Town Hall, where girls clad in pyjamas and bathing costumes hissed and booed whenever the accused man appeared with his police escort. Inside the court he told his story. He had returned to the basement flat in Park Crescent to find Violette Kaye dead, he said. Other men were in the habit of visiting her at which times he would keep out of the way, and he supposed that one of them had killed her. But he feared the police would not believe this on account of his bad record and mode of life in Brighton's underworld. Panic stricken he had bought a trunk, put the body in it, and conveyed it to the room in Kemp Street. Eventually Mancini was committed for trial at the next Sussex Assizes, due to be held in December.

While Mancini was in custody awaiting trial, his solicitor, a most astute local practitioner who had appeared for Mancini at the police court, telephoned Birkett's clerk and asked him whether Birkett would lead for the defence. It was a delicate matter since there was not much money available and in any event it was not Birkett's circuit, so that he would have to be briefed 'special'. Bowker travelled down to Brighton and talked the matter over with the solicitor. Eventually it was agreed that Birkett would accept the defence, his brief being marked at fifty guineas in addition to the usual one hundred guinea special fee and a daily 'refresher' of ten guineas.

'It's going to be a hard fight, isn't it?' Bowker remarked as he was leaving.

'Yes, pretty difficult,' replied the optimistic solicitor, 'but I'm certain we shall get a verdict.'

The trial of Cecil Lois England alias Toni Mancini alias Jack Notyre, began before Mr. Justice Branson at the Assize Court in Lewes on December 10, 1934, and lasted for five days. Mr. J. D. Cassels, K.C., later Mr. Justice Cassels, and Mr. Quintin Hogg, later Lord Hailsham, appeared for the Crown, while Birkett led Mr. John Flowers, K.C., and Mr. Eric Neve for Mancini.

The first substantive prosecution witness was Mr. Henry Snuggs, the landlord of the basement flat at 44 Park Crescent, who said he had let the flat to a man and woman in March of that year and he identified the prisoner in the dock as the man. 'I knew them as Mr. and Mrs. Watson,' he said. 'The prisoner said he was a clothes presser, and gave as his reason for leaving where he had been the fact that people objected to the banging of his iron. As far as I could see he and the woman were very friendly.'

'Affectionate?' queried Crown counsel.

'Yes.'

'Did you ever hear any quarrels?'

'No.'

'When did you last see the woman alive?'

'On Monday, May 7, when she paid the rent.'

Apart from a banging of the area gate one night in the following week by the prisoner who had run up and downstairs as if in a hurry, the witness had noticed nothing unusual. Then, on May 14, he saw Mancini with a young woman, whom the prisoner introduced as his sister. He said he would be giving up the tenancy of the flat as his wife had run away to France and he could not live there by himself.

'On the occasions on which you saw the prisoner and the woman,' Birkett began his cross-examination by asking, 'they appeared not merely to be friendly, but to be affectionate?'

'Yes.'

'I want to get this quite plainly before the jury. At no time, from start to finish, did you ever see anything of any kind to the contrary?'

'No, sir.'

Questioned about another man whom he had seen accompanying the dead woman down to the basement flat, the witness said he could not remember much about him, except that he was tall, wore a trilby hat and stayed about half an hour between ten and eleven at night. He also identified another caller, a bookmaker named Charles Moores, whom she called 'uncle' and who had got her a wireless.

Unfortunately Mr. Moores could not be called, as he was in a mental institution. There was a suggestion that he was a drug addict. But other witnesses went into the box, where they identified the trunk in which Violette Kaye's doubled-up body was found. There was the owner of a furniture stall in the Brighton market, who said he had sold the trunk to Mancini for 7s. 6d. Then there was the prisoner's fellow worker at the café, Thomas Capelin, who had helped him to move it from Park Crescent to Kemp Street.

'Was it something like that one there?' Cassels asked, pointing to the exhibit in the case.

'Yes,' replied Capelin, adding, 'I lifted the trunk up, but it was very heavy.'

'Was anything said as to what was inside it?'

'The accused said there was some china and some clothes in it.' Neither of them could carry it alone, the witness went on, and they both carried it out and into the Kemp Street house together.

The statement about the contents of the trunk gave Birkett his first opening, small though it was, against the prosecution's case, for the witness had given a different version of this incident at the police court. Birkett's cross-examination consisted of three short questions.

'I suppose you have read a great deal since then about this case?'

'Now and again I have.'

'Do you remember that you said, when you gave evidence before, "Nothing was said as to what was inside it"?'

'I am very sorry,' the witness admitted. 'I made a mistake.'

'Which do you mean is true—that nothing was said, or he said that there was china and clothes inside?'

'I mean nothing was said.'

From Thomas Kerslake, a motor driver, who was the last Crown witness to see Violette Kaye alive, when he had a short conversation with her in the basement doorway on the afternoon of May 10, Birkett elicited an important admission.

'Are you familiar with the effect of drugs on people?'

'Yes.'

'Would you say that the appearance of the woman was that of somebody who was under the influence of drugs?' Birkett went on to ask.

'Yes,' the witness replied, 'and drink. She appeared to be in a distressed condition over something or other.'

'Was she all agitated and twitching?'

'Yes.'

'Did she appear to you to be in an extremely frightened condition?'

'Yes.'

'Her condition was really very remarkable, was it not?'

'Yes.'

This witness swore he had also seen Charles Moores swallow a tablet, but he did not know what it was.

But on the whole Birkett found it difficult to shake the Crown witnesses, and with several he made no attempt. For instance, the dead woman's sister Olive Watts was handed the original of the telegram supposedly signed 'Vi' and asked by Mr. Cassels whether her sister's handwriting was anything like that. She replied that it was not and added that the address was spelled wrongly.

Then a fellow employee at the Skylark was asked whether he recognized the handwriting on a menu. 'Yes,' he replied. 'That is Toni's.' After which Mr. Gurrin, the handwriting expert, said that in his opinion the telegram and the menu were written by the same person.

Various people who had been in the basement room in Kemp Street when Mancini was living there spoke of the smell and of Mancini's explanation of it. To one he put it down to disinfectant, to another his landlady's refusal to open the window and to the landlady's husband the fact that 'his old football boots and football outfit and a lot of old junk were in the trunk'.

'You have no complaint to make about him?' Birkett asked the last witness.

'No,' was the reply. 'All the time he was living with us he was a perfect gentleman. I have no hesitation in saying that.'

Mrs. Phyllis Summers, who had identified Violette Kaye's body in the mortuary, said she had known her for about eleven years and at one time had been engaged professionally with her on the stage. She said she had met Mancini when he was living with Violette.

'During the time you saw them together,' Birkett asked her in cross-examination, 'did they always appear to you to be upon the most friendly and affectionate terms?'

'Yes.'

Miss Elizabeth Attrill, a waitress at the Skylark Café, related how Violette Kaye had come into the café with Mancini and had shown some annoyance at Mancini's familiarity with the witness whom he called 'Mate'. Some words passed between Mancini and Violette and he told the witness not to take any notice as Violette was jealous. Next day they went dancing together at Sherry's and Mancini told

Miss Attrill that Violette had gone to Paris. Later Miss Attrill and Mancini went to Park Crescent, where Mancini gave her some clothes which he said Violette had left behind, namely a green costume, a fawn hat and a coat.

'While you were friendly with him,' Mr. Cassels asked her, 'did you do anything for him?'

'Yes, his washing.'

Miss Attrill was handed a shirt which she recognized. 'I washed it,' she said.

'Did you notice anything about it?'

'Yes. It had a bloodstain.' She added that she asked Mancini about it and he told her that he had done it while shaving.

'About how big was the bloodstain?'

'The size of a farthing or something a little smaller.'

Replying to further questions from Crown counsel, Miss Attrill said she had gone with Mancini to Kemp Street.

'Did you notice anything about the room?'

'Yes, it smelt.'

'Was he just an ordinary casual boy friend to you?' Birkett asked her in cross-examination.

'Yes.'

'Just that?'

'Yes.'

'You were never in love with him, for example?'

'No.'

'The times you went out with him were quite short?'

'Yes,' she replied, adding that he had introduced her to Mr. Snuggs as his sister, to which she had made no objection.

Miss Joyce Golding, another Crown witness, who gave her occupation as a waitress but was really a prostitute, began by relating how she had met Mancini several times at a fair near Brighton pier called Aladdin's Cave. 'I asked about Violette,' she said, 'and he told me she had gone to Montmartre on a two years' contract. He said they had been quarrelling, and now she had gone there would be no more following him in the streets and calling him names.' She added that the prisoner had once asked her to live with him but she refused. Once he had told her that he had had a letter from Violette and that she was 'doing all right'.

'I have to suggest to you,' Birkett began his cross-examination of this witness, 'although I am sorry to do so, that most of your evidence is quite false?'

'It is all true,' Miss Golding replied, somewhat put out.

'Did you say you asked where Violette was almost every night?'

'Almost every time I saw Toni.'

'Why did you do that when you knew she was on a two years' contract?'

'Because I wanted to know how she was getting on.'

'How did you live?'

'The best way I could.'

'How was that?'

'On the streets.'

'I am sorry about this,' Birkett continued. 'I put it to you that it is a deliberate lie to say that the prisoner ever invited you to go and live with him?'

'He invited me,' Miss Golding replied, 'for the simple reason that he knew what I was.'

'Let me suggest that another matter is wholly false. He never suggested to you that he had quarrelled with his wife?'

'Yes, several times. I can bring witnesses to prove it. There is one here.'

'Who is that?'

'Mrs. Summers would tell you.'

Miss Golding had naturally been kept out of court with the other witnesses while Mrs. Summers was giving her evidence. Otherwise she might have been tempted to give a different reply.

'Do you know,' said Birkett, eyeing her sternly, 'that Mrs. Summers has sworn on oath that they were on affectionate terms?'

'It might have slipped her memory,' was all Miss Golding could reply.

'Do you realize this man is on trial for murder?'

'Yes.'

9

So far Birkett had only succeeded in shaking the Crown's case in minor particulars. He scored his first major success when he cross-examined the first medical witness. This was his old friend, Dr. Roche Lynch, the Home Office analyst. Various articles of the prisoner's clothing were produced as exhibits, two shirts, two pairs of trousers and a handkerchief. There were marks of blood which he identified on all of them. He had also examined the hammer, but could find no blood on it. If there had been any, according to this expert witness, the effect of the fire to which it had been subjected would be to destroy the marks completely. He had also examined the dead woman's organs and in some of them he had detected a minute trace of morphine. In view of the advanced state of decomposition, the fact that he had found any morphine at all, he said, indicated that a quantity was taken distinctly greater than a medicinal dose. The result of such a dose would be sleepiness, followed by a deep sleep and probably unconsciousness.

'Do you know that prostitutes are in the habit of taking opium or morphine?' Birkett asked.

'I do not know,' Dr. Lynch replied.

'I am not speaking of law abiding people. You will have known in the past that morphine was commonly used by prostitutes?'

'In the past, yes.'

'It may lead to sleep, and death in sleep?'

'Yes.'

'Are you clear in this case that there was not enough to cause death?'

'I am not prepared to answer that question.'

'Do you mean by more than a medicinal dose a fatal dose?'

'It may have been. It is absolutely impossible to say.'

'Is it a matter of speculation that it was more than a medicinal dose?'

'No.'

'If somebody has taken morphine—not a lethal dose, but sufficient to dull the faculties and cloud the senses—and that person receives a head injury, would the presence of the morphine accelerate or assist the death?'

'I don't think so, because it is a common treatment to give people, who have had a serious head injury, morphine.'

Birkett then turned to the question of blood groups and asked the analyst to tell the jury the importance of distinguishing these groups.

'Human blood is divided into four groups,' said Dr. Roche Lynch, 'and every member of the population belongs to one of those four groups. Its value in criminal work is that if an alleged murderer has blood on his clothing and the group of that blood is the same as his victim and different from his own blood group, he naturally has to make an explanation.'

'Is this the case with each of the articles you have dealt with that the group is impossible to distinguish?'

'Yes,' said the analyst, 'and further than that, owing to the decomposed state of the body, we were unable to discover the group of the dead woman.'

Birkett pointed to one of the two shirts, a brown one, lying with the other exhibits on the table. 'Do all the marks indicate that blood was splashed upon the shirt?'

'Yes.'

Replying to further questions about the brown shirt, the witness said that he did not know when it was bought and that he had no means of knowing.

'Suppose I were to put to you that that brown shirt was bought after the death of Violette Kaye, it would be clear, if I could prove that, that these stains did not come from her blood during life?'

'Certainly.'

Birkett broke off his cross-examination to turn for a few moments to the jury. 'I shall hope to show that that shirt was not in the prisoner's possession until after the death,' he told them.

Picking up a microscope, Birkett focused it on one of the pairs of trousers, and examined the blood stain on them intently.

'It's a very minute spot of blood, this, isn't it?'

'It is a small spot,' Dr. Roche Lynch agreed.

'Could it have been caused by a finger on the lining of the pocket?'

'Yes.'

'If I were to establish that these trousers were not in the prisoner's possession during the lifetime of the dead woman, it is clear that the blood could not have been hers?'

'Yes.'

Here the judge broke in. 'It does not require an expert to tell you that!'

Everyone laughed, including the man in the dock. But Birkett had got his point across to the jury, and he was to back it up with clear evidence.

A seventeen-year-old girl named Doris Saville, whom Mancini

had met on the same day he went to London, told how they had gone for a walk together and a ride on a bus. According to her account, he asked her whether she could keep a secret. When she said she could, he told her it was about a murder and if he happened to be caught she was to tell the police this story. 'He said I was supposed to have met him in Brighton on the sea front at the end of May. We were supposed to have gone to tea with a woman in Park Crescent, and she told us she was expecting three men to come and see her. He said we left her alone with the three men and went for a walk. When we came back we found the woman dead.'

'Did he tell you why he wanted you to give that story?' Mr. Cassels asked her.

'He said he wanted someone to stand by him and that I could save him.'

At the police court Miss Saville had told a rather different story. He had talked to her about a murder, she had said then, but he did not say what murder. 'He said that a murder was done, and that he was innocent of it, and that I was supposed to have met him.'

'You did not tell us that today,' Birkett said in cross-examining her. 'Do you intend to convey that he was saying, "There was a murder and I am innocent of it, and I want you to help me." Is that what it was?'

'Yes,' answered Miss Saville.

'Perfectly plain, is it not, based on the fact that he was innocent of it?'

'Yes.'

'Do you know what alibi means?'

'No.'

From the point of view of the defence, the two final Crown witnesses produced perhaps the most important admissions when Birkett came to cross-examine them. The first was Chief Inspector Donaldson of Scotland Yard, who was called in to help the Brighton police. He had taken part in the questioning of Mancini on July 14 and had himself questioned the prisoner about another matter, namely the original trunk murder.

'Are you satisfied, Chief Inspector,' Birkett asked him, 'that, so far as the prisoner is concerned, he had absolutely nothing whatever to do with Trunk Crime No. 1?'

'Yes,' replied the Inspector.

Birkett went on to ask about the prisoner's criminal record, an unusual course since a man's previous convictions are normally not disclosed at this stage. But Birkett's object soon became clear, as Inspector Donaldson recited the official record of the prisoner's misdoings. His first offence, for which he had been bound over, was stealing a quantity of silver. Subsequently he received sentences respectively of three months for loitering with intent to commit a felony and six months for stealing clothing from a dwelling house.

'Those are the only convictions?'

'Yes.'

'There is nowhere any record of a conviction for the crime of violence?'

'No, sir.' The Inspector was quite definite.

'Is it within your professional knowledge, doing your duty,' continued Birkett, 'that there have been any false statements in the press relating to this prisoner?'

'Yes, sir,' replied Inspector Donaldson. 'From the accounts I have read I am satisfied that many of the stories that were told in relation to this matter were untrue.'

Asked by Birkett whether he was able to say that a statement in an evening newspaper that Mancini had been involved in a scene in Soho in which a woman was stabbed was false, the inspector replied, 'Yes, there is no foundation for it at all.'

The last to give evidence for the prosecution was the famous pathologist Sir Bernard Spilsbury. Violette Kaye suffered a depressed fracture of the skull, he said, and to illustrate the nature and extent of the injury a human skull was produced in court and this macabre exhibit remained on the ledge of the witness box while he gave the rest of his evidence. Then, holding up a piece of bone, Sir Bernard said that this was the exact piece forming the fracture, which in his opinion had been caused by a violent blow with some blunt object. Either end of the hammer could have produced the wound. Beneath where the bone was situated there was an artery, and there must have been a considerable rush of blood as soon as the fracture was inflicted.

'What period would elapse between the fracture being inflicted and death taking place?' Mr. Cassels asked the pathologist.

'Probably no more than a few minutes,' Sir Bernard replied, 'and there would be complete unconsciousness during that time.'

Radio Times Hulton Picture Library

VIOLETTE KAYE

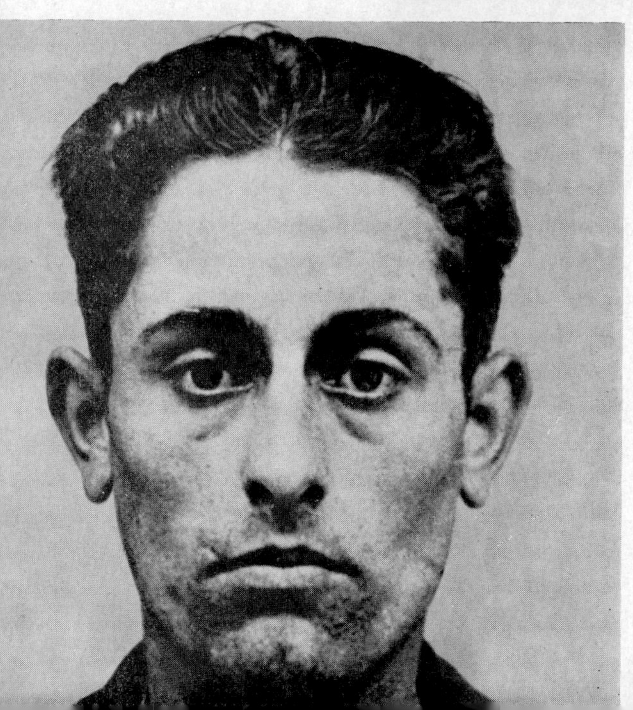

Radio Times Hulton Picture Library

TONY MANCINI

London News Agency Photos

DEFENDING MANCINI AT LEWES ASSIZES

Left to right: John Flowers, K.C., Eric Neve, Norman Birkett, K.C., and A. E. Bowke (Birkett's clerk).

'You know that a minute trace of morphine was found in the body. Did this woman die from morphine poisoning?'

'No.'

'Could you observe any signs on the body of any struggle on her part?'

'There was no evidence of it.'

Birkett began his cross-examination with a general question. 'Your views are rightly described as theory?'

'I am not quite sure that is right when my opinion is based on experience,' the pathologist replied.

'They are the results of your experience,' Birkett agreed, 'but without question they are mere theories?'

'They are in the sense that they are not facts.'

Birkett then proceeded to make the most of the fact that the prosecution had only produced the bone for the first time on the third day of the trial. 'Did it not occur to you that the defendant might have been informed that that small piece of bone was in your possession?'

'I am afraid it did not occur to me,' said Spilsbury. 'The bone was not ready to produce at the time I gave evidence in the police court.'

'For a piece of bone which has been in existence all this time to be produced on the third day of the trial does put the defence in some difficulty?'

'I do not think it would take anyone long to examine it and come to conclusions.'

Birkett handed the witness a plan and photograph of the entrance to the basement flat at Park Crescent with its stairway. Spilsbury agreed that that plan showed a stone brace at the top of the stairs and that it was possible for a person slightly drunk or under the influence of a drug to trip over it.

Next Birkett asked for the skull, which was handed to the witness who placed the piece of bone in its exact position on the skull and handed it back to Birkett, who examined it closely. It was then passed round the jury box.

Birkett turned to Spilsbury. Speaking very slowly and emphatically, he said, 'I am suggesting to you quite plainly that if some one fell from the top step of that flight or the second step or thereabouts with violence on to the iron rail at the bottom it could produce such a depressed fracture?'

'I think it is impossible,' said the pathologist.

'There was also a window ledge at the bottom of the stairs. If her head had struck this, could it not have produced a depressed fracture?'

Spilsbury did not think it could because the ledge would be too long.

'Are you really telling the members of the jury that if someone fell down that flight and came upon the stone ledge, he would not get a depressed fracture?'

'He could not get *this* fracture.'

'Could you get a depressed fracture of one-eighth of an inch, which was what this one was?'

'Yes.'

'The only thing in your mind is the shape of it?'

'Yes,' Spilsbury agreed, although he was careful to repeat that in his opinion the fracture was more likely to have been caused by the smaller end of the hammer. On resuming his seat, Birkett made a note of this admission about the hammer.

'If there had been a fall such as had been suggested in this case,' Mr. Cassels asked in re-examination, 'would you expect to find injuries only to the head and no injuries to other parts of the body?'

'No, I should certainly expect to find bruises on other projecting parts.'

Here the judge intervened with a question. 'Is it in your view possible for this woman, having received the injury which you saw, having gone through a period of unconsciousness, to recover sufficiently to walk to the bed and undress herself or do things of this sort?'

'It *is* possible to have happened after a depressed fracture,' the expert pathologist answered, 'but in this case it is quite clear it had not happened.' Spilsbury then went on to explain what he meant by this latter statement. 'If she had survived any extent of time, she would not have died from shock. She would have died from haemorrhage of the brain.'

Immediately Birkett was on his feet with a protest. 'This is the very first time that has been suggested in the whole history of the case.'

On this dramatic note the evidence for the Crown finished. Already Birkett had planted the idea in the minds of the jury that

Violette Kaye might have died from morphine poisoning, or she might have fallen down the steps leading to the basement at 44, Park Crescent, and fractured her skull. Alternatively, she might have been murdered by one or other of the men who visited her.

10

In opening the defence of Toni Mancini on the fourth day of the trial, Birkett quoted the well-known verse of *Omar Khayyam*:

> The moving finger writes, and having writ,
> Moves on; nor all thy piety nor wit
> Shall lure it back to cancel half a line,
> Nor all thy tears wash out a word of it.

'It would not be the first time that a man, overcome by feelings which may not commend themselves to you, members of the jury,' he continued, 'and once being committed irrevocably to that step, must go on. Once the crowning folly of that course is taken, there is no going back on that road.'

Before calling the prisoner into the witness box, Birkett referred to some of the evidence previously given, particularly that of the driver Kerslake. 'The Crown has done nothing to explain or illustrate the evidence of Kerslake, who says that on May 10—the day when the prisoner says he found the body—he (Kerslake) saw the dead woman in the late afternoon. He said that he suspected she was drunk or drugged. She was very frightened, leaning against the wall as though for support, her hands and face twitching, and in the basement flat were people whose voices he heard. Down those area steps at that self same moment went another man. I cannot prove she died by another hand: that is beyond my power. But I submit that you can never exclude it. If that is so, every single thing in the case falls into its true place.

'There has never been the slightest breath of motive. If you believe that evidence, I do not think you will have any doubt that the morphine in the body of Violette Kaye was morphine which, in one way or another, she herself had obtained. Every chemist shop in London and Brighton is known, and, with all the resources of the police, if the prisoner had bought a spot of morphine the last detail of it would be known to you.'

As the prisoner was taking the oath, he was seen to put his hand in his pocket and remove something. 'What did you take then out of your pocket?' the judge asked him. 'What is it?'

Mancini did not reply but held up the object. It was a black rosary.

'Are you a Roman Catholic?' Mr. Justice Branson questioned him again.

'I was,' the prisoner replied in a low voice.

At first, he answered his counsel's questions nervously and hesitantly but his confidence gradually increased and he turned out an unexpectedly good witness. His true name was England, he said. He had been born in Newcastle-on-Tyne and went to school in Hertfordshire. After serving two and a half years in the Air Force, he went to London where he became a waiter in a café in Leicester Square. It was there that he met Violette Kaye who was a customer. They got to know each other and first lived together for a week in London. Then they went to Brighton, where they lived together at various addresses.

'Where did she get money?' Birkett asked him.

'She was a loose woman and I knew it,' Mancini answered.

'Did men come to the flat?'

'Yes.'

'What did you do?'

'I walked out.'

'At 44, Park Crescent, Charlie Moores used to come. Were there any others you knew?'

'I have heard of one and have seen him. He was known as "Hoppy" because he was lame.'

'Were there occasions upon which she showed you money?'

'Yes. I would be in the room with her. There would be a knock at the door. She would open the door and I would hear her speaking to someone. She would say, "Go into the other room, quick. There is someone to see me." '

Then, turning to the judge, Mancini added, 'I know it was wrong, my Lord, but I would go. I would remain in the other room until this other man went. Then I would go back to the other room and she would show me money.'

Replying to further questions from Birkett, the prisoner said that all the time they were in Brighton, about nine months, until he obtained work at the Skylark Café, Violette provided all the money for food and pocket money.

'Did she appear to be in fear?' Birkett went on.

'Yes,' said Mancini. 'Some evenings I would be at home she would come home and say, "Quick, pack up your clothes, we have got to go." '

'Were there many times when she used to be in fear?'

'Yes. We were always moving, and she seemed to be in fear all the time.'

'What about Violette Kaye and the taking of drink?'

'She used to drink.'

'Were there many occasions when she was intoxicated?'

'Yes.'

'Did you ever buy morphine or give her morphine at any time?'

'Never.'

Birkett now posed a vital question to his client. 'During the whole time you lived with her as man and wife, how did you get on together?'

Mancini hesitated a moment, and then said in a low voice, 'Strange as it is, I used to love her. We were always on the most affectionate terms. There were no quarrels.'

'Did that cover the whole time?'

'Yes, every second she was alive.'

On May 9, a man called at the flat and remained nearly half an hour, said Mancini, in answer to further questions from his counsel. Afterwards Violette showed him (Mancini) fifty shillings. Next day she called at the Skylark Café. 'She staggered a little, as though affected by drink, or something.' When he went home that evening the front gate, which was usually closed, had been left open. 'I rang the bell and knocked at the door but got no answer. Nobody came. I waited. Then I opened the window and got through. I called out, "Are you here, Vi?" '

'Why did you do that?' Birkett asked.

'Because sometimes, if she was in, she used to hide behind the door and then spring out.'

Mancini continued his story. 'I went into the bedroom, and the first thing that met my eyes was her coat on the floor. I saw her lying on the bed, with her knees almost touching her chin. She was clutching a handful of sheets in one hand. I thought she was asleep and shook her. She was not cold and she was not warm. Then I saw blood on the pillow. I said to her, "Wake up!" Then I put my hands on her heart and it did not beat. I thought she must be dead.'

'When you realized she was dead, how did that affect your mind?'

Instead of answering his counsel direct, the prisoner turned to the judge. 'I was crazy, my Lord,' he said. Then he went on to recount how he picked up the coat and put it over her and saw a pool of blood between the door and the head of the bed.

'Why did you not go for the police?' Birkett asked.

Mancini replied as if deliberately choosing his words. 'I considered that a man who has been convicted never gets a fair and square deal from the police.'

'In what respect did you fear you would not get a square deal?' continued Birkett. 'Because of your convictions?'

'Because I thought they would say, "Very well, you must be the man. You have been living with her. She has been keeping you. You are a convicted man, and you found her".'

Mancini then described how he had put the body in a cupboard for the night, how he found Violette's bag with a letter from her sister to say she was coming down in a few days, how he sent her the telegram signed 'Vi' to say she had got a job so as to prevent her coming to the flat, how he bought the trunk and placed the body inside it and then moved to Kemp Street with Capelin's help.

Questioned by Birkett about his various alleged statements that he had given Violette Kaye the best hiding she had ever had, that it was 'no good knocking them about with your fists, you should use a hammer the same as I did', he stoutly denied that he had ever said anything of the kind. He similarly denied having asked Doris Saville to 'save' him by coming to his aid if he were charged with murder.

Then came Birkett's final questions of the examination-in-chief.

'Were you in any way responsible for the death of Violette Kaye?'

'I was not, sir.'

'Did you ever use the hammer which is an exhibit, in any way at all, let alone to hit a woman?'

'I have never seen it.'

'Had you anything to do in any way whatever with the death of the woman you lived with?'

This time Mancini's answer was loud and clear, 'No, sir.'

It was now the turn of Mr. Cassels to cross-examine for the prosecution, but throughout the prisoner stuck to his story and was quite unshaken by the Crown counsel's questions.

'When you knew she was dead, why did you not call assistance of any kind?'

'Because I was afraid, as it is now proved, I should be blamed for it.'

'Perhaps with reason?'

'There was no reason.'

'You say people convicted never get a square deal from the police?'

'Yes, it happens every day.'

'You suggest they would not have given you a square deal?'

'I am sure of it.'

'Are you saying they have not done so in this case?'

'That is not for me to say.'

Further questioned by Mr. Cassels, the prisoner said he thought Violette Kaye had been killed by one of the men who had visited her. Had he himself gone to the police, he would not have been believed, he said.

'Were you anxious to avoid the police for a reason?'

'No.'

'Were you not destroying useful evidence in disturbing the body and clearing up traces?'

'I did not think of that.'

'You were determined no eyes should ever see that body again if you could help it?'

'I knew one day it must come out.'

'You intended to disappear yourself?'

'*No, I trusted in God, as I do now.*'

Asked about Violette Kaye's callers, Mancini described how two men came to see her and he was sent out of the room. Shortly afterwards, she and Mancini shifted to a new address and the same two men again called there. Once, when he was walking with her along the Brighton front, a young man came across and slashed Mancini's face with a razor blade and tried to slash hers. 'Of course, I knocked him out,' Mancini added. 'He got up and ran.'

After a very brief re-examination,—'What you have told the members of the jury is the truth, is it?' 'It is true.'—Birkett called the next witness. This was a man named Kay Fredericks, who had been a professional dancing partner of the dead woman's. He swore that he had seen her taking tablets and that she seemed on occasions to be under the influence of drugs. The prisoner's mother, Mrs. Lydia England, also gave evidence. She told how her son and Violette Kaye had stayed for a week at her house in Catford about a year previously and how several times Miss Kaye appeared to be under the influence of drugs. Birkett called to other witnesses, one a tailor, to prove that the bloodstained articles of clothing worn by Mancini were not ordered until late in May, and not delivered until much later in June.

Having called evidence besides that of the prisoner, the rule of procedure required Birkett to address the jury before counsel for the prosecution made his closing speech. Birkett began his speech by referring to this rule, the effect of which in this case was that he did not know what Mr. Cassels would say. 'You may think, members of the jury,' he told them, 'that one of the reforms one day will be that counsel for the defence shall speak last, so that he can reply to everything that is said.'

The case for the Crown, said Birkett, was that Mancini took a hammer and killed Violette Kaye in the basement flat. 'I waited to hear some suggestion when Mancini was in the witness box as to why he had done it. There has not been a word upon this vital question. I submit that this vital omission in the case for the Crown destroys it. All the evidence before the death of Violette Kaye is that they were friendly, affectionate, had no quarrels or rows, no anger, no words of bitterness, no malice; none of those things which are concomitant with cruelty, or injury.'

On the questions of motive and morphine, ought not the jury to say that they had not been satisfied beyond all reasonable doubt? 'Is it not a most astounding thing that there was morphine in the body, that it was more than a medicinal dose—that it may have been a fatal dose? Is it not astounding that when Mancini was in the box he was not asked a single question about it? What part does morphine play in the theory of the Crown? Is he responsible for it? If it is to be suggested that he was, he should have been asked about it.'

Coming to the hammer, Birkett asked whether it might not have been scooped out of the dark place where the coal was kept, put on the fire with some coal, and taken out again with the ashes of the coal. 'But supposing a man had done this horrible thing,' Birkett went on, '—struck a woman with a hammer to kill her—don't you think he would have got rid of the hammer? Of course he would. He could go to the end of the pier at Brighton, or get a boat and row out and drop it into the depths of the sea where no human eye could ever see it again. Don't you think that he would? Doesn't that put doubt in your mind?'

When Sir Bernard Spilsbury gave evidence at the police court, he thought that the larger end of the hammer accorded with the size of the fracture. In this trial he said that the smaller end accorded with it. Sir Bernard also said that death came within two or three minutes of the blow. How could he tell? Then the other expert Crown witness, Dr. Roche Lynch, said that it looked as if the blood on the flannel trousers had been spattered as though from an artery. But it was clear that these trousers did not come into the prisoner's possession until June.

'I am not attacking the good faith of either Sir Bernard Spilsbury or Dr. Roche Lynch,' said Birkett. 'Men may have names and reputations, degrees, distinctions; but high and low, famous and obscure, known and unknown, men are all human and fallible. We have the firm fact clearly proved that those garments upon which the greatest stress was laid about blood being deposited from a distance were neither worn by the prisoner nor in his possession until after the death of this woman. The case for the Crown is simply riddled with doubt.'

Birkett then invited the jury to consider the other theories as to how Violette Kaye met her death. Did she fall down the area steps? Or did someone else kill her, if she was killed?

Birkett paused for a moment, adjusted his wig, then turned and pointed an outstretched arm towards the figure in the dock. 'This man lived upon her earnings,' he went on, 'and I have no word whatever to say in extenuation or justification. None.' Another pause, and he continued: 'You are men of the world. Consider the associates of these people. We have been dealing with a class of men who pay eightpence for a shirt and women who pay one shilling and sixpence or less for a place in which to sleep. It is an underworld that makes the mind reel. It is imperative that you should have it well in mind that this is the background out of which these events have sprung.'

Mancini had said that they had left their lodgings and went elsewhere hurriedly and in fear. He had spoken of an attempt made to cut the dead woman with a razor. 'Is it too much to say that you ought to consider gravely that the reasonable probability about it all was that in that unhappy woman's life, a dreadful and unspeakable life, blackmail may have formed a considerable part?'

And where were the men whose voices Kerslake had heard when he called on Violette Kaye on May 10? 'Somewhere in this world are the people who were heard speaking in the flat on that last occasion Violette Kaye was seen alive. The finding of the woman's body was proclaimed from the housetops. Those who were in the flat that day, they had a tale to tell. But not a word, never a word. Does not that put a doubt in your mind?'

Birkett had been speaking for close on an hour when he reached his peroration. His words were directed straight at the hearts as well as the minds of the jury. 'Defending counsel has a most solemn duty, as I and my colleagues know only too well,' he declared. 'We have endeavoured, doubtless with many imperfections, to perform that task to the best of our ability. The ultimate responsibility—that rests upon you—and never let it be said, never let it be thought, that any word of mine should seek to deter you from doing that which you feel to be your duty. But now that the whole of the matter is before you, I think I am entitled to claim for this man a verdict of Not Guilty. And, members of the jury, in returning that verdict, you will vindicate a principle of law, that people are not tried by newspapers, not tried by rumour, but tried by juries called to do justice and to decide upon the evidence. I ask you for, I appeal to you for, and I claim from you, a verdict of Not Guilty.'

He stopped as if about to sit down. But he remained on his feet for a few moments longer, during which time he allowed his eyes to rove up and down the length of the jury box. Then his voice rang out, as he gave the jury a last admonition. 'Stand firm.'

There was an almost reverent hush as Birkett resumed his seat, instead of the usual buzz of conversation and rustling of papers. Then the silence was broken by Mr. Cassels, who rose to his feet to begin his closing speech with a warm tribute to the way in which the defence had been conducted. He summarized the case for the Crown in a few sentences. 'Is not the outstanding feature of this case the concealment of the body from all eyes from that fatal evening of May 10? Is not such conduct contrary to human instincts and human nature, unless there is for such conduct the overwhelming reason of guilt?'

Mr. Justice Branson then summed up the evidence, and in this the prisoner was fortunate in having such a humane and sophisticated judge who began by reminding the jury that it was common ground that Violette Kaye—'the unfortunate woman', he called her—was of 'a certain class', and that she had been supporting Mancini by her immoral earnings. 'I shall say one word of warning,' the judge went on. 'This is not a court of morals but a court of law, and you must not allow the natural revulsion which one must feel against a man who so supports life to affect your judgment against this man. Do not feel any kind of resentment against him which would lead you to draw an inference against him which you would not draw against a man who had not spent his days in that kind of life.'

On the question of motive, which Birkett had made much of in his defence, the judge had this to say. 'It is no part of the law that the prosecution has to prove motive for murder before a jury can convict a prisoner. You cannot convict a man because he has a motive to kill another, and you do not acquit a man of murder simply because there is no motive brought before you, if the killing is otherwise proved. But the fact that there is no express evidence of motive called before you makes it necessary for you to scrutinize, with all the greater care, the other evidence brought before you in the endeavour to bring your minds to the conclusion that the prisoner is guilty.'

It took the jury nearly two-and-a-half hours to decide that Toni Mancini had not murdered Violette Kaye. When the foreman stood up and announced the verdict, 'Not Guilty,' the prisoner appeared dazed, as if he could not believe it. Waiting in a room outside was the prisoner's mother. 'Oh, my darling boy,' she gasped when they told her the news. 'My prayers have all been answered.' Then she fell down in a dead faint.

The first to congratulate Birkett on his spectacular win was Inspector Donaldson, who had been in charge of the case at Scotland Yard. He came over and shook hands with the victorious defence counsel.

Birkett then followed the discharged prisoner and his solicitor into an adjoining room. Mancini still looked dazed. All he could say, in stammering out a few words of thanks, was 'Not guilty, Mr. Birkett? Not guilty, Mr. Birkett?'

'Now go home and look after your mother,' said Birkett. 'She has stood by you and been a brick.'

Birkett's name made the headlines in every newspaper that evening and next morning throughout the country. Yet, as he told his cousin Henry, it was a victory which 'strangely enough has given me very little pleasure'. As for Mancini, 'he was a despicable and worthless creature. But the acquittal seems to have impressed the popular imagination.'

Among the many letters of congratulation he received was one from an old Birmingham friend named Musgrave Woodman, with whom he used to journey to the county courts twenty years previously. 'It will rank as one of the great defences in the annals of legal medical records and worthy of a Marshall Hall,' Woodman wrote.

CHAPTER X

FROM BAR TO BENCH

I

THE Mancini case marked the topmost height of Birkett's fame as an advocate. He was to have other successes during the next few years, before the outbreak of the Second World War put a stop to his practice, but none of these perhaps was to raise him higher in the public esteem than his achievement in the Brighton Trunk Murder. In a popularity poll organized at this time by 'William Hickey', the *Daily Express* columnist, who invited readers to write to the newspaper naming the public personalities they most liked reading about, it is noteworthy that Norman Birkett got into the first twenty, the result embodying the collective choice of a cross-section of the newspaper's readership. Lloyd George headed the list, closely followed by Winston Churchill and Lord Beaverbrook. The other popular favourites included Gracie Fields, Bernard Shaw, Franklin Roosevelt, Mussolini, Rudyard Kipling, Greta Garbo and the Aga Khan, with the last of whom incidentally Birkett tied for the final place among the first twenty. The twenty-first choice was Sir Bernard Spilsbury. 'What is it they all possess which attracts this searchlight of public interest?' the newspaper asked. 'Is it the ability they have in the jobs they perform? No, I don't think so. I think it is because besides doing whatever they choose to do well, they do it slightly differently from the others. There is a bit of colour about them and the way they do things.'[1]

Early in 1935, Birkett had the unusual experience of appearing for a fellow barrister and former leader of the Bar, who had been slandered by a Methodist minister. The plaintiff in the slander action was Sir John Simon, then Foreign Secretary, and such was Simon's

[1] *Daily Express*, February 1, 1935.

confidence in Birkett that he preferred him to any other member of his profession to represent him.

The defamatory words were uttered by the Rev. J. Whitaker Bond of East Dereham, Norfolk, at the annual meeting of the Dereham and District Free Church Council.

> What is the cause of warfare? The cause of warfare is your legislators, the men in your Cabinet, for their money is invested in armament firms.
>
> The reason why Sir John Simon has been running down the Peace Ballot promoted by the League of Nations is because his money is invested in armament firms.

At this point in the minister's speech, another delegate interjected, 'Can you prove it?'

'I can prove it,' the speaker replied, and proceeded: 'There is no truer statement in the whole Bible than "The root of all evil is the love of money". Your statesmen are prepared to make money out of warfare and bloodshed. We should make a stand on this question. I feel very strongly about it.'

The truth was, as Birkett put it in addressing the court, Sir John Simon did not possess one single investment in one single armament company, and the dreadful allegation that his conduct and attitude towards public affairs had been influenced by investments in armaments was 'ridiculous and utterly false'. However, for about five years Sir John had a small holding of 1,500 shares in Imperial Chemical Industries Ltd., which was promoted substantially for the production of chemicals. This investment was made on the advice of a chartered accountant. In February, 1933, there was an application to the Foreign Office in the ordinary way for a licence to export cartridges by a firm which the Foreign Secretary learned for the first time was a subsidiary or in some way connected with I.C.I. 'The matter was not dealt with by Sir John at all,' said Birkett, 'and on the next day, in order to avoid the theoretic possibility of any clash between public duty and private interest, every single share Sir John held was sold—incidentally at a loss.'

The Methodist minister was not the originator of the slanderous statements, which he merely repeated, and when he realized their falsity the Rev. Whitaker Bond withdrew what he had said and made an unqualified apology. Indeed the business so upset him that he became ill and in consequence was unable to come to court for the public vindication of the Foreign Secretary's character.

Sir John went into the witness box and was examined by Birkett. 'You have read what the defendant said. Is there one single word of truth in any of the matters alleged?'

'Every passage in that statement is untrue,' Simon replied; 'even the statement about the Peace Ballot. I have never denounced the Peace Ballot, but I have ventured to express the view that one of the questions it formulates is not very suitable for a "Yes" or "No" answer.'[1]

From time to time, during the past two years, Simon went on, he had been receiving in different forms imputations of that character, but not always in such violent terms.

'You have heard my statement as to the possible origin of this matter with Imperial Chemical Industries?'

'You have accurately put it,' said the Foreign Secretary. 'I did not in fact at that time know that the enterprise of Imperial Chemical Industries itself had any association with armaments, and I never had a personal knowledge until later. My experience of their litigation has been mostly about soda, fertilizers and that sort of thing.' He went on to point out that the investment was made when he was at the Bar and before he became Foreign Secretary. He added that, having regard to the defendant's position as a Nonconformist minister, a vocation he had a very special reason to hold in high honour—Simon's father had been a Congregational minister—he did not desire any damages or costs.

This gesture impressed the Lord Chief Justice, before whom the matter came for trial. 'Sir John has treated this defendant not only leniently but handsomely,' said Lord Hewart in announcing the settlement of the action. 'It is a shocking thing that an English statesman should be assailed in such a way, and the defendant ought to be thoroughly ashamed of himself. I hope this reverend gentleman, when he resumes his duties, will remember a text on which I have heard more than one sermon. It is: "*The tongue is a little*

[1] This ballot was organized by the National Declaration Committee, headed by Lord Cecil of Chelwood in association with the League of Nations, on the basis of an extensive house-to-house canvass. The answers to the questions were overwhelmingly pacifist, the results which were announced in June, 1935, showing the approval of over eleven millions.

member, and boasteth great things. Behold how great a matter a little fire kindleth." '[1]

Birkett represented another plaintiff in a slander action at this period, which deserves brief mention. A twenty-year-old society girl, the daughter of a titled lady, said of a young City man that he was suffering from venereal disease and that was why he had been 'dropped' by certain people. The slander was uttered in a night club and repeated next day in a hotel. 'You know how poison spreads,' said Birkett to the jury in this case, 'so that it can never be overtaken.' Here again the only issue for the jury was that of the amount of damages they should award the injured plaintiff, since the defendant had withdrawn her allegation and apologized. After his client had formally denied the charge from the witness box, Birkett again addressed the jury. 'Do not imagine that my client comes here to try to obtain a large sum of money,' he said. 'He does not. He comes here to get his good name established in open court that this poison shall be repressed.'[2]

The Lord Chief Justice, Lord Hewart, who tried the case, told the jury, that although the plaintiff did not ask for heavy damages, they should be such that it would be made plain to everybody that there was not the slightest foundation for the allegations. He added: 'Nothing more disgraceful, nothing more disgusting, nothing more repulsive it would be difficult to imagine.'

In the result, the jury awarded the slandered plaintiff £500, and the defendant also had to pay the costs of the action, the combined sum thus constituting a powerful anti-toxin to the poison spread through a few carelessly dropped words in a Mayfair night-club.

People with well-known names for whom Birkett appeared at this time included the son of an M.P., a peer of the realm who was a member of a distinguished banking family, and the Parliamentary Secretary to the Board of Trade.

In April, 1935, at Leeds Assizes, Birkett defended John Raphael Russell, the only son of Mr. Hamer Russell, Conservative M.P. for the Brightside Division of Sheffield, on the charge of attempting to murder a young woman, Miss Carol Leadbeater, to whom he had been secretly engaged for three years and who had been pregnant by

[1] Epistle of St. James, Chap. 3, verse 5.
[2] *Daily Express*, June 17, 1936.

him on several occasions. Russell, who was twenty-eight years old, the same age as his fiancée, and was formerly a popular figure in the social life of Sheffield, was also charged with conspiring with a woman hairdresser from Sheffield to procure a miscarriage by Miss Leadbeater.[1]

One evening Russell took the girl for a drive in his car and they sat for a while on the bank of the River Trent near Gainsborough. The prosecution alleged that, following a quarrel or an argument, the accused took the girl by the arms and pushed her into the river. She could not swim, but somehow she managed to scramble out and heard the car being driven off. Without attempting to raise the alarm or inform the police of the accident, Russell had driven home to Sheffield, a distance of nearly forty miles. In a statement Miss Leadbeater said that Russell had definitely pushed her in. ('I put out my hand, expecting him to pull me out, and he did not.') Russell, on the other hand, maintained that she fell in accidentally. 'I saw her floating down the river,' he said. 'I thought she was drowned, so I got in my car and drove away. I know it was a cowardly thing to do.'

Miss Leadbeater, who admitted at the trial to being still very much in love with the accused in spite of what had happened, had previously denied that he had pushed her, and she now repeated this denial in court in an attempt to shield her lover (so the prosecution alleged). 'I am not accusing Jack Russell of attempting to murder me,' she said in answer to a question from Birkett. 'He never attempted to murder me at all.'

'So far as you know, had he any part or lot in your falling in the river?'

'No.'

Russell confirmed this in the witness box. He did not push his fiancée into the river or cause her to go into the river. According to his account, she jumped in after they had an argument about marriage. He went into the water himself to try to save her. He caught his leg on a submerged stake, and it took him some moments before he got it free. When he did so, Miss Leadbeater had disappeared and he thought she was drowned. 'I was in a complete panic as to what had happened to the girl,' he said. 'I got into the car and drove away.'

'Did you remember on the way it would be a good plan to see if

[1] *Yorkshire Evening News*, April 1, 1935.

someone could rescue the poor girl left in the river?' Russell was asked in cross-examination.

'No.'

'Are you a member of St. John Ambulance Brigade, an officer?'

'Yes.'

'And you were so panicked that you drove straight back to Sheffield?'

'Yes.'

Asked by the judge, Mr. Justice Atkinson, if he was at any time in love with Miss Leadbeater, Russell replied: 'I may have been affectionate in the early stages of our friendship, but I was never sufficiently in love with her to desire to marry her.'

'She was a respectable girl except for her association with you?' queried Crown counsel.

'I should say so.'

Russell had unfortunately not made a good impression in the witness box, which added to Birkett's difficulty when he came to make his closing speech to the jury. 'There is much in the conduct of this young man that I do not stand here to defend,' said Birkett. 'To consort with a young woman, to get her into trouble, and to say, "I never intended to marry her," may, you think, merit the strongest condemnation. You may think it opposed to the standards of conduct of an ordinary English gentleman. But that is not the charge.' There were only two people in the world who could speak with anything approximating to first-hand knowledge of what took place—the girl and the man. And they both said that he did not do it. 'All this trouble has come from the fact that in a moment of panic the accused drove away.'

After an adverse summing up from Mr. Justice Atkinson, it took the jury only three quarters of an hour to find Russell guilty. Preparations were then made to try him with another jury on the abortion charges, to which he had pleaded Not Guilty, but in the meantime on Birkett's advice he changed his plea to Guilty. On the charge of attempted murder he was sentenced to five years penal servitude, and on the abortion charges to twelve months and nine months respectively, the latter to run concurrently.

In passing these sentences, Mr. Justice Atkinson used moderate language. 'I do not forget that the girl has forgiven you and that she does not desire your punishment,' he said to the man in the dock.

'I remember, too, the agony of mind which your parents must be suffering, and that fact and your knowledge of that fact would not be the least part of your punishment.' Then, as Russell turned to leave the dock, the judge added, in quiet tones: 'You must be conscious that your world is thinking very harshly of you. But remember always that the world is very generous to a man who, having paid the penalty for the wrong he has done, bravely tries to make it good.'

There was an appeal, which Birkett argued in the Court of Criminal Appeal, but it was dismissed. Lord Hewart remarked, in giving judgment, 'It is like the kind of case, about which one often hears, where the wife has been badly hurt by her husband but, in the pinch of the charge at the trial, she says she did not believe he intended to harm her.'[1]

The action for breach of promise of marriage, once relatively frequent, had become something of a rarity in Birkett's time. Indeed Birkett had only once been briefed in such an action before he appeared for Lord Revelstoke when the latter was sued by a film actress, and former 'Miss England' in an international beauty contest, called Ivy Dawkins, professionally known as Angela Joyce. She alleged that, when he was the Hon. Rupert Baring, shortly after he came of age, he had orally promised to marry her. In his defence Lord Revelstoke, who had meanwhile married someone else, maintained that he had never made any such promise. Because of the names and position of the parties the case attracted very considerable public interest, and the court room where the action was tried before Mr. Justice Rigby Swift and a special jury, was thronged with a fashionable and curious crowd of spectators. The action, as the judge reminded the jury, was one for damages for breach of contract. 'If it had been a contract for the sale of flour or a claim for damages for breach of an engagement to deliver a truck load of railway sleepers,' said Mr. Justice Swift, 'it would have excited less interest than it has done. . . . If this had been an action even for breach of promise of marriage, in which the plaintiff had been Miss Ivy Dawkins, a shop assistant, and the defendant had been Rupert Baring, a gas inspector, or something of that kind, little interest would have been taken in the case. But because the plaintiff is Miss Angela Joyce, a film actress, and because Rupert Baring is Baron Revelstoke, considerable interest

[1] *Daily Telegraph*, May 30, 1935.

appears to be taken in the matter, as you may observe by looking round the court or by reading the newspapers.'

Cross-examined by Birkett, the plaintiff declared that she had not brought the action for publicity, she had brought it for damages. She should have been Lady Revelstoke. 'I loved him,' she added, 'and I suffered mental torture which led to my physical breakdown. I have not worked since.'

'In the letters Lord Revelstoke wrote to you there is no word of marriage from start to finish?'

'Not actually the words, "I want to marry you." '

'Don't you think it likely, if a man has promised to marry someone, he should mention it in his letters to her?'

'Maybe sometimes, but not always.'

In opening the defence, Birkett remarked that the action was a cruel one which ought never to have been brought. Miss Joyce could not say that her life had been ruined by a callous, heartless defendant. There was no suggestion of any impropriety by word, act or deed, or that Miss Joyce had suffered any special damage. They were, therefore, left with an action, brought on, on Miss Joyce's own admission, for nothing but money. Lord Revelstoke's case was that for a short time, when he was an undergraduate at Cambridge, and still a minor, he had been infatuated with the plaintiff, but he had never promised to marry her. Nor had he ever bought her a ring, or mentioned marriage, although he had written her a number of affectionate letters, which had been read out in court. No man liked to have the effusions of his youth made public, said Birkett, but when the action was brought Lord Revelstoke decided that he would face it. At the time of his association with Miss Joyce, who was five years older, she had been a Beauty Queen in London and Paris, and she was obviously a woman with experience of the world.

'According to Lord Revelstoke,' said the judge in his summing up, 'the infatuation stopped because they both cooled off. You may think that that is not an unnatural explanation. These sort of infatuations do cool off, as your experience must have taught you. Very few men, I imagine, marry the woman that they first tell they love.'

It took the jury only half an hour to accept Lord Revelstoke's explanation, and judgment was accordingly entered for the defendant, with costs. After the verdict was announced, Birkett was happy to see his client leaving the court arm in arm with Lady Revelstoke, his wife.[1]

Towards the end of 1935, Birkett appeared for the Liberal M.P. and Parliamentary Secretary to the Board of Trade, Dr. Leslie Burgin, and other members of Dr. Burgin's firm of solicitors, in an action in which the latter were sued by a business promoter, Mr. Gwilym Owen, for breach of contract or alternatively fraudulent misrepresentation in connection with a £20,000,000 railway project in Yugoslavia. Briefly Mr. Owen's case was that Messrs. Burgin undertook to form an international trust to advance £20,000,000 to construct and equip railways from Belgrade to the Adriatic, after negotiations by Mr. Owen with the Yugoslav Government. The defendants denied that they were in any contractual relationship with Mr. Owen, but acted throughout as solicitors, professionally advising their own clients.

The plaintiff made serious charges against Dr. Leslie Burgin. It is not necessary to go further into the details of this case, except to state that in his cross-examination of the plaintiff Birkett forced him to admit that he had mis-stated certain facts in a letter he had written but had not disclosed to his own solicitors. The jury thereupon stopped the case against Dr. Burgin's firm before Dr. Burgin had an opportunity of going into the witness box and denying the allegations. 'As a public man and a Minister of the Crown, it is a matter of vital importance to him,' said Birkett to the judge, 'he was at all times ready and willing to go into the witness box.' To which the judge, Mr. Justice Talbot, replied, 'The jury quite appreciate that.'[2]

In gratitude for his efforts on their behalf, Dr. Burgin and the other members of his firm presented Birkett with a solid silver inkstand bearing the inscription:

Norman Birkett, Esq., K.C.,
Jugo Slavia, £20,000,000
17th October, 1935.

The inkstand was to remain on Birkett's desk in his chambers in Temple Gardens, and later, when he became a judge, he was to take it with him to his room in the Law Courts.

[1] *Daily Express*, May 15, 1935.
[2] *Daily Mail*, October 18, 1935.

2

After he had retired and not long before he died, Birkett was asked in the course of a television interview by Mr. John Freeman whether he had ever got a man or a woman acquitted of a murder charge whom he believed in his heart to be guilty. He replied that he had and he had no regrets about it. When the interviewer went on to ask him whether he had ever defended a person on a murder charge whom he *knew* to be guilty, Birkett drew a distinction between defending an accused person whom the barrister *believes* to be guilty and someone he *knows* to be guilty. 'How can you defend a man you know to be guilty?' he said. 'The answer is you never do. You are not permitted to do so. You may think that he is guilty, and of course it is really quite impossible for any man of sense to have a brief to defend some man, and read all about the facts without coming to some conclusion in his mind. But if he *thinks*, that is quite irrelevant. He is not the judge.'

As an illustration, Birkett liked to quote the example of Buck Ruxton, otherwise Bakhtyar Hakim, the thirty-seven-year-old Indian doctor, whom he defended at Manchester Spring Assizes in 1936 on a charge of murdering his wife, and also his children's nursemaid, as that of a lay client of whose guilt he gradually became convinced as he studied the depositions of the Crown witnesses. 'Nobody could read, as I read, all the facts the prosecution were going to prove,' Birkett admitted to John Freeman, 'without feeling that, well, this is a very difficult case. But it didn't make me any the less eager to do everything that I could for Dr. Ruxton.'

Buck Ruxton, or, to give him his real name, Bakhtyar Rustomji Ruttonju Hakim, belonged to a well-to-do Parsee family in Bombay. He held medical degrees from the University of Bombay and London, including that of Bachelor of Surgery. While taking a post-graduate course in medicine at Edinburgh University, when he was known as Gabriel Hakim, he used to go for meals to a restaurant in Princes Street. The manageress of this establishment, Isabella Kerr, had previously been married to a Dutch sailor named Van Est, but she had only lived with him for a short time before obtaining a divorce. In 1928, she went through a marriage ceremony with her Indian customer, who incidentally already had a Parsee wife living in India. Shortly afterwards he left for London where his 'common law wife' joined him, and he changed his name by deed poll to Ruxton. Two years later they appeared in Lancaster, where Dr. Ruxton bought a panel practice at 2, Dalton Square in that town.

Although they had three children, to whom they were devoted, the Ruxtons' life together was extremely tempestuous. They quarrelled incessantly, and on two occasions, Isabella Ruxton, fearing for her life, sought police protection. Excitable, jealous and suspicious, Ruxton habitually slept with a revolver under his pillow, and frequently abused and assaulted his 'wife', whom he believed to be consorting with other men. The mere sight of her dancing or even speaking to another man threw him into paroxysms of fury. 'I would be justified in murdering her,' he was heard to say on one occasion when he went to the local police station where she had taken refuge. He lost his temper again next day, when he shouted in the presence of a police officer, 'My wife has been unfaithful, and I will kill her if it continues.'

At the beginning of September, 1935, Mrs. Ruxton joined the family of a Mr. Edmondson, with whom she was friendly, on a motor trip to Edinburgh, and stayed the night in a hotel. Meanwhile Dr. Ruxton followed them by car to Edinburgh, returning to Lancaster with the idea firmly embedded in his mind that Mrs. Ruxton and Mr. Edmondson had spent the night together, for which incidentally there was not the slightest foundation in fact. Then, on September 14, Mrs. Ruxton motored over from Lancaster to Blackpool to see her two sisters who had come down on holiday from Edinburgh. Later they watched the illuminations together, and Mrs. Ruxton left in her husband's car to return home. That was the last time she was seen alive. She undoubtedly arrived home as the car was there next morning. To a woman called Roberts, who called at nine o'clock that morning with some newspapers, Dr. Ruxton, who unexpectedly opened the door, said, 'The maid is away with my wife in Scotland.' The nursemaid, whose name was Mary Rogerson, was also last seen alive on the previous evening.

Shortly after Miss Roberts had called, another woman Mrs. Hudson came with the milk. When Dr. Ruxton came to the door, she noticed that his right hand was bandaged. On asking him what he had done, he said, 'I have jammed it.' Later he said in answer to similar inquiries that he had cut his hand when opening a tin of peaches and the opener had slipped. But his wound was later shown to be a clean cut made by a sharp knife, probably a surgeon's knife, and not a tin opener.

The next caller was a newspaper boy, who brought a copy of the *Sunday Graphic*. The issue was dated September 15, and the edition was what was known as a 'slip' edition, that is one which contains a page of local news specially printed and included as being of interest to the district in which the newspaper circulates. This newspaper was to assume a particularly sinister significance at the trial.

The doctor next went to a garage with which he did not normally deal, and bought four gallons of petrol in tins. A little later he bought four more gallons from another garage and these were put in the petrol tank of his car.

Returning home, he met a patient, Mrs. Whiteside, who called about an operation that he had promised to perform on her son that morning. The doctor told her that he was sorry he could not perform the operation that day. 'My wife has run away to Scotland,' he added. 'There is just myself and my little maid, and we are busy taking the carpets up ready for the decorators in the morning.' After that he took the children to a neighbour's, Mrs. Anderson, the wife of a dentist with whom the Ruxtons were friendly, and left them with her to look after. She too expressed interest in his bandaged hand, and he explained he had cut it on a tin of peaches.

For the next four hours or so, no one saw Dr. Ruxton. But some time after four o'clock in the afternoon, he called on another patient, a Mrs. Hampshire, and asked her to come and help in cleaning the house as he had taken up the carpets and the decorators were coming in the morning. Mrs. Hampshire had never done any work in the house before, and before agreeing to come it was natural that she should ask, 'Where is the maid?' Dr. Ruxton assured her that she was on holiday, while his wife had gone to Blackpool.

When Mrs. Hampshire arrived at 2, Dalton Square, she found the hall and staircase littered with straw, there were no carpets on the floor, and the bathroom was in a dirty condition, while the bath was tinted a brownish-yellow colour, which one might expect if blood had been in it for some time. In the back yard Mrs. Hampshire noticed a quantity of carpet, a shirt and a number of surgical towels, all partly burnt and bearing traces of blood on them. She also found the linoleum in the house stained with blood, besides which two of the doors on the top landing were locked. She saw some carpets and a blue suit, which Dr. Ruxton gave her for her husband, saying as he did so, 'The suit is a good one. You can have it cleaned. I had it on this morning when I cut my finger and it is badly stained.' However, it was significant that Mrs. Hampshire, who went into the kitchen, did not see any tin of peaches there or anywhere else in the house, either opened or unopened.

Next morning, shortly after seven o'clock, Mrs. Oxley, the Ruxtons' regular charwoman, rang the doorbell of the house several times but could get no reply. About nine o'clock, however, Dr. Ruxton appeared at Mrs. Hampshire's house in his car to take her back to continue the cleaning. He was dressed in flannel trousers and a dirty old raincoat, he was unshaven and looked as if he had not slept. He told her that he had been up all night because his hand had caused him pain. Picking up the suit he had given her, he offered to have it cleaned, but she replied that as he had been good enough to give it to her she would be glad to pay for the cleaning. He then took up the coat and asked Mrs. Hampshire for a pair of scissors to cut out the tab with the maker's name on it. But, as he could not use the scissors, she did it for him and at his request threw the tab on the fire. Later Mrs. Hampshire swilled the carpet with thirty buckets of water, and as it came away she saw that the water was coloured red like blood.

Next day Mrs. Hampshire again went to the house in response to a message from Dr. Ruxton, but found there was no work to be done. 'I sent for you because you give me courage,' Dr. Ruxton remarked to her mysteriously. Again Mrs. Hampshire asked him why he had not sent for the mistress, and he replied that she was in London. But Mrs. Hampshire was suspicious. 'Doctor, you are telling me lies!' she said. 'Yes, dear, I am,' answered Dr. Ruxton. 'I will tell you the truth. My wife has gone away with another man and left me with the three children. A man comes to your house as a friend; you treat him as one; he eats from your table, and makes love to your wife behind your back. It is terrible. I can forgive extravagance or anything else, but infidelity—never!'

During the next day or two neighbours noted signs of burning in the doctor's backyard, and later the corporation dustmen remembered clearing away from the yard a quantity of burned carpets, clothes and rags, all of them bloodstained. Among these things was a blue silk dress with glass buttons which had been worn by the maid Mary Rogerson. At the same time, Mrs. Oxley, while she was working in the kitchen, heard Dr. Ruxton going up and down stairs several times, finally driving off in his car. After he had gone—and he was away for nearly seven hours—the doors, which the charwoman had seen were previously locked, were now open. Mrs. Oxley went into the doctor's bedroom where she noticed a foul smell. Another charwoman, Mrs. Smith, also employed on cleaning the staircase, observed that the rails, balustrade and stair rods were all spotted with blood.

Meanwhile Dr. Ruxton was endeavouring to pacify the families of the two women who had disappeared. He wrote to his wife's sisters in Edinburgh to the effect that his wife had left him and might have gone to Scotland. He then went to see Mrs. Rogerson, Mary's stepmother. 'Mary has been very different lately,' he told her. 'I think she has started going with boys. She has a laundry boy. Do you know she is pregnant?' Mrs. Rogerson replied that Mary was not pregnant so far as she knew. 'As a doctor I know she is,' said Dr. Ruxton. 'Mrs. Ruxton has taken her away to see if they can do anything about it.' Later the same day he repeated these words to the girl's father, who declared that he wanted his daughter back whatever her condition. He then threatened to go to the police and report that his daughter was missing unless she was home again by the following Saturday. 'Don't go to the police,' Dr. Ruxton begged. 'I will bring her back on Sunday.'

Four days later, on September 29, a Miss Susan Johnson, on holiday at Moffat in Scotland was crossing a bridge over a ravine on the Edinburgh-Carlisle road. She paused to study the wild countryside and her glance happened to light on what appeared to be a human arm protruding from a parcel at the bottom of the ravine. Looking more closely to make quite certain of what she saw, Miss Johnson hastened off to tell her brother, who confirmed that it was in fact a human arm. On opening the parcel, he found other human remains wrapped in a portion of a sheet. He immediately called the police, and following a search about thirty other parcels were discovered, all containing human remains in advanced stages of decomposition. Examination revealed that the limbs had been cut up with surgical skill and that the operator had taken pains to remove all possible marks of identification, severing fingers and thumbs, extracting teeth and scalping the head. The remains were sent to the anatomical department of Edinburgh University, and the experts pronounced that they belonged to two bodies. The sheet in which the remains in the original parcel were wrapped turned out to be of similar manufacture to a sheet on Dr. Ruxton's bed at 2, Dalton Square. Also, the remains in another parcel were found to be inside part of a 'slip' edition of the *Sunday Graphic* for September 15, which circulated in the Lancaster district. Other portions of the bodies were wrapped in a blouse which belonged to Mary Rogerson and a child's romper which had been given to her by a friend.

In consequence of these gruesome revelations, Dr. Ruxton was seen by the police and, after he had been questioned and cautioned, he was arrested and charged with the murder of Isabella Ruxton. A second charge of murdering Mary Rogerson was added to the indictment, but he was tried only on the first charge. He pleaded Not Guilty.

The trial began before Mr. Justice Singleton and an all-male jury at Manchester Assizes on March 2, 1936, and lasted for eleven days. Mr. J. C. Jackson, K.C., led Mr. David Maxwell-Fyfe, K.C. (afterwards Lord Kilmuir) and Mr. Hartley Shawcross (afterwards Lord Shawcross) for the Crown. Ruxton was defended by Birkett and Mr. Philip Kershaw, the leader being briefed 'special' as Manchester was not on Birkett's circuit.

The prosecution had suggested from the outset that there was a witness to the murder of Mrs. Ruxton, namely Mary Rogerson, and that was why she met her death. The death of both women, according to the prosecution, took place on the landing at the top of the staircase, outside the maid's bedroom, because from that point down the staircase, right into the bathroom, there were trails of enormous quantities of blood. 'The prisoner's wife had gone out for the evening and come back late,' was how Mr. Jackson put it in his opening speech to the jury. 'Remember the prisoner's violent temper and jealousy! What do you think was in his mind when she came home? There is a violent quarrel; he strangles his wife. Mary Rogerson caught him in the act and was killed. Her skull was fractured; she had received blows on the top of the head which would not kill her, and she was killed by other means, probably by a knife, because of the blood that was found on the stairs.'

It was clear that the case for the prosecution had involved the most detailed preparations. There were over two hundred exhibits in court, including a scale model of the prisoner's house complete with furnishings and the nameplate on the door. There were eighteen complete sets of photographs of the various parts of the bodies, comprising one hundred and thirty photographs to each set, and each member of the jury was given one for his own use. Then there was a long procession of witnesses, professors, pathologists, policemen, charwomen and dustmen, who came forward to tell their grim stories. Thus it was a truly formidable case that Birkett had to answer, and his task was not rendered any easier by the constant stream of notes, over one hundred in all, which reached him from the prisoner in the dock suggesting particular questions he should ask in cross-examination. Ruxton would scribble a note, then wave it across the dock rails to attract his counsel's attention, before passing it down to him. There were several dramatic moments too during the evidence, such as when Mrs. Hampshire fainted in the witness box and the court adjourned to enable her to recover outside, where by the judge's direction she was taken for a walk. 'She will be all right,' the prisoner exclaimed as the prostrate witness was carried from the box.

On the eighth day of the trial, when the prosecution's case was complete except for the medical witnesses, Birkett had to consider what evidence he would call for the defence. Accordingly he drew up a memorandum for his instructing solicitor to peruse and show the prisoner.

Re Evidence for Defence

1. The moment has come in this Case where a decision must be taken as to the Evidence to be called for the Defence.

   It falls into three divisions—

   (*a*) The Prisoner himself.

   (*b*) The evidence relating to the spotting of the suit by operatives.

   (*c*) The Medical Evidence.

   I disregard the evidence relating to Mrs. Ruxton and Mary Rogerson having been seen after September 15th as being so unreliable as to be fantastic and indeed ridiculous.

2. The Prisoner can give evidence if he so desires, when, of course, he would be subjected to cross-examination.

He may decline to give evidence, when, of course, the Judge, and the Judge alone can comment on this fact.

If we call further evidence, documentary or otherwise, we shall lose the last word to the Jury, which I regard of greater importance than anything else in this case.

We have considerable evidence already of the spotting of the suit, and we shall gain nothing by adding to it.

The Medical Evidence to be of any avail must deny the medical evidence of the Prosecution in its essential feature, i.e. these are the bodies of Mrs. Ruxton and Mary Rogerson, and I am informed by the Medical Experts that this is impossible. Contradictions on minor matters are useless, e.g. the true cause of death is really immaterial: and we must be content with cross-examination of the Experts for the Crown and endure any comment on the absence of medical evidence for the Defence rather than strengthen the case for the Crown.

In my clear and very strong view, if Dr. Ruxton desires to give evidence we should confine our evidence to him, and exercise our right of the last word to the Jury.

I particularly desire Dr. Ruxton's assent to this course, which is the best possible course in his interest.

Any other course, in my view, would be absolutely fatal.

NORMAN BIRKETT
10.iii.36

'I entirely agree with you,' the prisoner wrote to his counsel after he had seen this memorandum. 'I wish to give evidence on my own behalf, and I also note that it is not in the interest of defence that further evidence should be called.'

3

Following some formal evidence of finger prints on the morning of the ninth day of the trial, Mr. Jackson intimated that the case for the Crown was closed. Birkett thereupon rose and said in a quiet tone: 'I call the prisoner.' Dr. Ruxton thereupon left the dock and stepped quickly into the witness box, where he took the oath in a clear, precise voice and remained standing with his hands behind his back, as he answered his counsel's questions. At first he appeared nervous and once or twice seemed on the verge of tears. But gradually he developed confidence, and he gave his answers clearly and concisely and apart from a few nervous outbursts he turned out to be a remarkably good witness, both during his examination-in-chief and his cross-examination. Unfortunately for him, as will be seen, he was still being cross-examined by Mr. Jackson when the court rose for the day.

Birkett began his examination by remarking that he would ask a few general questions about the years from 1930 to 1935 and on evidence which had been called in the court.

'What do you yourself say about your relationship with Mrs. Ruxton during those years?'

'If I may put it in proper English,' Dr. Ruxton replied, 'we could not live with each other and we could not live without each other.'

Taking a handkerchief from his pocket, the prisoner dabbed his eyes with it, and then broke into French, quoting a French proverb: 'Who loves most chastises most.' He went on to explain himself. 'I am speaking in general parlance. My mentality thinks in French and you will have to excuse me while I translate into English.' Later he said that his counsel could ask him any questions he liked, and he would speak the truth.

Asked if there had been any quarrels between him and his wife, Dr. Ruxton said there had been, but they lasted hardly two or three hours. Every time a quarrel arose, he paid dearly for it, he said. 'And I can prove it.'

'After the quarrels had passed, what was the relationship then?'

'Oh, more than intimate.'

Explaining what he meant when he said that he had paid dearly for it, he declared that many a time Mrs. Ruxton would come into the surgery and smile and say, 'How do you think I would look in a suit or a costume or something like that?'

When the evidence of Inspector Thompson of the Lancaster Police was put to him that he had said his wife was unfaithful and he would kill her, he said that he did not 'exactly say the word "kill" '. He admitted, however, that he had 'unfortunately' accused his wife of being unfaithful. What he had really said in effect was, 'It makes my blood wild.'

Coming to the fateful night of September 15, Birkett asked the prisoner what happened when Mrs. Ruxton came home from her visit to Blackpool. He replied that Isabella came in and asked for the key of the garage to put the car away. After she had done this, she came back and as she passed his room she said, 'Good night, pa', and took the bunch of keys with her. She then went to bed in her own bedroom.

'I want to put the question plainly and directly,' said Birkett. 'It is suggested by the Crown that on the morning of Sunday after your wife had come back you killed her?'

At this question, Dr. Ruxton burst into tears. 'It is a deliberate fantastic story,' he sobbed. 'You might just as well say the sun was rising in the West and setting in the East!'

'It is suggested also that upon that morning you killed Mary Rogerson?' continued Birkett.

'It is absolute bunkum with a capital B, if I may say so,' the prisoner declared, still weeping. 'Why should I kill my poor Mary?'

What had happened, according to the prisoner, was that about 6.30 a.m. she came into his room and said, 'Let's go out for the day.' They had often done that on the spur of the moment. When he got up, he went to get the car, and on his return he found his wife and Mary in the living room. He went straight up to his bedroom and waited, as 'I do not like meddling myself with the lady folks of the house'. He then went into the bathroom, and while he was there 'my Belle' came in to make up in the looking glass, and as she was doing so she asked him if she minded if she went to Edinburgh that day instead of the following as she had planned.

'I got a little bit annoyed,' said Dr. Ruxton. 'I could not help getting annoyed, because I was asked to get up and to dress . . . I was annoyed at her making a monkey out of me by making me get up early and changing her mind at the last moment.'

However, the prisoner continued, he told his wife she could go, but she was not to take the car with her. As she was leaving, Mrs. Ruxton said that Mary was going with her, and indeed he saw them leave the house together between nine-fifteen and nine-thirty. He could not say whether they had taken anything with them in the way of clothes.

It was while he was looking for something to get the children for breakfast that he opened the kitchen cupboard and found a tin of peaches. He tried to open it with a tin opener but the blade was bent and would not go into the tin. He used a small sofa arm to knock it in, and that was how he injured his hand. The wound bled profusely, as he went up the three flights of stairs to the bathroom.

The prisoner offered various further explanations. Other bloodstains on the carpets might have happened when his wife had had a miscarriage some time previously. As for the bedroom doors, it was always his custom to keep them locked. Then again he was in the habit of buying petrol in tins as he often used this to burn rubbish and waste in the yard. The extra supply of petrol he got for the car was because his wife had used the car the day before for her visit to Blackpool. On the question of the suit of clothes he gave Mrs. Hampshire he denied that he had ever told her to cut off the tab and throw it in the fire. She received the suit in his house in the lounge where there was an electric fire. Nor did he have any conversation with her on the subject of his wife's infidelity. 'I never discussed it with strangers,' he added. 'I did say that Mrs. Ruxton was going north and south and was never at home, or something like that.' As for the foul smell in the house, he attributed this to the charwoman stripping the walls and washing off the glue used to affix the wallpaper, and this smell pervaded the house right up to the top landing. Finally, on the possibility of Mary Rogerson being pregnant, he said that the thought had crossed his mind one day while they had company at the house and he looked at her. He had persuaded the girl's father not to go to the police because of his position as a doctor. If the police had been notified and Mary had turned up a few days afterwards, 'it would have been something in the mouths of the people to speak about'.

'So far as Mrs. Ruxton is concerned,' Birkett asked in concluding his examination-in-chief, 'did you do any violence of any kind to her on the morning of Sunday, September 15?'

'Never, never, sir,' the prisoner answered excitedly.

'If she was strangled, had you any part or lot in it?'

'Sir, I have never done it.'

'So far as Mary Rogerson is concerned, did you do any violence to her?'

'Never. Let alone doing it, I never thought of it. She has always been a dear child to my heart.'

'If Mary Rogerson is dead, had you any part in bringing about her death?'

'Certainly not. A most ridiculous thing to suggest.'

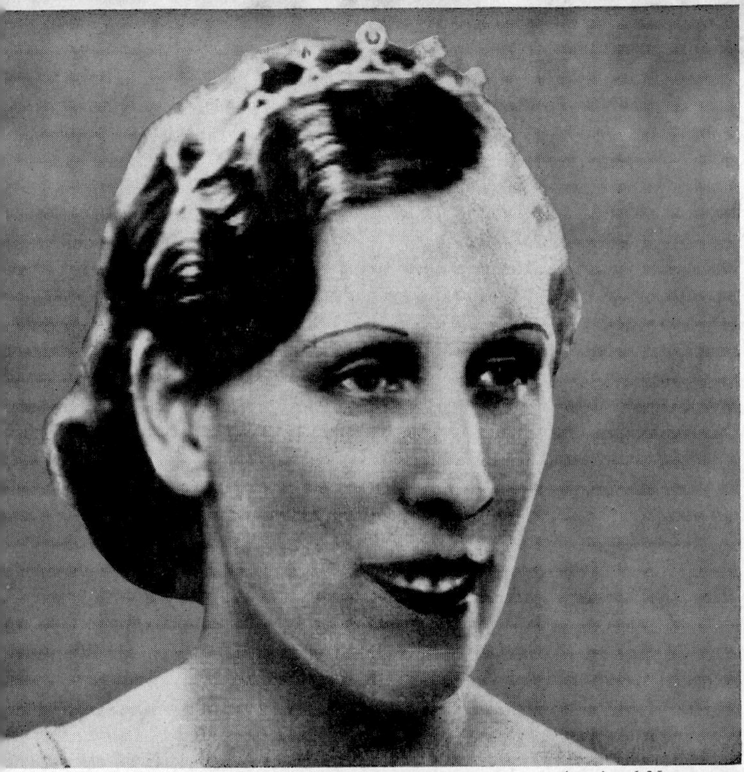

Associated Newspapers

ISABELLA RUXTON

[A]ssociated
[N]ewspapers

[R]UXTON
[A]ND HIS
[D]AUGHTER

Buckinghamshire Advertiser and County Gaze[tte]

IN HIS STUDY AT CHALLENS GREEN

'Apart from what you have told us about their departure on the morning of Sunday, September 15, do you know anything else about their disappearance?'

'No. I do not.'

Mr. Jackson for the Crown then began his cross-examination of Dr. Ruxton. 'I understand Mary was very dear to your heart?'

'Yes,' the prisoner agreed.

'You say she was a very loyal girl?'

'Yes. I would stake my reputation upon that.'

'One that would never allow any harm to come to her mistress?'

'She was not primarily meant for my Belle. She was loyal to everybody.'

'She was a girl who would have stood by her mistress and defended her if attacked."

'Yes. By anybody.'

'She would have stood by her master as well?'

'Yes, I am quite sure.'

'Why is she not standing by you today if she is alive?'

The prisoner paused for a few moments before replying. 'That is not a question I can answer.'

'Do you think your wife was unfaithful to you?' Crown counsel continued.

'Yes,' replied Dr. Ruxton. 'It has been going on since 1932.'

'You have for a considerable time thought your wife unfaithful?'

'She has done some silly things that would not have been done by sensible women—put it that way.' Dr. Ruxton added that by infidelity he did not mean misconduct of a sexual nature but in the sense of a transfer of affection. In the case of Mr. Edmondson he had no evidence of actual misconduct.

'Where do you say Mrs. Ruxton is today, if she is not dead?'

'Isabelle has done the trick often of going to Holland without a passport. If one can do that, there is no knowing where she may be.'

'If I understand your story, you were in the bathroom when she finally left the house, and she tapped on the door and said, "Well, we are off, dear"?'

'Yes, quite friendly.'

'Have you ever been able to find a single person who ever saw your wife or Mary Rogerson leave your house on that morning?'

'I myself and my solicitor have made inquiries, and a lady has written a letter?'

'Where is that person?'

The prisoner was heard to say something about his solicitor, when Birkett interrupted to say that, if counsel persisted in this line of cross-examination, he must object. After a comment by the judge, Mr. Jackson said he had not intended to take the point any further and passed on to other matters.

Questioned about the evidence of one witness who said she found the doctor holding his wife down on the bed fully dressed, Dr. Ruxton said he did not do it, and supposing he had, the witness could not have seen him from the position in which she was supposed to be standing. He also denied that the same witness ever entered the kitchen and heard Mrs. Ruxton say, 'He has had a knife at my throat.' He similarly denied the evidence of another witness who said she had heard him call Mrs. Ruxton 'a dirty prostitute'. But, he admitted, he might have said that she had the mind of a prostitute.

Asked why the stairs were washed down before the walls were stripped of paper, Dr. Ruxton said that the carpets had been taken up, and that the dust that had accumulated on the staircase made the place rather shabby.

The prisoner was still in the witness box when the court rose for the day. Had the cross-examination ended at this point, it is just conceivable that the jury would have given the accused the benefit of the doubts in their minds and acquitted him, since he had made quite a good showing and stood up well to the leading counsel for the Crown. But the cross-examination was not finished, and when it was resumed next morning the prisoner seemed a changed man. His self-confidence left him, he got more excited than ever, raving and weeping hysterically by turns, and quickly losing the sympathy of the jury to whom he seemed to become more and more of a lying hypocrite.

Mr. Jackson began his resumed cross-examination by asking about Miss Roberts who called at the house about nine o'clock on the morning of September 15. 'She says she rang three times and you opened the door a little way and she apologized for disturbing you?'

'I don't recall that.'

'She says you told her, "My maid is away in Scotland with my wife" ?'

'I don't recollect having told anything to Miss Roberts. I don't think I saw her at all.'

'She says you were agitated. What had you to be agitated about at nine o'clock in the morning?'

'Nine o'clock in the morning it could not be, because Belle left after nine o'clock.'

'She says you were very agitated,' counsel pressed the prisoner. 'It could not have been your wife leaving you that agitated you?'

'I am telling you that I have never seen Miss Roberts, if I may politely say so,' said the prisoner, rapidly losing his temper.

'May I suggest the reason why you took so long to answer the bell is that you were busy cutting up the bodies of your wife and Mary Rogerson?'

'May I respectfully suggest that the three children were in the house with me at that time,' retorted Dr. Ruxton angrily.

When the prosecuting counsel began to question the prisoner about the suit he had given to Mrs. Hampshire, there was an awkward surprise. The prisoner said that the blood was accumulated over several years as the result of his work, 'two or three years easily'. 'But surely,' said Mr. Jackson, 'that suit was sent to the cleaners in August and returned on August 17 perfectly clean?'

'My Belle does all the cleaning,' the prisoner stammered, obviously taken aback at this unexpected and unwelcome revelation. 'I know nothing about it. . . . I don't remember it. . . . I cannot say.'

Mr. Jackson then turned round and asked if there was a Mr. Cherry in court. A man rose from the seats at the back of the dock and came forward near the witness box. Counsel then asked the prisoner if he knew Mr. Cherry, a cleaner. 'I have never seen the gentleman before,' replied Dr. Ruxton.

Here Mr. Justice Singleton intervened to ask, 'If you have a suit which goes away to be cleaned, don't you notice the difference when it comes back?'

'Yes,' the prisoner admitted weakly, 'but I don't recollect this particular suit.' He added that his wife used her discretion in sending his suits to be cleaned.

'If it was cleaned, as I say,' Crown counsel continued, 'the whole of this blood has accumulated since August 17?'

'I could not do it that way,' was all Dr. Ruxton could say. 'I don't know how to answer the question.'

'Have you attended confinements in the suit?'

'Yes, sir, many a time.'

'Did you hear Dr. Glaister say that the suit was a potential source of infection?'

At this question the prisoner showed signs of becoming hysterical. 'Out of two hundred cases of confinement in Lancaster,' he shouted, 'Dr. Ruxton has never written a death certificate. Let us go by practical results and not by theories.'

Pressed further on this point, the prisoner continued to shout, 'Has my learned friend read the life of Jonathan Hunter the great surgeon?'

'It would be better for you and everyone,' the judge interrupted, 'if you listened to the questions and tried to answer.'

'I humbly beg your pardon,' said Dr. Ruxton, by this time in tears. 'You can imagine how I am feeling, everybody cornering me.'

The scene ended with Birkett rising and asking his client to be quiet and give his answers calmly. 'Would you remember this?' he added. 'I am watching the case in your interests and I will deal with all these matters.'

'I am grateful to you,' replied the prisoner, who had now calmed down.

But he did not remain calm. There were several further outbursts, as for instance when he exploded in reply to a question about his car, 'This is a court to give men justice, not to put a man on the gallows for nothing.' Again, when he was asked about Mrs. Hampshire using thirty buckets of water to clean the blood-saturated carpet, he exclaimed, 'I would like to know how much blood there would be, and why she counted the buckets. A fantastic story!' Then, in reply to a question as to whether he had been to Moffat, he answered contemptuously, 'It would require the speed of a racing motorist to go there, especially at night time. It is 110½ miles. Would I be taking a gruesome cargo driving with the left hand? Ask yourself a reasonable question!'

But Mr. Jackson's questions were not only reasonable but deadly, particularly the last, when he pointed to a portion of a sheet among the exhibits. 'If that is the sheet from your wife's bed, can you explain how it got round those bodies at Moffat?'

The prisoner could not explain it. All he could say was, 'How could it be, sir?'

In re-examination Birkett could do little more than reiterate his client's previous declaration of innocence.

'Did you at any time purport to give away or deal with any clothes of Mary Rogerson?'

'Never.'

'It is suggested that you have invented the idea of Mary Rogerson's pregnancy to account in some way for her going away?'

'If ordinarily anyone had suggested anything wrong about her, I should have felt like stabbing his face. It was from my observations.'

'Did you at any time do any act of violence to Mrs. Ruxton or Mary?'

'No. God is my judge.'

'Or did you make any journeys to dispose of the remains?'

'No.'

4

The remainder of the tenth day of this remarkable trial was occupied with the closing speeches of counsel. Mr. Jackson spoke first, since Birkett had called no evidence besides the prisoner himself. 'Were these bodies found in the ravine those of Isabella Buxton and Mary Rogerson?' he asked the jury. 'Once you are satisfied with that, I suggest you can have little doubt as to how they met their deaths.' To be precise, Dr. Ruxton, after having killed his wife by throttling her and when the maid came to the door, hearing a noise determined to get rid of her too, the one witness to his crime. 'That is why Mary Rogerson lost her life. She lost it simply because of the devotion and protection after she had come to her mistress because she was a loyal girl.'

The leading Crown counsel was answered by Birkett, who justifiably took every advantage of the last word with the jury, apart from the judge's summing up. 'It is the duty of the Crown to prove beyond all reasonable doubt the guilt of the person who stands at the bar as Dr. Ruxton stands today,' said Birkett. 'Suspicion is not enough, doubt is not enough, the accusing finger is not enough . . . the imaginative reconstructions of my learned friend are not enough.' He emphasized that even if the bodies found in the ravine were those of Mrs. Ruxton and Mary Rogerson, it did not prove the Crown's case, particularly if the prisoner's statement that they had left the house was true. 'Though their bodies were found in the ravine, though of a certainty those were the bodies, it has not been proved in the case against the prisoner. The Crown must prove the fact of murder.' Some other hand might have caused their death.

The case for the Crown, Birkett went on, was that on the morning of the Sunday, September 15, the prisoner's house was a house of murder. Yet into that house came Mrs. Oxley, Mrs. Hampshire and two other women, day after day, seeing the stairs, the wallpaper, the carpets, the yard, the petrol, the fire—and none of them thought at the time that there was a single suspicious circumstance. 'There are many features of this case which are mysterious, dark, and seemingly unfathomable,' he remarked. 'It is part of the Crown case that not only did Dr. Ruxton kill his wife, but that he drained the body of blood in the house, dismembered the body, and that on the night of Monday, the 16th September, he deposited those remains in the ravine at Moffat. But there is not a single shred of evidence of any journey to Moffat that night. We now know that the night of Monday was wet, but according to the evidence the car which he is said to have driven to Moffat was clean the next day. Furthermore, although he had these remains in the car, there was never a single spot of blood upon it.'

It was a valiant effort on the part of a defending counsel in whose mind there can now have been few if any doubts of the prisoner's guilt. And what lingering doubts there were in the minds of the jury were removed by the judge's careful and detailed summing up of the evidence on the eleventh and final day of this long drawn out trial. One by one Mr. Justice Singleton called for the exhibits to be brought into court. Bloodstained stair pads, the front panel of the bath, the childrens' rompers in which one of the heads found in the ravine had been wrapped, the blouse which had contained the other —all these were shown once more to the jury. 'I confess that I attach the greatest importance to these,' said the judge as he turned the stair pads over carefully in his hands. 'If you look at the blood on the one I am holding towards you, can you conceive that that is the result of a dripping hand?' Then he held up the stained rompers which had been established as belonging to one of the Ruxton children. 'Doesn't this establish the case for the prosecution as a case was rarely established before on circumstantial evidence?'

And so the judge went on, analysing the evidence piece by piece. At one point he drew the forefinger of his right hand across the palm of his left in a dramatic gesture, suggesting a link between the wound on the head believed to be that of Mary Rogerson and the cut on Dr. Ruxton's hand about which so much had been said. 'Perhaps his hand slipped—the hand of the person who was cutting up the bodies.'

It took the jury just one hour's reflection to find the prisoner guilty. Asked the customary question by the Clerk of Assize whether he had anything to say why sentence of death should not be passed according to law, Dr. Ruxton raised his right hand, palm forwards, in a kind of strange salute to the judge. Then he spoke a few words quickly and in a low voice. 'Subject to the point that I be allowed to appeal . . . in the administration of justice . . . I submit that to your Lordship and the jury . . . I want to thank everybody for the patience and fairness of my trial . . . I should like to hear whatever his Lordship has to say about it.'

'Buck Ruxton,' said Mr. Justice Singleton, after the Black Cap had been placed on his head, 'you have been convicted on evidence that can leave no doubt in the mind of anyone. The law knows but one sentence for the terrible crime which you committed.'

The judge, having assumed the Black Cap, proceeded to utter the time-honoured formula, and as his voice died away with the words, 'And may the Lord have mercy on your soul. Amen,' the figure in the dock again raised his hand and again saluted the judge. He then made a short bow and walked quickly out of the dock followed by two warders and looking strangely unmoved. Thus ended on a curiously bizarre note one of the longest and most horrible murder trials in English criminal history.

After consulting with Ruxton and his solicitor, Birkett lodged an appeal on the ground that the judge had misdirected the jury in that he omitted to direct them sufficiently as to the evidence of witnesses in regard to the clean condition of the car after the suggested run to Moffat, and the state of the weather at Moffat at the time. The appeal was heard in the Court of Criminal Appeal six weeks later, the court consisting of the Lord Chief Justice, Lord Hewart, Mr. Justice du Parcq and Mr. Justice Goddard.[1]

[1] *Evening News*, April 27, 1936.

Birkett's argument, to which Ruxton listened attentively, centred round the fact that the doctor's car was clean on the Monday, although it was raining at Moffat, and he argued that it was impossible that the car could have been driven more than two hundred miles across rain-sodden roads in wild moorland country. If the jury were satisfied that the car did not travel to Moffat on the Sunday night, then the whole structure of the case for the Crown came tumbling down. 'There was not a spot of blood on the car,' said Birkett. 'Isn't that a most remarkable thing? Is it not of outstanding moment in the case that the car which was to connect the murder at Dalton Square with the ravine had no spot of blood on it, and that, having travelled all those miles on such a night, there is no mud, no staining?' At the same time Birkett applied to call further evidence in the shape of two expert medical witnesses.

'Was that evidence available at the trial?' asked Lord Hewart.

'I am bound to say that it was,' Birkett replied, who went on to explain the reason for his request, which he knew must be refused. 'I am specially requested by the appellant to make this application. Therefore I am anxious to make it so that it shall be plainly made in the hearing of the appellant.'

Without calling on counsel for the Crown, the Court dismissed the appeal after consulting together for only a few moments. 'The evidence that the dismembered bodies were those of Mrs. Ruxton and Mary Rogerson was really overwhelming,' Lord Hewart declared. 'There is nothing in the summing-up that can be said even faintly to resemble misdirection. As for the application to call here witnesses who might have been called in the court below, it must be dismissed. The application is of a kind which the Court cannot grant.'

In spite of all the evidence which had been brought against the prisoner and the verdict of the two courts, many of Ruxton's fellow citizens were dubious of his guilt, judging by the petitions for his reprieve which were got up all over the country. In Lancaster alone there were six thousand signatories. But the Home Secretary refused to intervene, and Dr. Buck Ruxton was duly hanged.

On the night before his execution, the condemned man addressed the following letter to his counsel. Birkett carefully preserved it with other papers relating to the trial, including the numerous notes which Ruxton had scribbled from the dock.

Manchester Prison.
7.20 *p.m., Monday, May* 11,
1936.

Dear Mr. Birkett,

This letter will be forwarded to you by my solicitor and trustee Mr. C. F. Gardner of 31, Sun Street, Lancaster.

Thanks awfully, old man, for all you have done.

Please accept a trivial token of gratitude I have left you in my will. I am sure your wife will be delighted with it. Mr. C. F. Gardner will send it on to you in due course.

May I beg a favour of you? If there should be any litigation re my estate, will you kindly give your services as a favour to a dying man?

I am leaving three bonnie little mites behind.

If you can, please do be good to them. They are intelligent and good looking.

May you reach the highest pinnacle of the Legal Pedestal.

I'll bless you from above. Try your best to get in touch with Mr. Gardner now and again and do your best for my children.

God bless you and yours,

Yours very sincerely,
BUCK RUXTON

Norman Birkett, Esq., K.C.

The 'trivial token of gratitude' turned out to be a set of silver forks and fish knives with mother-of-pearl handles, which Ruxton had left in his will. But in the circumstances, understandably enough, Birkett felt unable to accept the bequest. But he did go to considerable trouble afterwards to arrange for the care and education of the murderer's three orphaned children.

At one time it was common practice at the coroner's inquest on the body of the executed criminal for the prison governor to reveal, usually in response to a juror's question, whether the condemned person had made any last-minute confession of guilt. But there had been a Home Office instruction against this practice, and for many years past, if such a confession was made, it was withheld from publicity. Thus a considerable sensation was caused when, on the

Sunday following Ruxton's execution, the *News of the World* published a signed confession by Ruxton in his own handwriting to the effect that he had killed both his wife and the maid. 'I killed Mrs. Ruxton in a fit of temper because I thought she had been with a man,' he wrote. 'I was mad at the time. Mary Rogerson was present at the time. I had to kill her.'

Lancaster.
14.10.35.

I killed Mrs Ruxton in a fit of temper because I thought she had been with a man. I was Mad at the time. Mary Rogerson was present at the time. I had to Kill her.

B Ruxton

Doctor Ruxton's confession

This remarkable document was dated from Lancaster, the day after Ruxton's arrest. Just before his arrest Ruxton had been visited in his surgery by a *News of the World* representative, who again came to see him when he had been taken into custody. On the latter occasion, Ruxton handed the representative a sealed envelope. 'Take great care of this,' he said. 'They have charged me with murder, and I, in turn, charge you to place this envelope in safety and security. On no account must it be opened until my death, if to die I am. If I am acquitted—and I think I must be acquitted—you will give it back to me.' He saw the newspaperman again, towards the end of the trial, reiterating his injunction and asking that in the event of his death the envelope should be handed unopened to the editor. This was done on the same day as Ruxton went to the gallows.

This sealed confession was unique, since never before, so far as is known, had a document of this character been entrusted to a newspaper by a man who was destined for the scaffold. It is said that Ruxton received £3,000 for it. Although Birkett did not know it at the time, whatever the sum was it helped to defray the very substantial costs of the defence. Of these Birkett's fees amounted to approximately £2,000.

Asked many years later by John Freeman, in the television interview already mentioned, what he thought of the practice which had since grown up of great newspapers paying for the defence of criminals in return for their 'confessions', Birkett made it clear that he did not disapprove of it, 'provided', to use his own words, 'counsel is left, as he ought to be left, entirely free to conduct the case as he ought to do.'

5

For Birkett the year 1936 was conspicuous for the number of murder trials in which he appeared. There were three others, besides Dr. Ruxton's, in two of which he defended the accused and in one of which he was for the prosecution. In the latter he prosecuted to conviction a woman nurse who was charged along with her lover with killing a woman patient by an overdose of morphine.

Dorothy Waddingham was an unregistered nurse, who had been left a widow with three young children and carried on a home in Nottingham for 'aged, medical and chronic cases'. One of her patients, a middle-aged cripple named Ada Baguley, drew up a will dated May 4, 1935, in which she left the whole of her estate, amounting to £1,600 to Nurse Waddingham and her handyman at the nursing home, who was suspected of being her lover. Miss Baguley had previously expressed her intention to leave her money in this way in consideration of Nurse Waddingham looking after her and her ninety-year-old mother for the rest of their lives. Mrs. Baguley died eight days later, and she was followed by her daughter four months afterwards. It was a strangely worded letter, admittedly written by the handyman and purporting to be signed by Miss Baguley, asking that she should be cremated and adding 'and my last wish is my relatives shall not know of my death', that aroused the suspicions of the local authorities. A *post-mortem* examination of Ada's remains was ordered and this revealed enough morphine to constitute a lethal dose. As a result Nurse Waddingham and the handyman were arrested and charged with murder. 'I have never given Miss Baguley any morphia,' said the nurse. 'I have never had any in the house. Apart from the medicine prescribed by the doctors and aspirins she had had no other medicine.' The mother's body was now exhumed and a *post-mortem* on her remains showed the presence of morphine in excess of a medicinal dose.[1]

The trial judge at Nottingham Assizes, Mr. Justice Goddard, ruled that there was no case to go to the jury in respect of the handyman and he was discharged. The doctors who gave evidence swore that they had never prescribed morphine for Ada, although they had done so for other patients at the home, and when Nurse Waddingham went into the witness box Birkett had no difficulty in eliciting from her answers that she must have administered the morphine from these other prescriptions, although she persisted in her story that the doctors had prescribed morphine for Miss Baguley.

Under cross-examination by Birkett, Nurse Waddingham admitted that she knew Miss Baguley had had a lot of medicine with morphia. Unfortunately she had thrown the remains of the medicine with the medicine glass into the dustbin because of the smell.

'Why did you say to the police, "I have never given Miss Baguley any morphia, I have never had any in the house"?'

'I had not had any. I had not given it on my own.'

'Did you know then that you had given her some on the doctor's instructions?'

'Yes.'

'Why did you not say so?'

'Because I was told not to say so.'

'By whom?'

'Dr. Manfield.'

'When?'

'Shortly after the *post-mortem*.'

'Why should Dr. Manfield tell you not to?'

To this last question the prisoner made no audible reply. The doctor, who had already given evidence, was then recalled to the witness box, where he repeated on oath that he had told Nurse Waddingham no such thing. Nor had he ever prescribed any morphine for her.

[1] *Nottingham Journal*, Feburary 25, 1936.

In convicting Nurse Waddingham of the murder of Ada Baguley, the jury added a strong recommendation to mercy. But this made no difference to her fate. After her appeal had been dismissed, the Home Secretary refused a reprieve and, although the youngest of her five children was only four months old, she was duly hanged. Presumably the Home Secretary's action was based on public policy, as in the case of Mrs. Major, murder by poison being regarded with special abhorrence by the authorities, in spite of the jury's recommendation to mercy.

In the two murder trials in which Birkett was for the defence, he secured acquittals. The first, which took place at Staffordshire Assizes, where Birkett was briefed 'special', the prisoner, a lorry driver named William Oakley, was charged with having murdered a young sailor's wife named Eliza Worton. Here the case for the Crown was that the woman was attacked and rendered unconscious at some distance from where her body was found in a canal, that she had been taken to the canal bridge in the accused's lorry, then carried to the towpath and drowned. Bloodstains found on Oakley's clothing were stated to belong to the same blood group as that of Mrs. Worton, with whom the accused was said to have spoken on the morning of her death. Some blood was also found on the lorry which Oakley was driving, which had been seen by two boys on the canal bridge. The boys said they had caught a glimpse of the driver's cap which had a shiny peak like a chauffeur's.

Oakley asserted that he had been at home on the night before the discovery of the body, at the hour the boys had said they saw the lorry on the bridge, and in opening the case for the Crown Mr. Cartwright Sharp, K.C., told the jury that if the prisoner was right then he had a perfect alibi. With Birkett's assistance, Oakley was able to prove just that. His wife and mother swore that he was in fact at home at the time. Then Birkett held up the cap the prisoner had worn, a greasy old brown cap, for the jury to see. 'Look at it,' he told them. 'This is Oakley's cap. There may be confusion in this world and there will be confusion till the end of time. But there can be no confusion between this and a shiny peak.'

There was no evidence of motive, no association, quarrel or threats, and Oakley had the reputation of being a model husband for the past fourteen years. True, there was the question of the bloodstains on his clothes and the lorry, but these he explained as due to bleeding from cuts or abrasions, which it was not unusual for him to sustain in the course of his work.

In this case the jury returned a verdict of Not Guilty. 'I knew I was innocent,' said Oakley afterwards, 'and I had every faith in British justice.' And, he might have added, in his counsel's advocacy. For just as Birkett's skilful use of a cap in the Winson Green murder largely convicted Power, so his use of Oakley's cap did much to secure his client's acquittal on that July day in the Stafford Shire Hall.[1]

Birkett's other success that year occurred when he interrupted his holiday to defend an elderly confectioner named Albert Hadfield, who came up at the September Sessions at the Old Bailey on the charge of murdering Mrs. Laura Mordaunt Chapman, a widow of independent means, who lived the life of a recluse in Twickenham. Mrs. Chapman was found dead at her home with over forty stab wounds on her body, which was lying under a heap of partly burned clothes. Hadfield, who helped her to manage her substantial property by collecting the rents, was arrested after he had telephoned the police asking for an officer to go to Mrs. Chapman's house in Hampton Road as 'there may be a body there'. In the bedroom was found a bloodstained postcard, which bore the impression of a thumb with a scar, and it so happened that Hadfield had a scar on his thumb.

In the witness box, Hadfield explained that he had indeed written Mrs. Chapman a postcard. He had also called to see her, and not getting any reply had left a note for her which he put under the window sash. Hearing nothing from her, he called again two days later and saw that his note was still there. He entered the house and seeing the bundle of clothes but no sign of Mrs. Chapman, he got agitated and telephoned the police. He denied that he had had anything to do with her murder, although he admitted that relations between them were strained from time to time owing to his complaining that she paid him insufficiently for his work for her.

At the conclusion of the Crown case, Birkett had submitted that there was no case to go to the jury, but this submission the judge, Mr. Justice Greaves-Lord, refused to accept. However, when he had heard Hadfield in the witness box, the judge intervened to ask the Crown counsel, 'Is it safe upon this evidence to put any one in

[1] *Wolverhampton Express and Star*, July 10, 1936.

jeopardy?' When counsel replied that in his opinion it would be very dangerous to do so, the judge stopped the trial and directed the jury to acquit the prisoner.[1]

Then, as he took off his wig and gown, Birkett commented calmly, 'Perhaps I can go back to my holiday now.' A few minutes later he was observed running down the steps of the Old Bailey like a happy schoolboy.

This was one of the very few cases, in which Birkett had secured an acquittal on a capital charge, where the accused person subsequently sent him a letter of thanks for what he had done. 'Please allow me the privilege of expressing my gratitude for your magnificent defence against the charge of that horrible crime,' wrote Mr. Hadfield. 'Also for your generosity in meeting my very limited resources.'

But Birkett did not get back to his holiday immediately. The firm of solicitors, in which his friend Dr. Leslie Burgin was a partner, took advantage of his presence in chambers during the Long Vacation to brief him in an urgent matter which came before the vacation judge in the King's Bench Division. This was an application on behalf of Warner Brothers, the American film company, for an interim injunction to restrain the actress, Miss Bette Davis, who was under contract with this company, from acting under any other management in breach of her contract with Warner Brothers. Miss Davis had recently come to England from the United States and repudiated her contract in a letter and had accepted an offer from another producer. In the ordinary course, Sir Patrick Hastings would have appeared for Warner Brothers, as he had a general retainer for them, but he was abroad and unable to return in time for the *ex parte* hearing. Birkett was accordingly instructed to appear instead, which he did, with the result that an interim injunction was granted pending the trial of the action, which was set down for hearing early in the following term. The solicitors assumed that in the circumstances Birkett would lead for the plaintiff company at the trial, and they were both somewhat surprised when Sir Patrick Hastings returned from his holiday and insisted on exercising his rights under the retainer, which could hardly be denied to a former Law Officer of the Crown. But Birkett received a brief as well; hence the unusual scene of his having his frequent opponent in the

[1] *Daily Telegraph*, September 25, 26, 1936.

courts as his 'leader' at the trial, a combination which had only once before occurred during his career at the Bar.

The hearing of the action of *Warner Brothers* v. *Nelson*—Miss Davis was sued under her married name—before Mr. Justice Branson calls for little comment, since Birkett was in effect a silent spectator of the proceedings which were entirely conducted by Hastings for the plaintiffs. The result of the case, which has since become a leading one in the law of contract, was that Miss Davis was restrained from giving her services to any other film or stage production for the next three years without the plaintiff's written consent, or during the currency of her contract with Warner Brothers, whichever period should be the shorter. It was also a case of very great importance to the film industry, since Miss Davis's contract was common form. 'If I had won,' she declared afterwards, 'lots of people would just walk out, as seventy-five per cent. of Hollywood contracts were like mine.'[1]

6

In October, 1936, Birkett was instructed to appear for the petitioner in an undefended divorce case. It was not an ordinary undefended case, although at first sight it might have appeared so, at least to the uninitiated who did not detect any particular significance about the cause of *Simpson* v. *Simpson*, which figured in the divorce list in the relatively obscure court of an English county town. However, the petitioner was Mrs. Wallis Simpson, the American wife of Mr. Ernest Simpson, former Guards officer and member of a shipping firm in the City, whom she now wished to divorce so that she could marry King Edward VIII.

Before the case came on, Birkett was summoned to a consultation at Fort Belvedere, the King's bachelor residence in Windsor Great Park. This was attended by the King and Mrs. Simpson and their legal advisers, Mr. Walter Monckton, K.C., Attorney-General to the Duchy of Cornwall, and Mr. George Allen, the King's solicitor, in addition to Birkett and Mr. Walter Frampton who had been briefed as the junior counsel in the case. Here Birkett, who in com-

[1] For a detailed account of this interesting case, see Hyde, *Sir Patrick Hastings*, pp. 312–17. The case has been reported in the Law Reports, *Warner Bros.* v. *Nelson* [1937] 1 K.B. 209.

mon with other newspaper readers had known of the King's growing friendship with Mrs. Simpson from photographs taken during their yachting cruise to Greece in the summer but had not realized its full implications, now learned the real significance of this friendship.

'Are you quite *sure*, Mrs. Simpson, that you want a divorce?' the King's solicitor asked her. Yes, she was, she said, and what is more had already filed her petition on the ground of her husband's misconduct with another woman. Indeed, she had written him the following letter from their London home.

> Dear Ernest,
>
> I have just learned that while you have been away, instead of being on business as you led me to believe, you have been staying at a hotel at Bray with a lady.
>
> I am sure you realize that is conduct which I cannot possibly overlook and I must insist that you do not continue to live here with me.
>
> This only confirms suspicions which I have had for a long time. I am therefore instructing my solicitors to take proceedings for divorce.
>
> WALLIS

Incidentally, the fact of her husband's infidelity had become known to Mrs. Simpson through what she was to describe as 'one of those coincidences that are stranger than fiction—a letter meant for Ernest that was inadvertently misaddressed to me.'[1] When he heard from his wife, Mr. Simpson complied with her request and moved out of their home in Bryanston Square to the Guards' Club.

In the normal course, since Mrs. Simpson lived in London, the case would have been heard in the Divorce Division of the High Court. The decision to bring it on in a small provincial town was not due to any desire on the part of the petitioner to avoid publicity, as has often been incorrectly stated, but simply because the lists in London were full up for a year or more, and Mrs. Simpson, not to mention the King himself, was anxious to have the matter disposed of before the Coronation, which had been fixed for the following June. Her solicitor, Mr. Theodore Goddard, thereupon discussed

[1] Duchess of Windsor. *The Heart Has Its Reasons* (1956), at p. 223.

with his partner, Mr. John Stenson, what Assize town reasonably near London would be most suitable in view of the time factor and the judges' circuit engagements. The choice lay between Reading on the Oxford Circuit and Ipswich on the South-Eastern, and eventually Ipswich was decided upon. For this purpose, it was necessary that Mrs. Simpson should acquire a local residence in order to come within the Assize Court's jurisdiction, and a house was conveniently discovered for her at the nearby seaside resort of Felixstowe, where she was reluctantly obliged to spend the weeks immediately preceding the hearing.

In the middle of October it became publicly known that the case had been set down for hearing in the undefended list at Ipswich towards the end of the month. Although the matter was briefly and most discreetly alluded to in the British press, largely at the instigation of the press lords, Beaverbrook and Rothermere, no such reticence was observed in some continental and American newspapers, where it was openly said that as soon as the divorce proceedings had gone through Mrs. Simpson would marry the King, thus becoming Queen. It was also pointed out that Mrs. Simpson had been previously divorced and that her first husband, an American, was still alive.

The Prime Minister, Mr. Stanley Baldwin, now sought an audience of the King, whom he saw at ten o'clock in the morning of October 20 at Fort Belvedere. Fortifying himself with a stiff whisky and soda, the Prime Minister produced a number of letters from various sources deprecating His Majesty's association with Mrs. Simpson and having pointed out the danger in which it seemed to him that the Monarchy stood because of this association and public feeling throughout the Empire, he begged the King to persuade her to withdraw her divorce petition. But that, said the King, is something he would not do, and he made it quite clear to his Prime Minister that he had no right to interfere with the affairs of an individual. The case must go forward, he said.

Thus it happened that one week later Birkett travelled down to Ipswich with his junior, Mr. Walter Frampton, to represent a lay client whose divorce was to form the prelude to an unprecedented constitutional crisis, which in turn was to lead to the King's abdication and his exile as Duke of Windsor. Special precautions were taken by the local police to control the admission of spectators, and none was allowed into the gallery facing Mrs. Simpson, only a handful being accommodated in the seats behind her. This arrangement, added to the general air of tense expectation and excitement in the court room, somewhat puzzled the judge, Mr. Justice Hawke, who observed irritably, as Birkett got up to address the court, 'How did the case come here?' After some whispers from the Clerk of Assize, the judge was heard to reply, 'Yes, yes, I see,' but he did not attempt to conceal his hostility when Mrs. Simpson went into the witness box. There she answered the few questions her counsel was obliged to put to her, with an understandable nervousness.

She said that she and her husband were married at Chelsea register office in 1928 and afterwards lived at addresses in Berkeley Street and Bryanston Court in London, W.1. There were no children of the marriage. Her case was that she lived happily with her husband until the autumn of 1935, when there was a change in his manner towards her. According to Mrs. Simpson, he became indifferent to her and stayed away at week-ends. She eventually consulted her solicitors, wrote the letter to her husband which has been quoted above and which Birkett now read out in court, and she subsequently received information upon which the petition was based. Evidence was also given by two waiters and the hall porter at the Hotel de Paris in Bray. The name of the woman concerned was not disclosed in open court.

'Well,' said Mr. Justice Hawke, when he had heard this recitation, 'I suppose I must come to the conclusion that there was adultery in this case.'

'I assume that is what your Lordship has in mind,' said Birkett.

Suddenly the judge's bored expression changed to one of palpable annoyance. 'How do you know what is in my mind?" he asked. 'What is it I have in my mind, Mr. Birkett?'

'I think, with great deference,' replied Birkett quietly, 'that your Lordship may have in mind what is known as "ordinary hotel evidence", where the name of the lady is not disclosed. I thought that might have been in your Lordship's mind.'

Again the judge's demeanour changed, as he became amenable to counsel's suggestion. 'That is what it must have been, Mr. Birkett. I am glad of your help.'

'The lady's name was mentioned in the petition, my Lord,'

continued Birkett, 'so now I ask for a decree nisi with costs against the respondent.'

'Yes, costs against the respondent, I am afraid,' the judge agreed with obvious reluctance and after some hesitation. 'I suppose I must in these unusual circumstances. So you may have it, with costs.'

'Decree nisi with costs?' Birkett repeated, to make sure.

'Yes, I suppose so,' said Mr. Justice Hawke.

Birkett escorted his client to her car, a chauffeur-driven Buick saloon belonging to the King, and while the police threw a cordon across the road to allow the car to get clear of curious press photographers and reporters, Mrs. Simpson hastened back to her new London house in Cumberland Terrace.

The rest of the story, culminating in the King's abdication, farewell broadcast, and departure as the Duke of Windsor to stay with Baron Eugene de Rothschild in Austria until Mrs. Simpson's divorce decree became absolute and they were free to get married, belongs to history and as such has no place in this book.

For Birkett Mrs. Simpson's divorce had a touching epilogue. He spent part of the ensuing Christmas Vacation at the Branksome Tower Hotel in Bournemouth, where he and his wife saw the New Year in together. A few nights later he was summoned to the telephone to hear a familiar voice thanking him for his successful efforts as counsel in helping Mrs. Simpson to obtain her freedom. 'I spoke to the Duke of Windsor in Austria last night from here and it was as clear as a local call,' Birkett wrote to his cousin Henry. 'It was strange to hear the voice that spoke to millions the other night just speaking to me. He was amusing about the Archbishops! I must tell you all about it sometime, but of course it is all *very private*. . . .'

7

With the exception of 1931, the year of economic crisis and depression, when his income from the Bar fell to a little below £19,000, Birkett's professional earnings averaged between £20,000 and £30,000 annually during the nineteen-thirties, even if his investments in the stock market did not invariably turn out to his satisfaction. But there were always other consolations. 'This year has been one of my best at the Bar, though I have lost many thousands in the slump in the Stock Exchange,' he wrote to his cousin at the end of 1937. 'I was made Master of my Worshipful Company [of Curriers], Sole Delegate [of the English Bar] to [the] Canad[i]a[n Bar Association], Chairman of the Inter-Departmental Committee on Abortion, J[ustice of the] P[eace] for Buckingham with a view to becoming Chairman of Quarter Sessions, and a few other things so it was a rich year. But Love and Friendship are still the greatest things, and I prize them more and more as Life advances.'

Four of the cases call for brief mention. In February, 1937, at Lincoln Assizes, he defended Mrs. Dora Teesdale, the twenty-eight-year-old wife of a butcher in Scunthorpe, on a charge of murdering her husband by shooting him with a revolver. Theirs was not a very happy marriage, since it appeared there were frequent quarrels owing to the husband's habit of staying out late at night and his liking for the company of other women. On the occasion which led to the fatality, he had stayed out the whole night, and on his refusing to say where he had been when they met at breakfast the following morning, Mrs. Teesdale threatened him with a revolver, which was kept in the house, in order, so she said, to make him tell. She did not think the gun was loaded and in fact he told her that there were only blanks in it at the time. But it did contain live cartridges and it went off, killing him. 'I had fired it off to the side of him,' she said afterwards in the witness box. 'I thought it would go between him and the table. I did not think it would do any harm as they were only blanks.'

'When you are dealing with the important question of intent,' Birkett told the jury, 'consider her attitude in the box. There was no venom. It was plain she never intended to do the slightest hurt or smallest harm to her husband. The atmosphere of that room was not threatening. The deceased man did say, "You cannot hurt me. They are only blanks." She did believe it.'

On the other hand, the prosecution argued that, on her own statement, the act of the accused was at least manslaughter, since there was no sense or meaning in firing the gun if she only intended to scare her husband and she thought they were blank cartridges. And this view was strongly supported by the trial judge, Mr. Justice Humphreys, in his summing up, who said there could not be the smallest question that Mrs. Teesdale had killed her husband unlawfully and instructed the jury in the clearest possible language that it would be wrong for them to find a verdict of Not Guilty because they felt sorry for a woman who had a very good case for a divorce or a separation from her husband. 'I tell you quite frankly that, in my opinion as a lawyer,' said the judge, 'I cannot understand how you can fail to say that this woman is guilty of manslaughter.'

Notwithstanding this admonition, the jury accepted Birkett's view, and acquitted Mrs. Teesdale both of murder and manslaughter, much to the disgust of the judge, who seemed to be surprised that there was no other charge against her. The only possible charge was being in unlawful possession of a firearm, but no doubt the police were satisfied that the weapon belonged to her husband and not to her. The acquittal, however, remained one of Birkett's most spectacular triumphs, secured as it was in the face of a deadly summing up against the prisoner by one of the most experienced criminal judges in the country.

In the same month, Birkett appeared for Baron Victor de Stempel in a long drawn out civil action brought by the Baron, a Russian aristocrat and naturalized British subject, against his wife's stepfather, Mr. Walter Dunkels. The Baron had been employed by a firm of diamond brokers controlled by the defendant's cousin, Mr. Otto Dunkels, and following on matrimonial differences between the Baron and his wife, he complained that the defendant had slandered him to his cousin, saying that 'Victor is a Jew hater' and was unfit to be employed in the business, and had thus procured his dismissal.

When the alleged slander was put to him by Birkett in cross-examination, Mr. Otto Dunkels said that it might be 'a plausible statement of a comment by a Russian aristocrat', but he did not believe it. 'I think that the Baron's views were the same as mine,' added the witness, '—that there are good Jews and bad Jews, just as there are good Christians and bad Christians.' At which Mr. Justice Swift characteristically observed from the Bench: 'No particular race has a monopoly of virtue.'

The jury found for Birkett's client, awarding him £200 damages for the slander and £6,000 for procuring the alleged breach of contract. But the judge held that the slander was not actionable without proof of special damage (of which no evidence had been offered), since the words complained of had nothing to do with the Baron's fitness for his job of buying and selling diamonds or his financial stability as a trader. But he got his £6,000 on the other claim. In this his self-confidence was rewarded since in the course of the case the defendant had offered to settle for a much smaller sum, which the Baron had refused saying he wanted £5,000 and this in turn had been refused by Birkett's client.[1]

An action of a more light-hearted nature was *Plumb* v. *Jeyes Sanitary Compounds Co. Ltd.*, in which a retired police constable, who had been photographed on point duty in the act of removing his helmet and mopping his brow, sued the defendant company for libelling him by publishing the photograph as an advertisement for their product, with the following caption: 'Phew! I am going to get my feet into a Jeyes' Fluid footbath.' The plaintiff who had been much twitted by his friends and others who recognized him in the picture, resented the implication that his feet were malodorous. Birkett appeared for the Jeyes' Fluid company.

'Do you seriously suggest,' Birkett asked the plaintiff in cross-examination, 'that anybody looking at this advertisement would say that you had got bad feet?'

'Yes,' replied the outraged Mr. Plumb. 'The advertisement for Jeyes' says it is good for feet or smelling feet.'

'Is anybody going to think the penny the worse of you because you have a foot-bath?'

'No, but this is associated with disinfectant. I would use a foot-bath because my feet ached and not because they were smelly.' He added that the advertisement had led to jokes which made him angry and 'caused bad feeling in the family'.

Addressing the jury for the defendants, Birkett said he had heard of families being broken up for many reasons, but never by Jeyes' Fluid.

A sense of humour does not seem to have been Mr. Plumb's strong point, a fact which was probably not lost on the jury. They found for the plaintiff, but they considered that his wounded feelings were only worth £100 damages. But Mr. Plumb got his costs, as well as some further publicity, which can have given him little pleasure.

In the same year Birkett prosecuted in what was to be the last murder trial in which he appeared for the Crown. This was the case of a ten-year-old schoolgirl, Mona Tinsley, who was abducted by a motor mechanic named Frederick Nodder after leaving the Wesleyan School in Newark, on a stormy afternoon in January. Nodder was first tried at the Warwick Winter Assizes in Birmingham on the abduction charge, in which Birkett also prosecuted, when he was

[1] *De Stempel* v. *Dunkels. The Times*, February 5, 6, 11, 12, 13, 24, 25, 26, 1937.

convicted and sentenced to seven years penal servitude by Mr. Justice Swift. While he was in custody, Mona Tinsley's body was recovered from the River Idle, where it had been dumped after Nodder had strangled her, having also apparently raped her. Nodder was brought up later in the year on the murder charge before Mr. Justice Macnaughton at Nottingham Assizes. He was again convicted and this time sentenced to death. He appealed, but his appeal was dismissed, the Home Secretary refused to reprieve him and he was duly executed.[1]

In May, 1937, Birkett was appointed Chairman of the Inter-Departmental Committee for Abortion, which was set up by the Home Secretary and the Minister of Health 'to enquire into the prevalence of abortion, and the law relating thereto, and to consider what steps can be taken by more effective enforcement of the law or otherwise to secure the reduction of maternal mortality and morbidity arising from this cause.' It was a mixed committee, consisting of fifteen members in addition to the Chairman and included Mrs. Baldwin, the Prime Minister's wife, Sir Rollo Graham-Campbell, the chief metropolitan magistrate, and Mr. Bentley Purchase, the London coroner. During the next two years, in the course of which the Committee had forty-seven meetings and examined fifty-five witnesses, Birkett put in a lot of hard work on the subject, besides writing most of the eventual report.[2]

[1] See Winifred Duke. *The Trials of Frederick Nodder* (1950).

[2] Ministry of Health. Home Office. *Report of the Inter-Departmental Committee on Abortion* (1939). 'The induction of abortion is on ethical, social and medical grounds essentially an undesirable operation, justifiable only in exceptional circumstances, and the Committee is strongly opposed to any broad relaxation of the law designed to make social, economic, and personal reasons a justification for the operation' (p. 123). At the same time, the Committee recommended that the law should be amended 'to make it unmistakably clear that a medical practitioner is acting legally, when in good faith he procures the abortion of a pregnant woman in circumstances which satisfy him that continuance of the pregnancy is likely to endanger her life or seriously impair her health.' It was also recommended that 'full opportunity of obtaining the most reliable contraceptive advice ought to be made available by Local Authorities to every married woman to whose health pregnancy would be detrimental, and the medical grounds should not be limited by too narrow an interpretation' (p. 122).

Mrs. Dorothy Thurtle, a member of the Committee who considered that these proposals did not go far enough, submitted a minority report, with which Birkett had some sympathy, as he subsequently wrote a Foreword to Mrs. Thurtle's book, *Abortion Right or Wrong* (1940), in which her recommendations were expanded. She favoured abortion in cases of (i) women who have had four pregnancies; (ii) rape, unlawful carnal knowledge, and incest; and (iii) mental and physical defectives.

He had originally intended to spend most of the Long Vacation working on this project, but his work was interrupted when he was invited to represent the English Bar at the annual meeting of the Canadian Bar Association, which was held at Toronto in August. On his arrival, he found that his fame had preceded him as Mrs. Simpson's counsel, but he resolutely refused to be drawn on this case. 'Not a word, not a word,' he told reporters wherever he went. But he did allow himself a comment on the recent Matrimonial Causes Act, which had placed wives on the same footing as husbands in divorce proceedings in England, besides extending the grounds to desertion. 'Frankly, I believe the reform of the British divorce law is a step in the right direction,' he admitted, adding that many people believed the reform should have gone further. But, in deference to the possible susceptibilities of his hosts, he did not say whether he included himself in this number. In Ottawa he delivered an address to the Canadian Club on the administration of criminal justice in England.

Birkett had hoped to be accompanied by his wife, but the illness of one of their children kept her at home. However, she was able to join him for the latter part of the visit, and they were able to see something of the country, including the scenic beauties of the Rockies. With characteristic hospitality the Canadians gave them free hotel accommodation and free passes on the railways.

But both Birkett and his wife seem to have gone down well wherever they went. 'What I like about Birkett,' the Chief Justice of Manitoba said of him in Winnipeg, 'is that he looks like a Canadian.' Retailing this remark afterwards to the Canada Club in Ottawa, Birkett caused some hilarity by commenting, 'I appreciate that, whether you do or not.'

In January, 1938, Mr. Justice Finlay, who was to have gone on the Midland Circuit, was unable to set out on the appointed date, as he was presiding over the Railway and Canal Commission in London, and it consequently became necessary to appoint a Commissioner of Assize to take the judge's place. By this time Birkett had become the circuit leader, and so the Lord Chancellor invited him to act as Commissioner, which he agreed to do. The first assize on the circuit was held at Aylesbury, near his home. Wearing his King's Counsel robes and full bottomed wig, he was attended by trumpeters, and all the customary ceremonial associated with the opening of an Assize;

he carried an Assize judge's three-cornered hat, white kid gloves and black cap, as he solemnly walked in procession from St. Mary's Church to the court house.

On the first day, he tried ten cases, one of which concerned a young insurance agent who was convicted of embezzling sixty pounds. 'I want you to regard today as a landmark when clemency was extended to you,' said Birkett to the young man when he came up for sentencing. The prisoner, who expected a term of imprisonment was so surprised when Birkett bound him over for two years that he fainted in the dock. But the Commissioner showed that he could be stern when he felt that the occasion called for more severe punishment. To a woman at the next Assize town, Northampton, who had pleaded guilty to two particularly bad charges of bigamy, having deserted her husband and four children, he said that bigamy in whatever circumstances must always remain a serious offence, having regard to the desirability of maintaining the marriage laws. 'I find the greatest desire in the world to be as lenient as possible,' he added. 'But I really cannot overlook the two offences to which you have pleaded guilty.' Accordingly he sentenced her to six months imprisonment on each of the counts, the sentences to run concurrently.

By the time the Commissioner reached Leicester, Mr. Justice Finlay had finished his work in London and was able to take over for the remainder of the circuit. Here Birkett was able to accept a brief to lead the defence in a murder trial, where the accused, a seventeen-year-old youth named Owen Meakin, had applied for legal aid under the Poor Prisoner's Defence Act. Meakin, who had admitted striking his father two blows with a hatchet while he was asleep, said to the police when he was arrested, that he had acted purely for what he thought was best for his mother. In the witness box the mother said that her husband drank, had a violent temper and treated his son cruelly from the age of eight. As for her son, he was as good a son as any mother could wish to have. 'When I suffered, he suffered too,' she said. Thus, as Birkett put it in his speech to the jury, 'the home of this family—if it can be called a home—was one where misery, long-drawn, reigned day in and day out. It is impossible to measure the slow corrosion of the years, and I ask you to think as the head and front of this matter that the dead man was the author of that misery. Here is this boy, not yet eighteen, whose only fault was this overmastering love for his mother whom he believed to be in danger.'

The jury acquitted the boy of murder, but found him guilty of manslaughter, as in view of his admission they were bound at least to do. Mr. Justice Finlay sentenced him to twelve months imprisonment in the second division. Then, before dismissing the jury, the judge remarked that Birkett and his instructing solicitor had rendered a public service. 'I rejoice, and everyone must rejoice,' added Mr. Justice Finlay, 'at the tribute to English justice, that the accused, having no means, has been defended in such an admirable and skilful manner.'[1]

Several other cases in which Birkett figured prominently at this time call for similar brief reference. In February, 1938, he defended one of the so-called 'Mayfair playboys', who were charged with conspiracy and robbery with violence. All four defendants in this case had been educated at well-known English public schools and belonged to respectable families, but had drifted into a life of idleness and lived largely by their wits. One afternoon in the previous December they had combined to lure Mr. Etienne Bellenger of Cartier's, the well-known jewellery firm in Mayfair, to Room 305 at the Hyde Park Hotel on the pretext of buying some valuable rings. There the unfortunate jeweller, at a sign from Birkett's client, was brutally bludgeoned by one of the other conspirators, who had hidden in an adjoining room, receiving six fractures and nine jagged wounds about the head. Indeed had it not been for the fact that Mr. Bellenger possessed an unusually thick skull, he must have died from his injuries. There was little that Birkett could do for his client, nor could any extenuating circumstances be pleaded. He and his three companions were all convicted, two of them, including Birkett's client, being sentenced by the Lord Chief Justice to be flogged with the cat-o'-nine tails besides receiving long prison terms.

It was the only occasion in his judicial career that Lord Hewart ever passed a sentence of flogging, and Birkett found it difficult not to agree with the general opinion that it was well deserved in this case. To a well-connected woman, who protested to Lord Hewart at some social gathering against his action in ordering the 'cat' for public school boys, the Lord Chief Justice angrily exclaimed:

[1] *The Times*, January 31, 1938.

'Scoundrels, all of them! They are lucky. They might easily have been on a capital charge. The fact that they are public school boys makes their crime all the worse. They should have known better.'

Two months later, Birkett was again briefed at the Old Bailey, when he appeared for John Stanley Phillips, a theological student at Wycliffe Hall, Oxford, who was charged with the murder of Harold Mathews, the college pantry boy. The boy's mutilated body was found on the roof of Wycliffe Hall, and it was proved that while it was there Phillips had gone to Holy Communion. Birkett asked for a verdict of 'Guilty but insane', and this was accepted by the jury, with the result that Phillips was ordered to be detained indefinitely in a mental institution. In the following sessions, in May, he defended Mrs. Casserly, wife of Mr. Percy Casserly, director and secretary of John Watney & Co. Ltd., the London brewers, on the charge of being an accessory to her husband's murder by her lover, Edward Chaplin. Chaplin was convicted of manslaughter, but there was no evidence that Mrs. Casserley had had anything to do with her husband's death and she was discharged. Her case aroused a good deal of public sympathy because she was pregnant by Chaplin, but the presiding judge, Mr. Justice Humphreys, discounted this when he described her as simply a participator in a vulgar and sordid intrigue. Finally, in July, at Bow Street Police Court, Birkett represented Count Kurt Haugwitz-Reventlow on the summons taken out against him by his wife, formerly Miss Barbara Hutton, the Woolworth heiress, on the ground that he had threatened and intended to cause her bodily harm. Fortunately Birkett was able to convince the Countess's counsel, Sir Patrick Hastings, that whatever his client might have said in the heat of the moment he had not the slightest intention of harming his wife, and as a result the Countess withdrew the charge, but not before a lot of dirty linen had been publicly aired.

In this year, in which he figured in so many squalid criminal cases, it was a relief and pleasure to Birkett when he was invited to propose the toast of 'The Immortal Memory of William Shakespeare' at the Shakespeare Birthday Luncheon at Stratford-upon-Avon on April 23rd. In his speech he emphasized that the bard was thought of as not only belonging to the world but also as a great Englishman and a most devoted lover of his native land. 'And today we think of him in that capacity,' he said, quoting *King Richard II* and *King Henry V*, when we remember:

> This precious stone set in the silver sea . . .
> This land of such dear souls, this dear, dear land.

And that immortal phrase when men were bound together, in the face of danger, into a common allegiance:

> We few, we happy few, we band of brothers.'[1]

Birkett was to recall these words when, less than eighteen months later, Britain and Europe were faced with another common danger, and he was called to play his part in meeting it.

8

The last case, in which Birkett's name made newspaper headlines before the outbreak of the Second World War, was one where, oddly enough, a woman litigant, who had achieved quite a reputation for conducting her cases in person, seemingly got the better of the distinguished King's Counsel in the witness box. Mrs. Elsie Borders and her husband, James Walter Borders, a taxi driver, wished to move from Brixton to the more salubrious air of the country. They bought a house on mortgage at West Wickham in Kent, but unfortunately they got into the hands of speculative builders who erect 'jerry built' property and make glowing representations about the material and workmanship. Mr. and Mrs. Borders found that the house showed a number of unexpected faults: cracks appeared in the ceilings, floors squeaked and plaster began to fall, and they consequently withheld the mortgage payments due to the building society concerned. The enterprising Mrs. Borders then formed a federation of tenants and tenants' associations, studied law in her spare time at the London School of Economics and began a campaign against the building societies, which she considered were in league with the speculative builders.

When her own building society brought an action against her for defaulting on the mortgage payments, she defended the action in person to save the expense of engaging a lawyer, and at the same time

[1] This speech was recorded at the time by the British Broadcasting Corporation, and part of it has been included in a record of Birkett's speeches made by the Decca Record Co. Ltd. (No. LXT. 6032).

she counter-claimed for £500, alleging misrepresentation on the value of the house. The judge dismissed both actions, which meant that, although she had lost on her counter-claim she was left with a clear title to the house. Soon some five hundred tenants deliberately defaulted, and Mrs. Borders became popularly known as 'The Tenants' K.C.'

Mr. James Borders now brought an action against solicitors to the building society, who, he alleged, had libelled him in a letter to the society when they wrote that the plaintiff was 'definitely a bad egg' and that 'no rope whatever should be given' to him as a borrower. At the trial Mrs. Borders gave evidence in support of her husband's claim.

'You are getting quite used to litigation?' Birkett, who was appearing for the solicitors, asked her in cross-examination.

'This is the first time I have had the pleasure of meeting you, Mr. Birkett,' replied Mrs. Borders.

'You have acquired the title of the "Tenants' K.C.".'

'I have heard of it.'

'All the world knows of it?'

'Thank you.'

'We'll forget the Tenants' K.C. You are a woman of strong, independent mind?'

'I would rather let the world say as to that.'

'You have a head for these things?'

'I have a head for many things.'

'A business head?' queried Birkett.

'I have always considered myself merely as a housewife,' retorted Mrs. Borders. Then, she added, to the accompaniment of roars of laughter: 'There may not be any difference between Mr. and Mrs. Birkett, but there is a difference between Mr. and Mrs. Borders!'

The laughter which this reply produced in court visibly annoyed Birkett, who rejoined sharply, 'Do you think it smart to introduce the name of my wife?'

'No,' said Mrs. Borders blandly. 'You were suggesting a particular relationship between husband and wife and I was trying to explain it.'

For the defence Birkett pleaded that the letter was privileged, as it was written by a firm of solicitors to their clients. But the jury found there was some evidence of malice, sufficient in fact to rebut the defence, and awarded Mr. Borders £150 damages. Birkett bore the redoubtable Mrs. Borders no ill-feeling for her behaviour in the witness box which admittedly carried the jury with her in her husband's favour.

A few weeks after war broke out, in September, 1939, Sir John Anderson, Home Secretary in the Chamberlain Government, invited Birkett to become Chairman of the Home Office Advisory Committee on appeals from internment orders made by the Minister under Regulation 18B of the Emergency Powers Act, which authorized him to detain persons without trial in the interests of national security. This involved all enemy aliens as well as persons of suspected Nazi and Fascist sympathies. The Committee sat in a room put at their disposal by the Civil Service Commissioners in their offices in Burlington Gardens in London, and during the next two years it examined and reported upon more than 1,500 cases.[1]

To Henry Birkett

Challens Green, October 13, 1939 . . I made my last appearance in the Courts today for some time, if not for always, because on Monday I begin my new work for the Home Secretary dealing with hundreds of appeals from Orders of Internment, British and foreign. I shall sit every day and the work will last for many months: and if it ever ends, a new job I expect will be given me. I get no remuneration and my princely income at the Bar ceases! Can you spare a dime?

The work is important of course, for on the decision the freedom or imprisonment of the individual depends: and it is fascinatingly interesting with the Secret Service at its best. . . .

There is a terrible grim satisfaction in thinking that Hitler is being faced at last and that his long cruel reign is likely to be over. Thousands in Germany I am sure and millions in the world live for the day when the Hitler gang is destroyed. But it is going to be a long and heart-breaking struggle: and the happy world will take many years to bring.

[1] See speech by Mr. Herbert Morrison in the House of Commons, November 26, 1941. The other members of the Committee were Sir Arthur Hazlerigg, later Lord Hazlerigg; Sir George Clerk, a retired diplomat; Professor W. E. Collinson, Professor of German in Liverpool University; Dr. J. J. Mallon, Warden of Toynbee Hall; and Miss Violet Malcolm.

But his enthusiasm for the Secret Service, as he called the Security Service, began to wane as his work increased.

> *Challens Green, December* 25 . . . You will have had your usual happy Christmas dispensing good cheer to all and sundry. We have had a quiet but blissfully happy time with the great shadow fended off for a few hours. The trouble about life at the moment is that there is nothing to look forward to: and in place of the usual expectations the thought of loss and disaster to thousands of simple folk.
>
> I resume my rather thankless task on January 2nd. I say thankless because M.I. 5 of the Secret Service want everybody interned, whilst I cannot bring myself to send some simple German girl for years of detention, when I am quite satisfied that she has been in the country in some household for years and is not the slightest danger to anybody.
>
> So we keep some small element of Justice alive in a world in which we are supposed to be fighting for it. . . .

'I miss my work at the Bar and the income,' he noted on the day he resumed his task in Burlington Gardens; 'but, if I am really doing some useful war work, I am content, for I have no relish for making money when so many are making supreme sacrifices. I have won the esteem of all my colleagues, evidenced by their letters to me at Christmas, and that is very gratifying.' But he hated going back to his flat each evening in the 'black out' which he found 'quite a nightmare'. ('It is an inconceivable world when people have to hide themselves lest fellow human beings should destroy them from the skies.')

He stayed in London for the first Saturday of the New Year in order to lunch with the Curriers Company and to see the company's former Master, Lord Hewart.

After lunch, Birkett wrote in the diary which he began to keep intermittently at this time:

> I attended my first Court of the Curriers Company at the Cordwainers Hall in Cannon Street since my recent election to the Court of Assistants. My membership of this Company has been a very great joy to me. I was elected Master in the year of the Coronation, after only 10 years in the Livery. My loving

London Express Pictures

MRS. ERNEST SIMPSON WITH HER HUSBAND AND AUNT, MRS. MERRYMAN

Bedfordshire Times

AT BEDFORD ASSIZES, 1943

> cups, which I presented bearing the 'We Band of Brothers', expresses what I feel.
>
> The Lord Chief Justice sat next to me at lunch. I proposed his health, for he will be 70 on Sunday next. . . .

A few days later, Birkett was invited to lunch with Sir Stephen Tallents, at that time Public Relations Controller in the B.B.C. The purpose of this meeting was to ask him if he would undertake to deliver a weekly broadcast talk after the 'News' each Friday evening by way of answering the German propaganda talks which were being broadcast from Hamburg by 'Lord Haw-Haw' (William Joyce) and which were known to reach a wide listening audience in Britain. Birkett willingly agreed. He broadcast his first talk on February 9, 1940, under the pseudonym, 'Onlooker'. However, it was not long before his anonymity, on which the B.B.C. somewhat foolishly insisted, was discovered, just as that of 'Lord Haw-Haw' was also; Birkett's voice was soon recognized by his friends in the Temple. He continued to give his weekly talks until the fall of France, when the B.B.C. decided to replace him by Mr. J. B. Priestley. Only once was he unable to get to Broadcasting House, when he was ill, but the B.B.C. obligingly installed a microphone by his bedside in Challens Green.

That the talks were an excellent booster for morale on the home front during the waiting period of the 'phoney war', with their quiet confidential fireside manner, was generally acknowledged. Of course, they had to conform to the policy directive of the Ministry of Information which was designed, mistakenly in the light of subsequent events, to drive a wedge between the German people and their leaders. 'So long as the war lasts it is conducted by the German people under their leaders, and must be met by all our resources without distinction of leaders or people,' he said in one talk. 'But if the belief is well founded that there are millions in Germany who long for release—who desire the peaceful way of living—the future, then, is not without hope. Of this, at any rate, there can be no doubt; there can be no enduring peace so long as the 'wicked men' and the Nazi Party are there. None. But once they are removed, and their evil doctrines destroyed, I for one like to think there would come a great release of spirit amongst millions of Germans, who would turn to their new world with hope—that oldest and wisest of counsellors—that hope which for so long has been denied them.'

Meanwhile Birkett continued to plod on with his work with the Home Office Advisory Committee, sitting throughout the Battle of Britain and the subsequent 'blitz', which incidentally destroyed his chambers in the Temple. In October, 1940, Lord Hewart retired, his place as Lord Chief Justice being taken by Lord Caldecote, formerly Sir Thomas Inskip, and there were some other judicial vacancies. Birkett's work was considered to be too important for him to be released, even to go on the Bench. Yet he was becoming increasingly dissatisfied with his work. At Christmas, he wrote: 'I have not earned a penny since October, 1939. I am glad I was taught the virtue of saving when I was young, because I followed it in all the big years so that Life can still go on. But it is interesting to recall in these days when I am earning nothing that once I earned £4,200 in a day and never opened my mouth. That kind of thing might have made me careless! But the work I do now, though very important, is beset with frustration, and I am very far from happy in it. The delays are grievous and many people are in prison this Christmas who have been there since last May without any trial or reasons given for their detention. I suffer in spirit daily.'

The eighteen months of unpaid work which Birkett put in on the Home Office Committee as well as his 'Onlooker' broadcasts were recognized in the next King's Birthday Honours List, when Mr. Winston Churchill, who had now become Prime Minister, submitted his name for a knighthood. The official announcement was made after Birkett had been consulted, and had intimated that he was willing to accept the honour. Of the hundreds of letters of congratulation which he received he kept one in particular, which came from Mr. Brendan Bracken, the Prime Minister's Private Secretary and an old personal friend.

10 *Downing Street*, *S.W.*1
13*th June*, 1941

Dear Norman,

There are Knights and Knights. In the roll of Knighthood perhaps the most chivalrous and heroic figure was Sir Philip Sidney. He had the lovely gift of courtesy, unselfishness, and devotion to his country. If I were told to find someone like him in our generation, I should unhesitatingly fix upon Norman Birkett.

> Sidney was a soldier, and you are a lawyer. You may say, how can you compare such men? The answer is that you, like Sidney, are a fighter. You have fought for good causes all the days of your life and, like Sidney, you have never failed in loyalty. Bless you.
>
> I was with my Master when the Honours List was settled. He was greatly pleased to submit your name to His Majesty.
>
> BRENDAN BRACKEN

Three weeks later, he attended at Buckingham Palace with his wife to receive the customary accolade at the hands of King George VI.

'I miss more than I can say the old companionship and excitements of the Bar,' he told another friend, who had written to congratulate him on becoming Sir Norman Birkett. 'For two years I have been away from it all, and the work on which I am engaged, though very important, is dull in comparison. What the future holds no man can say, but we must keep hope and resolution alive and, when the menace which covers the world is removed, we can be happy still, I am sure.'

Later the same year he paid his first visit to the United States, when he represented the English Bar at the annual meeting of the American Bar Association at Indianapolis. 'Your visit is a demonstration of the fellowship, understanding and essential unity of English and American lawyers,' Mr. Walter P. Armstrong, the President of the Association, cabled him in a farewell message. 'You have earned the respect, admiration and affectionate regard of all the members of our Association who saw or heard you. Our hearts are with you and your brethren of the Bar in this the time of their ordeal.'

He was also the guest of the Canadian Bar Association at their meeting in Toronto, where he was able to renew his previous acquaintance. The Canadian President, Mr. D. L. McCarthy, wrote to the English Lord Chancellor, Lord Simon, as Birkett's old friend and colleague had become: 'I want to bear witness to the tremendous success of Sir Norman's visit. His great powers as a speaker, his kindly disposition, and his friendliness, won everyone with whom he came in contact. He was called upon to fulfil numerous engagements of a varied character—he spoke to the boys at Upper Canada College,

Toronto, where a great many English boys are now being looked after and educated; he addressed our young lawyers that I was calling to the Bar in a most memorable address; he spoke at different clubs and organizations—in fact, he never spared himself, and the demands on his time were given willingly and ungrudgingly, in spite of the terrific strain it was upon him. . . . From my conversations with American lawyers I know that he did a great deal to strengthen the tie that binds lawyers all over the world, and more particularly during the present crisis, and I think I can state without fear of contradiction that you did a very great deed, under present conditions, in allowing Sir Norman to come as the representative of the English Bar, both to Canada and the United States, at this very critical time.'

On November 3, 1941, shortly after Birkett's return from America, the Lord Chancellor wrote to him, asking whether he might submit his name to the King to fill the vacancy among the King's Bench Judges caused by the death of Mr. Justice Hawke. 'It will be a very splendid satisfaction to me,' Lord Simon added, 'if I may add your name to the list of members of the High Court of Justice.'

'Edgar,' said Birkett to his clerk on the morning he got the Lord Chancellor's letter, 'I have been asked by Lord Simon to take a judgeship. In fact, it has been more or less put to me that it is my public duty to become one of His Majesty's judges.' Then, after a pause, he added rather wistfully, 'I am afraid this will mean the parting of the ways,' for he felt that he could not in all conscience ask Edgar Bowker to make the financial sacrifice involved in becoming a judge's clerk. He did not attempt to conceal his pleasure and gratitude when Bowker said, 'I'd like to stay with you, sir.'

After a day's reflection, Birkett decided that in the circumstances he must accept the Lord Chancellor's offer. As soon as he heard the news, Lord Simon wrote to Lady Birkett: 'My wife and I would like to send you a line about this great decision of Norman's today. I am very happy to have a hand in it, not only because of my admiration and friendship, but because the new career will give him the scope he needs. You know my wife's saying that until "human" and "humane" mean the same thing, the world will not be civilized. Norman will help to that, and now he is going to help not only clients but the whole community.'

A week later, Mr. Justice Birkett was sworn in at the House of Lords before the Lord Chancellor, promising that he would 'do right to all manner of people after the laws and usages of this Realm without fear or favour, affection or ill-will.'

The feelings of the Bar leaders had already been expressed by his old friend and professional adversary, Sir Patrick Hastings, who sent his good wishes, as did many others on this occasion.

> My dear Norman,
>
> I have just heard your news which makes me very sad. Never again to have the joyful battles for which I have been hoping for many a long day. However, for the sake of the Bench I am very glad. I know you will make a Judge of whom we shall all be proud, and above all one to whom we shall all be devoted, and amongst all those who may appear before you there will be none who will wish you greater happiness than
>
> Your devoted friend,
>
> PAT HASTINGS

Most of all, perhaps, he was touched by his faithful clerk's loyalty. 'Bowker has been *noble*,' he told a friend at the time. 'He has left the Bar after thirty-three years of work to take the salary of a Judge's Clerk in place of the larger fees he could easily earn. That is devotion I can never forget, and I am daily surrounded by such good will that indeed I am the most fortunate of men.'

CHAPTER XI

JUSTICE AT NUREMBERG

I

ON November 24, 1941, Mr. Justice Birkett took his seat for the first time as a judge of the High Court, in King's Bench Court VII in the Royal Courts of Justice. When the first case in the list was called, Mr. H. H. Maddocks, a junior counsel whom the new judge immediately recognized as the son of his old friend and leader on the Midland Circuit, Sir Henry Maddocks, rose and said, 'May I just say what a great pleasure it is for me personally to be engaged on the first case your Lordship has to try. I remember the kindness I have received from you over many years. My father always had a very great affection for your Lordship.'

After remarking that this was a 'delightful little irregularity', Birkett went on: 'I must say that I, too, remember your father with great affection. Your words are very acceptable to me, and I am very much obliged.' The judge then plunged straight into the business of trying the case which the young Mr. Maddocks proceeded to open, a prosaic action brought by a firm of valuers for its fees for work done.

At the end of his first week in court, his clerk wrote to Lady Birkett to tell her how the new judge had got on. 'Right up to standard' was Edgar Bowker's opinion, which echoed that of the Bar generally. 'Indeed he is going to set a very high standard. We have courtesy, dignity and patience, and I hear there is to be a scramble to get before him. Having watched them now for forty-three years and often wanted to get up and throw things at them, it is a great joy to be associated with the best appointment since Rufus Isaacs went up.'

But it was a wrench, and Birkett felt it keenly. 'I have a bruised feeling at the heart all the time I am away from the Bar,' he told his friend and former junior on the Midland Circuit, Richard Elwes, who was now in the army and had written to congratulate him. 'I realize now how much I loved it, the hopeless defences, the libels, the divorces, even the nullities. Opening War Weapons Week is a poor substitute!'

To Henry Birkett

> *Challens Green, December* 26, 1941. . . . I am beginning to settle down to the new life, and the exaggerated adulation with which a Judge is treated has no effect on me up to the present. 'M'Lord' means just nothing: and 'Norrie' means more, though I never hear it now!
>
> . . . I have quite enjoyed the work as a Judge in London during these last weeks because I am growing in confidence and getting accustomed to quelling the advocate in me.

In his youth, particularly when he was an undergraduate at Cambridge and afterwards when he was reading for the Bar, Birkett kept a diary. But he discontinued it when he began to practise, and during his twenty-eight years as a barrister he was too occupied to make even intermittent entries. But after his elevation to the Bench he decided to resume it. It is a most revealing document, and shows more than once how he yearned to go back to the Bar.

> 1 *January*, 1942. At home. Long past making Resolutions, but still think it would be good to keep a daily note, not only of events but of this changeful heart and temperament of mine.
>
> 2 *January*. Saw the Home Secretary at 10.30 about cases from 18B.
>
> Herbert Morrison always pleasant to me and has paid me some remarkable tributes in the House for which I am grateful.

Two days later, Birkett took the Canadian lawyer, Leonard Brockington, who was visiting England at this time as the personal representative of the Canadian Prime Minister, to lunch at Churt with the veteran Liberal leader, Lloyd George.

'L.G. said he didn't think I would take a judgeship,' Birkett noted. 'So many think this: but the letters of welcome I received were prodigious.'

5 *January*. . . . The 18B work has been arduous but worth while. This year will see three years of steady work; but nobody ever suggested I should do more important work in the war effort. . . .

Brockington told me that when he saw Beaverbrook, Beaverbrook said that he was sorry I had become a Judge, because he had such schemes of work for me: but they have never been hinted at before.

12 *January*. Term opened. Sat in Court. Judge's Meeting at 3.30. Profoundly depressed. Circuits selected. I go Leeds in spring and Liverpool and Manchester in summer.

17 *January*. Dreadful day of depression and illness. Filled with every kind of foreboding. Seemed that I had made the greatest mistake of my life in accepting Judgeship. All seemed dark.

20 *January*. Running down case. . . . Tried it well.

21 *January*. Gave judgment, but gave the girl only £650, when upon reflection I should have given £900.

This in my ill-state gave me profoundest depression and was the occasion of gloom and foreboding that I should fail as a Judge, after a glorious success as an advocate.

29 *January*. Went out to see Gordon Hewart at Totteridge. Found him very ill and he said he 'wished he was dead'. All this is very painful when one thinks of his great career of 18 years on the Bench as L.C.J. He has pernicious anaemia, and lacks all strength. . . .

Very much upset at seeing the poor 'Chief'. I have promised to see him again at Easter.

3 *February*. *Newcastle-upon-Tyne*. This is the first morning of my first Assize as a Judge. I have looked forward to it with very great trepidation. There are so many pitfalls. The question of sentences is always difficult. . . .

Opened both Commissions. Then heard pleas all day.

Found myself doing the work as to the manner born. All my cares and apprehensions dropped from me. Really believe that I did the work in first-class style. Most thankful in my heart....

4 *February*. Several pleas: then began hearing of my first trial, a motor manslaughter case. Listened to the evidence all day and left summing-up until Thursday morning. Comfortable day in Court. Must repress my tendency to be *too* genial, and make smart observations!

Much gratified to hear that I have been winning golden opinions for my conduct as a Judge. Spent the evening reviewing the evidence and looking up law for next day in a difficult manslaughter case of abortion. . . . Found myself telling [Mr. Justice] Hilbery how much better it was to be a Judge than at the Bar! *Me!*

5 *February*. My first summing-up. It was the motor manslaughter. I was quite pleased with the effort, and the Lord Mayor thought it very good indeed. So did Edgar whose opinion I value highly. Then began difficult abortion case....

6 *February*. Continued abortion case. Summed up in late afternoon for 1¾ hours, covering the difficult matter of corroboration and all other matters. Jury failed to reach agreement after a further direction. I was told by Edgar that a juryman told him afterwards it was 11 to 1 and the one was perverse and would never agree.

Felt depressed because I thought I had been too impartial and, as I never doubted it was a clear case of guilt, this woman, who has been regularly doing this thing, I am sure ought to have been convicted. But experience is slowly coming: and I shall gain confidence and strength....

On his return to London later that month, he met Brendan Bracken, who had become Minister of Information. Bracken told him that he had had several pressing telegrams from Lord Halifax, British Ambassador in Washington, asking that Birkett should go to the United States to speak about the war effort. He added that he had written to the Lord Chancellor to say that it was 'imperative' that he should go. 'I do not want to go again,' Birkett noted in his diary,

16*

'for the journey and the separation are hateful to me, and invade all my thoughts and make me miserable. But I expect I shall go out of a sheer sense of duty in the end.'

24 *February. York Assizes.* . . . Felt sad today and some of the old nostalgia for the Bar returned. I had to keep bracing myself to think the work of a Judge worth while. . . .

25 *February.* . . . Very depressed indeed all day: a recurrence of some of my bad moments after I had accepted judgeship. The truth is I like the limelight, and cannot bear now to be in obscurity!

26 *February.* Letter from Simon about my proposed American tour, written in the most 'schoolmastery' style, saying I could go, but be sure to be back by June, etc; and Judges of the High Court were not free to make these excursions, etc. He had seen Caldecote before writing it, and this precise pair of 'old men of Munich' were writing like this to me! Angrier than I have been for a long time.

27 *February.* Divorce cases at Court. One defended desertion. Sat till 5 o'clock. This is a dreary day, but very important to the poor people concerned. I tried them as though they were the most important cases in the list.

Still profoundly depressed. I begin to think some of it is physical, because it is exactly the depression of the early days, and for a spell it left me entirely at Newcastle and Durham and when I was at home for a week. . . .

At Leeds Assizes he found himself accommodated in Carr Manor, the former home of Lord Moynihan, the surgeon.

3 *March.* . . . Could not help but reflect on the strangeness of life, which allowed me to be a great friend of Moynihan's, and now he is gone, the brief glory is all departed and strangers live in his well-loved house and wreck his grounds. What a small thing life is, and how very soon it is over. . . .

5 *March.* More pleas at Assizes. Did the work well. Afflicted still with lack of confidence which I must correct

speedily. Inconsistencies in sentences still troubles me but each case must depend on its own facts, bigamy particularly. . . .

9 *March. Birmingham Assizes.* . . . Did my work well today with growing sense of power. Am beginning to eliminate the sense of having given up much for narrower sphere. . . .

10 *March.* . . . Find the question of appropriate sentences most difficult to determine. There are so many considerations, including the effect on the public mind.

12 *March.* Criminal work at Assizes. Hope I shall be liked by the Bar for courtesy if for nothing else. I hope I am not *too* polite for that would be a failing too.

21 *March. Leeds* . . . a girl barrister appeared before me who did her work perfectly. She was good to look at, a lovely voice, good gestures, and knew her job and although it was only a mitigation it rejoiced my heart to confound Hilbery who dislikes woman barristers by saying she was much better than any man on this circuit.

I find now that most people agree with me, but I went out of my way to say how admirably the task has been done.

23 *March.* Last day of Leeds Assizes. . . . Running down case. Stay of execution. So ended my first Assize as a Judge. On the whole, quite pleasant, and most successful.

I must record that Malcolm Hilbery was a most pleasant companion with crosswords and literary and Biblical talk.

The American visit, which occupied two months and which Birkett described to an audience in San Francisco as a 'here, there and back again goodwill tour', covered thirty thousand miles and took him to most of the States of the Union, as well as Canada. It made a great impression. On May 16, Maurice Bathurst of the British Information Service cabled Lady Birkett from Washington: 'Words cannot begin to tell Sir Norman's outstanding success at San Francisco and Philadelphia. He resumes his conquering tour tonight and wants you to know that he is very well and sends his love to you all.' One well-known American newspaper described the visitor as 'the finest Ambassador England has ever sent to the United States'.

Some time previously Birkett had consented to become Chairman of the Governors of the Leys School at Cambridge. The school had been evacuated for the duration of the war to Pitlochry in Scotland, and shortly after his return from America Birkett went to the school to distribute the prizes on Speech Day. 'Spoke well in open air', he noted in his diary. One story he told seems to have been a success with the boys. It was about a pleasant and helpful negro porter at a Middle Western airport who handled his luggage on his recent tour.

Birkett noticed that he had a long scar from his ear to his chin, and asked him how he came by it. 'Yes, sir, a razor,' the negro replied. 'I was talking instead of listening.'

> 13 *July*. Sat in Court of Criminal Appeal for first time, with L.C.J. and Wrottesley. Enjoyed it very much indeed. Delivered a fine judgment which everybody concurred in thinking very good indeed.

In October, 1942, Birkett sat for the first time as the principal trial judge at the Old Bailey. His first case was one of infanticide, when he bound over the mother, saying, 'I think you have suffered greatly.' The next prisoner he sentenced to two days' imprisonment; he was a soldier who had returned home on leave and stabbed his wife because he found her associating with another man.

This was the occasion of his first death sentence, subsequently carried out. The trial, which took place *in camera*, concerned a young British merchant seaman named Duncan Scott-Ford, who had sold information to the enemy relating to the movements of convoys in the North Atlantic with disastrous results for some of the vessels, although the sum he received for his treachery only amounted to eighteen pounds.

Birkett had always rather dreaded having to pass the capital sentence; but, when the actual moment came and the traditional Black Cap was placed on his head, he did so without the slightest trace of emotion.

> 16 *October*. Charge under Treachery Act, 1940, at Old Bailey. Tried it very well and pleased even myself. Jury found young seaman, Scott-Ford, guilty, quite rightly, and I passed sentence of death for the first time. I was strangely unmoved

for the prisoner could excite no sympathy, having sold naval information to the Germans for money. . . .

A fortnight later he was again at Newcastle, where he had to try a murder case and, as he told his wife, he consequently had 'the old anxieties that I have had all my life before doing an important case. Now the responsibility is so much greater for I have to watch everything, and not merely one side as I used to do'.

1 *December. Swansea.* Enjoyed my first day in Court with the Welsh advocates and the Welsh witnesses. . . .

I miss my home and my books and the lovely atmosphere of Challens Green. . . .

7 *December*. . . . The *Daily Herald* today said I was to be offered the Viceroyalty of India: and in consequence I've been having wires from papers in London asking whether I'm going to take it! Needless to say the offer has not come through yet! I expect that's what made the telephone go out of order at home!

18 *December*. Last case at Swansea Assizes. Left with good wishes from all concerned. Assistant Associate gave me a book in Welsh. I thanked Inspector of Police.

At the end of 1942, he wrote in his diary: 'Not bad year. America is a great success. Broadcasting also. Work as a Judge improving.'

Besides continuing his work as Chairman of the Home Office Advisory Committee on appeals under Defence Regulation 18B, Birkett also sat for a few weeks early in the New Year in the Court of Appeal in the Law Courts.

22 *January*, 1943. . . . Have quite enjoyed sitting in C. of A. I feel no human judgment can stand up against three critical and hostile minds. Wilfred Greene starts with a bias against the judgment being right. . . .

Much oppressed by the feeling that I act weakly at times because I do not desire to hurt people's feelings. Oppressed also by nameless fears this week. I must always have something to worry about!

At the beginning of February, he again set off to go to the North-Eastern Circuit, but after only a few days at Newcastle he became ill with a virus infection and was unable to continue with the Assizes. His wife came to fetch him and took him home, where he soon began to feel better.

> 19 *February*. Reading and walking, still improving.
>
> Get oppressed sometimes when I think of my age with the best of Life over. But when I am well, I am full of schemes for the future.
>
> I should still like to be Lord Chancellor, Ambassador to America or Governor-General of Canada.
>
> I am also eager to win a reputation as a wise humane judge.

A week later he felt well enough to return to work and went up to York to finish the Circuit there. But in reality he was far from well and he only just managed to last out the Assizes and came straight home to bed, where he was to remain for the next three months. His illness, which was a combination of heart trouble, pneumonia and other complications was to keep him away from the courts until the autumn. He was slowly nursed back to health at Challens Green by his wife, and in the circumstances he made a remarkable recovery.

To Mrs. Cruesmann

> *Challens Green. August* 14, 1943. I continue to make slow but solid progress to the complete restoration I am promised. My walking improves and I find myself looking forward to October 4th when I start work at Aylesbury surrounded by my friends of the Midland Circuit. My judicial duties have been rather broken into by my visits to Canada and the United States, and my illness, and I hope I may do the long Midland Circuit without any untoward interruption, and gain valuable experience to be gained in no other way.
>
> My weakness (if weakness it be, which I doubt) is to understand so well how frail mortality came too often to offend, that compassion is somehow stronger than vengeance or retribution or punishment. You will understand me, I am sure, when I say that sometimes it requires great strength of mind to be gentle

and merciful in the fulfilment of public duty. But crimes of cruelty and violence and pure avarice awaken such feelings that it is more than ever desirable to be calm and judicial. . . .

November 9. . . . The opening day at Aylesbury was a great day for me. As I lay helpless on my bed in the long nights of sleeplessness, I often thought with longing of the day when I should be well and be back in the world of men again. When the Recorder of the Midland Circuit made his simple speech of welcome, I was quite overcome with emotion where a more eloquent speech would have left me unmoved. It had in it again kindness and friendliness and great sincerity. I made, for me in the circumstances, quite a fitting reply, and referred to the fact that the Clerk of Assize sitting below me (George Bancroft) had been the Clerk of Assize when I was first called to the Bar. . . .

I am standing up to my work quite well, and have finished Buckingham, Bedford, Northampton, Leicester and Lincoln and go to Derby this afternoon. My wife came to Lincoln and I had a young Canadian army officer as my Marshal for three days. He was thrilled beyond measure, for he was invited to the dinner the Bar of the Midland Circuit gave me and he attended the State service in Lincoln Cathedral on the Sunday morning and heard the Assize Sermon and the glorious singing, and saw three days of the Crown Court in Lincoln Castle. I am taking another young Canadian army officer to Warwick; and both Marshals are Canadian lawyers and exceptionally interested. . . .

'George Bancroft says I'm the finest Judge on the Bench and will make history,' Birkett noted in his diary. 'It is pleasant to hear, if scarcely true!' These words were echoed by the old chambers clerk in Birmingham, George Newey, who told Lady Birkett that to come into his court was 'like coming into sunshine in these dark December days'.

31 *December*. . . . No emotion at the end of my sixtieth year, but an indwelling thankfulness that I survived my dreadful illness, and have set my face to a few more happy years.

I should like to be something more than one of His Majesty's Judges before I write the last chapter.

This year has deepened my pleasure in reading, and made me feel what a pleasant thing Life can be.

Birkett's illness had left him a prey to fits of nervous depression and irritability. He was inclined to distrust his abilities as a judge and to wonder whether he should not give up his judicial work altogether. Here are some typical entries in his diary for the year 1944, which fortunately ended on a more self-confident note than they began.

3 *January*, 1944. . . . Felt again that I must keep in reserve my thought of resigning from the Bench and devoting myself to literary and other work. I feel the charm of my home, and my great desire not to be away from it for any length of time, as I am compelled to be on Circuit. . . .

14 *March*. . . . Felt sad and depressed. I cannot bring myself to think that there is any compensation for giving up the Bar.

1 *April*. . . . Gerald Dodson, Recorder of London, said I should give up all outside activities, e.g. broadcasts, 'for health's sake'. He meant they were not consonant with the austere retirement from the world of a Judge! To hell with it. . . .

27 *April*. . . . Feel I shall never be the perfect Judge. I haven't enough impudence to believe that I am always right!

1 *September*. . . . I hate the thought of work again and I have always a feeling that the best has gone in Life, and now it is all looking to the western horizon.

21 *September*. Merchant Taylors Luncheon at Threadneedle Street. Oysters and champagne. It certainly was a pleasant ending to a Term which has gone well on the whole. . . . I have improved as a Judge very much: but still feel, who am I to sit in judgment on anybody?

2

Of the hundreds of cases which Birkett tried during these war years, three in particular call for some detailed mention, and by an odd coincidence his old antagonist in the courts. Sir Patrick Hastings, appeared before him in all three. The first, which was heard on June 19, 1944, without a jury in an improvised air-raid-shelter room in the Law Courts, was an action for damages brought by Mr. (later Sir) Learie Constantine, the well-known West Indian cricketer, afterwards Minister of Transport in the Federal Government of the West Indies, and High Commissioner in London, against Imperial London Hotels Limited on the ground that the defendants refused to receive and lodge him in The Imperial Hotel, Russell Square, London. Sir Patrick Hastings, K.C., led Miss Rose Heilbron for the plaintiff, and Mr. G. O. Slade, K.C., and Mr. Aiken Watson represented the hotel company.

The defendants' refusal to accommodate Mr. Constantine, as Hastings explained in his opening speech, was on the grounds that the hotel 'did not want to have niggers in the hotel'. If that expression was used, counsel pointed out, it would be grossly offensive and, in addition, would be in breach of the statutory duty of an innkeeper to offer board and lodging to a traveller. Mr. Constantine was a native of the West Indies, but he had lived in Lancashire for the past fifteen years. He worked in the Ministry of Labour in Liverpool as Welfare Officer in charge of West Indian technicians and trainees on Merseyside. In the previous July he had been asked to captain a West Indies cricket team to play against England at Lord's, the proceeds of the match being devoted to charity, and he obtained special leave to come to London for a few days. An inquiry was made at The Imperial Hotel about rooms for him and his wife and daughter and it was asked if there was any objection to them because of their colour. The reply made on behalf of the hotel was that there was not. Mr. Constantine and his family arrived at the hotel in the evening of July 30, 1943. As a result of what happened there they left the Imperial Hotel and went to another hotel, The Bedford, the name of which was given to them by the management of The Imperial.

The plaintiff's first witness was his superior officer at the Ministry. He said he arrived at the hotel on the same evening and found Mr.

and Mrs. Constantine looking 'most disconsolate and unhappy'. He told the manageress, 'You cannot turn Mr. Constantine and his party out of the hotel like this,' to which, according to the witness, the manageress replied, 'We won't have niggers in this hotel.' Asked why, she was alleged to have said, 'Because of the Americans.' The witness stated that he had pointed out that Mr. Constantine was a civil servant and a British subject. But, according to him the manageress declared: 'He is a nigger. We are not going to have these niggers in our hotel. He can stop the night, but if he does not go tomorrow morning, his luggage will be put outside and his door locked.' The witness added that he had thought it most undesirable that there should be a scene in the hotel, and he consequently advised Mr. Constantine to leave and go to the other hotel.

'I put it to you,' said Mr. Slade, in cross-examining this witness, 'that the manageress never used the word "nigger" to you throughout the interview?'

'She did, many times,' the man from the Ministry answered. 'I noticed the offensive way she used the word.'

The manager of the match to be played, Mr. W. C. Leatherbarrow, who was in the hotel with the Constantines at the time, testified that the manager, who also spoke to him, was more diplomatic than the manageress. According to Mr. Leatherbarrow, the plaintiff stressed the fact that he was a British subject, and that he saw no reason why Americans, who were aliens, should have any preference at the hotel over a British subject.

Mr. Constantine then went into the witness-box. There, as Mr. Justice Birkett was later to observe in giving judgment, he bore himself with modesty and dignity, and did not appear at all vindictive, but was obviously affected by the indignity and humiliation, which he had suffered. He said he had paid a deposit of two pounds for his rooms. When he and his family arrived at the hotel, it became immediately apparent to him that they were not welcome. He was asked to see the manager, who said, 'You may stop tonight; you cannot stop any longer.' 'I am here for four days, I do not know what you mean,' the plaintiff said he replied. 'You can go when you like,' the manager said. 'I can turn you out when I like.' Mr. Constantine added that he realized that there was colour prejudice.

'Colour prejudice is particularly in evidence in the United States?' Mr. Slade asked him, when he rose to cross-examine.

'Yes.'

'If an hotel had a large number of American guests, it would be justifiable to consider whether the prejudice would exist among the guests?'

'I don't know how to answer that, because I booked for four nights and they knew that I was coloured. They accepted the booking and must have known that they had four or five hundred Americans in.'

Evidence for the defence was given by the manageress of The Imperial Hotel and the managing director of Imperial Hotels Ltd., who had been referred to as the manager.

The manageress said she had told Mr. Leatherbarrow that The Imperial Hotel was full of American and colonial soldiers, and that it might be more congenial for Mr. Constantine and his party to stay at the company's Bedford Hotel, as she saw the possibility of a quarrel with the Americans and 'colonials' in the evening, and she had no staff to quell it. According to her, she had said nothing about the desire of the management. She was quite certain that she did not use the word 'nigger' or 'niggers', and she had taken particular care not to be offensive. She denied that she would not allow the Constantine family to stay more than one night.

Hastings asked the manageress one pertinent question in cross-examination.

'If you felt that there might be a riot in the hotel, you would not be very anxious for Mr. Constantine to stay, would you?'

'No.'

The managing director of Imperial Hotels Ltd., supported what the manageress had said in her evidence. He was sure that she did not use the word 'nigger'. If she had, it would have struck him as a very offensive word to use. He had not the slightest intention of offering any personal affront to Mr. Constantine. What he desired was to avoid friction and trouble in the hotel.

'Assuming that the evidence given by the plaintiff's witness was true,' Hastings asked, 'would you agree that Mr. Constantine was grossly insulted in your hotel?'

'Yes, if the evidence was true,' answered the witness; 'but it was not.'

After some further evidence, Mr. Slade for the defence submitted that the action, being in law what was known as 'an action on the case', was not maintainable, without allegation and proof of 'special damage', which had not been pleaded or proved.

Replying, Hastings said that it was not a correct proposition in law that 'special damage' was an essential element of 'an action on the case'. In some instances, he argued, the law presumed damage, and in others it did not. The only question was into which class a particular case came. Here it was the plaintiff's right to have access to the defendants' inn, and it was the duty of the defendants to receive him. If the plaintiff's right was denied to him, it followed that he had suffered inconvenience, for which he was entitled to damages.

Mr. Justice Birkett delivered a reserved judgment on June 28, 1944, to the accompaniment of flying-bombs passing overhead. First, he reviewed the evidence given on both sides. Regarding what took place in the hotel, he said that he accepted 'without hesitation' the evidence of the plaintiff and his witnesses, and rejected that given on behalf of the defendants. He found on the facts that the defendants did refuse to receive and lodge the plaintiff in their hotel 'without any just cause or excuse', and that Mr. Constantine did not leave voluntarily. He accordingly gave judgment for the West Indian cricketer, agreeing with Hastings that the action was maintainable without proof of special damage, since 'the plaintiff's right, founded in the common law, had been violated and denied, and in those circumstances the law afforded him a remedy'. But at the same time the judge said he felt he could not award exemplary damages because of the circumstances in which the denial of the plaintiff's right took place; Hastings had urged him to do so, in the light of the authorities and having regard to the exact nature of the action. He, therefore, awarded nominal damages only, which he assessed at five guineas. The plaintiff was also awarded his costs.[1]

Although the facts were clear enough, it was a difficult case in law to decide, and Birkett's judgment earned the admiration among others of the learned editor of Salmond's *Law of Torts* and Principal of Brasenose College, Oxford, Dr. W. T. S. Stallybrass.

The second case in which Sir Patrick Hastings was for the defence occurred at Chester Assizes in February, 1945, when Hastings defended several individuals who had been charged with 'black market' offences under the Defence Regulations. 'For two days the Court listened to Sir Patrick enthralled,' noted Birkett's clerk at the

[1] [1944] 2 All England Reports, 171.

time. 'Listening to him myself, as I had done over the years, I sat back and enjoyed every moment as he scored point after point without wasting a word. One realized what a fine advocate he was.'

At the end of the day, the judge noted in his diary: 'Summed up *very well* and paid tribute to Pat. All acquitted.' This is what he said to the jury:

> You will probably long remember this case for one reason. That reason is, how fortunate you have been to have had the privilege of listening to a masterly defence by the very brilliant and learned counsel who has appeared before you during the last two days, Sir Patrick Hastings. For myself, I could but wish that many young members of the Bar at present serving in His Majesty's Forces could have been here during the past few days to listen to Sir Patrick and learn how a case should be conducted.

In the other action, which was tried before Birkett, sitting alone; on July 10, 1945, Hastings, who appeared with Mr. Valentine Holmes, K.C., and Mr. R. T. Paget, was on the losing side. It was a libel action brought by Mr. Frederick Voigt, a well-known journalist and editor of *The Nineteenth Century and After*, and the proprietors and publishers of this periodical, against News Chronicle Limited, Daily News Limited, the publishers and promoters of the *News Chronicle*, and another journalist, Mr. Cedric Belfrage. The plaintiffs, who were represented by Mr. Richard O'Sullivan, K.C. and Mr. Frank Gahan, complained that they had been libelled in an article published in the *News Chronicle*, which Mr. Belfrage wrote. The passage complained of appeared in the issue of July 10, 1944, and was as follows:

> Lord Haw-Haw's Favourite Paper
>
> When the magazine, *The Nineteenth Century and After*, was described as the favourite paper of Lord Haw-Haw by Brendan Bracken on Friday, our Minister of Information paid over-due, if acid tribute to its long, pink, bespeckled, multilingual and prophetic editor—Frederick A. Voigt.
>
> It was not kind of Brendan Bracken to say that *The Nineteenth Century* is well named. Its views are the worst kind of reactionary opinion. 'Its great desire', he told the House of

Commons, 'is to create the maximum amount of mischief among the United Nations.'

The plaintiffs alleged in their pleadings that these words meant that throughout the war they had been consciously and continuously publishing a journal whose views were designed and calculated to win the approval of traitors and like-minded persons and to serve as propaganda on behalf of the enemy, and that their deliberate aim and desire was so far as possible to cause mischief and damage to the United Nations, to impede the war effort and to give aid and comfort to the enemy. The defendants denied that the words bore this meaning or indeed any meaning defamatory of the plaintiffs. They pleaded that the words were an accurate report of proceedings in the House of Commons on July 7, 1944, published in good faith and without malice, and were privileged; and that, in the alternative, they were fair comment on the parliamentary proceedings in question.

Mr. Voigt, giving evidence, said that he was one of the first journalists to disclose Nazi terrorism in Germany, and he had never withdrawn any word which he had written against Nazism and anti-Semitism. He had not changed his essential political opinions since 1938, and would describe himself as a Victorian Radical. So far as he knew, *The Nineteenth Century* was not Lord Haw-Haw's favourite paper. He denied that he had written anything against the Allied cause or that he had ever disseminated the views of the Goebbels Press.

'At any period of your life were you in favour of peace by negotiation?' his leading counsel asked him.

'Never,' said Mr. Voigt.

'Did you write against it?'

'I did.'

'Have you consistently been in favour of a dictated peace for Germany?'

'I have.'

Cross-examined by Hastings, the witness admitted that in October, 1941, he had written that the Russian campaign had shown that Hitler was a military genius and that Stalin was an amateur by comparison. Hastings then put to Mr. Voigt an article he wrote in 1943 on the power of the Russian State, and asked: 'Do you really think that it was trying to improve the relations between Marshal Stalin and this country?'

'Ultimately, yes,' answered the witness.

'Do you happen to know that it incensed the Russians and very much pleased the Germans?'

'I doubt it.'

'You do not like Russia very much?'

'I like Russia very much.'

'Are you frightened of Russia?'

'A little.'

'And are you anxious to keep on good terms?'

'Yes.'

Hastings got little change out of this witness. While admitting that it would be a disgraceful thing in time of war to discredit an allied government or an allied commander in the field, Mr. Voigt stoutly denied that he had ever done so in any of his writings, or that their effect had been to create mischief among the United Nations.

'Do you agree that anyone engaged in throwing discredit on an allied government or general would be doing a great disservice to the war effort?' asked Hastings.

'Yes,' replied Mr. Voigt. 'But it is a question rather like the "Have you stopped beating your wife?" question.'

'I don't think so,' was Hastings's comment, amid laughter, 'but my answer is "No".'

Evidence on Mr. Voigt's behalf was also given by Miss Ellen Wilkinson, the former Labour Minister, and Miss Rebecca West, the authoress, who both testified that they knew Mr. Voigt to be a conscientious journalist with the interests of Britain at heart.

It was useless for Hastings to call any evidence for the defence. All he could do was to attempt to argue that Mr. Voigt's articles, from which he quoted at length, were clearly calculated to create mischief among members of the United Nations. The real damage to Mr. Voigt, if any, in his submission, was caused by what the Minister of Information had said in the House of Commons, and the *News Chronicle* had merely quoted it.

Mr. Justice Birkett did not agree. Giving judgment for the plaintiffs, he said he did not think the defendants had *bona fide* cited an extract from *Hansard* and commented on it. He had come to the conclusion that they had taken Mr. Brendan Bracken's statements and had made them their own. It was no disparagement of a fearless critic to say that he was wrong. But to say that Mr. Voigt and the three plaintiffs had conducted a journal which could be described as 'Lord Haw-Haw's favourite paper' was entirely false. He therefore awarded £1,000 each to all three plaintiffs with costs.

'I feel very strongly this case about the unfairness of Bracken and the *Nineteenth Century*,' Birkett noted in his diary, 'but I controlled myself well, I think.' A second action brought by Mr. Voigt against Mr. Cedric Belfrage, the author of the offending article, was settled out of court and accepted by Birkett from the Bench. 'These were the best cases I have had,' he added in his diary, 'and on the whole I did them well, I think.'

3

On the last day of August, 1945, Birkett arrived back at his home in Buckinghamshire from Scotland, where he had been spending a holiday with his family, to find a letter from the Lord Chancellor, Lord Jowitt, inviting him to be the British Judge at the trial of the major German War Criminals, which was to open at Nuremberg in the autumn. The Chancellor explained that the Court was to be a military tribunal, and there were to be four Judges—a Russian, an American, a French, and a British.

> We obviously want a trained lawyer who will be able to steer the trial in collaboration with his colleagues so as to arrive at the truth. I was talking to the Prime Minister about this today, and we both felt that you were the man to take the job on, if you were willing.
>
> I do not pretend that it is going to be a pleasant or an easy task, and I do not know what arrangements they can make for your comfort at Nuremberg, but I do know that it is supremely important from the international point of view that this trial should be a model of fairness, and therefore, I ask you to look at it from that point of view in giving me your decision.

Birkett immediately telephoned to the Lord Chancellor's office and said he would go. At the same time, he made an appointment to see Jowitt in London and learn the details. 'It puts me in a ferment,' he noted in his diary the same night, 'but I have no doubt it is my duty to do it.' Next day, he wrote: 'It is a great honour to be selected and restores my confidence in myself.'

But when he saw the Lord Chancellor three days later he found to his dismay that there had been a hitch. It appeared that the Foreign Office wanted a Law Lord, especially as there was a strong likelihood of his being appointed President of the Tribunal. However, Jowitt went on to say, the Charter creating the Tribunal provided for four Alternate Judges, in addition to the four principals. They were to be present at all sessions and in the event of the illness or other incapacity of any of the principals to take his place. The Chancellor said that, in these circumstances, he hoped that Birkett would go as the British Alternate.

As it happened, no Law Lord was available. Hence Jowitt turned to the Court of Appeal and invited Lord Justice du Parcq, who was on the point of retiring from the Bench. Meanwhile the Prime Minister, then Mr. Attlee, wrote officially to Birkett, asking him to accept the appointment as Alternate Member to du Parcq.

Again Birkett felt it was his duty to accept, although he did so with considerably less enthusiasm than he had shown over the original proposal. 'I cannot record the secret anguish this has been to me,' he confided to his diary, 'to have been selected as Member and then asked to become Alternate merely because of the absurd snobbishness of the Foreign Office.'

As events turned out, Lord Justice du Parcq refused and in the end Lord Justice Lawrence, later Lord Oaksey, was appointed. Before the trial began in Nuremberg, a meeting of the Judges and Alternates took place in Berlin, which Birkett attended. The American Judge was Mr. Francis Biddle, a former U.S. Attorney-General; he was accompanied as Alternate by the Hon. John J. Parker, Senior Judge of the U.S. Circuit of Appeals. The French were represented by Professor Donnedieu de Vabres, a recognized authority on international law, and M. Robert Falco, a member of the Cour de Cassation, the highest court in France, and the Russians by Major-General I. T. Nikitchenko, Vice-Chairman of the Supreme Court of the U.S.S.R., and Lieut-Colonel A. F. Volchkov, member of the Soviet District Court, both of whom wore their military uniforms on the Bench.

At the first meeting Birkett noted that the Soviet judge, who arrived with his colleague two hours late, was 'very troublesome', while the French judge was 'most voluble and dramatic'. As had been anticipated, Lord Justice Lawrence was chosen President at this meeting.

Incidentally, at their first meeting Lawrence confused Francis Biddle with A. J. Drexel Biddle, who had been U.S. Ambassador to the exiled Governments in London during the war, remarking that he 'realized the advantage' of Francis Biddle's 'diplomatic training', whereas he himself was 'nothing but a simple barrister and judge'. Lawrence, who reminded his American opposite number of Galsworthy's Soames Forsyte, 'looked like John Bull—rubicund, healthy, a twinkling eye and pleasant English humour, friendly and attractive'—and they soon became close friends. 'Lawrence's alternate, Sir Norman Birkett, was very different,' Biddle noted. 'Lawrence was short and roundish, Birkett towered above him, six feet three, beak-nosed, reddish hair, lean, angular, hawklike. He had wit, was broadly read, particularly in poetry; was impulsive and generous. I liked Birkett at once. . . . I don't think the two men were close friends—temperamentally they were very different—but they appeared to get along well, their relationship marked by more than usually good manners.'[1]

The Indictment which charged the accused with the commission of (1) conspiracy for war, (2) crimes against peace, (3) war crimes, and (4) crimes against humanity, originally contained the names of twenty-four defendants. But before the trial opened the effective number was reduced to twenty-one, as Martin Bormann had disappeared; Robert Ley, the Nazi Labour Front leader, had contrived to strangle himself in his cell; and Gustav Krupp, the armaments manufacturer, was too ill to be brought before the Tribunal. The Americans were anxious that Krupp's son Alfred should take his father's place in the dock, because, in the words of Mr. Justice Robert Jackson, who led the American prosecuting team, 'this is a trial for posterity'. Birkett strongly opposed this suggestion, which he called 'shocking', and pointed out that this was not a game of football in which a reserve could be fielded without more ado. His British and French colleagues both agreed with him, and his view eventually prevailed—although, it may be noted, the Alternate Judges had no vote.

Since Nuremberg was in the U.S. military zone of occupation the

[1] Francis Biddle *In Brief Authority* (1962), pp. 379–80.

Americans were responsible for all security and other 'logistical' arrangements, including the custody of the prisoners. After the trial began, the Judges were given a dining-room to themselves in the court building, but in the early days Birkett queued up with everybody else in the cafeteria, paid his three Reichsmarks and had his lunch unceremoniously dumped on his aluminium tray. He was amused, too, by the American guard, who would carefully scrutinize his pass whenever he entered or left the court room and say, 'That's O.K., fella!'

Birkett recorded the slow progress of the preliminary sessions in his diary. There were lengthy arguments about procedure, such as what the judges should wear in court. Nikitchenko, the Russian judge, objected to black gowns, which he said reminded him of 'the medieval ages'. As a result the Russians stuck to their uniforms while the others wore their gowns, the French, with their jabots and lace ruffles looking like figures in a Daumier drawing.

> 10 *October*. Meeting of Judges. Better progress. Lunch in building. Lunch set for Eisenhower and Montgomery with peaches and grapes.
>
> Long sitting in afternoon. Tea with Americans who told me with what esteem I am regarded in the U.S.A.
>
> Dinner at American House at night. All the delegations and staffs present. Biddle presided. Wine, champagne, cocktails in great profusion. All the toasts of countries given.
>
> 14 *October*. . . . Long drive round Berlin to see the sights, in charge of a young American Lieutenant who gave us a 'brief orientation of the position'. Saw the Reichstag burnt out, the Chancellery, Hitler's last refuge, Goering's house and Goebbels' house and the Air Ministry etc. All in perfect shambles. Biddle and Parker to lunch.
>
> Long session until 11.30 p.m. when Soviet Delegate refused to have public meeting tomorrow. I spoke warmly and finally I drafted the Public Notice explaining the delay. . . .
>
> 18 *October*. . . . Public Session of Tribunal in Berlin. Russian General presided. I had done most of the drafting of the speeches delivered. Cinema and flashlight photographs galore. Indictment lodged and the trial fixed for November 20.

We could not go to Nuremberg as arranged because of fog at Nuremberg, but the Americans went.

We went on a drive to Wannsee and walked by the lake, and drove through the Grünewald and on the great autobahn to Cologne. Pitiful sight was to see elderly people and children gathering firewood for the winter.

Birkett eventually reached Nuremberg ten days later, having come home for a short break in the meantime.

27 *October*. . . . Left Hendon in V.I.P. Dakota at 9.15 and flew over Deal, Dunkirk, Coblenz, Frankfurt to Nuremberg. Very bumpy after Frankfurt and we had to turn back and land at Frankfurt at 12.20. Three hours wait for cars and then drove 160 miles to Nuremberg through Wartzburg and Furth. First two hours in daylight through woods and by rivers and quaint villages: last three hours in the dark.

Called at Grand Hotel and then to 16 Steilenstrasse where we stayed. Most uncomfortable. Pillows like iron, and no comforts. My house not ready which is rather humiliating.

28 *October*. . . . Tea with Americans at their house. Invited Biddle and Parker for Christmas which seemed to please them.

Dinner at villa and early bed. Made pillow of my underclothing and did not sleep too badly.

Cannot help sighing for peace of home, but realize that wherever I am I should be sighing for something else.

29 *October*. . . . Meeting of Tribunal at 9.30. Long day of work and procedure with much wasted time. . . .

Felt tired and depressed tonight, and longed exceedingly for home and quiet and peace. . . . But life leads inexorably on, and there might yet be a bright future.

A few days later Birkett returned to England to fetch his wife, leaving Bowker behind to prepare the house which had been found for him in Beethovenstrasse, a small modern villa in a suburb which, like the court house, had escaped the general destruction of Nuremberg by allied air bombing. It was a great relief for Birkett to be able to have his wife with him at this time, since at first there had been a ban on wives coming to Nuremberg, which was only lifted by the Lord Chancellor after the wives of the French judges had made their appearance.

18 *November*. Spent the morning doing a draft of the President's opening speech for Tuesday. . . .

A light lunch and then Billy,[1] Gavin[2] and I went for a lovely motor ride in the Bavarian sunshine through the surrounding hilly country. We saw two deer scamper into the woods. We were accompanied everywhere by a military guard carrying a tommy gun.

Back to tea and a quiet evening. The V.I.P.s (God save the Mark!) have arrived.

19 *November*. Draft speech approved. . . .

A last minute effort was made to postpone the Trial because Rudenko (the Soviet Prosecutor) was ill. This I do not think was true and it was another good illustration of what we have had to endure in the way of baseless reasons which all the argument in the world was powerless to overcome.

20 *November*. Opening of trial. Everything went well and after the short opening speech the day was spent in reading the Indictment. Everybody agreed the whole thing was most dignified.

The trial was held in the main courtroom of the Bavarian Central Courts of Justice, where just over a year previously the leading conspirators in the bomb plot on Hitler's life in July, 1944, had been tried by a ranting judge, with none of the courtesies and decencies which were to characterize the present Tribunal. The courtroom had been cleverly adapted to meet the requirements of the Tribunal, with seats for 200 press representatives, 150 visitors, enclosed and soundproofed boxes for cinema projectors, and space for the interpreters and the special apparatus which with the aid of microphones and earphones enabled the proceedings to be simultaneously translated into German, French, Russian and English, as might be required. Although this procedure is commonplace today at international gatherings, it was a novelty in 1945, and on the whole it worked smoothly. Without it, or with consecutive instead of simultaneous interpreting, the proceedings, lengthy as they were, must have lasted considerably longer.

The indictment took nearly two days to read, consisting as it did

[1] Lady Birkett.

[2] Captain Gavin Cliff Hodges, whom Birkett had appointed his Marshal. He subsequently married Birkett's daughter Linnéa.

of 24,000 words and having to be translated into four languages. When the reading was over the accused were called upon to plead to the indictment, and as the name of each was announced he rose from his seat and advanced to the microphone before the dock. All twenty defendants present—Kaltenbrunner, the Gestapo chief, was in hospital suffering from a brain haemorrhage—pleaded Not Guilty in varying terms. Goering tried to make a speech first and when pulled up by the President declared that he was 'not guilty in the sense of the indictment'. Hess followed with a hurried '*Nein*', which Lord Justice Lawrence, amid a ripple of laughter, said he would enter as a plea of 'Not Guilty'. And so on through the two rows of prisoners in the dock, most of whom followed Goering's formula, although Jodl declared, 'I have a clear conscience before God and my people.' Schacht, the banker, said he was 'Guilty in no respect'.

> 21 *November*. Pleas taken and all went well. Jackson of U.S.A. made a very fine opening speech on which it was a genuine pleasure to congratulate him, which I have done.[1]

Thus opened a trial, as the President put it in Birkett's words, 'unique in the history of the jurisprudence of the world, and of supreme importance to millions of people all over the globe'. The longer it lasted—and it was to last 284 days, with 403 open sessions—the more Birkett was conscious of his subordinate role in the proceedings although his voice and influence were strong behind the scenes.

> 30 *November*. Tribunal all day. Soviet dinner at night for Vyshinsky[2] by General Rudenko. 25 toasts: much vodka, cognac, champagne and cartloads of food.
>
> I drank nothing because I had felt so very well all day because of my abstemious night.
>
> I made a speech also.

One of the toasts which was proposed on this occasion by the

[1] Robert H. Jackson, Chief Counsel for the United States at Nuremberg, had been a Justice of the U.S. Supreme Court since 1941. He wrote *The Case Against the Nazi War Criminals* (1946) and *The Nuremberg Case* (1947). He died in 1954.

[2] Andrei Vyshinsky, lawyer and former professor in Moscow University, had been Chief Public Prosecutor during the great 'purge' trials in the 1930's. In 1945 he was Deputy Foreign Minister and principal Soviet delegate to the United Nations, in which roles, as later when he became Foreign Minister, he exerted no influence on Soviet policy, being merely a mouthpiece of Stalin and the Politburo. He died in 1955.

expansive and slightly bibulous guest of honour was, 'To the German prisoners. May they all be hanged!' But Vyshinsky spoke so fast in Russian that it was difficult for the interpreter to keep pace with him, and before the other guests fully appreciated what had been said they had raised their glasses to their lips. The American Judge Parker was very upset when he realized what he had done, apprehensive that some mischievous gossip columnist in Washington would get hold of the story. ('Can't you see the headline: "American judges drink to the death sentence of the men they are trying"?') and he derived little comfort from his colleague Francis Biddle's reassurance that the incident was a triviality which would be forgotten by next morning. The essential was their approach to the prisoners, Biddle told him, and so far that had been fair, a proposition with which Birkett heartily agreed and which he was determined should continue to operate.

Each of the four prosecuting teams took it in turns to open its case. The Americans, who began, were followed by the British, who were led by the Attorney-General, Sir Hartley Shawcross, K.C., M.P. But the brunt of the burden fell on Sir David Maxwell-Fyfe, K.C., M.P., since his parliamentary duties necessarily kept Shawcross in England for most of the time. The other members of the British team were Mr. G. D. ('Khaki') Roberts, K.C., and four junior barristers, Lieutenant-Colonel Mervyn Griffith-Jones, Major F. Elwyn Jones, M.P., Colonel H. J. Phillimore (later Mr. Justice Phillimore) and Captain J. Harcourt Barrington.

If Birkett was obliged for the most part to remain silent on the Bench, at least he had plenty of time to record his observations of the courtroom spectacle in his note book day by day.

> 4 *December*. Shawcross made good opening speech at trial. He came to dinner at night. . . .
>
> I think Shawcross is marked out for high distinction.
>
> 5 *December*. David Maxwell-Fyfe presented British Case re broken Treaties and Conventions. He presented a dull section with lucidity.
>
> 7 *December*. British case at Tribunal. G. D. Roberts did not shine. Griffith-Jones and Elwyn Jones were good: Phillimore I thought good. . . . Biddle said that Elwyn Jones was always relevant and lucid, and was of great assistance to the

Tribunal. He said to me that it was the best presentation we have yet heard.

14 *December*. . . . American case where one of the Prosecution began—'The voice you hear is the knocking of my knees. They haven't knocked so hard since I asked my wonderful little wife to marry me.'

The shocking taste is really almost unbelievable.

The Tribunal adjourned for ten days at Christmas, and Birkett flew home to England taking Biddle with him for the holidays. Lady Birkett had preceded them by a few days so as to have everything in readiness at Challens Green. On the day after their arrival, Birkett took his guest over to Chequers, the Prime Minister's official country residence in Buckinghamshire. There they found Mr. Attlee in residence. 'He was very pleasant and showed us all over the rooms,' noted Birkett in his diary. 'A great atmosphere in the house. . . .' Biddle later recalled that the weather at Chalfont St. Giles was all mud and rain and low heavy fog: 'But it would break for a bit, not quite come through while Linnéa and I slogged together for a walk before a rewarding tea. We spent our evening reading poetry aloud—Norman was a passionate poetry lover, like so many Englishmen; or lying round the library fire playing records.' On Christmas morning, without telling his guest beforehand, Birkett had arranged for a long-distance-call to Mrs. Biddle in Washington. 'He had that kind of thoughtfulness,' noted the American judge.

There followed a round of sight-seeing and entertaining for the visitor, ending up with a luncheon party at Claridge's Hotel in London, at which the guests included Jowitt, Simon, Lawrence, Patrick Hastings, Shawcross and other leading members of the English Bar, as well as Lord Greenwood, the Canadian industrialist and chairman of the Pilgrims, and A. P. Herbert, the writer, who gave Biddle a copy of *Uncommon Law*, a collection of his 'Misleading Cases', in which the Lord Chancellor jocularly scribbled, 'Don't be misled by anything that Herbert says.' Jowitt proposed the principal guest's health. Then, in Biddle's words, 'there were a dozen friendly little informal "speeches", bonds were renewed, fellowship exchanged, the sense of comradeship lingered. Once you are accepted by a Britisher there is nothing he will not do for you.'

ON THE BENCH AT NUREMBERG

The President of the International Military Tribunal, Lord Justice Lawrence, is in the background.

ON HOLIDAY IN LAKELAND

31 *December*, *Paris*. Night train to Frankfurt.

Perfectly lovely day at the Embassy which I enjoyed more than I can say. Lady Diana Cooper and Duff Cooper most delightful. The wine and food and the house and guests and conversation—all quite enchanting. Went to the Louvre and saw 'The Winged Victory of Samothrace', 'The Venus de Milo', and 'Mona Lisa', etc.

This has been another great year culminating in my being asked by the Lord Chancellor and the Prime Minister to be the British Member of the International Military Tribunal at Nuremberg trying the War Criminals.

The Foreign Office intervened and wanted a Lord and du Parcq L.J. was asked and refused. Then Lawrence was asked and I was asked by the P.M. to be the Alternate. . . .

4

The International Military Tribunal, to give the court its official title, resumed its sittings on January 2, 1946. The case presented by the British and American prosecuting teams was followed by the French and finally by the Russian, all of which occupied over two months, while the court continued to sit from 10 a.m. to 1.0 p.m. and from 2.0 p.m. to 5.0 p.m. from Mondays to Fridays and often on Saturday mornings as well.

On January 20, Birkett wrote to his friend Mrs. Cruesmann:

The thing that sustains me is the knowledge that this trial can be a very great landmark in the history of International Law. There will be a precedent of the highest standing for all successive generations, and aggressor nations great and small will embark on war with the certain knowledge that *if they fail* they will be called to grim account. To make the trial secure against all criticism it must be shown to be fair, convincing and built on evidence that cannot be shaken as the years go past. That is why the trial is taking so much time and why documents are being piled on documents.

There are, in truth, two trials going on at the same time, the trial of the Defendants in the dock and the greater trial of a whole nation and its way of thought. The world must be patient

17

(and so must I!) for what is being done now assuredly belongs to history. But it will be late summer at the earliest, I think, before the final acts.

The Court is an interesting place and the moods of the Defendants are full of perpetual speculation. Many of them must know that the sands of life are running out for them, and I watch them sometimes with a fascinated interest and would give much to know the secrecy of their thoughts. And you could certainly never tell from their faces that they have been guilty of the deaths of millions or had reduced millions of men and women to slavery.

The purpose in this book is not to give a day-to-day account of the proceedings or even to give a general account, which has already been done by various authoritative writers, but rather to show through Birkett's eyes, as evidenced by the detailed diary he kept on the Bench, supplemented by occasional letters to friends, how the trial developed and what he thought of its principal characters. The diary is a unique document, and it is the only one recorded by any of the eight judges of the Tribunal to have seen the light of day.

21 *January*, 1946. This is supposed to be, and no doubt is, the greatest trial in history. The historian of the future will look back to it with fascinated eyes. It will have a glamour, an intensity, an ever-present sense of tragedy that will enthrall the mind engaged upon its consideration.

But to have been present at every moment of it is to occupy a position of advantage given to but few.

If it were possible to capture the moment, and to record in imperishable form the changing moods of the Assembly, a contribution to History would be made of the highest value. But there are but few Gibbons in this world, and they are not usually to be found among His Majesty's Judges! Moreover the documents that have been produced in such profusion are there for all men to read.

What alone is missing is the emotion, the colour, the movement that characterizes these days. And how shall that be captured, and when captured, how shall it be recorded?

The Master Race on trial sounds dramatic enough, but the Master Race in the dock seems singularly like the dregs of

> humanity. Funk, for example, once a dictator in the economic sphere, is here presented as a broken heap of flesh, half-asleep during most of the days, apathetic and listless, and raising blinking eyes to the bright lights installed in the Court for the benefit of the cinematograph operators.

The camera men not only recorded the trial proceedings on film, but they also lowered the lights in the courtroom from time to time to show portions of captured German film of concentration camp scenes, the Warsaw Ghetto and other horrors, which were thus added to the other documentary and oral evidence. At the first showing of the concentration camp film, Schacht turned his back in the dock and refused to look, while Von Papen covered his face with his hands, likewise Ribbentrop and Doenitz, while Keitel and Jodl looked at the floor. When the showing was over, the eight judges filed out of the courtroom without a word. The prisoners moved uneasily in their places.

> 28 *January*. This evidence is building up a most terrible and convincing case of complete horror and inhumanity in the concentration camps. But from the point of view of this trial it is a complete waste of valuable time. The case has been proved over and over again. Neither does the world need it any more, for all over the world the evidence has been published and one volume has been put in evidence in this trial. But it seems impossible to stop it, or to check the volume of it.
>
> 5 *February*. The day was spent in reading very many documents relating to the expulsion of Jews from France in heartless fashion.
>
> This immense detail did not advance in any way the formidable case already presented, but no doubt will be useful in recalling to the French people the horrors of the German occupation. But one must take leave to observe that, if all the matters had been rigorously excluded which were repetitious or cumulative (as it has been inaccurately termed), this trial would certainly have been of shorter duration, the issues more clearly and lucidly defined, tempers would have been more equable, and general benefits would have resulted. . . .
>
> 6 *February*. This day, which is the 100th session of the Tribunal, the French counsel with a voice so toneless as to be

> without any meaning presents a completely useless exposé of the looting of art treasures in France.
>
> The work has been done completely by the Americans, and even then was a work of supererogation.
>
> But there is no disposition to stop him and with complete murder in my heart I am compelled to sit in suffering silence, whilst the maddening, toneless, insipid, flat, depressing voice drones on in endless words which have quite lost all meaning.
>
> Rosenberg, Goering, Keitel, Ribbentrop, Seyss-Inquart are the chief pillagers.
>
> 7 *February*. I regret to say that all the matters dealt with today have been largely repetition of matters already discussed by the other delegations. It is difficult to remain patient, but the prestige of France is somehow involved.
>
> But it is drawing to an end, and only the Soviet case remains when the case of Hess has been presented. The accumulation of evidence is not without some value, however, as a general picture of illegality, brutality and crime generally has been built up.

While the case against Hess was being presented, Birkett carefully observed the behaviour of the figures in the dock.

> Hess and Goering are the inseparable and loving friends of this trial, if appearances count for anything. They seem cordial and spontaneously considerate of each other.
>
> During this presentation, Goering has shown great interest and considerable animation, and has repeatedly conversed with Hess as the evidence has been unfolded. These conversations or comments are obviously of a humorous kind, judging from Hess's reception of them. Possibly caustic or satirical asides: and it is a remarkable thing that two men on trial for their lives who must inevitably have a growing feeling that their days are numbered can jest and smirk and smile in this way.
>
> Frank by contrast, spends long hours apparently communing with himself in a far-away brooding attitude, as though the full tragedy of what has happened to him and Germany had been most fully and most poignantly realized.
>
> It is indeed a sobering thought that these men, now sitting as closely guarded prisoners in every guise of dejection and

failure were a few brief years ago masters of their country in the fullest sense, and as they hoped, potential masters of the whole world.

13 *February*. Colonel Pokrovsky (Assistant Soviet Prosecutor), Violation of Laws and Customs of War relating to Prisoners of War.

The above was the extent of the note I made this day, and I cannot comment more forcefully on the waste of time. The Soviet ideas of legal procedure are extremely primitive.

15 *February*. The presentation of the case dealing with crimes against the civilian populations of various countries overrun by the German armies has been most detailed, and is contained for the most part in official documents which purport to record judicial hearings of the evidence. The impression created on my mind is that there has been a good deal of exaggeration, but I have no means of checking this. But no doubt can remain in any dispassionate mind that great horrors and cruelties were perpetrated.

I think, also, that there is a good deal of evidence to show that the Nazi hierarchy used calculated cruelty and terror as their usual weapons. But it is impossible to convict an army generally, and no doubt many of the terrible excesses were those of a brutal and licentious soldiery, to quote Gibbon.

The only importance of the evidence is to convict the members of the Cabinet and the military leaders of calculated cruelty as a policy. . . .

What is much more important is the form of the eventual judgment to be delivered next July. There must be a clear well expressed section dealing with the law applicable to the case. There is no doubt that the judgment will form a precedent of far-reaching importance in the field of International Law; and it is also of the highest importance that some popular misconceptions should be removed. The Charter is new in this: that for the first time it sets up an International Military Tribunal and clothes it with jurisdiction and power to try war crimes. It defines the crimes but does not create them. The crimes are crimes which existed at the time the acts were done either by domestic law or by existing international law. The only new thing is enforcement.

> The second equally important thing is to say a few pregnant words about the nature of the evidence in order to remove now and hereafter any suggestion that the Tribunal acted on evidence that was not worth the name. It will be important to speak of captured documents in German, of the affidavits, interrogatories, commissions, findings of courts martial, etc. Then it will be necessary to marshal the evidence on the indictment relating to conspiracy, and to deal with the case of each individual Defendant. A particularly difficult problem must be dealt with in connection with the organization, which the Prosecution desires to be declared criminal. This involves a definition of a criminal organization, and reasons for including those persons who are deemed to come within it.

Another month passed before the Prosecution's case was concluded. Then, shortly after two-thirty in the afternoon of March 13, 1946, the Defence was opened when Goering left his corner seat in the dock and walked boldly to the witness box, his baggy trousers falling over his high jack boots and a thick sheaf of papers under his arm.

It was soon apparent that Goering intended to use his position as a platform from which to justify the Nazi revolution in Germany and its achievements. No attempt was made by the Court to stop him making long-winded and rhetorical speeches from the box. ('The only motive which guided me was my ardent love for my people, their fortunes, their freedoms, their life. And for this I call on the Almighty and the German people as witness!')

Birkett was quick to perceive the dangers inherent in Goering's tactics. 'If this procedure is followed in the case of all the Defendants and long, detailed statements are made covering important and unimportant points alike,' he noted after the first day of the defence, 'then the time taken will be so great that the trial will be written down as a failure. It will have done more to restore German belief in their leaders, and the verdicts against the leaders will be regarded by the German people as excessively unjust.'

> 18 *March.* Goering reveals himself as a very able man who perceives the intent of every question almost as soon as it is uttered. He has considerable knowledge, and has an advantage over the Prosecution in this respect, for he is always on familiar

> ground. He has knowledge which many others belonging to both the Prosecution and the Tribunal have not.
>
> He has therefore quite maintained his ground, and the Prosecution has not really advanced its case at all. Certainly there has been no dramatic destruction of Goering as had been anticipated or prophesied. . . .

The first of the Prosecutors to cross-examine Goering was the American, Mr. Justice Jackson. Birkett's opinion of the American performance, and its effect upon the course of the trial, he set down at the end of the second day. It is one of the most revealing passages in his Nuremberg diary.

> In this long drawn-out trial of the major war criminals at Nuremberg, intense expectation was centred on the moment when Goering, the first of the Defendants named in the Indictment was cross-examined.
>
> It was, in a very real sense, the critical moment of the trial. If the leader of the surviving Nazis could be exposed and shattered, and the purposes and methods of the Nazi Government revealed in their horrible crudity, then the whole free world would feel that this trial had served its supreme purpose; but if, for any reason, that design should fail, then the fears of those who thought the holding of any trial to be a mistake would be in some measure justified. . . .
>
> Three months had been spent in stating the case for the Prosecution, and there had been great repetition of evidence, vast fields of irrelevancy, and the creation of the feeling that four nations were determined to have their part in the prosecution without regard to time or vain repetition. Consequently it was felt that the cross-examination of Goering might do something to retrieve the situation, and bring about the possibility of a more speedy end to the trial. The ability of Mr. Justice Jackson had been shown in some masterly addresses to the Tribunal, and the contest between him and Goering was felt to be crucial to a high degree. The utmost confidence was felt in his ability to achieve the desired end.
>
> At 12.15 on the morning of March 18, Mr. Justice Jackson rose to begin the long-awaited cross-examination. The Court filled quickly as the House of Commons fills when a speech of

great importance is to be made. The same air of suppressed excitement pervaded the Court room, but before the adjournment had been reached it was clear that all the high hopes were to be disappointed, and that so far from the cross-examination destroying the Nazi case, it was to be the means whereby the Defendants in the dock were to be stimulated and encouraged in the use made by Goering of the free platform granted to them to explain and expound their ideas and beliefs for future generations of Germans.

This deplorable situation was brought about by a combination of factors which ought to have been foreseen, but unfortunately was not. The great battle was lost, and once lost, there may be partial but never complete recovery. The position may be improved, but never quite redeemed.

The first factor creating this situation was the extraordinary personality of Goering himself. Throughout this trial the dead Hitler has been present at every session, a dreadful, sinister, and in some respects an inexplicable figure; but Goering is the man who has really dominated the proceedings, and that remarkably enough, without ever uttering a word in public up to the moment he went into the witness box. That in itself is a very remarkable achievement and illuminates much that was obscure in the history of the past few years. He has followed the evidence with great intentness when the evidence required attention, and has slept like a child when it did not; and it has been obvious that a personality of outstanding though possibly evil qualities, was seated there in the dock.

But nobody appears to have been prepared for his immense ability and knowledge, and his thorough mastery and understanding of the detail of the captured documents. He obviously studied them with greatest care and appreciated the matters which might assume the deadliest form.

The cross-examination had not proceeded more than ten minutes before it was seen that he was the complete master of Mr. Justice Jackson. Suave, shrewd, adroit, capable, resourceful, he quickly saw the elements of the situation, and as his confidence grew, his mastery became more apparent. His self-control, too, was remarkable, and to all the other qualities manifested in his evidence he added the resonant tones of his speaking voice and the eloquent but restrained use of gesture.

The second factor constituting the present situation was the undoubted fact that Mr. Justice Jackson, despite his great abilities and charm and his great powers of exposition had never learnt the very first elements of cross-examination as it is understood in the English courts. He was overwhelmed by his documents, and there was no chance of the lightning question following upon some careless or damaging answer, no quick parry and thrust, no leading the witness on to the prepared pitfall, and above all no clear over-riding conception of the great issues which could have been put with simplicity and power.

But perhaps the most important factor of all was the failure of the Tribunal to intervene when the situation developed and to retain control of the proceedings. Goering was allowed to make long statements in reply to almost every question, and with his combination of knowledge and ability, he was able to present at least a plausible case on almost every aspect of the matter.

It is impossible to say that these answers were wholly irrelevant. They were not. That was where the cleverness of Goering was fully shown. Having been informed by the Tribunal that he could answer 'Yes' or 'No' to the question and could then add any explanation he wished to make, he took the fullest advantage of the situation by making an answer to every question which consisted of cleverly constructed statements which were not strictly speaking answers to the questions at all. For almost two days he held the stage without interruption of any kind and no doubt performed the task he set himself to do.

If he had been informed (as I urged) in the severest way and reminded of it from time to time that the witness box was not to be used as though it were a platform from which speeches could be made to some outside audience, but was to be used solely for the purpose of giving evidence on matters relevant to the Indictment, he would certainly have been much more under control, and the lost confidence of Mr. Justice Jackson would have been restored for the ultimate benefit of all concerned in this trial.

But the new situation which has undoubtedly been created

> by the failure of the hopes to shorten the trial by the extinction of Goering, must be faced in all its implications. The trial will now take a very long time . . .

With the object of curbing Goering's lengthy harangues from the witness box, Birkett drafted a notice which he was anxious should be read out from the Bench at the opening of the following day's session. ('This trial is in danger of becoming unduly and unnecessarily prolonged because of the non-observance of the essential rules of giving evidence, and the Tribunal gives clear and firm notice that no irrelevancy in the answering of questions will be tolerated.') But, as Birkett noted at the time, 'Biddle and Judge Parker were against it—for reasons personal to Jackson, I think—and Geoffrey Lawrence acquiesced, although he had been strongly in favour of it in the morning: and therefore it was not used, a fatal mistake, I think, which will have profound effects on this trial.'

> 20 *March*. I drew up a Notice this morning to be read at the opening of the Court. This was not done, and in my opinion this was a very great mistake which cannot now be rectified. Public opinion, which is hardening against the procedure followed by the Tribunal, would have been to some extent reassured and the confidence of Jackson would have been restored.
>
> The trial from now on is really outside the control of the Tribunal, and in the long months ahead the prestige of the trial will steadily diminish. Public opinion will harden still more, and when the end comes, the interest will have gone out of it. For public opinion is already formed about what the end should be, but in reaching it, if too much licence is allowed, the end will not justify the means.

5

Goering was followed into the witness box by Ribbentrop, with the precise results which Birkett had foreseen.

> 30 *March*. The trial is now completely out of hand. The witness [Ribbentrop] continues to make very long answers on matters which are only indirectly relevant to the issues in the case.

There is no effective control of the witnesses at all, and mountains of useless documents are translated and put in.

Many months of this kind of thing are before us, largely due to the initial mistake of allowing Goering to make long speeches from the witness box without interruption or effective and instructed control.

2 *April.* Suggested interruption not made! 'I don't want to interrupt your cross-examination, General Rudenko, but many of these matters have already been gone into most exhaustively, and I am not sure how far a repetition of them is helpful to the Tribunal.'

Does the Tribunal really need any further evidence about the German attitude to Jews? It has been dealt with exhaustively. The truth is that very little cross-examination is needed: and all the Prosecutors should limit themselves most rigidly in the interests of time.

3 *April.* Dr. Nelte [Keitel's counsel] has just said according to the interpreter, 'The evaluation of judgment is always subjective.'

That is the sort of sentence which makes me despair of the record of this trial. I don't believe that Dr. Nelte really said it in the original German: and if he did, it contains nothing to my mind.

One of the tortures of this trial has been the language used by the interpreters into English (God save the mark!) There are some words which I vow never to use again while Life lasts. Here are one or two: clarify, concept, basic, ideology, subjective, objective, contact, evaluation, enquiry, controversy, applicable, etc., etc.

10 *April.* Yesterday, the 9th April, Mr. Justice Jackson came to the microphone to protest against the large number of useless documents put in by Rosenberg's counsel. The subject-matter was unimportant; but the manner of Jackson's appearance was revealing and disturbing. He is a thoroughly upset man because of his failure in cross-examining Goering from which so much was expected. He has taken it very badly indeed and his instinct is to run away from the scene of his failure. . . .

The trial is regarded as a spectacle, a kind of gladiatorial show, with the prominent Nazis like Goering taking the place of the wild beasts and prosecuting counsel as the gladiators and baiters. The enormous staffs think of the trial as a means of enjoying a good time, and as most of them are young this can be forgiven: but the fact remains that much more serious work ought to be going on in almost every field, and notably in connection with the final judgment.

11 *April.* Kaltenbrunner, the Chief of the Security Police and S.D., and a very sinister figure in the Nazi hierarchy, was an interesting figure in the witness box. He said that he realized that the hatred of the world was concentrated upon him, since Himmler, Muehler, Pohl and Heydrich were now dead. The dreadful crimes of the Gestapo are being visited on his head, and it is always difficult to imagine that one human person can have been the head and fount of such scenes of misery and bloodshed.

But Kaltenbrunner is making a vigorous defence, denying his signature to documents of a most incriminating nature, endeavouring to show that he was really without power or influence. He is a fluent speaker and speaks with great animation and uses much gesture. In some matters he is no doubt right and it is then that he grows animated. Some of the things attributed to him are no doubt exaggerated, but it is impossible to think of the position occupied by Kaltenbrunner and, at the same time, to believe that he was ignorant of so many matters.

On the same day as the above entry, Birkett expressed himself to Mrs. Cruesmann in a letter which went right to the core of the whole Nuremberg process:

The endless debates which have been hitherto carried on have centred round the question whether the trial should have been held at all or whether, the decision having been made to hold it, the trial could be made a means of exposing the evils of the Nazi system and of establishing a precedent of great value in international relations and international law. Then, as the years pass, it will be asserted with growing vehemence that this was a court of victorious belligerents alone, that no German and no neutral was upon the Bench.

Although great efforts have been made to show the world

that this is to be a fair trial, by the provision of counsel and full facilities for calling witnesses and producing documents, and in many other matters, I yet greatly fear that so far as the German people are concerned all these efforts will be in vain. It is difficult to see how the situation might be improved: but I think that if there had been a better Tribunal much might have been done. The standard of the court does not compare favourably with the highest Courts in England and there has been much weakness and vacillation, and, above all, a failure to appreciate that the trial is only in form a judicial process and its main importance is political. For that, of course, what was required was not only a knowledge of law but a knowledge of history, particularly German history, a knowledge of men and world affairs, and an instinct to apply these things at every stage of this most remarkable case.

Birkett's preoccupation with the repetitious use of certain words and expressions both by counsel and witnesses caused him to list several more which, as he jocularly noted in his diary, seemed to him in his 'tired state of mind' to be 'crimes against humanity', in addition to those with which the defendants were charged. In particular, he noted the following: argumentation, orientation, activated, motivation, finalize, objectivity, visualize, concrete observations, and reprivatization, i.e. land going back into private hands after public ownership. He was also critical of the interpreters.

23 *April.* The translators generally may know the outlines of both languages, German and English, but in general they have no sense at all of the meaning of words. For example, Frank has just said, 'I must clarify a misunderstanding', when I suppose he meant, 'I must remove a misunderstanding'.

26 *April.* Dr. Seidl [Frank's counsel] spoke with unusual passion when cross-examining Gisevius and suggesting he was working with foreign powers against Germany, although Gisevius had admitted quite frankly what he was doing against the Nazi regime.[1]

It was most revealing and showed the depth of national feeling whatever the evil of the record of the nation.

[1] Dr. Hans Gisevius, a member of the Gestapo, who worked for the German resistance and later came over to the Allies. He gave evidence for the prosecution at Nuremberg.

1 *May*. Jackson has come to the microphone twice this morning to protest against some of the questions. He has done this in a most petulant and aggressive manner, and is obviously suffering from frayed nerves. This is the result of his failure against Goering, and he seems to fear a similar failure against Schacht and he is anxious to prepare the way.

Despite the extremely flattering press notices of some of the cross-examination by the British, it yet remains true that a true cross-examination has not yet been given. It is cross-examination in name only, which consists of putting incriminating documents [to the witness]. The true art of cross-examination is something in a different plane altogether: and it has not yet been seen at Nuremberg in any shape or form.

2 *May*. Today at 3 p.m. Jackson began his cross-examination of Schacht. With the memory of the failure to crush Goering, some considerable interest was aroused in this second attempt. Schacht, of course, was an extremely able witness with great knowledge, complete self-control and mastery of the details of this long and complicated history.[1] But again quite soon the reasons for Jackson's weakness and, indeed, failure were made manifest. It may be of some slight interest to set them, or some of them, down.

1. Jackson has no real knowledge of the art of cross-examination. Almost the chief quality of a cross-examiner is to have a complete grasp of the case he proposes to make, so that he may attack the witness whenever a weak place appears, with the knowledge he carries in his head. If he is unsure of his case or his facts, so he stumbles or delays, the richest opportunity of the cross-examiner is lost. This is one of the first and main weaknesses of Jackson.

2. Jackson collects a great number of documents including the Interrogatories and then makes long quotations from them by way of questions. This is most ineffective and the effect of

[1] Dr. Hjalmar Schacht, German banker and economist, was President of the Reichsbank and Minister of Economics from 1934 to 1937, when he was relieved of his ministerial post by Hitler although he remained President of the Reichsbank until 1939. He was indicted on the conspiracy count since he had been the central figure in the financing of the German rearmament programme in the early days of the Nazi régime, but rearmament in itself was not a crime under the Charter and he could not be conclusively shown to have conspired with Hitler and his generals to wage an aggressive war.

the cross-examination is lost. The witness knows the documents and has plenty of time to make effective answers.

3. The quick thrust and parry of cross-examination is impossible in the circumstances.

4. In this particular contest between Schacht and Jackson, Schacht most certainly held his own. He was alert to every point, would not permit a point to pass which was not put beyond doubt as to his position and supported his answers with documents, knowledge and proof.

5. The central point of the Defence, which it was the task of Jackson to break down if he could, was that Schacht forsook the Nazi régime from the moment its evil tendencies were made known: and his earlier adherence was not really criminal. In particular, the purposes of the original re-armament was the main difficulty Schacht had to meet. But nothing occurred during the cross-examination other than a strengthening of Schacht's defence.

It is also a grave mistake in a criminal trial to make little jokes, or witticisms or smile or laugh, and allow the witness and the spectators to do so too.

3 *May*. Goering takes a savage delight in the discomfiture of Schacht when faced with awkward questions.

Hess is merely the devoted disciple of Goering, and shares all his emotions.

Jackson makes a mistake in questioning Schacht on banking and economic matters about which he is imperfectly instructed and knows little, when Schacht can overpower him on these topics at any moment.

When a perfectly futile cross-examination is combined with a translation which murders the English language, then the misery of the Bench is almost insupportable.

4 *May*. I begin to think that the ineffectiveness of most of the German counsel is due to the fact that they are taking part in a procedure which is strange to them. They have been unaccustomed to cross-examination, and certainly do not shine at examination-in-chief. But one would have thought that native common sense would tell you that the proper method is to ask the witness to deal with the precise charges which have been made.

All the German witnesses moreover cannot answer questions simply and directly but must needs make very long statements to almost every question, much of which seems quite beside the point.

23 *May*. The trial has now got to a stage when nobody makes any effort to consider time. (Sievers for Raeder goes on endlessly, repeating himself over and over again.) The Prosecution must cross-examine whether it serves any useful purpose or not, in order that each member of the team shall have a show and get the needful publicity.

When I consider the utter uselessness of acres of paper and thousands of words and that life is slipping away, I moan for this shocking waste of time.

I used to protest vigorously and suggest matters to save time, but I have now got completely dispirited and can only chafe in impotent despair.

For example, five minutes have just been spent in a dispute about the number of a quoted document which could have been ended in ten seconds by clear speech and firm handling.

4 *June*. Jodl, in his explanations, gives the impression that he was much more than a mere soldier. He shows considerable political knowledge, much ingenuity and remarkable shrewdness. He obviously knows the strength of the case made against him, and also the best lines on which to answer it.

12 *June*. Small incidents may be revealing. The American Member left the Bench obviously to go to the lavatory and Goering turned to the back row of the dock and made some comment apparently of a humorous nature to Raeder. An American guard tapped him on the shoulders to stop it as being against orders, and Goering most deliberately and carefully brushed his shoulders with his hand to get rid of the contamination!

Nothing could be more revealing as to Goering's attitude of mind!

18 *June*. The change in the appearance of some of the Defendants is getting rather marked as the days go by. Keitel noticeably has grown older, greyer and more grizzled. His

soldierly brightness has been succeeded by a lethargic dullness and his face wears always a troubled anxious look.

Doenitz seems to have fallen into despair: Frank sits for long hours in an attitude of brooding: and even Goering has long moods of apparent depression and gloom. Saukel, Kaltenbrunner and Streicher seems to be quite unchanged. Rosenberg writes continually. Raeder wears an air of wonderment as though he didn't quite understand all that goes on. Ribbentrop is a pitiable figure with the mainspring of his life broken.

Goering maintains the position as a defender of the system in all things, bridling at the use of abusive terms, rejoicing in the discomfiture of Defendants who seek to excuse themselves at the expense of Hitler or the system, and revealing himself as a Nazi to the end.

I must record my opinion of Dr. Kubuschok, the German counsel for Von Papen. My ordeal of the last few days demands it. He is not exactly to be described as a 'wind-bag', because that implies some powers of rhetoric and possibly eloquence. Of these qualities this man is strikingly bereft. He is however a great waster of time, and is highly gifted in the arts of circumlocution. He will never use one word when a dozen will do, and is quite incapable of uttering a simple sentence. Clouds of verbiage, mountains of irrelevance, and oceans of arid pomposity distinguish his every moment in the Court, and it is difficult to avoid the extremest forms of irritation with him. I have not avoided it, I regret to say!

He unites with this absence of merit a smug self-complacency, an indifference to ordinary emotions (such as diffidence in taking so much time), and quite obviously is making the most of a situation into which a blind Fortune (blind indeed!) has thrown him. But that this Court should have to suffer under him is a most bitter thing to endure. Incompetency and mediocrity are enthroned and with the despotism associated with power are enjoying their little day. May it soon end!

19 *June*. We are now enduring another spell of the dreadful Kubuschok. In England he would be hard put to it to maintain the lowest footing in any County Court: but here, with the written questions in front of him, he goes through

the form of examination with no insight or imagination at all. It is, to me, a torture of the spirit, a degradation of the arts of advocacy.[1]

20 *June*. When Fleischer [Speer's counsel] succeeded Kubuschok at the microphone, it became clear that there were lower depths of advocacy to be reached, unbelievable as it sounds.

Whilst Kubuschok sleeps in the court room, his fell work accomplished, Fleischer carries on the evil tradition with unashamed and unabated zeal.

21 *June*. The witness [Speer] is taken through a great mass of figures dealing with raw materials [in cross-examination by the Russian prosecutor]. The questions themselves are extremely difficult to follow, but they are most fearfully mangled in translation by the worst interpreter the world has ever known.

Oscar Wilde began *De Profundis* by asserting that 'suffering is one long moment'—and the truth of that assertion cannot be better exemplified than in this awful cross-examination, which the Tribunal is compelled to suffer and endure.

I do not think it will be possible to write down a coherent note of this cross-examination. The emotions are too deeply stirred. Irritation, I suppose, is the chief feeling, for not only is the whole proceeding a grave and wicked waste of time, but the illiterate translation is really a torture of the spirit. Time simply stands still, and at the moment at which I write there is almost half an hour to go, thirty minutes of sheer, unadulterated misery.

What a commentary on the greatest trial in history, when the great nations co-operate in concord and unite, and the nations of the world look on!

24 *June*. Then comes Leidinghausen [Von Neurath's counsel] tall, aristocratic, aloof, insensible to affront, with an extraordinary droning voice, and bearded like the poet. He loses himself in the maze of events, and produces an effect of complete and utter stupefaction.

[1] It is noteworthy that Von Papen thought rather more highly of his counsel. 'Kubuschok was an excellent defence counsel, with a keen intelligence which enabled him to master every situation. But even he found that the procedure adopted at the trial taxes the qualities of the most expert counsel.' Franz von Papen. *Memoirs* (1952), at p. 548.

29 *July*. Dubost is at the microphone again, making his final speech. He is robust and vigorous: but such is the irony of fate that he is being translated by a stout, tenor-voiced man with the 'refayned' and precious accents of a decaying pontiff. It recalls irresistibly a late comer making an apology at the Vicarage Garden Party in the village, rather than the grim and stern prosecution of the major war criminals.

But translators are a race apart—touchy, vain, unaccountable, full of vagaries, puffed up with self-importance of the most explosive kind, inexpressibly egotistical, and, as a rule, violent opponents of soap and sunlight. . . .

What Gibbon said of one of the dons of Magdalen College, Oxford, may be said with truth of one of the minor officials of this Tribunal—and more than one! 'Dr.—— remembered that he had a salary to draw, but forgot that he had a duty to perform.'

The background of this trial will not bear examination.

16 *August*. I am exceedingly weary today in consequence of a very late night at our party last night and a trifle too much indulgence in 'White Ladies'. Fellow sufferers in this last respect are General Nikitchenko and Colonel Volchkov of the Russian delegation.

I have the greatest difficulty in keeping awake and the documents which are being discussed by Dr. Servatius [Sauckel's counsel] are of such surprising dullness that the temptation to sleep is quite overpowering.

31 *August*. Morning Session. Today the Defendants are making their final statements.

For some of them it is the last public statement they will ever make: and that simple fact is enough to show the solemnity of the occasion. On the whole the Defendants have borne themselves with considerable dignity. Hess betrayed the signs of a disordered mind in almost every word he spoke, but the rest of the Defendants spoke with great feeling and force.

When one considers that these men have fallen from high place and power, that they now contemplate the ruins of everything for which they once cared and share the suffering and humiliation of the German people and, at the same time, they know that their persons, fortune and fate are being weighed in the balance, one cannot refrain from some admiration for their outward fortitude in such circumstances.

Keitel bore himself like a brave soldier and spoke bravely too. Funk faltered a little under the stress of emotion, but Schacht was in complete control of himself and spoke with great ability. Frank, strangely enough, was swayed by strong religious feeling, and laid the blame for the acknowledged evil on the nation's denial of God. Keitel, the soldier, and Schacht, the banker, made the two best speeches of the front row, despite the fact that Goering sits there.

This was a morning when the dignity of the Trial might have been impaired by unseemly scenes: as it turned out, the dignity of the Trial was enhanced by the Defendants themselves.

6

After the last of the twenty-one prisoners in the dock, Hans Fritzsche, the former head of the Broadcasting Division in Dr. Goebbels's Propaganda Ministry, had made his final plea, the President of the Tribunal announced that the court would adjourn until September 23 in order to consider the verdict in closed session. A further week was found necessary for this process, since the Tribunal could not complete its deliberations in the time originally anticipated. This was due partly to the attitude of the two Soviet judges who wanted all the accused to be convicted, and partly to a difference which developed between Birkett and the American judge Francis Biddle on the issue of criminal conspiracy. Biddle profoundly distrusted conspiracy counts in an indictment, which in his own country at least, as he remarked, were used too often by the government to catch anyone however remotely connected with the substantive crime. He felt that the prosecution theory of the conspiracy dating from the formation of the Nazi Party and drawing into the net almost anyone who was a German went too far from any reasonable point of view. In this he was strongly supported by the French judge, Donnedieu de Vabres, who argued that conspiracy was a crime unknown to international law, and furthermore that it violated a fundamental principle of French criminal law that a crime must be precisely defined. Birkett and the President, on the other hand, felt that the conspiracy counts were essential in order fully to bring home the defendants' guilt, and in this they were supported by the Russian judges, who foresaw that otherwise men like Schacht and Fritzsche would escape altogether.

'The British were upset by my stand—it was as if I had deserted them,' Biddle noted afterwards. 'The heart would be taken out, Birkett believed, if we rejected conspiracy. From the beginning the Nazis had planned and worked for war.'[1]

For a time there was a complete deadlock between the British and Russian judges on the one hand and the American and French judges on the other. It was eventually resolved by a compromise, which Biddle was assigned the task of putting into words. It was agreed that the conspiracy counts should stand, but that the conspiracy must be 'clearly defined in its criminal purpose' and 'not too far removed from the time of decision and action'. Thus it was held that the conspiracy definitely existed on November 5, 1937, when Hitler, with Goering, Von Neurath and the service chiefs made plans for the aggressive invasion of Europe, and the decision to seize Austria and Czechoslovakia was discussed in some detail, and it was decided to take action as soon as a favourable opportunity presented itself. In the words of that portion of the final judgment, which was drafted by Birkett and read out in open court by him on September 30, 'in the opinion of the Tribunal, the evidence established the common planning to prepare and wage war by certain of the defendants. It is immaterial to consider whether a single conspiracy to the extent and over the time set out in the indictment has been conclusively proved. Continued planning, with aggressive war as the objective, has been established beyond doubt.'

The most careful security precautions were taken while the judges were in closed session, the telephones were disconnected and the contents of the wastepaper baskets were subjected to particular scrutiny, and the clerical staff entrusted with making copies of the judgment were isolated in a villa outside Nuremberg, so that no hint of the verdict should be disclosed before the appointed day. Finally, for their journey to the court all the judges were provided with bullet proof cars. 'It has glass about an inch thick and weighs an incredible number of tons and is tiring to drive,' noted Lady Birkett. 'It's all very impressive, but very unnecessary and nothing could make us a likelier target than a great black car led by a

[1] Biddle. *In Brief Authority*, p. 468.

siren-screaming jeep and followed by another, if anyone felt like slinging a bomb or having a pot shot.'

The delivery of the judgment, a lengthy document running to some 50,000 words, occupied the whole of September 30 and the morning of October 1. Each of the eight judges took it in turns to read it. Afterwards, M. Falco, the French Alternate Judge, told Lady Birkett, who felt she could not face the occasion ('It seems too much like a Roman holiday for my liking') that her husband's voice had come through perfectly, and 'an elocution teacher couldn't have done it better'. In the result, eighteen out of the twenty-one defendants were convicted, on one or more of the counts in the indictment and three were acquitted, namely the banker Schacht, the diplomat Von Papen, and the propagandist Fritzsche. The verdict of the court was a majority one, the two Russian judges dissenting, no doubt on instructions from Moscow, and making it clear that in their opinion all the accused should have been found guilty and all should be executed.

In the afternoon, the convicted prisoners were brought up one by one to hear their sentences. It was a solemn moment when Goering, who was the first, appeared with his guards through the door at the back of the dock, took the pair of earphones which were offered to him and listened to the President's words. 'Defendant Hermann Wilhelm Goering. . . .' The expressionless voice of the interpreter began to translate into German, when Goering made agitated signs with both hands. He could hear nothing, as the sound relay system had broken down. A technician immediately hurried over and corrected the fault. The President began again. 'Defendant Hermann Wilhelm Goering. In accordance with the counts of the indictment, on which you have been convicted the International Military Tribunal sentences you to death by hanging.' The prisoner heard the sentence with bowed head, but showed no outward signs of emotion. He quickly removed the earphones, turned about smartly and left the dock.

Rudolf Hess, who followed a minute or two later—unlike Goering he had handcuffs—created a very different impression, brushing aside the proffered earphones, rolling his eyes, rocking on his feet and staring at the ceiling. His sentence was imprisonment for life, but he did not appear to hear it, as one of the guards had to tap him on the shoulder, before he slowly turned round and ambled out of the dock. Afterwards he told the prison psychiatrist, who was waiting for him in his cell below, that he had not heard the sentence and neither knew nor cared what it was.

Of the remaining prisoners, Ribbentrop, Keitel, Kaltenbrunner, Rosenberg, Frank, Frick, Streicher, Saukel, Jodl and Seyss-Inquart were also sentenced to death, and Funk and Raeder to life imprisonment; Von Schirach and Speer each received twenty years, Von Neurath fifteen and Doenitz ten. The same day Lady Birkett noted in her diary: 'Norman told me it had been a very dignified afternoon with the defendants coming up singly from the lift, putting on earphones, listening to their sentences without signs of emotion and then turning and going back into the lift and down. He also said that when Papen, Schacht and Fritzsche were acquitted, Speer had congratulated them with a very kindly smile.'

Except in the case of Goering, who had contrived to cheat the hangman's rope by taking a lethal dose of cyanide poison, a few hours earlier, the death sentences were carried out shortly after midnight on October 16 in the prison gymnasium, where three gallows had been erected. A smell of whisky, Nescafe and Virginia cigarettes pervaded the grim scene. The executions began about one o'clock in the morning with Ribbentrop and ended two hours later with Seyss-Inquart. The operation was under the charge of U.S. Army Master-Sergeant John C. Woods, who in his fifteen years experience as a military executioner had hanged 347 of his fellows, and on this occasion had two G.I. assistants. 'I hanged those ten Nazis and I am proud of it,' he was reported as saying afterwards. 'I wasn't nervous. A fellow can't afford to have nerves in this business. I want to put in a good word for those G.I.s who helped me. I am trying to get them a promotion. The way I look at this hanging job, somebody has to do it.' At the same time, he vigorously rebutted the charge made by two journalists who were present, one a veteran crime reporter from the London *Star*, that the business had been bungled. The *Star* man, Mr. Cecil Catling, had declared that there was not enough room for the men to drop, which meant that their necks had not been properly broken and that they had died of slow strangulation; he also charged that they had not been properly tied, with the result that their heads struck the platform as they went down, which accounted for the blood on their faces afterwards. As for the suggested suffocation, the executioner admitted that the men 'emitted certain sounds and made certain movements after their drop', but according to medical opinion this was 'merely a question of reflexes', while the fact of the bloodstained features bore a similar explanation. 'That is quite natural,' said the doughty Master-Sergeant. 'It happens when the condemned man opens his mouth at the moment of the drop and bites his tongue. He knows nothing about it. It is a thing which might happen in the course of any execution no matter how perfect it might be.'[1]

The Press had asked to be present at this gruesome spectacle and to take photographs. The President and Birkett opposed this request, but they were overruled by their American, French and Russian colleagues on the ground that, if the Press were to be excluded, it might be said in Germany that the condemned men had not really been hanged at all. Thus, besides a number of official witnesses, eight selected representatives of the Press were admitted, and also the Bavarian Prime Minister Dr. Wilhelm Hoegener, who was hastily summoned to Nuremberg as 'a witness of the people'.

After the executions were over, the bodies were placed on stretchers at the foot of the gallows, with the ropes still round their necks, Goering's body being added, and photographs were taken of each individual much to Birkett's disgust when he subsequently saw them, although the pictures were not allowed to be printed in the English Press. Then the bodies were secretly conveyed to Munich, where they were cremated and the ashes deposited in the River Isar, while the official announcement merely stated that the ashes had been scattered 'in a river somewhere in Germany at an undisclosed place to prevent a shrine being made of it at any time'. But, when the location of the spot subsequently became known, it was perhaps hardly surprising that no one should show any disposition to enshrine it.

On their arrival at Northolt airport, near London, the two British judges and the British prosecuting team were welcomed home by an impressive legal gathering headed by the Lord Chancellor, Lord Jowitt, and including the Lord Chief Justice, Lord Goddard, and the Law Lord and former Lord Chancellor, Lord Simon. Also waiting to greet Birkett and his wife was his daughter Linnéa with his marshal, Captain Gavin Cliff Hodges, to whom she was shortly to become engaged. Then came the good-byes and the Birkett

[1] Charles Duff. *A Handbook of Hanging* (1961), at pp. 132–3.

family reached Challens Green in time for lunch, after which, in Lady Birkett's words, 'Norman settled into his own big chair with his papers and letters as if he'd never been away, and I started unpacking and getting settled into the thousand and one jobs waiting to be done.'

Two warm tributes were paid to Birkett for his work at Nuremberg. The first came from Lord Simon. 'Sir Norman Birkett was an admirable choice,' Simon wrote at this time. 'He threw himself into all the difficult work behind the scenes and promoted harmonious co-operation and good understanding, utterly regardless of the fact that, as things worked out, he had himself small opportunity of speaking before the footlights. Mr. Justice Birkett's broad humanity and fervent devotion to peace are known to all who have heard him on the wireless. Justice, with him, is not divorced from mercy, but when he tries the bully he does not forget the victim. The country owes much to him, as well as to Lord Justice Lawrence, for vindicating our conceptions of an impartial trial under the rule of law.'[1]

The other assessment of Birkett's contribution to this historic trial came from his American opposite number as Alternate Judge. 'He realized thoroughly the importance of the business in which we were engaged,' Judge Parker declared afterwards; 'he was tireless in his efforts to draft a judgment which would not only do justice to those on trial, but would also commend itself to the wisdom of mankind and the dispassionate judgment of history. Although only an Alternate Member of the Tribunal without a vote, his voice was heard in all of its deliberations, his hand drafted a large and most important part of its judgment, and no one connected with the Tribunal, Member or otherwise, had a greater part than he in shaping the final result. If, as I confidently believe, the work of the Tribunal will constitute a landmark in the development of world order based on law, to Norman Birkett must go a large share of the credit for the success of the undertaking. To few men does the opportunity come to labour so mightily for the welfare of their kind.'[2]

[1] *Sunday Times*, October 6, 1946.

[2] From Judge Parker's Foreword to *Behind the Bar* by A. E. Bowker, Birkett's clerk.

7

Before leaving Nuremberg to fly home, Judge Parker invited Birkett and his wife to the annual conference of the American Bar Association in Atlantic City at the end of October and to stay with him later at his home in Charlotte, North Carolina. Birkett was also asked to be the speaker at the principal dinner of the Association. His acceptance of both invitations meant that he and his wife had only a fortnight in England before boarding the *Queen Elizabeth* on her maiden voyage as a passenger liner to New York. Their fellow passengers included Messrs. Molotov and Vyshinsky, the Soviet Foreign Minister and his Deputy, who were on their way to the United Nations Assembly, Sir Hartley Shawcross, the British Attorney-General who had been invited to represent the English Bar at the Atlantic City conference, and the Birketts' old friend Cecil Roberts, who had been editor of the *Nottingham Journal* when Birkett first stood for the House of Commons, and had since become a most successful novelist; with the two latter they spent most of their time on the voyage, very agreeably, as they found. Another passenger was the English theatrical producer, Mr. William Mollison, and as the ship was passing the Statue of Liberty at the entrance to New York harbour, Birkett was overheard by an astonished American reciting to Mr. Mollison the lines of verse inscribed on its base many years before by a Jewish woman immigrant, Emma Lazarus, for the benefit of those 'coming to the promised land'.

> Give me your tired; your poor
> Your huddled masses, yearning to breathe free,
> The wretched refuse of your teeming shore:
> Send these, the homeless, tempest-tossed to me:
> I lift my lamp beside the golden door.

'Why!' the American remarked to Birkett. 'I've lived in New York all my long life, and have to learn this from an Englishman!'

The octogenarian Senator George W. Pepper, who was to be their host in Philadelphia, met them at the quay side, and to Lady Birkett's incredulous delight whisked them off to the Hotel Pierre in a Port Authority car with a police motor cycle escort, with their sirens screaming as they sped through the Manhattan traffic. 'George Pepper is a most charming man and loves Norman and made me feel he'd include me in his affection too,' Lady Birkett noted in her diary. 'It was good to see the two of them so happy together.'

For his speech to the Bar Association, as might be expected, Birkett chose the trial of the war criminals as his subject.

As sometimes happens on these occasions there were too many preliminary speakers and they spoke for so long that it was 11.30 p.m. when Birkett was called upon, and everyone including himself was already feeling weary.

'Poor fellow, he made a noble effort and everyone sat up and took notice,' his wife noted afterwards, 'but the conditions gave him no chance to do what he could have done . . . poor Norman was so bitterly disappointed with himself and the evening generally. Not that he need have been for his speech stood out like a diamond in a bucket of dross.'

In his speech Birkett emphasized that the fate of the individual defendants was perhaps the least important result of the Nuremberg trial. What was of much greater significance was that nine months of evidence had revealed in the greatest detail the dreadful consequences which come to a great nation when the rights of the individual are disregarded. 'That record is now available,' said Birkett, 'not merely for the present generation, but for all generations to come.'

The advent of the secret police and the concentration camp and the resulting reign of fear and terror were the inevitable result of the abrogation of the rule of law, he went on. In the realm of international law it was certainly a step forward that a properly constituted court had for the first time branded aggressive war as an international crime, but it was only a step. Finally, he suggested that the moment was opportune for a further step forward in the framing of an international penal code. Certain salutary principles had already been set out in the Charter of the Tribunal which governed the proceedings. Certain crimes had been defined. The doctrine of the immunity of Heads of State had been denied and the defence of superior orders rejected. 'The United Nations would do well to take this opportunity of advancing still further,' he concluded. 'The attainment of peace is still the world's greatest need, and it may very well be that the trials at Nuremberg will come to be regarded as a distinct step towards its achievement.'

Back in England, he was heartened by the news that his old Cambridge college, Emmanuel, had elected him an Honorary Fellow. But he continued to be troubled by fits of melancholy. 'Have felt a growing oppression with the passing of the years,' he wrote in his diary at the end of the year. 'They go so swiftly and I have done so very little and have so much I would like still to do. I want to write my Memoirs at least before I go.'

Then, what he read in the New Year Honours List plunged him into the depths.

> 1 *January*, 1947. Today Geoffrey Lawrence was made a Baron for his work at Nuremberg: I was given nothing.

Next day he received a letter of condolence from Lord Jowitt, the Lord Chancellor, who incidentally had been made a Viscount. 'I am deeply conscious of the great debt which this country owes you for your work in 1946,' wrote Jowitt, 'and I wish that I could have secured some public recognition of this fact. . . . However these things have a habit of righting themselves, but whether they do or not, it must be a consolation to you to know that all your friends—and their name is legion—realize the great part you played.'

To Lord Jowitt

> *Challens Green. January* 2, 1947. . . . I must thank you too for the most kind and generous letter which was sent on to me here from the Courts this morning. It was more than welcome, for I confess to you and to nobody else, that I spent a day nursing my most grievous hurt. For it is idle to deny that I am hurt, deeply and grievously.
>
> I should like you to understand, and I think you do, that I never expected or desired any reward for my work at Nuremberg. I never thought that the distribution of honours for the regular work of a criminal trial could compare with the dignity of the procedure in the United States where the President thanked both the American judges publicly for their work for the country.
>
> But to announce publicly that one of the British judges at Nuremberg was worthy of a peerage, and (by implication) that

> the work of the other was unworthy of any public recognition of any kind is quite a different thing. It is, on any view of the facts, unkind and unjust, because it seems to imply to the public that his work was not acceptable, and may injure his public usefulness for the future.
>
> . . . You will understand therefore how all yesterday and today those familiar lines of poor Johnson kept running through my head:
>
> > 'I had done all I could; and no man is well pleased to have his all neglected, be it ever so little.'

Birkett was fortunate in having his wife at his side to sustain him during this trying period, and he paid her a well deserved tribute in his diary.

> 4 *January*. This has been a bad start for the New Year and I have never been so sad for a long time. Through it all my Billy has been a tower of strength, strong, courageous, sensible and radiant. The Honours of this world are very little beside that!

In the next Birthday Honours List Birkett was created a Member of His Majesty's Privy Council. The honour was announced on June 12, and Mr. Patrick Barry, K.C., (later Mr. Justice Barry), who happened to be in court when the new 'Right Honourable' took his seat on the Bench made what Birkett described as 'a neat speech of congratulation'. Then 'scores of wonderful letters' poured in upon him. 'It is really quite amazing to find myself so regarded by all sorts and conditions of men from Cabinet Ministers downwards —or upwards!'

Yet somehow he continued to feel dissatisfied. 'King's Counsel, Judge, Bencher, Honorary Fellow, Master, Privy Councillor—not a bad achievement really,' he mused, 'but yet I cannot feel content. John Simon thought it failure to be made Lord Chancellor when he wanted to be Prime Minister: and now of course he has lost even that! Jowitt has become Lord Chancellor, but I would like to know his inmost thoughts.'

8

Birkett continued to experience a sense of personal dissatisfaction, particularly when he was on circuit, which he disliked more and more because it separated him from his wife and home. 'I get easily depressed and dispirited these days,' he wrote when doing the Northern Circuit in October, 1947. 'I cannot recapture the joy of achievement I used to experience at the Bar. I am nervous of myself, without much confidence in my judgment and hesitant about sentences and damages and things of that kind. I have felt no glow of achievement in any summing up this circuit, though none of them has been bad.'

At Liverpool Assizes on this same circuit, Birkett had to try a remarkable case of seditious libel, the first prosecution of its kind to have been brought in England for over a century. The defendant, Mr. James Caunt, was the editor and publisher of a local newspaper, the *Morecambe and Heysham Visitor*, and the alleged libel consisted of an anti-Jewish attack in a leading article which, according to the prosecution, constituted an invitation to violence.

> If British Jewry is today suffering from the righteous wrath of British citizens, then they have only themselves to blame for their passive inactivity. Violence may be the only way of bringing them to a sense of their responsibility to the country in which they live.

It was also suggested in the article that the Jews only pretended to be ashamed of the terrorist acts being committed against the British forces in the mandated territory of Palestine.

Mr. Caunt admitted in evidence that he had meant to be offensive about the Jews, but he added that, rightly or wrongly, he had believed it was true that they had derived ill-gotten wealth through 'black market' activities, and he adhered to the opinion that there was a growing feeling that Britain was in the grip of the Jews.

'What did you intend to convey,' Mr. G. O. Slade, K.C., his counsel, asked him, 'by the passage to the effect that violence might be the only way of bringing the Jews to a sense of their responsibility?'

'I intended it to be a warning to the Jews of what would eventually happen to them if they did not mend their ways,' the defendant replied. 'It never entered my head that the passage could be interpreted as an invitation to violence.'

In cross-examination, the defendant agreed that he had charged the Jewish community with hypocrisy of the most unpleasant kind.

'You charged them with being heavily involved in the black market, and said in effect they were not concerned to earn a living as common tradesmen but rather to drift into industries where rackets thrived. That must have been extremely offensive to many people?'

'It was offensive. I intended the article to be offensive to the Jews.' Mr. Caunt went on to say that he did not think he was stirring up hostility or ill-will, not even against himself.

'Were you surprised that two Jews threatened you with personal violence?'

'I was not surprised then, and certainly not now, because I know the type.'

'You have built up an enormous mass of hatred in this article, haven't you, and been as offensive as possible?'

'Yes, but I do not think that a man reading the article as a whole would think that I was encouraging violence.'

Mr. Slade, addressing the jury for the defendant, said it would be a black day for freedom if they convicted Mr. Caunt. 'This prosecution is an attempt to put back the clock at least one hundred and fifty years.' Before 1792 it would not be unfair to say that seditious libel was anything which happened to be distasteful to the Government of the day. The well-known volumes of *State Trials* were disfigured by case after case of attempts to prevent free speech through prosecutions for seditious libel. Under Fox's Act of 1792, such cases were left to a jury to decide. 'This is not a matter of Jews and non-Jews,' continued defending counsel. 'It is a question of whether an editor has a right to say what he thinks and believes to be true without being hauled through the criminal courts by means of the antiquated weapon of seditious libel for over a hundred years.' What the prosecution was trying to do, he claimed, was precisely what was implied in the dictum of Cardinal Richelieu: 'Show me six lines written by the most honest man in the world and I will find enough in them to hang him.'

Summing up, Birkett said it was impossible to consider any

question affecting the Jews without strong emotions coming to the surface. 'There are some people who look upon the Jews with great compassion, who think that the ages have shown them to be the victims of martyrdom; on the other hand, there are people who feel very strongly incensed against the Jews because of alleged practices or matters of that kind. We will all do very wisely if we put aside any preconceived ideas whether sympathetic or the reverse, and look on this case with clear eyes and decide it on the evidence.' But, he went on, the issue of liberty of the press could not be overstated, and here he showed where his own sympathies lay, albeit reluctantly. 'It is in the highest degree essential—and I cannot over-emphasize its importance—that nothing should be done to destroy or weaken the liberty of the press.'

The same evening he wrote in his diary:

> 17 *November*, 1947. Seditious libel. *Rex* v. *Caunt*. Liverpool Assizes.
>
> I summed up quite well, though I wished I had had more time. There will be repercussions.
>
> Caunt was acquitted.

In fact, it only took the jury a quarter of an hour to find Caunt not guilty of seditious libel. The verdict was greeted with an outburst of cheering on the part of the spectators in court, which Birkett quickly suppressed. Unfortunately the defendant was not content with his acquittal and he afterwards chose to improve the occasion with a public statement outside the court, in which he put himself forward as the champion of the freedom of the press against a Government which 'appears to render lip-service to the Jewish community'. This action produced a strong leading article in next morning's edition of the Liberal *Manchester Guardian*, which Birkett cut out and preserved, as he was wholeheartedly in agreement with what it said about the case.

> All of us are for the freedom of the press, but we would prefer to be represented by any champion but Mr. Caunt. Freedom carries with it responsibilities as well as rights, and, like other precious things, it can be used well or ill. The jury decided that his leading article of August 6 did not constitute a seditious libel. It was a discreditable piece of work none the

less and the last thing we should wish to see held up as a sample of a free press. The writer has said that he meant it to be 'offensive to the Jews'. It was offensive to many others as well.

Throughout his time on the Bench, Birkett continued to be troubled by the question of sentences and what to pass in any particular case where there was a conviction. If he erred at all, it was almost invariably on the side of leniency. At Stafford Assizes in the same year, he noted in his diary: 'I find it hard to be severe on erring humanity, when the crime is not really serious, and cruelty is not involved.' This entry was prompted by an observation of the High Sheriff, Sir William Talbot, who had sat beside him on the Bench on the opening day of the Assizes and, according to Birkett, 'was much impressed by my conduct of the cases, saying I was humane and got the best out of everybody.'

An incident at Manchester Assizes, also in 1947, made an unforgettable impression upon a young police-sergeant, when Birkett was the trial judge in a manslaughter case. The accused had caused the death of a man during a brawl outside a public house in a South Lancashire colliery district by striking him savagely twice, with the result that the man fell down and died from striking the pavement. When charged at the police station by the Sergeant, who had arrested him, the accused replied, referring to the dead man, 'He kept moithering me.'

The police-sergeant had concluded his evidence at the trial and was about to leave the witness box, when Birkett said, 'Just one moment, Sergeant. I wonder if you could be good enough to help me. This word "moithering". What does it mean?'

'My Lord,' the Sergeant replied. 'It is a word which is commonly used in this part of Lancashire. It means—and I have no doubt that the accused intended it to mean when he used it—"to annoy persistently".'

The judge repeated the words 'to annoy persistently' slowly, wrote them down in his notes, and then looked up and said, 'I understand—I am most grateful to you, Sergeant.'

Of course, as a Lancashire man, Birkett was well aware of the meaning of this expression, and he could easily have aired his knowledge as some other judges had a habit of doing and told the jury its meaning. But it was not his method to show off in this way, and he preferred to make sure that the jury understood from the police witness whose evidence had impressed him. Incidentally, the prisoner was convicted of manslaughter, and Birkett noted afterwards in his diary: 'I gave him nine months, which he richly deserved.'

On another occasion he conspicuously tempered justice with mercy when the problems of three youths and three girls, all under twenty-one, were unfolded before him at Cambridge Assizes. The first case concerned an eighteen-year-old tractor driver, who was accused of having had unlawful carnal knowledge of a girl whose age was fifteen, and who had given birth to a baby. When he was told that the youth had subsequently married the girl, Birkett conditionally discharged him, saying: 'I have been impressed by the character you displayed during the girl's difficulty and the loyalty with which you stood by her. Now that you are man and wife, I hope you will be happy.'

The second case concerned a young soldier who was similarly charged in respect of a sixteen-year-old girl. Birkett was told by the man's counsel that he was anxious to marry the girl and that her parents were willing but that his parents would not give their consent and that an application was to be made to the court for permission to marry. 'It is a little outside my province to be a marriage broker, and there may be circumstances I am not aware of,' said Birkett in similarly discharging the soldier, 'but it seems a pity this bar should be put in their way, particularly where there is a child.'

The third case concerned an apprentice and a girl, aged fourteen. 'Do you think there is a chance they will marry?' Birkett asked the apprentice's father. 'It will be against my will if they do,' the father replied. 'I do not think they would be happy.'

'Well,' said Birkett to the young man, likewise binding him over, 'I am not here as a moralist, but you know what your duty should be.'

At the same time, the judge issued a general warning: 'If I have appeared to be lenient,' he said, 'no one must suppose I do not appreciate the importance of the Act of Parliament which must be observed. People should know that in appropriate cases the law will deal with offenders with the greatest possible severity.'[1]

[1] *News Chronicle*, May 17, 1950.

Indeed there were occasions when Birkett imposed an exemplary sentence. At the Old Bailey, in May 1947, he gave a gunman seven years and in addition ordered that he should receive six strokes of the 'cat'. 'Had a dreadful fight with myself to do this,' he noted in his diary afterwards, 'but I felt the public need demanded something dramatic to reassure them. It was as bad a case as possibly could be conceived.' So far as can be ascertained, this was the only occasion on which Birkett ever passed a sentence of corporal punishment, although on one other occasion he confided to his diary that he would have done so if the convicted man had been medically fit to be flogged or birched.

So far as the death penalty was concerned, Birkett felt that it might have a limited deterrent value and that, even after the passing of the Homicide Act of 1957, which restricted its scope, there might still be something to be said for its retention 'in certain isolated cases', such as the shooting of a policeman. At the same time, as he put it in his television interview with John Freeman in 1959, 'I have long thought that capital punishment was on the way out.' The first death sentence which he passed was in the treachery case during the Second World War, which has been noticed above. His second and only other capital sentence was in the trial, at the Old Bailey in May, 1948, of George Epton, an engineer, for the murder of Winifred Mulholland at his flat in Kensington. The prisoner was defended by Mr. Derek Curtis-Bennett, son of Birkett's old protagonist Sir Henry, and defence counsel raised a plea of insanity, but it was rejected by the jury after an hour's summing up by Birkett ('I think I covered everything but always have a most anxious time afterwards fearing I have not.'). Epton was found guilty and Birkett put on the Black Cap. But the condemned man was not executed, since the case was tried when the Criminal Justice Bill was before Parliament and, as an amendment to the Bill was brought forward abolishing the death penalty for murder, all convicted murderers were reprieved by the Home Secretary as a matter of policy during this period.[1] As events turned out, it was the last sentence of its kind which Birkett was called upon to pass.

A few of the civil actions which Birkett tried at this time may be mentioned here. In *Whiteford* v. *Hunter and Gleed*, which came

[1] After passing the Commons the amendment was rejected by the House of Lords in June, 1948. Executions were then resumed.

before him in the King's Bench Division of the High Court in July, 1948, without a jury, the plaintiff, an American consulting engineer practising in England, sued a medical specialist and a general practitioner for wrongly diagnosing inoperable cancer, as a result of which Mr. Whiteford gave up his flat, sold his business and belongings in England and returned to the United States. 'The facts are most unusual,' said Birkett in a reserved judgment which it took him four days to write and nearly two hours to deliver, 'and it is happily a rare occurrence for a man to be told that he is a victim of a dread disease, that nothing can be done for him, that in consequence he has a short time to live, and then, five months later, it is discovered that the diagnosis was wrong.' He described Mr. Hunter as a 'most distinguished surgeon', and referred to examinations carried out by him and Dr. Gleed, and said that they decided that Mr. Whiteford had extensive inoperable cancer. Later the plaintiff was seen by a surgeon in New York, Dr. Barringer, who found no evidence of cancer.

The judge went on to say that the evidence satisfied him that the case of each of the two defendants must be looked at separately if justice was to be done. He pointed out that Dr. Gleed was criticized for not using a cystoscope, but the general practitioner did not normally possess one, and that was one reason why a specialist was called in. On the evidence he found that Dr. Gleed had acted in accordance with the approved practice of the medical profession, and no negligence could be attributed to him. Therefore the action against him failed. On the other hand, he found that Mr. Hunter was negligent in not carrying out a microscopic examination or biopsy and in not using a cystoscope in his examination of Mr. Whiteford. 'If a cystoscopic examination and a sample had been taken for microscopic examination,' he said, 'in all probability the diagnosis of cancer would never have been made.' Having remarked that it was 'a dreadful ordeal' for a man to face and that 'to assess it in money was well-nigh impossible', Birkett awarded the plaintiff damages in all amounting to £6,300. These consisted of £2,000 general damages, including pain and suffering, and £4,300 special damages, covering Mr. Whiteford's fare to New York, his medical expenses in America, convalescence, and loss on the sale of his furniture and books, and loss of earnings.[1]

[1] *Evening Standard*, July 29, 1948.

Birkett's judgment in this case was reversed in the Court of Appeal, which held that, on the evidence, a finding that the surgeon was negligent in not carrying out a biopsy and not examining by cystoscope could not be supported. The patient then appealed to the House of Lords. 'I still think I was right,' Birkett noted afterwards, 'and I hope the House of Lords will say so.' But the House of Lords did not say so. On the contrary, their Lordships unanimously upheld the decision of the Court of Appeal. 'Nothing in the evidence showed that the surgeon was negligent not to use a cystoscope,' said Lord Porter, in delivering judgment. 'Even if Dr. Barringer's testimony were accepted in full, no specimen could have been taken by means of a cystoscope unless it were fitted with a rontgen attachment, and at the relevant date (1942) the instrument was rare in England and was not possessed by the defendant surgeon.'[1]

At Chelmsford Assizes, in June, 1950, Birkett had to try another unfortunate case, *Still* v. *Southend Borough Council*, in which he awarded damages of £2,500 to a schoolboy who lost the sight of one eye after a blow from a Bible. It had been thrown in a moment of temper by his mathematics master in the Southend High School for Boys in which the plaintiff was a pupil. Being the local education authority, the Southend Borough Council was joined as a defendant. It appeared that one day when the boy was putting away his books after class, the master had thrown the Bible at him with the remark, 'That will teach you to pay attention to your lessons!' The Bible struck the boy in the left eye. He subsequently underwent two operations, and besides losing the sight of the eye, the vision in the other eye was affected, so that he would always have to wear spectacles. The boy had intended joining the Merchant Navy, but had to abandon the idea, and was now studying music.

On the master's behalf, it was stated that no one regretted the accident more than he did. 'I have no doubt,' said Birkett in his judgment, 'that the master feels very deeply the tragic outcome of this rather foolish act which he committed in a moment of impatience, anger or irritation. I cannot help feeling that, if he had opened the book and read one or two passages, for example, from the Book of Proverbs, it would never have been thrown.'[2]

[1] [1950] *Weekly Notes*, 553.
[2] *Daily Telegraph*, June 30, 1950.

For one who always claimed to be and was no doubt rightly regarded as an advocate rather than a jurist, it is perhaps worth noting that relatively few of Birkett's decisions were reversed on appeal. Once, after he had awarded a sum of damages to a widow whose husband had been killed in an industrial accident, the Court of Appeal reduced the figure. This decision offended Birkett's deep and compassionate understanding of ordinary men and women, and he spoke of it with some feeling to a friend. 'If only I had been in a position to plead the case!' he remarked. But in another case, a particularly complicated one involving the construction of the Town and Country Planning Act, in which he quashed a compulsory purchase order of land made by the Minister, who subsequently took the case to the Court of Appeal and the House of Lords, his findings were upheld by both superior appellate courts,[1] although on the day he gave judgment he remarked in his diary that he was 'always filled with doubts whatever case I decide, whether I have decided it rightly'. Other notable judgments of his which were reported and now appear in the law books concerned rent restriction,[2] statute-barred debts,[3] a landlord's liability for dangerous property,[4] and a husband's right to deal with matrimonial assets.[5]

Nevertheless, he always missed the advocate's life and yearned for the old days. 'There is no satisfaction in work on the Bench at all comparable with the work one used to do at the Bar,' he wrote in his diary at this time. 'There is no scope for fine speaking or for playing on the emotions. I still have the power of dominating juries, however: they do whatever I wish.'

[1] *FitzWilliam Estates* v. *Minister of Town and Country Planning*, [1950] 2 A.E.R. 765; [1952] 1 A.E.R. 509.

[2] *Langford Property Co. Ltd.* v. *Goldrich* [1948] 2 A.E.R. 439.

[3] *Jones* v. *Belgrave Properties Ltd.* [1949] 1 A.E.R. 498.

[4] *Mount* v. *Good* [1950] 2 A.E.R. 1159.

[5] *Scott* v. *Scott* [1950] 2 A.E.R. 1154.

CHAPTER XII

COURT OF APPEAL

I

AT the beginning of the Michaelmas Law Sittings in 1948, Lords Justice Scott and Wrottesley resigned from the Court of Appeal, and Singleton and Denning JJ. were appointed, after Mr. Justice Lynskey had been offered the appointment and refused it. At the same time Lynskey was appointed Chairman of the Tribunal which had been set up to investigate certain corrupt practices in government circles. 'Denning and Lynskey both junior to me,' noted Birkett in his diary, 'so the painful truth is I have been passed over and I fear it is final. . . . A very sad day. . . .'

Just before the beginning of the Long Vacation in 1949, Birkett went down to the House of Lords and broached the subject directly with Jowitt.

> 30 *July*, 1949. . . . I have been depressed ever since I saw the Lord Chancellor. I can see that my advancement has been held up because of my career as an advocate, my facility in public speaking, etc., which detract from my reputation as a lawyer pure and simple.
>
> But I must acknowledge that I cannot give myself to a life which consists of reading Law Reports and cutting myself off from the main current of living. I have a mind which I can apply to any case which comes before me, and in this respect have much more judgment than either Jowitt or Simon.

Unfortunately Birkett had for some years been suffering from a duodenal ulcer originally developed during his arduous time considering appeals from internment orders made under Regulation 18B. The trouble came to a head on November 14, 1949, after a long day's sitting in the Court of Criminal Appeal followed by a broadcast on the work of the National Trust and a dinner at a London hotel. He was just sitting down at the table when 'something happened inside me which quite literally took my breath away'. The ulcer had perforated. After a quick diagnosis by a surgeon, he was taken off to the London Clinic where an emergency operation was performed. 'I don't ever remember pain so severe or prolonged,' the patient noted afterwards. 'Of the operation of course I knew nothing.' During the three weeks he remained in the clinic, 'there was a remarkable outpouring of good will for me which I am never likely to forget—flowers and letters in abundance'. He had many visitors and inquirers, including the Lord Chief Justice, Lord Goddard, and his old colleague on the Bench at Nuremberg, now Lord Oaksey. 'All my engagements had to go by the board, and to a man of my temperament it was hard to be laid aside.'

> 1 *January*, 1950. . . . I am improving every day, but am still absurdly nervous of myself fearing infection and indeed all the ills that flesh is heir to. . . . I hope for everybody's sake that I shall keep well and make 1950 the best year ever in achievement.

He returned to work in February, after an absence of three months, and was 'welcomed back by everybody'. The senior counsel in court, Mr. Scott Cairns, K.C., expressed the Bar's 'great pleasure' at his return. Birkett for his part apologized for the delay in giving judgment in a farm possession action, which he had tried in the previous November, when, as he put it, he was taken ill 'without warning, perhaps I should say, without proper or sufficient warning'.

He completed his convalescence during the Easter Vacation at the Swiss lakeside resort of Lugano and was back in the Law Courts at the beginning of the Summer Term, 'all eager to begin work'.

> 1 *May*. In my own Court again. Lunched in my room for my walking is none too good yet.
>
> 3 *May*. Walked to Bench at Inner Temple to lunch. Everybody most kind. . . .
>
> 6 *May*. . . . I have to see Lord Chancellor on Monday at 4.30, but what about I can only conjecture. Promotion?

8 *May*. . . . Saw Lord Chancellor. He offered me a Peerage, but without salary. I told him my finances could not permit me to accept.

Made Russell Vick certain of his Judgeship. . . .

His old friend and junior in the Midland Circuit, Richard Elwes, who had recently become a K.C., made his first appearance in Birkett's court in the same month. Birkett wrote to him:

I thought that I would send you this little note about your first appearance before me in the Front Row. I watched you with a most critical (if benevolent) eye, because it is so long ago now that I have seen you in action. My considered conclusion is that you ought to be the most outstanding success as a Silk, and that in due time, you will certainly ascend the Bench. First of all, you looked the part. This no doubt was Nature's doing, but none the less it is an asset of the most valuable kind. Again, through the kindness of Nature you have the most pleasing and attractive voice. It can be heard with perfect ease, and this again is an asset beyond price. Your Court manners in a somewhat exasperating case were of the best, and your courtesy to a somewhat trying opponent and his witnesses was good to see. In a word, (if you will allow a very old friend to say so without his appearing to be pontifical) you played your part as to the manner born. I felt that a word of this kind, if sincerely and honestly held, might be a stimulus and encouragement to you in these early days of your new life.

Birkett found his return to work, particularly on circuit, a great nervous strain.

29 *July*. I am at the end of my tether. I have worked very hard for twelve consecutive weeks, eight of them on Circuit, with many Speech Days, etc. I am jaded in mind and body. . . .

31 *August*. For the early part of the Vacation I was in poor shape, the term having taken a great deal out of me. My nerves were bad; I was oppressed by a thousand things—[the war in] Korea and all it might involve, my growing years. . . . But I gradually improved, and as I write this on the eve of our journey to Washington, I feel quite well and strong, although never free from some kind of worry or apprehension.

He had been invited with his wife to be the principal speaker at the Annual Dinner of the American and Canadian Bar Associations in Washington in September, and as he was on the point of leaving a letter arrived from the Lord Chancellor with the news he had so long hoped for. At last he was to go to the Court of Appeal and become Lord Justice Birkett. Again he quoted to himself Dr. Johnson's celebrated lines in his letter to Lord Chesterfield, noting them in his diary.

> The notice which you have been pleased to take of my labours, had it been early, had been kind; but it has been delayed till I am indifferent, and cannot enjoy it; till I am solitary, and cannot impart it; till I am known and do not want it.

The Prime Minister's official letter offering him the promotion reached him through the Embassy in Washington, and Birkett wired delightedly, 'Accept'.

At the dinner, which took place in the National Guard Armoury in Washington on September 21, and was attended by 3,100 members and guests, Birkett chose as his subject, 'Law and Literature'. But he was disappointed in his performance, although many people congratulated him. 'I thought the audience far too dispersed and too large to be on the intimate terms I would have liked,' he noted, 'and (I am afraid) I am a shade too literary for many of the audience.'

Here is a typical passage from his speech on this occasion:

> There has always been a long and honourable connection between law and literature. The books which lawyers have themselves written of the law and about the law are of course very many. I am glad to have upon my shelves at home many such American and Canadian books. But it is of course the life of the law in England that I know best. Some legal books have become the possession of the world. Blackstone's *Commentaries on the Laws of England* first published in the years 1765 to 1769 was one of the great events in legal history, and marked the first beginnings of true legal education in England. Jeremy Bentham said that book first taught jurisprudence to speak the language of the scholar and the gentleman.

But quite apart from what may be called law books, the contribution of law to literature has been immense. I happen to be a Bencher of the Inner Temple and whilst the former glories of the Inns of Court have in a large measure departed, some things abide through the centuries. Clarendon, who wrote *The History of The Great Rebellion*, was a member of the Middle Temple; Bacon with the *Essays* and the outpourings of that noble mind, is the glory of Gray's Inn; Sir Thomas More with his *Utopia* is the great son of Lincoln's Inn; and John Selden with his *Table Talk* belongs to the Inner Temple. Henry Fielding wrote *Tom Jones* in Pump Court; Cowper of the lovely Olney hymns came from the Middle Temple—Burke, Sheridan, De Quincy, Thomas More, R. D. Blackmore of *Lorna Doone*, Thackeray and a hundred others.

Charles Dickens was steeped in the traditions of the law and some of his books might even be made text-books. . . . Samuel Pepys had a very close connection with the Temple. In the famous diary for 1662 he records: 'I walked an hour in the Temple Garden recording my vows which it is a great content to me to see how I am a changed man in all respects since I took them.' And then he records the purchase of a very scandalous book from one whom he called 'my bookseller in the Temple', which book, says he, 'is a mighty lewd book, but yet not amiss for a sober man to read over to inform himself of the villainy of the world'.

The news of his appointment as Lord Justice Birkett was published in the newspapers during his homeward voyage in the *Mauretania* and more telegrams of congratulation reached him in mid-Atlantic. The Captain invited him to cocktails to celebrate and took him up to the bridge. He reached Southampton on the 1st October, where his son Michael met him with the news that he was to be sworn in by the Lord Chancellor at the opening of the Michaelmas Term on the following day, and they drove home together to Challens Green.

2 *October*. Sworn in before Lord Chancellor at House of Lords as Lord Justice of Appeal. Service in the Abbey where I went in my new gold robes: Chancellor's Breakfast and then Court of Appeal where I sat for the first time.

> 3 *October*. Sat with Bucknill and Singleton L.JJ. Felt quite at home.

2

Although his promotion satisfied his ambition and contributed to his peace of mind, since the judicial work kept him in London and he was relieved of the circuit duties, which had been his lot as a puisne judge, it would be wrong to pretend that Birkett really enjoyed sitting in the Court of Appeal. To tell the truth, he found the work dull, and its dullness increased as time went on. After fifteen months there, he wrote in a note on the year 1951 in his diary: 'The work in the Court of Appeal retained its dullness.'

The previous evening he had attended a dinner in the rebuilt hall of Gray's Inn to mark the retirement of the eighty-four-year-old Mr. Justice Humphreys, after nearly a quarter of a century on the Bench and forty years at the criminal Bar.

> 10 *January*, 1952. . . . Gray's Inn is now complete and is a perfect gem: it is the equal of the Middle Temple.

If Birkett delivered no outstanding reported judgments on points of law in the Court of Appeal, there was a marked feeling of humanity coupled with common sense in the way he applied his mind to the cases which came before him. 'Cannot feel confidence I am right in any matter of law,' he noted in his diary after he had attempted to apply the provisions of the Catering Wages Act, 'but on fact I always feel certain.'

A good example is afforded by his words in an action for false imprisonment which had been brought against a London department store by the mother of a girl caught shoplifting when accompanied by her mother, although there was no evidence to justify leaving the case of the mother to the jury. 'The questions that have been debated here are of the very greatest importance,' said Birkett in his judgment, 'affecting as they do the liberty of the subject and also the question of the respect which ought to be paid to the decision of juries.'[1] Other noteworthy judgments were delivered in a negligence case concerning boys vaulting in a school gymnasium, when he discussed the standard of care expected of the school authorities in the circumstances;[2] and also in a case involving the sale of a car with a defective speed indicator, silencer and braking system in the light of the Road Traffic Acts.[3] Perhaps his most notable judgment, however, was in an appeal by a wife petitioner in a divorce case where the trial judge had refused to grant a decree on the ground of the husband's cruelty. The court allowed the appeal, and this gave Birkett an opportunity of setting out what he conceived to be the duties of a judge.[4]

In this case the transcript of the shorthand note of the evidence showed quite plainly that all the witnesses were questioned by the judge in such a manner and to such an extent that the conduct of the case was virtually taken out of the hands of counsel altogether, and to Birkett's mind the trial was consequently most unsatisfactory.

> The duty of the judge to keep complete control of the proceedings before him is an essential part of the administration of justice in all our Courts. He has a duty to intervene by way of question or otherwise at any time that he deems it necessary to do so. He may wish to make obscurities in the evidence clear and intelligible; he may wish to probe a little further into matters that he deems important; and in a score of ways his interventions may be both desirable and beneficial. But it is safe to say that all his interventions must be governed by the supreme duty to see that a fair trial is enjoyed by the parties. His interventions must be interventions and not a complete usurpation of the functions of counsel. The task of eliciting the truth is assigned to counsel by the method of examination-in-chief, and perhaps particularly by cross-examination. In performing this task counsel may be gentle or stern, hostile or friendly, as the occasion and circumstances warranted. But the judge best serves the administration of justice by preserving the judicial calm and the judicial demeanour, aloof and detached from the arena of contention.

[1] *Turner* v. *John Lewis* [1951] 1 A.E.R. 814.
[2] *Wright* v. *Cheshire County Council* [1952] 2 A.E.R. 789.
[3] *Newall* v. *Howard* [1954] 1 A.E.R. 458.
[4] *The Times*, April 9, 1952.

In the present case, Birkett continued, the parties came from comparatively humble walks of life. They had received legal aid in order to come to the Courts at all. Such people were unaccustomed to the procedure of the Courts and they were likely to be overawed or frightened, or confused, or distressed when under the ordeal of prolonged questioning from the presiding judge. Moreover, when the questions took on a sarcastic or ironic note, as it was apt to do, or when it took on a hostile note, as was sometimes almost inevitable, the danger was not only that witnesses would be unable to present the evidence as they would wish, but the parties might begin to think, quite wrongly as it might be, that the judge was not holding the scales of justice quite evenly. 'In the kind of case before the Court, where the issues were of very great moment to the parties, touching their future welfare and happiness, it was peculiarly incumbent on the judge to exercise restraint, and to avoid the criticism made in this case that he had debarred himself from the exercise of the judicial faculty by the part he played at the hearing.'

During this period Birkett was constantly pressed to be the guest speaker at public dinners, literary luncheons, and school prize-givings, and to deliver presidential and other addresses on a variety of subjects, besides broadcasting and writing articles and reviews for newspapers and journals, besides forewords for other people's books.

In the summer of 1951, he broadcast three talks in the overseas service of the B.B.C. on the growth of international law, with particular reference to the work of the International Court of Justice, which had been set up under the United Nations Charter, and the protection of human rights. In November, 1952, he proposed the health of his old party political leader, Lord Samuel, at a dinner held in his honour at the National Liberal Club to mark the fiftieth anniversary of the veteran parliamentarian's first election to the House of Commons. 'In his long public life,' said Birkett, 'he has exhibited those qualities the English people most love to see in their leaders—courage, dignity, loyalty, integrity, and an unswerving devotion.'[1]

During the Michaelmas Term, 1953, Birkett celebrated his seventieth birthday, making more public speeches than ever before, 'some of them big ones'. One of the 'big ones' was an address on

[1] *The Times*, November 2, 1952.

'The Lawyer's Contribution to Society', which he delivered at the annual conference of the Law Society, the solicitors' professional organization in Scarborough. ('Spoke for an hour . . . very well received.') Among the societies of which he was President were the National Book League—in this capacity he opened the Festival of Britain Exhibition of Books at the Victoria and Albert Museum, London, in May, 1951—the Classical Association, the English Association, and the Holdsworth Club of the Law Faculty in the University of Birmingham. 'I lie awake at nights in order to appear spontaneous when I have an important speech to make,' he told his Cambridge contemporary, the Rev. Alfred Bellerby, at this time. 'I always have notes of the main headings in my pocket, but I never produce them, and the language always comes to clothe the ideas.'

To Henry Birkett

Challens Green, December 22, 1953. . . . We finished the term on Friday, and I have stood up to it quite well for one of 'the brave old boys'. When I think of Aunt Cissie I feel a youngster, and sometimes I feel a youngster anyhow, but the inexorable years tell their tale. I find that I fulfilled thirty-four engagements of one kind or another this term, and made more than twenty speeches also of one kind or another, that is good and bad.

I have been the chief guest of the Cricketers, the Footballers and the Golfers, and seeing that I never even batted at Tarn Close, or played on the Morecambe Road Ground, and struggled to the first hole on Outrake in twenty-four strokes (because of hitting the stone wall guarding the first green with persistent accuracy) I have the feeling that I am merely being colossally impudent. But nobody exposed me and I sat down to the usual 'Cheers and Laughter'.

The northern parson's opening prayer, 'Oh Lord, as thou wilt doubtless have seen in this morning's *Manchester Guardian* . . .' usually goes well at a cricket dinner when you link it with the exclusion of George Hirst from the Test team—'and in thy great mercy open the eyes of the Selectors. . . .' But one of the best little sayings I have picked up lately (which

> is infinitely adaptable) is that of the gentleman from California expatiating on the wonders of his State when he said, 'In California we are blessed with marvellous weather. We have 365 days of sunshine every year, *and that's a conservative estimate.*'
>
> Incidentally I get quite a lot of letters from visitors to Ulverston who say how much they regret the passing of the name BIRKETT'S from County Square. But all things change. Modern poetry has changed for the worse and I still go back to the music makers. The methods of succeeding at the Bar have changed, and there is nothing that remains unaffected unless it be the salaries of the judges. They are proposing to increase my salary from £5,000 to £8,000 and I am informed by the know-alls that my net increase will be £300. . . .

In his Presidential Address to the English Association on 'The Magic of Words', which he gave on June 21, 1953, with the second Earl of Birkenhead in the chair, Birkett remarked that, if ever he were left on a desert island and allowed one book, he would take the thirteen volumes of the *Oxford English Dictionary* and argue that they constituted a single volume. He went on to say:

> You cannot spend long years in the law, as I have done, without being conscious that the lawyer for many of his purposes—his Statutes and Wills and Conveyances and the like—must resolutely eschew the words that have colour and content himself with the 'hereinbefores' and 'aforesaids' in order to achieve precision. But the lawyer has moments when he, too, may employ the words of colour, as in that noble piece of English which made up the Oath of the Foreman of the Grand Jury in other days, or in the judgments of men like Lord MacNaghten, Lord Sumner, and the great and distinguished father of our distinguished Chairman today. . . .
>
> In a language like English it is sometimes said that there are no synonyms; there is the one perfect word for the occasion. But it yet remains true that we have many words in use where it is difficult to find any real difference of meaning, but there may be this tremendous difference in 'colour' or quality. It was said by that great authority, Jesperson, that when Canning wrote the inscription which appears on the monument to Pitt in Guildhall, an Alderman expressed grave displeasure at the

words Canning used, which were: 'He died poor'; and the Alderman wished them to be changed for the words 'He expired in indigent circumstances'. It approaches too nearly to a good joke for me to be quite satisfied of its truth, but it illustrates this use of words about which I am speaking.

It is my unfortunate lot to hear sometimes in cases concerning the Rent Act phrases such as 'He was evacuated to alternative accommodation', instead of 'He was sent to another home'. In one of the institutions with which I am concerned we had to consider certain plans which had been laid before us by the architect. Under certain rooms on the plan were the resounding words 'ablution cubicle' but it turned out to be an ordinary wash-room, which seemed a little disappointing after the promise of the original description. On that occasion I learnt further that 'long-term ablution' was the phrase used when you were speaking of a bathroom, and 'short-term ablution' when you were merely speaking of a wash-room.

So when I hear of targets, and overall targets, and global targets, and things being adumbrated or visualized, or finalized, or indeed envisaged, or circumstances eventuating or transpiring, I think of that other aim of this Association, 'To uphold the standards of English writing and speech', and I try to act accordingly when it lies in my power.

For his Presidential Address to the Holdsworth Club in Birmingham in May, 1954, Birkett chose his favourite subject of 'Advocacy', of which his own career at the Bar had been such a leading and successful exponent. Here is how he defined the advocate's art, as he saw it:

The first quality beyond all others in the advocate, whatever his particular type of advocacy may be, is that he must be a man of character. The Court must be able to rely on the advocate's word; his word must indeed be his bond; and when he asserts to the Court those matters which are within his personal knowledge, the Court must know for a surety that those things are as represented. The advocate has a duty to his client, a duty to the Court, and a duty to the State; but he has above all a duty to himself that he shall be, as far as lies in his power, a man of integrity. No profession calls for higher standards of honour and uprightness, and no profession, perhaps, offers greater temptations to forsake them; but whatever gifts an advocate may possess, be they never so dazzling, without the supreme qualification of an inner integrity he will fall short of the highest. . . .

The fact that the advocate is paid for his services ought not to blind the public to the true nature of the advocate's task; and indeed in a society where the administration of justice is recognized to be perhaps the most important thing affecting its welfare, it is essential that there should always be men of honour and uprightness who make the profession of the law their livelihood, trained to defend and to plead for the citizen, and zealously to guard his rights, his liberties, and, if need be, his life. . . .

It is clear that advocacy is made up of many elements. There is first of all, I repeat, the importance of the advocate himself. He should count himself exceedingly fortunate if he has been endowed with a good voice. But he must use it. He must speak so that he can be heard, and he must articulate clearly. He must try to acquire tone and modulation, so that his every sentence is pleasant to the ear. To the advocate, the spoken word is the breath of his life, and it is quite astonishing to me that so little thought is given to it. I would like to see it made a part of the training of the young advocate that he should be taught how to speak, and how to produce his voice to the best advantage. Go into any of the courts of law today, and you will see the distressing spectacle of men addressing judges or juries who quite obviously know nothing of voice-production, and who perpetually keep on taking sips of water from a tumbler to the complete distraction of those who listen to them.

An advocate like the late Sir Patrick Hastings would speak for a whole day and never once take his eyes away from the Bench or the jury-box and never once break the invisible and all-important link by stopping to call the usher to bring water to his aid.

Unfortunately, too, there are some qualities most desirable in the advocate about which he can do nothing. A commanding presence is a great asset, but if Nature has been careless about this, the advocate must do the best he can by making up for it in other directions. When Marshall Hall or Edward Carson came into Court everybody was conscious of their presence. There was a subtle change in the atmosphere, a tightening of the tension, an air of expectation, due in some measure to the extraordinary power of reputation, but mainly due to their physical presence. But on the other hand, an advocate like the late Mr. C. F. Vachell who practised in the Courts at Birmingham, so far from possessing a commanding presence possessed the most curious and gnome-like features and a comparatively insignificant body, yet he could enthral and enchain a jury by his wit and the power of his personality.

It is well if the advocate is possessed of a quick mind, alert to seize the unexpected opportunity, to adapt himself to the sudden changes which occur in the conduct of a case, and to be ready to deal with any interventions from the Bench, whether they be disconcerting or helpful. But more important than the quick mind is the understanding heart, the insight into human nature, the natural sympathy with all sorts and conditions of men, the intuitive recognition of what the particular situation demands.

It would be easy to enumerate many more qualities and attributes that it is desirable for the advocate to possess. He should be courageous, and ready at all times to maintain the independence of the Bar; he should be resolute, able to make up his mind and take decisions and to stand by them; he should be courteous and good-mannered; he should be able at all times to control his temper; he should be severe when severity is demanded, and he should be gentle when gentleness brings its own rich rewards. In a word, the advocate should bring all the qualities of his own personality to the great task of persuasion and employ them as the circumstances dictate.

But whether the advocate possessed all or any of these qualities, there are certain desirable things which it is in the power of all advocates to do. I will not presume to speak of the elementary things which have been written and spoken about for generations, but I will mention one or two of them lest it should be thought that I had overlooked them. In the conduct of any case, whether it be in the Magistrate's court or in the House of Lords, the advocate must have made himself master

> of all the facts; he must have a thorough understanding of the principles and rules of law which are applicable to the case and the ability to apply them on the instant; he must gauge with accuracy the atmosphere of the Court in which he pleads and adapt himself accordingly; he must be able to reason from the facts and the law to achieve the end he desires, and he must above all have mastered the art of expressing himself clearly and persuasively in acceptable English.

It was inevitable that speaking engagements such as these should take a toll of Birkett's health. On top of his duodenal ulcer, which had kept him away from the courts for three months in the winter of 1950–51, he developed heart trouble, which was to bother him intermittently for the remainder of his life. He was also subject to recurring fits of depression. 'I had a very good day free from all fibrillations or disturbance,' he noted on New Year's Day, 1953. 'But I get gloomy thoughts that the best of my life is over—with so little done.' Two days after returning from the Law Society's conference in September of the same year, he had a bad turn, which made him nervous, and a few days later he fainted for the first time in his life when going up some stairs at an exhibition which he opened in London, having sat in court and delivered two judgments earlier in the day. But he recovered quickly and next day spoke in the open air at the unveiling of a sign on the village green at Chalfont St. Giles, near his country home. He fainted on two other occasions in the first half of the following year, the second time on the railway station platform at Chalfont. 'The most serious thing is the effect on my nervous system, for I get most apprehensive of another fall,' he wrote in his diary afterwards. 'I have now had three—one last October, one on June 29th at Ashridge and one on July 19th. The two first are to be explained by going up a long flight of stairs after making a speech when I was nervously tense; the one at Ashridge by making a long walk uphill after speaking for 1½ hours; and the last one was due, I think, to my stomach being quite out of order and being generally overtired.'

After this experience, he seriously thought he would be obliged to resign his judgeship, but after three weeks' holiday in the South of France, at Agay near Saint Raphael, he returned to the new law term, feeling greatly refreshed. But his doctors told him that he must take things more easily, so while he was able to continue to sit in the Court of Appeal for the next two years he did reduce considerably his outside engagements. Among other interests which he was compelled to give up was his work as Chairman of the Governors of the Leys School.

To Henry Birkett

> *Challens Green. December* 25, 1954. . . . I have been pretty good this term and my doctor is very pleased with me, but you get to the stage when you find yourself saying, 'Of course he's only deceiving you to try and keep you from worrying.' But strange things happen. I was advised to take *quindine* to control auricular fibrillations, and a very eminent physician urged me to take strong doses. I did so for months, and such is the power of imagination, thought they were doing me good. When I went to Sir John Parkinson, the eminent heart specialist a month or so ago, he asked me if I took any drugs at all. I said with some pride, 'Quindine.' He said, 'Drop it at once and take nothing. You don't need anything at all.' Pale and shaken I dropped it and have never had a fibrillation since. But nerves and mind do make a very great difference. Confidence is the sovereign remedy.
>
> I have been cutting down outside engagements and have only made one after dinner speech this term, and that was a cricket one where I sat between Pelham Warner and Herbert Sutcliffe. Shades of Tarn Close and Fardy Robinson with his whip! When I sit in the pavilion at Lords as a member of the M.C.C., I expect old Fardy to come round with his whip and chase me into the cheap seats. Indeed at that cricket dinner I had a cable signed Bradman, Hassett and a dozen distinguished names saying they wished they could be present to hear me speak. I wish Fardy could have read that. . . .

Birkett made up his mind to retire from the Bench at the end of 1956, when he would have completed fifteen years as a High Court Judge. In the same year, the Inner Temple elected him its Treasurer. And so, on the last day of the term, just before Christmas, Lord Justice Birkett pushed back his chair on the Bench of No. 1 Appeal Court in the Law Courts and passed through the door to his room for the last time. 'The cordial good wishes of the profession will go with him,' remarked the *Law Journal* on the occasion, 'that he may long be able to enjoy all, or at least the first two of the recreations as listed in *Who's Who*, "Reading, gentle walking and occasional golf". . . . The profession will hope that in his retirement Sir Norman will find ease without idleness.' The expectation thus expressed in the professional journal of English lawyers was to be richly fulfilled.

Meanwhile Birkett found plenty to do that Christmas. 'I am receiving a very heavy post-bag,' he told his cousin, 'but it is good to think that so many people speak well of you and so many of them go out of their way to tell you. If I were not immune to vanity, I really believe that I should begin to fancy myself!'

3

'At last,' said Birkett when he was asked by press reporters how he felt about retiring from the law, 'at last I shall be able to watch a Test Match all through. It is one of my regrets that I never saw a Test from start to finish, because I was in court when I would like to have been at Lord's.' He admitted that he sometimes thought that he must have been born with a love of cricket, just as Gibbon and Macaulay seem to have been born with a love of reading. There was no other way to explain why some men developed a passion for the game while others were quite indifferent to it. 'I played it as a boy and a young man with great intensity, though not very well,' he went on to recall, 'and now I find my chief delight in watching cricket or reading about it. . . . I played cricket at Cambridge and I hope nobody will think me immodest if I say I went in first with a duty to lay a foundation and wear down the bowling. That was not the policy of the captain. We had a team that was composed of about seven "rabbits" and one or two good players and possibly a Blue. We sent the worst "rabbits" in first, so that the other side would probably have six of our wickets down for eight runs and think they were having an easy task—and in came the Blue and made 100, or 300, and then we declared. Those were the days when I went in first!'

If he never managed to see a Test Match through, Birkett did have Saturdays and what he called 'an occasional lucky day off'. And he had some wonderful memories. 'I shall always remember

Bradman coming down the Pavilion steps at Lord's under that great green cap with the fate of a Test Match on his shoulders, coming to the wicket and scoring off his very first ball.' He remembered, too, when he met Bradman, with the hero worship he had that day inside him and he would often think of the lines Browning wrote:

> Ah, did you once see Shelley plain,
>   And did he stop and speak to you?
> And did you speak to him again?
>   How strange it seems, and new!

Then there were Hammond and Paynter in their great stand at Lord's in 1938 when Hammond made 240 and Paynter was out at 99; Frank Woolley standing up to the 'quite murderous assault' of Gregory and Macdonald at Lord's in 1921 and scoring a near century in each innings; the fielding of Bradman and Fingleton, and particularly of C. E. Pellew, of Australia, 'racing along the boundary as fleet as a deer'; Patsy Hendren 'scampering his first run with a schoolboy's delight at having broken his duck'; Jack Hobbs at the wicket or fielding at cover-point. 'There they all are with scores of other memorable incidents stored in the memory and imagination for ever.' Incidentally, Birkett always considered Jack Hobbs to be the finest batsman that England ever produced, having scored no less than 61,237 runs between 1905 and 1934, despite the fact that he missed four cricket seasons because of the First World War. The best Test Match he recalled, although he did not see it, he had no hesitation in saying was Jessop's match at the Oval against the Australians in 1902, when England were left with 263 to get to win, with five wickets down for only 48 runs, and Jessop went in to score 104 out of 139 runs in 75 minutes. 'It was probably the greatest innings ever played in Test cricket.'

'The fascination of cricket is made up of many factors,' Birkett mused on the charm of the game, 'but I think that one of the reasons why cricket wins so many adherents is because of its setting. It is thought of as an essentially English thing, with its true home in the English countryside. After all, Broadhalfpenny Down and the Hambledon Club capture the thoughts and affections of all cricket lovers. And still today, when men speak of the charm of cricket, they are not thinking of the Test matches played on the historic grounds such as Lord's or the Oval. They are thinking of the lovely cricket grounds in the incomparable beauty of the English countryside, where they have spent many long summer days watching the cricket, and seeing the white clouds sailing by overhead and the shadows lengthening as the sun declines. . . . And so, when I think of cricket and cricketers, it is not to the lordly places that my mind turns first of all, but to a remote cricket field nestling among the Furness fells where I went as a boy to see the local heroes play. It lay outside the little country town of Ulverston, and you reached it by one of the steep, ancient ways which led to wonderful views of the Lakeland hills and the arm of the sea. But when you turned off the road into the cricket field, you were in the very heart of the English countryside. There was a little white pavilion and a primitive scoreboard, and wooden benches at intervals round the ground, and great trees at the boundary's edge. That quiet ground has represented for me all my life the charm and joy of the game of cricket, for I cannot help thinking that men played the game there just because they loved it.'

As Birkett surely appreciated, with his discriminating enthusiasm, cricket is outstandingly a connoisseur's game. To foreigners it is incomprehensible, but to its devotees whether Indian, Australian, South African, West Indian, or English, it inspires an affection which continues long after active playing days are over. And so it was with Norman Birkett. In 1955, the year before his retirement was announced, he wrote *The Game of Cricket* for the 'British Sports Past and Present' Series of books, beautifully produced and published by B. T. Batsford Ltd. The account which he gave of the game was equally compounded of his own experience as a player and as a spectator, and of his knowledge of cricketing history. The book was illustrated by a wide range of interesting historic pictures of the game and its players, from those of Paul Sandby and Francis Hayman in the eighteenth century to contemporary paintings of Lord's by Charles Cundall and Dennis Flanders, with notes by Miss Diana Rait Kerr, Librarian and Curator of the Marylebone Cricket Club where the originals are now preserved.

'The game of cricket is never likely to pass out of the national life,' was Birkett's conclusion, 'for it is sustained from age to age by those who rejoice to play the game and thus keep cricket ever young; and from age to age, too, the watchers of cricket and the readers about cricket continue to sing its praises, if not in the language of James Love of two hundred years ago, certainly in the same spirit.'

Hail, Cricket! glorious, manly British game!
First of all Sports! be first alike in Fame!
To my fir'd Soul thy busy transports bring
That I may feel thy Raptures, while I sing.

Birkett's other open-air interest, which lasted throughout his life, was the preservation of the English countryside. He gave practical expression to it by becoming Chairman of the Standing Committee on National Parks and also President of the Friends of the Lake District. In 1936, when the Elterwater Hall estate at Little Langdale came under the auctioneer's hammer, Birkett had bought one of the farms on the estate, comprising sixty-four acres, in order to protect this beautiful corner of Lakeland from falling into the hands of the 'development' builder. Then, nine years later, just at the end of the war, he had delivered the Rede Lecture at Cambridge University on 'National Parks and the Countryside', in which he drew attention to the lack of national parks in this country compared with the United States and Canada, and put forward some concrete proposals for the consideration of the Government in post-war planning:

> The countryside is commonly spoken of as a great national heritage, and so it is; but the literature of the countryside is a most noble heritage too, and of a range and power and beauty quite without equal. All the great names are there, and some of the very greatest, it is good to think, are in a very special sense the possession of this University. Herrick is ours, no less surely than Milton or Spenser. But the very greatest, down to the most lowly, give full and dutiful expression to that love of the country-side which is a national characteristic.
>
> And with all this, there are still no national parks! That wilderness of beauty the poets immortalized has become too often the wilderness of mean streets, the glory departed, and all the magic gone as though it had never been. In recent years, the beauty of the countryside has been destroyed on a very great scale, and that loss is now irremediable.
>
> The work of preservation has always been hard, and at times a little thankless, but latterly it has become quite heart-breaking. To save a footpath or a lonely moor or a piece of

common land from destruction, or to preserve some historic and beautiful spot, the voluntary societies established for this purpose, have had to toil and sweat, to cajole and implore, to plead and beseech, lead deputations to Ministers, waylay Members of Parliament, write letters to *The Times* and the *Manchester Guardian*, raise Defence Funds, and, in sheer desperation, employ counsel. And for all the comfort that the 'severe and sour-complexioned' men in Government departments (as Izaak Walton would have called them, and as they inevitably seem to be at such moments) can give, Wordsworth might never have written a line; 'Tintern Abbey' which Sir William Beach Thomas believes to contain the whole creed of the countryman, 'to be repeated aloud in places of beauty where altars are lifted to the north and south and east and west, and wherever the eyes are bent', might be quite without meaning, and that exceeding great army might never have been mobilized. Not that Government departments must be blamed too much. The burden lies heavily upon us all, and the blame must be much more widely distributed.

As things are at present, and as we have for so long allowed them to be, the harassed Minister and his advisers have a score of conflicting claims to harmonize, all put forward with zeal, and some with discretion.

The great city needs water, and water it must by all means have. The claims of the beauty lovers in the catchment areas, fearful of the impounding of lakes and tarns and rivers, with knowledge, maybe, of Thirlmere and Haweswater as they once were, no doubt seem at times to be a little remote from stern reality; and certainly, it may be conceded, the thirst of the body is more readily understandable than that divine thirst which from the soul doth rise. The country areas need electricity both for light and power, and overhead pylons seem to be a most regrettable necessity; but the indignant deputation to the Minister wrings its hands and speaks like Gordon Bottomley 'To an Ironmaster'.

On the one side are those who wish to 'develop' the land, as the official phrasing goes, those who wish to quarry and to mine with the almost unavoidable consequence of unsightly slag heaps and polluted and disfigured becks, those who wish to plaster the lovely and austere hills with ugly, monotonous conifer plantations, those who wish to drive great roads in the most unsuitable places, those who wish to take some remote and tranquil spot and use it for military purposes; and on the other side are those who wish to meet national needs in a practical way, but believe that this can be done without too much sacrifice of native beauty.

What, therefore, is the unhappy and tortured Minister to do? When the deputation, at long last, withdraws, he removes the expression of intense and sympathetic interest from his features, and turns, no doubt, to Hardy or Gilbert White for consolation, but all that he has permitted himself to say is that he is most grateful to the deputation, and the matter will have his most careful and earnest attention. Now the establishment of national parks will change all that for some at least of the most beautiful and precious parts of the land.

A National Parks Commission must be created, specially appointed and directed by Act of Parliament, administering a special National Parks Fund under parliamentary control, with a continuity of policy and power unaffected by the chances and changes of political life. The choice of areas for national parks, the definition of the boundaries, the nature and extent of every kind of development within the national park boundaries—all these matters would be in the hands of the Commissioners, who would be appointed by the Minister of Town and Country Planning, and the Minister would be answerable for the Commissioners in Parliament. The creation of such a Commission is regarded as quite fundamental, and it is apparent that the Government departments themselves would be very great gainers.[1]

It was a great satisfaction to Birkett when his proposals were eventually accepted by the Government and embodied in the National Parks and Access to the Countryside Act, which was placed on the Statute Book in 1949. Its most important feature was the setting up of a National Parks Commission, charged with designating the new National Parks and the Commissioners immediately designated the Lake District, the Peak District and Snowdonia, and some time later Dartmoor, all of which were confirmed by

[1] Sir Norman Birkett. *National Parks and the Countryside* (1945), pp. 10–13.

the Minister of Town and Country Planning, as extensive tracts of country of natural beauty, and offering opportunities for open-air recreation, where special measures should be taken to enhance their beauty and 'for the purpose of promoting their enjoyment by the public'.

Preservation of the countryside and access to the countryside were the key-notes of the Act, but they brought new problems with them, particularly in the matter of public behaviour. 'Go to some of the loveliest places in Britain, which are easily accessible,' Birkett remarked after the Act had been in operation for a year, 'and observe the discarded cigarette box, the chocolate wrappings, the remains of a meal with bottles and papers and sandwiches, gates to fields left open, old stone walls broken down, hay grass trampled, and many more matters of the like kind. No doubt, in a few cases offenders could be detected, and in certain cases, penalties could be enforced; but legislation however severe could not eradicate the evil. . . . The problem is to preserve the loveliest countryside in the world in its natural and characteristic beauty, and at the same time to provide opportunities for those who are so minded to visit in comfort and freedom. These two things are now nearer accomplishment than ever before. Long years of the most devoted labour are beginning to see some reward. It now remains to see that public behaviour in the countryside is such that the great advances made by the new Act should find their justification in the matter in which they are enjoyed. Public opinion, in the long run, will be the most effective weapon, and it is to public opinion that the efforts of all concerned with the countryside should be directed.'[1]

If it took twenty years of continuous agitation to establish National Parks in England and Wales, Birkett was to be made unpleasantly aware that a further continuous fight was needed to save them from the hand of the despoiler. But it was not so much the public behaviour of private individuals which formed the principal problem, although some of this was bad enough, as the intrusion into the area of the National Parks of many disfiguring elements as oil refineries, iron-ore stocking grounds, water reservoirs, electricity cables, atomic power stations and other industrial undertakings, both public and private. Tourism too brought renewed dangers in the shape of caravans and campers, noisy speed boats on the lakes, and

[1] *The Field* ('Problems of Behaviour in National Parks'), September 23, 1950.

congestion of motor traffic on the roads, and the consequent cry for more and bigger roads to carry still more traffic.

This was to be Birkett's main preoccupation during his few years of retirement, and it was to form the theme, as will be seen, of his last and, in the opinion of some, his greatest forensic triumph.

4

'Now that I have made the great decision and am retiring on January 5th,' Birkett had written to his cousin at Christmas, 1956, 'I hope to have a little more time to myself.' In particular, he hoped to be able to get on with the task of writing his memoirs, for which he now set about collecting material in earnest. He steadfastly refused lucrative offers from Sunday newspapers for articles on his life which would be 'ghosted' for him; he preferred to write his autobiography himself, as he did other articles on a variety of topical subjects, mostly connected with aspects of the law, which he was constantly being pressed to write.

Many years previously, a writer named Roland Wild had planned a book entitled *The Famous Cases of Norman Birkett*, which was announced for the autumn list of a well-known London publishing house in 1935. Birkett thereupon intervened through his solicitors to prevent its publication, pointing out that the work from its title, its cover and its contents was calculated to convey to the public that he approved of it and had even assisted in its preparation. 'You are, of course, aware of the rigid rules of etiquette that govern the Bar,' the solicitors had written to the prospective publishers, 'and professionally speaking it is highly improper for any member of the Bar to lend himself to self-advertisement'. The book was consequently withdrawn. But now the situation was changed, and, since Birkett had retired, anyone was free to write about his cases without consulting him, subject to the laws of libel and copyright.

To Henry Birkett

> *Challens Green. April* 20, 1957. . . . I now find myself continually looking back (a sure sign of age they tell me) and marking the change. I remember as vividly as if it were yesterday going down to Mr. Weaver at Ulverston station, where Smith's had their bookstall, to see if I had got 10/6 for an article in

> *T.P.'s weekly*. Now the Managing Director of W. H. Smith is a great personal friend of mine, and the *Star* and *Everybody's* pay me fifty guineas for 1,500 words—but it's scarcely worth writing for the money because it's all taken back in tax.
>
> It's a bit rich, too, the way newspapers write their series of 'Birkett's Famous Cases' without a word to me. . . .
>
> I am going to Ireland to give an address on 'Advocacy and Oratory' to the law students on May 17th, and the Benchers and all sorts of people are giving dinners, etc. so I rather wish that I had said 'No' to the invitation. . . . Then on June 6th I am speaking at a cricket dinner in Manchester to mark the centenary of Old Trafford. Viscount Monckton is proposing the toast of Old Trafford, and as a Vice-President of the Lancashire Club I am responding. There is a great centenary match with the M.C.C. . . .

A week or so after his return from Manchester, Birkett was asked by the Prime Minister, Mr. Macmillan, to become chairman of a small committee of Privy Councillors which it had been agreed by all three political parties in Parliament should hold an immediate inquiry into the exercise of the prerogative power by the Home Secretary of intercepting telephone communications, or telephone 'tapping', as it was commonly known. Public attention had recently been drawn to the practice in a criminal case where conversations between an accused person and his counsel had been 'tapped'. Besides the Liberal chairman, the other members appointed to the committee were Lord Monckton representing the Conservatives and Mr. Patrick Gordon Walker for the Labour Party. The committee were given the widest possible terms of reference, in particular to consider and report upon 'under what authority, to what extent and for what purposes this power has been exercised and to what use information so obtained has been put; and to recommend whether, how, and subject to what safeguards this power should be exercised and in what circumstances information obtained by such means should properly be used or disclosed'.[1]

The committee sat throughout the summer, holding in all seventeen meetings for the purpose of discussion and twelve meetings for the hearing of oral evidence. Their report, which Birkett himself

[1] *The Times*, June 29, 1957.

drafted, was presented to Parliament on its reassembly in the autumn. Its gist may be thus summarized:

(1) The right of the power to intercept communications can only be surmised, but the power has been exercised from very early times; and has been recognized by a succession of statutes covering the last 200 years or more.
(2) There is some difference of view on the authority to intercept telephone messages. On one view the power is identical with the power to open letters and rests on the ancient power to intercept communications. Another view is that the power rests on a comparatively modern statute, namely the Telegraph Act of 1868.
(3) The power to intercept communications is exercised for the prevention and detection of serious crime and for the preservation of the safety of the State.
(4) The power is now almost exclusively exercised by the Metropolitan Police, the Board of Customs and Excise and the Security Service. It is used with the greatest care and circumspection, under the strictest rules and safeguards, and never without the personal considered approval of the Home Secretary.
(5) The use of the power has been effective in detecting major criminals and preventing injury to national security.
(6) The exercise of the power in these limited spheres should be allowed to continue under the same strict rules and supervision and in the special circumstances set out above. The criminal and the wrongdoer should not be allowed to use services provided by the State for wrongful purposes quite unimpeded, and the Police, Customs, and the Security Service, ought not to be deprived of an effective weapon in their efforts to preserve and maintain order for the benefit of the community.
(7) The interference with the privacy of the ordinary law-abiding citizen or with his individual liberty is infinitesimal and only arises as the inevitable result of intercepting the communications of some wrongdoer. It has produced no harmful consequences.[1]

[1] *Report of the Committee of Privy Councillors appointed to inquire into the interception of communications.* Cmd. 283. (October, 1957). Mr. Gordon Walker, the Labour member, had some minor reservations, which were appended to the report as a separate

Besides the usual string of luncheons and dinners, his work at the University of London occupied much of his time. There was a great occasion when as Chairman of the University Court he had presided over the proceedings at which Queen Elizabeth the Queen Mother, who was Chancellor of the University, conferred an honorary degree upon her daughter Princess Margaret.

To Henry Birkett

Challens Green, December 8, 1957. . . . Everybody has been most kind, and the Queen Mother sent me a most charming letter. I am glad that you thought it was all right.

I had rather a full week. On Thursday I had the Society of Bookmen's dinner; on Friday I presided at the Dorchester for Foyle's Literary Luncheon to Lord Samuel; in the evening I proposed the toast of the Amersham Horticultural Society and quoted Bacon 'On Gardens' at them; and tonight I propose the Guests at the Centenary Dinner of the Savage Club. If I get a chance, I am going to quote the malicious Sydney Smith bidding farewell to the missionary who was going to the Cannibal Islands. 'Good-bye,' said he, 'and God Bless You! I hope you'll agree with the savages!'

Two days later an important looking envelope marked 'Urgent Personal and Confidential' and addressed to Birkett arrived at Challens Green. It was from the Prime Minister and its contents, which came as a surprise to Birkett, gave him particular pleasure.

Personal and Confidential 10 *Downing Street,*
Whitehall,
December 9, 1957.

Dear Sir Norman,

I have it in mind on the occasion of the forthcoming list of New Year Honours to submit your name to The Queen with a recommendation that Her Majesty may be graciously pleased to approve that the dignity of a Barony of the United Kingdom be conferred on you.

note. He wished that for the detection of crime telephones should only be 'tapped' in 'unusual and extraordinary cases of the utmost urgency, in which there would be no doubt that the use of the power would carry overwhelming public support' and then only on a sworn information or affidavit.

Universal Pictorial Press and Agency

LORD JUSTICE OF APPEAL

Outside the House of Lords after being sworn in.

British Broadcasting Corporation

WITH MARGARET LANE IN THE STUDIO FOR HIS LAST BROADCAST

I should be glad to know if this would be agreeable to you, and I will take no steps until I have your reply.

Yours very sincerely,

HAROLD MACMILLAN

The honour was indeed acceptable to Birkett, and he immediately wrote back to the Prime Minister to this effect. And so, on New Year's Day, 1958, Birkett's name appeared at the head of the 'Prime Minister's List' of New Year Honours.

To Henry Birkett

Challens Green, January 2, 1958. . . . It's a long time since I did stocktaking at County Square and wrote on some of the boards inside the dress cloths things like 'The Right Honourable Sir Norman Birkett' as I remember doing; but I don't remember that I ever got as high as a Lord! But it's nice to head the whole list, didn't you think?

Well, as Father and you have made BIRKETT OF ULVERSTON quite a name in the countryside, that is the name I am going to tell Garter King of Arms, who has written to me, that I am going to take. . . . Lord Birkett of Ulverston in the county of Lancaster has a pleasant sound at any rate. . . .

I am going to sit in the Judicial Committee of the Privy Council in Downing Street on January 14th for about three weeks to hear appeals from Ceylon.

And I am supposed to be a retired Lord Justice!

Seven weeks later, on February 20, he took his seat in the House of Lords, his sponsors being two fellow lawyers, Lord Morton of Henryton and Lord Evershed, Master of the Rolls. Meanwhile Birkett had been asked by Garter about a coat of arms for his escutcheon, and he had jokingly suggested 'A pair of scissors rampant on a yard of calico couchant!' Actually the arms he chose were, in heraldic language, 'Gules three full bottom wigs argent,' with the motto '*Lex mea lux*'. (The law is my light.)

Other tokens of public recognition followed in this year. He already possessed honorary degrees from the Universities of London, Birmingham and Hull. Now his *alma mater* proposed to confer upon him the degree of Doctor of Laws, *honoris causa*. 'This is a great honour,' he told his cousin Henry, 'and they cannot know of that country lad that crept to Ulverston Station to go to Cambridge for the Entrance Examination for Emmanuel, knowing that if he failed he would have to come all the way back!' The degree was duly conferred by the Chancellor of the University, Lord Tedder, as well as upon seven other distinguished men, including Mr. Dean Acheson, the former American Secretary of State, and the late Mr. Dag Hammarskjöld, the United Nations Secretary-General. In presenting him for the degree, the Public Orator made the customary speech in Latin in which he said that Lord Birkett was endowed with such a voice as Cicero declared to be the first requisite of an orator. To this he had added all the qualities of eloquence and in our own time there had been no one more skilled in swaying the mind of a jury. Nor was his reputation confined to the courts. His fund of anecdote and wide knowledge of literature made him the best of after-dinner speakers (*tanta copia inest fabellarum, litterarum tanta cognitio*). 'To literature indeed he has contributed much himself, both as a writer and an encourager of writers.'[1]

While he continued to sit on appeals before the Judicial Committee of the Privy Council and also the House of Lords,—'I thought it typical of the highest court in the land that most of the Lords of Appeal were deaf, and the learned counsel for the most part inaudible. *Fiat justitia!*'—he decided to give up the chairmanship of Buckingham Quarter Sessions, over which he had presided for the past twelve years. He had grown tired of the work at Aylesbury, although it only occurred four times a year, 'admonishing young offenders', as he put it, 'and sending old lags to preventive detention for ten years (think of it!).' At the same time, he admitted on reflection, 'there must always be a tinge of sadness at the end when you think of all the way you have come, and the people you have known.'[2] Indeed he experienced more than a tinge when he went back to Ulverston to receive the town's official congratulations on his peerage, recorded on a silver tray presented to him by the local Urban District Council as 'Ulverston's most distinguished son' and he recalled his boyhood and told the people of Ulverston, in his speech of thanks, how he had carried with him the image and memory of those early days, and how at every stage of his career he was stimulated and encouraged by the kindly feelings of the

[1] *The Times*, *Cambridge Daily News*, June 6, 1958.
[2] *Evening News*, June 24, 1958.

townsfolk of his birthplace. 'During my life I have learned you can buy or acquire many things,' he added, his voice near to breaking point. 'You can buy an ermine mantle, but the things that are of the most value are never to be bought or acquired. They are, in fact, bestowed and I regard tonight's presentation to me as one of the great bestowals, one of those things which are beyond all price.[1]

'I am not pretending that my own retirement was a terrible wrench,' he wrote about this period, 'for it is much alleviated by my being allowed to sit in the Judicial Committee of the Privy Council and the Appellate Committee of the House of Lords on occasion. But if you have enjoyed your work, the parting from it is not easy. Whatever the life and whatever the experience I doubt whether any man says farewell to it without some emotion.' And then, as he found, 'in retirement, how the great moments stand out'. That first brief, in the Magistrate's Court at Birmingham; that great moment when the Clerk of Assize on the Midland Circuit, the beloved George Bancroft, 'almost reverently' laid in his hands his first Poor Prisoner's Defence on a charge of murder at Bedford Assizes; the day when he stood at the end of the line of new 'silks' waiting to be called within the Bar, and caught the encouraging smile of 'that great man', Lord Justice Scrutton; the sadness it was to leave the Bar for the Bench; the 'wonderful companionship' of the members of the Court of Appeal, which compensated in some degree for what one of them, Lord Justice Asquith, called 'plain black robes and grinding work'. All these things, and countless others, came back so vividly to Birkett that it was difficult to think that some of them had happened 'a great while since, a long, long time ago'. But they had 'and one of the more satisfactory pleasures of retirement is to have occasional moments in which to think about them and to live again the great days in the distance enchanted'.[2]

5

Birkett again re-lived some of the past when, in February 1959, he appeared before the television cameras in the first of the B.B.C. series 'Face to Face', subsequently made famous by the interviewer, Mr. John Freeman. This initial venture was generally acclaimed a

[1] *Lancashire Evening Post*, October 9, 1958.
[2] Lord Birkett. 'Reflections in Retirement', in *The Oxford Lawyer*, Vol. 2, No. 1 (1959).

great success, in which Birkett's candour and fluency and his shrewd, benign manner were well matched by the thorough yet polite probing of the interviewer on matters of conscience, law and detailed record. 'It's a long time since half an hour went so quickly,' remarked the *Sunday Times* television critic after the performance.[1]

'Lord Birkett,' Mr. Freeman began, 'you are known to the world, I suppose, as one of the three or four greatest criminal lawyers of this century, and perhaps one of the three or four greatest cross-examiners of all time. Now, I want you to tell me, face to face, what manner of man you really are. First, then, about the law. Do your murder trials stand out in your memory as great dramatic high-lights?'

'One or two of them do, I think,' Birkett answered carefully as if searching the recesses of his mind. 'I think there's a danger of rather exaggerating their importance. The number of murder trials, or indeed criminal trials, that one takes part in are a very small part of one's work. But one or two of them do stand out as very dramatic—for example, Dr. Ruxton at Manchester, or the Rouse trial down at Northampton—both struck me as being very dramatic indeed.'

'Do you happen to remember how many successful murder defences you undertook in your career at the Bar?'

'If it doesn't sound immodest,' replied Birkett with a chuckle, 'it's easier to remember those in which I failed!'

'Well, how many did you fail in?'

'Well, three, I think.'

'Out of many dozens?'

'Yes.'

'Now,' continued Mr. Freeman. 'I want to ask you, did you yourself always believe in the innocence of your clients when you defended them?'

'To be quite, quite frank, no,' said Birkett. 'I think I just ought to say this, that you know, whatever your belief is, you're not allowed to state it in the court. I once remember a man saying, "Now, m'Lord, I lay aside my wig. I speak as a man," and the judge said, "And I shall stop you if you do." You're allowed to speak as an advocate, but you mustn't give your opinion.'

'Did you personally ever have any qualms about defending some-one on a murder charge, whom you believed to be guilty?'

[1] *Sunday Times*, February 8, 1959.

'None,' Birkett was at pains to explain. 'You see, the view I took of the advocate's duty,—and I think it's the right one—is this. He's there to present one side only, and he must do it to the very best of his ability, and do for the man what he himself would do, had he the ability to do it; and what he thinks really is irrelevant, as Dr. Johnson said.'

But when Mr. Freeman went on to ask whether he thought it was his duty as counsel 'to use every possible trick within the law to get a man acquitted', Birkett rejected the word 'trick'. He made it clear that he was against tricks of all kinds, but if he were asked whether he regarded it as his duty to do everything within his *power*, within the *rules*, to get him acquitted, he would agree.

'And that would include, perhaps, bamboozling a jury?'

'Well, shall I say, *persuading* a jury,' Birkett put it with his customary courtesy. 'I wouldn't *bamboozle* them. You know, the common complaint that "he threw dust into the eyes of the jury" is a very ancient one, and no counsel is supposed to throw dust into the eyes of the jury. What you *do* is to try and persuade them to your point of view.'

In answer to further questions, Birkett admitted that he had indeed got a prisoner acquitted on a murder charge when he believed that prisoner to be guilty, and he went on to draw the distinction, which has already been noticed, between defending a client whom the advocate believes to be guilty and defending one whom he knows to be guilty.[1]

'Did you ever refuse a brief because of moral certainty that the person who offered it to you was guilty?'

'Never.'

'Have you ever felt sure that someone convicted on a capital charge was innocent?'

'Never.'

'So that you know of no case where a man has gone to the gallows wrongly?'

'Never,' repeated Birkett. 'Indeed, I'd like to say I think possibly I could recall one case during the war where a young man was convicted who ought not to have been convicted, at least in my opinion, but it's so rare that that's about the only case that stands out in my mind.'

[1] See above, p. 428.

'Did that particular person go to the gallows?'

'No. He went to penal servitude.'

'You would never refuse a brief because you disliked the kind of offence which was alleged?' Mr. Freeman persisted.

'Oh, no indeed,' said Birkett, with some emphasis. 'Oh, no indeed. Otherwise one would refuse half the cases. But I think I still ought to point out that the criminal side of one's practice is comparatively small compared with the civil.'

'Nevertheless, you would surely agree that a great deal of your public reputation was based on your exploits in the criminal courts?'

'Yes, I think so.'

'More so, perhaps, than many other leading counsel of your day?'

'I think so, too, yes.'

'Now, what was it that particularly attracted you, because it is true, isn't it, that many lawyers affect to look down a little on criminal practice?'

'They do, yes.'

'Now, why did a man of your ability find this so attractive?'

'Well I found a very great fascination in winning twelve people to my point of view. There is a very great attraction and fascination in the exercise of persuasive speech; and I daresay, if one began to analyse it, that was one of the factors.'

'It's always said of you by many of your friends and those who have followed you that your great asset in persuasive speech was the appearance of sincerity. Do you agree with that?'

'Well, if so,' Birkett replied, 'it wasn't so to speak a piece of acting. It's quite impossible to persuade a jury by talking nonsense and the thing that you say must at least have the appearance of sound sense; otherwise it's no good. And when you're presenting that to the jury, you must certainly give the impression that you are sincere.'

'Even in those cases where your own private belief was that your client was guilty?'

'Yes,' said Birkett, and proceeded to give as an illustration the case of Dr. Ruxton, of whose guilt he gradually became convinced as the case went on, but this did not make him any the less eager to do what he could for the accused.

Passing on to his education and family background, the interviewer asked him about his schooling and boyhood experience.

'Did you ever regret not having been to a public school?'

'Yes,' replied Birkett. 'I'm not sure that it was a wise regret, but I've often said—the way I put it—I'd like to have made a century for Harrow at Lord's or something of that kind. But on reflection I'm not at all sure that there weren't very many compensations; by the time I went to Cambridge and took part in the debates at the Union I was a fairly practised speaker.'

'Did you send your son to a public school?'

'Yes, he went to Stowe.'

'What sort of upbringing did you have in childhood?' Mr. Freeman continued his line of questioning. 'I mean, were your family puritanical and stern?'

'Well, my father and mother, they were Wesleyan Methodists,' Birkett answered, 'and I suppose one would say they were very, very devoted people. I shall always be grateful for my home life and for the chapel life to which they led me. My knowledge of the Authorized Version and the hymns of Wesley and Watts are certainly some of my very greatest possessions, and at the most formative period of my life I shall never cease to be grateful for the training I had in religious things.'

'Do you still hold these beliefs yourself?'

'No. You know, as one grows older one rather grows out of certain ideas, and, although I have my own very strong views about the conduct of life and the qualities which are necessary for the conduct of life, the great doctrinal things rather perplex me and trouble me.'

Mr. Freeman now posed a most pertinent question.

'Would you in fact describe yourself as a Christian, or not?'

Birkett paused for a moment or two before replying. 'I would call myself a Christian,' he said, 'but, of course, as it was once said, you've got to define your terms. If you mean, do I believe in what are called *Christian* qualities, I most certainly do.'

'But not perhaps in the Thirty Nine Articles?'

'I sometimes would like to say that I called myself a Christian agnostic,' said Birkett to this question, 'but I don't know whether that term is permissible.'

'Well, it is to me,' commented Mr. Freeman, 'but I'm not sure whether it would be to many Christians!'

The interviewer then turned to Birkett's professional career.

'Looking back on your life now—you've had this terribly busy life—you were an M.P. for a time, you've been one of the leading counsel at the Bar—would you choose such a busy life, if you had your time over again?'

'Yes, I think so, I think so,' Birkett answered. 'My life at the Bar certainly was the happiest period of my life. It stands well out in my mind as compared with being a judge, or a Lord Justice, or anything else. It was a really happy time, though every moment of one's day, and almost night, was spent in that work.'

'Exactly. But then what about your family life? Did you, for instance, have enough time to supervise the upbringing of your children?'

'No, I wouldn't say I did, myself. We had, of course—I was earning a lot of money—we had opportunity of good nurses, and household staff, and things of that kind, but I'm bound to say that so far as the children were concerned, I didn't do very much in the way of personal supervision.'

The mention of money brought Mr. Freeman to the question of Birkett's earnings at the Bar. While admitting that he was 'a bit shy about giving figures, perhaps it would be enough for me to say that when I became a judge, at £5,000 a year, it was a terrible financial sacrifice'. He agreed, when pressed by the interviewer, that his income at the height of his career averaged round £30,000 a year, 'sometimes below it, sometimes above it.'

'Were you—and are you, indeed—a thrifty man?' Mr. Freeman continued. 'Did you save and invest your money?'

'Yes,' said Birkett. 'You see, one of the advantages was in my day that you could save a little. I paid very large sums in taxation. But I was always a thrifty man in that sense, largely because of my upbringing, I suppose, and I did save.'

'During the whole of your busiest practice at the Bar, how many poor people's defences did you undertake?'

'Well, I always as a matter of principle took on so many a year. Very many of the murder cases, about which you spoke, were done under the Poor Persons' Rules, because I always felt it as a kind of duty. It was Bacon, I think, who said, "Every man is a debtor to his profession and ought to make some kind of return", and that was the way I thought of it. The profession has been very good to me, and I thought, well, I can make some slight return—and I did.'

Mr. Freeman then asked Birkett about his career on the Bench, his views on capital punishment, and the War Crimes Trials at Nuremberg.

FREEMAN: You did eventually become a judge in, I think, 1941. Had you ever turned down the opportunity before?

BIRKETT: Yes.

FREEMAN: Why did you do that?

BIRKETT: Because I wasn't really drawn to the judicial office. I loved the Bar so much. It wasn't the money, but I loved the life of the Bar, and I think, you know, the life of a judge, and I've proved it since, is a bit remote and a little lonely. You're necessarily withdrawn from the ordinary life of the Bar, and it's—as I say, I turned it down.

FREEMAN: And the remark you've just made means that you did in fact pine for the Bar when you were on the Bench?

BIRKETT: Well, pine is a strong word, but shall I say I had slight yearnings that way.

FREEMAN: Because it was dull, or because it was isolated, or——?

BIRKETT: Well, I felt as a matter—To be quite honest, sometimes when I listened to cases being conducted, I felt how much I would like to be down there doing it.

FREEMAN: In other words, you missed the chance of appealing to the twelve men, that you were talking about earlier.

BIRKETT: That's right. That's right, yes.

FREEMAN: Do you remember when you gave your first death sentence?

BIRKETT: Yes, quite well.

FREEMAN: Did that move you very much?

BIRKETT: No. Quite contrary to my expectation—I'd always rather dreaded it, but when the actual moment came, I did it without the slightest trace of emotion.

FREEMAN: What sort of case was it?

BIRKETT: It was a case during the war, and it was a case where a young sailor had betrayed the position of a convoy to the Germans, and the Germans attacked and sank the convoy, and the charge I think was under the Treachery Act, I think—the Treachery Act or something of that kind. At any rate, when the moment came for me to sentence him to death, I did it without any emotion at all.

FREEMAN: Do you yourself now believe in capital punishment?

BIRKETT: Well, I think the Homicide Act of 1957 has really rather solved that problem. I have long thought that capital punishment was on the way out. I'm not sure that the Act of 1957 doesn't raise equally difficult problems, but I think, for example, that where you have an element of deterrence, if such there be, that there may still be something to be said for capital punishment in certain isolated cases. For example, it's a capital offence for a man to shoot a policeman, and of course if that deters people—the fact that that is a capital offence—well, I don't see very much harm in retaining that.

FREEMAN: You, at any rate, never felt any personal qualms about sentencing a man to death?

BIRKETT: No.

FREEMAN: Never any doubt that you were doing it justly?

BIRKETT: No. You see, it's a very curious thing that when you sit in the seat of justice how impartial you become. I won't say you become inhuman. That would be quite wrong. You must keep your human sympathies, and your human faculties all alert, but I think you do get a detached, dispassionate outlook upon things which permits you to do your duty. I think so.

FREEMAN: Well now, in the world outside this country, I suppose that you're perhaps best known as being one of the judges at the Nuremberg war crimes trial, and I'd like to ask you a bit about that. First of all, I never saw the accused who were present at that trial. You did. What did you make of men like Goering and Hess and the rest of them?

BIRKETT: Well, of course, I saw them about the distance—little more than I am from you at the moment, for twelve months, every day, in every possible situation. Goering, for a very long time, simply dominated the court. He was a man of very great personality, and when he came to give evidence in the witness box he did very well indeed.

FREEMAN: Well, I was going to ask—did you at any time have the feeling that you'd sort of got on terms with any of the accused? You warmed a little to Goering, did you?

BIRKETT: No. I never did to Goering, largely because I knew his history and I knew the kind of man he was. The kind of man for whom I felt a little sympathy was a man like Speer, who was only brought in by Hitler towards the end, and was involved in all this, not in creating aggressive war or anything of that kind, but because he took part in the Sauckel policy, of bringing all these people from the other satellite countries.

FREEMAN: Did this extraordinary polyglot team of judges, and barristers, and barristers' clerks and everything else that was assembled at Nuremberg—did you in fact manage to work together as a unified team?

BIRKETT: Ultimately, yes. There was a little difficulty at first with regard to the Russian judges. I sat next to General Nikitchenko throughout the hearings and we became the greatest possible friends, and it's much to my regret that when we left Nuremberg, and he promised to keep in touch with me, I've never heard from him since, though I've inquired. But at first the Russian judges were very recalcitrant; if a proposal was raised by one of the German counsel in favour of the defence they were against it, without any argument at all, and one had to try and persuade them to come to one's point of view. But it was very, very difficult. But ultimately we worked together.

FREEMAN: Just by the way—have you ever written to him?

BIRKETT: Yes, indeed. My wife sent him and the other judges a wonderful album of photographs covering the whole time we were there, and fountain pens and all sorts of things. Never any acknowledgement.

FREEMAN: Now did any of the accused at Nuremberg take the trial seriously—that is to say, did they behave as if they thought there was any possibility of their being acquitted?

BIRKETT: Yes, I think so. I think Schacht did. And he was, of course, acquitted. I think Schacht did. I think a good many of the other people thought, well, this is merely the victors trying the vanquished.

FREEMAN: Well, wasn't it?

BIRKETT: Well, it was in truth, but I don't see how that was to be avoided, but the only question I think that can really be asked about Nuremberg: was it a fair trial? and I think it was.

FREEMAN: Well, I would like to ask another question. I don't doubt that, but I'd like to ask you a different question. Looking back on it, do you think that justice was in the end served by staging a trial without really the existence of a law?

BIRKETT: Well, there was. You see, that's commonly stated, which is quite wrong. There was a law. The Charter of 1945 which governed all the activities of the tribunal, certainly set down the law as it existed. It was not a creation of law, it was international law as it existed.

FREEMAN: Well, now, could we just look into that for one moment, because you see the soldier now is presented with a very remarkable dilemma, because none of the soldiers were allowed to plead that they were ordered to do what they did by their superior officers.

BIRKETT: Well, but there was nothing new about that. You see, after the First World War there was the *Llandovery Castle*, where the Leipzig Court, a German court, wouldn't allow the defence of superior orders. And in the Charter of 1945 it was expressly stated that superior orders shall not be a defence, but it may be a mitigation. Well, that's always been the law. It's quite true that in our manual of military law there was a mistake, which was amended in 1944, but the true position is that the soldier is bound to obey orders that are not manifestly unlawful. But if he does take part in unlawful activities that really can be no defence.

FREEMAN: Well, I hope soldiers will feel comfortable in this dilemma.

BIRKETT: Well, you see, I know there's been trouble about this. It was because of Keitel and Jodl. You see, Field-Marshal Keitel and General Jodl were both convicted and hanged, but if you examine the Nuremberg records you will find that they weren't just merely acting under superior orders. Take the murder of fifty airmen—the *murder* of fifty airmen:—because that's what it was. They were taken out and shot. And Keitel was very largely responsible for it as indeed Goering was. Well, is anybody going to say that they could say well, you mustn't blame me, because Hitler told me to do it?

The interview came to an end with an interesting exchange on the combination of the Bar with politics. 'The real disappointment in my life,' Birkett admitted with a wry smile, 'was that, being a Liberal, the Liberal Party, when I was ready to take part in Elections, was on the decline, and therefore I could never be a Law Officer of the

Crown, because you must be in Parliament and your Party must be in power. That was really one of the disappointments, because when one goes to the Bar one rather hopes that politics and the Bar together will lead one a good long way.'

'It is, of course, often said, and experience bears this out, that politics and the Bar *don't* mix awfully well in most cases. Now, why is that?' Freeman asked. 'Is there some quality which is needed for politics, which the lawyer doesn't have?'

'Yes,' Birkett agreed. 'You see, in the law, the barrister, the advocate, has all the preparatory work done for him by the solicitor, and he's merely got to get it up and have it firmly in his mind. But in politics he must be rather more original; and I think that's one of the very great difficulties—that where the barrister can do his job because somebody has put all the material before him, he finds it a little more difficult in the political sphere, when he's got to do the work for himself.'

'And this, therefore, is your lost ambition?' Mr. Freeman finally queried.

'Well, in a sense,' said Birkett. 'At the time I was in the House of Commons, I was far too busy to attend to the House of Commons. That was the trouble. I never got down there until about five o'clock in the evening, and then I had to get up all the briefs for next day. It was that kind of life, and I think that the very busy man really cannot combine the two.'

From the chorus of praise which greeted the interview in the press, two tributes may be mentioned. 'It was a superb interview of a superb character who could afford to wear his heart on his sleeve,' wrote Colin Frame in the *Star*, '—and did so to our delight.' Or, as the *New Statesman* put it, 'many viewers must have felt like a coach-party visiting Chatsworth who suddenly realize that they are being shown round by the Duke in person.'[1]

[1] *Star*, February 5; *New Statesman*, February 14, 1959.

CHAPTER XIII

HOUSE OF LORDS

I

IF Birkett had been 'far too busy' to attend the House of Commons punctually and regularly, when he was an M.P., his many interests in retirement prevented him from putting in more than an occasional appearance in the House of Lords. Indeed, he waited for over a year after taking his seat before he made his maiden speech in that assembly, and he was only to address the Upper House on three other occasions during the remainder of his life.

The occasion of Birkett's maiden speech was a motion moved by the Labour peer, Lord Pakenham, later Earl of Longford, on April 8, 1959, calling attention to crime in Great Britain 'at the present time'. Birkett spoke sixth in the debate, immediately following Lord Nathan, who as Chairman of the Trustees of the Isaac Wolfson Foundation had announced to the House that on behalf of the Foundation he had offered to the University of Cambridge, and the University had accepted, the sum of £150,000 for the purpose of founding a Chair of Criminology in association with the recently established Institute of Criminology at Cambridge. As one of the trustees, Birkett had warmly supported the gift and he now made use of the opportunity to express his views on the subject of crime and penal practice in the context of the newly created university institute.

> For over forty years now I have been associated in one capacity or another with the administration of the criminal law, first of all as a practitioner in the courts, and in my very early days mostly in the magistrates' courts. As your Lordships know, there the bulk of the criminal work of this country is

conducted, a fact which ought never to be overlooked. It is the court in which the ordinary member of the public is most likely to come into contact with the law, and the necessity for the right type of magistrate and the right type of education to be given to the magistrate is all important. I am glad to think that in my early days I had a very wide and prolonged acquaintance with the work of the magistrates' courts.

Then I became in due course a Judge of Assize, and have been for many years a Judge of Quarter Sessions. I know—and I want to relate this to the Institute of Criminology—that there is a feeling that Judges are averse to penal reform, I think it is largely a legacy from the past. As your Lordships know, there was a time when William Pitt and the Lord Chancellor, Lord Loughborough, publicly announced that there should be no reform of the criminal law unless it originated from the Judges or, alternatively, the proposal had been considered by the Judges and approved by them. When Sir Samuel Romilly, in the early part of the nineteenth century, began his noble work of reform and introduced his three Bills—one of which was to abolish the death penalty for stealing forty shillings in a house, or the death penalty for stealing five shillings worth of goods in a shop—it was defeated in this House, although it had passed the other place, by Lord Eldon, the Lord Chancellor, and Lord Ellenborough, the Lord Chief Justice, rising in their places and saying on behalf of all the Judges that that humane proposal, as we now think it, would simply demoralize the structure of society and forthwith ought to be defeated—as it was, with the assistance of many of the right reverend Prelates.

I wanted to say that for this reason. This Institute of Criminology, if it is to do any good at all, must win the co-operation of every kind of worker in the field of criminal administration, or of penal reform. The Judiciary, the Executive, the medical profession, the psychiatrists, the social psychologists, the Prison Commissioners, the probation officers, must all be brought into the great work which the Institute can do. The modern Judges of this country—I am now in a position to speak quite freely, whereas a few years ago I should not have been able to do so—are concerned with the administration of the law in a just and humane way, and I think it is of the utmost importance that they, too, should co-operate in the fullest way with the methods of research to be instituted by the Institute referred to by the noble Lord.

I hope I may be forgiven for saying that, because I think it is important. Judges of the present day at least can say—and I speak here with personal knowledge—that they have brought the administration of our criminal law to such a standard that in all the English-speaking communities of the world, and in many communities which do not speak our tongue, the administration of British justice is the admiration of the world. Therefore, I think the Institute starts off well. . . .

It is a most lamentable thing that at this time crime was never higher, that all the remedial and redemptive agencies were never better, and that the question of punishment was never more reasonable. I will not suggest by a sentence that you should alter the policy, but when it is said that there are in prison people who ought not to be there, I begin to be a little sceptical—for this reason. Out of every four persons under the age of twenty-one who are convicted on indictment of an indictable offence, one is put upon probation; and out of every one hundred people convicted on indictment from twenty-one and below that age, one or two only go to prison; sixty-five go to probation; twenty are fined, and the remainder go to remand homes, detention centres or approved schools and the like. I am not suggesting for a single moment that there should be severer sentences, except to say this: that there are occasions—we have had evidence of it in the immediate past—where proper severity, at the proper time, at the appropriate place, can be a most marvellous instrument in dealing with certain forms of crime.

I come to the last thing I want to say on this point. When we find the public mind greatly exercised, with people calling out for severer penalties, some calling for the reinstitution of flogging, it is well to remember that nearly every deterrent element has gone from our system of punishment. I will not discuss capital punishment. The Homicide Act of 1957 was a clear compromise. In my own opinion the day will come when capital punishment will go altogether. Flogging, corporal punishment, has entirely gone since the Departmental Com-

> mittee recommended that it should be so. The only thing left is a severe sentence of imprisonment. The Acts of Parliament give Judges proper power to impose penalties, but out of ten thousand sentences of imprisonment imposed last year on people convicted upon indictment only eight hundred were sentences of four years or more. It is, therefore, a very lamentable thing that there should be in the public mind this feeling that we must go back to severer methods; and it is on such a matter that the new Institute of Criminology can, I think, render a great public service, by satisfying the public mind; because I am satisfied, quite satisfied, that we can never prevent crime or repress crime by severity alone. The eighteenth century demonstrated it. The death penalty was as common then as a magistrate's imposing a fine of forty shillings today, and yet people cried out for severer punishment. Women were burned alive at the stake and they still cried out for severer punishment, and crime persisted. I do not think that if you send somebody to prison that, of itself, however severe the sentence, is going to do much in the way of reformation.

After Birkett sat down two notes were passed along the red benches to him. One was from Lord Pakenham, who had opened the debate. 'Many many congratulations!' it read. 'A magnificent effort—deeply appreciated by me and, I know, by everyone.' The other was from his co-trustee on the Isaac Wolfson Foundation, Lord Nathan. 'What a leg-up you've given the I.W.F.! You had of course a triumph—as was predestined: all your past proclaimed your future. And no one rejoices more than a very old friend.' These words were echoed by the Lord Chancellor, Lord Kilmuir, who spoke next. 'We go back to Erskine, to Russell, to Carson, to Isaacs,' he said, in adding his congratulations, 'and now we have gained among our numbers one of the greatest forensic orators of the twentieth century.'

A few weeks later, Birkett was asked to move the second reading of the Obscene Publications Bill in the House of Lords. This was a Private Members' Bill, which had been largely evolved by a committee of the Society of Authors, consisting of authors, publishers, M.P.s and others under the chairmanship of Sir Alan Herbert, and which had passed the House of Commons with all-Party support. In its present form, the Bill was really the result of a compromise between the Herbert Committee, who considered that some recent court decisions had seriously jeopardized literary freedom, and the Home Office and police, who wished to strengthen the law as regards the sale of 'dirty' books and pictures. In agreeing to sponsor the measure in the Upper House, Birkett hoped that it would, in the words of its title, provide for the protection of literature, as well as strengthen the law concerning pornography.

If the existing legal test of obscenity were rigorously applied, Birkett pointed out in his speech, Chaucer's *Reeve's Tale*, *Romeo and Juliet*, Pepys's *Diary* and *Tristram Shandy*, 'examples taken at random', were liable to be condemned. 'It is enough for me to say that it has been widely felt that, while it is important that pornography should be struck at with vigour, and everybody would support such action,' he observed, 'we ought to be extremely careful not to injure true literature. In my submission to your Lordships, the freedom to write is a great freedom. Your English writer must be free and permitted to depict the thoughts and feelings, the customs, the prejudices and the weaknesses which form the complexity of human behaviour, the ideas which are current in all sorts and conditions of men—he must be able to set them down not only for his own generation but, it may be, for the generations that are still to come.'[1]

One of the changes in the law which the Bill contained applied to orders for forfeiture and destruction of allegedly obscene matter sought by the Director of Public Prosecutions. Formerly neither the author nor anyone else concerned with the work was permitted to give evidence. Under the new measure he or she could be heard and indeed must be heard on the ground that they were defending the article against the charge of obscenity. In this context Birkett recalled his defence of *The Well of Loneliness* in 1928, when the authoress, the publishers and a large number of expert witnesses were excluded from giving evidence at Bow Street Magistrates' Court in support of her case.

> In a case involving a publication called *The Well of Loneliness* in which many years ago I appeared as counsel for the defence, the book had been written by a Miss Radclyffe Hall. The case, under the Act of Lord Campbell, came before Sir

[1] Hansard. *Official Report*, June 2, 1959.

> Chartres Biron in the courts, and the authoress had no voice whatever. When she attempted to speak she was sternly told by the magistrate that she would be ejected if she said another word. I may add that I had to read that book several times before I could discover the alleged obscenity, and it is now on sale in almost every bookseller's shop. That case shows that the extension of the doctrine of the Obscene Publications Act went to the theme, as it did in *The Well of Loneliness*; for the book was destroyed on the ground, not that there was a word of obscenity in it, not that there was an offensive expression from start to finish, but because of the theme of the book and Miss Radclyffe Hall had not condemned it.[1]

The most important section in the Bill was that which stated that in future no one could be convicted of writing or publishing an obscene work and no order for forfeiture should be made 'if it is proved that publication of the article in question is justified as being for the public good on the ground that it is in the interests of science, literature, art, or learning, or of other objects of general concern'.

> The promoters of this Bill believe that to be a very valuable thing. It is designed in the true interests, not of the author or of the publisher but of literature in general. The value of the work in question will now have to be considered from a literary point of view, from a scientific point of view, from an educational point of view or from the point of view of any other merits. If there be passages in the book which are objectionable, or are felt to be objectionable, it must be considered as a whole; consideration must be given to whether those passages are relevant to the author's purpose and to the question whether he could have depicted the life he desired to depict in any other way. . . .
>
> So, my Lords, I present this Bill for its three purposes; the proper amendment of the law of obscenity; for the work it does in protecting that which is perhaps among the most valuable things which our country can possess, its literature, extending through very many centuries; and, finally, to strengthen the law against that evil thing which ought to be most sternly suppressed, pornography.

[1] See above, p. 255.

After Lord Pethick-Lawrence had given the Bill his blessing for the Labour Opposition and the Lord Chancellor for the Government, and before the House proceeded to give it a second reading without a division, Lord Birkett wound up with some words of thanks to those speakers who had contributed to the debate. Then, remembering his experience in *The Well of Loneliness* case, he added: 'I am bound to say that I have a wild feeling of regret that it is not possible for me to appear as counsel and speak to the jury about Clause 4 (the defence of public good) in the first case brought before the courts.'

The first such case was the prosecution of Penguin Books, Ltd., for publishing a cheap paperback edition of *Lady Chatterley's Lover* by D. H. Lawrence. This trial took place in October, 1960, at the Old Bailey, scene of some of Birkett's past triumphs. But on this occasion he had to be content with reading about the case. At the same time, however, the case inspired him to write a stimulating essay on the law of obscene publications, which appeared in a collection of similar essays edited by C. H. Rolph under the title, *Does Pornography Matter?* 'The new Act of 1959 made great and beneficial changes in the law,' he wrote in this essay. 'The protection of any individual citizen is clearly a matter of the first importance. The author and the publisher have suffered too long from the rigour of an outmoded law unduly hampering their activities. But the Act of 1959 in reshaping the law relating to obscenity and pornography has done something even more important than remedying injustices to individuals. It has set up what I hope will prove to be a real protection for literature. . . . Despite all the changes in taste in the past and all the rigours of past legislation, it is something to be thankful for that we can still enjoy Rabelais, Chaucer, Shakespeare, Dryden, Pepys, Sterne, and a hundred others who might have fallen under the ban if the law as it existed up to 1959 had been strictly enforced. It is no little satisfaction that the writers of the future may breathe an ampler air.'[1]

In private, however, Birkett expressed the opinion that there would never be a satisfactory law in England about obscenity. As he put it in a letter to the distinguished American lawyer, Morris Ernst, 'our 1959 Act in Clause 4 is the best we have yet done. Its real value is that it frightens off the intending prosecutor but permits

[1] C. H. Rolph (ed.) *Does Pornography Matter?* (1961), pp. 9–10.

pornography to be attacked. But with us the Roman Catholics regard a handbook about birth control as obscene and also pornographic. And how do you *prove* that reading tends to deprave and corrupt?'

A matter of some difficulty and delicacy which Birkett hoped to raise in the House of Lords but which, as will be seen he was prevented from doing by circumstances beyond his control, concerned a remarkable case of espionage. In May, 1961, George Blake, a member of the British Secret Intelligence Service, pleaded guilty at the Old Bailey to an indictment containing five counts under the Official Secrets Act. Since much of the proceedings took place behind doors closed to the press and the public, the details of the offences with which Blake was charged remained largely a secret. Although it was known that he had passed secret information to the Russians, all the public gathered was when next day, in answer to questions in the House of Commons, the Prime Minister, Mr. Macmillan, stated that he could assure the House that 'Blake's disclosures will not have done irreparable damage. In particular he did not have access to secret information on defence, nuclear or atomic matters'. But that his crime was of a heinous character appeared from the remark made by the Lord Chief Justice, Lord Parker, in passing a sentence of unprecedented severity in this century, that it was 'one of the worst that can be envisaged in time of peace'. On each of five counts Blake received the maximum sentence of fourteen years' imprisonment, the first three terms to run consecutively. This amounted in effect to a sentence of forty-two years, which as Mr. Jeremy Hutchinson, who defended Blake, put it in appealing against this sentence in the Court of Criminal Appeal, meant that Blake would be an octogenarian by the time he was released. The Court of Criminal Appeal, presided over by Mr. Justice Hilbery, dismissed the appeal.[1]

Until two months before the Blake case, when the Soviet spy known as Gordon Lonsdale was sentenced to twenty-five years for his part in the Portland navy case, no convicted prisoner had received a longer sentence than twenty years, apart from life sentences, but in practice 'lifers' never served more than twenty years, and frequently much less. Indeed, apart from one sentence of twenty-seven years passed in 1887, where the prisoner served twenty years, no sentence of more than twenty years was ever passed in this

[1] *The Times*, June 20, 1961.

country until Lonsdale's. Therefore when Blake was sentenced to forty-two years, Birkett felt very strongly that the sentence was really 'administrative', even 'political' in character, rather than strictly judicial. It offended against all his liberal principles, not to mention the Bill of Rights which provided that 'cruel and unjust punishments should not be inflicted'. Even Dr. Klaus Fuchs, the atom spy, had only been given fourteen years and had been released after he had served nine, when he had gone straight off to East Germany to resume work for the Russians, whereas Blake had ceased to be of any value to his former Soviet employers. After Blake's appeal had been dismissed, Birkett wrote to his counsel, Mr. Hutchinson: 'I would most willingly see you to discuss the George Blake sentence though I doubt whether there is much that one can do of a direct kind at the moment. What must be done, I think, is to keep public attention alive such as by letters to *The Times*, questions in the House, a debate in the Lords on sentencing policy arising out of the Streatfield Committee's Report, etc.' A few days later Birkett called at the counsel's chambers.

To Jeremy Hutchinson

> *Challens Green. September* 28, 1961. . . . I have had the case of Blake continually in my mind since our conversation together, and I had a talk with [Lord] Longford in the House of Lords about it. He suggested that perhaps a good method would be to put down a Motion, but it is a little difficult to put down a Motion on so simple a matter which would be debated in a very short time.
>
> The question of sentencing in the Courts might be introduced by a reference to the recent Report on the conditions in the Courts which was produced, you will remember by Geoffrey [Mr. Justice] Streatfield. But I am merely writing to acknowledge your letter and to say that if the opportunity serves I will certainly raise the matter in the House of Lords, and would then be very grateful for all the material which you have gathered together. However, I must first be satisfied that I can get a Motion that would really interest the House of Lords, and on the mere question of whether forty-two years is a proper thing or not is too sharp an issue for the House of Lords to make a debate covering several hours.

I will certainly think about the matter, and will write to you again.

Birkett did write again, some weeks later, when he received a batch of papers on the case from Mr. Hutchinson. As will be seen, he was working on these at the time of his death. So far as the matter went, however, all he had been able to do was to make a brief intervention when another peer, Earl Winterton, asked the Government if, in view of the criticisms which had appeared in some quarters about sentences imposed by the courts—he evidently had in mind the disparity of sentences imposed by magistrates for motoring and similar offences—that the judiciary had the sole right to impose such sentences and 'cannot be subjected to outside influences'. The Lord Chancellor, Lord Kilmuir, agreed that it was desirable that the Court's exercise of this discretion should be completely free.

'Is it not a dangerous thing to suggest, if the question did suggest, that judges are immune from criticism?' Birkett asked by way of a supplementary question. 'Is it not the right of every citizen to criticize a sentence imposed by a judge, or any other act done in the judicial capacity, provided it is done respectfully and without any imputation of improper motives? If a citizen, for example, thinks that a sentence of imprisonment of forty years is an intolerable thing he should be entitled to say so?'

After the Lord Chancellor had pointed out that he thought Birkett was thinking of an entirely different matter from Lord Winterton, he quoted the late Lord Atkin to the effect that justice was not a cloistered virtue and the administration of it was subject to criticism just as everything else in society. 'I hope,' he added, 'that Lord Birkett will not be interpreted as justifying outside influence and pressure on the judiciary in coming to their decision.'[1]

Birkett resented the implied rebuke in this remark. Indeed it was the very last thing he would have attempted to justify.

2

Shortly after piloting the Obscene Publications Bill through the House of Lords, a further opportunity of rendering public service was afforded to Birkett. This was provided by the invitation from the

[1] Hansard. *Official Report*, July 19, 1961.

interested parties in an industrial dispute affecting the whole of the printing trades to be the independent chairman in an endeavour to find a settlement between the employers and the unions. The dispute which began in June, 1959, and was the most serious industrial stoppage since the General Strike of 1926, involved more than 120,000 printing operatives, over 1,000 newspapers and more than 4,000 member firms of the British Federation of Master Printers.

At the beginning of 1959, ten unions affiliated to the Printing and Kindred Trades Federation had made application to the British Federation of Master Printers and Newspaper Society for a reduction of the working week from 43½ to 40 hours, for a 10 per cent. wages increase and other adjustments. During protracted negotiations the employers refused to improve on a first offer of a 42½ hour week and a 2½ per cent. wages increase linking with them the acceptance of proposals on labour supply, demarcation of work and the introduction of new processes. These proposals (which the employers said were their final offer) were unacceptable to the unions and it was decided to impose sanctions which included a ban on overtime. The British Federation of Master Printers advised their member-firms to give two weeks 'protective notice' to their employees and this was accepted by the unions as notice of termination of employment. By June 20 work had ceased throughout the greater part of the industry, the only major section not being involved were the national newspapers covered by a separate employers' organization.

As weeks went by the stoppage had an ever-widening effect on industry and commerce. There were no signs of a resumption of negotiations and there was a widespread feeling in the country that the dispute was being allowed to drag on. There was also considerable criticism of what was considered to be the ineffective role of the Minister of Labour, Mr. Iain Macleod. Parliament became increasingly anxious and, at their invitation, Mr. G. G. Eastwood, General Secretary of the Printing and Kindred Trades Federation, addressed the Parliamentary Labour Party at the House of Commons. This was followed by a debate on July 6 when, from the Opposition Front Bench, Mr. Alfred Robens, 'Shadow' Minister of Labour, vigorously urged upon the Government the 'real necessity of getting negotiations going again between the two sections'. He pressed the Ministry of Labour to follow a T.U.C. suggestion that negotiations should be re-opened under an independent chairman who, said Mr. Robens, 'should be an eminent person sitting there, holding the reins, helping and guiding'.

Immediately following this debate joint discussions between the printing trade leaders on both sides went on at the Ministry of Labour until midnight and the result was the acceptance of a formula for a resumption of negotiations under a chairman whose functions should be to 'advise, guide and control the discussions to achieve a negotiated settlement'. At first it was hoped to secure the services of Lord Monckton, a former Minister of Labour, as independent chairman. But he was not available, and the unions suggested Birkett, to which the employers' side readily agreed.

When this news was conveyed to the Minister, he telephoned Birkett and asked him to take on the job, offering him payment according to the length of time the discussions took. Birkett promptly accepted the offer to act as chairman of the resumed negotiations but declined to accept any remuneration for his services, saying he gladly undertook the job 'as a public duty'. Birkett accepted the invitation on July 11, and two days later he met Mr. Iain Macleod, who endorsed his role. Birkett was thus a conciliator, not an arbitrator—each side referred to him as 'our friend'—although both employers and unions agreed that, if they failed to reach agreement on any point, Birkett's recommendations as independent chairman on such points should be submitted to their constituents as part of the final settlement to be accepted or refused.[1]

The first meeting between the parties took place at the Ministry of Labour on July 14. Little progress was made, the venue of the Ministry in St. James's Square was inconvenient and available conference rooms inadequate. The talks were therefore adjourned to the offices of the British Federation of Master Printers at 11, Bedford Row, where the facilities were better for the preparation of documents and communications with the various union headquarters. Here six working parties were immediately set up to examine questions of productivity, increased efficiency and individual unions' domestic claims. Meanwhile one conference room was set aside for the forty or so trade union representatives, while another room just inside the front entrance bore the label 'Lord Birkett'.

Throughout the next seventeen days the talks went on, often well

[1] *The Times*, July 13, 1959.

into the night. Birkett never left the building while the talks were in progress, eating a sandwich lunch each day from an improvised office canteen. After a fortnight's almost continuous discussions, a settlement appeared in sight, when a sudden difficulty was encountered. This was due to the possibility that one or two unions might vote against the terms, in which case none of them would have been entitled to the improved conditions. The deadlock was eventually broken when the union representatives—there were ten unions in all—undertook to make a joint recommendation to their members in favour of acceptance of the proposed terms. On this understanding it was agreed that, if one or two unions did vote against acceptance, there would be a further period of time after that allowed for the ballot, during which it was hoped that the union or unions concerned would decide to come into line with the rest. The terms, which were suggested by Birkett himself and were in fact generally accepted throughout the industry, provided for a standard working week for day workers in all departments of 42 hours. (Except in daily newspapers, 43½ hours had previously been the rule.) The maximum number of hours of overtime permitted under existing arrangements were to be increased by an hour and a half a week or its equivalent, while the basic wage rates were to be increased by 4½ per cent. with appropriate percentages for apprentices and learners. The agreement which was to continue in force for three years, and provided for a 'staged' reduction of working hours to 40 by the middle of 1962, was announced at the final meeting on July 31. 'Nobody outside this room,' Birkett told the negotiating parties, 'can possibly appreciate the magnitude and complexity of the task you have completed today.' It was estimated that the stoppage cost the country in all about £30 millions and was the most expensive of its kind in British industrial history.[1]

'The best thing for an independent chairman to do is to keep the sides talking and try to narrow the points of view,' Birkett told newspaper reporters immediately afterwards. 'The last thing I wanted to do in the printing dispute was to reach the stage where I had to make a recommendation. Success depends on the goodwill of both sides. I was exceedingly fortunate in having it over the printing dispute. Praise is not for me but for the two parties.'[2]

[1] *The Times*, August 1, 1959.
[2] *Daily Mail*, August 1, 1959.

But praise was lavished on Birkett's achievement both publicly and privately. While the press throughout the country united to laud Birkett's efforts, both unions and employers expressed their feelings likewise. Here is what the General Secretary of the Printing and Kindred Trades Federation wrote:

> Lord Birkett soon gained the negotiators' confidence, and as the talks ran into increasing difficulties, they saw the mind of this distinguished lawyer at work. He re-drafted clauses and got both sides out of difficulties, he had many separate talks with both the employers and ourselves; he presided over full sessions of the negotiating teams and over smaller sectional meetings; and all the time he was ever-ready to advise and guide and to put his views frankly and with clarity. He made many suggestions that bridged gaps which at times seemed insurmountable. Those who took part in the 'marathon' negotiations, will always remember Lord Birkett for his ready understanding of the problems, for his infinite patience, and for a charm and graciousness which never left him even during the most stressful and trying moments. Perhaps they will remember him most for his humanity. He never forgot, or allowed the negotiators to forget, that whilst they argued interminably, over a hundred thousand families continued to suffer from the effects of the stoppage, and that it was affecting industry and the nation, too, in many ways. He was ever anxious for an honourable and negotiated settlement, but, as he put it, he did not want the dispute to go on 'one minute longer than necessary'.

On the employers' side the President of the British Federation of Master Printers wrote to the Minister of Labour:

> *Westhanger,*
> *Cleeve,*
> *near Bristol.*
> *2nd August*, 1959.
>
> Dear Mr. Macleod,
>
> I am writing to you as President of the British Federation of Master Printers, first to thank you for having appointed Lord Birkett to preside over the negotiations in the printing dispute, and then to place on record our appreciation of the magnificent way in which he has carried out that task.

His success was due to his patience, his humour and his remarkable impartiality, which enabled him to gain and keep the confidence of both sides.

The last three weeks were a great strain to all who took part, but the strain on him, with all the responsibility that rested on his shoulders must have been tremendous. He has the satisfaction of having brought to an end the hardship suffered by many thousands in the industry and to do that was I know his foremost concern.

Many people outside the industry have suffered loss and inconvenience from the unfortunate dispute. I am not entitled to speak for them but I am sure I may speak for everyone in the industry in expressing our very deep gratitude to Lord Birkett for all he has done for us.

Yours sincerely,

PETER G. CARDEW

'I certainly cannot recall a more complimentary tribute by the employers concerned in an industrial dispute,' the Minister wrote to Birkett in sending him this letter, 'and it is deeply satisfying that everybody is so content with the outcome.'

Although he had refused any remuneration from the Minister, Birkett was prevailed upon to accept from the parties to the dispute as a token of their appreciation a beautifully bound copy of *The Oxford Dictionary of Quotations*, itself a fine example of British typography and craftsmanship, containing the signatures of the principal representatives of both sides of this ancient industry. 'I think,' he said after it was all over, 'the outcome of this dispute is the most satisfying success of my career.'

3

Ever since he had first visited the United States in 1937, Birkett had been an enthusiastic admirer of that country and its people. His war-time speaking tour had established his success, and his continuing popularity has been demonstrated by the frequent invitations he had received for over a quarter of a century to be the guest of honour at American functions, particularly of the American Bar Association. He liked the Americans, whose democratic and freedom-loving way of life appealed to him, and in particular he had a profound respect for the United States Supreme Court, having made a careful study of the judgments of such great jurists as Oliver Wendell Holmes and Benjamin Cardozo. He had made many friends there during his visits and also when he was thrown much into the society of the American judges and prosecuting team at Nuremberg. His interest in promoting good relations between the two countries and the hospitable welcome which he and his wife regularly gave American visitors to England at Challens Green, were so widely and generally known that when Lord Halifax resigned the office of President of The Pilgrims in July, 1957, Birkett was the obvious and natural successor.

The name of this celebrated society dedicated to the cause of Anglo-American understanding had been suggested by its first President, Field Marshal Earl Roberts, when it was founded at the turn of the century, the suggestion having arisen from a remark made by one of its American founders, Mr. George Wilson, in London. 'It will be composed of Americans like ourselves who have made the pilgrimage over here and have received and have appreciated British hospitality,' said Mr. Wilson, 'and there will be English members who have made the pilgrimage to the United States and have discovered that we are not all Red Indians.' The early dinners of the society took place at the old Carlton Hotel, but since the building of the Lancaster Room on the former site of an open courtyard in the Savoy Hotel in 1904, for the primary purpose of accommodating the Pilgrims, the dinners have always been held in the Savoy. Meanwhile, the sister society, The Pilgrims of the United States, had come into being in New York, its dinners customarily taking place at the Waldorf-Astoria Hotel there.

Birkett was the seventh President of The Pilgrims to occupy the chair since the society's inauguration in 1902.[1] The first occasion on which he presided was a domestic affair, a dinner given to mark the retirement of Sir Campbell Stuart as Chairman of the Executive Committee of The Pilgrims in October, 1958. After enumerating Sir Campbell's record of ten years as Chairman and forty years of devoted service, Birkett went on to speak of his 'greatest memorial'

[1] The others were Earl Roberts (1902–14), Viscount Bryce (1915–17), H.R.H. the Duke of Connaught (1917–42), the Earl of Derby (1945–8), Viscount Greenwood (1948), and the Earl of Halifax (1950–4).

in the shape of the statue to President Franklin Roosevelt in Grosvenor Square, for the erection of which his efforts had been largely responsible.

> That is almost the most enduring thing that The Pilgrims have done, and for this reason. It is comparatively easy for the heads of state in one country to come in contact with the heads of state in another country, but what is so desirable and so difficult is to get the great body of the people in one country in touch with the great body of the people in another country. The nearest thing that we have done to that as Pilgrims was in this great venture in Grosvenor Square.
>
> Under the Presidency of Lord Derby, it is an open secret that Sir Campbell had much to do with the inception of the idea, the obtaining of the site from the Duke of Westminster and the quite brilliant idea of refusing all American money, which would have poured in for the venture, and saying 'We will take it in small sums of five shillings', with the remarkable result that in five days it was all subscribed and people had to be told to stop sending money. All that is due in very large measure to the insight and enthusiasm, the devotion and the knowledge of Sir Campbell Stuart.
>
> That, perhaps, reveals his secret. If I may use the term, the genius that he has employed in the service of The Pilgrims lies here. He had the wit and the insight to recognize that a great organization, a great institution, like The Pilgrims, is not a mere mechanical thing but is composed of warm-hearted human people who have made the institution what it is, and who have become part of its history. To them there has been handed down from generations that have gone, great ideals, great traditions and imperishable memories; and so long as a society or an institution like The Pilgrims maintains the traditions, and holds fast to the memories, and yet allows them to be strengthened and maintained by a perpetual reaching out for the highest fulfilment or its essential purpose then the institution survives from age to age, and a kind of immortality descends upon it. Sir Campbell's great genius about this matter was that he perceived all this and in the great achievement of Grosvenor Square he gave visible form to the ideals of The

Pilgrims so that when we are all gone, *that* will remain; nation speaking to nation, and people speaking to people.

An interesting link with the past was provided at this dinner by the eighty-five-year-old Sir Harry Brittain, who had been one of the founder members of The Pilgrims with Lord Roberts and had been effective head of the society for the first seventeen years of its existence. Called upon by the President to speak before the guest of the evening, Sir Harry recalled that he had recently opened a two-day conference at Westminster Hospital on the subject of work study and its application to the hospital service. 'I found that uphill business,' he said, 'but not half so difficult as attempting to follow Lord Birkett on anything in the way of expression. I am a Yorkshireman, and very proud of my native county, but following Lancaster's most eloquent son let me say that at this particular job the White Rose gives way to the Red.'

A month later, Birkett presided at his first function in honour of an outside guest, when The Pilgrims gave a luncheon for Mr. Richard Nixon, then Vice-President of the United States. Among the speakers on this occasion was the British Foreign Secretary, Mr. Selwyn Lloyd, who said this:

> This is the first Pilgrims' function since the resignation of Lord Halifax as President. We are very sorry indeed that he is not with us today, and I think we should like to say how much we appreciated all that he did for The Pilgrims and for their services. The fact that you, Sir, have agreed to succeed him is some consolation to us.
>
> Lord Birkett, this is not the first occasion upon which I have appeared before you. In my present task I think somewhat nostalgically of the days of the Northern Circuit and the Liverpool Assizes where one very soon learned the magic words, 'If your Lordship pleases', said with smug contentment if you thought the judge was with you and with cold severity if you thought he was against you; or, as was much more likely, if you were not sure which, like a hand held out in the dark as if trying for some sort of hand-rail. I have long wanted the opportunity to say to a high judicial personality, 'Whether your Lordship pleases or not'. I do so today; whether your Lordship pleases or not, we are delighted to welcome you and we know

> quite well that you will be a most worthy President of The Pilgrims.

Other distinguished guests who were entertained by The Pilgrims at the Savoy during Birkett's term of office as President included Mr. Eugene Black, President of the World Bank; Mr. Hugh Bullock, President of The Pilgrims of the United States; and the two United States Ambassadors in London and the two British Ambassadors in Washington at this period, Mr. John Hay Whitney, Mr. David K. E. Bruce, Sir David Ormsby Gore (later Lord Harlech) and Sir Harold Caccia. It was during this period, too, that Birkett paid his last visit to the United States, when he was the guest of honour with Lady Birkett at a dinner of The Pilgrims of the United States in New York.

The three hundred or so members of the sister society who sat down to dinner under their President, Hugh Bullock, in the Waldorf-Astoria on November 9, 1960, had the pleasure of listening to Birkett in his happiest vein. They were greatly moved by some of the things he said.

> Mr. President, our two societies have now enjoyed sixty years of existence and still grow in strength and in influence and in power, and I think that in this family gathering of the Pilgrims the reason for that continued growth ought not to be lost upon us.
>
> There is only one means by which societies like ours can survive, only one means by which they can put on a kind of immortality, for The Pilgrims of the United Kingdom, and The Pilgrims of the United States are certainly not impersonal abstractions. Our two societies are composed of men who have common aims and common aspirations and so long as The Pilgrims of the present day and those of the next sixty years will follow the imperishable traditions and the associations which those who went before have handed down, and will allow them to be permeated and revivified by the struggle for all that is best, then our societies will never grow old but will rather continue and go from strength to strength.
>
> It has been ordained that old men shall dream dreams and that young men shall see visions. And it is easy enough, far, far too easy to dream of a world that is purged of all its evil, with the want and the hunger and the loneliness and the hatred all

Westminster Press Provincial Newspapers

BEFORE THE DEBATE, FEBRUARY 8, 1962

irkett died two days after this picture was taken at the entrance to the House of Lords.

BIRKETT FELL, OVERLOOKING ULLSWATER *The Times*

'He loved Ullswater. He strove to maintain its beauty for all to enjoy.'

driven away, and the vision of the Prophet Micah fulfilled with the world at peace. Easy to dream, but we have long been awakened by the very stern realities of the world in which we live.

That is why I say in this Pilgrims gathering that to The Pilgrims there must be the vision of the young man. Without vision it is said that people perish, but with vision linked with indomitable purpose, then those ideals which have been handed down can still be carried on from generation to generation, not merely for our own benefit but as I think, for the benefit of all mankind. . . .

We are still living in a dangerous world, a frustrating world, but a world in which as it seems to me, it is all the more necessary that we should stand together through fair weather and through foul, and that we should be inspired by the great men who have laid down for us in this noble language our great ideals, and that we should remember at all times the rock from which we are hewn.

So, Mr. President, may I now turn for a moment to just one of the great ties which bind us to each other. I am, of course, not unmindful of the manifold ties which bind our two societies and our two great countries to each other, ties of history, ties of blood, ties of literature, ties of language, all binding us together in pursuit of our common purposes.

These things have been spoken about so many times, proclaimed in particular by the great ambassadors which you have sent to our country from time to time. I think particularly of men like Joseph Choate—and John W. Davis—those great masters of the spoken word. I never heard Mr. Choate, but I heard John W. Davis, and they always preached this self-same doctrine, friendship between the nations, co-operation in our enterprises.

It was Mr. Choate, as a matter of fact, who revealed to his audiences in Britain that when his president, President McKinley, gave him his letter of credence to the Court of St. James's he gave him one instruction only and that was to cultivate in the highest degree the closest friendship and co-operation between the two countries. And right nobly did Mr. Choate do it.

When he was about to end his sixth year of labour in

London, he was, first of all, given a great banquet by the Bench and Bar of England in the ancient hall of Lincoln's Inn, and a very few days later by the Lord Mayor and the Corporation of the City of London; and on both those occasions he simply took the opportunity to repeat what he had been preaching during the six years, the vast importance, not merely for the safety and the security of our two countries, but for the true welfare of the world, that the two countries should stand together and pursue their purposes at all times together. And so you will understand that whilst I do not refer to all those ties again tonight, I am not unmindful of them.

In particular, Mr. President, I am not unmindful of the many reminders in England that we have which have been given by this country. Nearly every day of my working life for many, many years I passed through the great hall of the Royal Courts of Justice in the Strand. There is the great statue of Blackstone, the author of the *Commentaries on the Laws of England* which was read much more in this country than in our own and which did a great deal to help forward the administration of justice in the growing republic, and that statue was given by the lawyers of America as a symbol of the uniting quality of the Common Law, common to our country, common to yours.

And I saw that statue almost every day. I like to think, too, of that brooding figure of Abraham Lincoln in Parliament Square where he looks out, if you remember, to Westminster Hall and the House of Commons and the House of Lords and to the great Abbey of Westminster; and I never pass it but I think of that great affirmation 'Fourscore and seven years ago, our Fathers brought forth on this continent a new nation' and mark the nobility of the idea 'conceived in liberty', conceived in liberty and dedicated to the proposition that all men are created equal.

Although he enjoyed such visits as this to America and also occasional jaunts to the European continent, Birkett always disliked being away from home for long. As he told his friend Cecil Roberts, who was an inveterate world traveller, 'Three weeks is enough for me at any one time. After that I pine for England and Challens Green. I love all the changing seasons, the winter with the snow making all the trees so beautiful and of course those wonderful days of February when the sun begins to shed a little warmth and the daffodils are getting ready, and the summer days by the swimming pool. And London with all its fascination at all times. But I envy you your power to travel the world round and to enjoy it all as if you were still one and twenty.' And this was how the years of retirement swiftly passed. He had seen his two children happily married and settled, and he could now watch his grandchildren growing up, while in his own home he enjoyed the companionship of his devoted wife, who had meant so much to him in his career. Then there were public speeches, and broadcasts and articles, which took up much of his time. Like his life-long hero Dr. Johnson, he believed in keeping his friendships in repair, and he would type long letters on his portable typewriter to a wide range of correspondents.

One of these correspondents, who used to come to England from time to time, was the veteran New York lawyer, Morris Ernst, whose defence of *The Well of Loneliness* in the American courts had been as spirited as Birkett's had been before the Chief Magistrate at Bow Street. Birkett shared Ernst's liberal views on censorship and literature, and they corresponded on this and a variety of other legal topics. One feature of the American scene which intrigued Birkett was the success of lawyers in politics like Mr. Richard Nixon, who had become Vice-President of the United States and later Republican candidate for President, and whose professional achievements contributed to their political careers. This prompted Birkett to write to Ernst:

> Your country is very different from mine. I do not think that a lawyer, *as such*, will ever lead Britain. Lawyers are not popular, and for the most part don't deserve to be, and don't desire to be. Judges may not appear on television and counsel may not advertise. The language of the law will never be the language of the people. The real trouble with our lawyers is that they are not truly cultivated men. . . .
>
> When I was at the Bar I accepted many criminal briefs when I could have got ten times as much by refusing them and accepting civil cases. But I was plagued by a sense of service and duty and have never quite lost it. I actually did briefs for nothing, which was exceedingly unprofessional. John Simon and

> Edward Clarke thought the law was merely a way by which poor men might become politicians; and men like Asquith became statesmen but they were not regarded as lawyers leading the nation. To be a lawyer was to have a handicap in the House of Commons.

There remained always the abiding joy of reading good literature, both old favourites and new works, including such excerpts as appeared in *The Law as Literature*, an anthology selected and introduced by Mr. Louis Blom-Cooper, to which Birkett contributed a Foreword.

To Louis Blom-Cooper

> . . . I have returned the proof of the Foreword today, and all the correction I found it necessary to make was to remove a comma. It made me think of A. E. Housman and his sleepless nights over commas.
>
> I am a great admirer of Bowen and Macnaghten. John Simon finished his *Retrospect* with a summary of a speech delivered by Bowen in Balliol Hall but I think Simon was mistaken for there is no record of any such speech. But Bowen made the comparison *somewhere* between life at the Bar and a journey by train, concluding with the train running into the terminus and the inexorable official asking for your ticket. It ought to be unearthed and reproduced. Have you the little volume published by the late Macnaghten J. containing a selection from the speeches of his father? Some of them have already gone into the anthologies. In Kenny's *Outlines of Criminal Law* there is a case reported early in the volume about the law of homicide. It dates from Charles I and reports a householder aroused in the night thrusting his rapier into the darkness of the buttery where a servant had hidden a friend to avoid discovery. It is a perfect piece of prose.
>
> These are merely suggestions for the Second Volume.
>
> . . . It has been a great pleasure to write the Foreword and when I saw it in print I was not dissatisfied with it. It is a curious thing but almost always after a little interval I find myself quite enjoying my own writings which seems wrong somehow!

The following is an extract from the Foreword which Birkett wrote for Mr. Blom-Cooper's book:

> Lawyers need no reminding from me that law and literature have been long and closely associated. Words are said to be the raw material of the legal profession, and the assiduous study of words, and the proper use of words have always been part of the lawyer's most desirable accomplishments. Many of our judges have been great masters of the spoken and the written word, and the Law Reports are not only a great treasury of law but they are a great treasury of literature. More than three hundred years ago the judges were called in to advise the House of Lords in a peerage claim when the Earl of Oxford died without issue. The famous speech delivered by Chief Justice Crewe has always been regarded as a superb piece of English prose with its magnificent opening and its majestic conclusion—
>
> > 'And yet Time hath its revolutions; there must be a period and an end to all temporal things—an end of names, and dignities and whatsoever is terrene, and why not of De Vere? For where is Bohun? Where is Mowbray? Where is Mortimer? Nay, which is more and most of all, Where is Plantagenet? They are entombed in the urns and sepulchres of mortality. And yet let the name and dignity of De Vere stand so long as it pleaseth God.'

In an article on the pleasures of reading which he wrote for *The Times* a few days before Christmas, 1961, Birkett recalled Charles Lamb having blessed his stars 'for a taste so catholic, so unexcluding'.[1]

> I like to think I have something in common with Lamb (apart from our devotion to the Inner Temple) for I, too, have been a great lover of reading and esteem it one of the major pleasures of life. Nowadays I confess, I enjoy occasional reading in bed, with the bolster and the pillows properly arranged, with the bed lamp at the right angle, and one or two clear hours before it is time to put out the light. But to make my pleasure quite complete I must have behind me a day of activity which can give me the feeling that the heavenly quietude of the day's closing hours is not wholly unearned.

[1] *The Times*, December 21, 1961.

Birkett's reference to reading in bed touched off an interesting and diverse correspondence on how this could best be achieved in the British arctic winter without contracting frostbite. It was of course unquestioningly assumed by everyone that central heating, that strange, unhealthy American custom, would be an un-British solution. 'It would be a great service to those of us who do not enjoy central heating,' wrote the gentleman who initiated the correspondence, 'if Lord Birkett, or any kind reader, could suggest how this can be done without hands and shoulders becoming numb with cold.'

'I can only say that I have no central heating in my bedroom,' Birkett replied, 'but I find that one bar of an electric fire and a thick sweater defeat the coldest nights. The important thing is to warm the bed with a hot water bottle or an electric blanket before getting into it.' (Only a puritan, commented the London *Evening Standard*, would begrudge him the sybaritic indulgence of that single bar.)

The leisure of the Christmas holiday brought many letters to *The Times* office, mainly from the scholarly readers of that journal. 'After years of experience in this field,' said one fellow sufferer, 'I find the following equipment most desirable: a woollen ski cap, a Shetland shawl, mittens secured at the wrists by means of rubber bands.' The Bishop of Ripon advised learning Braille and reading under the bedclothes; Professor Basil Ward, the well-known architect, suggested 'a thick cardigan got into the wrong way round and pulled well up under the chin'; and from Cambridge University a clergyman and don in Jesus College reported: 'The reader tucks himself in. He then holds the book in one hand with perhaps a thumb and two fingers protruding. If they get cold he then turns over and uses the other hand.'

'As long as Britain can produce inventiveness of this character,' wrote the *Evening Standard* reassuringly, 'the challenge of a scientific age should not defeat us.'[1] The correspondence caused considerable amusement in the Birkett household, culminating as it did with a contribution from a champion of male supremacy in the home. 'A fig for dressing up! The sole requirement is a literate wife with a melodious voice.' But after several weeks, even the indefatigable *Times* correspondents began to show signs of tiring of this chilly subject, and after one reader had begged, 'Lights out, please!', the

[1] *Evening Standard*, January 6, 1962.

editor brought the correspondence to a close with a sense of relief.

But it was as a broadcaster, both on television and sound radio, that Birkett became during his retirement most widely known to viewers and listeners. His famous interview with John Freeman which launched the 'Face to Face' series on B.B.C. television has already been noticed. Then, on sound, he wound up a popular series of talks in the B.B.C. 'Woman's Hour', in which twenty-five eminent men and women briefly recounted what they had 'learned from life'. Here are his concluding observations.[1]

> I have seen a good deal of human nature in my time. I spent long years in the Courts of Law as Counsel and then as a Judge, and that experience has taught me that men and women can shape their own lives by their own efforts and determination.
>
> I've seen many a young man pull himself together and forsake evil ways by his resolute purpose and endeavour. I am not forgetting the enormous part that heredity and environment play—the special equipment with which people are born, or the state of life to which they are called—and whilst these things may determine the ultimate course of life, I yet hold firmly to the belief that what men and women make of their lives depends very largely upon themselves.
>
> The world has changed a great deal in my lifetime and we must all adapt ourselves to change if we can; but I still think there are some changeless things in the world that make or mar our happiness. Let me therefore conclude with a few of the ideas I have learned from my own life. I think that men and women who can choose their job, and find a daily pleasure in doing it are fortune's favourites; that a happy home life is the very greatest of human blessings; that there is infinite wisdom in the old words 'Whatsoever thy hand findeth to do, do it with thy might'; that it is wise to have a hobby of some kind, and if it's a useful hobby, so much the better; that it is the highest wisdom to make friends, and to take every kind of trouble to keep the friendships in repair, particularly as you grow older; that excess in *all* things is to be avoided; that it is wise to keep one's word, and not break promises; that a sense of public duty should be cultivated, if only as a safeguard against selfishness; and that

[1] Madge Hart (ed.) *Learned from Life* (1959), pp. 110–11.

> it is wise to keep the mind alert by reading and by all the agencies, such as Television and Radio, that now exert themselves for our benefit. I think it is wise to realize the value of a margin in *all* things, and not only in money matters; and not to spend too much time on seeking mere pleasure; and not to live for the moment only.... In the end, it is Life that teaches us all.

A little later, Birkett was invited by the B.B.C. to contribute a series of talks on six great advocates and to wind up the series with a general talk on the art of advocacy. The advocates he chose were Sir Edward Marshall Hall, Sir Patrick Hastings, Sir Edward Clarke, Sir Rufus Isaacs (later Lord Reading), Sir Charles Russell (later Lord Russell of Killowen) and Thomas Erskine (later Lord Erksine). The talks which were broadcast on seven Sunday evenings in the Home Service in April and May, 1961, lasted for thirty minutes each and, in Birkett's words, 'were written and delivered in the hope that they might provide entertainment and pleasure by recalling some of the great figures at the English Bar and some of the cases by which they are best remembered'. He admitted afterwards that he felt a 'particular pleasure' in writing and speaking of those advocates he had known and admired such as Marshall Hall and Patrick Hastings, 'and an almost equal pleasure in speaking of those advocates whose fame, almost legendary with lawyers, is handed on from generation to generation'. These talks, like the television interview with John Freeman, were a great success and brought a flood of letters from listeners asking that they should be published. At first Birkett hesitated, as he had always felt the truth of Hazlitt's famous essay 'On the Difference between Speaking and Writing', but when a well-known firm of paperback publishers offered to bring them out, Birkett agreed.[1] Some time later, the talk on advocacy was also made available as a long-playing record, so that the melody of his voice expounding his favourite professional theme has been preserved for posterity.[2]

4

New Year, 1962, began with the usual round of speaking engagements. On January 10, Birkett presided at a dinner of The Pilgrims

[1] Lord Birkett. *Six Famous Advocates.* Penguin Books, 1961.
[1] *Decca Mono.* LXT. 6032.

—for the last time, as it turned out—in honour of Sir Harold Caccia, the retiring British Ambassador in Washington. The toast of the principal guest on this occasion was proposed by the Archbishop of Canterbury, Lord Fisher of Lambeth, and in doing so the speaker recalled how he had 'learnt by a bitter lesson never to controvert Lord Birkett'. The incident which the Archbishop recalled had taken place at another dinner where Birkett had quoted from the New Testament, naming the Book from which he was quoting, and was later publicly corrected by the Archbishop who told him he was wrong. 'I thought that was a good evening,' said Lord Fisher, 'but two or three days later I got a letter from Lord Birkett drawing my attention to the fact that he was right, as indeed he was.'

When he came to wind up the proceedings of the evening, Birkett, who had somewhat naturally resented the correction which His Grace had previously administered, told Lord Fisher how much his speech had been enjoyed by his fellow Pilgrims and himself.

> I was particularly grateful that he made public the little incident that occurred at a dinner given by the Dean and Chapter of St. Paul's, and I must add, so that my conduct on that occasion will not be misunderstood, that it was an audience composed almost entirely of clergymen. There were a handful of laymen, and the Dean of St. Paul's kindly asked me if I would respond to the toast of 'The Guests'. I said that of course I would. When the Dean proposed the toast, he used the phrase, 'This is really a dinner given in honour of St. Paul'. It occurred to me—I was seeking to curry favour with the clerical audience—that I might show a little knowledge of the New Testament, and I thereupon said that I thought that was a delightful thing because it was St. Paul, was it not, who in the Epistle to the Romans used that great phrase (which I observe has gone from the new translation of the New Testament, I am sorry to see) 'a man given to hospitality'—which I thought and still think a lovely phrase. When Lord Fisher, the Archbishop as he then was, corrected me before this audience, you can imagine the contrition with which I expressed my apologies for being so bold as to refer to the New Testament before such an audience. When I got home, I looked up the passage, and there, in the Epistle to the Romans, was the very phrase that I had used. So I had the

> intense satisfaction of writing a letter, which I trust is still in the archives at Lambeth, and the very gracious way in which Lord Fisher referred to it tonight relieved my mind very much indeed.

A few days later found Birkett at the Metropole Hotel in Brighton responding to the toast of the Bench at the annual dinner of the Sussex Law Society. The solicitor who had instructed him in the Brighton Trunk Murder nearly thirty years before, was amongst his audience, also his old clerk Edgar Bowker, who had retired and was living in the neighbourhood. Neither of them knew, nor did any one else who heard him, that it was to be the last legal occasion at which Birkett was to speak. And on this particular evening Birkett was at his most brilliant and witty and profound, as he spoke of the contribution of the law to English society.

> In my view the contribution the law makes in all its branches, the judiciary, the two branches of the legal profession, is, in a word, they are creating order, and without the law creating that necessary order none of the other professions could survive or flourish at all. If you look at our history, Magna Charta, the Petition of Right, the Bill of Rights, the Habeas Corpus Act, these great milestones of our history, the very signs of freedom have all got one basis, that the English people said we desire to be governed by law and not by whim or caprice, and every day and all day through the centuries the lives of men and women have been governed by law. Most people when they think of the law think of the dramatic case in the Assize Court, which is in a sense the failure of law; but very few people stop to think that from the moment they rise in the morning to the moment they go back to their bedroom at night every single act they do is controlled by law.

From the lawyers of Sussex to a fashionable girls' school, Heathfield, where Birkett, versatile as ever, presented the prizes on Speech Day and at the same time unlocked the literary treasures of a new school library. He left behind him some thoughts for the pupils to ponder over.

> On a Speech Day people usually expect the visiting speaker just to add a special word of his own. And if I were asked the

kind of message I would like to leave with the girls of this school it would be this. I would say two things are well worth doing: One is to cultivate a sense of beauty, and the other to cultivate a sense of duty. And when I say a sense of beauty—music, art, natural beauty, wherever it is to be found—to cultivate those qualities that appreciate beauty. And, in particular—that is why I use it—the beauty in our own English tongue.

I was delighted to see the emphasis laid upon English and English literature and the books which the girls had selected for themselves because I believe that this marvellous, flexible English tongue of ours is the most lovely language in the world—and I say it with some knowledge, some little knowledge, and with much experience. I don't forget Greek and I don't forget Latin: I don't forget Italian, or Spanish, or German, or French. I still say that the English tongue, made up as it is with its wonderful power, because of its flexibility, its mixture from every source, is a thing of infinite beauty, and every girl will find it an advantage all her life through to use that language as it ought to be used, and to use it well. . . . And therefore I would say to you this afternoon, cultivate the sense of beauty, and particularly the beauty to be found in our English tongue.

And one last word: cultivate a sense of duty. Now I am one of those who believe that people naturally do think about themselves; it's no good saying we must think of others and not think of yourself. People do think about themselves, and there's no real conflict between the two; you can think of yourself and think of others. But what I venture to say about the sense of duty is this: that if you want to achieve anything like happiness in this world, it's never, never going to come by being selfish—never! Never just by thinking only of yourself. And the real pleasure in life is to have friends that are bound to you by loyalty and by kinship, and because of the bond of service that lies between you.

Back at home for the week-end, Birkett set about preparing two major speeches which he had to deliver in the following week. One was at a dinner to mark the hundred and fiftieth anniversary of the birth of Charles Dickens on February 7. The other was a motion in the House of Lords which he had consented to move on the following day, rejecting that part of the Manchester Corporation Bill which sought to augment the city's water supply from Ullswater by a scheme which he and others interested in preserving the beauties of the Lakes considered would seriously threaten to spoil them if it were carried out.

To Henry Birkett

> *Challens Green.* [*February* 4, 1962.] I went to a Speech Day at a girls' school at Harrow on Thursday last and they gave me a presentation key with which to open the new library. . . .
>
> I have become great friends with Lord Lonsdale who is a very nice chap and fighting like a Briton for Ullswater. I hope to win a lot of support on Thursday as I make the first speech in opposition. But the Government is not treating us fairly; and I have arranged to see the Minister in charge, Dr. Charles Hill, with Lord Lonsdale on Wednesday. . . .
>
> On the Wednesday night I propose 'The Immortal Memory of Charles Dickens' at the Birthday Dinner. I am going to Edinburgh in March to preside at the Walter Scott dinner, though I am told a man simply *cannot* love Dickens and Scott at the same time.

On the eve of the Dickens birthday celebrations, Birkett was invited by the B.B.C. to have an informal broadcast discussion with a fellow Dickensian, Miss Margaret Lane, the novelist and critic, in private life Lady Huntingdon, who was a former President of the Dickens Fellowship. They met in the studio at Broadcasting House, where they were photographed in a happy and relaxed attitude before going on the air. For Birkett it was to be his last radio performance, and he felt thoroughly happy and at ease in it.

'I've often thought what a wonderful lawyer Dickens would have made,' he said. 'He had a marvellous use of the English tongue, and moreover, what people don't give him credit for, he had a marvellous knowledge of the law. Lawyers to this day speak with admiration of the trial scene in *Pickwick*, of Mrs. Bardell and Pickwick's breach of promise case. Every detail of that famous case is accurate. When Trollope started to write about the law, he fell into error on almost every page. But Dickens—never! . . . I think as a speaker, a man with a love of language, a man with a knowledge of law, a man above all with sympathy, and insight, and understanding, he would have carried every jury completely away.'

'And, of course,' Miss Lane broke in, 'he had the talents of a very good actor in him, which you must very well know is essential to every great advocate. He could spellbind as well as plead.'

'Yes,' agreed Birkett. 'It is a very interesting speculation, that kind of thing. Dickens himself used to say, "Well, you know I might have been a different man if I'd had a different education", and he spoke about the miseries of the blacking factory, and how his family hadn't treated him quite well, and so on. But you know, I still think that for a man such as Dickens was to be, the training he had was just the perfect training for him. He'd got a knowledge of life, and of the poor, the life of the poor, of all sorts and conditions of men, and he had what I sometimes call, though I can never quite define it, he had the "common touch". He could bring all these things so clearly and lucidly before the reading public. If Dickens had gone to a public school, to a university and all the rest of it, I don't think we should have that wonderful output of books that we have had.'

'I'm sure you are right,' said Miss Lane. 'Nor can I believe that his imagination would have been stimulated in the way it was by the life of the poor and the criminal.'

'No,' Birkett rejoined. 'That element of his life in which he exposed the social evils of the day is one of the great contributions that Dickens, I think, made to our public life. Dickens was by no means a perfect man, and nobody would pretend that he was. He had many shortcomings and many weaknesses. But in this particular respect he had the power of exposing social evils in a manner which made the whole nation think.'

Birkett expanded this tribute at the Dickens Birthday Dinner, where he expressed in the words of the Honorary Secretary of the Dickens Fellowship, Mr. John Greaves, 'as only he could express his great love of the works of the famous novelist'. This task completed, he began to brace himself for the struggle against the promoters of the obnoxious waterworks clauses of the Manchester Corporation Bill, which he was convinced would be an ugly blot on the face of his beloved Lakeland. As he entered the House of Lords in readiness for the debate on the controversial measure, he obligingly posed for a press photographer. He looked smiling and confident.

Although it was strictly speaking a Private Bill promoted by the Manchester Corporation, the measure had the blessing of the Government. The case for it was put by Lord Jessel, who moved the Second Reading and invited the House to reject Birkett's motion. It boiled down to the fact that the big city of Manchester needed more water and it had to get it from somewhere. Industrial demand was increasing and by 1970 the situation for industry might well become critical, said Lord Jessel, when an additional forty or fifty million gallons a day would have to be provided. The scheme involved the construction of an impounding reservoir at Bannisdale, two weirs, a treatment works to purify the water, an intake below the surface of Ullswater and an underground pumping chamber beneath the surface of the land which abuts on the lake, and an underground aqueduct, for which purpose the Corporation was to be given powers for the compulsory purchase of land in the neighbourhood.

By the time Birkett rose to move his motion, both the red leather benches on the floor of the House and the seats in the galleries were unusually crowded for a Lords debate. There had been a good deal of lobbying by the opponents of the Bill and such organizations as the National Trust, the Friends of the Lake District, and the Ullswater Preservation Society had seen to it that their Lordships were well briefed in advance on the dangers of the Bill, besides which their arguments had already been to some extent canvassed in the press, so that public interest in the Manchester scheme had been aroused far outside the confines of the northern city. It was the fullest House that Birkett had ever addressed, perhaps the fullest since the debate on the Death Penalty Bill in 1957, for there is nothing like a controversial non-party subject with strong emotional overtones to fill a British legislative chamber. Birkett was much heartened by the sight as he began to speak.

To those who heard him on this memorable February afternoon, Birkett's utterance may have appeared a little hesitant compared with what it once was. But his voice was still of such beauty, his enunciation so pure and clear, so polished and yet so unaffected, and his manner and gestures so perfect that he appeared altogether as persuasive as in the days when he so successfully cast his spell over juries in the court room. There was a note of scorn in his voice as he accused the Manchester Corporation, which did not need the additional water until 1970, of coming to the House and pleading as a matter of 'urgency' that there should be no delay, otherwise the Corporation could not fulfil the obligations which Parliament had laid upon its members in the matter of supplying water, saying that the Lake District was their only hope. 'I have heard some specious pleading in my time, and made it, I freely acknowledge,' he said, 'but that has also given me the experience to recognize it when I see it. . . . They do not need the water until 1970. If they get the forty million or fifty million gallons under this Bill, and it begins to be expended in 1970, by 1985 or thereabouts they will want more water. Where are they going for that? Ullswater? The Chairman of the Waterworks has given an undertaking, I understand, that they will seek no more from Ullswater. It is like the extemporary speech of which Lord Hewart used to speak—it is not worth the paper it is written on. The Manchester Corporation can no more bind its successors than anyone else can.'

> We have only to look at Thirlmere as it is today; we have only to look at Haweswater as it is today. Both lovely lakes have been murdered. They are now dead water reservoirs: no human life; sterile shores; why, even the afforestation of the Manchester Corporation prevents proper access to the Fell-side until invention is made in that behalf.
>
> And they come to this House with this Bill now and say, 'We are only going to destroy a valley, if you can call it destruction; in Bannisdale, we are going to build a huge reservoir with a mighty dam; but it is a secluded valley, very few people go there'—as though seclusion and solitude was not one of the things people wanted! They say, 'We are only going to take up our weir from Ullswater: we are not going to damage the amenities; you need have no fear.' Whereas we know in truth and in fact that if you raise the level of the lake, and hold it there fifteen days, there may be a flood. . . .
>
> Under this Bill it can be taken for a certainty—everybody with any experience of Lakeland knows it—that these lovely shores of Ullswater, where people picnic, where the ponies come down, will be just sterile shores like one sees at Thirlmere.

The question which the House had to decide was a simple one of principle, Birkett went on. It was whether Manchester Corporation should be permitted to invade Lakeland for the third time, to impound its waters, to pour them into its aqueducts, or not. 'What we are debating is principle,' he urged; 'and the great overriding principle which never operated in the case of Thirlmere or in the case of Haweswater arises now—namely, are we going to allow this in a National Park?'

> The National Parks were set up so that the scenic beauty should be preserved and that the enjoyment of the parks should be for all people in all times. That is the principle which is before your Lordships here this afternoon. To say 'There have been many invasions there. Here is one more', is a pitiful argument. Your Lordships could, I think—and before I sit down I shall make one plea that your Lordships will—assert that Parliament has said that these areas, few though they be in our land shall be preserved inviolate; that they shall not be invaded by this or the other undertaking; that that principle shall be maintained in its fullness by the Members of this House.
>
> I know perfectly well what people feel about it. We are unaccustomed to use words such as
>
> 'This precious jewel set in the silver sea.'
>
> We think it but rarely say it. I am greatly tempted when it comes to defending the beauty of the English Lakelands—so small, so lovely, so vulnerable upon that account—to call to aid the great Wordsworth, the great men who have lived there and who have had the power to set down upon the printed page what scenic beauty can mean to the individual life and to the life of the nation. So far from saying in this House 'It has been done many times. Let it be done once more,' surely the argument should be 'It has been done too many times already: do not let us add to it'. That is the point of principle which is involved in the procedure which I am suggesting here this afternoon.

Birkett was careful to emphasize in his speech that the opposition to the Bill were not saying that Manchester should not have the water. On the contrary, it was agreed that Manchester should have it. 'So I want to make clear to every Member of this House that the opposition are not seeking to deprive Manchester of water which it will need in days to come, and which it must have in days to come,' he said. 'It may very well be that some will have to come from the north-west of England. But it ought not to come at the present time.' Meanwhile he urged the authorities concerned to look into the question of the distillation of seawater for industrial and domestic purposes which was already being done in an American plant and might be 'something which is just around the corner'.

He had been on his feet for about half an hour when he brought his speech to a close with these words:

> My Lords, I suppose that today we have a House which is as full as any I have had the privilege of addressing, and I suppose this would be the moment for what I would call my peroration. I leave it on one side: I do not feel equal to a peroration on a theme like this at this moment, and will content myself by saying this. Your Lordships will have a great opportunity this evening when the Division is taken—it may be late I am afraid, but their devotion to this cause might persuade Members to undergo a little inconvenience in order to stay and vote—the first opportunity you will have had on this matter, to vindicate the right of the House to say on any measure such as this. 'Thus far and no farther. Go away. Come again another day, if you will. But in the meantime, do that which ought to have been done before. Produce the hydrological data on which the House can come to a proper decision. Until that is done you have no right whatever to invade the sanctity of a National Park.' That principle will be invaluable if it is established by the House. And it involves this other principle too. It will urge upon the Government the immediate necessity of producing that national scheme which, in the words of the noble Lord, Lord Morrison of Lambeth, will give natural justice to every interest.

Among those who heard him from the gallery was Lady Birkett, who had also witnessed so many of his triumphs in the courts. She had to leave, shortly after he sat down, to go back to their country home, because, like the good wife she was, she liked to have everything ready and comfortable for his return. Before she left, she scribbled a note to her husband on the back of the day's Order Paper and gave it to one of the doorkeepers to deliver. 'Darling,' she wrote, 'it was a splendid effort, and I shall be surprised if the House does not carry your motion. . . . I am going off to catch the five train but thought you'd like to know how well it went.'

In the lively debate which followed, Birkett was strongly supported by the Bishop of Carlisle and Lords Lonsdale, Rea, Rochdale, Chorley, MacAndrew, Conesford and Huntingdon, while from the Government Front Bench the measure was commended to the House by Lord Jellicoe, the Parliamentary Secretary to the Ministry of Health and Local Government, and by Lord Hailsham, the Lord President of the Council and Leader of the House. In doing so, the leader went out of his way to pay a graceful tribute to Birkett.

'His deeply felt and highly eloquent speech is still fresh in our minds,' said Lord Hailsham in winding up the debate from the Government side. 'One who has known him, as I, though a much younger man, have known him for more than thirty years now, cannot speak of his powers without deep feeling. At the Bar, he was one of the greatest of English advocates. One of my earliest and most dramatic memories is of hearing him in one of those great cases which secured a verdict that one had almost thought to be impossible.[1] On the Bench, if he will allow me to say so, I felt for him not only admiration but the kind of gratitude which only counsel can feel for a learned judge who not only makes it a pleasure to appear before him but also, by numerous acts of personal kindness, has completely won one's heart. If I differ from him on this matter, it ought not to be thought, nor even suspected, that I desire to diminish in any way the immense reputation which he nationally enjoys.'

In the course of his speech, Lord Hailsham remarked that he had a rooted objection to trying cases before the evidence had been heard, and until that afternoon he had supposed that Birkett had shared his prejudice. 'I am wondering whether he was not more the advocate than the judge on this occasion,' he went on. 'Small shame to him if he was, because this is a matter about which he feels so sincerely and deeply.'

When he came to reply, Birkett good-humouredly twitted Lord Hailsham on this remark. 'One of the tragedies of my own life,' he

[1] Lord Hailsham evidently had in mind the case of *R.* v. *Mancini* (The Brighton Trunk Murder), in which he was junior counsel for the Crown. See above, p. 397.

said, 'has been that, when I have espoused a cause in court, opposing counsel was accustomed to deprecate it by saying that it was pure advocacy. I never expected it in this House; but I must say with all affection—I hope I may use that term of the noble Leader—when he talks to me about advocacy, "Physician, heal thyself!" '

When the laughter which greeted this remark had died down, Birkett continued:

> I do not propose to re-argue the matter. I hope the House will support me in this: that when I made my speech this afternoon I tried to make it clearly; I tried to make it forcibly, and I restrained myself from saying anything unkind about Manchester.
>
> I had intended to say some very kind words about Manchester, because I am proud to be a Lancastrian, and Manchester, in my view, has been a great city and a great leader in many matters with which I myself am deeply concerned. I have for the great city of Manchester nothing but admiration, and I hope that that will be taken to my credit here today. When the noble Viscount said, 'You should not decide a case until you have heard the evidence,' I would reply (although I dislike the character of the man who used the words) 'All these things have I observed from my youth up.' And the last thing that I need telling is that you should hear both sides before making your decision. I was at pains to say that at some length. We were not debating the merits of this matter here in this House this evening. What I suggested was that the point of principle was within the procedure of the House, the constitutional procedure of the House, that it was right and proper in these circumstances that where a great corporation had not had the requisite consultation with the authorities, where it was seeking to do something in a National Park which Parliament had said ought not to be violated but ought to be preserved for the enjoyment of all generations—when these matters were propounded by sponsors of the Bill, I ventured to say this was one of the occasions on which this House might very well rely upon its great power and say they will not permit it.

It was past ten o'clock when Birkett formally put his motion and the House divided. He and Lord Lonsdale acted as tellers, and as the peers trooped through the lobbies it soon became evident that Birkett and his supporters had carried the day. A few minutes later the Lord Chancellor announced the figures from the Woolsack—70 for the motion, 36 against.

An outburst of cheers greeted the result of the division, as Birkett's motion was formally agreed to and, in parliamentary language, 'ordered accordingly'. His friends crowded round to congratulate him and shake his hand. No wonder he was in a jubilant mood when he left the House to catch the train for home. His wife, who had meanwhile heard the news on the radio, met him with the car at Chalfont station. 'He was like a schoolboy in his delight and told me all about everything I hadn't heard,' Lady Birkett later recalled.

It was to be his final achievement as an advocate. Some people, notably those who shared his belief in the preservation of the unspoiled English countryside, thought it was the greatest speech of his career. It may well have been that he thought so himself on that day, which his wife was to describe as 'one of his fittest, happiest and most satisfactory days of his life when he saved his lovely Lakeland'. For Norman Birkett there could have been no better swansong.

5

Next day he had breakfast in bed and spent a leisurely and happy morning reading the laudatory newspaper reports on his speech as well as the telegrams and letters of congratulation which had begun to arrive. Towards lunch time he complained of a touch of lumbago and said he would stay in bed. His wife, who was an expert therapist, gave him some infra-red heat treatment and as this did not seem to ease the trouble she sent for the doctor. His heart seemed normal and the doctor thought that the long day on the upright benches in the House of Lords might have caused the lumbago. After the doctor had left, Lady Birkett went downstairs for a short time, and on returning to the bedroom a little later found Birkett lying on the floor, looking very white and obviously in pain. Somehow she got him back into bed and the doctor was again summoned, also a specialist, followed by an ambulance to take him to the London Clinic, where he had previously been a patient. He was given some morphia to make him more comfortable, and as he was being carried downstairs to the ambulance he remarked with an air of distinct surprise, 'What is so astonishing is the calm way I am taking this!'

His wife travelled with him to the clinic and saw him tucked up in bed, looking and feeling somewhat better, after more specialists had examined him. He had a good night, and next morning, Saturday, February 10, Lady Birkett returned with a further batch of telegrams and letters which she read to him, from the Westmorland and Cumberland County Councils, the National Trust, the Friends of the Lake District and similar bodies. Even the Parliamentary Secretary to the Ministry of Housing and Local Government sent his congratulations. 'I hope you will not feel it impertinent if I write to tell you how much I enjoyed, and indeed admired, your speech, even though it did not have quite the effect I would have liked,' wrote Lord Jellicoe. 'I think we will all have to scratch our heads pretty hard now in order to try and work out a sensible and generally acceptable scheme. I do hope you will feel quite free to offer us any suggestions which may occur to you from time to time.'

Most of all the letters he received he was touched by one from a secondary girls school in the town where he had received the elements of his own education seventy years before.

Alfred Barrow Secondary School for Girls,
Barrow-in-Furness,
Lancashire.
9th February, 1962.

Dear Lord Birkett,

We, the Fifth Years of Alfred Barrow Girls' School, would very much like to thank you for all you have done in saving Ullswater. It was a great relief to us, for we have been following the reports and debates steadily in the newspapers and on television. For the first time in our experience, we have been personally interested in the workings of Parliament, and are quite thrilled at the outcome of our first contact with it.

We have had notices and pictures posted all round the corridors on the topic in question, and have also a flourishing Rambling Club to which many girls belong. As regularly as possible they visit different parts of the Lake District, and sidetrack the main roads as much as they can in search of the 'Solitude and Seclusion' of which you spoke.

We were more excited than ever this morning when we learnt that you have been the main person responsible for getting this plan rejected, for we have already talked about you in our lessons this week in connection with the 150th Anniversary of Dickens's birth, and the celebration dinner given at the Dorchester Hotel at which you were the chief speaker.

We think you are interested in the things that matter, and should like to tell you so.

Yours sincerely,
THE FIFTH FORM

Birkett slept quietly during the afternoon and when he woke up he was glad to see his son Michael at his bedside; he had been out of London and returned just in time to have a talk with his father. For the doctors and surgeons had told Lady Birkett that an immediate operation was imperative, and he now had to be prepared for it. Shortly afterwards she saw him gradually eased into unconsciousness with another injection. The operation took place at eleven o'clock that night and it confirmed the doctors' fears that he was suffering from a fatal impairment of a vital blood vessel. At the most he could have survived for only a few days under drugs. It was therefore a merciful relief for him and his family and those closest to him when his heart failed while he was still unconscious under the anaesthetic, and, in his wife's words, he was allowed to slip away with the minimum of pain and the minimum of worry. 'It was the way for him to go on the very crest of the wave,' said Lady Birkett, 'and whatever terrible gaps in companionship and love have to be got over, I don't wish it differently for a minute.'

At his express wish, Birkett's remains were cremated, and there were no funeral or memorial services. Only his son attended the cremation ceremony.

Meanwhile tributes public and private reached Lady Birkett from all over the country and also from America. The President of the Pilgrims of the United States, Mr. Hugh Bullock, cabled, 'Seldom has an Englishman won so much affection combined with infinite respect from all our countrymen who knew him,' while Mr. David Bruce, the American Ambassador in London, wrote: 'In my opinion, he was the most engaging and graceful orator to whom I ever listened. In addition, his personal conversation, when I was lucky enough to sit next to him was a delight. Kindness, benevolence, wit and humour seemed to flow naturally from him.'

The feelings of the English judiciary were expressed by Lord Denning at the sitting of the Judicial Committee of the Privy Council two days after his death. 'As an advocate he was fair and fearless and as a judge wise and good,' said Lord Denning. 'He was a master of the English tongue, eloquent and persuasive.' And, in a private letter of sympathy to Lady Birkett, Lord Denning added: 'He held strongly that the law must be in accord with public opinion and by his speeches and broadcasts he did more than anyone to give the people some knowledge of it and respect for it.'

Another of the many tributes which touched Lady Birkett came from Sir Douglas Logan, the Principal of the University of London, who had worked with Birkett for the past fourteen years in the University Senate. 'It is only rarely that one gets an opportunity of working closely with a great man—and he certainly was that,' wrote the Principal. 'But he was more than that. He was unassuming, kind and considerate for others and these were the qualities which won universal affection for him. But you, better than anyone else, knew how rich and varied were his qualities and the break must be a tragic one. I have never been in a house which was so obviously happy as yours. And, if I may say so, I admired the way you let him live his life to the full, even in retirement, though his activities may have shortened his life a little.'

But surely the most charming, if not the truest, tribute to the memory of Norman Birkett came in a personal letter to Lady Birkett from Princess Margaret. She remembered the kind words he had spoken to her when he was Chairman of the Court of the University of London and she had received an honorary degree. 'Lord Birkett had that unique quality of making people feel that everything was all right if he was there.'

Birkett had made a will, which, when admitted to probate revealed the value of his estate as approximately £43,000.[1] It may have been wondered why he did not leave more, seeing that for many years his income at the Bar had averaged between £20,000 and £30,000. But taxation had taken its toll, as with his colleague Sir Patrick Hastings, who died worth considerably less, and like Hastings, too, Birkett

[1] The actual probate figures were £43,294 gross, £42,526 net (duty paid £11,955). *The Times*, May 17, 1962.

had been generous with his family and friends, and others in need.

When a man dies as suddenly and unexpectedly as Birkett did, it is inevitable that he should leave behind a certain amount of unfinished business. Apart from public engagements such as presiding over the dinners of The Pilgrims and taking the chair at the annual dinner of The Edinburgh Sir Walter Scott Club which would necessarily involve some preparation, there was another matter which Birkett was considering at the time of his death and which had been causing him concern for several months past. This was the unfortunate Blake espionage case which he planned to raise in the House of Lords in the general context of the policy of judicial sentencing by the courts. That he had been working on it to the last was evident from the papers on the case which were found on his desk.[1] But if he could do nothing further in the Blake matter, he had at least succeeded over his beloved Lakeland, and it was in this connection that a permanent memorial to him came into being. The proposal was made to Lady Birkett by the Ullswater Preservation Society that a plaque should be placed on a rock promontory on the lake shore and at the same time that a fell nearby known as the Nameless Fell should be named or rather renamed Birkett Fell. 'I can think of nothing that would have pleased my husband more,' said Lady Birkett, in giving her permission. 'He would have been very proud to have his name permanently associated with one of the lakes in that part of the country which he regarded as home and loved so dearly. I personally think it is a wonderful, understanding and imaginative idea.'

The idea was carried into execution eighteen months later. The plaque made of Westmorland green slate from a local quarry and covered with a Union Jack had been set into the rock face of Kailpot Crag, near Howtown, on the eastern shore of Ullswater, and it was unveiled in the presence of two hundred guests including Lady Birkett and her two children, and Birkett's cousin Henry, assembled on one of the lake steamers, at a signal from the chairman of the Ullswater Preservation Society, Major E. W. Hassell. The new Lord Birkett spoke a few words of thanks for the Birkett family. 'My father had many great triumphs in his life and achieved many of his dearest ambitions,' he said, 'but nothing in the world could have given him

[1] These were returned to Mr. Jeremy Hutchinson who had defended Blake at his trial and with whom Birkett had been in consultation on the case. See above, p. 587.

greater pleasure if he could have known of this commemoration of him. . . . It is more than a great and gracious memorial. It is something of which his family will be proud for many generations to come.' Then the Bishop of Penrith, the Right Rev. S. C. Bulley, dedicated the tablet in memory of one 'by whose vision and labours the values of this beautiful spot were discerned, defined and defended to the common welfare of all who seek here refreshment of body, mind and spirit.'

The actual installation of the plaque was largely the work of the staff and boys of the nearby Outward Bound Mountain School. They also built a cairn on the top of the 2,290 ft. fell, which lies a short

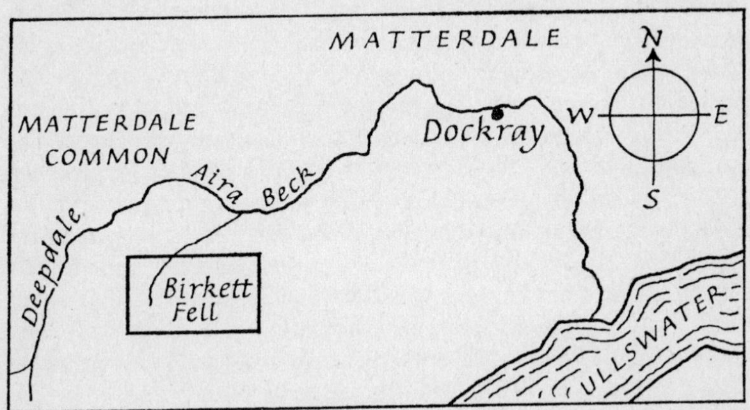

distance to the north-east of the summit of Helvellyn, with a name plate bearing the words 'Birkett Fell' enclosed by the cairn, which also contained some stones carried up from the lake shore. As the steamer sailed back to Glenridding Pier and the fell came into view, a party of the school personnel fired Very lights from the fell top, thus symbolizing the commemoration, the first time a mountain in Britain had been renamed in five centuries.

It was altogether a simple yet remarkably moving ceremony which took place that July afternoon, partly in sunshine and partly in mist so characteristic of the lakes and fells. It was well matched, too, by the simplicity of the wording of the inscription on the plaque by the lake shore. 'He loved Ullswater. He strove to maintain its beauty for all to enjoy.'[1]

[1] *The Times*, July 3; *Cumberland and Westmorland Gazette*, August 4, 1963.

Long after the dust has settled on the barrister's briefs and the judge's law books, and the voice of the advocate has been stilled and the causes which he pleaded in the courts are a distant memory, his last cause had been permanently enshrined. It is by that, perhaps most of all, that the name of Norman Birkett will be lovingly remembered.

BIBLIOGRAPHY

THE principal MS. sources for the life of Lord Birkett are the private papers in the possession of Ruth, Lady Birkett. They consist of diaries, letters, press cutting books, notebooks and the uncompleted holograph draft of what was intended to be the first chapter of Birkett's memoirs. Mr. Henry F. Birkett also possesses an important collection of letters. Other correspondents are mentioned in the Preface.

The following printed sources have been classified as (*A*) published writings of Lord Birkett, and (*B*) secondary authorities.

A. Published Writings of Lord Birkett

(*in chronological order*)

Furness Railway. English Lake Land Guide. Ulverston, 1916.

'The War and Liberty'. (Address to the Birmingham Liberal Association.) Birmingham, 1917.

Foreword to *Lakeland Passes* by John B. Barker and George Atkinson. London, 1934.

Preface to *Abortion Right or Wrong* by Mrs. Dorothy Thurtle. London, 1940.

National Parks and the Countryside. (The Rede Lecture.) Cambridge, 1945.

'The Future of National Parks' in *Countrygoer's Heritage* (ed. Cyril Moore). London, 1945.

The English Circuit System. (Address to Canadian Bar Association.) Toronto, 1947.

The Art of Advocacy. (Address to Lawyers Club of Toronto.) Toronto, 1947.

Contribution of Law in Literature. (The Cavendish Lecture.) London, 1948.

Foreword to *Judge Jeffreys* by H. Montgomery Hyde. London, 1948.

Foreword to *Brightly Fades the Don* by J. H. Fingleton. London, 1949.

Foreword to *The National Parks and Access to the Countryside Act, 1949*. London, 1949.

Foreword to *Alphabet of Life* by Edward Hulme. London, 1949.

Foreword to *Trial of Nikolaus von Falkenhorst* (ed. E. K. Stevens). London and Edinburgh, 1949.

Memoir in *Stay Me With Flagons* by Maurice Healy. London, 1949.

Use and Abuse of Reading. Cambridge, 1951.

Foreword to *Advice on Advocacy in the Lower Courts* by F. J. O. Coddington. Chichester, 1951.

Foreword and Introduction to *The English Lake District in Pictures*. London, 1951.

The Newgate Calendar. London, 1951.

'Books and the General Reader' in *Books are Essential*. London, 1951.

Foreword to *The Table Talk of Samuel Marchbanks* by Robertson Davies. London, 1951.

Introduction to *The Quest for Corvo* by A. J. A. Symons. London, 1952.

'On the Singing of Hymns' in *Spectator Harvest*. London, 1952.

Article on 'The Essay' in *Cassell's Encyclopedia of Literature* (ed. S. H. Steinberg). London, 1953.

Findlay Memorial Lecture. Cardiff, 1953.

The Lawyer's Contribution to Society. (Annual Address to Law Society.) London, 1953.

The Magic of Words. (Presidential Address to the English Association.) Oxford, 1953.

Contribution to *This I Believe* (ed. Edward P. Morgan). London, 1953.

Foreword to *So Far So Good* by Morris L. Ernst. London, 1953.

Foreword to *They Have Their Exits* by Airey Neve. London, 1953.

Advocacy. (Presidential Address to Holdsworth Society.) Birmingham, 1954.

Introductory Essay in *The Game of Cricket*. London, 1955.

Introduction to *Test Matches of 1956* by E. W. Swanton. London, 1956.

Address at Opening of Sterling Library, University of London. London, 1956.

'Law and Literature' in *The Lawyer's Treasury* (ed. Eugene C. Gerhart). New York, 1956.

The Decay of Oratory. (Address to Convocation, University of London.) London, 1956.

Address on Conferring of Honorary Degree of Doctor of Music on Princess Margaret, University of London. London, 1957.

Foreword to *National Parks for Britain* by Henry Chessell. Birmingham, 1957.

Foreword to *Village Cricket* by A. J. Forrest. London, 1957.

On the *Owning and Borrowing of Books.* (Library Association Annual Lecture.) Brighton, 1958.

Foreword to *Teach Them to Live* by Frances Banks. London, 1958.

Foreword to *The Testing Years* by Gordon Ross. London, 1958.

Preface to *Mainly Personal.* (Articles from Court Page of *The Times.*) London, 1958.

'The Importance of Little Things' in *My Philosophy of Life* (ed. Lord Inman). London, 1958.

'The Love of Cricket' in *Wisden's Cricketer's Almanack* (ed. Norman Preston). London, 1958.

Foreword to *Mystery of Life* (ed. Kenneth Ullyett). London, 1958.

Our Heritage of Freedom. (Ford Lecture to Youth.) Dagenham, 1959.

'Reflections in Retirement' in *The Oxford Lawyer.* Oxford, 1959.

'The Lake District' in *Britain's National Parks* (ed. Harold M. Abrahams). London, 1959.

Contribution to *Learned from Life* (ed. Madge Hart). London, 1959.

Prefatory Word in *The Murder and the Trial* by Edgar Lustgarten. London, 1960.

Foreword to *Sir Patrick Hastings: His Life and Cases* by H. Montgomery Hyde. London, 1960.

Introduction to *The Verdict of the Court* (ed. Michael Hardwick). London, 1960.

The Newgate Calendar. New Edition. London, 1960.

Foreword to *Relax with a Smile.* (Anthology for After Dinner Speakers.) London, 1960.

'The Unfading Genius of Rudyard Kipling' in *The Kipling Journal.* London, March, 1961.

'Some Reflections on Advocacy'. (Address to the New York Bar Association.) New York, 1961.

Foreword to *Inside the Real Lakeland* by A. H. Griffin. Preston, 1961.
'On After Dinner Speaking' in *Catalyst* 7 (ed. G. H. Metcalfe).
Foreword to *Topolski's Legal London* by Francis Cowper. London, 1961.
Six Great Advocates. Penguin Books Ltd. Harmondsworth, 1961.
Foreword to *Forensic Fables* by Theobald Mathews. London, 1961.
Foreword to *Laughter at Law* by Stanley Jackson. London, 1961.
Contribution to *Does Pornography Matter?* (ed. C. H. Rolph). London, 1961.
Foreword to *The Law as Literature* by Louis Blom-Cooper. London, 1961.
'The Changing Law' in *To Deprave and Corrupt* (ed. John Chandos). London, 1962.

B. Secondary Authorities

Bancroft, George P. *Stage and Bar*. London, 1939.
Bardens, Dennis. *Lord Justice Birkett*. London, 1962.
— —*Famous Cases of Norman Birkett, K.C.* London, 1963.
Biddle, Francis. *In Brief Authority*. New York, 1962.
Birkett, Henry F. *The Story of Ulverston*. Kendal, 1949.
Bowker, A. E. *Behind the Bar*. London, 1947.
— — *A Lifetime with the Law*. London, 1961.
Blundell, R. H., and Wilson, G. Haswell, *Trial of Buck Ruxton*. London and Edinburgh, 1937.
Browne, Douglas G. *Sir Travers Humphreys*. London, 1960.
Chandos, John. Five Articles on Lord Birkett in *Sunday Telegraph*, May 13, 20, 27; June 3, 10, 1962.
Craddock, Percy. *Recollections of the Cambridge Union*. Cambridge, 1953.
Duke, Winifred. *Trials of Frederick Nodder*. London and Edinburgh, 1950.
Gardiner, A. G. *Life of George Cadbury*. London, 1923.
Hyde, H. Montgomery. *United in Crime*. London, 1955.
— — *Sir Patrick Hastings: His Life and Cases*. London, 1960.
— — 'The Private Papers of Norman Birkett' in *Sunday Times*, March 31; April 7, 14, 1963.

Jackson, Robert. *The Chief: The Biography of Gordon Hewart.* London, 1959.
Marjoribanks, Edward. *The Life of Sir Edward Marshall Hall, K.C.* London, 1929.
Normanton, Helena. *Trial of A. A. Rouse.* London and Edinburgh, 1931.
Pollock, George. *Mr. Justice McCardie.* London, 1934.
Ward, Arthur. *Stuff and Silk.* Ramsey, 1949.
All England Law Reports.
The Birmingham Post.
The Daily Mail.
The Daily Telegraph.
The Nottingham Guardian.
The Nottingham Journal.
The Times.

INDEX

21